Craig
Marc
Nigel
Matt Winkler

Windows Communication Foundation

UNLEASHED

SAMS | 800 East 96th Street, Indianapolis, Indiana 46240 USA

Windows Communication Foundation Unleashed

Copyright © 2007 by Sams Publishing

All rights reserved. No part of this book shall be reproduced, stored in a retrieval system, or transmitted by any means, electronic, mechanical, photocopying, recording, or otherwise, without written permission from the publisher. No patent liability is assumed with respect to the use of the information contained herein. Although every precaution has been taken in the preparation of this book, the publisher and author assume no responsibility for errors or omissions. Nor is any liability assumed for damages resulting from the use of the information contained herein.

ISBN-10: 0-672-32948-4

ISBN-13: 978-0-672-32948-7

Library of Congress Cataloging-in-Publication Data

Windows communication foundation unleashed / Craig McMurtry ... [et al.].

   p. cm.

  Includes index.

  ISBN 0-672-32948-4

  1. Application software–Development. 2. Electronic data processing–Distributed processing. 3. Microsoft Windows (Computer file) 4. Web services. I. McMurtry, Craig.

QA76.76.A65W59 2007

005.4'46–dc22

2007004268

Printed in the United States of America

First Printing: March 2007

10   09   08   07   4   3   2

Trademarks

All terms mentioned in this book that are known to be trademarks or service marks have been appropriately capitalized. Sams Publishing cannot attest to the accuracy of this information. Use of a term in this book should not be regarded as affecting the validity of any trademark or service mark.

Warning and Disclaimer

Every effort has been made to make this book as complete and as accurate as possible, but no warranty or fitness is implied. The information provided is on an "as is" basis. The author and the publisher shall have neither liability nor responsibility to any person or entity with respect to any loss or damages arising from the information contained in this book.

Editor-in-Chief
Karen Gettman

Senior Acquisitions Editor
Neil Rowe

Development Editor
Mark Renfrow

Managing Editor
Patrick Kanouse

Project Editor
Seth Kerney

Copy Editor
Mike Henry

Indexer
Ken Johnson

Proofreader
Leslie Joseph

Technical Editor
John Lambert

Publishing Coordinator
Cindy Teeters

Book Designer
Gary Adair

Contents at a Glance

Table of Contents

Part IV   Integration and Interoperability

11   Legacy Integration   385

12   Interoperability   413

Tell Us What You Think!

As the reader of this book, you are our most important critic and commentator. We value your opinion and want to know what we're doing right, what we could do better, what areas you'd like to see us publish in, and any other words of wisdom you're willing to pass our way.

As a senior acquisitions editor for Sams, I welcome your comments. You can fax, email, or write me directly to let me know what you did or didn't like about this book—as well as what we can do to make our books stronger.

Please note that I cannot help you with technical problems related to the topic of this book, and that due to the high volume of mail I receive, I might not be able to reply to every message.

When you write, please be sure to include this book's title and author as well as your name and phone or fax number. I will carefully review your comments and share them with the author and editors who worked on the book.

Email: feedback@samspublishing.com

Fax: (317) 428-3310

Mail: Neil Rowe, Senior Acquisitions Editor
             Sams Publishing
             800 East 96th Street
             Indianapolis, IN 46240 USA

Foreword

I started working on the Windows Communication Foundation in 2001 (then known as "Indigo"), when we were a small team—I was perhaps the 20th person to join. In my tenure on the team, I served as lead program manager for storage, manageability, reliable messaging, and queuing. The team had a great vision of facilitating the next generation of Web services by creating a foundation for Web services that could be practically applied to a breadth of distributing computing problems. We wanted to ensure that Web services could be implemented for businesses that enable secure communication—confidentiality, signing, federation—so distributed computing customers could use Web services for communication in the real world. We wanted to make sure that Web services could participate in transactions in the ACID model, ensuring that practical interactions with data-driven systems, or with which "all or nothing" computing is essential. We wanted to ensure that Web services could be written in a way that lossiness of the WAN didn't inhibit development of meaningful distributed applications—where you could actually count on messages getting where you sent them, and in the order you sent them. In retrospect, these "basic plumbing" goals seem almost quaint, but in 2001 we accepted, for the most part, the need to "do it ourselves" when building distributed systems.

We also understood that most computing environments are heterogeneous, with systems from many vendors coexisting with each other, so we wanted to ensure interoperability through great technical web service standards. We made a deep commitment to interoperability, and executed relentlessly on that commitment. WS-Security, WS-AtomicTransactions, WS-ReliableMessaging, WS-Management, WS-Policy, WS-Transfer, WS-Eventing and others were essential for broad interoperability at the "basic plumbing" level—but none existed when we kicked off this project (all were made possible in greater or lesser part by colleagues on the WCF team). Looking back, we might say "Of course we want to work with other systems with broadly accepted composable Web service standards"—but again, in 2001 this was a lofty goal.

We wanted to support a single programming model so developers wouldn't face a new learning curve if they wanted to shift from message-oriented to remote procedural paradigms, or to go from TCP to HTTP or queuing protocols such as MSMQ. In the face of .Net Remoting, ASMX, Sockets, MSMQ, and other programming models, a unified API to accomplish what any of its predecessors could seemed difficult—we were trying to forge one from many. We wanted to support extensibility, so that each new message exchange pattern, protocol, or encryption mechanism wouldn't force yet-another programming paradigm.

For my part as a lead program manager, I helped champion manageability—the idea that anything that should be left to the IT pro (protocol du jour, encryption mechanisms, service addresses, monitoring aspects, and so on), could be. Here again we had lofty goals—we wanted best-of-breed tracing, intrinsic monitoring and control of applications built with WCF, ease of use through great configuration and tracing tools, and integration with all the Windows management assets through WMI. The goal was simply that applications built with WCF would be intrinsically more manageable with less effort than those built on other frameworks.

And perhaps most ambitiously, we wanted it to be *easy* and *fun* to build great distributed applications for use in the real world. We wanted it to intuitively lead developers to build applications that followed the best practices of distributed systems. As Steve Swartz, one of the greatest champions of "easy and fun" told me, our goal was to build a framework such that "if you set a ball at the top of a hill and let it roll down, it would just naturally stop in a place where you had a well factored Service that helped you avoid all the mistakes distributed systems developers have made in the last 20 years."

So how did we do? Looking at the finished product that shipped as part of .Net 3.0 in Vista and on the Web, I think we actually did pretty darned well. WCF is a unified, extensible framework that does in fact help you build secure, reliable, interoperable, manageable real world distributed applications in a unified framework that is, by gum, actually fun (well, at least for those of us who enjoy programming). It took us six years, but we hit all our key goals. In fact, I like the product so well that my NEW job is focused on building new products for Microsoft to sell that bet entirely on the facilities that WCF provides (and I'm having a blast). This book is on every developer and PM's shelf in the team—it is the "go to" reference for those of us who either provide or consume Web services in the product—which is basically all of us (including several developers and PMs who actually helped build WCF!).

A few words about Craig. Craig and I met while he was serving as the technical evangelist for WCF. His energy and enthusiasm for the product was infectious—he was a great champion of the vision. About 90% of the time, when a question came up about "Can we support that scenario?" Craig would chime in with "Oh yeah, I did that last week—here's the prototype." In his role, he was able to see the "gestalt" of the product in a way that those of us who were heads down on specific features didn't. His candid feedback, technical depth, and enthusiasm were instrumental in making WCF what it is today. I believe his comprehensive knowledge of and enthusiasm for WCF shines through every chapter—I am sure you'll find the book as enjoyable, enlightening, and plain useful as we do here on our team.

—Alex Weinert

Group Program Manager, Microsoft Corporation

Introduction

The Windows Communication Foundation, which was code-named *Indigo*, is a technology that allows pieces of software to communicate with one another. There are many other such technologies, including the Component Object Model and Distributed Component Object Model, Remote Method Invocation, Microsoft Message Queuing (MSMQ), and WebSphere MQ. Each of those works well in a particular scenario, not so well in others, and is of no use at all in some cases. The Windows Communication Foundation is meant to work well in any circumstance in which a Microsoft .NET assembly must exchange data with any other software entity. In fact, the Windows Communication Foundation is meant to always be the very best option. Its performance is at least on par with that of any other alternative and is usually better; it offers at least as many features and probably several more. It is certainly always the easiest solution to program.

Concretely, the Windows Communication Foundation consists of a small number of .NET libraries with several new sets of classes that it adds to the Microsoft .NET Framework class library, for use with the second version, the 2.0 version, of the .NET Common Language Runtime. It also adds some facilities for hosting Windows Communication Foundation solutions to the 5.1 and later versions of Internet Information Services (IIS), the web server built into Windows operating systems.

The Windows Communication Foundation is distributed free of charge as part of a set that includes several other technologies, including the Windows Presentation Foundation, which was code-named *Avalon*, Windows CardSpace, which was code-named *InfoCard*, and the Windows Workflow Foundation. Prior to its release, that group of technologies was called *WinFX*, but it was renamed the *.NET Framework 3.0* in June 2006. Despite that name, the .NET Framework 3.0 is still primarily just a collection of classes added to the .NET Framework 2.0 for use with the 2.0 version of the .NET Common Language Runtime, along with some enhancements to the Windows operating system, as shown in Figure I.1.

One can install the .NET Framework 3.0 on Windows XP Service Pack 2, Windows Server 2003, and Windows Server 2003 R2. The runtime components are pre-installed on Windows Vista. On the successor to Windows Server 2003, which is code-named *Windows Server "Longhorn,"* one can add the .NET Framework 3.0 via the Server Configuration Wizard. Only a very small number of features of the .NET Framework 3.0 will be available exclusively on Windows Vista and later operating systems.

This book does not serve as an encyclopedic reference to the Windows Communication Foundation. Instead, it provides the understanding and knowledge required for most practical applications of the technology.

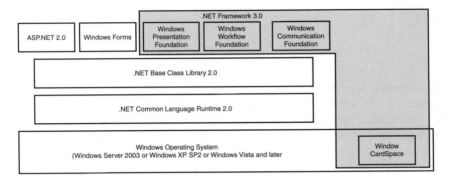

FIGURE I.1   The .NET Framework 3.0.

The book explains the Windows Communication Foundation while showing how to use it. So, typically, each chapter provides the precise steps for building a solution that demonstrates a particular aspect of the technology, along with a thorough explanation of each step. Readers who can program in C#, and who like to learn by doing, will be able to follow the steps. Those who prefer to just read will get a detailed account of the features of the Windows Communication Foundation and see how to use them.

To follow the steps in the chapters, one should have installed any version of Visual Studio 2005 that includes the C# compiler. Free copies are available at http://msdn.microsoft.com/vstudio/express/. One should also have IIS, ASP.NET, and MSMQ installed.

The .NET Framework 3.0 is also required, as one might expect. One can download it from http://www.microsoft.com/downloads/. The instructions in the chapters assume that all the runtime and developer components of the .NET Framework 3.0 have been installed. It is the runtime components that are preinstalled on Windows Vista, and which can be added via the Server Configuration Wizard on Windows Server "Longhorn." The developer components consist of a Software Development Kit (SDK) and two enhancements to Visual Studio 2005. The SDK provides documentation, some management tools, and a large number of very useful samples. The enhancements to Visual Studio augment the support provided by IntelliSense for editing configuration files, and provide a visual designer for Windows Workflow Foundation workflows.

To fully utilize Windows CardSpace, which is also covered in this book, one should install Internet Explorer 7. Internet Explorer 7 is also available from http://www.microsoft.com/downloads.

Starting points for the solutions built in each of the chapters are available for download from the book's companion page on the publishers' website, as well as from http://www.cryptmaker.com/WindowsCommunicationFoundationUnleashed. To ensure that Visual Studio does not complain about the sample code being from a location that is not fully trusted, one can, after due consideration, right-click the downloaded archive, choose Properties from the context menu, and click on the button labeled Unblock, shown in Figure I.2, before extracting the files from the archive.

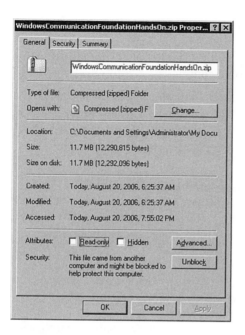

FIGURE I.2   Unblocking a downloaded source code archive.

Note that development on the Vista operating system will be supported for Visual Studio 2005 with an update that will ship after Service Pack 1. Developers working with an earlier version of Visual Studio 2005 on the Vista operating system should anticipate some compatibility issues. To minimize those issues, they can do two things. The first is to disable Vista's User Account Protection feature. The second is to always start Visual Studio 2005 by right-clicking on the executable or the shortcut, selecting Run As from the context menu that appears, and selecting the account of an administrator from the Run As dialog.

This book is considerably different from its predecessor, *Windows Communication Foundation Hands On!* Naturally, the text and samples are up to date with the object model of the final released version of the Windows Communication Foundation. There are also several new chapters, though.

Most significantly, there are two chapters dedicated to the Windows Workflow Foundation and to how to use it with the Windows Communication Foundation. The authors have found that the requirement to have the two technologies work together is commonplace, but know that accomplishing the feat is still quite challenging in the .NET Framework 3.0. Making it simple to do is an important objective only for the next release, which is currently referred to within Microsoft as the *.NET Framework 3.5*.

Whereas the earlier book had just one chapter on Windows CardSpace, this book sports two. Their author, Nigel, once described CardSpace in an internal email as *a sleeping giant of a technology*. It is sleeping because we find that it is the least well-known of the facilities included in .NET Framework 3.0. Yet it is a giant because it is not only the one technology of which consumers are most likely to become aware, but it is also the one that promises to have the most impact by tangibly improving most people's computing experience and further accelerating the growth of electronic commerce.

In terms of coverage of the Windows Communication Foundation itself, several new chapters have been added. Those chapters provide better coverage of the security features and the extensibility points, as well as offering a passel of recommendations for designing and building Windows Communication Foundation applications gleaned from the authors' work with early adopters.

Many people contributed to this book. The authors would like to thank Joe Long, Eric Zinda, Angela Mills, Omri Gazitt, Steve Swartz, Steve Millet, Mike Vernal, Doug Purdy, Eugene Osvetsky, Daniel Roth, Ford McKinstry, Craig McLuckie, Alex Weinert, Shy Cohen, Yasser Shohoud, Kenny Wolf, Anand Rajagopalan, Jim Johnson, Andy Milligan, Steve Maine, Ram Pamulapati, Ravi Rao, Mark Garbara, Andy Harjanto, T. R. Vishwanath, Doug Walter, Martin Gudgin, Marc Goodner, Giovanni Della-Libera, Kirill Gavrylyuk, Krish Srinivasan, Mark Fussell, Richard Turner, Ami Vora, Ari Bixhorn, Steve Cellini, Neil Hutson, Steve DiMarco, Gianpaolo Carraro, Steve Woodward, James Conard, Nigel Watling, Vittorio Bertocci, Blair Shaw, Jeffrey Schlimmer, Matt Tavis, Mauro Ottoviani, John Frederick, Mark Renfrow, Sean Dixon, Matt Purcell, Cheri Clark, Mauricio Ordonez, Neil Rowe, Donovan Follette, Pat Altimore, Tim Walton, Manu Puri, Ed Pinto, Erik Weiss, Suwat Chitphakdibodin, Govind Ramanathan, Ralph Squillace, John Steer, Brad Severtson, Gary Devendorf, Kavita Kamani, George Kremenliev, Somy Srinivasan, Natasha Jethanandani, Ramesh Seshadri, Lorenz Prem, Laurence Melloul, Clemens Vasters, Joval Lowy, John Justice, David Aiken, Larry Buerk, Wenlong Dong, Nicholas Allen, Carlos Figueira, Ram Poornalingam, Mohammed Makarechian, David Cliffe, David Okonak, Atanu Banerjee, Steven Metsker, Antonio Cruz, Steven Livingstone, Vadim Meleshuk, Elliot Waingold, Yann Christensen, Scott Mason, Jan Alexander, Johan Lindfors, Hanu Kommalapati, Steve Johnson, Tomas Restrepo, Tomasz Janczuk, Garrett Serack, Jeff Baxter, Arun Nanda, Luke Melton, and Al Lee.

A particular debt of gratitude is owed to John Lambert for reviewing the drafts. No one is better qualified to screen the text of a book on a programming technology than an experienced professional software tester. Any mistakes in the pages that follow are solely the fault of the writers, however.

The authors are especially grateful for the support of their wives. They are Marta MacNeill, Kathryn Mercuri, Sylvie Watling, and Libby Winkler. Matt, the only parent so far, would also like to thank his daughter, Grace.

PART I

Introducing the Windows Communication Foundation

IN THIS PART

Prerequisites

Introduction

To properly understand and work effectively with the Windows Communication Foundation, one should be familiar with certain facilities of the 2.0 versions of the .NET Framework and the .NET common language runtime. This chapter introduces them: partial types, generics, nullable value types, the Lightweight Transaction Manager, and Role Providers. The coverage of these features is not intended to be exhaustive, but merely sufficient to clarify their use in the chapters that follow.

Partial Types

Microsoft Visual C# 2005 allows the definition of a type to be composed from multiple partial definitions distributed across any number of source code files for the same module. That option is made available via the modifier partial, which can be added to the definition of a class, an interface, or a struct. Therefore, this part of the definition of a class

```
public partial MyClass
{
    private string myField = null;

    public string MyProperty
    {
        get
        {
```

```
            return this.myField;
        }
    }
}
```

and this other part

```
public partial MyClass
{
    public MyClass()
    {
    }

    public void MyMethod()
    {
        this.myField = "Modified by my method.";
    }
}
```

can together constitute the definition of the type MyClass. This example illustrates just one use for partial types, which is to organize the behavior of a class and its data into separate source code files.

Generics

"Generics are classes, structures, interfaces, and methods that have placeholders for one or more of the types they store or use" (Microsoft 2006). Here is an example of a generic class introduced in the System.Collections.Generic namespace of the .NET Framework 2.0 Class Library:

```
public class List<T>
```

Among the methods of that class is this one:

```
public Add(T item)
```

Here, T is the placeholder for the type that an instance of the generic class System.Collections.Generic.List<T> will store. In defining an instance of the generic class, one specifies the actual type that the instance will store:

```
List<string> myListOfStrings = new List<string>();
```

Then one can use the Add() method of the generic class instance like so:

```
myListOfStrings.Add("Hello, World");
```

Evidently, generics enabled the designer of the List<T> class to define a collection of instances of the same unspecified type; in other words, to provide the template for a type-safe collection. A user of List<*T*> can employ it to contain instances of a type of the user's choosing, without the designer of List<*T*> having to know which type the user might choose. Note as well that whereas a type that is derived from a base type is meant to derive some of the functionality it requires from the base, with the remainder still having to be programmed, List<*string*> comes fully equipped from List<*T*>.

The class, System.Collections.Generic.List<*T*>, is referred to as a *generic type definition*. The placeholder, *T*, is referred to as a *generic type parameter*. Declaring

List<string> myListOfStrings;

yields System.Collections.Generic.List<*string*> as a *constructed type*, and *string* as a *generic type argument*.

Generics can have any number of generic type parameters. For example, System.Collections.Generic.Dictionary<*TKey*,*TValue*> has two.

The designer of a generic may use constraints to restrict the types that can be used as generic type arguments. This generic type definition

public class MyGenericType<*T*> where *T*: new(), IComparable

constrains the generic type arguments to types with a public, parameter-less constructor that implements the IComparable interface. This less restrictive generic type definition

public class MyGenericType<*T*> where *T*: class

merely constrains generic type arguments to reference types.

Both generic and nongeneric types can have generic methods. Here is an example of a nongeneric type with a generic method:

```
using System;

public class Printer
{
    public void Print<T>(T argument)
    {
        Console.WriteLine(argument.ToString());
    }

    static void Main(string[] arguments)
    {
        Printer printer = new Printer();
        printer.Print<string>("Hello, World");
        Console.WriteLine("Done");
        Console.ReadKey();
    }
}
```

In programming a generic, it is often necessary to determine the type of generic argument that has been substituted for a generic type parameter. This revision to the preceding example shows how one can make that determination:

```
public class Printer
{
    public void Print<T>(T argument)
    {
        if(typeof(T) == typeof(string))
        {
            Console.WriteLine(argument);
        }
        else
        {
            Console.WriteLine(argument.ToString());
        }
    }

    static void Main(string[] arguments)
    {
        Printer printer = new Printer();
        printer.Print<string>("Hello, World");
        Console.WriteLine("Done");
        Console.ReadKey();
    }
}
```

A generic interface may be implemented by a generic type or a nongeneric type. Also, both generic and nongeneric types may inherit from generic base types.

```
public interface IMyGenericInterface<T>
{
    void MyMethod<T>();
}

public class MyGenericImplementation<T>: IMyGenericInterface<T>
{
    public void MyMethod<T>()
    {
    }
}

public class MyGenericDescendant<T> : MyGenericImplementation<T>
{
}

public class MyNonGenericImplementation : IMyGenericInterface<string>
{
```

```
    public void MyMethod<T>()
    {
    }
}

public class MyNonGenericDescendant : MyGenericImplementation<string>
{
}
```

Nullable Value Types

According to the Common Language Infrastructure specification, there are two ways of representing data in .NET: by a value type or by a reference type (Ecma 2006, 18). Although instances of value types are usually allocated on a thread's stack, instances of reference types are allocated from the managed heap, and their values are the addresses of the allocated memory (Richter 2002, 134–5).

Whereas the default value of a reference type variable is null, indicating that it has yet to be assigned the address of any allocated memory, a value type variable always has a value of the type in question and can never have the value null. Therefore, although one can determine whether a reference type has been initialized by checking whether its value is null, one cannot do the same for a value type.

However, there are two common circumstances in which one would like to know whether a value has been assigned to an instance of a value type. The first is when the instance represents a value in a database. In such a case, one would like to be able to examine the instance to ascertain whether a value is indeed present in the database. The other circumstance, which is more pertinent to the subject matter of this book, is when the instance represents a data item received from some remote source. Again, one would like to determine from the instance whether a value for that data item was received.

The .NET Framework 2.0 incorporates a generic type definition that provides for cases like these in which one wants to assign null to an instance of a value type, and test whether the value of the instance is null. That generic type definition is System.Nullable<T>, which constrains the generic type arguments that may be substituted for T to value types. Instances of types constructed from System.Nullable<T> can be assigned a value of null; indeed, their values are null by default. Thus, types constructed from System.Nullable<T> may be referred to as *nullable value types*.

System.Nullable<T> has a property, Value, by which the value assigned to an instance of a type constructed from it can be obtained if the value of the instance is not null. Therefore, one can write

```
System.Nullable<int> myNullableInteger = null;
myNullableInteger = 1;
if (myNullableInteger != null)
{
```

```
    Console.WriteLine(myNullableInteger.Value);
}
```

The C# programming language provides an abbreviated syntax for declaring types constructed from System.Nullable<*T*>. That syntax allows one to abbreviate

```
System.Nullable<int> myNullableInteger;
```

to

```
int? myNullableInteger;
```

The compiler will prevent one from attempting to assign the value of a nullable value type to an ordinary value type in this way:

```
int? myNullableInteger = null;
int myInteger = myNullableInteger;
```

It prevents one from doing so because the nullable value type could have the value null, which it actually would have in this case, and that value cannot be assigned to an ordinary value type. Although the compiler would permit this code,

```
int? myNullableInteger = null;
int myInteger = myNullableInteger.Value;
```

the second statement would cause an exception to be thrown because any attempt to access the System.Nullable<*T*>.Value property is an invalid operation if the type constructed from System.Nullable<*T*> has not been assigned a valid value of *T*, which has not happened in this case.

One proper way to assign the value of a nullable value type to an ordinary value type is to use the System.Nullable<*T*>.HasValue property to ascertain whether a valid value of *T* has been assigned to the nullable value type:

```
int? myNullableInteger = null;
if (myNullableInteger.HasValue)
{
    int myInteger = myNullableInteger.Value;
}
```

Another option is to use this syntax:

```
int? myNullableInteger = null;
int myInteger = myNullableInteger ?? -1;
```

by which the ordinary integer myInteger is assigned the value of the nullable integer myNullableInteger if the latter has been assigned a valid integer value; otherwise, myInteger is assigned the value of -1.

The Lightweight Transaction Manager

In computing, a transaction is a discrete activity—an activity that is completed in its entirety or not at all. A resource manager ensures that if a transaction is initiated on some resource, the resource is restored to its original state if the transaction is not fully completed. A distributed transaction is one that spans multiple resources and therefore involves more than a single resource manager. A manager for distributed transactions has been incorporated into Windows operating systems for many years. It is the *Microsoft Distributed Transaction Coordinator.*

.NET Framework versions 1.0 and 1.1 provided two ways of programming transactions. One way was provided by ADO.NET. That technology's abstract `System.Data.Common.DbConnection` class defined a `BeginTransaction()` method by which one could explicitly initiate a transaction controlled by the particular resource manager made accessible by the concrete implementation of `DbConnection`. The other way of programming a transaction was provided by Enterprise Services. It provided the `System.EnterpriseServices.Transaction` attribute that could be added to any subclass of `System.EnterpriseServices.ServicedComponent` to implicitly enlist any code executing in any of the class's methods into a transaction managed by the Microsoft Distributed Transaction Coordinator.

ADO.NET provided a way of programming transactions explicitly, whereas Enterprise Services allowed one to do it declaratively. However, in choosing between the explicit style of programming transactions offered by ADO.NET and the declarative style offered by Enterprise Services, one was also forced to choose how a transaction would be handled. With ADO.NET, transactions were handled by a single resource manager, whereas with Enterprise Services, a transaction incurred the overhead of involving the Microsoft Distributed Transaction Coordinator, regardless of whether the transaction was actually distributed.

.NET 2.0 introduced the Lightweight Transaction Manager, `System.Transactions.TransactionManager`. As its name implies, the Lightweight Transaction Manager has minimal overhead: "...[p]erformance benchmarking done by Microsoft with SQL Server 2005, comparing the use of a [Lightweight Transaction Manager transaction] to using a native transaction directly found no statistical differences between using the two methods" (Lowy 2005, 12). If only a single resource manager is enlisted in the transaction, the Lightweight Transaction Manager allows that resource manager to manage the transaction and the Lightweight Transaction Manager merely monitors it. However, if the Lightweight Transaction Manager detects that a second resource manager has become involved in the transaction, the Lightweight Transaction Manager has the original resource manager relinquish control of the transaction and transfers that control to the Distributed Transaction Coordinator. Transferring control of a transaction in progress to the Distributed Transaction Coordinator is referred to as *promotion of the transaction.*

The System.Transactions namespace allows one to program transactions using the Lightweight Transaction Manager either explicitly or implicitly. The explicit style uses the System.Transactions.CommitableTransaction class:

```
CommitableTransaction transaction = new CommittableTransaction();
using(SqlConnection myConnection = new SqlConnection(myConnectionString))
{
        myConnection.Open();

        myConnection.EnlistTransaction(tx);

        //Do transactional work

        //Commit the transaction:
        transaction.Close();

}
```

The alternative, implicit style of programming, which is preferable because it is more flexible, uses the System.Transactions.TransactionScope class:

```
using(TransactionScope scope = new TransactionScope)
{
        //Do transactional work:
        //...
        //Since no errors have occurred, commit the transaction:
        scope.Complete();
}
```

This style of programming a transaction is implicit because code that executes within the using block of the System.Transactions.TransactionScope instance is implicitly enrolled in a transaction. The Complete() method of a System.Transactions.TransactionScope instance can be called exactly once, and if it is called, then the transaction will commit.

The System.Transactions namespace also provides a means for programming one's own resource managers. However, knowing the purpose of the Lightweight Transaction Manager and the implicit style of transaction programming provided with the System.Transactions.TransactionScope class will suffice for the purpose of learning about the Windows Communication Foundation.

Role Providers

Role Providers are classes that derive from the abstract class System.Web.Security. RoleProvider. That class has the interface shown in Listing 1.1. Evidently, it defines ten simple methods for managing roles, including ascertaining whether a given user has been assigned a particular role. Role Providers, in implementing those abstract methods, will read and write a particular store of role information. For example, one of the concrete implementations of System.Web.Security.RoleProvider included in the .NET Framework 2.0 is System.Web.Security.AuthorizationStoreRoleProvider, which uses an Authorization Manager Authorization Store as its repository of role information. Another concrete implementation, System.Web.Security.SqlRoleProvider, uses a SQL Server database as its store. However, because the System.Web.Security.RoleProvider has such a simple set of methods for managing roles, if none of the Role Providers included in the .NET Framework 2.0 is suitable, one can readily provide one's own implementation to use whatever store of role information one prefers. Role Providers hide the details of how role data is stored behind a simple, standard interface for querying and updating that information. Although System.Web.Security.RoleProvider is included in the System.Web namespaces of ASP.NET, Role Providers can be used in any .NET 2.0 application.

LISTING 1.1   System.Web.Security.RoleProvider

```
public abstract class RoleProvider : ProviderBase
{
    protected RoleProvider();

    public abstract string ApplicationName { get; set; }

    public abstract void AddUsersToRoles(
                string[] usernames, string[] roleNames);
    public abstract void CreateRole(
                string roleName);
    public abstract bool DeleteRole(
                string roleName, bool throwOnPopulatedRole);
    public abstract string[] FindUsersInRole(
                string roleName, string usernameToMatch);
    public abstract string[] GetAllRoles();
    public abstract string[] GetRolesForUser(
                string username);
    public abstract string[] GetUsersInRole(
                string roleName);
    public abstract bool IsUserInRole(
                string username, string roleName);
    public abstract void RemoveUsersFromRoles(
                string[] usernames, string[] roleNames);
    public abstract bool RoleExists(string roleName);
}
```

The static class, System.Web.Security.Roles, provides yet another layer of encapsulation for role management. Consider this code snippet:

```
if (!Roles.IsUserInRole(userName, "Administrator"))
{
  [...]
}
```

Here, the static `System.Web.Security.Roles` class is used to inquire whether a given user has been assigned to the Administrator role. What is interesting about this snippet is that the inquiry is made without an instance of a particular Role Provider having to be created first. The static `System.Web.Security.Roles` class hides the interaction with the Role Provider. The Role Provider it uses is whichever one is specified as being the default in the configuration of the application. Listing 1.2 is a sample configuration that identifies the role provider named MyRoleProvider, which is an instance of the `System.Web.Security.AuthorizationStoreRoleProvider` class, as the default role provider.

LISTING 1.2   Role Provider Configuration

```
<configuration>
  <connectionStrings>
    <add name="AuthorizationServices"
    `connectionString="msxml://~\App_Data\SampleStore.xml" />
  </connectionStrings>
  <system.web>
    <roleManager defaultProvider="MyRoleProvider"
      enabled="true"
      cacheRolesInCookie="true"
      cookieName=".ASPROLES"
      cookieTimeout="30"
      cookiePath="/"
      cookieRequireSSL="false"
      cookieSlidingExpiration="true"
      cookieProtection="All" >
      <providers>
        <clear />
          <add
            name="MyRoleProvider"
            type="System.Web.Security.AuthorizationStoreRoleProvider"
            connectionStringName="AuthorizationServices"
            applicationName="SampleApplication"
            cacheRefreshInterval="60"
            scopeName="" />
      </providers>
    </roleManager>
  </system.web>
</configuration>
```

Summary

This chapter introduced some programming tools that were new in .NET 2.0 and that are prerequisites for understanding and working effectively with the Windows Communication Foundation:

- The new `partial` keyword in C# allows the definitions of types to be composed from any number of parts distributed across the source code files of a single module.

- Generics are templates from which any number of fully preprogrammed classes can be created.

- Nullable value types are value types that can be assigned a value of `null` and checked for `null` values.

- The Lightweight Transaction Manager ensures that transactions are managed as efficiently as possible. An elegant new syntax has been provided for using it.

- Role Providers implement a simple, standard interface for managing the roles to which users are assigned that is independent of how the role information is stored.

References

Ecma International. 2006. *ECMA-335: Common Language Infrastructure (CLI) Partitions I–VI.* Geneva: Ecma.

Lowy, Juval. *Introducing System.Transactions.* http://www.microsoft.com/downloads/details.aspx?familyid=aac3d722-444c-4e27-8b2e-c6157ed16b15&displaylang=en. Accessed August 20, 2006.

Microsoft 2006. *Overview of Generics in the .NET Framework.* http://msdn2.microsoft.com/en-us/library/ms172193.aspx. Accessed August 20, 2006.

Richter, Jeffrey. 2002. *Applied Microsoft .NET Framework Programming.* Redmond, WA: Microsoft Press.

The Fundamentals

Background

Dealing with something as an integrated whole is self-evidently easier than having to understand and manipulate all of its parts. Thus, to make programming easier, it is commonplace to define classes that serve as integrated wholes, keeping their constituents hidden. Doing so is called *encapsulation*, which is characteristic of what is known as *object-oriented programming*.

The C++ programming language provided syntax for encapsulation that proved very popular. In C++, one can write a class like this one:

```
class Stock
{
private:
    char symbol[30];
    int number;
    double price;
    double value;
    void SetTotal()
    {
        this->value = this->number * this->price;
    }
public:
    Stock(void);
    ~Stock(void);
    void Acquire(const char* symbol, int number, double
price);
    void Sell(int number, double price);
};
```

The class hides away its data members—symbol, number, price, and value—as well as the method SetTotal(), but exposes the methods Acquire() and Sell() for use.

Some refer to the exposed surface of a class as its *interface,* and to invocations of the methods of a class as *messages.* David A. Taylor does so in his book *Object-Oriented Information Systems: Planning and Integration* (1992, 118).

Using C++ classes to define interfaces and messages has an important shortcoming, however, as Don Box explains in *Essential COM* (1998, 11). There is no standard way for C++ compilers to express the interfaces in binary format. Consequently, sending a message to a class in a dynamic link library (DLL) is not guaranteed to work if the calling code and the intended recipient class were built using different compilers.

That shortcoming is significant because it restricts the extent to which the class in the DLL can be reused in code written by other programmers. The reuse of code written by one programmer within code written by another is fundamental not only to programming productivity, but also to software as a commercial enterprise, to being able to sell what a programmer produces.

Two important solutions to the problem were pursued. One was to define interfaces using C++ abstract base classes. An *abstract base class* is a class with pure virtual functions, and, as Box explained, "[t]he runtime implementation of virtual functions in C++ takes the [same] form[...]in virtually all production compilers" (1998, 15). You can write, in C++, the code given in Listing 2.1.

LISTING 2.1   Abstract Base Class

```
//IStock.h
class IStock
{
public:
    virtual void DeleteInstance(void);
    virtual void Acquire(const char* symbol, int number, double price) = 0;
  virtual void Sell(int number, double price) = 0;
};

extern "C"
IStock* CreateStock(void);

//Stock.h
#include "IStock.h"

class Stock: public IStock
{
private:
  char symbol[30];
  int number;
  double price;
  double value;
  void SetTotal()
  {
```

LISTING 2.1   Continued

```
        this->value = this->number * this->price;
    }
public:
    Stock(void);
    ~Stock(void);
    void DeleteInstance(void);
    void Acquire(const char* symbol, int number, double price);
    void Sell(int number, double price);
};
```

In that code, IStock is an interface defined using a C++ abstract virtual class. IStock is an abstract virtual class because it has the pure virtual functions Acquire() and Sell(), their nature as pure virtual functions being denoted by having both the keyword, virtual, and the suffix, = 0, in their declarations. A programmer wanting to use a class with the IStock interface within a DLL can write code that retrieves an instance of such a class from the DLL using the global function CreateStock() and sends messages to that instance. That code will work even if the programmer is using a different compiler than the one used by the programmer of the DLL.

Programming with interfaces defined as C++ abstract virtual classes is the foundation of a Microsoft technology called the *Component Object Model*, or *COM*. More generally, it is the foundation of what became known as *component-oriented programming*.

Component-oriented programming is a style of software reuse in which the interface of the reusable class consists of constructors, property getter and setter methods, methods, and events. Programmers using the class "…follow[] a pattern of instantiating a type with a default or relatively simple constructor, setting some instance properties, and finally, [either] calling simple instance methods" or handling the instance's events (Cwalina and Abrams 2006, 237).

Another important solution to the problem of there being no standard way for C++ compilers to express the interfaces of classes in binary format is to define a standard for the output of compilers. The Java Virtual Machine Specification defines a standard format for the output of compilers, called the *class file format* (Lindholm and Yellin 1997, 61). Files in that format can be translated into the instructions specific to a particular computer processor by a Java Virtual Machine. One programmer can provide a class in the class file format to another programmer who will be able to instantiate that class and send messages to it using any compiler and Java Virtual Machine compliant with the Java Virtual Machine Specification.

Similarly, the Common Language Infrastructure Specification defines the Common Intermediate Language as a standard format for the output of compilers (ECMA International 2005). Files in that format can be translated into instructions to a particular computer processor by Microsoft's Common Language Runtime, which is the core of Microsoft's .NET technology, as well as by Mono.

Despite these ways of making classes written by one programmer reusable by others, the business of software was still restricted. The use of COM and .NET is widespread, as is the use of Java, and software developed using Java cannot be used together easily with software developed using COM or .NET. More importantly, the component-oriented style of software reuse that became prevalent after the introduction of COM, and which was also widely used by Java and .NET programmers, is grossly inefficient when the instance of the class that is being reused is remote, perhaps on another machine, or even just in a different process. It is so inefficient because, in that scenario, each operation of instantiating the object, of assigning values to its properties, and of calling its methods or handling its events, requires communication back and forth across process boundaries, and possibly also over the network.

> "Since [the two separate processes] each have their own memory space, they have to copy the data [transmitted between them] from one memory space to the other. The data is usually transmitted as a byte stream, the most basic form of data. This means that the first process must marshal the data into byte form, and then copy it from the first process to the second one; the second process must unmarshal the data back into its original form, such that the second process then has a copy of the original data in the first process." (Hohpe and Woolf 2004, 66).

Besides the extra work involved in marshalling data across the process boundaries,

> "...security may need to be checked, packets may need to be routed through switches. If the two processes are running on machines on opposite sides of the globe, the speed of light may be a factor. The brutal truth is that that any inter-process call is orders of magnitude more expensive than an in-process call—even if both processes are on the same machine. Such a performance effect cannot be ignored." (Fowler 2003, 388).

The Web Services Description Language (WSDL) provided a general solution to the first restriction, the problem of using software developed using Java together with software developed using COM or .NET. WSDL provides a way of defining software interfaces using the Extensible Markup Language (XML), a format that is exceptionally widely adopted, and for which processors are readily available. Classes that implement WSDL interfaces are generally referred to as *services*.

Concomitantly, an alternative to component-oriented programming that is suitable for the reuse of remote instances of classes became progressively more common in practice, although writers seem to have had a remarkably difficult time formalizing its tenets. Thomas Erl, for instance, published two vast books ostensibly on the subject, but never managed to provide a noncircuitous definition of the approach in either of them (Erl 2004, 2005). That alternative to component-oriented programming is service-oriented programming.

Service-oriented programming is a style of software reuse in which the reusable classes are services—classes that implement WSDL interfaces—and the services are designed so as to minimize the number of calls to be made to them, by packaging the data to be transmitted back and forth into messages. A message is a particular kind of data transfer object. A *data transfer object* is

> "…little more than a bunch of fields and the getters and setters for them. The value of [this type of object] is that it allows you to move several pieces of information over a network in a single call—a trick that's essential for distributed systems. […] Other than simple getters and setters, the data transfer object is […] responsible for serializing itself into some format that will go over the wire." (Fowler 2003, 401—403).

Messages are data transfer objects that consist of two parts: a header that provides information pertinent to the operation of transmitting the data and a body that contains the actual data to be transmitted. Crucially, the objects into which the content of a message is read on the receiving side are never assumed to be of the same type as the objects from which the content of the message was written on the sending side. Hence, the sender and the receiver of a message do not have to share the same types, and are said to be *loosely coupled* by their shared knowledge of the format of the message, rather than *tightly coupled* by their shared knowledge of the same types (Box 2004). By virtue of being loosely coupled, the sender and the receiver of the message can evolve independently of one another.

A definition of the term *service-oriented architecture* is warranted here for the sake of disambiguation. *Service-oriented architecture* is an approach to organizing the software of an enterprise by providing service facades for all of that software, and publishing the WSDL for those services in a central repository. The repository is typically a Universal Description Discovery and Integration (UDDI) registry. Having interfaces to all the software of an enterprise expressed in a standard format and catalogued in a central repository is desirable because then, in theory, its availability for reuse can be known. Also, policies defining requirements, capabilities, and sundry other properties of a service can be associated with the service using WSDL or by making suitable entries in the registry. That fact leads enterprise architects to anticipate the prospect of the registry serving as a central point of control through which they could issue decrees about how every software entity in their organization is to function by associating policies with the services that provide facades for all of their other software resources. Furthermore, measurements of the performance of the services can be published in the registry, too, so the registry could also serve as a monitoring locus.

Note that *service-oriented architecture* does not refer to the process of designing software that is to be composed from parts developed using service-oriented programming. There are at least two reasons why not. The first is simply because that is not how the term is actually used, and Ludwig Wittgenstein established in his *Philosophical Investigations* that the meaning of terms is indeed determined by how they are customarily used by a community (Wittgenstein 1958, 93). The second reason is that the community really could not use the term to refer to a process of designing software composed from parts developed using service-oriented programming because the process of doing that is in no way distinct from the process of designing software composed using parts developed in some other fashion. More precisely, the correct patterns to choose as guides in designing the solution would be the same regardless of whether or not the parts of the solution were developed using service-oriented programming.

Now, Microsoft provided support for service-oriented programming to COM programmers with the Microsoft SOAP Toolkit, and to .NET programmers with the classes in the System.Web.Services namespace of the .NET Framework Class Library. Additions to the latter were provided by the Web Services Enhancements for Microsoft .NET. Java programmers can use Apache Axis for service-oriented programming.

Yet service-oriented programming has been limited by the lack of standard ways of securing message transmissions, handling failures, and coordinating transactions. Standards have now been developed, and the Windows Communication Foundation provides implementations thereof.

So, the Windows Communication Foundation delivers a more complete infrastructure for service-oriented programming than was available to .NET software developers. Providing that infrastructure is important because service-oriented programming transcends limits on the reuse of software between Java programmers and COM and .NET programmers that had been hampering the software business.

Today, even with the Windows Communication Foundation, service-oriented programming is still suitable only for interactions with remote objects, just as component-oriented programming is suitable only for interacting with local objects. A future goal for the team that developed the Windows Communication Foundation is to extend the technology to allow the service-oriented style of programming to be equally efficient for both scenarios.

Even so, to understand the Windows Communication Foundation as merely being Microsoft's once and future infrastructure for service-oriented programming severely underestimates its significance. The Windows Communication Foundation provides something far more useful than just another way of doing service-oriented programming. It provides a software factory template for software communication.

The concept of software factory templates is introduced by Jack Greenfield and Keith Short in their book *Software Factories: Assembling Applications with Patterns, Models, Frameworks, and Tools* (Greenfield and others 2004). It provides a new approach to model-driven software development.

The notion of model-driven software development has been popular for many years. It is the vision of being able to construct a model of a software solution from which the software itself can be generated after the model has been scrutinized to ensure that it covers all the functional and nonfunctional requirements. That vision has been pursued using general-purpose modeling languages, the Unified Modeling Language (UML) in particular.

A serious shortcoming in using general-purpose modeling languages for model-driven software development is that general-purpose modeling languages are inherently imprecise. They cannot represent the fine details of requirements that can be expressed in a natural language such as English. They also are not sufficiently precise to cover things such as memory management, thread synchronization, auditing, and exception management. If they were, they would be programming languages, rather than general-purpose modeling languages, yet memory management, thread synchronization, auditing, and exception management are precisely the sorts of things that bedevil programmers.

Greenfield and Short argue that progress in model-driven development depends on eschewing general-purpose modeling languages in favor of *domain-specific languages*, or DSLs. A DSL models the concepts found in a specific domain. DSLs should be used in conjunction with a corresponding class framework, a set of classes specifically designed to cover the same domain. Then, if the DSL is used to model particular ways in which those classes can be used, it should be possible to generate the software described in the model from the class framework (Greenfield and others 2004, 144).

The combination of a DSL and a corresponding class framework constitute the core of a software factory template (Greenfield and others 2004, 173). Software factory templates serve as the software production assets of a software factory from which many varieties of the same software product can be readily fabricated.

A fine example of a software factory template is the Windows Forms Designer in Microsoft Visual Studio .NET and subsequent versions of Microsoft Visual Studio. In that particular case, the Windows Forms Designer is the DSL, the Toolbox and Property Editor being among the terms of the language, and the classes in the `System.Windows.Forms` namespace of the .NET Framework Class Library constitute the class framework. Users of the Windows Forms Designer use it to model software that is generated from those classes.

Programmers have been using the Windows Forms Designer and tools like it in other integrated development environments for many years to develop software user interfaces. So, Greenfield and Short, in introducing the concept of software factory templates, are not proposing a new approach. Rather, they are formalizing one that has already proven to be very successful, and suggesting that it be used to develop other varieties of software besides user interfaces.

The Windows Communication Foundation is a software factory template for software communication. It consists of a DSL, called the *Service Model*, and a class framework, called the *Channel Layer*. The Service Model consists of the classes of the `System.ServiceModel` namespace, and an XML configuration language. The Channel Layer consists of the classes in the `System.ServiceModel.Channel` namespace. Developers model how a piece of software is to communicate using the Service Model, and the communication components they need to have included in their software are generated from the Channel Layer, in accordance with their model. Later, if they need to change or supplement how their software communicates, they make alterations to their model, and the modifications or additions to their software are generated. If they want to model a form of communication that is not already supported by the Channel Layer, they can build or buy a suitable channel to add to the Channel Layer, and proceed to generate their software as usual, just as a user of the Windows Forms Designer can build or buy controls to add to the Windows Forms Designer's Toolbox.

That the Windows Communication Foundation provides a complete infrastructure for service-oriented programming is very nice because sometimes programmers do need to do that kind of programming, and service-oriented programming will likely remain popular for a while. However, software developers are always trying to get pieces of software to communicate, and they always will need to do that because software is reused by sending and receiving data, and the business of software depends on software reuse. So, the fact that the Windows Communication Foundation provides a software factory template for generating, modifying, and supplementing software communication facilities from a model is truly significant.

The Service Model

The key terms in the language of the Windows Communication Foundation Service Model correspond closely to the key terms of WSDL. In WSDL, a piece of software that can respond to communications over a network is called a *service*. A service is described in an XML document with three primary sections:

▶ The service section indicates where the service is located.

▶ The binding section specifies which of various standard communication protocols the service understands.

▶ The third primary section, the portType section, lists all the operations that the service can perform by defining the messages that it will emit in response to messages it receives.

Thus, the three primary sections of a WSDL document tell you where a service is located, how to communicate with it, and what it will do.

Those three things are exactly what you specify in using the Windows Communication Foundation Service Model to model a service: where it is, how to communicate with it, and what it will do. Instead of calling those things *service*, *binding*, and *portType*, as they are called in the WSDL specification, they are named *address*, *binding*, and *contract* in the Windows Communication Foundation Service Model. Consequently, the handy abbreviation *a*, *b*, c can serve as a reminder of the key terms of the Windows Communication Foundation Service Model and, thereby, as a reminder of the steps to follow in using it to enable a piece of software to communicate.

More precisely, in the Windows Communication Foundation Service Model, a piece of software that responds to communications is a service. A service has one or more endpoints to which communications can be directed. An endpoint consists of an address, a binding, and a contract. How a service handles communications internally, behind the external surface defined by its endpoints, is determined by a family of control points called *behaviors*.

This chapter explains, in detail, how to use the Windows Communication Foundation Service Model to enable a piece of software to communicate. Lest the details provided obscure how simple this task is to accomplish, here is an overview of the steps involved.

A programmer begins by defining the contract. That simple task is begun by writing an interface in a .NET programming language:

```
public interface IEcho
{
    string Echo(string input);
}
```

It is completed by adding attributes from the Service Model that designate the interface as a Windows Communication Foundation contract, and one or more of its methods as being included in the contract:

```
[ServiceContract]
public interface IEcho
{
    [OperationContract]
    string Echo(string input);
}
```

The next step is to implement the contract, which is done simply by writing a class that implements the interface:

```
public class Service : IEcho
{
    public string Echo(string input)
    {
        return input;
    }
}
```

A class that implements an interface that is designated as a Windows Communication Foundation contract is called a *service type*. How the Windows Communication Foundation conveys data that has been received from the outside via an endpoint to the service type can be controlled by adding behaviors to the service type definition using the ServiceBehavior attribute:

```
[ServiceBehavior(ConcurrencyMode=ConcurrencyMode.Multiple)]
public class Service : IEcho
{
    public string Echo(string input)
    {
        return input;
    }
}
```

For example, the concurrency mode behavior attribute controls whether the Windows Communication Foundation can convey data to the service type on more than one concurrent thread. This behavior is set via an attribute because it is one that a programmer, as opposed to an administrator, should control. After all, it is the programmer of the service type who would know whether the service type is programmed in such a way as to accommodate concurrent access by multiple threads.

The final step for the programmer is to provide for hosting the service within an application domain. IIS can provide an application domain for hosting the service, and so can any .NET application. Hosting the service within an arbitrary .NET application is easily accomplished using the ServiceHost class provided by the Windows Communication Foundation Service Model:

```
using (ServiceHost host = new ServiceHost(typeof(Service))
{
    host.Open();

    Console.WriteLine("The service is ready.");
    Console.ReadKey(true);

    host.Close();
}
```

Now the administrator takes over. The administrator defines an endpoint for the service type by associating an address and a binding with the Windows Communication Foundation contracts that the service type implements. An editing tool, called the *Service Configuration Editor,* shown in Figure 2.1, that also includes wizards, is provided for that purpose.

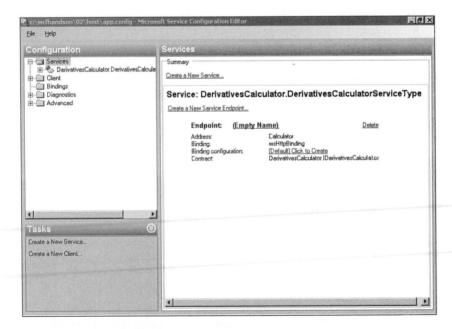

FIGURE 2.1   Defining an address and a binding.

Whereas the programmer could use attributes to modify the behaviors that a programmer should control, the administrator, as shown in Figure 2.2, can use the Service Configuration Editor to modify the behaviors that are properly within an administrator's purview. All output from the tool takes the form of a .NET application configuration file.

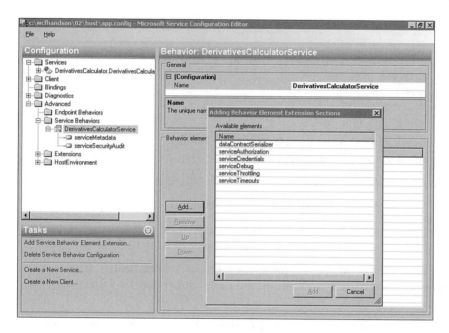

FIGURE 2.2   Adding behaviors to a service.

Now that the address, binding, and contract of an endpoint have been defined, the contract has been implemented, and a host for the service has been provided, the service can be made available for use. The administrator executes the host application. The Windows Communication Foundation examines the address, binding, and contract of the endpoint that have been specified in the language of the Service Model, as well as the behaviors, and generates the necessary components by which the service can receive and respond to communications from the Channel Layer.

One of the behaviors that the administrator can control is whether the service exposes WSDL to describe its endpoints for the outside world. If the administrator configures the service to do so, the Windows Communication Foundation will automatically generate the WSDL and offer it up in response to requests for it. A programmer developing an application to communicate with the service can download the WSDL, and generate code for exchanging data with the service, as well as an application configuration file with the endpoint information. That can be done with a single command

```
svcutil http://localhost:8000/EchoService?wsdl
```

wherein svcutil is the name of the Windows Communication Foundation's Service Model Metadata Tool, and http://localhost:8000/EchoService?wsdl is the address from which the metadata of a service can be downloaded. Having employed the tool to produce the necessary code and configuration, the programmer can proceed to use them to communicate with the service:

```
using(EchoProxy echoProxy = new EchoProxy())
{
  echoProxy.Open();

  string response = echoProxy.Echo("Hello, World!");

  echoProxy.Close();
}
```

The preceding steps are all that is involved in using the Windows Communication Foundation. In summary, those simple steps are merely these:

1. The service programmer defines a contract using a .NET interface.

2. The service programmer implements that interface in a class, a service type.

3. The service programmer optionally modifies Windows Communication Foundation behaviors by applying attributes to the service type or to its methods.

4. The service programmer makes provisions for the service to be hosted. If the service is to be hosted within a .NET application, the programmer develops that application.

5. The service administrator uses the Service Configuration Editor to configure the service's endpoints by associating addresses and bindings with the contracts implemented by the service type.

6. The service administrator optionally uses the Service Configuration Editor to modify Windows Communication Foundation behaviors.

7. The programmer of a client application uses the Service Model Metadata Tool to download WSDL describing the service and to generate code and a configuration file for communicating with the service.

8. The programmer of the client application uses generated code and configuration to exchange data with the service.

At last, the promise of model-driven development might have actually yielded something tangible: a software factory template by which the communications system of an application can be manufactured from a model. The value of using this technology is at least threefold.

First, developers can use the same simple modeling language provided by the Service Model to develop solutions to all kinds of software communications problems. Until now, a .NET developer would typically use .NET web services to exchange data between a .NET application and a Java application, but use .NET Remoting for communication between two .NET applications, and the classes of the `System.Messaging` namespace to transmit data via a queue. The Windows Communication Foundation provides developers with a single, easy-to-use solution that works well for all of those scenarios. Because, as will be shown in Part V, "Extending the Windows Communication Foundation," the variety of bindings and behaviors supported by the Windows Communication Foundation is indefinitely extensible, the technology will also work as a solution for any other software communication problem that is likely to occur. Consequently, the cost and risk involved in developing solutions to software communications problems decreases because rather than expertise in a different specialized technology being required for each case, the developers' skill in using the Windows Communication Foundation is reusable in all of them.

Second, in many cases, the administrator is able to modify how the service communicates simply by modifying the binding, without the code having to be changed, and the administrator is thereby able to make the service communicate in a great variety of significantly different ways. The administrator can choose, for instance, to have the same service communicate with clients on the internal network they all share in a manner that is optimal for those clients, and can also have it communicate with Internet clients in a different manner that is suitable for them. When the service's host executes again after any modifications the administrator has made to the binding, the Windows Communication Foundation generates the communications infrastructure for the new or modified endpoints. Thus, investments in software built using the Windows Communications Foundation yield increased returns by being adaptable to a variety of scenarios.

Third, as will be shown in Part VII, "The Lifecycle of Windows Communication Foundation Applications," the Windows Communication Foundation provides a variety of powerful tools for managing applications built using the technology. Those tools reduce the cost of operations by saving the cost of having to develop custom management solutions, and by reducing the risk, frequency, duration, and cost of downtime.

The foregoing provides a brief overview of working with the Windows Communication Foundation Service Model. Read on for a much more detailed, step-by-step examination. That account starts right from the beginning, with building some software with which one might like other software to be able to communicate. To be precise, it starts with developing some software to calculate the value of derivatives.

A Software Resource

A *derivative* is a financial entity whose value is derived from that of another. Here is an example. The value of a single share of Microsoft Corporation stock was $24.41 on October 11, 2005. Given that value, one might offer for sale an option to buy 1,000 of those shares, for $25 each, one month later, on November 11, 2005. Such an option, which is known as a *call*, might be purchased by someone who anticipates that the price of the shares will rise above $25 by November 11, 2005, and sold by someone who anticipates that the price of the shares will drop. The call is a derivative, its value being derived from the value of Microsoft Corporation stock.

Pricing a derivative is a complex task. Indeed, estimating the value of derivatives is perhaps the most high-profile problem in modern microeconomics.

In the foregoing example, clearly the quantity of the stock and the current and past prices of the Microsoft Corporation stock are factors to consider. But other factors might be based on analyses of the values of quantities that are thought to affect the prices of the stock, such as the values of various stock market indices, or the interest rate of the U.S. Federal Reserve Bank. In fact, one can say that, in general, the price of a derivative is some function of one or more quantities, one or more market values, and the outcome of one or more quantitative analytical functions.

Although actually writing software to calculate the value of derivatives is beyond the scope of this book, one can pretend to do so by following these steps:

1. Open Microsoft Visual Studio 2005, choose File, New, Project from the menus, and create a new blank solution called DerivativesCalculatorSolution in the folder C:\WCFHandsOn\Fundamentals, as shown in Figure 2.3.

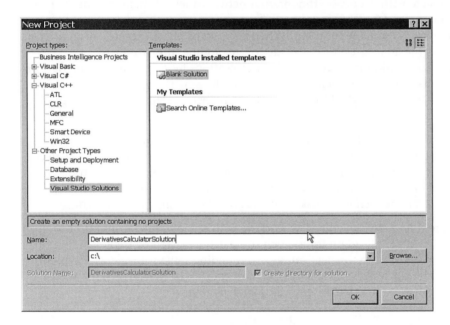

FIGURE 2.3   Creating a blank Visual Studio solution.

2. Choose File, New, Project again, and add a C# Class Library project called DerivativesCalculator to the solution, as shown in Figure 2.4.

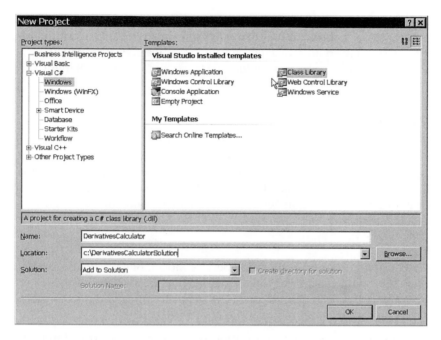

FIGURE 2.4   Adding a Class Library project to the solution.

3. Rename the class file Class1.cs in the DerivativesCalculator project to
   Calculator.cs, and modify its content to look like this:

```
using System;
using System.Collections.Generic;
using System.Text;

namespace DerivativesCalculator
{
    public class Calculator
    {
        public decimal CalculateDerivative(
string[] symbols,
decimal[] parameters,
string[] functions)
        {
            //Pretend to calculate the value of a derivative.
            return (decimal)(System.DateTime.Now.Millisecond);
        }
    }
}
```

This simple C# class purports to calculate the value of derivatives, and will serve to represent a piece of software with which one might like other software to be able to communicate. Certainly, if the class really could calculate the value of derivatives, its capabilities would be in extraordinary demand, and one could quickly earn a fortune by charging for access to it.

Building a Service for Accessing the Resource

To allow other software to communicate with the class, one can use the Windows Communication Foundation Service Model to add communication facilities to it. One does so by building a Windows Communication Foundation service with an endpoint for accessing the facilities of the derivatives calculator class. Recall that, in the language of the Windows Communication Foundation Service Model, an endpoint consists of an address, a binding, and a contract.

Defining the Contract

In using the Windows Communication Foundation Service Model, one usually begins by defining the contract. The contract specifies the operations that are available at the endpoint. After the contract has been defined, the next step is to implement the contract, to actually provide the operations it defines.

Defining and implementing Windows Communication Foundation contracts is simple. To define a contract, one merely writes an interface in one's favorite .NET programming language, and adds attributes to it to indicate that the interface is also a Windows Communication Foundation contract. Then, to implement the contract, one simply programs a class that implements the .NET interface that one has defined:

1. Choose File, New, Project from the Visual Studio 2005 menus again, and add another C# Class Library project to the solution, called DerivativesCalculatorService.

2. Rename the class file `Class1.cs` in the DerivativesCalculatorService project to `IDerivativesCalculator`.

3. Modify the contents of the `IDerivatesCalculator.cs` file to look like so:

```csharp
using System;
using System.Collections.Generic;
using System.Text;

namespace DerivativesCalculator
{
    public interface IDerivativesCalculator
    {
        decimal CalculateDerivative(
            string[] symbols,
            decimal[] parameters,
            string[] functions);
```

```
        void DoNothing();
    }
}
```

IDerivativesCalculator is an ordinary C# interface, with two methods,
CalculateDerivative() and DoNothing(). Now it will be made into a Windows
Communication Foundation contract.

4. Choose Project, Add Reference from the Visual Studio 2005 menus. Select
   System.ServiceModel from the assemblies listed on the .NET tab of the Add
   Reference dialog that appears, as shown in Figure 2.5, and click on the OK button.
   System.ServiceModel is the most important of the new .NET class libraries included
   in the Windows Communication Foundation.

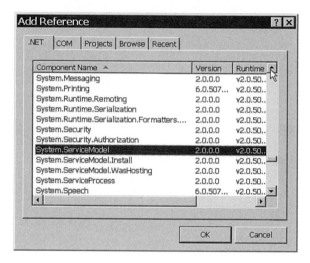

FIGURE 2.5   Adding a reference to the System.ServiceModel assembly.

5. Modify the IDerivativesCalculator interface in the IDerivativesCalculator.cs
   module to import the classes in the System.ServiceModel namespace that is incorporated in the System.ServiceModel assembly:

```
using System;
using System.Collections.Generic;
using System.ServiceModel;
using System.Text;

namespace DerivativesCalculator
{
    public interface IDerivativesCalculator
    {
```

```
            decimal CalculateDerivative(
                string[] symbols,
                decimal[] parameters,
                string[] functions);

        void DoNothing();
        }
    }
```

6. Now designate the `IDerivativesCalculator` interface as a Windows Communication Foundation contract by adding the `ServiceContract` attribute that is included in the `System.ServiceModel` namespace:

```
using System;
using System.Collections.Generic;
using System.ServiceModel;
using System.Text;

namespace DerivativesCalculator
{
    [ServiceContract]
    public interface IDerivativesCalculator
    {
        decimal CalculateDerivative(
            string[] symbols,
            decimal[] parameters,
            string[] functions);

        void DoNothing();
    }
}
```

7. Use the `OperationContract` attribute to designate the `CalculateDerivative()` method of the `IDerivativesCalculator` interface as one of the methods of the interface that is to be included as an operation in the Windows Communication Foundation contract:

```
using System;
using System.Collections.Generic;
using System.ServiceModel;
using System.Text;

namespace DerivativesCalculator
{
    [ServiceContract]
    public interface IDerivativesCalculator
    {
```

```
[OperationContract]
decimal CalculateDerivative(
    string[] symbols,
    decimal[] parameters,
    string[] functions);

    void DoNothing();
  }
}
```

By default, the namespace and name of a Windows Communication Foundation contract are the namespace and name of the interface to which the ServiceContract attribute is added. Also, the name of an operation included in a Windows Communication Foundation contract is the name of the method to which the OperationContract attribute is added. You can alter the default name of a contract using the Namespace and Name parameters of the ServiceContract attribute, as in

```
[ServiceContract(Namespace="MyNamespace",Name="MyContract")]
public interface IMyInterface
```

You can alter the default name of an operation with the Name parameter of the OperationContract attribute:

```
[OperationContract(Name="MyOperation")]
string MyMethod();
```

8. Returning to the derivatives calculator solution in Visual Studio 2005, now that a Windows Communication Foundation contract has been defined, the next step is to implement it. In the DerivativesCalculatorService project, choose Project, Add, New Class from the Visual Studio 2005 menus, and add a class called DerivativesCalculatorServiceType.cs to the project, as shown in Figure 2.6.

9. Modify the contents of the DerivativesCalculatorServiceType.cs class file to look like this:

```
using System;
using System.Collections.Generic;
using System.Text;

namespace DerivativesCalculator
{
    public class DerivativesCalculatorServiceType: IDerivativesCalculator
    {
        #region IDerivativesCalculator Members
        decimal IDerivativesCalculator.CalculateDerivative(
            string[] symbols,
```

```
            decimal[] parameters,
            string[] functions)
    {

        throw new Exception(
           "The method or operation is not implemented.");
    }


    void IDerivativesCalculator.DoNothing()
    {
        throw new Exception(
           "The method or operation is not implemented.");
    }
    #endregion
}
}
```

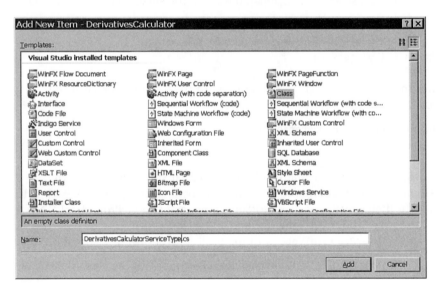

FIGURE 2.6   Adding a class to a project.

As mentioned earlier, in the language of the Windows Communication Foundation, the name *service type* is used to refer to any class that implements a service contract. So, in this case, the DerivativesCalculatorServiceType is a service type because it implements the IDerivativesCalculator interface, which has been designated as a Windows Communication Foundation service contract.

A class can be a service type not only by implementing an interface that is a service contract, but also by having the ServiceContract attribute applied directly to the class. However, by applying the ServiceContract attribute to an interface and then implementing the interface with a class, as in the foregoing, one yields a service contract that can be implemented with any number of service types. In particular, one service type that implements the service contract can be discarded in favor of another. If the service contract attribute is instead applied directly to a class, that class and its descendants will be the only service types that can implement that particular service contract, and discarding the class will mean discarding the service contract.

10. At this point, the DerivativesCalculatorServiceType implements the IDerivativesCalculator interface in name only. Its methods do not actually perform the operations described in the service contract. Rectify that now by returning to the DerivativesCalculatorService project in Visual Studio 2005, and choosing Project, Add Reference from the menus. Select the Projects tab, select the entry for the DerivativesCalculator project, shown in Figure 2.7, and click on the OK button.

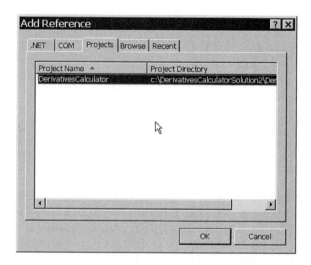

FIGURE 2.7   Adding a reference to the DerivativesCalculator project.

11. Now program the CalculateDerivative() method of the DerivativesCalculatorServiceType to delegate the work of calculating the value of a derivative to the Calculator class of the DerivativesCalculator project, which was the original class with which other pieces of software were to communicate. Also modify the DoNothing() method of the DerivativesCalculatorServiceType so that it no longer throws an exception:

```
using System;
using System.Collections.Generic;
using System.Text;

namespace DerivativesCalculator
{
```

```
public class DerivativesCalculatorServiceType: IDerivativesCalculator
{
    #region IDerivativesCalculator Members
    decimal IDerivativesCalculator.CalculateDerivative(
        string[] symbols,
        decimal[] parameters,
        string[] functions)
    {
        return new Calculator().CalculateDerivative(
            symbols, parameters, functions);
    }

    void IDerivativesCalculator.DoNothing()
    {
        return;
    }
    #endregion
}
}
```

12. Choose Build, Build Solution from the Visual Studio 2005 menu to ensure that there are no programming errors.

Hosting the Service

Recall that the purpose of this exercise has been to use the Windows Communication Foundation to provide a means by which other software can make use of the facilities provided by the derivatives calculator class written at the outset. That requires making a Windows Communication Foundation service by which the capabilities of the derivatives calculator class are made available. Windows Communication Foundation services are collections of endpoints, with each endpoint consisting of an address, a binding, and a contract. At this point, the contract portion of an endpoint for accessing the facilities of the derivatives calculator has been completed, the contract having been defined and implemented.

The next step is to provide for hosting the service within an application domain. Application domains are the containers that Microsoft's Common Language Runtime provides for .NET assemblies. So, in order to get an application domain to host a Windows Communication Foundation service, some Windows process will need to initialize the Common Language Runtime on behalf of the service. Any .NET application can be programmed to do that. IIS can also be made to have Windows Communication Foundation services hosted within application domains. To begin with, the derivatives calculator service will be hosted in an application domain within a .NET application, and then, later, within an application domain in IIS:

1. Choose File, New, Project from the Visual Studio 2005 menus, and add a C# console application called Host to the derivatives calculator solution, as shown in Figure 2.8.

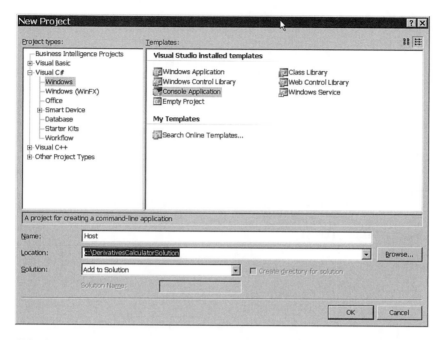

FIGURE 2.8   Adding a host console application to the solution.

2. Select Project, Add Reference from Visual Studio 2005 menus, and, from the .NET tab of the Add Reference dialog, add a reference to the `System.ServiceModel` assembly, as shown earlier in Figure 2.5. Add a reference to the `System.Configuration` assembly in the same way.

3. Choose Project, Add Reference from the Visual Studio 2005 menus, and, from the Projects tab, add a reference to the DerivativesCalculatorService project.

4. Modify the contents of the `Program.cs` class module in the Host project to match Listing 2.2.

LISTING 2.2   A Host for a Service

```
using System;
using System.Collections.Generic;
using System.Configuration;
using System.ServiceModel;
using System.Text;

namespace DerivativesCalculator
{
    public class Program
    {
```

LISTING 2.2   Continued

```
    public static void Main(string[] args)
    {
        Type serviceType = typeof(DerivativesCalculatorServiceType);

        using(ServiceHost host = new ServiceHost(
            serviceType))
        {
            host.Open();

            Console.WriteLine(
                "The derivatives calculator service is available."
            );
            Console.ReadKey(true);

            host.Close();
        }
    }
  }
}
```

The key lines in that code are these:

```
using(ServiceHost host = new ServiceHost(
    serviceType))
{
    host.Open();

    ...
    host.Close();
}
```

ServiceHost is the class provided by the Windows Communication Foundation
Service Model for programming .NET applications to host Windows
Communication Foundation endpoints within application domains. In Listing 2.2, a
constructor of the ServiceHost class is given information to identify the service
type of the service to be hosted.

5. Choose Build, Build Solution from the Visual Studio 2005 menu to ensure that there
   are no programming errors.

Specifying an Address and a Binding

A Windows Communication Foundation endpoint consists of an address, a binding, and
a contract. A contract has been defined and implemented for the endpoint that will be

used to provide access to the derivatives calculator class. To complete the endpoint, it is necessary to provide an address and a binding.

Specifying an address and a binding for an endpoint does not require writing any code, and is customarily the work of an administrator rather than a programmer. Providing an address and a binding can be done in code. However, that would require having to modify the code in order to change the address and the binding of the endpoint. A key innovation of the Windows Communication Foundation is to separate how software is programmed from how it communicates, which is what the binding specifies. So, generally, one avoids the option of specifying the addresses and bindings of endpoints in code, and instead specifies them in configuring the host.

As indicated previously, an editing tool, the Service Configuration Editor, is provided, by which administrators can do the configuration. The use of that tool is covered in detail in Chapter 19, "Manageability." Here, to facilitate a detailed understanding of the configuration language, the configuration will be done by hand:

1. Use the Project, Add Item menu to add an application configuration file named `app.config` to the DerivativesCalculatorService project, as shown in Figure 2.9.

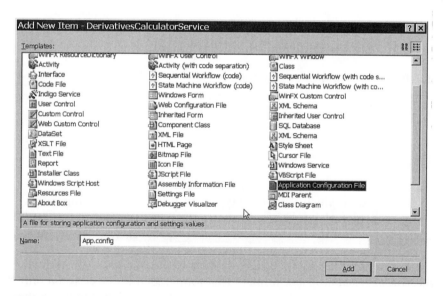

FIGURE 2.9   Adding an application configuration file.

2. Modify the contents of the `app.config` file to look as shown in Listing 2.3.

LISTING 2.3   Adding an Address and a Binding

```xml
<?xml version="1.0" encoding="utf-8" ?>
<configuration>
    <system.serviceModel>
      <services>
        <service name=
```

LISTING 2.3   Continued

```
"DerivativesCalculator.DerivativesCalculatorServiceType">
        <host>
          <baseAddresses>
          <add baseAddress=
              "http://localhost:8000/Derivatives/"/>
            <add baseAddress=
              "net.tcp://localhost:8010/Derivatives/"/>
          </baseAddresses>
        </host>
        <endpoint
          address="Calculator"
          binding="basicHttpBinding"
          contract=
"DerivativesCalculator.IDerivativesCalculator"
          />
        </service>
      </services>
    </system.serviceModel>
</configuration>
```

2. Choose Build, Build Solution from Visual Studio 2005.

In the XML in Listing 2.3,

```
<service name=
"DerivativesCalculator.DerivativesCalculatorServiceType">
```

identifies the service type hosted by the Host application to which the configuration applies. By default, the name by which the service type is identified in the configuration file is matched to the name of a .NET type compiled into the host assembly. In this case, it will be matched to the name of the `DerivativesCalculatorServiceType` class in the `DerivativesCalculator` namespace.

Why isn't the service type identified by the name of a type in the standard .NET format, which is called the *assembly-qualified name* format? That format identifies a class not only by its name and namespace, but also by the display name of the assembly containing the type. Those assembly display names consist of the name of the assembly, the version number, a public key token, and a culture identifier. So, the assembly-qualified name of a class might look like this (.NET Framework Class Library 2006):

```
TopNamespace.SubNameSpace.ContainingClass+NestedClass, MyAssembly,
Version=1.3.0.0, Culture=neutral, PublicKeyToken=b17a5c561934e089
```

The assembly-qualified names for types are the standard mechanism for unambiguously identifying a type to be loaded by reflection from any assembly that the Common Language Runtime Loader can locate. Also, they are commonly used in .NET configuration languages for identifying types. Nonetheless, assembly-qualified names are terribly unwieldy to use, for they are not only long, difficult to remember, and easy to mistype, but any errors in entering them also go undetected by the compiler. So, it is a blessing that the Windows Communication Foundation has mostly eschewed their use in its configuration language, and it is to be hoped that the designers of other .NET libraries will follow that example. Furthermore, although the names used to identify service types in the Windows Communication Foundation configuration language are matched, by default, to the names of types, they are really just strings that custom service hosts can interpret in any fashion, not necessarily treating them as the names of .NET types.

This section of the configuration supplies base addresses for the service host in the form of Uniform Resource Identifiers (URIs):

```
<host>
        <baseAddresses>
                <add baseAddress=
                "http://localhost:8000/Derivatives/"/>
                <add baseAddress=
                "net.tcp://localhost:8010/Derivatives/"/>
        </baseAddresses>
</host>
```

The addresses provided for the service's endpoints will be addresses relative to these base addresses. The term preceding the initial colon of a URI is called the *scheme*, so the schemes of the two URIs provided as base addresses in this case are http and tcp. Each base address provided for Windows Communication Foundation services must have a different scheme.

The configuration defines a single endpoint at which the facilities exposed by the service type will be available. The address, the binding, and the contract constituents of the endpoint are all specified:

```
<endpoint
        address="Calculator"
        binding="basicHttpBinding"
        contract=
"DerivativesCalculator.IDerivativesCalculator"
/>
```

The contract constituent is identified by giving the name of the interface that defines the service contract implemented by the service type. That interface is IDerivativesCalculator.

The binding constituent of the endpoint is specified in this way:

```
binding="basicHttpBinding"
```

To understand what that signifies, one must understand Windows Communication Foundation bindings. A Windows Communication Foundation binding defines a combination of protocols for communicating with a service. Each protocol is represented by a single binding element, and a binding is simply a collection of binding elements. Binding elements are the primary constituents provided by the Windows Communication Foundation's Channel Layer.

One special category of binding element consists of those that implement protocols for transporting messages. One of those is the binding element that implements the Hypertext Transport Protocol (HTTP). Another is the binding element that implements the Transmission Control Protocol (TCP).

Another special category of binding element consists of those that implement protocols for encoding messages. The Windows Communication Foundation provides three such binding elements. One is for encoding SOAP messages as text. Another is for encoding SOAP messages in a binary format. The third is for encoding SOAP messages in accordance with the SOAP Message Transmission Optimization Mechanism (MTOM), which is suitable for messages that incorporate large quantities of binary data.

Examples of Windows Communication Foundation binding elements that are neither transport protocol binding elements nor message-encoding binding elements are the binding elements that implement the WS-Security protocol and the WS-ReliableMessaging protocol. One of the most important ways in which the capabilities of the Windows Communication Foundation can be extended is with the addition of new binding elements that might be provided by Microsoft, or its partners, or by any software developer. Later chapters show how to program custom binding elements, including custom message-encoding binding elements and custom transport protocol binding elements.

A Windows Communication Foundation binding is a set of binding elements that must include at least one transport protocol binding element and zero or more other binding elements. If no message-encoding binding element is specified, the transport protocol binding element will apply its default message-encoding protocol.

Bindings can be defined by selecting individual binding elements, either in code or in configuration. However, the Windows Communication Foundation provides several classes that represent common selections of binding elements. Those classes are referred to as the *predefined bindings*.

One of the predefined bindings is the `BasicHttpBinding`. The `BasicHttpBinding` represents the combination of the HTTP transport binding element and the binding element for encoding SOAP messages in text format. The `BasicHttpBinding` class configures those binding elements in accordance with the WS-I Basic Profile Specification 1.1, which is a combination of web service specifications chosen to promote interoperability among web services and consumers of web services on different platforms.

All the current predefined bindings are listed in Table 2.1. They each derive, directly or indirectly, from the class `System.ServiceModel.Channels.Binding`.

TABLE 2.1   Windows Communication Foundation Predefined Bindings

Name	Purpose
BasicHttpBinding	Maximum interoperability through conformity to the WS-BasicProfile 1.1
WSHttpBinding	HTTP communication in conformity with WS-* protocols
WSDualHttpBinding	Duplex HTTP communication, by which the receiver of an initial message will not reply directly to the initial sender, but may transmit any number of responses over a period
WSFederationBinding	HTTP communication, in which access to the resources of a service can be controlled based on credentials issued by an explicitly identified credential provider
NetTcpBinding	Secure, reliable, high-performance communication between Windows Communication Foundation software entities across a network
NetNamedPipeBinding	Secure, reliable, high-performance communication between Windows Communication Foundation software entities on the same machine
NetMsmqBinding	Communication between Windows Communication Foundation software entities via Microsoft Message Queuing (MSMQ)
MsmqIntegrationBinding	Communication between a Windows Communication Foundation software entity and another software entity via MSMQ
NetPeerTcpBinding	Communication between Windows Communication Foundation software entities via Windows Peer-to-Peer Networking

This specification, in the configuration of the endpoint for the DerivativesCalculatorService in Listing 2.3

```
binding="basicHttpBinding"
```

identifies the BasicHttpBinding as the binding for that endpoint. The lowercase of the initial letter, b, is in conformity with a convention of using camel-casing in configuration files.

You can adjust the settings of a predefined binding by adding a binding configuration to the definition of the endpoint like so:

```
<system.serviceModel>
  <services>
    <service type=
"DerivativesCalculator.DerivativesCalculatorServiceType">
      <endpoint
        address="Calculator"
        binding="basicHttpBinding"
```

```
        bindingConfiguration="bindingSettings"
        contract=
"DerivativesCalculator.IDerivativesCalculator"
        />
      </service>
    </services>
    <bindings>
      <basicHttpBinding>
        <binding name="bindingSettings" messageEncoding="Mtom"/>
      </basicHttpBinding>
    </bindings>
  </system.serviceModel>
```

In this case, the settings for the predefined BasicHttpBinding are adjusted so as to use the MTOM message-encoding binding element rather than the default text message-encoding binding element.

The address specified for the endpoint in the configuration of the DerivativesCalculatorService in Listing 2.3 is Calculator. That address for the endpoint is relative to a base address. Which of the base addresses defined for a service is the base address for the endpoint? It is determined based on the scheme of the base address and the transport protocol implemented by the transport-binding element of the endpoint, as shown in Table 2.2. The transport protocol implemented by the transport-binding element of the endpoint is the HTTP protocol, so, based on the information in Table 2.2, the base address for the endpoint is http://localhost:8000/Derivatives/. Therefore, the absolute address for the endpoint is http://localhost:8000/Derivatives/Calculator.

TABLE 2.2   Mapping of Base Address Schemes to Transport Protocols

Base Address Scheme	Transport Protocol
http	HTTP
net.tcp	TCP
net.pipe	Named Pipes
net.msmq	MSMQ

Anyone who would like to know the complete Windows Communication Foundation configuration language should study the XML Schema file containing the definition of the configuration language. Assuming that the "Orcas" Development Tools that are among the multiple constituents of the .NET Framework 3.0 have been installed, that XML Schema file should be \Program Files\Microsoft Visual Studio 8\Xml\Schemas\DotNetConfig.xsd, on the disc where Visual Studio 2005 is installed. If that file seems to be missing, search for a file with the extension .xsd, containing the expression system.serviceModel.

Deploying the Service

Now an address, a binding, and a contract have been provided for the Windows Communication Foundation endpoint at which the facilities of the derivatives calculator class will be made available. An application domain for hosting the service incorporating that endpoint has also been provided, or, to be more precise, it will be provided as soon as the Host console application is executed:

1. Execute that application now by right-clicking on the Host entry in the Visual Studio 2005 Solution Explorer, and selecting Debug, Start New Instance from the context menu. After a few seconds, the console application window of the host should appear, as in Figure 2.10.

FIGURE 2.10   The Host console application running.

The Windows Communication Foundation has examined the code in the Host and DerivativesCalculatorService assemblies, as well as the contents of the Host assembly's configuration file. The code and the configuration use the Windows Communication Foundation's Service Model to define a service for accessing the derivatives calculator class. From that code and that configuration, the Windows Communication Foundation generates and configures the service using the programming framework constituted by the classes of the Channel Layer. In particular, it employs the binding element classes used by the BasicProfileBinding class that was selected as the binding for the service. Then the Windows Communication Foundation loads the service into the default application domain of the Host console application.

This is the step at which folks using the Vista operating system with a version of Visual Studio 2005 that does not have the Vista compatibility update installed could run into difficulty. They might encounter a namespace reservation exception, due to their service being denied the right to use the address they have specified for its endpoint. In that case, it will be necessary for them to grant permission to have a service use the address to the NETWORK SERVICE user account. The official tool for that purpose is Microsoft's Httpcfg.exe. A more usable one is Steve Johnson's HTTP configuration utility, which, unlike the Microsoft tool and several others for the same job, sports a graphical user interface. His utility is available at http://www.StevesTechSpot.com.

2. Confirm that the Windows Communication Foundation service for accessing the capabilities of the derivatives calculator class is available by directing a browser to the HTTP base address that was specified for the service in the host's application configuration file: `http://localhost:8000/Derivatives/`. A page like the one shown in Figure 2.11 should be opened in the browser.

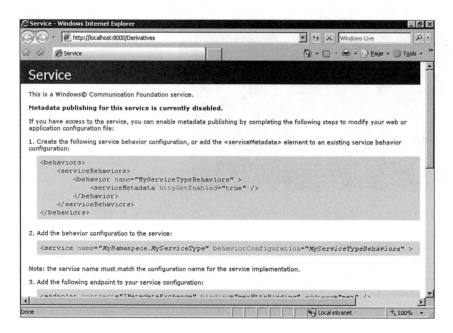

FIGURE 2.11   Help page for a service.

A similar page can be retrieved for any Windows Communications Foundation service with a host that has been provided with a base address with the scheme `http`. It is not necessary that the service have any endpoints with addresses relative to that base address. Note, though, that the page cautions that metadata publishing for the service is disabled. Metadata publishing is disabled by default for the sake of maximizing security so that nothing is made known about a service except what is deliberately chosen by its developers and administrators. To deliberately opt to have the service publish its metadata, it will be necessary to reconfigure it.

3. Choose Debug, Stop Debugging from the Visual Studio 2005 menus to terminate the instance of the Host console application so that its configuration can be modified.

4. The configuration needs to be modified to include a behavior setting by which metadata publishing is activated. Edit the app.config file in the Host project of the DerivativesCalculator Solution so that its content matches that of Listing 2.4.

LISTING 2.4   Enabling Metadata Publication

```xml
<?xml version="1.0" encoding="utf-8" ?>
<configuration>
  <system.serviceModel>
    <services>
      <service name=
"DerivativesCalculator.DerivativesCalculatorServiceType"
        behaviorConfiguration=
          "DerivativesCalculatorService">
        <host>
          <baseAddresses>
            <add baseAddress=
              "http://localhost:8000/Derivatives/"/>
            <add baseAddress=
              "net.tcp://localhost:8010/Derivatives/"/>
          </baseAddresses>
        </host>
        <endpoint
          address="Calculator"
          binding="basicHttpBinding"
          contract=
"DerivativesCalculator.IDerivativesCalculator"
          />
      </service>
    </services>
    <behaviors>
      <serviceBehaviors>
        <behavior name=
          "DerivativesCalculatorService">
          <serviceMetadata
            httpGetEnabled="true" />
        </behavior>
      </serviceBehaviors>
    </behaviors>
  </system.serviceModel>
</configuration>
```

The additions to the configuration of the Windows Communication Foundation service signify that behaviors that apply to a service, rather than to one of its endpoints, are being modified:

```
<behaviors>
        <serviceBehaviors>
            . . .
        </serviceBehaviors>
</behaviors>
```

The modification is made to the service's ServiceMetadata behavior, and the nature of the modification is to have the service generate its metadata in response to a request for it in the form of an HTTP GET:

```
<serviceMetadata httpGetEnabled="true" />
```

To associate this behavior configuration with the DerivativesCalculator service, the behavior is given a name

```
<behavior name="DerivativesCalculatorService">
        . . .
</behavior>
```

and identified by that name as a behavior configuration that applies to the service:

```
<service name=
"DerivativesCalculator.DerivativesCalculatorServiceType"
 behaviorConfiguration="DerivativesCalculatorService">
        . . .
</service>
```

5. Execute the Host console application again by right-clicking on the Host entry in the Visual Studio 2005 Solution Explorer, and selecting Debug, Start New Instance from the context menu.

6. Add the query wsdl to the URI at which the browser is pointing, by aiming the browser at http://localhost:8000/Derivatives/?wsdl, as in Figure 2.12, and the WSDL for the service should be displayed.

Using the Service

Now a Windows Communication Foundation service is available for accessing the facilities of the derivatives calculator class. The Windows Communication Foundation can be employed to construct a client for the derivatives calculator, a software entity that uses the facilities of the derivatives calculator via the service. Different ways to build the client with the Windows Communication Foundation are shown, as well as ways to build a client in Java for the same Windows Communication Foundation service.

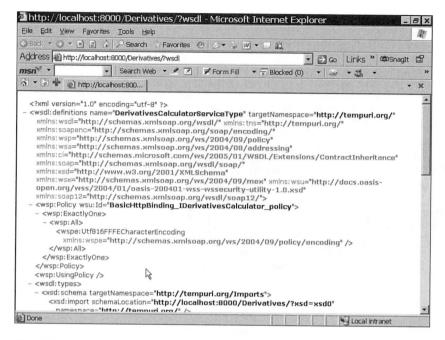

FIGURE 2.12   Examining the WSDL for a service.

Using the Service with a Windows Communication Foundation Client

For the following steps, access to the tools provided with the Windows Communication Foundation from a .NET command prompt will be required. Assuming a complete and normal installation of the Microsoft Windows SDK for the .NET Framework 3.0, that access is provided by a command prompt that should be accessible from the Windows Start menu by choosing All Programs, Microsoft Windows SDK, CMD Shell. That command prompt will be referred to as the *SDK Command Prompt*. From that prompt, the Windows Communication Foundation's Service Metadata Tool, SvcUtil.exe, will be used to generate components of the client for the derivatives calculator:

1. If the Host console application had been shut down, start an instance of it, as before.

2. Open the SDK Command Prompt.

3. Enter

   ```
   C:
   ```

   and then

   ```
   cd c:\WCFHandsOn\Fundamentals\DerivativesCalculatorSolution
   ```

   at that prompt to make the derivatives calculator solution folder the current directory.

4. Next, enter

```
svcutil http://localhost:8000/Derivatives/ /out:Client.cs /config:app.config
```

The output should be as shown in Figure 2.13.

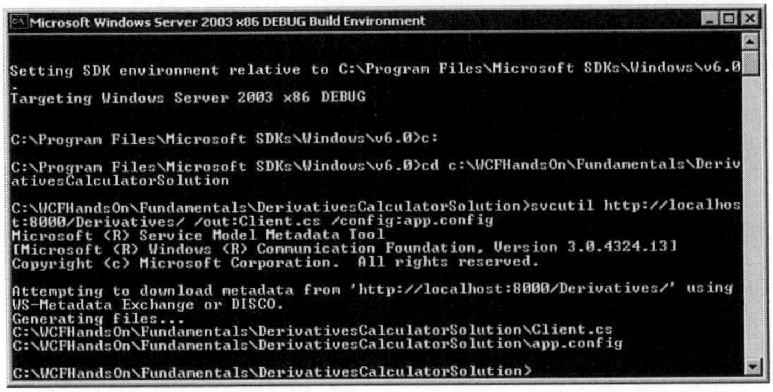

FIGURE 2.13   Using the Service Metadata Tool.

The command executes the Windows Communication Foundation's Service Metadata Tool, passing it a base address of a service that has the scheme http. In this case, it is passed the base address of the derivatives calculator service constructed by the earlier steps in this chapter. Given a base address of a Windows Communication Foundation service, provided it is an address with the scheme http, and provided metadata publishing via HTTP GET is enabled for the service, the Service Metadata Tool can retrieve the WSDL for the service and other associated metadata. By default, it also generates the C# code for a class that can serve as a proxy for communicating with the service, as well as a .NET application-specific configuration file containing the definition of the service's endpoints. The switches /out:Client.cs and /config:app.config used in the foregoing command specify the names to be used for the file containing the C# code and for the configuration file. In the next few steps, the output from the Service Metadata Tool will be used to complete the client for the derivatives calculator.

5. Choose Debug, Stop Debugging from the Visual Studio 2005 menus to terminate the instance of the Host console application so that the solution can be modified.

6. Select File, New, Project from Visual Studio 2005 menus to add a C# Console Application project called Client to the DerivativesCalculator solution.

7. Choose Project, Add Reference from the Visual Studio 2005 menus, and add a reference to the Windows Communication Foundation's System.ServiceModel .NET assembly to the client project.

8. Select Project, Add Existing Item from the Visual Studio 2005 menus, and add the files `Client.cs` and `app.config`, in the folder `C:\WCFHandsOn\Fundamentals\ DerivativesCalculatorSolution`, to the Client project, as shown in Figure 2.14. Those are the files that should have been emitted by the Service Metadata Tool.

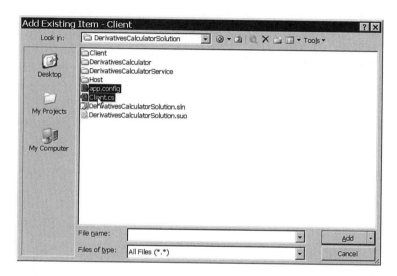

FIGURE 2.14   Adding output from the Service Metadata Tool to a project.

9. Alter the code in the `Program.cs` file of the Client project of the derivatives calculator solution to use the class generated by the Service Metadata Tool as a proxy for communicating with the derivatives calculator service. The code in the `Program.cs` file should be the code in Listing 2.5.

LISTING 2.5   Using the Generated Client Class

```
using System;
using System.Collections.Generic;
using System.Text;

namespace Client
{
    public class Program
    {
        public static void Main(string[] args)
        {
            Console.WriteLine("Press any key when the service is ready.");
            Console.ReadKey(true);

            decimal result = 0;
            using (DerivativesCalculatorProxy proxy =
```

LISTING 2.5   Continued

```
            new DerivativesCalculatorProxy(
                "BasicHttpBinding_IDerivativesCalculator"))
        {
            proxy.Open();
            result = proxy.CalculateDerivative(
                new string[] { "MSFT" },
                new decimal[] { 3 },
                new string[] { });
            proxy.Close();
        }
        Console.WriteLine(string.Format("Result: {0}", result));

        Console.WriteLine("Press any key to exit.");
        Console.ReadKey(true);


    }
  }
}
```

In Listing 2.5, the statement

```
DerivativesCalculatorProxy proxy =
            new DerivativesCalculatorProxy(
                "BasicHttpBinding_IDerivativesCalculator"))
```

creates an instance of the class generated by the Service Metadata Tool to serve as a proxy for the derivatives calculator service. The string parameter passed to the constructor of the class, BasicHttpBinding_IDerivativesCalculator, identifies which definition of an endpoint in the application's configuration file is the definition of the endpoint with which this instance of the class is to communicate. Therefore, an endpoint definition in the configuration file must be named accordingly.

The app.config file added to the Client project in step 8 should contain this definition of an endpoint, with a specification of an address, a binding, and a contract:

```
<client>
        <endpoint
                address="http://localhost:8000/Derivatives/Calculator"
                binding="basicHttpBinding"
                bindingConfiguration="BasicHttpBinding_IDerivativesCalculator"
                contract="IDerivativesCalculator"
                name="BasicHttpBinding_IDerivativesCalculator" />
</client>
```

Notice that the name provided for this endpoint definition matches the name that is passed to the constructor of the proxy class.

The binding configuration named `BasicHttpBinding_IDerivativesCalculator` to which this endpoint configuration refers, explicitly specifies the default values for the properties of the predefined `BasicHttpBinding`:

```
<basicHttpBinding>
    <binding
        name="BasicHttpBinding_IDerivativesCalculator"
        closeTimeout="00:01:00"
        openTimeout="00:01:00"
        receiveTimeout="00:10:00"
        sendTimeout="00:01:00"
        allowCookies="false"
        bypassProxyOnLocal="false"
        hostNameComparisonMode="StrongWildcard"
        maxBufferSize="65536"
        maxBufferPoolSize="524288"
        maxReceivedMessageSize="65536"
        messageEncoding="Text"
        textEncoding="utf-8"
        transferMode="Buffered"
        useDefaultWebProxy="true">
        <readerQuotas
                    maxDepth="32"
                    maxStringContentLength="8192"
                    maxArrayLength="16384"
            maxBytesPerRead="4096"
            maxNameTableCharCount="16384" />
        <security mode="None">
            <transport
                        clientCredentialType="None"
                        proxyCredentialType="None"
                realm="" />
            <message
                        clientCredentialType="UserName"
                        algorithmSuite="Default" />
        </security>
    </binding>
</basicHttpBinding>
```

Those default values were left implicit in the service's configuration of the endpoint. The Service Metdata Tool diligently avoided the assumption that the configuration of the binding that it derived from the metadata is the default configuration.

10. Prepare to have the client use the derivatives calculator by modifying the startup project properties of the derivatives calculator solution as shown in Figure 2.15.

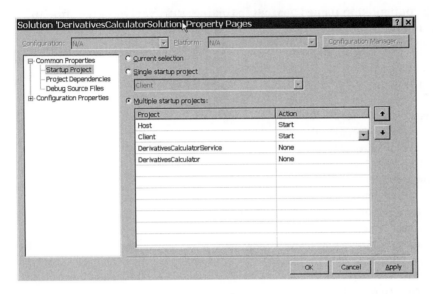

FIGURE 2.15   Startup project properties of the derivatives calculator solution.

11. Choose Debug, Start Debugging from the Visual Studio 2005 menus.

12. When there is activity in the console for the Host application, enter a keystroke into the console for the Client application. The client should obtain an estimate of the value of a derivative from the derivatives calculator service, as shown in Figure 2.16. Note that the value shown in the Client application console might vary from the value shown in Figure 2.16 due to variations in prevailing market conditions over time.

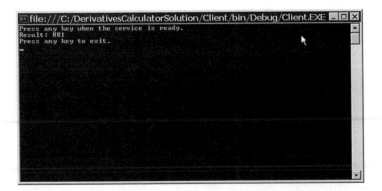

FIGURE 2.16   Using the derivatives calculator via a service.

13. In Visual Studio 2005, choose Debug, Stop Debugging from the menus.

Different Ways of Coding Windows Communication Clients

In the preceding steps for building a client for the derivatives calculator service, the code for the client was generated using the Windows Communication Foundation's Service Metadata Tool. The generated code consists of a version of the IDerivativesProxy interface, and the code of a proxy class for communicating with the derivatives calculator service. The latter code is in Listing 2.6.

LISTING 2.6   Generated Proxy Class

```
[System.Diagnostics.DebuggerStepThroughAttribute()]
[System.CodeDom.Compiler.GeneratedCodeAttribute(
        "System.ServiceModel", "3.0.0.0")]
public partial class DerivativesCalculatorClient :
        System.ServiceModel.ClientBase<IDerivativesCalculator>,
        IDerivativesCalculator
{

    public DerivativesCalculatorClient()
    {
    }

    public DerivativesCalculatorClient(
            string endpointConfigurationName) :
        base(endpointConfigurationName)
    {
    }

    public DerivativesCalculatorClient(
            string endpointConfigurationName,
            string remoteAddress) :
        base(endpointConfigurationName, remoteAddress)
    {
    }

    public DerivativesCalculatorClient(
            string endpointConfigurationName,
            System.ServiceModel.EndpointAddress remoteAddress) :
        base(endpointConfigurationName, remoteAddress)
    {
    }

    public DerivativesCalculatorClient(
            System.ServiceModel.Channels.Binding binding,
            System.ServiceModel.EndpointAddress remoteAddress) :
```

LISTING 2.6   Continued

```
                base(binding, remoteAddress)
    {
    }

    public decimal CalculateDerivative(
                string[] symbols,
                decimal[] parameters,
                string[] functions)
    {
        return base.Channel.CalculateDerivative(
                    symbols,
                    parameters,
                    functions);
    }
}
```

Naturally, one can write such a class instead of generating it with the Service Metadata
Tool. To do so, one simply defines a class that inherits from the Windows
Communication Foundation's ClientBase<T> generic, and that implements the contract
for the service:

```
[ServiceContract]
public interface IDerivativesCalculator
{
    [OperationContract]
    decimal CalculateDerivative(
            string[] symbols,
            decimal[] parameters,
            string[] functions);
    ...
}

public partial class DerivativesCalculatorProxy :
    ClientBase<IDerivativesCalculator>,
    IDerivativesCalculator
{
    ...
}
```

Then, in the class's implementations of the contract, one simply delegates to the methods
of the Channel property of ClientBase<T>:

```
public partial class DerivativesCalculatorProxy :
    ClientBase<IDerivativesCalculator>,
    IDerivativesCalculator
{
    public decimal CalculateDerivative(string[] symbols,
        decimal[] parameters,
        string[] functions)
    {
        return base.Channel.CalculateDerivative(symbols,
            parameters,
            functions);
    }
}
```

This way of writing a Windows Communication Foundation client for the derivatives calculator service is one of at least three ways of doing so. The other way of writing a client for the service, given a definition of the IDerivativesCalculator contract, would simply be to write

```
IDerivativesCalculator proxy =
new ChannelFactory<IDerivativesCalculator>("BasicHttpBinding_IDerivativesCalcula-
tor").
    CreateChannel();
proxy.CalculateDerivative(... );
((IChannel)proxy).Close();
```

The ChannelFactory<T> generic is defined in the System.ServiceModel.Channels namespace. Whereas the first method for writing clients yields a reusable proxy class, this second method merely yields a proxy variable.

A third option for writing the client would be to program it in such a way that it downloads the metadata for the service and configures a proxy in accordance with that metadata while executing. Listing 2.7 shows how to do that using the Windows Communication Foundation's MetadataExchangeClient class. A MetadataExchangeClient object is provided with a location for the metadata for the derivatives calculator service, the same metadata shown earlier in Figure 2.12. Then the GetMetadata() method of the MetadataExchangeClient object is used to download that metadata, which is represented in the form of a MetadataSet object. A WsdlImporter object is constructed from that MetadataSet object. A collection of ServiceEndpoint objects that describe the service endpoints defined in the metadata is obtained using the WsdlImporter object's ImportAllEndpoints() method. Each ServiceEndpoint object is used to configure a proxy variable that can then be used for communicating with the service.

LISTING 2.7   Retrieving Metadata Dynamically

```
using System;
using System.Collections.Generic;
using System.ServiceModel;
using System.ServiceModel.Channels;
using System.ServiceModel.Description;
using System.Text;

namespace Client
{
    class Program
    {
        static void Main(string[] args)
        {
            Console.WriteLine("Press any key when the service is ready.");
            Console.ReadKey(true);

            MetadataExchangeClient metadataExchangeClient =
                new MetadataExchangeClient(
                new Uri(
                    "http://localhost:8000/Derivatives/?wsdl"),
                MetadataExchangeClientMode.HttpGet);

            MetadataSet metadataSet =
                metadataExchangeClient.GetMetadata();
            WsdlImporter importer =
                new WsdlImporter(metadataSet);
            ServiceEndpointCollection endpoints =
                importer.ImportAllEndpoints();
            IDerivativesCalculator proxy = null;
            foreach (ServiceEndpoint endpoint in endpoints)
            {
                proxy = new ChannelFactory<IDerivativesCalculator>(
                    endpoint.Binding, endpoint.Address).CreateChannel();
                ((IChannel)proxy).Open();
                Console.WriteLine(proxy.CalculateDerivative(
                    new string[] { "MSFT" },
                    new decimal[] { 3 },
                    new string[] { }));
                ((IChannel)proxy).Close();
            }
```

LISTING 2.7   Continued

```
        Console.WriteLine("Press any key to exit.");
        Console.ReadKey(true);
    }
  }
}
```

Using the Service with a Java Client

The service by which the facilities of the derivatives calculator class are made available for use by other software entities, is configured to use the Windows Communication Foundation's predefined BasicProfileBinding. That binding conforms to the WS-I Basic Profile Specification 1.1. Therefore, the service can be used not only by clients built using the Windows Communication Foundation, but by any clients that can consume services that comply with that specification.

The Apache Foundation provides a web services development toolkit for Java programmers called *Axis*. Axis incorporates a tool called *WSDL2Java*, which, like the Windows Communication Foundation's Service Metadata Tool, will download the WSDL for a service and generate the code of a class that can be used as a proxy for the service. Whereas the Windows Communication Foundation's Service Metadata Tool can generate code in the C#, Visual Basic .NET, VBScript, JScript, JavaScript, Visual J#, and C++ programming languages, the WSDL2Java tool generates code only in the Java programming language.

You can download Axis from http://ws.apache.org/axis/. After it has been installed correctly, and the Host console application of the derivatives calculator solution is running, one can issue this command from a command prompt:

java org.apache.axis.wsdl.WSDL2Java http://localhost/Derivatives/?wsdl

That command should cause WSDL2Java to download the WSDL for the Windows Communication Foundation derivatives calculator service and generate Java code for accessing the service.

The quantity of that code will be much larger than the quantity of code emitted by the Windows Communication Foundation's Service Metadata Tool. The code for a proxy class for the derivatives calculator service generated by the WSDL2Java tool is 18KB in size, whereas the code for a proxy class for the same service emitted by the Windows Communication Foundation's tool is about 3KB in size.

Given the code emitted by the WSDL2Java tool, one can write a Java application to use the derivatives calculator service. The code for such an application is in Listing 2.8. Figure 2.17 shows the application executing within the Eclipse 3.1 development environment, which is available from http://eclipse.org/downloads/.

LISTING 2.8   WSDL2Java Proxy

```java
import org.tempuri.*;
import java.math.*;

public class Client
{
    public static void main(String[] arguments)
    {
        try
        {
            String[] symbols = new String[1];
            symbols[0] = "MSFT";

            BigDecimal[] parameters = new BigDecimal[1];
            parameters[0] = new BigDecimal(3);

            String[] functions = new String[1];
            functions[0] = "TechStockProjections";

            DerivativesCalculatorServiceTypeLocator locator =
                new DerivativesCalculatorServiceTypeLocator();
            IDerivativesCalculator stub =
                locator.getBasicHttpBinding_IDerivativesCalculator_port();
            BigDecimal[] values = new BigDecimal[1];
            values[0] = stub.calculateDerivative(symbols,parameters,functions);


            System.out.println(String.format("Result: %f", values));
        }
        catch(Exception e)
        {
            System.out.println("Error: " + e.getMessage());
        }

        try
        {
            System.in.read();
        }
        catch(Exception e)
        {
        }
    }
}
```

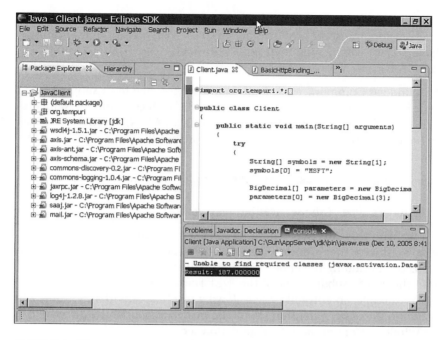

FIGURE 2.17   Using the derivatives calculator service using a Java Client.

Hosting the Service in IIS

Recall that IIS can be made to provide application domains for hosting Windows Communication Foundation services. Having IIS provide hosts for Windows Communication Foundation services is beneficial for several reasons:

▶ IIS is a scalable host. Its scalability features include central processing unit (CPU) affinity and web gardening.

▶ IIS is a reliable host. Its reliability features include health management, process isolation, and application domain isolation.

▶ IIS is a fault-tolerant host. If an unhandled exception occurs in a service, IIS automatically restarts it.

▶ The security of IIS has been arduously tested, found wanting, and reinforced. Although IIS is notorious for having been the victim of a number of successful attacks in the past, it now incorporates lessons learned from that experience, making it far more trustworthy than untried alternatives.

Only services of which all the endpoints have HTTP bindings can be hosted within IIS 5.1 and IIS 6. Those are the versions of IIS provided for Windows XP and Windows Server 2003. IIS 7 incorporates a new facility, called the *Windows Activation Service*, for routing messages received using any transport protocol to hosted .NET assemblies. Thus, Windows

Communication Foundation services can be hosted within IIS 7 regardless of their transport protocols. Even custom transport protocols added to the Windows Communication Foundation's Channel Layer can be supported in IIS 7 through customizations to the Windows Activation Service.

To have IIS host a Windows Communication Foundation service, one must simply identify the service type of the service to IIS. That is done in a file with content very similar to the contents of the .asmx file that you would use in creating an ASP.NET web service. For example, to have the derivatives calculator service hosted within IIS, one would use a file containing this directive

```
<%@ServiceHost Service="DerivativesCalculator.DerivativesCalculatorServiceType" %>
```

which identifies the service type of the service that IIS is to host.

Now, by default, a file with this directive, telling IIS to host a Windows Communication Foundation service, must have the extension .svc. However, one can specify any number of alternative extensions by adding the appropriate entry to the system's web.config file, which should be in the CONFIG subdirectory of the .NET Framework subfolder of the system directory. For example, an entry like the following would specify that not only the .svc extension, but also the .asmx extension should be treated as containing directives for the hosting of Windows Communication Foundation services:

```
<system.web>
        <compilation>
                <compilation debug="true">
                        <buildProviders>
                                <remove extension=".asmx"/>
                                <add extension=".asmx"
                                    type="System.ServiceModel.ServiceBuildProvider,
                                    System.ServiceModel,
                                    Version= 3.0.0.0,
                                    Culture=neutral,
                                    PublicKeyToken= b77a5c561934e089" />
                        </buildProviders>
                </compilation>
        </compilation>
</system.web>
```

Having files with the .asmx extension treated as files with directives for hosting Windows Communication Foundation services would be useful in rewriting ASP.NET web services as Windows Communication Foundation services. You could rewrite the ASP.NET services as Windows Communication Foundation services and have clients of the original services still be able to refer to those services using URIs with paths containing the .asmx extension.

Up to this point, the Windows Communication Foundation service for accessing the facilities of the derivatives calculator class has been hosted within a console application. The steps for hosting the service within IIS begin with these steps for creating an IIS virtual directory by which IIS will map a URI to the location of the derivatives calculator service:

1. Choose Control Panel, Administrative Tools, Internet Information Services (IIS) Manager from the Windows Start menu.

2. Expand the nodes of the tree control in the left pane until the node named Default Web Site becomes visible.

3. Right-click on that node, and choose New, Virtual Directory from the context menu that appears.

4. In the Virtual Directory Creation Wizard, enter **DerivativesCalculator** in the Virtual Directory alias screen.

5. Enter

   ```
   c:\WCFHandsOn\Fundamentals\DerivativesCalculatorSolution\
   ➥DerivativesCalculatorService
   ```

   as the path on the Web Site Content Directory screen of the wizard.

   Select the Read, Run Scripts, and Execute permissions on the wizard's Virtual Directory Access Permissions screen; then click Next and follow the instructions to exit the wizard.

   Right-click on the node representing the new DerivativesCalculator virtual directory under the Default Web Site node, and choose Properties from the context menu that appears. Select the ASP.NET tab, and ensure that the ASP.NET version chosen for the virtual directory is 2.0.50727 or higher, as shown in Figure 2.18.

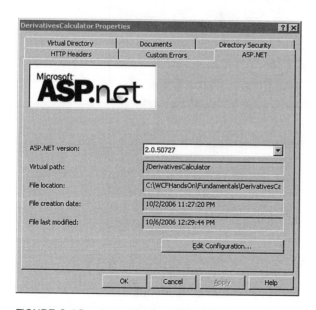

FIGURE 2.18   Selecting the .NET 2.0 Common Language Runtime for use with a virtual directory.

The creation of the IIS virtual directory is complete. These next few steps deploy the Windows Communication Foundation service in that virtual directory:

1. Add a text file named `Service.svc` to the DerivativesCalculatorService project.

2. Add content to that file so that it looks like this:

```
<%@ServiceHost Service=
➥"DerivativesCalculator.DerivativesCalculatorServiceType" %>
```

This directive tells IIS to host the Windows Communication Foundation service type `DerivativesCalculator.DerivativesCalculatorServiceType`. IIS will be looking for that type among the assemblies in the `bin` subdirectory of the folder in which the file referring to the assembly is located. Therefore, it is necessary to ensure that the asssembly is located there. The next two steps will accomplish that task.

3. Select the DerivativesCalculatorService project of DerivativesCalculatorSolution in the Visual Studio 2005 Solution Explorer. Choose Project, DerivativesCalculatorService Properties from the Visual Studio menus. Select the Build tab, and set the value of the Output path property to refer to the `bin` subdirectory of the project directory, as shown in Figure 2.19.

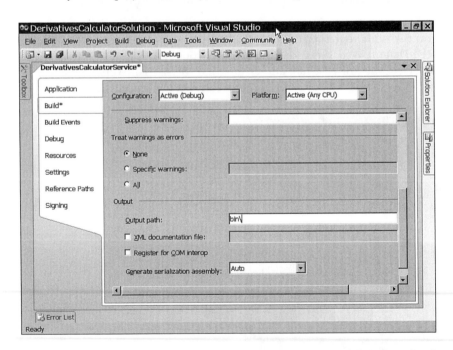

FIGURE 2.19   Altering the build properties of the DerivativesCalculatorService project.

4. Select Build, Build Solution from the Visual Studio 2005 menus.

The remaining two steps are for configuring the service. In hosting the service within the Host console application, the configuration for the service was incorporated into the configuration file for that application. Now that the service is to be hosted within IIS, the configuration information must be a configuration file named Web.config in the same directory as the file with the directives telling IIS to host the service. Follow these steps to create the configuration file:

1. Add an application configuration file named Web.config to the DerivativesCalculatorService project in the derivatives calculator solution.

2. Modify the contents of that file in this way, before saving the file:

```
<?xml version="1.0" encoding="utf-8" ?>
<configuration>
        <system.serviceModel>
                <services>
                        <service name=
"DerivativesCalculator.DerivativesCalculatorServiceType"
 behaviorConfiguration="DerivativesCalculatorService">
                                <endpoint
                                        address="Calculator"
                                        binding="basicHttpBinding"
                                        contract=
"DerivativesCalculator.IDerivativesCalculator"
                                />
                        </service>
                </services>
                <behaviors>
                        <serviceBehaviors>
                                <behavior name="DerivativesCalculatorService">
                                        <serviceMetadata httpGetEnabled="true" />
                                </behavior>
                        </serviceBehaviors>
                </behaviors>
        </system.serviceModel>
</configuration>
```

There is just one difference between this configuration information and the information that was in the application configuration file of the Host console application: no base addresses are specified. Base addresses are not required because the base address of a Windows Communication Foundation service hosted within IIS is the URI of the file containing the directives telling IIS to host the service.

The work required for hosting the derivatives calculator service in IIS is now complete. To confirm the availability of the service, follow these steps:

1. Choose Run from the Windows Start menu, and enter

   ```
   http://localhost/DerivativesCalculator/Service.svc
   ```

   Internet Explorer should open and display a page similar to the one shown earlier in Figure 2.11. Now that the service is available, the client can be modified to use the derivatives calculator service hosted within IIS.

2. Modify the app.config file in the Client project of the derivatives calculator solution to refer to the address of the endpoint hosted within IIS by changing this entry in the file

   ```
   address="http://localhost:8000/Derivatives/Calculator"
   ```

   to this:

   ```
   address="http://localhost/DerivativesCalculator/Service.svc/Calculator"
   ```

3. Choose Build, Build Solution from the Visual Studio 2005 menus.

4. Right-click on the Client entry in the Visual Studio 2005 Solution Explorer, and select Debug, Start New Instance from the context menu.

5. When the console application window of the host appears, enter a keystroke into the console. The client obtains an estimate of the value of a derivative from the derivatives calculator service hosted in IIS, with output like that shown earlier in Figure 2.16. Note, again, that the value shown in the Client application console might vary from the value shown in Figure 2.16 due to variations in prevailing market conditions over time.

6. Close the Client executable.

Changing How the Service Communicates

This chapter has introduced the Windows Communication Foundation as a software factory template that provides a simple modeling language, the Service Model, for describing how a piece of software is to communicate. The key terms of that language are *address*, *binding*, and *contract*. The Windows Communication Foundation examines the software communication model provided for an application using those terms, and builds runtime components from the Windows Communication Foundation Channel Layer to implement the model when the application prepares to communicate. The binding included in the model specifies the transmission protocols by which the application can send and receive messages. The claim was made that by simply changing the binding, you can alter the transmission protocols that the application uses, and, moreover, that the alteration can be made solely within the configuration for the application, without any code having to be changed. That claim will now be corroborated.

The steps that follow will have the client communicating with the derivatives calculator service hosted within the .NET application. Prepare for that by altering the client application's configuration file so that the client directs its transmissions to the appropriate address by following these steps:

1. Modify the `app.config` file in the Client project of the derivatives calculator solution to refer to the address of the endpoint hosted within the .NET application by changing this entry in the file

   ```
   address="http://localhost/DerivativesCalculator/Service.svc/Calculator"
   ```

   back to this:

   ```
   address="http://localhost:8000/Derivatives/Calculator"
   ```

2. Choose Build, Build Solution from the Visual Studio 2005 menus.

These next steps will serve to capture the communications directed to the service hosted by the .NET application, making use of just one of the Windows Communications Foundation's many features for administering services: its facility for logging messages.

1. Provide an empty folder to which the Windows Communication Foundation can log messages. In the following steps, that folder will be assumed to be `c:\logs`.

2. Modify the `app.config` file of the Host project of the derivatives calculator solution to look as shown in Listing 2.9, which configures a standard .NET diagnostics trace listener to listen for trace information emanating from the Windows Communication Foundation's message-logging facility, `System.ServiceModel.MessageLogging`. The configuration also turns that logging facility on with the diagnostics element within the `System.ServiceModel` element.

LISTING 2.9   Message Logging Configuration

```xml
<?xml version="1.0" encoding="utf-8" ?>
<configuration>
        <system.diagnostics>
                <sources>
                        <source
                                name="System.ServiceModel.MessageLogging"
                                switchValue="Verbose">
                                <listeners>
                                        <add
                                        name="xml"
                                type="System.Diagnostics.XmlWriterTraceListener"
                                        initializeData="c:\logs\message.log" />
                                </listeners>
                        </source>
                </sources>
                <trace autoflush="true" />
```

LISTING 2.9   Continued

```
        </system.diagnostics>
        <system.serviceModel>
            <diagnostics>
                <messageLogging logEntireMessage="true"
                                maxMessagesToLog="300"
                                logMessagesAtServiceLevel="false"
                                logMalformedMessages="false"
                                logMessagesAtTransportLevel="true" />
            </diagnostics>
            <services>
                <service name=
"DerivativesCalculator.DerivativesCalculatorServiceType"
 behaviorConfiguration="DerivativesCalculatorService">
                    <host>
                        <baseAddresses>
                            <add
    baseAddress="http://localhost:8000/Derivatives/"/>
                            <add
    baseAddress="net.tcp://localhost:8010/Derivatives/"/>
                        </baseAddresses>
                    </host>
                    <endpoint
                        address="Calculator"
                        binding="basicHttpBinding"
                        contract=
"DerivativesCalculator.IDerivativesCalculator"
                    />
                </service>
            </services>
            <behaviors>
                <serviceBehaviors>
                    <behavior name="DerivativesCalculatorService">
                        <serviceMetadata httpGetEnabled="true" />
                    </behavior>
                </serviceBehaviors>
            </behaviors>
        </system.serviceModel>
</configuration>
```

3. Build the solution.

4. Start an instance of the Client executable, and enter a keystroke into the console for the Client application. The client should obtain an estimate of the value of a derivative from the derivatives calculator service, as shown earlier in Figure 2.16.

5. Enter a keystroke into the console of the client application to terminate it.

6. Enter a keystroke into the console of the service's host application to terminate it.

7. Open the file `c:\logs\Message.log` in Notepad. Search for the string MSFT, which, as should be apparent from Listing 2.5, is a stock symbol that the client transmits to the server in its request to calculate the value of a derivative. That string will be found in the file because the communications are being transmitted in accordance with the WS-I Basic Profile 1.1, which stipulates the sending of plain text XML via HTTP.

8. Delete the file `c:\logs\Message.log`.

9. Use Notepad to open the file `Host.exe.config`, which should be in the folder `C:\WCFHandsOn\Fundamentals\DerivativesCalculatorSolution\Host\bin\Debug`.

10. Make a single modification to that file, changing

    ```
    binding="basicHttpBinding"
    ```

    to

    ```
    binding="netTcpBinding"
    ```

11. Save the file.

12. Use Notepad to open the file `Client.exe.config`, which should be in the folder `C:\WCFHandsOn\Fundamentals\DerivativesCalculatorSolution\Client\bin\Debug`.

13. Modify the endpoint configuration in that file so that it looks like this:

    ```
    <endpoint address="net.tcp://localhost:8010/Derivatives/Calculator"
        binding="netTcpBinding"
        contract="IDerivativesCalculator"

        name="BasicHttpBinding_IDerivativesCalculator"/>
    ```

14. Save the file.

15. Start an instance of the Client executable, and enter a keystroke into the console for the Client application. The client should obtain an estimate of the value of a derivative from the derivatives calculator service as usual.

16. Enter a keystroke into the console of the client application to terminate it.

17. Enter a keystroke into the console of the service's host application to terminate it.

18. Open the file `c:\logs\Message.log` in Notepad. Search for the string MSFT. That string will not be found in the file because this time the protocol used for transmission was the Windows Communication Foundation's own TCP protocol, which encrypts messages by default.

Thus, without even recompiling either the client or the service, the manner in which those applications communicate with each other has been altered considerably. The only changes that were made were to the description of the endpoints in the Service Model's configuration language.

Summary

The Windows Communication Foundation provides a software factory template for software communication, consisting of a modeling language called the Service Model, and a programming framework called the Channel Layer. The Service Model incorporates a class library and a configuration language by which services are described simply as collections of endpoints defined by an address, a binding, and a contract. Descriptions of software communication solutions expressed in the language of the Service Model are used as input for generating the components of the solution from the lower-level class library that is the Channel Layer. Using the software factory template for communication among applications that the Windows Communication Foundation provides, one can quickly adapt code to new scenarios. For instance, as demonstrated in the foregoing, one can host the same service within a .NET console application or within IIS without modifying the code for the service at all. One can also easily change how a client and a service communicate, making the communication between them confidential, for example. Being able to adapt software to diverse scenarios with little effort has always been the promise of model-driven development. With the Windows Communication Foundation, that promise is realized for software communications.

References

Box, Don. 1998. *Essential COM*. Reading, MA: Addison-Wesley.

_____. 2004. Code Name Indigo: A Guide to Developing and Running Connected Systems with Indigo. *MSDN Magazine* (January).

Cwalina, Krzysztof and Brad Abrams. 2006. *Framework Design Guidelines: Conventions, Idioms, and Patterns for Reusable .NET Libraries*. Upper Saddle River, NJ: Addison Wesley.

Erl, Thomas. 2004. *Service-Oriented Architecture: A Field Guide to Integrating XML and Web Services*. Upper Saddle River, NJ: Prentice Hall.

_____. 2005. *Service-Oriented Architecture: Concepts, Technology, and Design*. Upper Saddle River, NJ: Prentice Hall.

Fowler, Martin. 2003. *Patterns of Enterprise Application Architecture*. Boston, MA: Addison Wesley.

Greenfield, Jack, Keith Short, Steve Cook, and Stuart Kent. 2004. *Software Factories: Assembling Applications with Patterns, Models, Frameworks, and Tools*. Indianapolis, IN: Wiley.

Hohpe, Gregor, and Bobby Woolf. 2004. *Enterprise Integration Patterns: Designing, Building and Deploying Messaging Solutions*. Boston, MA: Addison-Wesley.

.NET Framework Class Library. 2006. S.v. "Type.AssemblyQualifiedName Property." http://msdn2.microsoft.com/en-us/library/system.type.assemblyqualifiedname.aspx. Accessed October 1, 2006.

Taylor, David A. 1992. *Object-Oriented Information Systems: Planning and Implementation*. New York, NY: Wiley.

Wittgenstein, Ludwig. 1958. *Philosophical Investigations*. Oxford: Blackwell.

CHAPTER 3

Data Representation

Background

The Windows Communication Foundation provides a language, called the Service Model, for modeling software communications. Software executables can be generated from models expressed in that language using the classes of a lower-level programming framework called the Channel Layer.

In the language of the Service Model, a piece of software that responds to communications over a network is a *service*. A service has one or more endpoints to which communications can be directed. An endpoint consists of an address, a binding, and a contract.

The role of the address component is simple. It specifies a unique location for the service on a network in the form of a uniform resource locator.

The binding specifies the protocols for communication between the client and the server. Minimally, the binding must provide a protocol for encoding messages and a protocol for transporting them.

A contract specifies the operations that are available at an endpoint. To define a contract, one merely writes an interface in one's preferred .NET programming language, and add attributes to it to indicate that the interface is also a Windows Communication Foundation contract. Then, to implement the contract, one simply writes a class that implements the .NET interface that one defined.

This contract was used to define the operations of a derivatives calculator service in Chapter 2, "The Fundamentals."

```
[ServiceContract]
public interface IDerivativesCalculator
{
```

```
[OperationContract]
decimal CalculateDerivative(
    string[] symbols,
    decimal[] parameters,
    string[] functions);


    [...]
}
```

One way of writing code for a client of that service which is to use the CalculateDerivative() operation would be to write this:

```
string[] symbols = new string[]{"MSFT"};
decimal[] parameters = new decimal[]{3};
string[] functions = new string[]{"TechStockProjections"};

IDerivativesCalculator proxy =
  new ChannelFactory<IDerivativesCalculator>(
        "CalculatorEndpoint").CreateChannel();
proxy.CalculateDerivative(symbols, parameters, functions);
((IChannel)proxy).Close();
```

When the statement

```
proxy.CalculateDerivative(symbols, parameters, functions);
```

is executed, the data being provided by the client as input to the operation is added to an instance of the Message class of the Windows Communication Foundation's Channel Layer. Within the Message class, the data is represented in the form of an XML Information Set, commonly referred to as an *InfoSet*. When the data is ready to be transported from the client to the service, the message-encoding protocol specified in the binding will determine the form in which the Message object containing the data provided by the client will be represented to the service. The message-encoding protocol could conceivably translate the message into a string of comma-separated values, or into the JavaScript Object-Notation Format, or any format whatsoever. However, all the standard bindings specify encoding protocols by which the Message object will continue to be represented as an XML InfoSet. Depending on the encoding protocol of the predefined binding, that XML InfoSet might be encoded using one of the standard XML text encodings, or the standard MTOM protocol, or using a binary format proprietary to the Windows Communication Foundation.

When a transmission is received by a Windows Communication Foundation service, it is reassembled as a Message object by a message-encoding binding element, with the data sent by the client being expressed within the Message object as an XML InfoSet, regardless of the format in which it was encoded by the client. The Message object will be passed to the dispatcher component of the Windows Communication Foundation. The dispatcher extracts the client's data items from the XML InfoSet. It invokes the method of the service that implements the operation being used by the client, passing the client's data items to the method as parameters.

The XmlSerializer and the DataContractSerializer

From the foregoing, it should be apparent that data being sent from the client to the service is serialized to XML within the client, and deserialized from XML within the service. There are two XML serializers that the Windows Communication Foundation can use to accomplish that task.

One is the System.Xml.Serialization.XmlSerializer that has always been included in the System.Xml assembly of the .NET Framework Class Library. The other is a new XML serializer provided with the Windows Communication Foundation. It is the System.Runtime.Serialization.DataContractSerializer class within the System.Runtime.Serialization assembly. The System.Runtime.Serialization.DataContractSerializer class is the XML serializer that the Windows Communication Foundation uses by default.

Given a type like the one defined in Listing 3.1, one could make the type serializable by the System.Runtime.Serialization.DataContractSerializer by adding System.Runtime.Serialization.DataContract and System.Runtime.Serialization.DataMember attributes as shown in Listing 3.2. The representation of instances of a class in XML that is implied by the addition of the System.Runtime.Serialization.DataContract attribute to the class, and the System.Runtime.Serialization.DataMember attribute to its members, is commonly referred to as a *data contract* in the argot of the Windows Communication Foundation.

LISTING 3.1   DerivativesCalculation Class

```
public class DerivativesCalculation
{
        private string[] symbols;
        private decimal[] parameters;
        private string[] functions;

        public string[] Symbols
        {
            get
            {
                return this.symbols;
            }

            set
            {
                this.symbols = value;
            }
```

```
        }

        public decimal[] Parameters
        {
            get
            {
                return this.parameters;
            }

            set
            {
                this.parameters = value;
            }
        }

        public string[] Functions
        {
            get
            {
                return this.functions;
            }

            set
            {
                this.functions = value;
            }

        }
}
```

LISTING 3.2   DerivativesCalculation Data Contract

```
[DataContract]
public class DerivativesCalculation
{
        [DataMember]
        private string[] symbols;
        [DataMember]
        private decimal[] parameters;
        [DataMember]
        private string[] functions;

        public string[] Symbols
        {
```

LISTING 3.2   Continued

```csharp
            get
            {
                return this.symbols;
            }

            set
            {
                this.symbols = value;
            }
        }

        public decimal[] Parameters
        {
            get
            {
                return this.parameters;
            }

            set
            {
                this.parameters = value;
            }
        }

        public string[] Functions
        {
            get
            {
                return this.functions;
            }

            set
            {
                this.functions = value;
            }
        }

    }
}
```

Although the System.Runtime.Serialization.DataContractSerializer is the default XML serializer of the Windows Communication Foundation, the Windows Communication Foundation can also be configured to do XML serialization using the System.Xml.Serialization.XmlSerializer class. To exercise that option, add the

`System.ServiceModel.XmlSerializerFormat` attribute to the definition of a Windows Communication Foundation contract, like so:

```
[ServiceContract]
[XmlSerializerFormat]
public interface IDerivativesCalculator
{
    [OperationContract]
    decimal CalculateDerivative(
        string[] symbols,
        decimal[] parameters,
        string[] functions);

    [...]
}
```

The option of using the `System.Xml.Serialization.XmlSerializer` class for XML serialization can also be selected just for individual operations:

```
[ServiceContract]
[XmlSerializerFormat]
public interface IDerivativesCalculator
{
    [OperationContract]
    [XmlSerializerFormat]
    decimal CalculateDerivative(
        string[] symbols,
        decimal[] parameters,
        string[] functions);

    [...]
}
```

The `System.Xml.Serialization.XmlSerializer` provides very precise control over how data is to be represented in XML. Its facilities are well documented in the book *.NET Web Services: Architecture and Implementation,* by Keith Ballinger (2003).

The `System.Runtime.Serialization.DataContractSerializer`, on the other hand, provides very little control over how data is to be represented in XML. It allows you to specify only the namespaces and names used to refer to data items in the XML, and the order in which the data items are to appear in the XML, as in this case:

```
[DataContract(Namespace="Derivatives",Name="Calculation")]
public class DerivativesCalculation
{
        [DataMember(Namespace="Derivatives",Name="Symbols",Order=0)]
        private string[] symbols;
```

```
    [DataMember(Namespace="Derivatives",Name="Parameters",Order=1)]
    private decimal[] parameters;
    [...]
}
```

Unlike the `System.Xml.Serialization.XmlSerializer`, which, by default, serializes all public data items to XML, the `System.Runtime.Serialization.DataContractSerializer` requires one to be explicit about which data items are to be serialized, by adding the `System.Runtime.Serialization.DataMember` attribute to them.

By not permitting any control over how the data items that are to be serialized will be represented in XML, the serialization process becomes highly predictable for the `System.Runtime.Serialization.DataContractSerializer` and, thereby, more amenable to optimization. So, a practical benefit of the `System.Runtime.Serialization.DataContractSerializer`'s design is better performance, approximately 10% better performance.

The XML Fetish

One might wonder whether the gain in performance is worth the loss of control over how data is represented in XML. That is most certainly the case, and understanding why serves to highlight the brilliance of the design of the Windows Communication Foundation.

A practice that is most characteristic of service-oriented programming is commonly referred to as *contract-first development*. Contract-first development is to begin the construction of software by specifying platform-independent representations for the data structures to be exchanged across the external interfaces, and platform-independent protocols for those exchanges.

Contract-first development is a sound practice. It helps one to avoid such unfortunate mistakes as building software that is meant to be interoperable across platforms, but that emits data in formats for which there are only representations on a particular platform, such as the .NET DataSet format.

However, the sound practice of contract-first development has become confused with one particular way of doing contract-first development, by virtue of which people become excessively concerned with XML formats. That particular way of doing contract-first development is to use an XML editor to compose specifications of data formats in the XML Schema language, taking care to ensure that all complex data types are ultimately defined in terms of XML Schema data types. Now, as a software developer, one's sole interest in contract-first development should be in defining the inputs and outputs of one's software, and in ensuring that, if necessary, those inputs and outputs can be represented in a platform-independent format. Yet practitioners of contract-first development, working in the XML Schema language in an XML editor, tend to become distracted from those core concerns and start to worry about exactly how the data is to be represented in XML. Consequently, they begin to debate, among other things, the virtues of various ways of encoding XML, and become highly suspicious of anything that might inhibit them from seeing and fiddling with XML. The XML becomes a fetish, falsely imbued with the true virtues of contract-first development, and, as Sigmund Freud wrote, "[s]uch substitutes are with some justice likened to the fetishes in which savages believe that their gods are embodied" (1977, 66).

With the System.Runtime.Serialization.DataContractSerializer, the Windows Communication Foundation not only restores the focus of software developers to what should be important to them, namely, the specification of inputs and outputs, but also relocates control over the representation of data to where it properly belongs, which is outside of the code, at the system administrator's disposal. Specifically, given the class

```
public class DerivativesCalculation
{
    public string[] Symbols;
    public decimal[] Parameters;
    public string[] Functions;
    public DataTime Date;
}
```

all one should care about as a software developer is to be able to say that the class is a data structure that may be an input or an output, that particular constituents of that structure may be included when it is input or output, and also, perhaps, valid ranges of values for the constituents when the structure is used as an input. The System.Runtime.Serialization.DataContract and System.Runtime.Serialization.DataMember attributes provided for using the System.Runtime.Serialization.DataContractSerializer to serialize data allow one to say that the class is a data structure that may be an input or an output, and to say which constituents of the structure may be included when it is input or output:

```
[DataContract]
public class DerivativesCalculation
{
    [DataMember]
    public string[] Symbols;
    [DataMember]
    public decimal[] Parameters;
    [DataMember]
    public string[] Functions;
    public DataTime Date;
}
```

It is by configuring the encoding protocol in the binding of an endpoint that one can control exactly how data structures are represented in transmissions.

Now there are two scenarios to consider. In the first scenario, the organization that has adopted the Windows Communication Foundation is building a service. In the other scenario, the organization that has adopted the Windows Communication Foundation is building a client.

Building a Service

In the first of these scenarios, the Windows Communication Foundation developers define the data structures to be exchanged with their services using the System.Runtime.Serialization.DataContract and System.Runtime.Serialization.DataMember attributes. Then they generate representations of those structures in the XML Schema language using the Service Metadata Tool, introduced in Chapter 2. They provide those XML Schema language representations to developers wanting to use their services. The designers of the Windows Communication Foundation have expended considerable effort to ensure that the structure of the XML into which the System.Runtime.Serialization.DataContractSerializer serializes data should be readily consumable by the tools various vendors provide to assist in deserializing data that is in XML. Therefore, anyone wanting to use the services provided by the Windows Communication Foundation developers in this scenario should be able to do so, despite the Windows Communication Foundation developers never having necessarily looked at, or manipulated, any XML in the process of providing the services.

What if the developers wanted to constrain the valid ranges for values used as inputs to their services, though? The XML Schema language has much richer facilities for expressing such constraints than the .NET programming languages do, and the System.Runtime.Serialization.DataContract and System.Runtime.Serialization.DataMember attributes provide no means of doing so. Not only would the XML Schema language allow the developers of the services to communicate the valid ranges of values to developers wanting to use the services, but the XML representations of the inputs could be validated against XML Schema documents to detect any deviations including values outside of the valid ranges.

Now suppose that the developers of the services were to spend many hours carefully hand-crafting XML Schema language expressions into the metadata for their services, using all the facilities of that language to express the constraints that they hoped to convey to their counterparts developing client applications. Unfortunately, their efforts would likely prove to be for naught. The developers of the client applications will probably use a tool to generate the code for communicating with the services, because, after all, being able to generate such code from the metadata of a service is one of the principal benefits afforded by service-oriented programming technologies. Well, the tool will very likely simply ignore all the XML Schema language expressions that the developers of the services wrote to define valid ranges of input values. The Microsoft Schemas/DataTypes support utility, xsd.exe, which has been used for generating .NET data types from XML schemas since the initial release of Microsoft .NET certainly would ignore all of those expressions. For example, from this XML Schema document,

```xml
<?xml version="1.0" encoding="utf-8" ?>
<xsd:schema xmlns:xsd="http://www.w3.org/2001/XMLSchema" >
  <xsd:complexType name="BookOrderType">
    <xsd:sequence>
      <xsd:element name="quantity" >
        <xsd:simpleType >
```

```
    <xsd:restriction base="xsd:positiveInteger">
      <xsd:minExclusive value="100"/>
      <xsd:maxExclusive value="1000"/>
    </xsd:restriction>
   </xsd:simpleType>
  </xsd:element>
 </xsd:sequence>
 </xsd:complexType>
<xsd:element name="BookOrder" type="BookOrderType"/>
</xsd:schema>
```

the Microsoft Schemas/DataTypes support utility yields this class definition,

```
[Serializable]
[XmlRootAttribute("BookOrder",Namespace="",IsNullable=false)]
public class BookOrderType
{
    private string quantityField;

    [XmlElement(
        Form=System.Xml.Schema.XmlSchemaForm.Unqualified,
        DataType="positiveInteger")]
    public string quantity
    {   get
        {
            return this.quantityField;
        }
        set
        {
            this.quantityField = value;
        }
    }
}
```

which not only omits any reference to the constraint expressed in the XML Schema language that quantity values should range between 100 and 1000, but even ignores the constraint that the values should be positive integers, defaulting to representing the quantity value as a string.

Suppose, next, that the developer of a client application, who had not pored over the XML Schema language incorporated in the metadata for a service, ran afoul of some constraint expressed in the metadata that had not been evident in the code generated from it. If that violation was to be detected by validating the incoming data against XML

Schema documents, the errors that the developer of the client application would see would typically be difficult to interpret, and, moreover, the process of validating the incoming data against XML Schema documents is notoriously inefficient.

A far more practical way of conveying and implementing constraints on input values would simply be to use expressive names

```
[DataContract]
public class BookOrderType
{
    [DataMember]
    public int QuantityValueBetween100And1000;
}
```

to test the values explicitly in code, and to return deliberate exceptions if the values fall outside of the proper ranges.

Building a Client

What about the case where Windows Communication Foundation developers want to use the Service Metadata Tool to generate code for using a software service that might or might not have been developed using the Windows Communication Foundation? If the XML representations of the inputs and outputs of that service deviate from the way in which the System.Runtime.Serialization.DataContractSerializer represents data in XML, the code generated by the Service Metadata Tool will include the switch for using the XmlSerializer instead of the System.Runtime.Serialization.DataContractSerializer for serializing data to XML. That code should allow the Windows Communication Foundation developers to use the service, and, once again, they will not have had to look at or manipulate any XML to do so.

Succumbing to the Urge to Look at XML

Should the fetish for XML prove too overwhelming, and one is compelled to look at the XML Schema language that defines how a class will be represented within XML, the Windows Communication Foundation does make provision for that. Executing the Service Metadata Tool in this way,

```
svcutil /datacontractonly SomeAssembly.dll
```

where SomeAssembly.dll is the name of some assembly in which a data contract is defined for a class, will yield the XML Schema language specifying the format of the XML into which instances of the class will be serialized.

The Case for the DataContractSerializer

The question being considered is whether the gain in performance yielded by the System.Runtime.Serialization.DataContractSerializer is adequate compensation for its providing so little control over how data is represented in XML. The answer that should be apparent from the foregoing is that control over how data is represented in

XML is generally of no use to software developers, so, yes, any gain in performance in exchange for that control is certainly welcome.

Using the DataContractSerializer

To become familiar with the System.Runtime.Serialization.DataContractSerializer, open the Visual Studio solution associated with this chapter downloaded from http://www.cryptmaker.com/WindowsCommunicationFoundationHandsOn. The solution contains a single project, called Serialization, for building a console application. All the code is in a single module, Program.cs, the content of which is shown in Listing 3.3. Note that there is a using statement for the System.Runtime.Serialization namespace, and also that the project references the System.Runtime.Serialization assembly.

LISTING 3.3   Program.cs

```
using System;
using System.Collections.Generic;
using System.Data;
using System.IO;
using System.Runtime.Serialization;
using System.ServiceModel;
using System.ServiceModel.Channels;
using System.Text;

namespace Serialization
{
    [DataContract(Name="Calculation")]
    public class ServiceViewOfData: IExtensibleDataObject
    {
        [DataMember(Name = "Symbols")]
        private string[] symbols;
        [DataMember(Name = "Parameters")]
        private decimal[] parameters;
        [DataMember(Name = "Functions")]
        private string[] functions;
        [DataMember(Name="Value")]
        private decimal value;

        private ExtensionDataObject extensionData;

        public string[] Symbols
        {
            get
            {
                return this.symbols;
            }
        }
```

LISTING 3.3   Continued

```
        set
        {
            this.symbols = value;
        }
    }

    public decimal[] Parameters
    {
        get
        {
            return this.parameters;
        }

        set
        {
            this.parameters = value;
        }
    }

    public string[] Functions
    {
        get
        {
            return this.functions;
        }

        set
        {
            this.functions = value;
        }

    }

    public decimal Value
    {
        get
        {
            return this.value;
        }

        set
        {
```

LISTING 3.3   Continued

```
                this.value = value;
        }
    }

    #region IExtensibleDataObject Members

    public ExtensionDataObject ExtensionData
    {
        get
        {
            return this.extensionData;
        }

        set
        {
            this.extensionData = value;
        }
    }

    #endregion
}

[DataContract]
public class Data
{
    [DataMember]
    public string Value;
}

[DataContract]
public class DerivedData : Data
{
}

[DataContract(Name = "Calculation")]
public class ClientViewOfData : IExtensibleDataObject
{
    [DataMember(Name = "Symbols")]
    public string[] Symbols;
    [DataMember(Name = "Parameters")]
    public decimal[] Parameters;
    [DataMember(Name="Functions")]
    public string[] Functions;
    [DataMember(Name="Value")]
```

LISTING 3.3   Continued

```
        public decimal Value;
        [DataMember(Name = "Reference")]
        public Guid Reference;

        private ExtensionDataObject extensionData;


        public ExtensionDataObject ExtensionData
        {
            get
            {
                return this.extensionData;
            }

            set
            {
                this.extensionData = value;
            }
        }


    }




[ServiceContract(Name = "DerivativesCalculator")]
[ServiceKnownType(typeof(DerivedData))]
public interface IServiceViewOfService
{
    [OperationContract(Name="FromXSDTypes")]
    decimal CalculateDerivative(
        string[] symbols,
        decimal[] parameters,
        string[] functions);

    [OperationContract(Name="FromDataSet")]
    DataSet CalculateDerivative(DataSet input);

    [OperationContract(Name = "FromDataContract")]
    ServiceViewOfData CalculateDerivative(ServiceViewOfData input);
```

LISTING 3.3   Continued

```
    [OperationContract(Name = "AlsoFromDataContract")]
    Data DoSomething(Data input);

}

[ServiceContract(Name="DerivativesCalculator")]
[ServiceKnownType(typeof(DerivedData))]
public interface IClientViewOfService
{
    [OperationContract(Name = "FromXSDTypes")]
    decimal CalculateDerivative(
        string[] symbols,
        decimal[] parameters,
        string[] functions);

    [OperationContract(Name = "FromDataSet")]
    DataSet CalculateDerivative(DataSet input);

    [OperationContract(Name = "FromDataContract")]
    ClientViewOfData CalculateDerivative(ClientViewOfData input);

    [OperationContract(Name = "AlsoFromDataContract")]
    Data DoSomething(Data input);
}

public class DerivativesCalculator : IServiceViewOfService
{
    #region IDerivativesCalculator Members

    public decimal CalculateDerivative(
        string[] symbols,
        decimal[] parameters,
        string[] functions)
    {
        return (decimal)(System.DateTime.Now.Millisecond);
    }


    public DataSet CalculateDerivative(DataSet input)
    {
        if (input.Tables.Count > 0)
        {
            if (input.Tables[0].Rows.Count > 0)
            {
```

LISTING 3.3   Continued

```
                    input.Tables[0].Rows[0]["Value"] =
                        (decimal)(System.DateTime.Now.Millisecond);
                }
            }
            return input;
        }

        public ServiceViewOfData CalculateDerivative(ServiceViewOfData input)
        {
            input.Value = this.CalculateDerivative(
                input.Symbols,
                input.Parameters,
                input.Functions);
            return input;
        }

        public Data DoSomething(Data input)
        {
            return input;
        }

        #endregion
    }

    public class Program
    {
        public static void Main(string[] args)
        {
            using (ServiceHost host = new ServiceHost(
                typeof(DerivativesCalculator),
                new Uri[] {
                    new Uri("http://localhost:8000/Derivatives") }))
            {
                host.AddServiceEndpoint(
                    typeof(IServiceViewOfService),
                    new BasicHttpBinding(),
                    "Calculator");
                host.Open();

                Console.WriteLine("The service is available.");

                string address =
                    "http://localhost:8000/Derivatives/Calculator";
                ChannelFactory<IClientViewOfService> factory =
```

LISTING 3.3   Continued

```
                    new ChannelFactory<IClientViewOfService>(
                        new BasicHttpBinding(),
                        new EndpointAddress(
                            new Uri(address)));
                IClientViewOfService proxy =
                    factory.CreateChannel();

                decimal result = proxy.CalculateDerivative(
                    new string[] { "MSFT" },
                    new decimal[] { 3 },
                    new string[] { "TechStockProjection" });
                Console.WriteLine("Value using XSD types is {0}.", result);

                DataTable table = new DataTable("InputTable");
                table.Columns.Add("Symbol", typeof(string));
                table.Columns.Add("Parameter", typeof(decimal));
                table.Columns.Add("Function", typeof(string));
                table.Columns.Add("Value", typeof(decimal));

                table.Rows.Add("MSFT", 3, "TechStockProjection",0.00);

                DataSet input = new DataSet("Input");
                input.Tables.Add(table);

                DataSet output = proxy.CalculateDerivative(input);
                if (output != null)
                {
                    if (output.Tables.Count > 0)
                    {
                        if (output.Tables[0].Rows.Count > 0)
                        {
                            Console.WriteLine(
                                "Value using a DataSet is {0}.",
                                output.Tables[0].Rows[0]["Value"]);
                        }
                    }
                }

                ClientViewOfData calculation =
                    new ClientViewOfData();
                calculation.Symbols =
                    new string[] { "MSFT" };
                calculation.Parameters =
                    new decimal[] { 3 };
```

LISTING 3.3   Continued

```
                     calculation.Functions =
                         new string[] { "TechStockProjection" };
                     calculation.Reference =
                         Guid.NewGuid();

                     Console.WriteLine(
                         "Reference is {0}.", calculation.Reference);

                     ClientViewOfData calculationResult =
                         proxy.CalculateDerivative(calculation);
                     Console.WriteLine("Value using a Data Contract {0}.",
                         calculationResult.Value);

                     Console.WriteLine(
                         "Reference is {0}.", calculationResult.Reference);

                     DerivedData derivedData = new DerivedData();
                     Data outputData = proxy.DoSomething(derivedData);

                     MemoryStream stream = new MemoryStream();
                     DataContractSerializer serializer =
                                                new
➥DataContractSerializer(typeof(ClientViewOfData));
                     serializer.WriteObject(stream, calculation);
                     Console.WriteLine(
                         UnicodeEncoding.UTF8.GetChars(stream.GetBuffer()));

                     Console.WriteLine("Done.");

                     ((IChannel)proxy).Close();

                     host.Close();

                     Console.ReadKey();

                 }
             }
         }
}
```

In this code, an endpoint, with its address, binding, and contract, is added to the service programmatically, rather than through the host application's configuration, as was done in the preceding chapter:

```
using (ServiceHost host = new ServiceHost(
    typeof(DerivativesCalculator),
    new Uri[] {
        new Uri("http://localhost:8000/Derivatives") }))
{
    host.AddServiceEndpoint(
        typeof(IServiceViewOfService),
        new BasicHttpBinding(),
        "Calculator");
    host.Open();

    Console.WriteLine("The service is available.");

    [...]
}
```

Similarly, the client code directly incorporates information about the service's endpoint, rather than referring to endpoint information in the application's configuration:

```
string address =
    "http://localhost:8000/Derivatives/Calculator";
ChannelFactory<IClientViewOfService> factory =
    new ChannelFactory<IClientViewOfService>(
        new BasicHttpBinding(),
        new EndpointAddress(
            new Uri(address)));
IClientViewOfService proxy =
    factory.CreateChannel();
```

This imperative style of programming with the Windows Communication Foundation is used here for two reasons. The first is simply to show that this style is an option. The second and more important reason is to make the code that is discussed here complete in itself, with no reference to outside elements such as configuration files.

The contract of the service is defined in this way:

```
[ServiceContract(Name = "DerivativesCalculator")]
[...]
public interface IServiceViewOfService
{
    [...]
}
```

The client has a separate definition of the contract of the service, but the definition used by the client and the definition used by the service are semantically identical:

```
[ServiceContract(Name="DerivativesCalculator")]
[...]
public interface IClientViewOfService
{
    [...]
}
```

In both the client's version of the contract and the service's version, there is this definition of an operation:

```
[OperationContract(Name="FromXSDTypes")]
decimal CalculateDerivative(
    string[] symbols,
    decimal[] parameters,
    string[] functions);
```

When the client uses that operation, like this,

```
decimal result = proxy.CalculateDerivative(
    new string[] { "MSFT" },
    new decimal[] { 3 },
    new string[] { "TechStockProjection" });
```

its attempt to do so works, which can be verified by running the application built from the solution. In this case, the inputs and outputs of the operation are .NET types that correspond quite obviously to XML Schema data types. The `System.Runtime.Serialization.DataContractSerializer` automatically serializes the inputs and outputs into XML. Other types besides the .NET Framework's built-in value types that the `System.Runtime.Serialization.DataContractSerializer` will automatically serialize include byte arrays, `System.DateType`, `System.TimeSpan`, `System.GUID`, `System.XmlQualifiedName`, `System.XmlElement`, `System.XmlNode`, and various array and collection classes including `System.Collections.Generic.List<T>`, `System.Collections.Generic.Dictionary<K,V>`, and `System.Collections.Hashtable`.

The next operation defined in both the client's version of the contract and the service's version is this one:

```
[OperationContract(Name="FromDataSet")]
DataSet CalculateDerivative(DataSet input);
```

The client uses that operation with this code:

```
DataTable table = new DataTable("InputTable");
table.Columns.Add("Symbol", typeof(string));
table.Columns.Add("Parameter", typeof(decimal));
```

```
table.Columns.Add("Function", typeof(string));
table.Columns.Add("Value", typeof(decimal));

table.Rows.Add("MSFT", 3, "TechStockProjection",0.00);

DataSet input = new DataSet("Input");
input.Tables.Add(table);

DataSet output = proxy.CalculateDerivative(input);
[...]
Console.WriteLine(
  "Value using a DataSet is {0}.",
  output.Tables[0].Rows[0]["Value"]);
```

In this case, the input and output of the operation are both .NET System.Data.DataSet objects, and the .NET System.Data.DataSet type does not obviously correspond to any XML Schema data type. Nevertheless, the System.Runtime.Serialization.DataContractSerializer automatically serializes the input and output to XML, as it will for any .NET type that implements System.Runtime.Serialization.ISerializable. Of course, passing .NET System.Data.DataSet objects around is a very bad idea if you can anticipate a non–.NET client needing to participate, and it is never wise to rule that out as a possibility.

In the service's version of the contract, this operation is included:

```
[OperationContract(Name = "FromDataContract")]
ServiceViewOfData CalculateDerivative(ServiceViewOfData input);
```

The input and output of this operation is an instance of the ServiceViewOfData class, which is defined like so:

```
[DataContract(Name="Calculation")]
public class ServiceViewOfData: IExtensibleDataObject
{
    [DataMember(Name = "Symbols")]
    private string[] symbols;
    [DataMember(Name = "Parameters")]
    private decimal[] parameters;
    [DataMember(Name = "Functions")]
    private string[] functions;
    [DataMember(Name="Value")]
    private decimal value;

    [...]
}
```

The client's version of the contract defines the corresponding operation in this way:

```
[OperationContract(Name = "FromDataContract")]
ClientViewOfData CalculateDerivative(ClientViewOfData input);
```

Here, the input and output are of the `ClientViewOfData` type, which is defined in this way:

```
[DataContract(Name = "Calculation")]
public class ClientViewOfData : IExtensibleDataObject
{
    [DataMember(Name = "Symbols")]
    public string[] Symbols;
    [DataMember(Name = "Parameters")]
    public decimal[] Parameters;
    [DataMember(Name="Functions")]
    public string[] Functions;
    [DataMember(Name="Value")]
    public decimal Value;
    [DataMember(Name = "Reference")]
    public Guid Reference;

    [...]

}
```

The service's `ServiceViewOfData` class and the client's `ClientViewOfData` class are used to define data contracts that are compatible with one another. The data contracts are compatible because they have the same namespace and name, and because the members that have the same names in each version of the contract also have the same types. Because of the compatibility of the data contracts used in the client's version of the operation and the service's version, those operations that the client and the service define in different ways are also compatible with one another.

The client's version of the data contract includes a member that the service's version of the data contract omits: the member named `Reference`. However, the service's version implements the Windows Communication Foundation's `System.Runtime.Serialization.IExtensibleDataObject` interface like so:

```
[DataContract(Name="Calculation")]
public class ServiceViewOfData: IExtensibleDataObject
{
    [...]

    public ExtensionDataObject ExtensionData
    {
        get
        {
```

```
        return this.extensionData;
    }

    set
    {
        this.extensionData = value;
    }
}
}
```

By implementing the System.Runtime.Serialization.IExtensibleDataObject interface, the class sets aside some memory that the System.Runtime.Serialization.DataContractSerializer can use for storing and retrieving the values of members that other versions of the same contract might include. In this case, that memory is named by the variable called extensionData. Thus, when a more advanced version of the same data contract is passed to service, with members that the service's version of the data contract does not include, the System.Runtime.Serialization.DataContractSerializer is able to pass the values of those members through the service. In particular, when the client calls the service using this code

```
ClientViewOfData calculation =
    new ClientViewOfData();
calculation.Symbols =
    new string[] { "MSFT" };
calculation.Parameters =
    new decimal[] { 3 };
calculation.Functions =
    new string[] { "TechStockProjection" };
calculation.Reference =
    Guid.NewGuid();

Console.WriteLine(
    "Reference is {0}.", calculation.Reference);

ClientViewOfData calculationResult =
    proxy.CalculateDerivative(calculation);
Console.WriteLine("Value using a Data Contract {0}.",
    calculationResult.Value);

Console.WriteLine(
    "Reference is {0}.", calculationResult.Reference);
```

not only is the System.Runtime.Serialization.DataContractSerializer able to serialize the custom type, ClientViewOfData, to XML for transmission to the service, but the member called Reference that is in the client's version of the data contract, but not in the service's version, passes through the service without being lost.

Two things should be evident from this case. First, the System.Runtime.Serialization.DataContract and System.Runtime.Serialization.DataMember attributes make it very easy to provide for the serialization of one's custom data types by the Windows Communication Foundation's System.Runtime.Serialization.DataContractSerializer. Second, implementing the Windows Communication Foundation's System.Runtime.Serialization.IExtensibleDataObject interface is always a good idea because doing so allows different versions of the same data contract to evolve independent of one another, yet still be usable together.

The last operation defined for the service is this one, which is defined in the same way both in the code used by the service and in the code used by the client:

```
[OperationContract(Name = "AlsoFromDataContract")]
Data DoSomething(Data input);
```

The input and output of the operation are of the custom Data type, which is made serializable by the System.Runtime.Serialization.DataContractSerializer through the use of the DataContract and DataMember attributes, like so:

```
[DataContract]
public class Data
{
  [DataMember]
 public string Value;
}
```

The client uses that operation with this code:

```
DerivedData derivedData = new DerivedData();
Data outputData = proxy.DoSomething(derivedData);
```

That code passes an instance of the DerivedData type to the service, a type that is derived from the Data class, in this way:

```
[DataContract]
public class DerivedData : Data
{
}
```

What will happen in this case is that the System.Runtime.Serialization.DataContractSerializer, in deserializing the data received from the client on behalf of the service, will encounter the XML into which an instance of the DerivedData class had been serialized, when it will be expecting the XML into which an instance of the Data class has been serialized. That will cause the System.Runtime.Serialization.DataContractSerializer to throw an exception.

However, both the service's version of the endpoint's contract and the client's version have a `System.ServiceModel.ServiceKnownType` attribute that refers to the `DerivedData` class:

```
[ServiceContract(Name = "DerivativesCalculator")]
[ServiceKnownType(typeof(DerivedData))]
public interface IServiceViewOfService
{
    [...]
}

[ServiceContract(Name="DerivativesCalculator")]
[ServiceKnownType(typeof(DerivedData))]
public interface IClientViewOfService
{
    [...]
}
```

That attribute prepares the `System.Runtime.Serialization.DataContractSerializer` to accept the XML for a `DerivedData` object as a parameter whenever it is expecting the XML for an instance of any type from which the `DerivedData` class derives. So, by virtue of that attribute being added to the definition of the service's contract, when the `System.Runtime.Serialization.DataContractSerializer` encounters XML for a `DerivedData` object when it is expecting XML for a `Data` object, it is able to deserialize that XML into an instance of the `DerivedData` class. It follows that if one was to define an operation in this way,

```
[OperationContract]
void DoSomething(object[] inputArray);
```

one should add to the service contract a `System.ServiceModel.ServiceKnownType` attribute for each of the types that might actually be included in the input parameter array. Whereas the `System.ServiceModel.ServiceKnownType` attribute allows for the substitution of a parameter of a derived type for a parameter of a base type in the invocation of operations, the similar `System.Runtime.Serialization.KnownType` attribute is provided to allow a data member of a derived type to be substituted for a data member of base type:

```
[DataContract]
[KnownType(typeof(string))]
[KnownType(typeof(int))]
public class MyDataContract
{
    [DataMember]
    object[] MyArrayOfThings;
}
```

That the `System.ServiceModel.ServiceKnownType` attributes is required in order for parameters of derived types to be substituted for parameters of base types in the invocation of operations implies that one should avoid using inheritance as a way of versioning data contracts. If a base type is expected, but a derived type is received, serialization of the derived type will fail unless the code is modified with the addition of the `System.ServiceModel.ServiceKnownType` attribute to anticipate the derived type.

The Windows Communication Foundation uses the `System.Runtime.Serialization.DataContractSerializer` invisibly. So, these remaining lines of client code in the sample simply show that it can be used separately from the rest of the Windows Communication Foundation for serializing data to XML:

```
MemoryStream stream = new MemoryStream();
DataContractSerializer serializer =
        new DataContractSerializer(typeof(ClientViewOfData));
serializer.WriteObject(stream, calculation);
Console.WriteLine(
    UnicodeEncoding.UTF8.GetChars(stream.GetBuffer()));
```

Exception Handling

Data contracts also assist in being able to notify clients of exceptions that may occur in a service. To see how that works, follow these steps:

1. Add this class to the `Program.cs` module of the Serialization project referred to previously:

   ```
   public class SomeError
   {
     public string Content;
   }
   ```

2. Create a data contract from that class using the `System.Runtime.Serialization.DataContract` and `System.Runtime.DataMember` attributes:

   ```
   [DataContract]
   public class SomeError
   {
     [DataMember]
     public string Content;
   }
   ```

   This yields a data contract that specifies the format of a simple error message that the service might send to the client.

3. Add an operation to the `IServiceViewOfService` interface that defines the service's version of the service's contract:

```
[OperationContract(Name="Faulty")]
decimal DivideByZero(decimal input);
```

4. Add a fault contract to the operation, using the `System.ServiceModel.FaultContract` attribute, to inform clients that they should anticipate that, instead of returning the expected result, the service might return an error message of the form defined by the `SomeError` data contract:

```
[OperationContract(Name="Faulty")]
[FaultContract(typeof(SomeError))]
decimal DivideByZero(decimal input);
```

5. Add an implementation of the `DivideByZero()` method to the `DerivativesCalculator` class, which is the service type that implements the `DerivativesCalculator` service contract defined by the `IServiceViewOfService` interface:

```
public class DerivativesCalculator : IServiceViewOfService
{
    [...]
    public decimal DivideByZero(decimal input)
    {
        try
        {
            decimal denominator = 0;
            return input / denominator;
        }
        catch (Exception exception)
        {
            SomeError error = new SomeError();
            error.Content = exception.Message;
            throw new FaultException<SomeError>(error);
        }
    }
}
```

By virtue of this code, when the service traps an exception in the `DivideByZero()` method, it creates an instance of the `SomeError` class to convey selected information about the exception to the caller. That information is then sent to the caller using the Windows Communication Foundation's generic `System.ServiceModel.FaultException<T>`.

6. Because of the `System.ServiceModel.FaultContract` attribute on the `DivideByZero()` method, if the metadata for the service was to be downloaded and

client code generated from it using the Service Metadata Tool, the client's version of the contract would automatically include the definition of the DivideByZero() method and its associated fault contract. However, in this case, simply add the method and the fault contract to the client's version of the contract, which is in the IClientViewOfService interface:

```
[ServiceContract(Name="DerivativesCalculator")]
[KnownType(typeof(DerivedData))]
public interface IClientViewOfService
{
    [...]
    [OperationContract(Name = "Faulty")]
    [FaultContract(typeof(SomeError))]
    decimal DivideByZero(decimal input);
}
```

7. Now have the client use the Faulty operation by adding code to the static Main() method of the Program class, as shown in Listing 3.4. Because receiving an error message from an attempt to use the operation should be anticipated, as the FaultContract for the operation indicates, the client code is written to handle that possibility. That is accomplished using the Windows Communication Foundation's System.ServiceModel.FaultException<T> generic, which was also used in the code for the service to convey information about an exception to the client. The Detail property of the System.ServiceModel.FaultException<T> generic provides access to an instance of T, which, in this case, is an instance of the SomeError class that the client can interrogate for information about the error that occurred.

LISTING 3.4   Anticipating a Fault

```
public class Program
{
  public static void Main(string[] args)
  {
    using (ServiceHost host = new ServiceHost(
      typeof(DerivativesCalculator),
        new Uri[] {
          new Uri("http://localhost:8000/Derivatives") }))
    {
      host.AddServiceEndpoint(
        typeof(IServiceViewOfService),
        new BasicHttpBinding(),
        "Calculator");
      host.Open();

      Console.WriteLine("The service is available.");
```

LISTING 3.4   Continued

```
    string address =
      "http://localhost:8000/Derivatives/Calculator";

    ChannelFactory<IClientViewOfService> factory =
      new ChannelFactory<IClientViewOfService>(
        new BasicHttpBinding(),
          new EndpointAddress(
            new Uri(address))));
    IClientViewOfService proxy =
      factory.CreateChannel();

    [...]

    try
    {
      Decimal quotient = proxy.DivideByZero(9);
    }
    catch (FaultException<SomeError> error)
    {
      Console.WriteLine("Error: {0}", error.Detail.Content);
    }

    [...]

  }
 }
}
```

8. To see the effect of the changes, choose Debug, Start Without Debugging from the Visual Studio 2005 menus.

9. Enter a keystroke into the application's console to terminate it.

The approach to handling exceptions shown here has multiple virtues. It allows the developers of services to easily define the structure of the error messages that they want to transmit to client programmers. It also allows them to advertise to client programmers which operations of their services might return particular error messages instead of the results they would otherwise expect. The service programmers are able to easily formulate and transmit error messages to clients, and client programmers have a simple syntax, almost exactly like ordinary exception-handling syntax, for receiving and examining error messages. Most important, service programmers get to decide exactly what information about errors that occur in their services they want to have conveyed to clients.

However, the design of the Windows Communication Foundation does anticipate the utility, solely in the process of debugging a service, being able to return to a client complete information about any unanticipated exceptions that might occur within a service. That can be accomplished using the IncludeExceptionDetailInFaults property of the behavior System.ServiceModel.Description.ServiceDebugBehavior. The properties of that behavior can be set through configuration, and this configuration of a service will result in any unhandled exceptions being transmitted to the client:

```xml
<?xml version="1.0" encoding="utf-8" ?>
<configuration>
        <system.serviceModel>
                <services>
                        <service
                                name=
"DerivativesCalculator.DerivativesCalculatorServiceType,
DerivativesCalculatorService"
                                behaviorConfiguration=
"DerivativesCalculatorBehavior">
            <endpoint
                address=""
                binding="basicHttpBinding"
                contract=
"DerivativesCalculator.IDerivativesCalculator "
                                />
                                </service>
        </services>
        <behaviors>
                        <serviceBehaviors>
                                <behavior
                                        name="DerivativesCalculatorBehavior"
/>
                                <serviceDebug
includeExceptionDetailInFaults="true"/>
                                </behavior>
                        </serviceBehaviors>
        </behaviors>
    </system.serviceModel>
</configuration>
```

To reiterate, this configuration could be very useful for diagnosis in the process of debugging a service, but it is dangerous in production because transmitting all the information about an exception to a client might expose information about the service that could be used to compromise it. To diagnose problems with services in production, use the tracing and logging facilities described in Chapter 19, "Manageability."

Summary

Data being sent from a Windows Communication Foundation client to a service is serialized to XML within the client, and data received from clients by Windows Communication Foundation services is deserialized from XML within the service. There are two XML serializers that the Windows Communication Foundation can use to accomplish the serialization to XML and deserialization from XML. One is the `System.Xml.Serialization.XmlSerializer` class that has been a part of the .NET Framework class library from the outset. The other is the `System.Runtime.Serialization.DataContractSerializer` class that is new with the Windows Communication Foundation. Whereas the `System.Xml.Serialization.XmlSerializer` provides precise control over how data is represented as XML, the `System.Runtime.Serialization.DataContractSerializer` provides very little control over that. It provides little control over how data gets represented in XML in order to make the serialization process very predictable, and, thereby, easier to optimize. As a result, the `System.Runtime.Serialization.DataContractSerializer` outperforms the `System.Xml.Serialization.XmlSerializer`.

Allowing the `System.Runtime.Serialization.DataContractSerializer` to serialize one's custom types is very simple. One merely adds a `System.Runtime.Serialization.DataContract` attribute to the definition of the type, and `System.Runtime.DataMember` attributes to each of the type's members that are to be serialized.

Implementing the `System.Runtime.Serialization.IExtensibleDataObject` interface in any type that is to be serialized using the `System.Runtime.Serialization.DataContractSerializer` is wise. It allows for different versions of the same way of representing the data in XML to evolve independently of one another, yet still be usable together.

References

Ballinger, Keith. 2003. *.NET Web Services: Architecture and Implementation*. Reading, MA: Addison-Wesley.

Freud, Sigmund. 1977. *Three Essays on Sexuality*. In *On Sexuality: Three Essays on Sexuality and Other Works*, ed. Angela Richards. The Pelican Freud Library, ed. James Strachey, no. 7. London, UK: Penguin.

CHAPTER 4

Sessions, Reliable Sessions, Queues, and Transactions

Introduction

This chapter covers an assortment of facilities that the Windows Communication Foundation provides for making systems more robust. Those features are Reliable Sessions, session management, queued delivery, and transaction flow. Besides introducing each feature, this chapter shows how to use them together to properly implement distributed, transactional systems.

Reliable Sessions

The Windows Communication Foundation's Reliable Sessions facility is for providing assurances at the binding level that messages will be delivered exactly once, and in order. When communicating with the Transmission Control Protocol (TCP), a measure of reliability is ensured by the protocol itself. However, those assurances are strictly at the packet level and between just two points. The Windows Communication Foundation's Reliable Sessions feature provides assurances against the possibility of messages being lost in transmission, duplicated, or received out of order, and it provides those assurances at the message level, across any number of intermediate nodes, and independent of the transport protocol. Furthermore, with Reliable Sessions enabled, the Windows Communication Foundation will attempt to re-establish dropped connections, and free the resources associated with a session if attempts at reconnection fail. It will also attempt to compensate for network congestion by adjusting the rate at which messages are sent.

To use the Windows Communication Foundation's Reliable Sessions facility, one must select a binding that supports it. The predefined bindings that support the feature are the WSHttpBinding, the WSDualHttpBinding, the WSFederationBinding, the NetTcpBinding, and the NetNamedPipesBinding. In the case of the WSHttpBinding, the WSDualHttpBinding, and the WSFederationBinding, the option of using Reliable Sessions is turned off by default, whereas it is turned on by default on the other bindings. Toggling reliable sessions on or off is done by customizing the binding in the usual way:

```
<system.serviceModel>
        <services>
          <service
                <endpoint
                        binding="wsHttpBinding"
                        bindingConfiguration="MyReliableConfiguration"
                        [...]
                        />
          </service>
        </services>
        <bindings>
          <wsHttpBinding>
                <binding name="MyReliableConfiguration">
                  <reliableSession
                        enabled="true"
                        ordered="true" />
                </binding>
          </wsHttpBinding>
        </bindings>
</system.serviceModel>
```

The Reliable Sessions facility can also be added to custom bindings by including the binding element, System.ServiceModel.Channels.ReliableSessionBindingElement:

```
<system.serviceModel>
        <services>
                <service name="[...]">
                        <endpoint
                                [...]
                                binding="customBinding"
                                bindingConfiguration="MyReliableCustomBinding">
                        </endpoint>
                </service>
        </services>
        <bindings>
                <customBinding>
                        <binding name="MyReliableCustomBinding">
                                <reliableSession ordered="false"  />
```

```
                    <httpTransport />
                </binding>
            </customBinding>
        </bindings>
</system.serviceModel>
```

Windows Communication Foundation developers can indicate that their code relies on some assurances about the delivery of messages. In particular, they can specify that they are assuming that the messages will be delivered in the order in which they were sent:

```
[ServiceContract(SessionMode = SessionMode.Required)]
[DeliveryRequirements(RequireOrderedDelivery = true)]
public interface IMyServiceContract
```

Adding this specification to a service contract will cause the Windows Communication Foundation to confirm that, for any endpoint that includes the service contract, a binding that supports Reliable Sessions has been selected and appropriately configured to ensure ordered delivery.

Reliable Sessions in Action

To see the effect of using the Windows Communication Foundation's Reliable Sessions facility, follow these steps:

1. Copy the code associated with this chapter downloaded from http://www.crypt-maker.com/WindowsCommunicationFoundationUnleashed to the folder C:\WCFHandsOn. The code is all in a folder called ReliableSessionsQueuesAndTransactions, which has two subfolders, one of which is called ReliableSessions.

2. Open the solution C:\WCFHandsOn\ ReliableSessionsQueuesAndTransactions \ReliableSessions\ReliableSessions.sln. The solution, which was the brainchild of Windows Communication Foundation program manager Shy Cohen, consists of four projects. The Sender project is for building a Windows application that sends a picture to the Windows application that is built by the Receiver project. In so doing, it breaks the picture being transmitted down into 100 parts and sends each part to the receiver as a separate message. The RouterController project is for controlling the likelihood of messages getting lost en route between the Sender and the Receiver.

3. Choose Debug, Start Debugging from the Visual Studio 2005 menus. The Sender, Receiver, and Router Controller applications should all start.

4. Click the Sender application's Open button, select the C:\WCFHandsOn\ReliableSessionsQueuesAndTransactions\ReliableSessions\Seattle. jpg file in the Open dialog that appears, and click the Open button on that dialog. A picture of the Seattle skyline should be displayed in the Sender application's window.

5. Click the Sender application's Send button. The picture displayed in the Sender application's window will evidently be transferred via 100 separate messages to the Receiver application.

6. Click the Clear button on the Receiver application.

7. Click the Clear button on the Router Controller application.

8. Move the Network Message Loss gauge on the Router Controller application all the way over to the right, so that it indicates that about 10% of the messages transferred are to be lost in transmission.

9. Click the Sender application's Send button. This time, only some of the picture displayed in the Sender application's window will be reproduced in the Receiver application's window.

10. Choose Debug, Stop Debugging from the Visual Studio 2005 menus.

11. Open the App.config file in the Receiver project and uncomment the line

    ```
    <!--<reliableSession ordered="false"  />-->
    ```

    so that the custom binding configured in that file now includes the `System.ServiceModel.Channels.ReliableSessionBindingElement` that provides the Windows Communication Foundation's Reliable Session facility:

    ```
    <bindings>
          <customBinding>
                  <binding name="ServiceBinding">
                          <reliableSession ordered="false"  />
                          <tcpTransport />
                  </binding>
          </customBinding>
    </bindings>
    ```

12. Open the App.config file of the Sender project and uncomment the line

    ```
    <!--<reliableSession ordered="false"  />-->
    ```

    so that the custom binding element configured in that file now also includes `System.ServiceModel.Channels.ReliableSessionBindingElement`:

    ```
    <customBinding>
          <binding name="ClientBinding">
                  <reliableSession ordered="false" />
                  <MyCustomBindingElement/>
                  <tcpTransport/>
          </binding>
    </customBinding>
    ```

13. Choose Debug, Start Debugging from the Visual Studio 2005 menus.

14. Click the Sender application's Open button, select the C:\WCFHandsOn\ ReliableSessionQueuesAndTransactions\ReliableSessions\Seattle.jpg file in the Open dialog that appears, and click the Open button on that dialog. A picture of the Seattle skyline should be displayed in the Sender application's window.

15. Move the Network Message Loss gauge on the Router Controller application so that it indicates that about 4% of the messages transferred are to be lost in transmission.

16. Click the Sender application's Send button, and watch the Receiver application's window carefully. It will be apparent that messages are being lost en route. Now, however, with Reliable Sessions enabled, the lost messages are being detected and re-sent so that all the parts of the picture sent by the Sender application are received at their destination.

17. Choose Debug, Stop Debugging from the Visual Studio 2005 menus.

Session Management

The session management capabilities of the Windows Communication Foundation are different from the Reliable Sessions feature. Reliable Sessions are for providing assurances of messages being delivered. Session management allows a Windows Communication Foundation application to treat a message that it receives as part of a session—as part of a unified sequence of messages exchanged with another application.

Therefore, developers of Windows Communication Foundation applications can write the code for processing one message in such a way that it depends on information from an earlier message. If they find themselves having to do that, they can indicate that they are doing so by assigning the value System.ServiceModel.SessionMode.Required to the SessionMode parameter of the System.ServiceModel.ServiceContract attribute:

```
[ServiceContract(SessionMode=SessionMode.Required)]
public interface IMyServiceContract
```

Doing so will cause the Windows Communication Foundation to verify that the binding chosen for any endpoint in which that contract is included can support a session and can support incorporating information into the messages to identify the session. The prede-fined bindings that do so are WSHttpBinding, WSDualHttpBinding, WSFederationBinding, NetTcpBinding, NetNamedPipesBinding, and NetMsmqBinding.

Developers can store and retrieve data pertaining to a session in instance context sessions:

```
public class MyExtension: IExtension<InstanceContext>
{
        public string sessionIdentifier = null;
        public MyDataType MyData = null;
}
```

```
public void FirstRequest(MyDataType myData)
{
        MyExtension extension = new MyExtension();
        extension.sessionIdentifier = OperationContext.SessionId;
        extension.MyDataType = myData;
        OperationContext.InstanceContext.Extensions.Add(myData);
}

public MyDataType SubsequentRequest()
{
        Collection<MyExtension> extensions =
          OperationContext.InstanceContext.Extensions.FindAll<MyExtension>();
        foreach(MyExtension extension in extensions)
        {
                if(string.Compare(
             extension.sessionIdentifier,OperationContext.SessionId,true)==0)
                        return extension.MyData;
        }
        return null;
}
```

To better manage the resources associated with a session, developers can stipulate which operation may be invoked to initiate a session and which operations signal the end of a session:

```
[ServiceContract(SessionMode=SessionMode.Required)]
public interface IMyServiceContract
{
        [OperationContract(IsInitiating=true)]
        void StartSession();
        [OperationContract(IsTerminating=true)]
        void StopSession();
}
```

Queued Delivery

The assurances provided by Reliable Sessions extend only to the lifetime of the host application domain. If a message is lost en route to its destination but the application domain from which the message was sent terminates before the loss of the message is detected, when the application domain is restored, it will be unaware of the message having been lost. In fact, it will have lost the context of the session in which the message went missing.

The Windows Communication Foundation's capability of sending messages via Microsoft Message Queuing (MSMQ) queues provides message delivery guarantees that are independent of the lifetime of the sending and receiving application domains. The queues store messages from a sending application on behalf of a receiving application. At some point after the message has been placed on the queue, the receiving application gets the message.

Using queues to convey messages yields a considerable number of benefits. First, if the receiving application is unavailable, perhaps because of an issue with that application or possibly due to a breakdown in connectivity, the sending application can still transmit messages and continue its work. The messages will be held on the queue until the receiving application is ready to accept them. Second, the speed and capacity of the network between the sending and the receiving application is mostly of no consequence, the sole limitation being that MSMQ can only accommodate messages up to 4MB in size. Third, the receiving application cannot be overwhelmed by unanticipated spikes in the frequency and volume of requests. It can consume them from the inbound queue at its own rate. Finally, MSMQ is a familiar technology for most administrators, and a Microsoft Management Console Snap-In is provided with Windows operating systems for them to use in managing MSMQ.

Queues can be used for communication between two Windows Communication Foundation applications, as well as between a Windows Communication Foundation application and a non–Windows Communication Foundation application that uses MSMQ. This chapter focuses on the case in which queues are used for exchanging messages between two Windows Communication Foundation applications. Exchanging messages between Windows Communication Foundation applications and other MSMQ applications is covered in Chapter 11, "Legacy Integration."

To have a message go from one Windows Communication Foundation application to another via an MSMQ queue, select the predefined `NetMsmqBinding`:

```
<services>
        <service name="Fabrikam.TradeRecorder">
                <host>
                        <baseAddresses>
                          <add baseAddress="net.msmq://localhost/private/"/>
                          </baseAddresses>
                </host>
                <endpoint
                        address="EndpointAddress"
                        binding="netMsmqBinding"
                        [...]/>
        </service>
</services>
```

The absolute address of the endpoint in this example is net.msmq://localhost/private/EndpointAddress. For an endpoint that uses the predefined `NetMsmqBinding`, the `net.msmq` scheme is mandatory. The next segment of the address, which in this case is `localhost`, identifies the host on which the queue resides. The segment `private` is mandatory if the queue is a private one. The last segment, which is the address of the endpoint itself, must be the name of a transactional MSMQ queue on the specified host.

A service that is configured to receive messages via an MSMQ queue must be deployed on the same machine as the queue itself. That restriction is due to MSMQ allowing remote reads only from nontransactional queues, and the Windows Communication Foundation allowing services to receive messages only via the `NetMsmqBinding` from transactional queues.

Multiple instances of a service can be configured to receive messages from the same queue. In that case, the most available application will receive the next available message.

When an endpoint is configured with a predefined binding by which messages are received from a queue, the Windows Communication Foundation will confirm that all the operations of the endpoint's contract are explicitly one-way:

```
public interface IMyServiceContract
{
    [OperationContract(IsOneWay=true)]
    void FirstOperation(string input);
    [OperationContract(IsOneWay = true)]
    void SecondOperation(string input);
}
```

The developers of a Windows Communication Foundation application can add an attribute to a service contract to indicate that the developer expects the application to receive messages via a queue:

```
[ServiceContract(SessionMode=SessionMode.Required)]
[DeliveryRequirements(QueuedDeliveryRequirements
    = QueuedDeliveryRequirementsMode.Required)]
public interface IMyServiceContract
```

If the developer does so, the Windows Communication Foundation will confirm that the binding of any endpoints that include those service contracts is a binding by which messages are delivered to the service via a queue.

Enhancements in Windows Vista

There are some enhancements to MSMQ in Windows Vista and later operating systems from which Windows Communication Foundation applications that communicate via MSMQ can benefit. Those enhancements concern dead-letter and poison queues.

Dead-Letter Queues

MSMQ messages have a configurable time to reach their destination queues and a configurable time to be received from the destination queues. When either of those times expires, the message is placed in a system queue called the dead-letter queue. In addition, if a message was sent to a transactional queue and the queue manager on the sending host does not receive positive confirmation that the message was read from the destination queue, the message will be moved to a transactional dead-letter queue.

On Windows Vista and later operating systems, it is possible to create a queue and designate it as the dead-letter queue for another specified queue. The Windows Communication Foundation provides support for that enhancement by allowing one to specify, for an application that is to send or receive messages from a queue, another queue that is to serve as the dead-letter queue:

```
<client>
        <endpoint
                address="net.msmq://localhost/private$/EndpointAddress"
                binding="netMsmqBinding"
                bindingConfiguration="QueuedBinding"
                [...]/>
</client>
<bindings>
  <netMsmqBinding>
    <binding
     name="QueuedBinding"
     deadLetterQueue="Custom"
     customDeadLetterQueue="net.msmq://localhost/private$/myDeadLetterQueue">
    </binding>
  </netMsmqBinding>
</bindings>
```

Poison Queues

A poison message is a message on a transactional queue that cannot be processed by the receiving application. When the message is read from the queue and the receiving application fails to process it, the application rolls back the transaction by which the message was read, and the message is thereby restored to the queue. The application will then proceed to read the message again, and the cycle of reading and rolling back the poison message could continue indefinitely.

Prior to Windows Vista, MSMQ left one to one's own devices in detecting and coping with poison messages. The Windows Communication Foundation renders assistance by allowing one to specify values for the ReceiveRetryCount and ReceiveErrorHandling properties.

```
<services>
        <service name="Fabrikam.TradeRecorder">
                <host>
                        <baseAddresses>
                         <add baseAddress="net.msmq://localhost/private/"/>
                         </baseAddresses>
                </host>
                <endpoint
```

```
                    address="EndpointAddress"
                    binding="netMsmqBinding"
                    bindingConfiguration="QueuedBinding"
                    [...]/>
        </service>
</services>
<bindings>
  <netMsmqBinding>
    <binding
          name="QueuedBinding"
          receiveRetryCount="0"
       receiveErrorHandling="Fault">
    </binding>
  </netMsmqBinding>
</bindings>
```

The value of the ReceiveRetryCount property serves to define what constitutes a poison message—it is one that is rolled back onto the queue a number of times exceeding the value of ReceiveRetryCount property. The value of the ReceiveErrorHandling property is used to signify what is to be done with the poison message. The options are to move the receiving service into a faulted state so that it cannot receive any further messages or to ignore the poison message.

On Windows Vista and later operating systems, there is a richer set of options. Poison messages can be sent back to their source by assigning the value Move to the ReceiveErrorHandling property. In that case, they will end up on the dead-letter queue there. Otherwise, by assigning the value Reject to the ReceiveErrorHandling property, they can be moved to a poison subqueue of the receiving queue. For a queue named net.msmq://localhost/private/EndpointAddress, the address of the poison subqueue is net.msmq://localhost/private/EndpointAddress;Poison.

Being able to designate a custom dead-letter queue and being able to dispatch poison messages to a poison subqueue raises interesting design possibilities. In particular, one could have Windows Communication Foundation services configured to read messages from the dead-letter queue and the poison subqueue and programmed to take actions to compensate for the problem messages.

Transactions

The Windows Communication Foundation implements both the standard WS-AtomicTransaction (WS-AT) protocol and Microsoft's proprietary OleTx protocol in certain predefined bindings. Those protocols are for conveying information about the state of transactions in messages. Windows Communication Foundation developers can indicate that the code for a given operation is written so as to execute within the scope of a transaction:

```
[ServiceContract]
public interface IMyServiceContract
{
    [OperationContract(IsOneWay = false)]
    [TransactionFlow(TransactionFlowOption.Required)]
    void MyMethod();
}

public class MyServiceType: IMyServiceConract
{
    [OperationBehavior(TransactionScopeRequired=true)]
    void MyMethod()
    {
      […]
    }
}
```

Any operation that the developer indicates must execute within the scope of a transaction cannot also be marked as a one-way method because information about the state of the transaction at the end of the operation must be transmitted back to the caller.

The developer can also indicate that the Windows Communication Foundation should automatically vote on behalf of the operation to commit the transaction if no exception occurs:

```
public class MyServiceType
{
    [OperationBehavior(TransactionScopeRequired=true,TransactionAutoComplete=true)]
    void MyMethod()
    {
      […]
    }
}
```

If the developer would rather vote to commit the transaction deliberately, it can be done via the Windows Communication Foundation's static System.ServiceModel.OperationContext object:

```
public class MyServiceType
{
    [OperationBehavior(
      TransactionScopeRequired=true,
      TransactionAutoComplete=false)]
    void MyMethod()
    {
```

```
        //Work gets done here
        OperationContext.Current.SetTransactionComplete();
    }
}
```

If a developer specifies that the operations of a service must execute within the context of
a transaction, the Windows Communication Foundation will confirm that the service has
been configured with a binding that supports sending information about the state of
transactions within messages. The predefined bindings that provide that support are
WSHttpBinding, the WSDualHttpBinding, WSFederationBinding, NetTcpBinding, and
NetNamedPipesBinding. The last two allow one to choose between using the WS-AT protocol and the OleTx protocol, whereas the others use the standard WS-AT protocol only.

```
<bindings>
  <netTcpBinding>
    <binding
                name="..."
                transactionFlow="true"
                transactionProtocol="OleTransactions"/>
  </netTcpBinding>
  <wsHttpBinding>
    <binding
                name="..."
                transactionFlow="true"/>
  </wsHttpBinding>
</bindings>
```

Developers of Windows Communication Foundation clients can use the syntax provided
by the System.Transactions namespace to include service operations within the scope of
a transaction.

```
ServiceClient client = new ServiceClient("MyServiceEndpointConfiguration");
using(TransactionScope scope =
        new TransactionScope(TransactionScopeOption.RequiresNew))
{
        client.DoSomething([...]);

        scope.Complete();
}
client.Close();
```

If those service operations support transactions, and the binding is configured to convey
information about the state of the transaction, the client's transaction will not commit
unless the service operations vote to commit. Conversely, any actions performed by the
service on transactional resources within the scope of the client's transaction will be
rolled back if the client does not vote to commit.

Designing a system in this way is generally unwise, though. The operations of the service and its resources will be tied up while a remote client decides what action to take. Even if the client can be trusted to decide expeditiously, the latency entailed by the very fact that the components are distributed will cause some delay. As a general principle, one should avoid extending transactions across boundaries of trust.

A smarter way of implementing distributed transactions with the Windows Communication Foundation is depicted in Figure 4.1. This approach combines the support for session management, queued delivery, and transactional messaging.

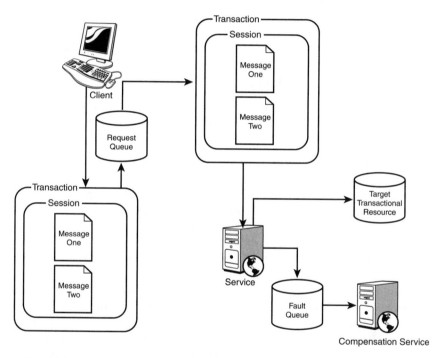

FIGURE 4.1   Distributed transactions.

The service shown in the diagram is configured to receive messages from clients via a queue. A client initiates a transaction and then a session, and sends a series of messages to the service. The client completes the session, and if and only if the client commits its transaction will the messages that it sent go onto the queue. The separate messages that the client sent will appear on the queue as a single item. On the service's side, the Windows Communication Foundation detects the item on the queue and initiates a transaction and then a session. It decomposes the single item on the queue into the separate messages that were sent by the client, and delivers each of those messages to the service. If all goes well, the service closes the session and commits the transaction. If something goes awry in processing any of the messages, the transaction can be aborted, in which case anything done in the processing of any of the messages on a transactional resource will be rolled back. The batch of messages is transferred to the poison message queue, where a service charged with compensating for the failure picks up the messages. That service could alert an administrator, or even notify the client application, that processing failed and that action to compensate should be taken.

By virtue of this design, operations on the client and the server are not held up by one another or by the latency of the connection between them. The client's transaction and the server's transaction commit independently. The client's transaction ensures that the client is always in a consistent state, and the server's transaction ensures that the server is always in a consistent state. If the client fails in the scope of its transaction, the server is unaffected because messages sent by the client as part of that transaction are never delivered to the server's queue. If the server fails to process messages sent by the client, although the client will be in a consistent state and the server will be in a consistent state, the client's state and the server's state will not be mutually consistent. In that case, some actions to compensate for the inconsistency will have to be taken. However, one might be able to confirm that such cases occur only infrequently.

To see an implementation of this design and to witness the Windows Communication Foundation's support for session management, queued delivery, and transacted messaging in action, follow these steps:

1. Assuming that the code associated with this chapter has been downloaded and copied to the folder C:\WCFHandsOn, as instructed previously in this chapter, proceed to open the solution, ComposingSessionsQueuesAndTransactions.sln in the ComposingSessionsQueuesAndTransactions subdirectory of the ReliableSessionQueuesAndTransactions folder. There are four console application projects in the solution. The Sender project is for building the client application, and the Receiver project is for building the Windows Communication Foundation service to which the client application sends messages via a queue. The Target project is for building another Windows Communication Foundation service that also receives messages via a queue. That application represents the transacted resource that the Receiver service performs operations on in response to the client's messages. Imagine, then, that the Target project represents a database, although, unlike a database, it is easier for readers to install and the effects of the operations performed on it will be more obvious. The fourth project in the solution, the Compensator project, is for building the service that initiates compensatory action when the server fails in processing messages received from the client.

2. Look at the service contract in the IMyServiceContract.cs file of the Receiver project. It defines a session consisting of a sequence of two operations.

```
[ServiceContract(SessionMode=SessionMode.Required)]
[DeliveryRequirements(QueuedDeliveryRequirements
    = QueuedDeliveryRequirementsMode.Required)]
public interface IMyServiceContract
{
    [OperationContract(IsOneWay=true,IsInitiating=true)]
    void FirstOperation(string input);
```

```
[OperationContract(IsOneWay = true,IsTerminating=true)]
void SecondOperation(string input);
}
```

3. Study the code of the Sender application in the Program.cs file of the Sender project. The code starts a transaction and, by virtue of how the contract is defined, implicitly initiates a session. The client invokes the two operations provided by the service in the proper sequence, and then, if no errors have occurred, commits the transaction.

```
using (TransactionScope transaction =
            new TransactionScope(TransactionScopeOption.Required))
{
    MyClient client = new MyClient("MyService");

    client.Open();

    client.FirstOperation("First set of data");

    client.SecondOperation("Second set of data");

    if (fail)
    {
        throw new Exception("Something bad.");
    }

    client.Close();

    transaction.Complete();
}
```

4. See how the service is configured to receive messages from the client by studying the configuration in the App.config file of the Receiver project, shown in Listing 4.1. The service is to receive messages via the predefined NetMsmqBinding. By virtue of the values assigned to the ReceiveRetryCount and ReceiveErrorHandling properties, messages that cannot be processed will be immediately removed from the queue.

LISTING 4.1   Service Configuration

```
<system.serviceModel>
        [...]
      <services>
      <service
            name="Compensation.MyService">
            <host>
```

LISTING 4.1   Continued

```
                        <baseAddresses>
                            <add baseAddress="net.msmq://localhost/private/"/>
                        </baseAddresses>
                </host>
            <endpoint
                address="MyService"
                binding="netMsmqBinding"
                bindingConfiguration="MyQueuedBinding"
                contract="Compensation.IMyServiceContract" />
        </service>
    </services>
    <bindings>
        <netMsmqBinding>
            <binding
                name="MyQueuedBinding"
                receiveRetryCount="0"
                receiveErrorHandling="Drop">
                <security mode="None" />
            </binding>
        </netMsmqBinding>
    </bindings>
</system.serviceModel>
```

5. Examine how the service is programmed to process messages received from the client. The relevant code is in the MyService.cs file of the Receiver project and is reproduced in Listing 4.2. In processing either of the two messages that may be received from the client, the service sends a message to the Target service. If an error occurs, the service sends the messages that it has received to the compensation service. The processing of messages from the client takes place in the context of a transaction.

LISTING 4.2   Service Processing

```
[OperationBehavior(
        TransactionScopeRequired = true,
        TransactionAutoComplete = false)]
public void FirstOperation(string input)
{
    try
    {
        MyClient targetClient = new MyClient("TargetService");
        targetClient.Open();
```

LISTING 4.2   Continued

```
            targetClient.FirstOperation(input);
            targetClient.Close();


    }
    catch (Exception exception)
    {
        this.Compensate(extension);

        throw exception;
    }



}

[OperationBehavior(
        TransactionScopeRequired = true,
        TransactionAutoComplete = true)]
public void SecondOperation(string input)
{
    try
    {
        MyClient targetClient = new MyClient("TargetService");
        targetClient.Open();
        targetClient.SecondOperation(input);
        targetClient.Close();


    }
    catch (Exception exception)
    {
        this.Compensate(extension);

        throw exception;
    }
}

private void Compensate(MyExtension extension)
{
    using (TransactionScope transaction =
                new TransactionScope(TransactionScopeOption.RequiresNew))
    {
        [...]
```

LISTING 4.2 Continued

```
        CompensationClient compensationClient =
                        new CompensationClient("CompensationService");
        compensationClient.Open();

        compensationClient.Compensate(Message.CreateMessage(
                        MessageVersion.Soap12WSAddressing10,
                        "*",
                        buffer == null ? string.Empty : buffer.ToString()));
        compensationClient.Close();
        transaction.Complete();
    }
}
```

6. Look again at the configuration of the service in the App.config file of the Receiver project to see how the service is configured to send messages to the target service. Those messages are to be sent using the predefined NetMsmqBinding. And because that binding has messages delivered via a transacted queue, in sending messages to the Target service, the Receiver service is performing operations on a transacted resource.

```
<system.serviceModel>
        <client>
                <endpoint
                        name="TargetService"
                        address="net.msmq://localhost/private/MyTarget"
                        binding="netMsmqBinding"
                        bindingConfiguration="MyQueuedBinding"
                        contract="Compensation.IMyServiceContract"/>
                [...]
        </client>
        [...]
</system.serviceModel>
```

To see the solution in action, do the following:

1. Right-click on the Sender project, and choose Debug, Start New Instance from the context menu. A console for the Sender application should appear.

2. Enter a keystroke into the Sender application's console. After a few moments, the output in the console window should confirm that the application has transmitted messages to the service.

3. Choose Debug, Stop Debugging from the Visual Studio 2005 menus.

4. Open Administrative Tools from the Windows Control Panel, and choose Computer Management.

5. Expand the Services and Applications node in the left pane.

6. Expand the Message Queuing subnode.

7. Select the Private Queues subnode.

8. Look at the number of messages shown to be on the `myservice` queue through which the Sender application communicates with the Receiver service. There should be just one MSMQ message containing both of the Windows Communication Foundation messages sent by the Sender application as part of one session.

9. Choose Debug, Start Debugging from the Visual Studio 2005 menus to start the Receiver, the Target, and the Compensator applications, as well as the Sender. In spite of not having been running when the Sender dispatched messages to the Receiver, the Receiver receives the Sender's messages, which were held on the queue, and the output in the Target application console should indicate that the Receiver passed the messages from the Sender along.

10. Choose Debug, Stop Debugging from the Visual Studio 2005 menus.

11. Open the App.config file of the Sender application and modify the entry

```
<add key="Succeed" value="true"/>
```

to instead read

```
<add key="Succeed" value="false"/>
```

That change will cause the Sender application to fail in its processing.

12. Choose Debug, Start Without Debugging from the Visual Studio 2005 menus.

13. Enter a keystroke into the console of the Sender application. It should show that messages were sent to the Receiver application, but that an error occurred in the Sender application. Because the transaction in which the Sender dispatched the messages aborted, the Receiver application is unaffected, and the Sender and the Receiver are both in a consistent state and consistent with one another.

14. Close the consoles of the four applications.

15. Reverse the change made to the App.config file of the Sender application so that the entry that now reads

```
<add key="Succeed" value="false"/>
```

once again reads,

```
<add key="Succeed" value="true"/>
```

16. Now cause the Receiver application to fail by modifying the App.config file in the Receiver project so that the entry

```
<add key="Succeed" value="true"/>
```

instead reads

```
<add key="Succeed" value="false"/>
```

17. Choose Debug, Start Without Debugging from the Visual Studio 2005 menus.

18. Enter a keystroke into the console of the Sender application. It should show that messages were sent to the Receiver application. The output in the console of the Receiver application should show that it received both messages but that an error occurred in processing the second. There should be no output in the console of the Target application, which is very important. That shows that although the Receiver application will have passed the first message from the Sender along to the target, it did so in the context of a transaction that was rolled back due to the failure in processing the second message. Therefore, the Receiver application and its resources are left in a consistent state. The output in the console of the compensator application should indicate that it has been notified of the problem messages, in which case it could initiate efforts to restore the Sender application to a state that is consistent with the Receiver's state.

Summary

This chapter covered the Windows Communication Foundation's Reliable Sessions feature, which provides assurances that messages will be delivered in order and exactly once. The chapter also dealt with the Windows Communication Foundation's session management, queued delivery, and transacted messaging facilities. It showed how those features can be used together to yield efficient distributed transaction processing.

PART II

Introducing the Windows Workflow Foundation

IN THIS PART

CHAPTER 5

Fundamentals of the Windows Workflow Foundation

Introduction

This text mainly focuses on the creation of services using Windows Communication Foundation. The various chapters discuss the definition, security, structure, and customization of services. One aspect not covered in many discussions about Windows Communication Foundation is the actual implementation of the services. To realize the value of an service-oriented architecture (SOA), services must expose valuable functionality. The primary representation of application logic has been in code. Irrespective of language, one distills the actions of an application—from data retrieval to processing logic—in a programming language. The Windows Workflow Foundation brings the power of a model-based, declarative process execution engine into the .NET Framework in order to move the experience of developing the functionality of services beyond writing lines and lines of code.

What Is Windows Workflow Foundation?

Windows Workflow Foundation is a component of the .NET 3.0 Framework for developing workflow-enabled applications. It is a technology used within Microsoft in products such as Microsoft Office SharePoint Server 2007, Microsoft Speech Server 2007, and in the next wave of Microsoft Dynamics products. This same technology is available to ISVs and software developers who use the .NET Framework. There are three core components to Windows Workflow Foundation:

▶ Activity Framework

▶ Runtime Environment

▶ Workflow Designer

What Windows Workflow Foundation Is Not

The term, *workflow*, is quite overloaded within the software development industry and the larger business community. It is important to clearly state how Windows Workflow Foundation fits into those popular conceptions of workflow.

▶ Windows Workflow Foundation is not a server, although one could centralize workflow functionality and expose it as a server for other applications to utilize.

▶ Windows Workflow Foundation is not a Business Process Management (BPM) tool, although one could build a BPM tool using Windows Workflow Foundation as the workflow execution engine.

▶ Windows Workflow Foundation is not targeted at business analysts, although one could expose functionality using the rehostable designer to allow business analysts to build their own workflow. The flexibility of Windows Workflow Foundation allows that to be incorporated into the analysts' familiar environments. If the included designer does not work, one could also create a custom workflow designer.

▶ Windows Workflow Foundation is not an enterprise application integration tool, although one could encapsulate third-party system functionality into activities and compose those into workflows.

▶ Windows Workflow Foundation, however, is not a toy. It has been designed to operate to enterprise scale, in a redundant server-farm environment, with high performance. It is ready to be used by enterprise-class applications today, as evidenced by its usage with SharePoint Server. Windows Workflow Foundation by itself, however, is not an enterprise-class application; it is a developer toolkit.

▶ That said, Windows Workflow Foundation is not only for server-based deployments. It can be used with a Windows Forms application to execute any of the application logic, from service coordination, to UI customization. It can be used within a web application to manage process state. In short, it can be used as code to provide logic anywhere one can write .NET code.

Activities

Activities are the building blocks of Windows Workflow Foundation. From providing complex execution logic to executing an update against a SQL database, that behavior is encapsulated into discrete units of work called activities. An *activity* is any class that ultimately derives from `System.Workflow.ComponentModel.Activity`. There are two aspects to an activity:

▶ Runtime behavior

▶ Design-time behavior

Runtime behavior is the code executed when the activity is used within a workflow. This might include calling a web service or executing a chunk of code, as well as coordinating the execution of child activities. One question often asked is, "How well does Windows Workflow Foundation perform?" At the activity level, the answer is simple: An activity executes as fast as the same piece of code residing in a .NET assembly. This is because an activity is simply a compiled .NET assembly that contains a class derived from `Activity`. It will execute just as fast (or as slow) as the .NET code contained within. That is the individual activity; overhead is then incurred for managing the lifecycle of an activity, as outlined in Figure 5.1.

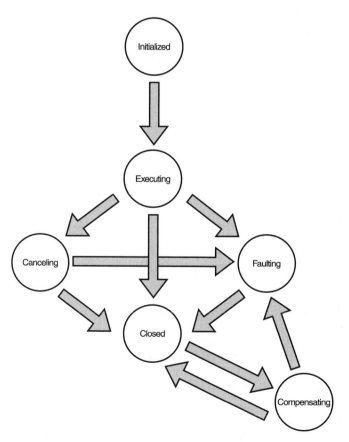

FIGURE 5.1   The lifecycle of an activity.

An activity is initialized when the workflow it is contained within is created, and remains in the Initialized state. That is, when `CreateInstance` is called and the workflow instance is created, all the activities are initialized. An activity is then moved into the Executing state when scheduled for execution. The normal path is then for the activity to move to the Closed state, where it should gracefully rest in peace, its work done.

There are complications, of course, which can occur along the way. An activity can encounter an error, entering the Faulting state on its way to closing. The activity might be progressing nicely, but it might be cancelled by another activity, entering its Canceling state prior to moving into the Closed state. Finally, an activity might be required to be awakened from its Closed state and move the Compensating state in cases where the activity has defined a way to roll back or compensate for its execution, and for some reason, an error, or maybe a cancellation of the process, needs to invoke that compensation logic.

That is a brief summary of the runtime behavior of an activity. An activity also has a design experience that is important when building workflows. An activity might require a special representation on the design surface in order to convey to the developer what the activity is doing. This might be something quite simple (an icon, logo, color or shape attached to the activity when it is displayed) or a complex layout that mimics the execution behavior of the activity. An example of an activity that benefits from a strong design component is the `Parallel` activity, as shown in Figure 5.2.

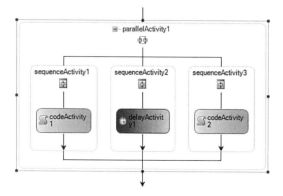

FIGURE 5.2   A `Parallel` activity.

Beyond the graphical representation of the activity, there might be validation behavior one would like as part of the design experience. Perhaps a `PlaceOrder` activity is not configured correctly until it contains both a ship-to address and a deliver-by date. The validation components allow one to specify the exact criteria required for the activity to be used within a workflow. This could be as simple as ensuring that a property has a value assigned to it, or as complex as a calculation and database lookup to determine whether a property value or values fall within a specified tolerance. Design and validation are topics discussed later in this chapter.

Out of the Box Activities

The activities that are shipped with Windows Workflow Foundation are often referred to as the *out of the box activities*. They are a collection of fundamental activities, many structural, that can be used to create simple workflows and compose new activities. Table 5.1 is a brief summary of each of these activities.

TABLE 5.1   Out of the Box Activities

Activity	Description
CallExternalMethod	Invokes method in host
Code	Executes code defined in code beside
Compensate	Invokes target activity's compensation
CompensatableSequence	Sequence activity with capability to define compensation
ConditionedActivityGroup	Rule-based activity group
Delay	Pauses workflow execution for a period of time
EventDriven	Sequence whose execution is triggered by an event
EventHandlingScope	Executes child activities while listening for events
FaultHandler	Composite activity that executes on exception in workflow
HandleExternalEvent	Waits and receives message from host
IfElse	Conditional branching activity
InvokeWebService	Calls a web service
InvokeWorkflow	Asynchronously initiates another workflow
Listen	Waits for the first of a set of events
Parallel	Schedules parallel execution of child branches
Policy	Executes a rules policy
Replicator	Spawns a dynamic number of execution contexts for the contained sequence
Sequence	Enables the sequential execution of child activities
SetState	Sets the next state to be entered (used only in a state machine workflow)
State	Represents a state in a state machine workflow (used only in a state machine workflow)
StateFinalization	Occurs before transitioning to a new state (used only in a state machine workflow)
StateInitialization	Occurs when the State activity starts running (used only in a state machine workflow)
Suspend	Suspends workflow execution
SynchronizationScope	Serializes execution of contained activities to control access to shared variables
Terminate	Halts the workflow with an error
Throw	Raises an exception within the workflow
TransactionScope	Sequence activity executing within a transaction

5

TABLE 5.1   Continued

Activity	Description
CompensatableTransactionScope	Transaction scope with a defined compensation sequence
WebServiceInput	Exposes a workflow as a web service
WebServiceOutput	Returns a value when exposed as a web service
WebServiceFault	Returns a fault when exposed as a web service
While	Loops based on rule condition

Creating Custom Activities

The activities included with Windows Workflow Foundation exist to provide a strong starting point for creating a workflow. However, it will be a very common activity (no pun intended) for a workflow developer to need to create a custom activity. From encapsulating frequently used functions to creating a custom composite activity to model a new pattern of execution, developers will need to start a workflow project by thinking about the activities needed. As time progresses, these activities can be reused, composed into higher-level activities, and handled just as common objects are today.

Basic

The most basic way to create a custom activity is to simply inherit from System.Workflow.ComponentModel.Activity. This will create all the basic machinery for an activity, except for the actual logic implemented by the activity. To do this, one should override the Execute() method, as shown in Listing 5.1.

LISTING 5.1   A Basic Activity

```
public class BasicActivity: Activity
{
        public BasicActivity()
        {
                this.Name = "BasicActivity";
        }
        protected override ActivityExecutionStatus Execute
            (ActivityExecutionContext executionContext)
        {
            Console.WriteLine("Basic Activity");
            return ActivityExecutionStatus.Closed;
        }
}
```

The Execute() method performs the work of the activity and is required to notify the runtime its status. In this case, a status of Closed is returned, indicating the activity has completed its work. A more complex pattern would be to return a status of Executing while waiting for some long-running work to complete. On completion of the long-running work, such as a manager approving an expense report, the activity notifies the runtime it has been completed. While waiting, the workflow instance might be idled and persisted awaiting the completion of the long running work.

As activities form the building blocks of a workflow, this pattern shows how one can very quickly wrap existing functionality inside an activity. An existing code library or component call can be wrapped inside of an activity with very little work. In Chapter 6, "Using the Windows Communication Foundation and the Windows Workflow Foundation Together," this technique will be used to encapsulate calls to Windows Communication Foundation services. The activity shown earlier is not particularly interesting, nor does it expose any useful customization. This might work if one is wrapping an API consisting completely of hard coded or parameter-less functions. One usually wants to control some parameters that will affect the behavior to provide a useful activity. The simplest way to expose that capability is to add a property to the activity class, as shown in Listing 5.2.

LISTING 5.2   Adding a Property

```
public string TextToPrint
{
     get { return textToPrint; }
     set { textToPrint = value; }
}
protected override ActivityExecutionStatus Execute
     (ActivityExecutionContext executionContext)
{
     Console.WriteLine("Text To Print: {0}", TextToPrint);
     return ActivityExecutionStatus.Closed;
}
```

By adding this property, the activity can be configured when the workflow is designed, as shown in Figure 5.3.

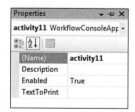

FIGURE 5.3   A standard property on the property grid.

When declaratively creating workflows in XAML (Extensible Application Markup Language), the XML representation of the workflow, these properties are set as attributes on the activity, as in Listing 5.3.

LISTING 5.3   Properties in XAML

```
<SequentialWorkflowActivity x:Class="SampleWFApplication.Workflow1"
  x:Name="Workflow1" xmlns:ns0="clr-namespace:SampleWFApplication"
  xmlns:x="http://schemas.microsoft.com/winfx/2006/xaml"
  xmlns="http://schemas.microsoft.com/winfx/2006/xaml/workflow">
  <ns0:BasicActivity TextToPrint="Hello World"
    x:Name="basicActivity1" />
</SequentialWorkflowActivity>
```

This allows the properties to be set in the designer to customize the behavior of the activity. But it remains fairly static, limited to the value input at design time. What if the scenario called for passing in a customer object that the workflow was created to evaluate? This is accomplished through the use of dependency properties. Dependency properties are similar to the standard .NET properties described earlier, but differ in declaration and usage. There is a built-in code snippet to create these in Visual Studio, but the general pattern is given in Listing 5.4.

LISTING 5.4   Creating a DependencyProperty

```
public static DependencyProperty OrderAmountProperty = System.Workflow.
➥ComponentModel.DependencyProperty.Register("OrderAmount",
➥typeof(int), typeof(BasicActivity));
[Description("This property holds the amount of the order")]
[Category("Order Details")]
[Browsable(true)]
[DesignerSerializationVisibility(DesignerSerializationVisibility.Visible)]
public int OrderAmount
{
    get
    {
        return ((int)(base.GetValue(BasicActivity.OrderAmountProperty)));
    }
    set
    {
        base.SetValue(BasicActivity.OrderAmountProperty, value);
    }
}
```

This slightly longer declaration appears to have some elements of a property, but also contains a static DependencyProperty declaration. A *DependencyProperty* is a special type of property that is attached to a DependencyObject, one of the classes that Activity inherits from. A DependencyProperty differs from a traditional property in that it supports three special use cases:

▶ Activity binding

▶ Metadata, assigning a value *only* at design time that is immutable during run-time

▶ Attached properties; dynamically adding a property to an activity

The most common scenario is using dependency properties to support activity binding. The advantage gained by using dependency properties is additional design-time behaviors. Dropping the activity onto the design surface and inspecting its properties yields a new icon next to the property just declared, as shown in Figure 5.4.

FIGURE 5.4   `DependencyProperty` in grid.

Clicking on that new icon raises a new dialog, the bind dialog, as shown in Figure 5.5.

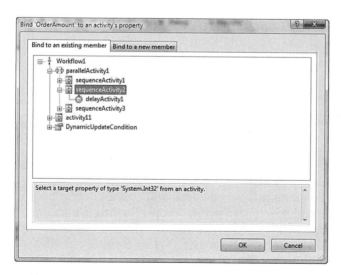

FIGURE 5.5   The Bind dialog.

The Bind dialog allows the value of the property to be dynamically bound to another value in the workflow. This could be a property on the workflow passed in at the time of workflow creation or this could be a property on another activity. At design time, the activity is told where to look for the value of this property. By selecting another value in the workflow of the same type (and this can be a custom type), a binding expression now appears in the property grid as the value of the property. It looks something like this:

```
Activity=Workflow1, Path=WorkflowOrderAmount
```

The first part allows for the source (in this case, the parent workflow) and then the property on that activity to be resolved. Dot notation can be used here, so if the desired value to be bound is a few layers beneath a property, it can be reached.

Of course, with a dependency property, the value can still be hard-coded. In the previous example, there would be nothing to prevent one from inputting a fixed number, say 42, into the property grid.

Within the Bind dialog is a Bind to a New Member tab, as shown in Figure 5.6.

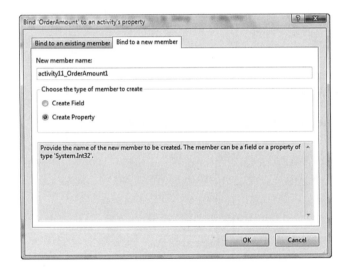

FIGURE 5.6   Property promotion via binding to a new member.

This dialog lets a dependency property of an activity be "promoted" to be a member of the containing activity. In this case, binding to a new member will create a dependency property (or public member) on the workflow and insert the proper binding syntax for the activities value. This lets the property of an activity contained within a composite activity to bubble up to a property on the containing activity. When creating activities through composition, this is a useful way to mimic the polymorphism of inheritance. The containing activity can expose the properties of a contained activity as if it had inherited them from that activity.

Composition

The second way to create an activity, and the one Visual Studio defaults to, is through composition. The activity class definition of a newly created activity in Visual Studio looks like this:

```
public partial class ACompositeActivity: SequenceActivity
```

This inherits from `SequenceActivity`, the fundamental activity for building sequential workflows. The `Execute()` method of `SequenceActivity` is responsible for scheduling the execution of each contained child activity in sequence. By inheriting, that behavior *is not overwritten*, it is desired. Additionally, the design behavior of the `SequenceActivity` is preserved. This allows an activity developer to create a new activity by dragging and dropping other activities into the new activity, thus creating an activity out of existing activities. This is a powerful tool for creating new units of work, activities to be used inside of a workflow. This means that given a powerful enough set of basic activities implemented in code, perhaps wrapping an existing API, one can very rapidly create those units of functionality into new, higher-level units of functionality. To drive this concept home, consider the following activities:

- ▶ SendEmail
- ▶ LookupManager
- ▶ WaitForResponseToEmail

With these activities, along with some of the structural activities provided by the out of the box activities, one can compose an arbitrarily complex approval activity, and then expose that activity out as "the" approval activity to use in any workflow (see Figure 5.7).

As higher-order activities are created, such as `Approval`, these too can be composed again and again into additional activities, allowing process of arbitrary sophistication to be created. A `NewProductIdeaGeneration` activity might consist of a parallel activity containing a set of cross-departmental feedback requests that each need an approval. This activity could then be used in a `New Product Creation` workflow with the workflow developer unaware of the many layers of implementation detail there are behind the NewProductIdeaGeneration activity. This developer just knows that the NewProductIdeaGeneration activity will execute, and when it completes, it will be populated with a set of vetted, approved ideas to be used elsewhere in the workflow. As mentioned earlier, properties of contained activities can be promoted to be properties on the containing activity, allowing the useful customization properties to be exposed to users of the containing activity.

It is in these higher-level, composition-based activities where many organizations look to have nondevelopers arrange them into workflows. Consider the document approval activity created earlier. By providing that activity and a parallel activity, a business analyst could create the approval workflow for a given class of documents. This is the approach exposed through SharePoint Designer and Microsoft Office SharePoint Server, which allows a business analyst or power user to create and customize document workflows in

SharePoint. The challenge of providing a repository where activities can be referenced across an enterprise or department, and their characteristics expressed for other developers and analysts to reference, is left as an exercise to the reader.

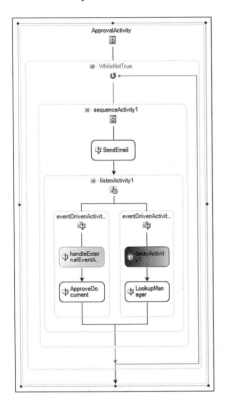

FIGURE 5.7   An Approval activity composed of more basic activities.

Custom Composite Activities

There exists an additional type of activity one can create—a custom composite activity. A *composite activity* is one that contains child activities, and its Execute() method is responsible for scheduling the execution of those child activities. Out of the box, examples of composite activities are Sequence, While, and Parallel.

Those activities, however, express only a few types of execution semantics. There exist many other ways in which one might want to execute the child activities, such as a priority execution where child activities are executed in some type of prioritized ordering. One might want to have an activity that executes in parallel but allows the developer to set a looping variable on each branch, so that not only does it executes in parallel, but also executes each branch a specified number of times.

The implementation of such activities deals with some advanced intricacies of activity execution. Shukla and Schmidt's "Essential Windows Workflow Foundation" is recommended to explore the details of activity execution and ways to create advanced, custom composite activities.

The composite activity executes by scheduling execution of its child activities and subscribing to those child activities' completed event. The activity then returns the Executing status, indicating to the runtime to continue by executing the next activity scheduled. On receiving the child completed event, the composite can proceed scheduling other activities or evaluate if it can close. When all of the activities complete or the composite decides enough has been done, the composite will return a state of Closed, indicating it has completed. The workflow runtime will enforce a restriction that all child activities must be Closed before allowing the parent activity to close.

Communicating with Activities

Workflows do not operate in a purely isolated environment; rather, they will frequently need to interact with the host application to communicate messages out to the host or to wait to receive a message from the host. Two out of the box activities are designed to support this: HandleExternalEvent and CallExternalMethod. These activities communicate with the host via a contract shared between the host and the workflow. The implementation of this contract is provided to the runtime ExternalDataExchangeService as a local service.

To clarify what is going on here, an example of each of the activities follows based on the scenario of surveying employees. First, create a contract to be shared between the host and workflow, and decorate with the ExternalDataExchange attribute as shown in Listing 5.5.

LISTING 5.5   Interface for Workflow Communication

```
using System;
using System.Workflow.ComponentModel;
using System.Workflow.Activities;

namespace ExternalEventSample
{
    [ExternalDataExchange()]
    public interface ISurveyResponseService
        {
        void SurveyEmployee(string employee, string surveyQuestion);
        event EventHandler<SurveyEventArgs> SurveyCompleted;
        }


    [Serializable]
    public class SurveyEventArgs : ExternalDataEventArgs
    {
        private string employee;
using System;
using System.Workflow.ComponentModel;
using System.Workflow.Activities;
namespace ExternalEventSample
{
```

LISTING 5.5   Continued

```
[ExternalDataExchange()]
public interface ISurveyResponseService
{
    void SurveyEmployee(string employee, string surveyQuestion);
    event EventHandler<SurveyEventArgs> SurveyCompleted;
}
[Serializable]
public class SurveyEventArgs : ExternalDataEventArgs
{
    private string employee;
    public string Employee
    {
        get { return employee; }
        set { employee = value; }
    }
    private string surveyResponse;
    public string SurveyResponse
    {
        get { return surveyResponse; }
        set { surveyResponse = value; }
    }
    public SurveyEventArgs(Guid instanceId,
                        string employee, string surveyResponse)
        : base(instanceId)
    {
        this.employee = employee;
        this.surveyResponse = surveyResponse;
    }
}
```

This interface defines an event, a custom event arguments class, and a public method. Next, provide an implementation of the interface, as in Listing 5.6. This will be used by the host to expose the functionality to the workflow.

LISTING 5.6   Implementation of Interface

```
using System;

namespace ExternalEventSample
{
    class SurveyResponseService : ISurveyResponseService
    {
        public void SurveyEmployee(string employee, string surveyQuestion)
        {
            // here we would notify and display the survey
            Console.WriteLine("Hey {0}, what do you think of {1}?",
            employee, surveyQuestion);
```

LISTING 5.6   Continued

```
        }
        public event EventHandler<SurveyEventArgs> SurveyCompleted;
        public void CompleteSurvey(Guid instanceId, string employee,
                                        string surveyResponse)
        {
            // the host will call this method when it wants
            // to raise the event into the workflow.
            // Note that the workflow instance id needs to be passed in.
            EventHandler<SurveyEventArgs> surveyCompleted =
            this.SurveyCompleted;
            if (surveyCompleted != null)
            {
                surveyCompleted(null,
                new SurveyEventArgs(instanceId, employee, surveyResponse));
            }
        }
    }
}
```

Now, add the `ExternalDataExchange` service to the runtime and add an instance of the interface implementation as a local service, as in Listing 5.7. Additionally, use the `OnWorkflowIdled` event as the opportunity to send the response to the host. An assumption is made in this sample that only one workflow type will be executing, and the only time it will go idle is while waiting for a survey response.

LISTING 5.7   Configure the Host for Communication

```
using System;
using System.Collections.Generic;
using System.Text;
using System.Threading;
using System.Workflow.Runtime;
using System.Workflow.Runtime.Hosting;
using System.Workflow.Activities;

namespace ExternalEventSample
{
    class Program
```

LISTING 5.7   Continued

```
{
    static SurveyResponseService surveyService;
    static void Main(string[] args)
    {
        using (WorkflowRuntime workflowRuntime = new WorkflowRuntime())
        {
            // add the local service to the external data exchange service
            surveyService = new SurveyResponseService();
            ExternalDataExchangeService dataService =
                new ExternalDataExchangeService();
            workflowRuntime.AddService(dataService);
            dataService.AddService(surveyService);
            AutoResetEvent waitHandle = new AutoResetEvent(false);
            workflowRuntime.WorkflowCompleted +=
             delegate(object sender, WorkflowCompletedEventArgs e)
              { waitHandle.Set(); };
            workflowRuntime.WorkflowTerminated +=
               delegate(object sender, WorkflowTerminatedEventArgs e)
               {
                  Console.WriteLine(e.Exception.Message);
                  waitHandle.Set();
               };
            workflowRuntime.WorkflowIdled += OnWorkflowIdled;
            WorkflowInstance instance =
               workflowRuntime.CreateWorkflow(typeof
               (WorkflowConsoleApplication13.Workflow1));
            instance.Start();
            waitHandle.WaitOne();
        }
    }
    static void OnWorkflowIdled(object sender, WorkflowEventArgs e)
    {
        surveyService.CompleteSurvey(e.WorkflowInstance.InstanceId,
        "Matt", "Very Satisfied");
    }
}
}
```

Moving to the workflow, drag the `CallExternalMethod` activity onto the design surface. Note that the smart tag validation indicates that neither the interface type nor the method name has been defined. Clicking on the `InterfaceType` property will bring up a standard type browser that will allow the selection of the proper interface (see Figure 5.8). The method can then be selected from the drop-down list of the `MethodName` property. After the method is selected, additional properties will be added that correspond to the input parameters as well as the output as defined by the interface, as shown in Figure 5.9.

When the `CallExternalMethod` activity executes, it gets access to the implementation of the contract via the `ActivityExecutionContext.GetService` and calls the method.

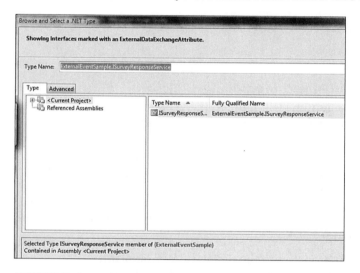

FIGURE 5.8   Browsing for the interface to use.

FIGURE 5.9   The post-binding property page; note the new property.

To use the `HandleExternalEvent` activity, the first thing that has to be done is provide a way for the host application to raise the event for the workflow runtime to receive and route the message. This is accomplished by calling the method on the service implementation:

```
public void CompleteSurvey(Guid instanceId, string employee,
➥ string surveyResponse
{
        EventHandler<SurveyEventArgs>surveyCompleted = this.SurveyCompleted;
        if (surveyCompleted != null)
        {
            surveyCompleted(null, new SurveyEventArgs(instanceId,
➥employee, surveyResponse));
        }
}
```

This will raise an event which the runtime will route to the workflow instance based on the `workflowId` parameter that has been passed in. Internally, the `HandleExternalEvent` activity creates a queue and subscribes to messages placed on the queue. When the event is received, the runtime places that message on the queue waiting for that type of message. It is possible to have multiple queues listening for the same type of message— imagine waiting for multiple employees to complete a survey. In this case, the granularity of which queue (and therefore, which activity) an event will be routed to can be specified by using correlation. A more thorough treatment of correlation can be found in the documentation contained in the Windows SDK.

To use `HandleExternalEvent`, first drop it onto the design surface. Similar to `CallExternalMethod`, an interface type must be specified, and then the event itself (see Figure 5.10).

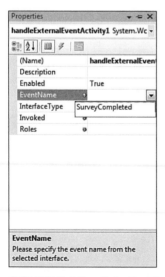

FIGURE 5.10   Selecting the event type.

When the workflow reaches the `HandleExternalEvent` activity, it will set up a queue to listen for the specified event type, and then will either go idle, or will process other activities that are scheduled for execution (if, for instance, the `HandleExternalEvent` activity occurs inside a `Parallel` activity).

Many times, a workflow needs to have a timeout while listening for an event. In the earlier sample, the workflow will listen indefinitely for the event to be received. It might be that the process should wait for an hour, or two days, or three weeks, but at some point, additional logic has to be executed, such as sending a reminder email out. The `Listen` activity can be used to facilitate this. The `Listen` activity has many branches, each of which must start with an activity that implements `IEventActivity`. The `HandleExternalEvent` activity is one of these activities; another is the `Delay` activity. The `Delay` activity exposes a `TimeSpan` property to set the `Delay` duration. In this way, the `Listen` activity can be used to model a timeout while waiting for input. In one branch is the `HandleExternalEvent` activity, and in the other a `Delay` activity, as shown in Figure 5.11.

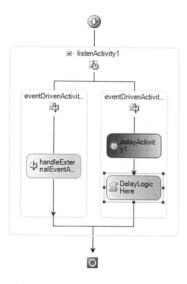

FIGURE 5.11   Using the `Listen` activity to model a timeout.

In the Windows SDK, there is a tool called wca.exe that can be pointed at an existing interface to create strongly typed activities for sending and receiving messages. This allows activities to be created that correspond to frequently used communications and increases the performance by generating a strongly typed activity. For each event declared on the interface, a derivative of HandleExternalEvent will be created; for each method, a derivative of `CallExternalMethod` will be created.

Design Behavior

It is the job of the workflow activity developer to define both the runtime and the design-time characteristics of an activity. Just as a Windows Forms control can have special design time functions, an activity can present the workflow developer with a special user interface to set up a complex set of properties, display itself in such a way that the intent or usage of the activity is clear (a red color for an exception activity), or ensure that the inputs to the activity are valid.

The design characteristics of an activity are defined in special classes outside the activity declaration itself. An activity is declared, and that declaration is decorated with attributes for design-time characteristics. This allows for multiple activities to share a designer class, and keeps the code of the activity focused on the execution behavior.

There are two major types of design behavior that can be specified. The first is the actual design and display of the activity on the workflow design surface. The second is validation, specifying the valid and invalid ways an activity can be used. This validation can be structural (a transaction scope cannot be nested in another transaction scope) or logical (a PlaceOrder activity must have an order amount greater than 0). Design-time behavior is a complicated topic and beyond the scope of this introductory chapter. The reader is encouraged to explore the Windows SDK for samples and documentation on the topic of activity design.

Validation

Validation is an important aspect to the design behavior of an activity. To validate an activity, there are two steps:

▶ Create a validator class that derives from ActivityValidator

▶ Apply the ActivityValidator attribute to the Activity class

An ActivtyValidator object implements one important method:

```
public ValidationErrorCollection Validate
➥(ValidationManager manager, object obj)
```

This method evaluates any and all possible validation conditions and returns a collection of the errors that occurred. In addition, there are two types of errors: errors and warnings. An error will stop compilation of the workflow; a warning will allow compilation to complete, but will output a warning message. An example of this might be on a ShipItem activity: One might not be required to put a postal code on the shipping label, however, it is important enough that its absence should be called to someone's attention at compile time. It might be the desired behavior not to provide a postal code, but most of the time, one should be provided, so a warning will alert the developer of the potential error.

Activity validators are also called when a workflow is loaded from an XmlReader in order to ensure that a valid workflow has been handed to the runtime to execute. In this case, a failed validation will result in an error during the attempted loading of the workflow.

A sample validator follows in Listing 5.8, this code checks to ensure that a value has been entered for the TransactionAmount property:

LISTING 5.8   Sample Validator

```
private class CustomValidator : ActivityValidator
{
    public override ValidationErrorCollection Validate
                    (ValidationManager manager, object obj)
    {
        ValidationErrorCollection errorCollection =
            base.Validate(manager, obj);
        DemoActivity demoActivity = obj as DemoActivity;
        if (obj.TransactionAmount <= 0)
        {
            errorCollection.Add(new ValidationError
                ("Transaction Amount must be greater than 0",8675309, false));
        }
        return errorCollection;
    }
}
```

The constructor for ValidationError has a few overloads, allowing an error number to be specified, a Boolean for determining whether this is a warning, and a property name if a specific property is responsible for the error. The property name, if specified, will allow the designer to set focus to that property in the property grid if the validation error is clicked on in the designer.

When an error collection is retuned, the developer is notified of this through the smart tag that appears adjacent to the activity. Clicking on the smart tag allows the developer to review the different errors that were returned by the executing validator, as shown in Figure 5.12.

FIGURE 5.12   Validation results displayed in a smart tag.

The validator is applied to an activity by decorating the definition of the class with the ActivityValidator attribute, as shown in the following code.

```
[ActivityValidator(typeof(CustomValidator))]
public partial class DemoActivity : SequenceActivity
```

Transactions and Compensation

Vital parts of any process are the ability to make sure that work is accomplished, and to be able to handle situations where the work at any given step needs to be undone.

Windows Workflow Foundation supports two different constructs aimed at solving those problems.

Over the short term of execution, it makes sense to have an *ACID (atomic, consistent, isolated, and durable)* transaction. If multiple database updates are occurring and transactional objects are being modified, it is desirable to make sure that all or none of the changes occur. The .NET Framework 2.0 provides a very nice model for this in the System.Transactions namespace. By wrapping a series of transaction-aware calls in a transaction scope, the developer gets transaction support, while System.Transactions manages the complexities of involving resource managers and escalating transactions (see Listing 5.9).

LISTING 5.9   Using System.Transactions

```
using (TransactionScope ts = new TransactionScope())
{
    // do transactional work here
    ts.Complete();
}
```

This is the model of transactions that is supported by the TransactionScope and CompensatableTransactionScope activities included in Windows Workflow Foundation. The TransactionScope activity functions in the same way that the using statement in Listing 5.9 wraps a series of calls in a single transaction. Any action taken by activities on transaction-aware objects, such as updates to a SQL database, will occur within an ACID transaction managed by System.Transactions. To ensure that the workflow state and the transaction state are consistent, the call to the persistence service to persist the workflow following the transaction scope will be included in the transaction as well. In this way, the entire transaction indicating scope completion as well as individual changes made by the contained activities will either commit or fail, so there is never an inconsistency of workflow state and transaction state.

Transactions work very well when executed over a short period of time. In a long-running process, the mechanics of an ACID transaction begin to break down. It is not feasible to maintain a lock on a row in SQL for a period of weeks during an expense-reporting process. This is where the concept of *compensation* comes in.

Compensation is the set of actions that need to be taken if a completed, closed activity has to be rolled back. This model gives the flexibility needed to offer fine-grained control that is specific to an individual activity. In the case of expense reporting, it might be desirable if the entire process is cancelled, and that the initial records of the expense report are kept in the database but are marked with a "cancelled" status. It might also be the case that the need is to delete those rows. Either one of those behaviors, or any other, can be implemented as the compensation for a given activity. Compensation can be defined for a specific activity by implementing ICompensatableActivity as shown in Listing 5.10.

LISTING 5.10   Compensatable Activity

```
public ActivityExecutionStatus Compensate
➡ (ActivityExecutionContext executionContext)
{
    // un-do the activity
    return ActivityExecutionStatus.Closed;
}
```

This allows the developer to define the specific behaviors required by the individual activity when it is told to compensate. Compensation will occur in the following cases:

▶ An unhandled exception occurs within the workflow

▶ By using the CompensateActivity to provide more fine-grained control over which activities compensate

It is important to note that the compensation will occur for every instance of an activity marked as ICompensatableActivity that has completed. This means that if such an activity is placed within a while loop that executes 10 times, the compensation logic will be executed for each instance of the activity; in this case, 10 times. This is accomplished by tracking the context in which the activity executed and keeping this as part of the state of the workflow.

There are also compensation scope activities, which allow compensation behavior to be modeled as a sequential workflow around a group of arbitrary activities. The CompensatableSequence and CompensatableTransactionScope surface this functionality when one right-clicks on the activity and selects View Compensation Handler, which will display a sequential activity to define the specific compensation behavior for that group of activities as seen in Figures 5.13 and 5.14. This is very useful in scenarios where compensation behavior needs to be defined for a group of activities.

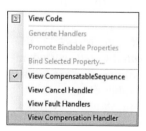

FIGURE 5.13   CompensatableSequence context menu.

The CompensatableTransactionScope functions in the same way, except that the contained activities will execute within a System.Transactions transaction to ensure ACID behavior in the short term, and will define a rollback if the sequence needs to be undone in three weeks if an error occurs.

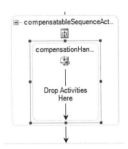

FIGURE 5.14   CompensationHandler sequence.

Workflow Models

A single activity, on its own, is not much to look at. It performs a task, and it executes that task in a nice, controlled fashion, but a single activity is comparable to a single method call on a class. Useful, but it is not until those method calls are composed that the purpose of the application becomes apparent.

It is the arrangement of work, of activities, that is the definition of a workflow. Fundamentally, a *workflow* is the arrangement of work. This loose concept leads to the many overloaded uses of the term. In the case of Windows Workflow Foundation, the works arranged are activities. An activity might perform a very narrow, specific function, such as inserting a row into a database, or it might be very structural, allowing the parallel execution of the contained activities.

In Windows Workflow Foundation, the arrangement of activities into workflows is accomplished in a fashion consistent with the remainder of the model, by composing activities into a containing activity that defines the execution behavior of the contained workflows. So, to say this another way, the runtime of the Windows Workflow Foundation only knows how to execute activities—that is the primary job it is tasked with. By providing different root activities, the execution behavior is in turn determined by that activity.

Moving beyond the abstract, there are two out of the box models of workflow in Windows Workflow Foundation, and each of these models corresponds to a special activity type. These are sequential and state machine workflows. A *sequential workflow* is what many people traditionally associate with workflow: a flowchart defining linear execution. A *state machine*, a concept familiar to many developers, defines a number of states an application can be in (and the application can be in one and only one state at any time), the events to listen for, and any logic to execute on receipt of those events including changing state. This by no means limits the execution pattern to these two types; on the contrary, any execution behavior that can be defined in the code of the Execute() method can be a workflow model. Jon Flanders, a Windows Workflow Foundation developer, wrote such a model that would randomly execute contained activities. Although this might describe business processes that need workflow, it shows the spectrum of execution patterns one could implement.

Sequential Workflows

A *sequential workflow*, without relying too heavily on recursive definitions, is simply the sequential execution of the contained activities, henceforth referred to as *activities*. The most basic sequential workflow would be a linear arrangement of activities, as shown in Figure 5.15.

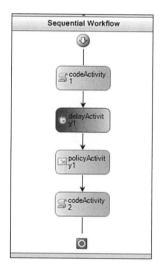

FIGURE 5.15   A basic sequential workflow.

Windows Workflow Foundation contains activities that can be used to provide greater flexibility in sequential execution. The two most frequently used are the `IfElse` and `Parallel` activities. Another commonly used activity is the `ConditionedActivityGroup` (CAG), which is described in detail in the "Rules Engine" section of this chapter. As mentioned elsewhere throughout this chapter, it is possible to compose these activities to arbitrary depth; that is, a branch in a parallel can contain an `IfElse` with a branch using a CAG, which has a path of execution using a `Parallel` activity.

IfElse **Activity**

When just sketching a process, not many boxes will be drawn until the inevitable decision diamond appears, indicating some choice that needs to be made. When drawing, the criteria is often written inside the diamond, indicating the criteria that defines the condition, as shown in Figure 5.16.

Inside of a workflow, when a decision needs to be made, the `IfElse` activity is used. The `IfElse` activity contains at least a single child branch, an activity of type `IfElseBranchActivity`. An `IfElseBranchActivity` is a sequential composite activity with a special property, `Condition`. It is the condition that determines whether the activities contained inside the `IfElseBranchActivity` are to be executed or ignored. The `IfElse` activity can contain an arbitrary number of branches, each having a defined condition. The `IfElse` activity defined last, or appearing to the rightmost side in the designer, will not require a condition. This activity is the `else` branch inside the `if` statement. Within the designer, to add an additional branch, right-click on the `IfElse` activity and select the Add Branch item that appears on the context menu, as shown in Figure 5.17. The result is seen in Figure 5.18.

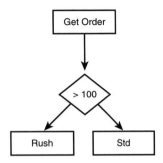

FIGURE 5.16   Napkin workflow with decision diamond.

FIGURE 5.17   `IfElse` context menu.

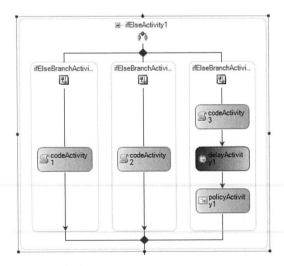

FIGURE 5.18   Multiple branch `IfElse` activity.

The validators on the `IfElseBranchActivity` require a condition be assigned unless it is the `Else` branch. However, there is no enforcement of exclusivity of conditions. That is, there might be three branches: The first defines a condition x > 5 and the second defines a condition x > 10. The validators do not look to see that there is a collision (namely, if x > 10, the condition on both branches would be satisfied). The `IfElse` activity will evaluate the conditions in a left-to-right sequence and will execute the first branch, and *only* the first branch, whose condition evaluates to true. If all the conditions evaluate to false and there is an `Else` branch, the `Else` branch will be executed. The different types of rule conditions and their use are discussed later in this chapter in the "Rules Engine" section.

Parallel Activity

Within the process, there might be a time when multiple activities need to execute simultaneously. There might also be a time where one wants to ensure that some number (*n*) of activities have completed before moving on to the next activity. The activities arranged in parallel might all execute over roughly the same amount of time, or the time might be radically different; one branch calling quickly to a web service to retrieve the credit limit of a customer, while another branch is waiting for a call-center representative to complete an over the phone survey of the same customer. Hopefully, the web service containing credit limit information would return well before the phone survey occurs. The model of this process can be seen in Figure 5.19

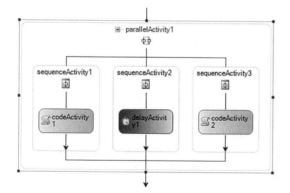

FIGURE 5.19   A simple parallel activity.

The `Parallel` activity is designed for this scenario. The `Parallel` activity consists of at least two `Sequence` activities. Additional branches can be added by selecting the `Parallel` activity, right-clicking, and selecting Add Branch in the same way that one adds branches to the `IfElse` activity. This leads to the very important conversation regarding the execution order of items contained inside a `Parallel` activity, which first must start off with the statement that the `Parallel` activity is not multithreaded.

This point bears repeating: The `Parallel` activity is not multithreaded. This stems primarily from the design decision made by the team that a workflow instance will run on one and only one thread at a given time. This decision was made to keep the simple, compositional nature of the Windows Workflow Foundation programming model, in a word, simple. In the words of the architects themselves:

> One big advantage of a single-threaded execution model is the simplification of activity development. Activity developers need not worry about concurrent execution of an activity's methods. Locking, preemption, and other aspects of multi-threaded programming are not a part of Windows Workflow Foundation activity development, and these simplifications are important given Windows Workflow Foundation's goal of broad adoption by .NET developers (from *Essential Windows Workflow Foundation* by Shukla and Schmidt).

Multithreaded programming is complicated, and the ability to reuse activities in multiple workflow types makes activity-hardening a very tough task when the concerns of multithreading are added. Additionally, this is not to say that the runtime engine is single-threaded. On the contrary, by default the engine will schedule workflow instances to execute on as many threads as it has been programmed to use to execute workflows. A workflow instance is tied to a single thread while it is executing, but the usual use of workflow is that there will be multiple instances of that workflow running at any one time, each on its own thread. Workflows can execute in parallel on multiple threads, but a single workflow instance will use one thread.

The question inevitably is raised, "What about my <tricky bit of computation> that requires me to multithread or else my performance will be horrible?" Again, going back to Shukla and Schmidt:

> Computations that benefit from true concurrency are, for Windows Workflow Foundation programs, best abstracted as features of a service; the service can be made available to activities... In this way, the service can be executed in an environment optimized for true concurrency, which might or might not be on the machine on which the Windows Workflow Foundation program instance is running.

In other words, if one has such a computation, the best way to leverage it from a workflow is to expose it as a service, using many of the techniques described elsewhere in this book. Chapter 6 will deal with integrating Windows Communication Foundation services with Windows Workflow Foundation programs.

Consider the following workflow that contains a parallel activity in three branches. Each of the activities will output the branch they are in and the position in which they appear in the branch, as shown in Figure 5.20.

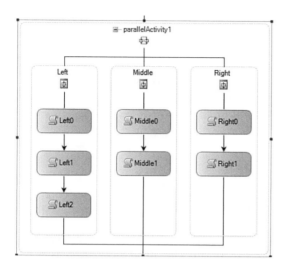

FIGURE 5.20   A parallel activity with three branches.

The output of this workflow will be the following:

Output of Parallel Execution

```
Left 0
Middle 0
Right 0
Left 1
Middle 1
Right 1
Left 2
```

To understand the earlier interleaved sequence, one must understand how the activities are actually being executed. A workflow instance maintains a schedule of activities to execute. As the parallel activity executes, it schedules each of the child activities (these are `Sequence` activities) for execution. This is scheduled by placing a delegate to the `Execute()` method onto the execution queue used by the runtime. The `Parallel` activity has scheduled the `Left`, `Middle`, and `Right` `Sequence` activities to execute, in that order. The execution queue now looks as shown in Figure 5.21.

FIGURE 5.21   Execution queue as scheduled by the `Parallel` activity.

The first activity to execute is `Left Sequence`. It is responsible for executing its contained activities, so it adds its activity to the execution queue. The queue now looks as shown in Figure 5.22.

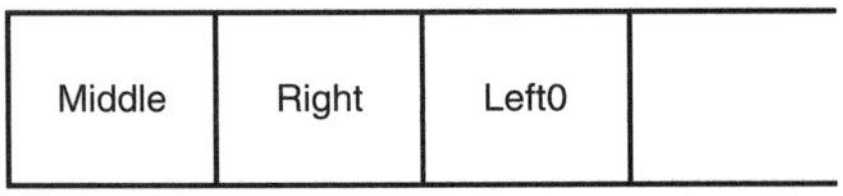

Middle	Right	Left0	

FIGURE 5.22   The execution queue after the `Left Sequence` activity executes.

Execution continues until the queue looks as shown in Figure 5.23.

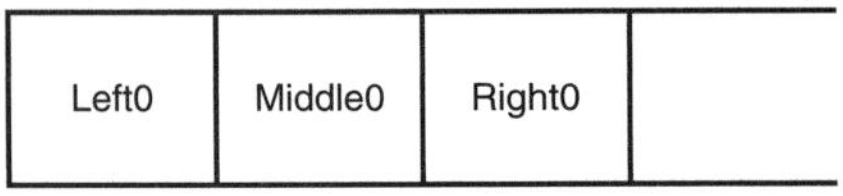

Left0	Middle0	Right0	

FIGURE 5.23   The execution queue with code activities scheduled.

When the `left0` activity completes, the event handler of the `Left Sequence` activity is called and schedules the next activity, `left1`, for execution. The queue now looks as shown in Figure 5.24.

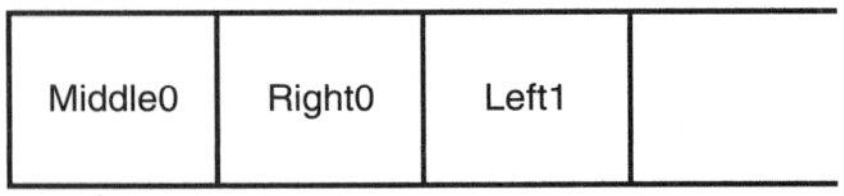

Middle0	Right0	Left1	

FIGURE 5.24   The execution queue after `left0` executes.

This pattern continues until all the `Sequence` activities have completed. Then the `Parallel` activity completes and the workflow moves on.

The workflow developer can have finer-grained control over the execution sequence by using the `SynchronizationScope` activity. `SynchronizationScope` is a composite activity one can use to serialize the execution of a group of activities. In the workflow just shown, assume that the right branch must execute only after the left branch has completed fully. It might be that the business process describes these two branches as parallel, but due to implementation, it is necessary that one execute prior to another (note to the process consultant, this might be a bottleneck to look at!). A `SynchronizationScope` activity has a `SynchronizationHandles` property that is used to determine the way in which the various `SynchronizationScope` activities interact with one another. The `SynchronizationHandles` property is a collection of strings used as handles on a shared resource. When a `SynchronizationScope` executes, it attempts to obtain a lock on each of the handles and will not execute until it obtains the lock. If the handle is locked by another `SynchronizationScope`, the other `SynchronizationScope` activities will wait to acquire the lock. In this way, access to these handles, and the activities within, can be serialized.

This is best shown by the workflow in Figure 5.25, which is the example shown earlier modified to contain three `SynchronizationScope` activities. The left most synchronization activity has a synchronization handle of a, the middle b, and the right a, b, or both of them. In plain language, the right branch activity will not execute until both the left and middle branch have completed.

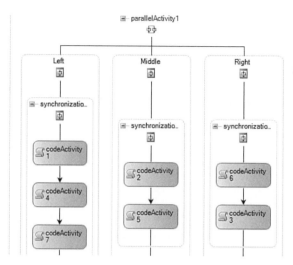

FIGURE 5.25   A parallel activity with `SynchronizationScope` activities on each branch.

Listing 5.11 expresses this in XAML.

LISTING 5.11   SynchronizationScope Example

```
<SequentialWorkflowActivity x:Class="WCFHandsOne.SynchronizationWithParallel"
  x:Name="SynchronizationWithParallel"
  xmlns:x="http://schemas.microsoft.com/winfx/2006/xaml"
  xmlns="http://schemas.microsoft.com/winfx/2006/xaml/workflow">
  <ParallelActivity x:Name="parallelActivity1">
    <SequenceActivity x:Name="sequenceActivity1">
      <SynchronizationScopeActivity
        x:Name="synchronizationScopeActivity1" SynchronizationHandles="a">
        <CodeActivity x:Name="codeActivity1"
          ExecuteCode="codeActivity1_ExecuteCode" />
        <CodeActivity x:Name="codeActivity4"
          ExecuteCode="codeActivity1_ExecuteCode" />
        <CodeActivity x:Name="codeActivity7"
          ExecuteCode="codeActivity1_ExecuteCode" />
      </SynchronizationScopeActivity>
    </SequenceActivity>
    <SequenceActivity x:Name="sequenceActivity2">
      <SynchronizationScopeActivity
        x:Name="synchronizationScopeActivity2" SynchronizationHandles="b">
        <CodeActivity x:Name="codeActivity2"
          ExecuteCode="codeActivity2_ExecuteCode" />
        <CodeActivity x:Name="codeActivity5"
          ExecuteCode="codeActivity2_ExecuteCode" />
```

LISTING 5.11   Continued

```
      </SynchronizationScopeActivity>
    </SequenceActivity>
    <SequenceActivity x:Name="sequenceActivity3">
      <SynchronizationScopeActivity
        x:Name="synchronizationScopeActivity3" SynchronizationHandles="a, b">
        <CodeActivity x:Name="codeActivity6"
          ExecuteCode="codeActivity3_ExecuteCode" />
        <CodeActivity x:Name="codeActivity3"
          ExecuteCode="codeActivity3_ExecuteCode" />
      </SynchronizationScopeActivity>
    </SequenceActivity>
  </ParallelActivity>
</SequentialWorkflowActivity>
```

With the code beside in Listing 5.12:

LISTING 5.12   SynchronizationScope Code Beside

```
public partial class SynchronizationWithParallel: SequentialWorkflowActivity
{
      private int i,j,k;
      private void codeActivity1_ExecuteCode(object sender, EventArgs e)
      {
          Console.WriteLine("Left {0}", i);
          i++;
      }
      private void codeActivity2_ExecuteCode(object sender, EventArgs e)
      {
          Console.WriteLine("Middle {0}", j);
          j++;
      }
      private void codeActivity3_ExecuteCode(object sender, EventArgs e)
      {
          Console.WriteLine("Right {0}", k);
          k++;
      }
}
```

It is insightful to trace through the execution of this workflow. Earlier, the behavior of the Parallel activity was discussed, assume that the execution queue is as shown in Figure 5.26.

The left SynchronizationScope will attempt to lock on the handle a, and will be successful. It will schedule its first child activity for execution, yielding the queue shown in Figure 5.26.

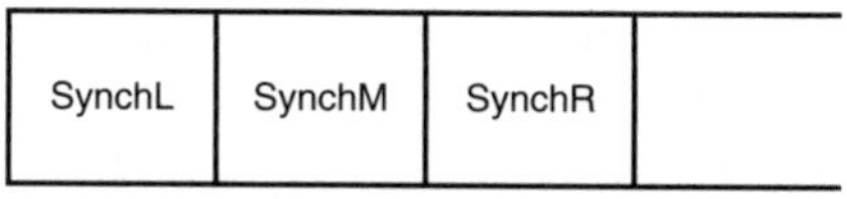

SynchL	SynchM	SynchR	

FIGURE 5.26   Execution queue scheduling of `SynchronizationScope` activities.

SynchM	SynchR	Left0	

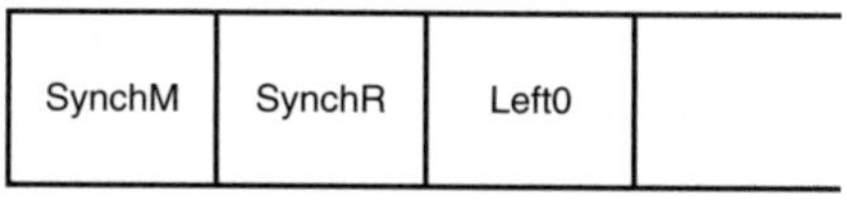

FIGURE 5.27   The execution queue following the left `SynchronizationScope` successfully locking its handle, A.

The middle `SynchronizationScope` will successfully lock its handle, b, and will schedule `middle0` for execution. When the right `SynchronizationScope` executes, it will attempt to obtain locks on a and b and will fail to obtain them. The left and middle `SynchronizationScope` activities will execute in an interleaved fashion until the right `SynchronizationScope` can obtain locks on both A and B. Therefore, its execution output would look like this:

Execution Output of Synchronization Scope Workflow

```
Left 0
Middle 0
Left 1
Middle 1
Left 2
Right 0
Right 1
```

One can also imagine the use of long-running activities in the braches, those activities that do some work and then await a message to conclude execution, such as a `RequestApproval` activity. In these scenarios, when an activity yields control, such as by returning a status of Executing while it waits for some message, the `Parallel` activity will continue executing the other branches. If an activity does a long-running amount of CPU-intensive work and never yields control back to the scheduler (by return Executing or Closed), the `Parallel` activity will not continue with the other items. This makes sense because the workflow instance is single threaded, so if one activity is continuing to do work, another activity cannot execute.

State Machine Workflows

One of the most important things an application might do is track the state of some process. Whether it is orders moving through an e-commerce website, or determining what actions are valid steps to perform inside of a Windows Forms application, knowing the current state and how to move from state to state are vital to any complex application. A state machine workflow can help to solve such a problem.

A state machine workflow consists formally of *n*-states, which include the current state of the application, an initial state, and a completed state. A *state* consists of actions to be performed on entering the state, actions to be performed before leaving the state, and a set of EventDriven activities. The EventDriven activities define some event for which they listen and the set of actions to be performed on receiving the event. The EventDriven activities require a single IEventActivity to be placed as the first child activity. Common examples of IEventActivity are the HandleExternalEvent and Delay activities. One of the subsequent actions should be a SetState activity that will initiate a state transition from the current state to a new state.

Within the designer, one sees two views of a state machine. The first is of the states themselves. The second view is inside one of the groups of actions described earlier, either the StateInitialization and StateFinalization activities or within EventDrivenActivity. One moves between these two views in the designer by double-clicking on the group of actions to view more detail (see Figure 5.28), or within the group of actions by clicking on the state to return to the state view (see Figure 5.29).

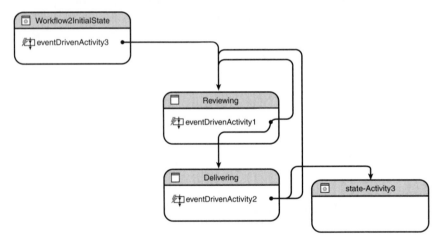

FIGURE 5.28   A state machine–based workflow.

A state machine workflow is completed when the current state is the state defined as the CompletedStateName on the root state machine workflow. The execution pattern is determined by the combination of states and potential transitions. This allows for a very nondeterministic execution pattern. Because of this, state machines are often used to model human-based processes. Consider a document approval process: The number of drafts a document might go through cannot easily be planned for. Additionally, a document might move all the way to an AlmostPublished state when the facts change and the document moves all the way back to the JustStarted state.

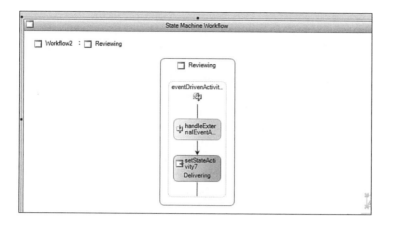

FIGURE 5.29   Inside The `EventDriven` activity on the state.

A state machine is not limited, though, to human-based processes. Manufacturing processes lend themselves to a state machine workflow because there are many, many different states the process can be in and minimal work that needs to be done between the transitions. For instance, after a car rolls out of the `PaintDryingState` on the `PaintDried` event, a notification might need to be sent to the shipping system that an additional vehicle will be ready for transport. The state machine provides a useful model for this process, especially because there might be instances when a car is in the same state multiple times, based on the customization criteria.

The decision between choosing a state machine or a sequential workflow model (or something custom) ultimately depends on how accurately the model (the workflow) represents the reality of the process. It is possible to represent the earlier document-routing scenario in a sequential workflow, with a series of `while` loops to indicate all the potential branches of retrying and routing back to the beginning. Similarly, many sequential workflows could be represented as state machines. This is not to be so bold as to claim there is an isomorphism between the two sets, but rather to suggest that many problems could be solved with either approach—the criterion has to be how naturally the model represents reality. In the case where neither a sequential nor a state machine approach models the workflow well, one can always create a custom root activity to define one's own workflow type.

Custom Root Activities

One is not limited to the execution semantics of the two root activities previously described. The role of any composite activity is to manage the execution of its child activities. By creating a custom root activity, one can implement any execution behavior desired (provided its logic can be somehow expressed in code). As with creating custom activities, a thorough treatment of the topic is outside of the scope of this introductory chapter. The reader is encouraged to reference Shukla and Schmidt for additional information in this area.

Workflow Hosting

Much has been written of the activity model and the ways to compose workflows. Those two things alone would not result in much, outside of a nice graphical representation of a business process. A runtime environment is crucial for turning that model into an executing application. The Windows Workflow Foundation runtime is remarkable in its achievement of minimal overhead and maximal extensibility. As the following sections will illustrate, almost any runtime behavior can be customized, including the threading model. At the same time, the runtime can be executed within a Windows Forms application or a web application to provide the logic behind the user interface anywhere access to a .NET application domain is available. That engine can then scale up to be the core of the workflow engine within Microsoft Office SharePoint Server 2007.

Hosting the Runtime

The base case of workflow hosting is the model that is included in the Visual Studio 2005 Extensions for Windows Workflow Foundation. When one selects a new workflow project (sequential or state machine), a very basic hosting environment is created. Listing 5.13 is the default program.cs that is included when tone creates a new workflow project.

LISTING 5.13   Console Based Workflow Host

```
static void Main(string[] args)
{
    using(WorkflowRuntime workflowRuntime = new WorkflowRuntime())
    {
        AutoResetEvent waitHandle = new AutoResetEvent(false);
        workflowRuntime.WorkflowCompleted +=
            delegate(object sender, WorkflowCompletedEventArgs e)
            {waitHandle.Set();};
        workflowRuntime.WorkflowTerminated +=
            delegate(object sender, WorkflowTerminatedEventArgs e)
            {
                Console.WriteLine(e.Exception.Message);
                waitHandle.Set();
            };
        WorkflowInstance instance = workflowRuntime.CreateWorkflow
            (typeof(WorkflowConsoleApplication1.Workflow1));
        instance.Start();
        waitHandle.WaitOne();
    }
}
```

The first thing that is done is the instantiation of the workflow runtime:

```
WorkflowRuntime workflowRuntime = new WorkflowRuntime()
```

This creates the execution environment for the workflows to execute within. Some house-keeping occurs to ensure that the console application will not exit prematurely when the main method finishes prior to the workflow completing. Remember, the workflow instance will be created on a separate thread (using the default scheduler service). Two events are wired up using anonymous delegates to ensure that errors are reported to the console, and successful completion of the workflow allows the console application to exit gracefully:

```
workflowRuntime.WorkflowCompleted += delegate
 (object sender, WorkflowCompletedEventArgs e) {waitHandle.Set();};
workflowRuntime.WorkflowTerminated += delegate
 (object sender, WorkflowTerminatedEventArgs e)
{
    Console.WriteLine(e.Exception.Message);
    waitHandle.Set();
};
```

Then a workflow instance is created by specifying the type of the workflow to be created. How this method is overridden to provide other workflow creation behavior will be discussed later.

```
WorkflowInstance instance = workflowRuntime.CreateWorkflow
(typeof(WorkflowConsoleApplication1.Workflow1));
```

Finally, the workflow instance is scheduled to begin execution, which will occur on a separate thread from the console application. The console application will patiently await the workflow's completion.

```
instance.Start();
```

The following are the tasks required by a simple workflow host:

1. A workflow runtime is created and made available.

2. Handlers are wired to events of interest; in this case, completion and termination.

3. An instance is created.

4. An instance is started.

This pattern is followed inside of any hosting environment, with the possible addition of step 1.5, the addition of runtime services to the WorkflowRuntime. This step is optional because

▶ Services might not be needed at all.

▶ Services can be configured declaratively within app.config.

This last point might seem familiar to readers who have completed some of the chapters focusing on the Windows Communication Foundation. The ability to define behaviors in code or in configuration is a theme present in both of these frameworks. The configuration option is more flexible, allowing services to be configured at deployment, whereas the code option insures certain behavior is implanted irrespective of deployment-time decisions.

Runtime Services

The flexibility of the runtime comes from its delegation of responsibility to a set of well-defined runtime services. This pluggable model of runtime services that have nothing to do with Windows Communication Foundation services lets a workflow developer choose to have file-based persistence while executing in a Windows Forms application and a SQL-based persistence while executing in the context of an ASP.NET application, with the workflow being none the wiser. There are a number of core problems identified as general areas where a suggested solution would be provided while remaining flexible for an implementation tailored and tuned for a specific scenario. These include persistence, tracking, and scheduling.

Persistence Services

A defining feature of a workflow system is its capability to enable long-running work. *Long-running work* generally refers to a pattern of request-response activities, with the time span between request and response a suitably long duration (minutes, hours, days). Windows Workflow Foundation provides this ability to workflow developers, and makes the task of persisting workflows while they wait transparent. This is accomplished through a persistence service. When a workflow is idled or is required to persist, the workflow runtime provides access to a persistence service. If a persistence service is not available, the workflow will not be persisted and will remain in-memory while awaiting its eventual resumption.

The persistence service is responsible for storing all the information about the workflow state to some location outside the workflow runtime. When an event occurs that requires that specific workflow instance, the workflow runtime will first check in memory to see whether that workflow is already executing. If it is not, it uses the persistence service to load the workflow instance back into memory. What is important to note is that the workflow can be reloaded into memory weeks after the last time it did anything. Additionally, the workflow could be reloaded onto a completely different machine than the one that initially persisted it. It is through a persistence service that one can obtain scalability by hosting workflow within a farm setting. The runtime will attempt to persist the workflow in the following situations:

- The host calls `WorkflowInstance.Unload()`

- The workflow instance completes or terminates

- The workflow instance goes idle (no activities scheduled to execute)

- Completion of an atomic transaction

- Completion of an activity marked `PersistOnClose`

To force persistence at a point within the workflow, an "empty" activity decorated with the `PersistOnClose` attribute could be used to ensure persistence.

Out of the box, Windows Workflow Foundation provides a default implementation of a persistence service: `SqlWorkflowPersistenceService`. To use `SqlWorkflowPersistenceService`, the following steps are necessary:

- Create the database using the scripts found at Windows\Microsoft.NET\Framework\v3.0\Windows Workflow Foundation\SQL\EN\SqlPersistenceService_Schema.sql and Windows\Microsoft.NET\Framework\v3.0\Windows Workflow Foundation\SQL\EN\SqlPersistenceService_Logic.sql

- Attach the persistence service to the workflow runtime

The last step is done either in code or within the application configuration file. The approaches are outlined in Listing 5.14 and Listing 5.15, respectively.

LISTING 5.14   Adding the Persistence Service in Code

```
using (WorkflowRuntime workflowRuntime = new WorkflowRuntime())
{
    WorkflowPersistenceService persistenceService =
        new SqlWorkflowPersistenceService(
        "Initial Catalog=SqlPersistenceService;Data Source=localhost;
➥Integrated Security=SSPI;",
        false,
        new TimeSpan(1, 0, 0),
        new TimeSpan(0, 0, 5));
    workflowRuntime.AddService(persistenceService);
...

}
```

LISTING 5.15   Adding the Persistence Service via Config

```
<configuration xmlns="http://schemas.microsoft.com/.NetConfiguration/v2.0">
        <configSections>
                <section name="WorkflowRuntime"
➥ type="System.Workflow.Runtime.Configuration.WorkflowRuntimeSection,
➥ System.Workflow.Runtime, Version=3.0.00000.0, Culture=neutral,
➥ PublicKeyToken=31bf3856ad364e35" />
        </configSections>
        <WorkflowRuntime Name="WorkflowServiceContainer">
                <Services>
```

LISTING 5.15   Continued

```
                            <addtype="System.Workflow.Runtime.Hosting.
➥SqlWorkflowPersistenceService, System.Workflow.Runtime, Version=
➥3.0.00000.0, Culture=neutral, PublicKeyToken=31bf3856ad364e35"
➥connectionString="Initial Catalog=WorkflowPersistenceStore;Data
➥Source=localhost;Integrated Security=SSPI;" UnloadOnIdle="true"/>
                </Services>
        </WorkflowRuntime>
...
</configuration>
```

In the second case, the persistence service is being configured with the `UnloadOnIdle` flag set to true. This forces the runtime to persist the workflows whenever they are reported as idle. `SqlWorkflowPersistenceService` is also responsible for managing the tracking of timers. If an expense-reporting workflow has a timeout of one week before the approval must escalate, something needs to keep track of that timer in order to load the workflow in the case where nothing happens for a week. `SqlWorkflowPersistenceService` stores the timer expiration within its SQL tables. When the runtime is started and the service is loaded, one of the first actions it performs is a scan of the timer expirations to determine whether any were "missed" while the host was unavailable. In this way, the persistence service ensures that even if the host was down, on resuming, any workflows whose timers have expired will be processed. There are a number of other features in `SqlWorkflowPersistenceService` that pertain specifically to scaling out in a farm setting. The reader is encouraged to explore the documentation further to investigate that scenario.

> **NOTE**
>
> Creating a custom persistence service is a relatively straightforward endeavor. An example of a file system persistence service is available within the Windows SDK.

Tracking Services

While a workflow is executing, there are many potentially interesting pieces of data one might want to collect. How long did an activity take? When did the workflow start and when did it finish? What was the value of the purchase order that went through the system? All of these questions can be answered via the information recorded by the tracking service. The *tracking service* is used by the workflow runtime to output various pieces of data to some kind of external store.

The mechanics of the tracking service are relevant to understand here. The runtime will call the `TryGetProfile()` method of the tracking service to obtain a tracking profile, if it exists, for the currently executing instance. If a profile exists, it describes what information should be sent via the tracking channel. The tracking service itself does not determine what data gets tracked; it provides a profile to the runtime, which in turn decides when to track. This design does not rely on a tracking service author to provide a high performance implementation of event filtering.

Tracking Profiles   A tracking profile defines on what events the workflow runtime should send a message to the associated tracking channel. It allows a developer to shape the data that is recorded from a workflow execution. A tracking profile can be defined within code, and the object serializes to XML for a more portable representation of the tracking profile. There are three types of events for which the tracking profile can be configured. *Workflow events* are those that pertain to the lifecycle of a workflow, from its creation to termination. *Activity events* are those pertaining to the lifecycle of an activity. Finally, *user events* are those emitted from an activity during its execution when the TrackData() method is called from the base Activity class.

A *tracking profile* is a collection of tracking points, of the types WorkflowTrackPoint, ActivityTrackPoint, or UserTrackPoint. Each of these tracking points consists of MatchingLocations, ExcludedLocations, Extracts, and Annotations. The locations are defined by a type (on what activity does the location apply?), the ExecutionStatusEvents (on what events does the location apply?), and the conditions (under what criteria should the location apply?). ExcludedLocation explicitly defines when tracking should not occur. Extracts define what data should be tracked, either as a property of the activity or the workflow, expressed in dot notation. Finally, Annotations are a set of strings that should be included in the tracking record if a record is sent.

The Windows SDK contains a number of samples related to tracking. The Tracking Profile Object Model sample provides an example of declaring a tracking profile in code and then outputting the tracking profile in its serialized XML form, which the reader might find more instructive. The XML output is contained in Listing 5.16.

LISTING 5.16   XML Tracking Profile

```xml
<?xml version="1.0" encoding="utf-16" standalone="yes"?>
<TrackingProfile xmlns="http://schemas.microsoft.com/
➥winfx/2006/workflow/trackingprofile" version="1.0.0">
    <TrackPoints>
        <ActivityTrackPoint>
            <MatchingLocations>
                <ActivityTrackingLocation>
                    <Activity>
                        <TypeName>activityName</TypeName>
                        <MatchDerivedTypes>false</MatchDerivedTypes>
                    </Activity>
                    <ExecutionStatusEvents>
                        <ExecutionStatus>Initialized</ExecutionStatus>
                        <ExecutionStatus>Executing</ExecutionStatus>
                        <ExecutionStatus>Canceling</ExecutionStatus>
                        <ExecutionStatus>Closed</ExecutionStatus>
                        <ExecutionStatus>Compensating</ExecutionStatus>
```

LISTING 5.16   Continued

```
                        <ExecutionStatus>Faulting</ExecutionStatus>
                    </ExecutionStatusEvents>
                    <Conditions>
                        <ActivityTrackingCondition>
                            <Operator>Equals</Operator>
                            <Member>memberName</Member>
                            <Value>memberValue</Value>
                        </ActivityTrackingCondition>
                    </Conditions>
                </ActivityTrackingLocation>
            </MatchingLocations>
            <ExcludedLocations>
                <ActivityTrackingLocation>
                    <Activity>
                        <TypeName>activityName</TypeName>
                        <MatchDerivedTypes>false</MatchDerivedTypes>
                    </Activity>
                    <ExecutionStatusEvents>
                        <ExecutionStatus>Compensating</ExecutionStatus>
                    </ExecutionStatusEvents>
                </ActivityTrackingLocation>
            </ExcludedLocations>
            <Annotations>
                <Annotation>Track Point Annotations</Annotation>
            </Annotations>
            <Extracts>
                <WorkflowDataTrackingExtract>
                    <Member>Name</Member>
                </WorkflowDataTrackingExtract>
            </Extracts>
        </ActivityTrackPoint>
    </TrackPoints>
</TrackingProfile>
```

This follows the pattern discussed earlier by defining a track point by setting a location—namely all executions of activityName on all of its status transitions—and then excluding when it would be in the compensating status. Additionally, the location will be valid only when the condition is Activity.memberName == memberValue. An annotation is added so that if the criterion is set, a tracking record will be created that includes the text Track Point Annotations. Finally, the data to be extracted is defined; in this case, the Name property from the workflow. By specifying WorkflowDataTrackingExtract, one can obtain access to the properties of the root activity of the workflow. If one were to specify ActivityDataTrackingExtract, one could obtain a tracking record that contains the data of the associated activity.

`SqlTrackingService`   As with the persistence service, a default implementation is provided that leverages SQL Server in order to store the information. The following steps will enable tracking within an application:

- ▸ Create the database using the scripts found at Windows\Microsoft.NET\Framework\v3.0\Windows Workflow Foundation\SQL\EN\Tracking_Schema.sql and Windows\Microsoft.NET\Framework\v3.0\Windows Workflow Foundation\SQL\EN\Tracking_Logic.sql

- ▸ Attach the persistence service to the workflow runtime

- ▸ Specify a tracking profile to receive only the desired events

Similar to `SqlWorkflowPersistenceService`, the service can be added to the runtime either in code or by the configuration file. In the case of the tracking service, it is possible that multiple tracking services could be configured, each returning a different profile of events for a given workflow. An example is when the `SqlTrackingService` is used for general reporting on the process, but highly critical errors need to be routed through an `EventLogTrackingService` to surface in the existing management tools. The `TryGetProfile()` method on the `EventLogTrackingService` might return a profile that specifies a location of the `OrderProcessing` activity, but might listen only for the `FaultingEvent`.

The Windows SDK contains a sample profile designer that can be used to analyze a workflow and specify the tracking points. It will then generate a serialized, XML form of the tracking profile that can then be used within code or within the tracking database to provide a profile for a given type.

Querying the Tracking Store   `SqlTrackingService` stores the tracking information within the tracking database throughout a number of different tables. There are stored procedures designed to access this data, but there is also a querying object model that was designed to help sift through the data stored within the database. The `SqlTrackingQuery` can be used to return a specific workflow instance by using the `TryGetWorkflow()` method, which will return a `SqlTrackingWorkflowInstance`, an object that mimics the `WorkflowInstance` with methods added to query against the different types of tracking data available.

For finer-grained control over the query, `SqlTrackingQuery` also has the `GetWorkflows()` method, which has an optional parameter of type `SqlTrackingQueryOptions` that allows the specification of types of workflow, status of workflows, and maximum and minimum time for the workflow to have been in that status. Additionally, a collection of `TrackingDataItemValue` objects can be specified to return only those records that specifically match the criteria that one is looking for. For advanced querying, such as querying on a range of these extracted values, a query will need to be written against the stored procedures and views included with the tracking database. The views `vw_TrackingDataItem` and `vw_ActivityExecutionStatusEvent` are good starting points to begin designing such a query.

Scheduler Services

The scheduler service is responsible for providing threads to the runtime in order to actually perform the execution of workflows. As noted in the discussion of the Parallel activity, a single instance of a workflow executes on only one thread. The engine itself can schedule multiple threads to be executing different workflow instances at the same time. It is quite probable that the number of executing workflow instances will be greater than the number of threads available to the application. Therefore, the runtime has to marshal threads to workflow instances in some fashion, and the way that is implemented is via the scheduler service.

DefaultWorkflowSchedulerService is, as its name implies, the default behavior of the runtime. It uses the .NET thread pool to provide threads for the executing workflows. It has one configuration setting of note, MaxSimultaneousWorkflows, which specifies how many threads will be used to execute workflow instances at the same time. By default, MaxSimultaneousWorkflows is set to a multiple of the number of processors on the machine. One is free to change this setting, but there are some words of caution. The scheduler service itself uses a single thread, so setting MaxSimultaneousWorkflows = Max Threads would be very bad, possibly resulting in a deadlock as the scheduler service is starved out of ever getting a thread. Additionally, the thread pool used by the default scheduler is the system thread pool, so there are plenty of other things that could take those threads. Operations such as transactions involving the Distributed Transaction Coordinator (DTC) might involve additional threads, so setting MaxSimultaneousWorkflows close to the maximum number of threads is generally not recommended. As with any performance tuning, it is best to experiment with this setting at a stage of development where the process is well defined, and the experiment can be repeated in order to truly understand the impact of turning this control knob.

There are also times in which multithreading is not desirable. Consider a workflow used by an ASP.NET page. Spawning additional threads within IIS takes away from the number of threads IIS has to serve additional incoming requests. The solution to this seems obvious enough: The ASP.NET page is not going to complete executing until the workflow does some work and then reaches an idle state or completes, so why not use that thread? This is precisely the scenario ManualWorkflowSchedulerService was created for.

ManualWorkflowSchedulerService provides a thread for the workflow to execute on by donating the currently executing thread to the workflow. Put another way, ManualWorkflowSchedulerService says, "Hey, I'm waiting here until the workflow is done, so why don't you use this thread I'd just be hogging anyway?" Therefore, control on the host is blocked until the workflow yields that thread, namely by completing or by going idle. Because the workflow will use the current thread, just calling WorkflowInstance.Start() is not enough to execute the workflow; doing so simply places the workflow in the running state where it awaits a thread in order to begin executing.

To hand the thread to the workflow, call ManualWorkflowSchedulerService.RunWorkflow(). This assigns the current thread of execution to the workflow to handle the next item on the queue, namely, the execution of the workflow. When the workflow completes, terminates, or goes idle, the call to RunWorkflow() will complete and return control to the host. Similarly, after sending a message to an idled workflow in this environment, the message will not be processed until RunWorkflow() is called again. This is similar to kicking a can down the street. It will roll and do some work, but it will reach a point at which it stops and waits to be kicked again in order to continue down the street. In Listing 5.17, note that the workflow will not process the event raised by the local service until RunWorkflow() has been called. RunWorkflow() will give the current thread to the runtime in order to execute a specific instance of the workflow until that instance completes or goes idle.

LISTING 5.17   Using the Manual Scheduler Service

```
public bool OrderProcess(Order order)
{
    ManualWorkflowSchedulerService schedulerService =
    workflowRuntime.GetService<ManualWorkflowSchedulerService>();
    orderLocalService.RaiseProcessing(order.WorkflowID);
    schedulerService.RunWorkflow(order.WorkflowID);
    // RunWorkflow completes when the workflow completes or goes idle
    return true;
}
```

Other Built-in Services

The persistence, tracking, and scheduler services are the most common services a work-flow developer will encounter. Writing a scheduler service is not a common task, but the choice between the default and manual services is one that will be frequently encountered. The persistence and tracking services have been optimized for the general scenario, and it is not uncommon to find developers writing a custom version of one or both of these services. In the case of the tracking service, the services can be "stacked" on top of one another, allowing multiple means of tracking. The persistence service is more funda-mental to the operation of the runtime, so only one of those is allowed. The runtime services do not stop there, however; a developer might encounter a number of other services, and in some scenarios, want to customize them.

Loader Service   The loader service is responsible for transforming an incoming XML stream into a workflow definition for execution. DefaultLoaderService operates on the assumption that the incoming XML stream is XAML. This service is invoked when one of the alternative WorkflowRuntime.CreateWorkflow() methods is called with an XmlReader passed in as the parameter (as opposed to the type passed in the default case). Creating a custom loader service is an effective way to map from an existing XML description of a process into the workflow definition. A workflow simply consists of a tree of activities, so by parsing the XML file according to its structure, one can quickly create such a tree of activities to return to the runtime for execution. For developers looking to leverage an existing process design tool with its own XML process representation, a custom loader service can be used to directly execute that unknown representation of activity arrange-ment.

Queue Services   WorkflowQueuingService is the one runtime service that cannot be over-ridden. It is responsible for managing the queues used by a workflow instance. The Windows Workflow Foundation runtime uses these internal queues as the basis for all communication with workflows and activities. The activities discussed in the "Communicating with Activities" section are abstractions built on top of this queuing mechanism. Fundamentally, those activities map to the creation of queues and the place-ment of messages onto those queues in order to deliver messages and continue execution. Within activity execution, it can access this service via the ActivityExecutionContext to create queues as well as to gain access to queues in order to retrieve or place messages onto the queues. An activity can also subscribe to the QueueItemAvailable event in order to process a message when it arrives on that queue.

SharedConnectionWorkflowCommitWorkBatchService   In addition to its status as one of the longest class names in the .NET Framework, SharedConnectionWorkflowCommitWorkBatchService handles the special case where the SQL tracking service and SQL persistence service are configured to use the same database. In this case, SharedConnectionWorkflowCommitWorkBatchService will perform both track-ing and persistence database queries using the same database connection, allowing a simple SQL transaction to be used to commit the update. This allows us to bypass the transaction escalation that would occur with the System.Transaction used in the default WorkflowCommitBatchService, thus avoiding the overhead of involving the Microsoft Distributed Transaction Coordinator to manage updates to two different databases within a single transaction.

This base class is used to combine a series of calls to be performed all at once throughout workflow execution. The most common example of this is a group of calls to TrackData() in the tracking service. These will be batched together to execute at the first workflow idle point. The runtime is responsible for initiating the commit, but it will pass WorkflowCommitBatchService a delegate to allow the service to add additional tasks, the batch, to be added into the transaction.

Listing 5.18 is an example of using SharedConnectionWorkflowCommitWorkBatchService inside of the configuration file to provide batching of persistence and tracking transac-tions to the same database. This will optimize the performance of the database writes in a scenario where tracking and persistence share the same database.

LISTING 5.18   Using the SharedConnectionWorkflowCommitWorkBatchService in Configuration

```xml
<?xml version="1.0" encoding="utf-8"?>
<configuration>
    <configSections>
        <section name="WorkflowServiceContainer"
➥type="System.Workflow.Runtime.Configuration.WorkflowRuntimeSection,
➥ System.Workflow.Runtime, Version=1.0.0.0, Culture=neutral,
➥ PublicKeyToken=31bf3856ad364e35" />
    </configSections>
    <WorkflowServiceContainer Name="Container Name" UnloadOnIdle="true">
```

LISTING 5.18   Continued

```
        <CommonParameters>
            <add name="ConnectionString" value="Initial Catalog
➥=WorkFlowStore;Data Source=localhost;Integrated Security=SSPI;" />
        </CommonParameters>
        <Services>
            <add type="System.Workflow.Runtime.Hosting.
➥DefaultWorkflowSchedulerService, System.Workflow.Runtime,
➥Version=1.0.0.0, Culture=neutral, PublicKeyToken=31bf3856ad364e35" />
            <addtype="System.Workflow.Runtime.Hosting.
➥SharedConnectionWorkflowTransactionService, System.Workflow.Runtime,
➥Version=1.0.0.0, Culture=neutral, PublicKeyToken=31bf3856ad364e35" />
            <add type="System.Workflow.Runtime.Tracking.SqlTrackingService,
➥ System.Workflow.Runtime, Version=1.0.0.0, Culture=neutral,
➥ PublicKeyToken=31bf3856ad364e35"/>
            <add type="System.Workflow.Runtime.Hosting.
➥SqlWorkflowPersistenceService, System.Workflow.Runtime, Version=
➥1.0.0.0, Culture=neutral, PublicKeyToken=31bf3856ad364e35"/>
        </Services>
    </WorkflowServiceContainer>
    <system.diagnostics>
    </system.diagnostics>
</configuration>
```

Custom Services

As a workflow developer, one is not limited to the runtime services provided; one can create additional services to add to the runtime. The scenarios for this include abstracting behavior out of the activity itself and providing access to a shared resource across multiple workflow instances. The WorkflowRuntime.AddService() method takes in an object—any object. This object acts as a service within the runtime, and is available to any executing activity by calling ActivityExecutionContext.GetService<T>(), where T is the type of object one looks to get back. The activity can then call any of the methods on that service. An example might provide some additional clarity.

Consider an activity that mimics the Policy activity, except that it needs to acquire the rule set from an external source. The implementation of how the rule set is provided is not relevant to the activity's execution. It can rely on a service in the runtime to provide the rule set prior to execution. This allows a workflow developer to simply use the activity within the workflow, and then select the appropriate runtime service to match the deployment scenario. In the case of a Windows Forms application, this might come from the file system; in a server environment, there might be a sophisticated cache-from-database pattern that the service follows. The point is that custom runtime services provide a nice layer of abstraction to insulate the execution of an activity from trivial implementation details, such as where to acquire the rule set from. By defining an abstract base service class, details of the implementation can be customized by providing different derived classes, as detailed in Listings 5.19 and 5.20. The base class can simply be an object, or it can inherit from WorkflowRuntimeService. By inheriting from WorkflowRuntimeService, one can take advantage of the Start and Stop methods to perform initialization or tear down work when the runtime itself is started or stopped.

LISTING 5.19   Base RuleSetProviderService

```
using System;
using System.Collections.Generic;
using System.Text;
using System.Workflow.Runtime;
using System.Workflow.Runtime.Hosting;
using System.Workflow.Activities.Rules;

namespace CustomService
{
        public abstract class  RuleSetProviderService :WorkflowRuntimeService
        {
        protected override void Start()
        {
            //implement startup logic here
        }

        protected override void Stop()
        {
            //implement shutdown logic here
        }

        public abstract RuleSet GetRuleSet(string rulesetName);
        }
}
```

LISTING 5.20   Implementation of RuleSetProvider

```
public class SqlRuleSetProviderService : RuleSetProviderService
{
    public override RuleSet GetRuleSet(string rulesetName)
    {
        // get the RuleSet from Sql and return
        return new RuleSet();
    }
}
```

By adding this to the runtime, either in code or in configuration, our activity (see Listing 5.21) can now access this service.

LISTING 5.21   DynamicRuleSetActivity

```
protected override ActivityExecutionStatus Execute(
                ActivityExecutionContext executionContext)
{
    RuleSetProviderService rspService = executionContext.
        GetService<RuleSetProviderService>();
    RuleSet ruleset = rspService.GetRuleSet(ruleSetName);
    // remainder of execution logic
    return ActivityExecutionStatus.Closed;
}
```

The activity requests a service that is of the type RuleSetProviderService, the abstract type. This allows the developer to substitute various implementations of the service at deployment time.

Rules Engine

Three things are important when one defines application logic. The first is simple; it is the ability to define the logic in code. The second is the runtime environment to execute. With these two alone, one can implement application logic, but does so by hard-coding aspects of the logic that are likely to change the rules. In addition to providing the object model to construct workflows and the runtime environment in which to execute them, Windows Workflow Foundation contains a rules engine. This allows for the separation of rules from process. Consider the expense-reporting scenario. One defines the process of order processing, which might look something like the example in Figure 5.30.

This process might change infrequently in terms of its structure of deciding the approval route, the approval by a manager, and the ultimate notification and disbursement of goods. This process might change only if an optimization is discovered or a compliance standard forces a different approval path. One thing would change with greater frequency: the condition that determines the approval path. Initially, this limit might be set to something purely currency based; for example, if the total is greater than $75. As business changes and expenses garner extra scrutiny, a simple total amount might not be enough. Suppose that the analysis of which approval process should be used now depends on a much more complicated condition such as the following:

```
If ((Customer.Category == Silver or Gold) AND
Expense.Submitter.LeadingAverageSimilarExpenses > $75) THEN ...
```

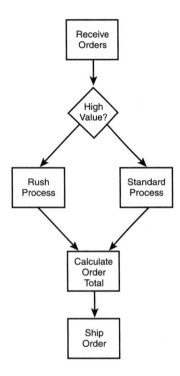

FIGURE 5.30   A Visio order-processing example.

It is important to note here that the process has not changed. What has changed is the condition used by the process. The process remains ignorant of the mechanics of the condition; it simply asks that a condition be evaluated. The separation of rules from process is important in enabling agility in a process, and is a natural extension of the declarative programming model embraced by Windows Workflow Foundation.

In addition to the execution being flexible, the rules designer is re-hostable inside a Windows Forms application, allowing a rule set to be edited outside of Visual Studio. Scenarios in which this would be useful include allowing power users or business analysts to design the rules to be executed inside of a process or allowing rule configuration inside of a management tool, where a full installation of Visual Studio is not desirable. It is also possible to create completely custom rule-authoring environments that construct the rule set.

TIP

There is a sample application that allows the customization of the rule set by assigning risk scoring to an Excel spreadsheet. The rule set is then executed against the balance sheet information entered in the first sheet. This sample is available at http://wf.netfx3.com/files/folders/rules_samples/entry313.aspx.

Rules as Conditions

The first place one will likely encounter the Windows Workflow Foundation rules engine is in the condition property of an activity, such as the IfElse activity. In the scenario described earlier, there is a branching activity, such as IfElse, that requires the output of a condition to determine the proper flow of execution. Other activities that use this type of property are the While activity and ConditionedActivityGroup. Custom activities can also leverage conditions to determine their execution path. An example of this would be an activity similar to the IfElse activity, but functioning as a switch statement and evaluating which of the branches should execute. (As an aside, this behavior can be achieved using the CAG activity.)

There are two types of rule conditions:

▶ Code condition

▶ Declarative rule condition

The type of condition determines how the rule condition is constructed and executed. In the case of the code condition, the condition is expressed in code file of the workflow. The condition is implemented as in Listing 5.22, with the return value of the condition set by the Result property of the ConditionalEventArgs parameter passed into the method.

LISTING 5.22   Code Condition

```
private void BigOrderCondition(object sender, ConditionalEventArgs e)
{
        if (Order.Amount > 100)
        {
            e.Result = true;
        }
        else
        {
            e.Result = false;
        }
}
```

A code condition gives one flexibility in implementation of the condition: Anything that can be expressed in .NET code can be used to evaluate the condition. The downside is the tight coupling of the condition code to the workflow itself. This makes the previously mentioned separation of rules from process near impossible. The solution is to externalize the rules into a rules file, an XML serialization of the rules, and load that file along with the workflow. The activity contains a reference to which condition it needs to evaluate, but then relies on the condition to be provided from this rules store.

A declarative rule condition is used in the following way:

1. Add an activity requiring a condition, and view its properties.

2. Select Declarative Rule Condition as the condition type. Doing so will cause the grid to expand with additional options.

3. Click the ellipsis icon next to the Condition Name property. This will bring up the condition selector, which lists all the previously created declarative rule conditions in this workflow.

4. Click the New button to create a new condition. Doing so will display the Rules Editor window.

5. Begin typing the condition, and see the IntelliSense-like drop-downs that appear to guide one through selecting the terms to evaluate.

The code being typed in might look like C#, but it is actually translated into an XML representation of the rule and is stored in the .rules file associated with the current workflow. Looking inside the .rules file in Listing 5.23, one can see the same structure of the condition defined, albeit slightly more verbosely than anticipated.

LISTING 5.23   .rules XML

```
<RuleExpressionCondition Name="Condition1">
  <RuleExpressionCondition.Expression>
    <ns0:CodeBinaryOperatorExpression Operator="GreaterThan"
      xmlns:ns0="clr-namespace:System.CodeDom;Assembly=System,
        Version=2.0.0.0, Culture=neutral, PublicKeyToken=b77a5c561934e089">
      <ns0:CodeBinaryOperatorExpression.Left>
        <ns0:CodeFieldReferenceExpression FieldName="Amount">
          <ns0:CodeFieldReferenceExpression.TargetObject="">
            <ns0:CodeFieldReference Expression="" FieldName="order">
              <ns0:CodeFieldReferenceExpression.TargetObject="">
                <ns0:CodeThisReferenceExpression="" />
              </ns0:CodeFieldReferenceExpression.TargetObject>
            </ns0:CodeFieldReference Expression>
          </ns0:CodeFieldReferenceExpression.TargetObject>
        </ns0:CodeFieldReferenceExpression>
      </ns0:CodeBinaryOperatorExpression.Left>
      <ns0:CodeBinaryOperatorExpression.Right>
        <ns0:CodePrimitiveExpression>
          <ns0:CodePrimitiveExpression.Value>
```

LISTING 5.23   Continued

```
              <ns1:Int32 xmlns:ns1="clr-namespace:System;Assembly=mscorlib,
                 Version=2.0.0.0, Culture=neutral,
                 PublicKeyToken=b77a5c561934e089">
                    50
              </ns1:Int32>
           </ns0:CodePrimitiveExpression.Value>
        </ns0:CodePrimitiveExpression>
      </ns0:CodeBinaryOperatorExpression.Right>
    </ns0:CodeBinaryOperatorExpression>
  </RuleExpressionCondition.Expression>
</RuleExpressionCondition>
```

When workflows are compiled into assemblies, the rules are compiled alongside the work-flow into the assembly. In the case where a declarative approach is being used, the `CreateWorkflow()` method contains overloads that take a second `XmlReader` parameter that points to the rules file. This allows the rules to be managed separately from the process itself. If that flexibility is desired in the compiled case, the rules can be deserial-ized from the rules file and a dynamic update can be used to insert the updated rules into the workflow instance as shown in Listing 5.24.

LISTING 5.24   Dynamic Update of `RuleDefintions`

```
WorkflowChanges workflowchanges = new
  WorkflowChanges(workflowInstance.GetWorkflowDefinition());
CompositeActivity transient = workflowchanges.TransientWorkflow;
RuleDefinitions newRuleDefinitions = // acquire new rules defintion here...
transient.SetValue(RuleDefinitions.RuleDefinitionsProperty,
  newRuleDefintions);
workflowInstance.ApplyWorkflowChanges(workflowchanges);
```

The SDK also contains a sample of using the dynamic update capability to target and update an individual rule.

The `ConditionedActivityGroup` **Activity**

The `CAG` is a composite activity that can be used to create highly dynamic execution patterns, as shown in Figure 5.31.

FIGURE 5.31   The ConditionedActivityGroup.

The CAG is designed by creating any number of child activities (which could include a sequence activity for multiple steps), and defining the rules that govern those activities' execution. The idea is best understood within the context of an example. Consider a grocery–order-processing scenario in which there are multiple activities that can be performed on an order, depending on the type of items it contains. The rules might be as follows:

▶ If an item is fragile, use the fragile-packing process.

▶ If an item is perishable, package it within dry ice.

▶ If an item is from the baby-food category, insert an upcoming event flyer.

The other logic is that all the items in the order must be looped through to properly evaluate this.

One might ask, "Can't I just do this in a normal sequential workflow?" The answer is usually, yes, it is possible, but how would that problem be solved in a sequential workflow?

The problem would be solved with a number of looping constructs to ensure reconsidering additional execution of individual branches. This quickly becomes a spaghetti workflow, with loops becoming the primary means of control flow, requiring a new developer to spend quite some time understanding how the application works, as well as creating a large cost (in terms of development and testing) to modify the process. Contrast that to the logic in Figure 5.32.

Here, the individual branches of execution have been defined and the decision to execute a branch is controlled by a set of rules, accessible from the CAG itself. This pattern allows for centralization of the rules (to outside the workflow) and the definition of discrete branches of functionality without focusing on how to nest the loops correctly to enable the execution behavior desired.

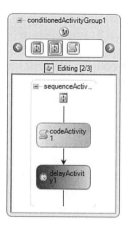

FIGURE 5.32   A `ConditionedActivityGroup` with three activity groupings.

An additional feature of the `CAG` is the model of repeated execution. If the value of `UntilCondition` is set to true, the `CAG` will not continue to execute any additional branches. If the `UntilCondition` is set to true, the `CAG` will take the step to cancel the currently executing activities in other branches, allowing the `CAG` to close and relinquish control to the next available activity.

Rules as Policy

In the previous sections, rules have been looked at as a simple `if <condition>` statement to serve as a gate around some other action. In the simple case of `IfElse`, the branch to execute is determined by the evaluation of the condition. A `While` activity depends on the condition to determine the number of times it needs to loop. There is another way to use rules, and that is in the execution of a rule policy.

In a rule policy, a `RuleSet` is built out of a collection of rules. A rule is defined as *both* a condition and an action to be performed. In the previous case, the first half of the rule is utilized, and the action is determined by the activity depending upon the condition. In a `RuleSet`, the action is defined as part of the individual rule. The `RuleSet` is then executed against an arbitrary object. It is against this object that the conditions are evaluated (is the order greater than $100?) and the actions are performed (set the discount to 22%). A `RuleSet` lets one group gather a collection of rules related to some processing task and evaluate all the rules together. The rules engine also supports prioritization of rules as well as a fine grained control over the chaining behavior of the rules.

Consider yet again the example of order processing. At some point in the execution of the process, the discount must be calculated. For most organizations the discount is not calculated simply by assigning a fixed number, it is usually a complex combination of conditions: How big is the order? How much has the customer ordered over the last year? Are the items being ordered in high demand? and so on. This list can begin to grow and become quite complicated, and it can quickly become difficult to continue to model these as an increasingly complicated series of `if/else` statements or `switch` statements in code.

As the number of rules increases beyond three or four, it becomes increasingly difficult to code all the various permutations and dependencies of those rules. As an example, insurance companies might have thousands of rules involved in their risk-scoring applications. The overhead to create, maintain, and debug such a rule set in code becomes unwieldy and defeats the flexibility that rules-based processing can provide. Within a workflow, `PolicyActivity` is used to provide these capabilities.

Forward Chaining

As rule sets become increasingly complicated, there will inevitably exist dependencies between rules. Rule 4 might base the discount on the expected profit from the order. Rule 10 might perform an analysis of the customer's delinquency rate and change the expected profit based on a new probability that the customer might not pay. Now that this expected profit has changed, what becomes of rule 4? It might be that the business requirement is that this rule should be evaluated again. This is referred to as the *forward-chaining behavior* of a rules engine. The rules engine is responsible for detecting such dependencies and selectively re-executing rules based on changes to the facts that the conditions depend on. Consider the rule set in Table 5.2.

TABLE 5.2   Sample Rule Set

Rule Number	Rule
1	If Order.Total > 1000 then Discount = 12%
2	If Order.Shipping > 0 then Discount = Discount + 3%
3	If Order.ShipToState = 'WA' then Shipping = 25

For inputs, `Order.Total = 1200`, `Shipping = 0`, and `ShipToState = 'WA'`.

The execution of this rule set is as shown in Table 5.3.

TABLE 5.3   Rule Set Execution

Step	Execution
1	Rule 1 evaluates to true; Discount set to 12%
2	Rule 2 evaluates to false
3	Rule 3 evaluates to true; Shipping set to 25
4	Rule 2 evaluates again (Shipping changed); Discount increased

As rule sets contain more rules, the evaluation pattern will become increasingly complicated. Consider modeling this execution behavior in code, especially the ability to re-evaluate rules when the facts it depends on change. This code would quickly spiral out of any state of maintainability and not easily allow new rules to be added. Something such as a pricing policy might be extremely flexible, and rule-based calculation enables that flexibility.

Forward chaining can be used to evaluate across a collection of objects as well. Consider an `Order` object with an array of `OrderItem` objects. Additionally, consider a counter variable, `i`, an integer initialized to `0`. Using the following rule set:

Rule Number	Rule
1	`If i < Order.Items.Length then ProcessItem(i), i=i+1`

With this single rule, the `ProcessItem()` method will be called for each item. The execution is easy to trace: evaluate initially, process the item for the counter, and then increase the counter. Increasing the counter changes the fact the rule depends on, forcing its re-evaluation. To make this more robust, a higher priority rule should be executed that initializes the counter to `0`.

External Policy Execution

The previous examples have focused on rules executing within the context of a workflow, with the object being operated on as the workflow class. But this is simply a matter of how the functionality is surfaced. A rule set can execute against any .NET object, any custom class that one creates may be the target of a rule set. The following steps are necessary to execute rules against an arbitrary object:

1. Deserialize the rule set into a `RuleSet` object.

2. Validate the rule set against the type (this ensures that if a rule mentions `object.foo`, the type contains `foo`).

3. Create a `RuleExecution` object that stores the state of execution.

4. Call `RuleSet.Execute`.

The code in Listing 5.25 does this.

LISTING 5.25   External Rule Execution

```
RuleExecution ruleExecution;
WorkflowMarkupSerializer serializer = new WorkflowMarkupSerializer();
XmlTextReader reader = new XmlTextReader(new StringReader(ruleSetXmlString));
RuleSet ruleSet = serializer.Deserialize(reader) as RuleSet;
//check that rules are valid
RuleValidation ruleValidation =
➥ new RuleValidation(executionObject.GetType(), null);
if (!ruleSet.Validate(ruleValidation))
{
    // handle errors
}
else
{
    ruleExecution = new RuleExecution(ruleValidation, executionObject);
}
ruleSet.Execute(ruleExecution);
```

This can be generalized to scenarios where processing occurs on many clients, but it is desirable to have a central rule store to ensure that all the clients are always using the same rule policies.

Summary

The chapter has provided an introduction to the major concepts of the Windows Workflow Foundation. The activity model, designer, and runtime are tools that can be used to create declarative processes for use inside of any .NET application. There is a substantial amount of extensibility built into Windows Workflow Foundation that enables it to be used in a wide variety of scenarios. Additionally, Windows Workflow Foundation includes a rules engine to allow declarative rules to be executed within a .NET application. Chapter 6, "Using the Windows Communication Foundation and the Windows Workflow Foundation Together," will look at how to integrate Windows Workflow Foundation with Windows Communication Foundation.

References

Shukla, Dharma and Bob Schmidt. 2006 *Essential Windows Workflow Foundation*. Addison-Wesley.

Using the Windows Communication Foundation and the Windows Workflow Foundation Together

Introduction

The Windows Communication Foundation and the Windows Workflow Foundation are naturally complementary to one another. The Windows Communication Foundation provides an elegant way to expose functionality as services, across an enormous number of different protocols and transports, while allowing the developer to focus on the message. Windows Workflow Foundation provides a way to rapidly compose application logic in a declarative fashion, allowing rapid expression of execution logic. Windows Workflow Foundation is a fantastic way to implement the services that the Windows Communication Foundation exposes. The compositional, activity-based model of development also provides a simple way to compose calls to Windows Communication Foundation services.

This chapter will focus on the basic problem of consuming Windows Communication Foundation services within Windows Workflow Foundation, as well as exposing processes implemented in Windows Workflow Foundation as Windows Communication Foundation services. There will also be a discussion of the built in activities designed to expose a workflow as an .asmx, WS-I Basic Profile 1.1 web service, and to consume those services as well.

Consuming Services

Readers of the previous chapter are aware of the fundamental building block of a workflow, the activity. Activities can perform any task that can be coded in their `Execute()` method, or, in the case of composite activities, execute other activities. As such, the delightfully simple answer to the question, "How do I consume the Windows Communication Foundation services discussed elsewhere in this book?" is, "Just as one would consume them from code, albeit wrapped inside of an activity."

The Simple Case

There exists an even easier way to consume web services from within a workflow, but it has the limitation that the web service must be one that implements the WS-I Basic Profile 1.1 or `.asmx` web services. If one consumes an `.asmx` web service, or more generally, a web service that implements WS-I Basic Profile 1.1, the InvokeWebService activity can be used.

Dropping the InvokeWebService activity onto the workflow design surface invokes the familiar Add Web Reference dialog within Visual Studio as shown in Figure 6.1. Inside this dialog, one points to an existing web service, acquires the Web Service Definition Language, and generates a simple proxy class to call the service. Properties that correspond to the input parameters as well as the output parameter are then added to the activity as shown in Figure 6.2. These properties are dependency properties and can be bound to other activity properties or workflow properties.

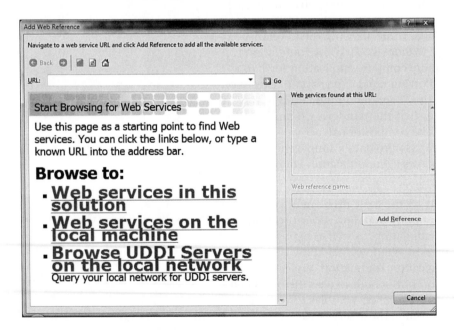

FIGURE 6.1   The Add Web Reference dialog.

FIGURE 6.2   The property grid for InvokeWebService after selecting a web service and method.

The InvokeWebService activity also exposes a URL property that allows the workflow developer to point the activity to the correct address.

This works with a Windows Communication Foundation service exposed as a WS-I Basic Profile 1.1 web service, as well as exposing the metadata exchange (MEX) endpoint.

The General Case

The majority of services will not implement the WS-I Basic Profile 1.1. Rather, as evidenced by the rest of this book, they will use many different transports, with different types of security, across the endless spectrum of bindings. Fortunately, the model that serves Windows Communication Foundation developers well works equally as well when consumed within a service. Consider the contract in Listing 6.1, which describes a system to return the pricing of stock options.

LISTING 6.1   Simple Interface for WF Consumption of WCF

```
[ServiceContract(Namespace="http://wcfunleashed/optionsInWFandWCF")]
public interface IOption
{
    OptionListing[] GetOptionChain(string symbolName);
}
```

Listing 6.2 shows the definition of OptionListing.

LISTING 6.2   OptionListing Definition

```csharp
[DataContract]
public class OptionListing
{
    string symbol;
    string optionSymbol;
    int expirationMonth;
    int expirationYear;
    double strikePrice;
    double optionPrice;
    int dailyVolume;

    [DataMember]
    public string Symbol
    {
        get { return symbol; }
        set { symbol = value; }
    }
    [DataMember]
    public string OptionSymbol
    {
        get { return optionSymbol; }
        set { optionSymbol = value; }
    }
    [DataMember]
    public int ExpirationMonth
    {
        get { return expirationMonth; }
        set { expirationMonth = value; }
    }
    [DataMember]
    public int ExpirationYear
    {
        get { return expirationYear; }
        set { expirationYear = value; }
    }
    [DataMember]
    public double StrikePrice
    {
        get { return strikePrice; }
        set { strikePrice = value; }
    }
    [DataMember]
    public double OptionPrice
    {
```

LISTING 6.2   Continued

```
        get { return optionPrice; }
        set { optionPrice = value; }
    }
    [DataMember]
    public int DailyVolume
    {
        get { return dailyVolume; }
        set { dailyVolume = value; }
    }
}
```

This contains all the information one would like to retrieve about a specific option contract (apologies for the overloaded term). Calling GetOptionChain() and passing in a stock symbol, such as MSFT, retrieves all the options currently available.

A simple proxy is generated as well, in this case by hand in Listing 6.3, but the svcutil.exe tool could be used.

LISTING 6.3   Simple IOption Proxy

```
public class OptionServiceProxy: ClientBase<IOption>, IOption
{
    public OptionServiceProxy(string config) : base(config)
    {
    }
    public OptionListing[] GetOptionChain(string symbolName)
    {
        return this.Channel.GetOptionChain(symbolName);
    }
}
```

All that is left to do is to encapsulate this proxy call inside the Execute() method of an activity. Dependency properties are created to allow the parameters and results to be bound to other values in the workflow as seen in Listing 6.4.

LISTING 6.4   GetOptionChainActivity

```
public class GetOptionChainActivity: Activity
{
  public GetOptionChainActivity()
  {
    this.Name="GetOptionChainActivity";
  }

  public static DependencyProperty SymbolNameProperty =
```

LISTING 6.4   Continued

```
  System.Workflow.ComponentModel.DependencyProperty.Register(
    "SymbolName",
    typeof(string),
    typeof(GetOptionChainActivity));


[Description("SymbolName")]
[Category("Input")]
[Browsable(true)]
[DesignerSerializationVisibility(
  DesignerSerializationVisibility.Visible)]
public string SymbolName
{
  get
  {
    return ((string)(base.GetValue(
      GetOptionChainActivity.SymbolNameProperty)));
  }

  set
  {
    base.SetValue(
      GetOptionChainActivity.SymbolNameProperty,
      value);
  }
}

public static DependencyProperty OptionListingsProperty =
  System.Workflow.ComponentModel.DependencyProperty.Register(
    "OptionListings",
    typeof(OptionsService.OptionListing[]),
    typeof(GetOptionChainActivity));

[Description("Option Listings")]
[Category("Output")]
[Browsable(true)]
[DesignerSerializationVisibility(
  DesignerSerializationVisibility.Visible)]
public OptionsService.OptionListing[] OptionListings
{
  get
  {
    return((OptionsService.OptionListing[])(
      base.GetValue(
```

LISTING 6.4   Continued

```
          GetOptionChainActivity.OptionListingsProperty)));
  }

  set
  {
    base.SetValue(
      GetOptionChainActivity.OptionListingsProperty,
      value);
  }
}

protected override ActivityExecutionStatusExecute(
  ActivityExecutionContext executionContext)
{
  using (OptionsService.OptionServiceProxy prox =
    new OptionsService.OptionServiceProxy("OptionsConfig"))
  {
    OptionListings = prox.GetOptionChain(SymbolName);
  }
  return ActivityExecutionStatus.Closed;
}
}
```

The Execute() method wraps the call to the proxy (and ensures its proper disposal) and then returns a status of closed.

Activities can be quickly built to encapsulate and leverage Windows Communication Foundation services. The activity model gives the activity developer the ability to wrap a more advanced user interface around the configuration of the service parameters, as well as to provide validation of the activity, potentially allowing a "client-side" validation of the parameters during design time. The application will provide the configuration settings for the proxy as needed.

Orchestrating Services

The ability to invoke a single remote service is interesting, but it does not provide much of an advantage beyond simply using the proxy in code. The power of the declarative model begins to surface as one uses the workflow to orchestrate the calls to a number of different services. Imagine that every service one wants to consume is wrapped into an activity. It now becomes easy to create a composition of those services:

▶ Arrange execution of the service calls in a parallel fashion, proceeding only after all service calls have been made

▶ Logically determine which service to call using rules

▶ Aggregate the results of a number of calls to similar services

▶ Chain together a number of related service calls and potentially couple that with user interaction in the process

In a case where services are one-way (that is, a message is sent but no reply is required), a case for workload distribution is possible where the workflow is the coordinator of tasks performed by a farm of other services. There have been some interesting applications in high-performance computing of this approach. The workflow in this case is responsible for assigning tasks in discrete chunks of work to processing machines. By using a one-way messaging pattern, the workflow can assign the entire work up-front, throttle based on detected load of machines in the environment, handle task timeouts and work reassignment, as well as aggregate the results. This is an interesting application of Windows Workflow Foundation that will be investigated further in the future. The references section at the end of this chapter lists an article by Paventhan, Takeda, Cox, and Nicole on the topic of Windows Workflow Foundation and high-performance computing.

The reader is encouraged to see Hohpe, Woolf for a more thorough discussion of patterns that relate to service composition in enterprise integration patterns, especially the message-routing patterns.

Exposing Workflows as Services

If workflows are used to compose services, it becomes quite useful to in turn expose those workflows as services for others to consume or to compose. Just as a simple set of activities can be composed into more powerful activities, so too can services. The experience around exposing a workflow as a service involves more work than consuming an already-existing service. What follows are some guidelines to make that a little easier.

Ultimately, the pattern of hosting a workflow as a service is really no different than hosting the workflow as a process within another application. In this case, the host is responsible not just for creating workflows, routing messages to the workflow, and monitoring their execution status, but also for handling the exposure as a service. In this way, the host application and its service implementation become a thin façade, receiving messages from the service calls and in turn routing them to the workflow.

The HandleExternalEvent activity ends up sitting directly behind each of the service calls specified by the interface. When the host receives a message for that service call, it sends a message to the (hopefully) awaiting HandleExternalEvent activity in the form of the expected event type. This pattern gives an additional layer of abstraction where the host layer can perform some additional tasks, such as looking up the workflow identifier based on some of the contents of the inbound message.

Publishing as a Web Service

As in the case of service consumption, there is support in the out of the box activity set to expose a workflow as an .asmx-based web service. The only requirement to do this is a contract describing the methods exposed by the service. The WebServiceInput and

WebServiceOutput activities can then be used to receive the input, process the message in the form of a workflow, and return the output.

The following steps will expose a workflow as a web service:

1. Craft an interface defining the methods to be called.

2. Create a new Sequential Workflow Library project type.

3. Make sure that the new project can reference the interface created.

4. Drag a WebServiceInput activity to the workflow and set the IsActivating property to true.

5. Specify the InterfaceType (as seen in Figure 6.3) and MethodName; notice that the property grid now displays the inputs to the web service (Figure 6.4).

6. Create the remainder of the workflow, which is able to reference the input parameters through binding.

7. Place a WebServiceOutput activity in the process and set the InputActivityName to the corresponding WebServiceInput activity.

8. Notice the (ReturnValue) property (in Figure 6.5). This value has to be set in the workflow.

9. Right-click on the workflow project file in the Solution Explorer and select Publish as Web Service (in Figure 6.6).

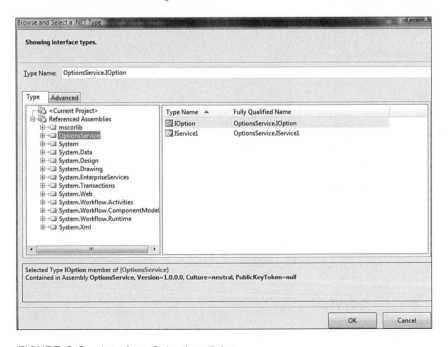

FIGURE 6.3   Interface Selection dialog.

FIGURE 6.4   The property grid of WebServiceInput.

FIGURE 6.5   The property grid of WebServiceOutput.

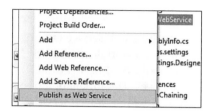

FIGURE 6.6   Context menu to publish as web service.

Selecting Publish as Web Service will not result in one being asked any questions. It will insert an ASP.NET Web Service project into the solution with a web.config file and an .asmx file. The .asmx file is very simple and points to a class defined in an included assembly. This does not provide any room for customization, including specifying a namespace that is not tempuri.org. This occurs because the file generated to create the assembly is deleted as part of the Publish as Web Service process. At the time of writing, there is discussion of publishing a tool that would allow customization of the .cs file that generates the assembly easier. By configuring a persistence service, the workflow will be able to persist to the persistence store and be picked up whenever the next call gets made. In a load-balanced setting in which multiple application servers expose the same work-flow as a web service, this negates the need for providing "sticky sessions," where there is an enforced affinity to a given server.

The WebServiceInput and WebServiceOutput activities can be used in more complex scenarios than the one described earlier. By chaining a series of these activities, the inter-actions with the various steps in a process can be modeled and exposed as a web service. In an ordering process, there could be a variety of steps that have to occur:

▶ Place order

▶ Confirm items in stock

▶ Ship the order

At each stage of the process, the workflow relies on various third-party systems notifying the workflow that each step has been completed. This process can be modeled with a series of web service inputs and outputs. In this way, not only can the details of a service be specified on a method level, the modeling specifies the valid order in which the methods may be called. This can give a system the capability to focus on modeling the process and enforce the desired method call semantics external to the process.

The problem becomes slightly more difficult because something is needed to route subse-quent messages back to the proper workflow instance. In the case of the WebServiceInput and WebServiceOutput activities, provided the client supports cookies to maintain some session information inside the caller's knowledge, subsequent calls to the web service can use the cookie that contains the workflow instance identifier and other information needed to successfully route the message back into the executing workflow. This cookie can be saved and used by other clients to send later messages to the workflow instance.

Hosting Inside a WCF Service

The approach just described is a useful approach to quickly generate a web service environment to host the workflow runtime and expose the functionality of a workflow as a web
service. But for a number of reasons very dear to readers of this book, WS-I Basic Profile 1.1
or .asmx web services do not provide the right way to expose services. The model described
earlier is a very nice, contract-first way to model a process and expose it as a web service,
but there is no way to specify the use of a TCP, socket-based transport with message-level
encryption. The ideal model would be to keep the same, contract-first approach just
described, but to decouple it by not exposing the workflow via an .asmx web service.

To do this, the pattern described in the introduction to this section must be used. This
approach calls for a very thin hosting layer acting as a façade to route messages received
by a service call to the waiting workflow. There are two primary issues: how messages are
routed into the workflow and where the runtime is hosted.

Message Routing

Putting aside the discussion of where to host the runtime, the issue of how to route
incoming messages to the workflow is the area where the most consideration needs to be
paid in terms of workflow design.

The simple case is the first call, which needs to initialize the workflow and commence its
execution. Here the workflow host receives a message, extracts the relevant parameters,
gets the runtime, and initiates the workflow. There are two patterns for making sure that
the caller will know the workflow instance identifier created. The first approach is to
return the workflow instance identifier to the caller after calling `CreateWorkflow()`. In a
situation using one-way messaging, the caller can submit a `Guid` as one of the service
parameters and use the overload of `CreateWorkflow()`, where the last parameter sets the
`WorkflowInstanceId` rather than allowing it to be set by the workflow runtime. Care must
be given that a workflow instance cannot be created with the same identifier. In this case,
it is not the best idea to use the `order` identifier because of the potential that the workflow might get started again for the same order, causing a conflict. The code sample in
Listing 6.5 shows how to use the overload to pass in the workflow identifier.

LISTING 6.5   Initiating a Workflow

```
public void PlaceOrder(Order order)
{
    if (Guid.Empty.Equals(order.WorkflowID))
    {
        order.WorkflowID = Guid.NewGuid();
    }
    Dictionary<string, object> paramDict = new Dictionary<string, object>();
    paramDict.Add("IncomingOrder", order);
    WorkflowInstance instance = workflowRuntime.CreateWorkflow
➥(typeof(ProcessOrder), paramDict, order.WorkflowID);
    instance.Start();
}
```

Subsequent method calls will need to contain enough information to route the message to the workflow. One way to accomplish this is to include the workflow instance identifier as a parameter on the method. This allows the event to be created directly from the submitted workflow instance identifier. This does add additional information to the messages that need to be sent, and in some cases, one may not have control over the structure of the message. Additional work may also have to be completed prior to raising the message to the workflow. A common scenario is one in which properties of the message arriving on the service are used to query a database to determine the workflow instance identifier. This commonly occurs because the system sending the message to the service has no idea that a workflow is executing behind this service, and has no reason to be aware of a workflow identifier. The order delivery system might simply drop a message onto a Microsoft Message Queuing (MSMQ) queue that contains the order number and the delivery time. It is the responsibility of the service to translate this into an event that the workflow runtime can use by correlating the facts of the message with the workflow instance identifier.

One design decision is the nature of the methods themselves. Does the method need to send a message to the workflow and wait for some signal from the workflow before returning a response to the client? Does the method need to simply raise the event and return a void or limited response to the client? The decision made here will influence the design of how a message is routed into the workflow.

The case in which the method needs to raise the event and return to the client without a response from the workflow is the easier of these two scenarios to code. In this case, the method implementation obtains the workflow runtime and raises the event. This is not very different from the pattern seen in the HandleExternalEvent discussion in the last chapter. To refresh, the HandleExternalEvent activity is configured to wait for an event handler (defined in the interface) to receive an event. It is the responsibility of the host to create this event and raise it into the workflow. In Listing 6.6, there is a reference to the local service added to the ExternalDataExchangeService that is used to raise events into the workflow itself. This is used inside the method to easily raise the message to the workflow.

LISTING 6.6   Raising an Event and Returning

```
public void OrderDelivered(Order order)
{
    orderLocalService.RaiseDelivered(order.WorkflowID, order.DeliveryTime);
}
```

This is the easiest approach, but there are scenarios in which one wants to wait for the workflow to output some response to the submitted event, such as a partial result based on the processing or the result of a query that occurs at that stage of the workflow. If the result has to wait for the workflow to be idle, that is, waiting for the next event, the ManualWorkflowSchedulerService provides a clean way to implement this. As discussed in the previous chapter, the ManualWorkflowSchedulerService executes the workflow on the

thread of the caller as opposed to on a new thread. Therefore, the call to the workflow
will block as the workflow executes. On reaching an idle point, control will be yielded
back to the caller; in this case, the service. At this point, any additional work can be done,
including querying the tracking store for information specific to the workflow to return.

LISTING 6.7   Using ManualWorkflowSchedulerService to Wait to Return a Value

```
public bool OrderProcess(Order order)
{
    ManualWorkflowSchedulerService schedulerService =
    workflowRuntime.GetService<ManualWorkflowSchedulerService>();
    orderLocalService.RaiseProcessing(order.WorkflowID);
    schedulerService.RunWorkflow(order.WorkflowID);
    // RunWorkflow completes when the workflow completes or goes idle
    return true;
}
```

In the preceding code, the `RaiseProcessing()` method simply raises a processing event
into the workflow runtime for the workflow instance to pick up. Note that while using
the ManualWorkflowSchedulerService, raising an event into the workflow will not cause it
to execute. Because it relies on being given a thread to execute on, it will not process the
event until the `RunWorkflow()` method is called.

A special case of this pattern would be when the workflow is expected to run until
completion. In the WorkflowCompleted event, one of the properties of the event arguments passed are output parameters of the workflow. It might be desirable to access these
parameters and return them as part of the last service call. The WorkflowCompleted event
handler will be executed as the last part of the `RunWorkflow()` method if the workflow
does in fact complete. This could be used to place the output parameters into member
variables that the service method could then access to perform meaningful work, such as
returning the completed order information or the detailed history of a document
approval process.

If one is not using the ManualWorkflowSchedulerService, in order to get the behavior
described earlier, the service method would need to wait to return. The workflow, which
is executing on a separate thread, will do its work and send some signal back to the
service method that it is safe to continue, either through an event like WorkflowIdled or
by using the CallExternalMethod activity. This approach, although more complicated and
involves coordinating multiple threads, affords a greater flexibility within the service
method. Using the ManualWorkflowSchedulerService puts the service at the mercy of the
workflow. If the implementation changes and suddenly a long-running activity is placed
in the workflow, there is no recourse, no way to send a response to the service method,
except to wait for the workflow to go idle. In the case where the service method is waiting
to be signaled to continue, there are other behaviors that could be programmed, such as a
timeout after some number of seconds, at which point a "Work Pending" message could
be sent back as the response. Because the workflow instance is executing on a separate

thread, there is no harm in returning a response and freeing up the thread the service method was executing on.

Runtime Hosting Options

Prior to this section, it has been assumed that a reference to the WorkflowRuntime itself will be available as these service methods execute. Furthermore, the *same* WorkflowRuntime needs to be made available; otherwise multiple runtimes are being used inside the same application domain, consuming resources and introducing additional, unneeded overhead. Even if overhead was a complete non-issue, additional management would be needed to prevent error conditions where two different runtimes were trying to send messages to the same workflow. In the case of a single runtime, the messages will be delivered in the order they are received by the runtime. In the case of multiple runtimes, the second message could be delivered only if the workflow had processed the first message, gone idle waiting for the second, and persisted to the persistence store. Otherwise, the second runtime will try to deliver the event and discover that the first runtime still has the workflow instance locked.

The singleton pattern is the simplest and best way to solve the problem of ensuring that there is only one runtime handling requests per instance of a service. The conversation quickly becomes one of the instancing behavior of the ServiceModel. There is a very simple model for enforcing singleton behavior on the service itself by applying the ServiceBehavior attribute to the service:

LISTING 6.8   Specifying a Singleton Service

```
[ServiceBehavior(InstanceContextMode = InstanceContextMode.Single,
➥ ConcurrencyMode = ConcurrencyMode.Multiple)]
```

The WorkflowRuntime can then be added as a private member of the class, and can be accessed knowing the same instance will always be accessed. That said, ConcurrencyMode.Multiple allows multiple threads to call the service object at the same time, so thread safety and concurrency are left to the developer. In the scenario discussed here, most operations with the workflow runtime are communications based, the underlying representations of which are internal queues to deliver the messages. Internally, the operations accessing those queues are thread-safe, minimizing the need for the developer to focus on concurrency issues involving the shared workflow runtime. If additional granularity is required to ensure thread safety—for instance to ensure that two events raised without any potential interruption by another thread—then typical concurrency constructs can be used to marshal access to the runtime. Listing 6.9 is an example of an entire service implementation.

LISTING 6.9   Singleton Service with Shared Workflow Runtime

```
[ServiceBehavior(
  InstanceContextMode = InstanceContextMode.Single,
  ConcurrencyMode = ConcurrencyMode.Multiple)]
public class OrderService : IOrderService
```

LISTING 6.9   Continued

```
{
  private WorkflowRuntime workflowRuntime;
  private OrderLocalService orderLocalService
    = new OrderLocalService();
  public OrderService()
  {
    if (null == workflowRuntime)
    {
      workflowRuntime = new WorkflowRuntime();
      ExternalDataExchangeService dataService =
        new ExternalDataExchangeService();
      workflowRuntime.AddService(dataService);
      dataService.AddService(orderLocalService);
      dataService.AddService(cdnws);
      workflowRuntime.WorkflowCompleted +=
        new EventHandler<WorkflowCompletedEventArgs>(
          workflowRuntime_WorkflowCompleted);
      workflowRuntime.WorkflowTerminated +=
        new EventHandler<WorkflowTerminatedEventArgs>(
          workflowRuntime_WorkflowTerminated);
      workflowRuntime.WorkflowAborted +=
        new EventHandler<WorkflowEventArgs>(
        workflowRuntime_WorkflowAborted);
    }
  }

  void workflowRuntime_WorkflowAborted(
    object sender,
    WorkflowEventArgs e)
  {
    throw //handle aborted event
  }

  void workflowRuntime_WorkflowTerminated(
    object sender,
    WorkflowTerminatedEventArgs e)
  {
    //handle terminated event
  }

  void workflowRuntime_WorkflowCompleted(
    object sender,
    WorkflowCompletedEventArgs e)
  {
```

LISTING 6.9   Continued

```
    Console.WriteLine(
      "Workflow {0} of type {1} has completed",
      e.WorkflowInstance.InstanceId,
      e.WorkflowDefinition.QualifiedName);
  }


  public void PlaceOrder(Order order)
  {
    if (Guid.Empty.Equals(order.WorkflowID))
    {
      order.WorkflowID = Guid.NewGuid();
    }
    Dictionary<string, object> paramDict =
      new Dictionary<string, object>();
    paramDict.Add("IncomingOrder", order);
    WorkflowInstance instance =
      workflowRuntime.CreateWorkflow(
        typeof(ProcessOrder),
        paramDict,
        order.WorkflowID);
    instance.Start();
  }

  public void OrderDelivered(Order order)
  {
    dnwls.RaiseDelivered(order.WorkflowID, "Order Delivered");
  }
}
```

In cases in which the service itself cannot be declared as a singleton, other methods are required to encapsulate the workflow runtime as a singleton for the Windows Communication Foundation service methods to access.

The previous paragraphs focused on how one can access the WorkflowRuntime to create and interact with workflows. The larger question of where to host the Windows Communication Foundation service itself is outside the scope of this chapter. However, the use of workflow as the implementation of the logic of the service does not restrict where the service can be hosted.

Looking Ahead

This chapter discussed ways to incorporate the synergy between Windows Communication Foundation and Windows Workflow Foundation. At the time of this writing, the Windows Communication Foundation and Windows Workflow Foundation teams have joined together. This team is responsible for developing the future versions of this technology, and one of the highest priority items for the next release is the integration of the two technologies. Many of the techniques discussed in this chapter will be abstracted into activities and into the runtime to further enhance the productivity of service and workflow developers.

This is not to discourage developers from using the two technologies together today. The patterns shown in this chapter can be used today to both consume services from workflow, as well as to host workflows as services. Indeed, this is the focus of many of the customer engagements the authors have been involved in to date.

The next release of Visual Studio, codenamed "Orcas," will contain enhancements to Windows Workflow Foundation and Windows Communication to allow developers to more easily create workflow-enabled services. These are Windows Communication Foundation services that have an underlying implementation written using Windows Workflow Foundation. This allows developers to take advantage of the infrastructure present in Windows Workflow Foundation, such as persistence, tracking, and a declarative process model, while maintaining the flexibility in service endpoints and other advantages Windows Communication Foundation offers.

The "plumbing" to create workflow-enabled service consists of the same elements discussed earlier in this chapter—a set of activities to send and receive messages, and an environment to host these workflows and take care of issues such as instancing and message routing. The remainder of this chapter will focus on what is currently planned for inclusion in the Visual Studio "Orcas" release. The screenshots and code samples are based on the March community technology preview (CTP) and are subject to change before the final version is released.

The two activities related to creating workflow-enabled services are the Send and Receive activities. The Send activity is used to consume another service, and the Receive activity is used to either instantiate a workflow when a message arrives, or to wait at some point in the workflow for a message to arrive. To be more precise, the Send activity sends a request message and then receives a response message (in the case of a one-way contract, it will simply send the request), and the Receive activity receives a request and then sends a response back to the caller. Both activities require the developer to select the contract and the operation being consumed or implemented. Based on the details of the contract being implemented, dependency properties will be added that correspond to the parameters and the return value (if applicable).

The Send activity requires two pieces of information: the operation to which it will send a message, and the name of the endpoint configuration that should be used. After dropping the Send activity onto the design surface, as seen in Figure 6.7, it can be double-clicked to bring up a dialog to select the operation, as in Figure 6.8.

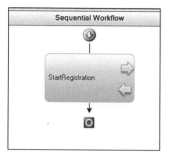

FIGURE 6.7   A sequential workflow containing the Send activity.

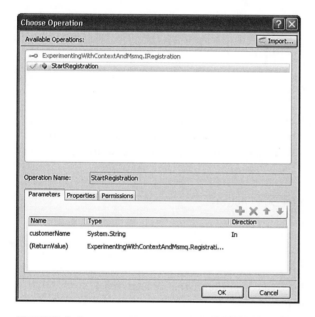

FIGURE 6.8   Dialog to select the contract and operation.

After the operation is selected, dependency properties are added and can be bound to values elsewhere in the workflow, or a property can be promoted. The final configuration for the Send activity is to select the endpoint used. This will need to be an endpoint named in the configuration file or set programmatically. The completed properties pane is seen in Figure 6.9. The ReturnValue parameter is a strongly typed dependency property that corresponds to the type and value returned by the service.

FIGURE 6.9　Send activity completed property pane.

The workflow will be created in the typical fashion; by creating a workflow runtime and then calling CreateWorkflow passing in the type of the workflow to create. The application configuration file can then be used to store the endpoint details. A sample configuration file for this is in Listing 6.10.

LISTING 6.10　Configuration Information for Send Activity

```
<configuration>
  <system.serviceModel>
    <client>
      <endpoint
          address="http://localhost:8998/Register/RegistrationService"
          binding="wsHttpContextBinding"
          contract="RegistrationContracts.IRegistration"
          name="httpBinding" />
    </client>
  </system.serviceModel>
</configuration>
```

The only detail contained in this endpoint definition unfamiliar to Windows Communication Foundation developers is the binding value of wsHttpContextBinding. This is a binding that includes a context channel that is responsible for managing the context information of the workflow. This is the mechanism that allows the runtime to properly route messages to the correct workflow instances. At the most basic level, the context being transmitted includes the workflow instance identifier. In scenarios in which the workflow instance identifier and the operation are not enough to route the message to the correct Receive activity, such as a parallel set of Receive activities, the context will need to contain additional information to route that message.

The other binding currently included is the `netTcpContextBinding`, which uses the TCP transport to exchange the context information. In the case in which the `wsHttpContextBinding` and the `netTcpContextBinding` are not appropriate, one can create a custom binding by mixing in the context channel into the custom binding definition.

The Receive activity requires only one piece of information to configure—the operation it implements. Similar to the Send activity, double-clicking displays a dialog that allows one to choose the operation. In addition to importing a contract, this dialog also allows a developer to define the contract and the details of the operation. This dialog is seen in Figure 6.10. The contract definition tool allows one to define the input parameters and types, as well as the return value.

FIGURE 6.10   Dialog to select or define the contract and operation.

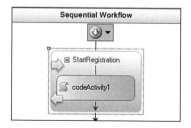

FIGURE 6.11   The Receive activity in a sequential workflow.

After the operation is selected, dependency properties are added to the activity so one can promote the properties to member variables or to bind to another value in the workflow. As seen in Figure 6.11, the Receive activity is a composite activity. The implementation details of the operation are expressed as the activities arranged within the Receive activity. The developer will want to create the return value within these activities. In Figure 6.11, a Code activity is used to create the ReturnValue. The property pane for the Receive activity is displayed in Figure 6.12.

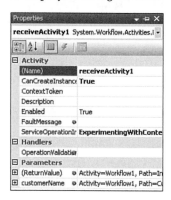

FIGURE 6.12   The property pane for a Receive activity.

The CanCreateInstance property indicates whether a workflow should be instantiated when a message is received without a context for that operation. If a message arrives with a context, the host will route that message to the existing instance as specified in the context. The host will inspect the workflow being hosted, and will look for activities with CanCreateInstance set to true to know when a workflow should be created. Typically, the first Receive activity in a workflow will have this set to true.

The other aspect of hosting a workflow-enabled service is the host itself. As discussed earlier in this chapter, there is a fair amount of "plumbing" within the host required to instantiate and route messages to workflows. This functionality is found within the WorkflowServiceHost, a sub-class of the ServiceHost used to create host a Windows Communication Foundation service. The WorkflowServiceHost can create a host based on a type passed in, or a string of XAML containing the workflow definition. The code in Listing 6.11 shows a simple WorkflowServiceHost.

LISTING 6.11   A Simple WorkflowServiceHost

```
using System;
using System.Collections.Generic;
using System.Text;
using System.Threading;
using System.Workflow.Runtime;
using System.Workflow.Runtime.Hosting;
using System.ServiceModel;
```

LISTING 6.11   Continued

```
namespace WCFUnleashed
{
    class Program
    {
        static void Main(string[] args)
        {
            WorkflowServiceHost wsh =
                new WorkflowServiceHost(typeof(Workflow1));
            wsh.Open();
            Console.WriteLine("Press <Enter> to quit the application");
            Console.ReadLine();
            wsh.Close();
        }
    }
}
```

This is very similar to the simple hosts of a Windows Communication Foundation service. The implementation has been created within the workflow type passed into the constructor. The configuration is needed to match the mechanics of the messaging with the Receive activities contained within the workflow. The configuration file listed in Listing 6.12 shows the configuration required.

LISTING 6.12   WorkflowServiceHost Configuration

```
<?xml version="1.0" encoding="utf-8" ?>
<configuration>
  <system.serviceModel>
    <services>
      <service name="WCFUnleashed.Workflow1"
                      behaviorConfiguration="WorkflowServiceBehavior" >
        <host>
          <baseAddresses>
            <add baseAddress="http://localhost:8998/
                      WCFUnleashed/Workflow1.svc" />
          </baseAddresses>
        </host>
        <endpoint address="ContextOverTcp"
                binding="wsHttpContextBinding"
                contract="WCFUnleashed.IRegistration" />
      </service>
    </services>
    <behaviors>
      <serviceBehaviors>
        <behavior name="WorkflowServiceBehavior"   >
```

LISTING 6.12   Continued

```
            <serviceMetadata httpGetEnabled="true"
                        httpGetUrl="http://localhost:8999/myMetaData" />
            <serviceDebug includeExceptionDetailInFaults="true" />
            <workflowRuntime name="WorkflowServiceHostRuntime"
                        validateOnCreate="true"
                        enablePerformanceCounters="true">
          <services>
            <add
              type="System.Workflow.Runtime.Hosting.
                      SqlWorkflowPersistenceService, System.Workflow.Runtime,
                      Version=3.0.00000.0, Culture=neutral,
                      PublicKeyToken=31bf3856ad364e35"
              connectionString="Data Source=localhost\sqlexpress;
                      Initial Catalog=NetFx35Samples_ServiceStore;
                      Integrated Security=True;Pooling=False"
              LoadIntervalSeconds="1" UnLoadOnIdle="true"   />
          </services>
        </workflowRuntime>
      </behavior>
    </serviceBehaviors>
  </behaviors>
 </system.serviceModel>
</configuration>
```

This configuration file creates an endpoint using the wsHttpContextBinding and defines the WorkflowServiceBehavior. Within the WorkflowServiceBehavior definition, one could add and configure additional runtime services. The WorkflowServiceHost also exposes a public property, WorkflowRuntime, which allows one to access the workflow runtime programmatically. Here the host could subscribe to the events raised by the runtime or interact directly with the workflow runtime.

The model in Visual Studio codename "Orcas" simplifies the work described earlier in this chapter by providing the WorkflowServiceHost and the Send and Receive activities, which allow one to work with services. This approach makes Windows Workflow Foundation a natural fit to both consume and implement services using Windows Communication Foundation. The capability for Windows Communication Foundation to interoperate with services implemented in other technologies means that Windows Workflow Foundation can be used by any technology that communicates with Windows Communication Foundation. This further expands the set of scenarios in which Windows Workflow Foundation can deliver value by allowing developers to focus on the details of the process and leave the rest (persistence, tracking, instancing, communications) to configuration.

References

Paventhan A., Takeda K., Cox, S. J., and Nicole, D. A., 2006, "Leveraging Windows Workflow Foundation for Scientific Workflows in Wind Tunnel Applications," IEEE Workshop on Workflow and Data Flow for Scientific Applications (SciFlow'06), Atlanta, GA.

Hohpe, Gregor, and Bobby Woolf. 2004. *Enterprise Integration Patterns: Designing, Building and Deploying Messaging Solutions*. Boston, MA: Addison-Wesley.

PART III

Security

IN THIS PART

Introduction

This first chapter on the security facilities provided by the Windows Communication Foundation (WCF) is meant to do two things. First, it is intended to show how to use those facilities to accomplish basic tasks in securing communications. Then the chapter will explain how the various security mechanisms in the Windows Communication Foundation fit together conceptually as part of an ingenious, extensible, and pioneering whole.

Basic Tasks in Securing Communications

Here are the basic tasks involved in securing communication among software entities:

▶ The sources of transmissions must be identified, and so must the receivers. The process of determining the identity of a sender or receiver is generally referred to as *entity authentication* (Tulloch 2003a, 31).

▶ Transmissions must be kept safe from interception, viewing, or copying by parties other than the intended receiver. In a word, they must be kept confidential (Tulloch 2003b, 66).

▶ The receiver must be assured of the integrity of the transmission; that the data received is the data sent by the identified source (Tulloch 2003c, 147).

▶ Entity authentication together with data integrity make a transmission nonrepudiable, providing undeniable evidence that the received data was sent by the identified source (Tulloch 2003d, 216).

▶ In responding to a received transmission, the receiving entity might be required to perform operations on behalf of the identified source. In doing so, the receiving entity is said to be *impersonating* the source (Tulloch 2003e, 141).

▶ Communications among software entities invariably have consequences: data gets stored, altered, sent, or deleted. Therefore, it is necessary to ensure that the identified source of a transmission is indeed entitled to cause those effects. The process of doing so is called *authorization* (Microsoft Press Computer Dictionary 1997, 36).

The Windows Communication Foundation has two primary layers: the Service Model and the Channel Layer. The Service Model translates data items that are to be transmitted into the form of a message, and passes the message to the Channel Layer, which will send the message to its destination. At the destination, the message is received by the Channel Layer and passed to the Service Model.

The Channel Layer of a sending entity authenticates the receiver, provides for the confidentiality and integrity of a message, and facilitates the receiver authenticating the sender. It also grants or denies permission for the receiver to impersonate the sender. The Channel Layer of a receiving entity facilitates the sender authenticating the receiver, confirms the confidentiality and integrity of a message, and authenticates the sending entity. The Service Model on the receiving side does the authorization and, if necessary, the impersonation.

Transport Security and Message Security

The Channel Layers of the sending and receiving entities, which ensure the confidentiality and integrity of messages and which authenticate one another, can be configured to delegate that work to the medium over which the message is transmitted. That option is referred to as *transport security*. They can also be made to perform operations on the messages themselves to ensure the confidentiality and integrity of the messages and to authenticate the sender and receiver. That option is referred to as *message security*.

Transport security works more quickly. It is also more widely supported across software communication systems, so if it is necessary to secure communications between a Windows Communication Foundation application and an application that does not use the Windows Communication Foundation, transport security is the approach most likely to work.

Message security can be maintained across any number of intermediate points between the original sender of a message and its ultimate recipient, whereas transport security maintains the security of a transmission only between one point and the next. Message security also provides more options than transport security provides for authenticating the source of a transmission. In particular, it facilitates the federated security scenario described in Chapter 8, "Using Windows CardSpace to Secure Windows Applications."

Using Transport Security

The Windows Communication Foundation uses the Secure Sockets Layer (SSL) protocol. According to that protocol, a client connecting to a server provides a list of encryption algorithms it supports. The server responds by returning a copy of its certificate, and selects an encryption algorithm from among those that the client claimed to support. The client extracts the server's public key from the server's certificate, and uses that key to authenticate the server. The client also uses that key to derive a session key from the server's response, and the session key is used to encrypt all the data exchanged between the client and the server for the remainder of the session, thereby ensuring its confidentiality (Tulloch 2003f, 299).

Installing Certificates

From the foregoing, it should be apparent that in order to use transport security with the Windows Communication Foundation, it will be necessary to install a certificate. The following steps are for installing certificates for use in the remainder of this chapter, as well as in Chapter 8. The initial steps are for executing a batch file that will create two certificates: one for an organization called FabrikamEnterprises and another for an organization called Woodgrove. The batch file will also make the certificates accessible to the Windows Communication Foundation.

1. Copy the code associated with this chapter downloaded from http://www.cryptmaker.com/WindowsCommunicationFoundationUnleashed to the folder C:\WCFHandsOn. The code is all in a folder called SecurityBasics. The SecurityBasics folder has a subfolder called Certificates.

2. Open the SDK Command Prompt by choosing All Programs, Microsoft Windows SDK, CMD Shell.

3. Use the cd command at the prompt to make the Certificates subfolder of the SecurityBasics folder the prompt's current directory.

4. On Windows Server 2003 or Windows Vista and later operating systems, execute setup.bat from the prompt. On Windows XP SP2, execute setupxp.bat.

Both of the certificates created by the batch file executed in the preceding step were issued by an organization called Root Agency. For the certificates to be trustworthy, a certificate for Root Agency itself must be installed in the machine's Trusted Root Certification Authority Certificate Store. These next few steps are for accomplishing that task. The procedure will be to export one of the new certificates along with the certificate for Root Agency that is included in its chain of certification, and then to import the exported certificates into the Trusted Root Certification Authority Store.

1. Open the Microsoft Management Console by choosing Run from the Windows Start menus, and entering

   mmc

2. Choose File, Add/Remove Snap-In from the Microsoft Management Console menus.

3. Click Add on the Add/Remove Snap-In dialog that opens.

4. Choose Certificates from the list of available standalone snap-ins presented, and click the Add button.

5. Select Computer Account on the Certificates snap-in dialog, and click the Next button.

6. Accept the default on the Select Computer dialog and click the Finish button.

7. Click the Close button on the Add Standalone Snap-In dialog.

8. Click the OK button on the Add/Remove Snap-In dialog.

9. Expand the Certificates node that now appears in the left panel of the Microsoft Management Console.

10. Expand the Personal child node of the Certificates node.

11. Select the Certificates child node of the Personal node.

12. Right-click on the FabrikamEnterprises certificate that should now have appeared in the right panel, and choose All Tasks, Export from the context menus.

13. Click Next on the first dialog of the Certificate Export Wizard.

14. Elect to export the private key on the next dialog.

15. Choose Personal Certificate Exchange as the format on the Export File Format dialog, and do be certain to choose the option of including all certificates in the certification path. That option will permit access to the Root Agency certificate.

16. Click Next to advance to the Password dialog.

17. Leave the password fields blank and simply click Next.

18. Use the Browse button on the next dialog to select the WCFHandsOn\SecurityBasics\Certificates folder, and enter **FabrikamEnterprises.pfx** as the name of the file to which the certificate is to be exported. Confirm the replacement of any existing file, if necessary.

19. Click Next to advance to the final dialog of the Certificate Export Wizard.

20. Click Finish, and then OK on the Export Confirmation dialog.

21. Right-click on the Trusted Root Certification Authorities node under the Certificates node in the left pane of the Microsoft Management Console, and select All Tasks, Import from the context menus.

22. Click Next on the first dialog of the Certificate Import Wizard.

23. On the next dialog, browse for the FabrikamEnterprises.pfx file to which certificates were exported in step 18. Note that the Open dialog that will be presented does not show files with the .pfx extension by default, so it is necessary to select Personal Certificate Exchange from the list of file type options that it offers in order to see the file.

24. Click Next to advance to the Password dialog.

25. Click Next to advance to the Certificate Store dialog.

26. Click Finish to complete the wizard, and then OK on the Import Confirmation dialog.

27. The preceding steps will have served to import both the FabrikamEnterprises certificate and the Root Agency certificate into the Trusted Root Certification Authorities Store. The former certificate does not belong there. Delete it by expanding the Trusted Root Certification Authorities node in the left pane of the Microsoft Management Console, selecting its Certificates subnode, right-clicking on the FabrikamEnterprises certificate in the list of the certificates in the right pane, and choosing Delete from the context menus.

If the preceding steps were completed successfully, the Fabrikam and Woodgrove certificates created earlier now have valid certification paths. Confirm that with these steps:

1. Select the Certificates child node of the Personal node in the left pane of the Microsoft Management Console.

2. Right-click the FabrikamEnterprises certificate in the right panel, and choose Open from the context menus.

3. Select the Certification Path tab.

4. Confirm that the certificate is OK in the Certificate Status field at the bottom of the tab.

5. Click OK to close the Certificate dialog.

6. Close the Microsoft Management Console.

Identifying the Certificate the Server Is to Provide

Now some certificates have been installed. The next step is to specify a certificate that the server is to present to clients that initiate SSL connections. The process of doing so differs according to whether the server is a Windows Communication Foundation service hosted in IIS (Internet Information Services), or a Windows Communication Foundation service hosted in a .NET application. For a Windows Communication Foundation service hosted in IIS, it is necessary to identify a certificate that IIS is to use for SSL exchanges. For Windows Communication Foundation services hosted in .NET applications that are to use SSL over HTTP, it is necessary to identify a certificate that HTTP.SYS is to use for SSL. HTTP.SYS is the Windows kernel mode driver for HTTP that the Windows Communication Foundation's HTTP transport channel relies on. For Windows Communication Foundation services hosted in .NET applications that are to use SSL over a transport other than HTTP, a certificate to use for SSL can be identified directly in the Windows Communication Foundation configuration of the service.

Identifying a Certificate for IIS to Use for SSL Exchanges

To specify a certificate that IIS is to use for SSL exchanges, follow these steps:

1. Choose Control Panel, Administrative Tools, Internet Information Services (IIS) Manager from the Windows Start menus.

2. Expand the nodes of the tree control in the left pane until the node named Default Web Site becomes visible.

3. Right-click on that node, and choose Properties from the context menus that appear.

4. Select the Directory Security tab.

5. Click the Server Certificate button.

6. Click Next on the first dialog of the Web Service Certificate Wizard.

7. Select Assign an Existing Certificate, and click Next.

8. Select the FabrikamEnterprises certificate from the list of available certificates and click Next.

9. Click Next on the SSL Port dialog.

10. Click Next on the Certificate Summary dialog.

11. Click Finish to complete the wizard.

12. Click OK on the Web Site Properties dialog.

13. Close the IIS Manager.

Identifying a Certificate for HTTP.SYS to Use for SSL Exchanges

The easiest tool to use to configure HTTP.SYS is Steve Johnson's HTTP configuration utility, which has a graphical user interface. His utility is available at http://www.StevesTechSpot.com. Follow these steps to use that tool to identify the certificate that HTTP.SYS is to use for SSL exchanges:

1. Start the HTTP Configuration Utility.

2. Choose the SSL Certs tab.

3. Click the Add button.

4. On the SSL Configuration dialog, enter **127.0.0.1** in the IP Address field and **8020** in the Port field.

5. Click the Browse button and select the FabrikamEnterprises certificate in the Select Certificates dialog, and click OK.

6. Click the OK button on the SSL Configuration dialog.

7. Click OK on the main window of the HTTP Configuration Utility to close it.

Configuring the Identity of the Server

Remember that according to the SSL protocol, the client uses the certificate provided by the server to authenticate the server to confirm that the server is indeed the server that the client believes it to be. The FabrikamEnterprises certificate has been identified as the certificate that the server will offer to the client. For that certificate to be useful in confirming the identity of the server, it is necessary to make the identity of the server correspond to the name of the certificate. Do that now by executing these steps:

1. Use Notepad to open the hosts file in the System32\drivers\etc subfolder of the system directory.

2. By default, that file contains this single entry:

   ```
   127.0.0.1        localhost
   ```

   Add an additional entry like so:

   ```
   127.0.0.1        localhost
   127.0.0.1        fabrikamenterprises
   ```

3. Save the hosts file.

4. Close the hosts file.

Transport Security in Action

Follow these steps to observe the application of transport security to the transmission of messages by the Windows Communication Foundation:

1. Open the Visual Studio 2005 solution, TransportSecurity.sln, in the folder WCFHandsOn\SecurityBasics\TransportSecurity. This solution is very similar to the one constructed in Chapter 2, "The Fundamentals." A derivatives calculator is exposed for use by a client application via a Windows Communication Foundation service. Hosted in IIS, the service will expose an endpoint for communication with SSL over HTTP. Hosted within a .NET application that is named Host, it will expose another endpoint for SSL communication over HTTP, as well as an endpoint for SSL communication over TCP.

2. Deploy the service into IIS by creating a virtual directory called SecurityBasics that uses WCFHandsOn\SecurityBasics\TransportSecurity\DerivativesCalculatorService as its content directory. The steps for creating a virtual directory for hosting a Windows Communication Foundation service were provided in Chapter 2.

3. Examine the code in the static Main() function in the Program.cs file of the Client project of the TransportSecurity solution. It has the client invoke the derivatives calculator hosted by the .NET host application first using the endpoint for SSL over HTTP, and then using the endpoint SSL over TCP. The code ten has the client invoke the derivatives calculator hosted within IIS using SSL over HTTP.

```
using (DerivativesCalculatorClient proxy =
    new DerivativesCalculatorClient("SelfHostedHTTPSService"))
{
    [...]
}
...
using (DerivativesCalculatorClient proxy =
    new DerivativesCalculatorClient("SelfHostedTCPService"))
{
    [...]
}
...
using (DerivativesCalculatorClient proxy =
    new DerivativesCalculatorClient("WebHostedHTTPSService"))
{
    [...]
}
```

4. Look in the app.config file of the Client project of the TransportSecurity solution to see how the client is configured to invoke the calculator using SSL over HTTP. The pertinent elements of the configuration are shown in Listing 7.1. The address of the service has the HTTPS scheme, which is commonly used for SSL over HTTP. The client is configured to use the predefined BasicHttpBinding. That predefined binding is customized, though, to use transport security, and to identify the client to the server with NTLM credentials. NTLM is used here for the sake of readers whose computers are not attached to any domain. Clients on computers that are attached to a Windows 2000 or later domain could offer Kerberos credentials if the client credential type was set to Windows rather than Ntlm, although a matching change would be required in the configuration of the services.

LISTING 7.1   Client Configuration for SSL over HTTP

```
<?xml version="1.0" encoding="utf-8"?>
<configuration>
    <system.serviceModel>
        <client>
            <endpoint
                address=
"https://fabrikamenterprises:8020/Derivatives/Calculator"
                    binding="basicHttpBinding"
                    bindingConfiguration="SecureTransport"
                    behaviorConfiguration="HTTPSEndpoint"
                    contract="DerivativesCalculator.IDerivativesCalculator"
                    name="SelfHostedHTTPSService"/>
        </client>
        <bindings>
```

LISTING 7.1   Continued

```
                    <basicHttpBinding>
                        <binding name="SecureTransport">
                            <security mode="Transport">
                                <transport clientCredentialType="Ntlm"/>
                            </security>
                        </binding>
                    </basicHttpBinding>
                </bindings>
                <behaviors>
                    <endpointBehaviors>
                        <behavior name="HTTPSEndpoint">
                            <clientCredentials>
                                <windows allowNtlm="true"
                            </clientCredentials>
                        </behavior>
                    </endpointBehaviors>
                </behaviors>
            </system.serviceModel>
</configuration>
```

5. Also see, in the app.config file of the Client project, how the client is configured to use SSL over TCP. The pertinent elements of the configuration are reproduced in Listing 7.2. The client is configured to use the predefined NetTcpBinding, but that binding is customized to include transport security. In this case, the client is configured to not offer any credentials by which it can be authenticated to the server. Clients on computers that are attached to a Windows 2000 or later domain could offer Kerberos credentials if the client credential type was set to Windows rather than None, although, again, a matching change would be required in the configuration of the service. A behavior is used to control the client's authentication of the service, bypassing the default check to determine whether the certificate presented by the server to identify itself has been revoked.

LISTING 7.2   Client Configuration for SSL over TCP

```
<?xml version="1.0" encoding="utf-8"?>
<configuration>
    <system.serviceModel>
        <client>
            <endpoint
                address=
"net.tcp://fabrikamenterprises:8010/Derivatives/Calculator"
                binding="netTcpBinding"
                    bindingConfiguration="SecureTransport"
                    behaviorConfiguration="TCPEndpoint"
```

LISTING 7.2   Continued

```
                              contract="DerivativesCalculator.IDerivativesCalculator"
                              name="SelfHostedTCPService"/>
              </client>
              <bindings>
                    <netTcpBinding>
                          <binding name="SecureTransport">
                                <security mode="Transport">
                                      <transport clientCredentialType="None"/>
                                </security>
                          </binding>
                    </netTcpBinding>
              </bindings>
              <behaviors>
                    <endpointBehaviors>
                          <behavior name="TCPEndpoint">
                                <clientCredentials>
                                      <serviceCertificate>
                                            <authentication revocationMode="NoCheck"
/>
                                      </serviceCertificate>
                                </clientCredentials>
                          </behavior>
                    </endpointBehaviors>
              </behaviors>
        </system.serviceModel>
</configuration>
```

6. Examine the app.config file of the Host project of the TransportSecurity solution to
   see how a service's endpoint may be configured to receive SSL requests over HTTP.
   The configuration is reproduced in Listing 7.3. The address for the endpoint has a
   base address with the scheme HTTPS, which signifies SSL over HTTP. The endpoint
   is configured to use the predefined BasicHttpBinding. However, that binding is
   customized to use transport security, and to anticipate clients presenting NTLM
   credentials by which they can be authenticated. On computers that are attached to
   a Windows 2000 or later domain, the clients and the service could be configured to
   use Kerberos credentials instead of NTLM credentials by setting the client credential
   type to Windows rather than Ntlm.

LISTING 7.3   Service Configuration for SSL over HTTP

```
<?xml version="1.0" encoding="utf-8" ?>
<configuration>
  <system.serviceModel>
    <services>
      <service
```

LISTING 7.3   Continued

```
          name=
"DerivativesCalculator.DerivativesCalculatorServiceType"
      <host>
        <baseAddresses>
          <add
baseAddress="https://localhost:8020/Derivatives/"/>
        </baseAddresses>
      </host>
      <endpoint
        address="Calculator"
        binding="basicHttpBinding"
        bindingConfiguration="SecureTransport"
        contract=
"DerivativesCalculator.IDerivativesCalculator"/>
      </service>
    </services>
    <bindings>
      <basicHttpBinding>
        <binding name="SecureTransport">
          <security mode="Transport">
            <transport clientCredentialType="Ntlm"/>
          </security>
        </binding>
      </basicHttpBinding>
    </bindings>
  </system.serviceModel>
</configuration>
```

7. Also study the app.config file of Host project to see how a service's endpoint can be configured to receive requests via SSL over TCP. The relevant parts of the configuration are reproduced in Listing 7.4. The address for the endpoint has a base address with the scheme, net.tcp, which is the scheme that must be used in conjunction with the Windows Communication Foundation's predefined NetTcpBinding. That predefined binding is indeed the one that is specified as the binding for the endpoint in this case, and it is customized to use transport security. The customization specifies that the service will not require clients to present credentials by which the service may authenticate them. On computers that are attached to a Windows 2000 or later domain, the clients and the service could be configured so that the clients would present Kerberos credentials that the service would use to authenticate the clients. That modification could be made by setting the value of the clientCredentialType attribute to Windows rather than None. Notice that the service is configured with a behavior that identifies the FabrikamEnterprises certificate as the certificate that the service is to present to the client to authenticate itself.

LISTING 7.4   Service Configuration for SSL over TCP

```xml
<?xml version="1.0" encoding="utf-8" ?>
<configuration>
  <system.serviceModel>
    <bindings>
      <netTcpBinding>
        <binding name="SecureTransport">
          <security mode="Transport">
            <transport clientCredentialType="None"/>
          </security>
        </binding>
      </netTcpBinding>
    </bindings>
    <services>
      <service
        name="DerivativesCalculator.DerivativesCalculatorServiceType"
        behaviorConfiguration="DerivativesCalculatorService">
        <endpoint
          address="Calculator"
          binding="netTcpBinding"
          bindingConfiguration="SecureTransport"
          contract="DerivativesCalculator.IDerivativesCalculator" />
        <host>
          <baseAddresses>
            <add baseAddress="net.tcp://localhost:8010/Derivatives/"/>
          </baseAddresses>
        </host>
      </service>
    </services>
    <behaviors>
      <serviceBehaviors>
        <behavior name="DerivativesCalculatorService">
          <serviceCredentials>
            <serviceCertificate
              findValue="CN=FabrikamEnterprises" />
          </serviceCredentials>
        </behavior>
      </serviceBehaviors>
    </behaviors>
  </system.serviceModel>
</configuration>
```

8. Now look at the code of the service type, which is in the DerivativesCalculatorServiceType file of the DerivativesCalculatorService project of the TransportSecurity solution. As shown in the following snippet, the service type retrieves the identity of the client using the Windows Communication Foundation's static `System.ServiceModel.Security.ServiceSecurityContext` class. It outputs that identity to the screen, thereby signifying that the task of authenticating the client's identity has been accomplished.

```
decimal IDerivativesCalculator.CalculateDerivative(
    string[] symbols,
    decimal[] parameters,
    string[] functions)
{
    WindowsIdentity identity =
            ServiceSecurityContext.Current.WindowsIdentity;
    if (identity != null)
    {
        string name = identity.Name;
        if (!(string.IsNullOrEmpty(name)))
        {
            Console.WriteLine("User is {0}.", name);
        }
    }
    return new Calculator().CalculateDerivative(
        symbols, parameters, functions);
}
```

9. Choose Build, Build Solution from the Visual Studio 2005 menus.

10. Execute TransportSecurity\Host\bin\Host.exe.

11. Execute TransportSecurity\Client\bin\Client.exe. In doing so, it would be more effective to right-click on the executable, choose Run As from the context menus that appears, and opt to run the application with the credentials of some user who has permission to log in locally, but who is not the user that is currently logged in.

12. When the output in the console of the Host application signifies that the service is ready, enter a keystroke into the console of the Client application. The Client application will display results retrieved, first via communication with SSL over HTTP with the service provided by the Host application, and then via communication with SSL over TCP with the same service, and finally via communication with SSL over HTTP with the service hosted in IIS. For cases in which the client is using SSL over HTTP, the client is configured to present credentials to the service, so the output in the console for the Host application will identify the user under whose account the Client application was run.

13. Close both consoles.

Using Message Security

Message security is the default option for securing messages with all the Windows Communication Foundation's predefined bindings with one exception: the BasicProfileBinding. Message security is not an option at all with the BasicProfileBinding because that binding implements the WS-I Basic Profile 1.1, which makes no provision for message security.

The WS-Security specification provides a basis for the message security facilities of the Windows Communication Foundation. That specification defines a way of incorporating into SOAP (Simple Object Access Protocol) messages information that can be used to authenticate the senders. The specification also defines how SOAP messages can be encrypted to preserve their confidentiality. The specification provides, too, for the sender of a SOAP message signing the message with a private key so that the receiver can validate the integrity of the message by reproducing the signature from the contents of the message with the sender's public key.

The Windows Communication Foundation also implements the WS-SecureConversation protocol. That protocol defines how the senders and receivers of SOAP messages can use WS-Security to negotiate the use of session-specific keys for securing their substantive messages.

Here are some steps to follow to see how to make use of the Windows Communication Foundation's message security capabilities:

1. Open the Visual Studio 2005 solution, MessageSecurity.sln, in the folder WCFHandsOn\SecurityBasics\MessageSecurity. This solution consists of a derivatives calculator service like the one constructed in Chapter 2, as well as a .NET console application for hosting that service, and another .NET console application to serve as the client.

2. Examine the code in the static Main() function in the Program.cs file of the Client project of the MessageSecurity solution. It has the client invoke the derivatives calculator service twice, using a different endpoint each time. In calling the second endpoint, it offers credentials in the form of a username and password:

```
decimal result = 0;
using (DerivativesCalculatorClient proxy =
    new DerivativesCalculatorClient("DerivativesCalculatorServiceWindows"))
{
    proxy.Open();
    result = proxy.CalculateDerivative(
    [...]
    proxy.Close();
}
[...]
using (DerivativesCalculatorClient proxy =
    new DerivativesCalculatorClient("DerivativesCalculatorServiceUserName"))
{
```

```
        proxy.ClientCredentials.UserName.UserName = @"don";
        proxy.ClientCredentials.UserName.Password = @"hall";
        proxy.Open();
        result = proxy.CalculateDerivative(
        [...]
        proxy.Close();
    }
```

3. Look at the app.config file of the Client project in the MessageSecurity solution to
    see how the first endpoint is configured. The pertinent elements of the configura-
    tion are reproduced in Listing 7.5. The endpoint is configured to use the predefined
    WSHttpBinding. That binding provides message security by default, using Kerberos or
    NTLM credentials to identify the senders, to sign and encrypt the messages, and to
    negotiate session-specific keys for a secure conversation.

LISTING 7.5   Client Configuration for Message Security with Windows Credentials

```xml
<?xml version="1.0" encoding="utf-8"?>
<configuration>
  <system.serviceModel>
    <client>
      <endpoint
        address="http://localhost:8000/Derivatives/Calculator"
        binding="wsHttpBinding"
        contract="DerivativesCalculator.IDerivativesCalculator"
        name="DerivativesCalculatorServiceWindows" />
    </client>
  </system.serviceModel>
</configuration>
```

4. Also examine the app.config file of the Client project in the MessageSecurity solu-
    tion to see how the second endpoint is configured, the endpoint for which a user-
    name and password are provided. The relevant portions of the configuration are in
    Listing 7.6. The predefined WSHttpBinding is used once again, but this time it is
    customized so as to present for authentication what the WS-Security specification
    refers to as a *UsernameToken*: a combination of a username and password (Kaler
    2002). Because passing the username and password credentials unencrypted from
    the client to the service would compromise their security, the Windows
    Communication Foundation requires that whenever usernames and passwords are
    used for authentication, the service must provide an X.509 certificate for encrypting
    them or be configured to use transport security. The behavior that is incorporated
    into the configuration in Listing 7.6 waives the check that the Windows
    Communication Foundation would otherwise perform automatically to determine
    whether the certificate offered by the service had been revoked by the issuer.

LISTING 7.6   Client Configuration for Message Security with a Username and Password

```xml
<?xml version="1.0" encoding="utf-8"?>
<configuration>
    <system.serviceModel>
        <client>
            <endpoint
                address=
"http://FabrikamEnterprises:8000/Derivatives/AnotherCalculator"
                binding="wsHttpBinding"
                bindingConfiguration="SecureMessageUserName"
                behaviorConfiguration="UserName"
                contract="DerivativesCalculator.IDerivativesCalculator"
                name="DerivativesCalculatorServiceUserName"/>
        </client>
        <bindings>
            <wsHttpBinding>
                <binding name="SecureMessageUserName">
                    <security mode="Message">
                        <message clientCredentialType="UserName"/>
                    </security>
                </binding>
            </wsHttpBinding>
        </bindings>
        <behaviors>
            <endpointBehaviors>
                <behavior name="UserName">
                    <clientCredentials>
                        <serviceCertificate>
                            <authentication
                                revocationMode="NoCheck"/>
                        </serviceCertificate>
                    </clientCredentials>
                </behavior>
            </endpointBehaviors>
        </behaviors>
    </system.serviceModel>
</configuration>
```

5. Look in the app.config file of the Host project of the MessageSecurity solution to see
    how the service endpoint that uses Kerberos or NTLM credentials to identify the
    users of clients is configured. The pertinent elements of that configuration are
    shown in Listing 7.7. The endpoint is simply configured to use the predefined
    WSHttpBinding, which, by default, anticipates users presenting Kerberos or NTLM to
    identify themselves.

LISTING 7.7   Service Endpoint Configuration for Message Security with Windows Credentials

```xml
<?xml version="1.0" encoding="utf-8" ?>
<configuration>
  <system.serviceModel>
    <services>
      <service
name="DerivativesCalculator.DerivativesCalculatorServiceType">
        <endpoint
          address="Calculator"
          binding="wsHttpBinding"
          contract="DerivativesCalculator.IDerivativesCalculator"/>
        <host>
          <baseAddresses>
            <add
              baseAddress="http://localhost:8000/Derivatives/"/>
          </baseAddresses>
        </host>
      </service>
    </services>
  </system.serviceModel>
</configuration>
```

6. Also examine the app.config file of the Host project to see how the service endpoint that employs username and password combinations to identify the users of clients is configured. The relevant parts of the configuration are in Listing 7.8. This configuration also uses the predefined WSHttpBinding, but customizes it to use usernames and passwords to authenticate the users of clients, rather than Kerberos or NTLM credentials. A behavior is used to specify that the FabrikamEnterprises certificate is the certificate that the server is to provide for encrypting the transmission of username and password combinations from the client to the service. The behavior also specifies that a custom class for validating username and password combinations will be used, and identifies that class as the DerivativesCalculator.MyUserNamePasswordValidator class in the Host assembly. Ordinarily, the Windows Communication Foundation validates user names and passwords against Windows account information, but the option of identifying a custom class to validate those credentials against some other store is provided.

LISTING 7.8   Service Endpoint Configuration for Message Security with a Username and Password

```xml
<?xml version="1.0" encoding="utf-8" ?>
  <configuration>
    <system.serviceModel>
      <services>
        <service
```

LISTING 7.8   Continued

```xml
              name="DerivativesCalculator.DerivativesCalculatorServiceType"
              behaviorConfiguration="DerivativesCalculatorService">
              <endpoint
                address="AnotherCalculator"
                binding="wsHttpBinding"
                bindingConfiguration="SecureMessageUserName"
                contract="DerivativesCalculator.IDerivativesCalculator"/>
              <host>
                <baseAddresses>
                  <add
                    baseAddress="http://localhost:8000/Derivatives/"/>
                </baseAddresses>
              </host>
            </service>
          </services>
          <bindings>
            <wsHttpBinding>
              <binding name="SecureMessageUserName">
                <security mode="Message">
                  <message clientCredentialType="UserName"/>
                </security>
              </binding>
            </wsHttpBinding>
          </bindings>
          <behaviors>
            <serviceBehaviors>
              <behavior name="DerivativesCalculatorService">
                <serviceCredentials>
                  <userNameAuthentication
                    userNamePasswordValidationMode="Custom"
                    customUserNamePasswordValidatorType=
"DerivativesCalculator.MyUserNamePasswordValidator,Host"/>
                    <serviceCertificate
                      findValue="CN=FabrikamEnterprises"/>
                </serviceCredentials>
              </behavior>
            </serviceBehaviors>
          </behaviors>
        </system.serviceModel>
</configuration>
```

7. Look at the code for the custom class for validating user names and passwords in the MyUserNamePasswordValidator file of the Host project. The class derives from the abstract base, `System.IdentityModel.Selectors.UserNamePasswordValidator`, and overrides that base class's sole abstract method, `Validate()`. That method is passed the username and password offered by the client. If the validation of the credentials fails, the `Validate()` method is expected to throw a `System.IdentityModel.Tokens.SecurityTokenException`. Otherwise, the client is presumed to have been authenticated by the credentials.

```
public class MyUserNamePasswordValidator : UserNamePasswordValidator
{
    public override void Validate(string userName, string password)
    {
        if ([...])
        {
            throw new SecurityTokenException("Unknown user.");
        }
        Console.Write("Credentials accepted. \n");
    }
}
```

8. Study the code of the service type, which is in the DerivativesCalculatorServiceType file of the DerivativesCalculatorService project. As the following snippet shows, if the credentials offered by the user map to a Windows account, the service prints out the name of the user of the client before responding to the client's request.

```
decimal IDerivativesCalculator.CalculateDerivative(
    string[] symbols,
    decimal[] parameters,
    string[] functions)
{
    WindowsIdentity identity = ServiceSecurityContext.Current.WindowsIdentity;
    if (identity != null)
    {
        string name = identity.Name;
        if (!(string.IsNullOrEmpty(name)))
        {
            Console.WriteLine("User is {0}.", name);
        }
    }
    return new Calculator().CalculateDerivative(
        symbols, parameters, functions);
}
```

9. Choose Build, Build Solution from the Visual Studio 2005 menus.

10. Execute MessageSecurity\Host\bin\Host.exe.

11. Execute MessageSecurity\Client\bin\Client.exe. Once again, it would be more effective to do so under a different account from the one that is currently logged-in. To do so, right-click on the executable, choose Run As from the context menus that appears, and run the application with the credentials of some user who has permission to log in locally, but who is not the user that is currently logged in.

12. When the output in the console of the Host application signifies that the service is ready, enter a keystroke into the console of the Client application. The Client application will display results retrieved, first after offering Windows credentials to the service, and then after offering a username and password combination. In the first case, in which the client offers Windows credentials, the output in the console for the Host application will identify the user under whose account the Client application was executed.

13. Close both consoles.

Impersonation and Authorization

Earlier it was explained that the Windows Communication Foundation's Channel Layer does the work of entity authentication, ensuring the confidentiality of messages, and confirming their integrity, whereas the Service Model layer on the receiving side does the authorization and the impersonation. Then various options were demonstrated for configuring Windows Communication Foundation bindings to control how the Channel Layer authenticates clients, and preserves the confidentiality and integrity of messages. Now the Service Model's facilities for impersonation and authorization will be shown.

Impersonation

Impersonation is possible only when the user of the client has been authenticated as a Windows user—when that user's Windows account has been identified. In addition, the client must have been configured to grant permission to the service to impersonate the user of the client. To see a Windows service impersonate the user of a client application, follow these steps:

1. Open the Visual Studio 2005 solution, Impersonation.sln, in the folder WCFHandsOn\SecurityBasics\Impersonation. Like the solutions used earlier in this chapter, this one contains a .NET console application that uses a derivatives calculator service. That service is hosted, as usual, within a .NET console application called Host. However, the service actually delegates its work of calculating the values of derivatives to another derivatives calculator service hosted by a second .NET console application, which is called BackOfficeHost.

2. See how the client is configured by examining the app.config file in the Client project of the Impersonation solution. The configuration is shown in Listing 7.9. It incorporates a behavior associated with the endpoint that grants the service permission to impersonate the user of the client. The binding specified for the endpoint is

the predefined WSHttpBinding, which by default will identify the user of the client to the service using Windows credentials.

LISTING 7.9   Client Configuration to Permit Impersonation

```xml
<?xml version="1.0" encoding="utf-8"?>
<configuration>
  <system.serviceModel>
    <client>
      <endpoint
        address="http://localhost:8000/Derivatives/Calculator"
        binding="wsHttpBinding"
        contract="DerivativesCalculator.IDerivativesCalculator"
        behaviorConfiguration="Windows"
        name="DerivativesCalculatorServiceWindows"/>
    </client>
    <behaviors>
      <endpointBehaviors>
        <behavior name="Windows">
          <clientCredentials>
            <windows
              allowedImpersonationLevel="Impersonation"/>
          </clientCredentials>
        </behavior>
      </endpointBehaviors>
    </behaviors>
  </system.serviceModel>
</configuration>
```

3. Look at the code of the derivatives calculator service hosted by the Host application. The code for that service is in the DerivativesCalculatorServiceType.cs file in the Host project of the solution. The important parts of the code are in Listing 7.10. This code handles requests from the client, and delegates them to the derivatives calculator service hosted by the BackOfficeHost. The key element of the code is the Impersonation parameter passed to the System.ServiceModel.OperationBehavior attribute. The value of that parameter is set to System.ServiceModel.ImpersonationOption.Required, which signifies that the operation needs to impersonate the user of the client to access resources that it needs. Therefore, the binding of any endpoint that incorporates a contract implemented using this operation must have clients present Windows credentials for the service to authenticate their users because impersonation is possible only when the user of the client has been authenticated as a Windows user. If the binding does not conform to this requirement, the service will not start. Furthermore, in order for a client to invoke this operation through the Windows Communication Foundation, the client must permit the service to impersonate the user of the client.

LISTING 7.10   Having a Service Operation Impersonate a Client User

```
[OperationBehavior(Impersonation=ImpersonationOption.Required)]
decimal IDerivativesCalculator.CalculateDerivative(
    string[] symbols,
    decimal[] parameters,
    string[] functions)
{
    [...]

    decimal result = 0;
    using (DerivativesCalculatorClient proxy =
        new DerivativesCalculatorClient("BackOfficeDerivativesCalculator"))
    {
        proxy.Open();
        result = proxy.CalculateDerivative(
            new string[] { "MSFT" },
            new decimal[] { 3 },
            new string[] { });
        proxy.Close();
    }
    return result;
}
```

4. Check how the service hosted by the Host application is configured to use the service that is hosted by the BackOfficeHost application. The configuration is in the app.config file of the Host project, and shown in the following snippet. The predefined WSHttpBinding is used, which, by default, will offer Windows credentials to authenticate the caller. In this case, the intermediary service will be offering the Windows credentials of the user of its own client, who it will be impersonating.

```
<client>
    <endpoint
        address="http://localhost:8020/Derivatives/Calculator"
            binding="wsHttpBinding"
        contract="DerivativesCalculator.IDerivativesCalculator"
        name="BackOfficeDerivativesCalculator"/>
</client>
```

5. Look at the code of the derivatives calculator service hosted by the BackOfficeHost application. That code is in the DerivativesCalculatorServiceType.cs file of the BackOfficeHost project. The pertinent elements are in this next snippet. The CalculateDerivative() method that will be invoked by the intermediary service hosted by the Host application has a System.Security.Permissions. PrincipalPermission attribute that restricts access to one particular user.

```
[PrincipalPermission(
    SecurityAction.Demand,
    Name = @"ws2k3r2082006\DonHall")]
[OperationBehavior(Impersonation=ImpersonationOption.Allowed)]
decimal IDerivativesCalculator.CalculateDerivative(
    string[] symbols,
    decimal[] parameters,
    string[] functions)
{
    [...]
    return new Calculator().CalculateDerivative(
        symbols, parameters, functions);
}
```

6. Modify the System.Security.Permissions.PrincipalPermission attribute so that the name specified for the sole authorized user is that of a valid user on the computer that has been granted the right to log on locally, but is not the user that is currently logged on.

7. Choose Build, Build Solution from the Visual Studio 2005 menus.

8. Choose Debug, Start Debugging from the Visual Studio 2005 menus to start the Host application and the BackOfficeHost application.

9. Execute Impersonation\Client\bin\Client.exe, and do so as the user that was selected as the sole user permitted to access the service hosted by the BackOfficeHost in step 6. Right-click on Impersonation\Client\bin\Client.exe, choose Run As from the context menus, and select that user on the Run As dialog and enter that user's credentials.

10. When the output in the consoles of the Host and BackOfficeHost applications indicates that the services hosted by those applications are available, enter a keystroke in the console of the Client application. The Client application should request that the service hosted by the Host application calculate the value of a derivative. That service should delegate the work of doing the calculation to the service hosted by the BackOfficeHost application, and the Client application should get a response. Evidently, the intermediary service hosted by the Host application is impersonating the user of the Client application because no other user is authorized to use the service Hosted by the BackOfficeHost application.

11. Close the consoles of all three applications.

Authorization

In addition to showing how to have the Windows Communication Foundation do impersonation, the foregoing exercise has also demonstrated the first option that the Windows Communication Foundation provides for authorization. That option is to add

`System.Security.Permissions.PrincipalPermission` attributes to the methods by which the operations of a service are implemented. Those attributes can restrict access to individual users, or, as they are more commonly employed, to restrict access to users in particular roles.

By default, the roles referred to by `System.Security.Permissions.PrincipalPermission` attributes are, in fact, Windows groups, rather than application-specific roles. So, the management of authorization for an application gets tied to the assignment of Windows users to groups, which is awkward. The Windows Communication Foundation allows that problem to be circumvented using Role Providers.

Role Providers where introduced in Chapter 1, "Prerequisites." Listing 7.11 shows the configuration of a Windows Communication Foundation service that has been configured to use a Role Provider to evaluate role membership requirements specified in `System.Security.Permissions.PrincipalPermission` attributes.

LISTING 7.11   Configuring a Service to Use a Role Provider

```xml
<?xml version="1.0" encoding="utf-8" ?>
<configuration>
  <system.serviceModel>
    <services>
      <service
name="DerivativesCalculator.DerivativesCalculatorServiceType"
        behaviorConfiguration="Authorization" >
        <endpoint
          address="Calculator"
          binding="wsHttpBinding"
          contract="DerivativesCalculator.IDerivativesCalculator"
         />
        <host>
          <baseAddresses>
            <add
            baseAddress="http://localhost:8000/Derivatives/" />
            <add
            baseAddress="net.tcp://localhost:8010/Derivatives/"/>
          </baseAddresses>
        </host>
      </service>
    </services>
    <behaviors>
      <serviceBehaviors>
        <behavior name="Authorization">
          <serviceAuthorization
 principalPermissionMode="UseAspNetRoles"
```

LISTING 7.11   Continued

```
roleProviderName="AuthorizationStoreRoleProvider" />
          </behavior>
        </serviceBehaviors>
      </behaviors>
    </system.serviceModel>
    <system.web>
    <roleManager
      defaultProvider="AuthorizationStoreRoleProvider"
      maxCachedResults="0"
      enabled="true"
      cacheRolesInCookie="false"
      cookieName=".ASPROLES"
      cookieTimeout="1"
      cookiePath="/"
      cookieRequireSSL="false"
      cookieSlidingExpiration="true"
      cookieProtection="All" >
    <providers>
      <clear />
      <add
        name="AuthorizationStoreRoleProvider"
        type="System.Web.Security.AuthorizationStoreRoleProvider"
        connectionStringName="AuthorizationServices"
        cacheRefreshInterval="1"
        applicationName="RoleProvider" />
     </providers>
    </roleManager>
  </system.web>
  <connectionStrings>
    <add
      name="AuthorizationServices"
      connectionString=
"msxml://C:\WCFHandsOn\[...]\AuthorizationStore.xml" />
    </connectionStrings>
</configuration>
```

A set of behaviors with the arbitrary name Authorization is associated with the service. That set of behaviors includes a System.ServiceModel.Description.ServiceAuthorization behavior that is configured so that its PrincipalPermissionMode property is assigned the value System.ServiceModel. Description.PrincipalPermissionMode.UseAspNetRoles. Its RoleProviderName property is assigned the name of a Role Provider that is defined elsewhere in the configuration and in the way that Role Providers are usually defined. By virtue of this configuration, the service would use the specified Role Provider to evaluate the role membership requirements of `System.Security.Permissions.PrincipalPermission` attributes like the one applied to this operation:

```
[PrincipalPermission(SecurityAction.Demand, Role = "QuantitativeAnalyst")]
decimal IDerivativesCalculator.CalculateDerivative(
    string[] symbols,
    decimal[] parameters,
    string[] functions)
{
    return new Calculator().CalculateDerivative(
        symbols, parameters, functions);
}
```

The role identified by the attribute need not be a Windows group. It refers to a role that the Role Provider will look for in whatever store it uses as a repository for role information. Because the Role Provider that is identified by the configuration happens to be of the `System.Web.Security.AuthorizationStoreRoleProvider` class, that Role Provider will be looking for the role and the users assigned to it in an Authorization Manager authorization store. The particular Authorization Manager authorization store that will be queried is identified by the connection string that is also included in the configuration. Administrators could use the Authorization Manager Management Console snap-in to control which users are assigned to the role.

The option of using Role Providers to evaluate authorization demands expressed by `System.Security.Permissions.PrincipalPermission` attributes offers the flexibility of defining authorization requirements in terms of roles that may be defined in any repository of role information—not just in terms of membership in Windows groups. Still, any reliance on `System.Security.Permissions.PrincipalPermission` attributes for authorization has shortcomings. Because the `System.Security.Permissions.PrincipalPermission` attributes are in the code for the application, that code has to be modified to widen authorization to include users in additional roles or to restrict authorization to users in a smaller number of roles. In addition, `System.Security.Permissions.PrincipalPermission` attributes can only be used to evaluate the authorization of Windows accounts.

The Windows Communication Foundation offers a far better way of authorizing access than `System.Security.Permissions.PrincipalPermission` attributes can provide. To explore that option, follow these steps:

1. Open the Visual Studio 2005 solution, Authorization.sln, in the folder WCFHandsOn\SecurityBasics\Authorization. The solution contains a .NET console application called Client that uses a derivatives calculator service hosted within another .NET console application called Host. The solution also contains a class library called `CustomServiceAuthorizationManager`.

2. Notice that the definition of the service's contract, which is in the
   IDerivativesCalculator.cs file of both the Host and Client projects, exercises the
   option of explicitly providing a value for the `Action` parameter of the sole
   `System.ServiceModel.OperationContract` attribute applied to any of its methods:

```
[OperationContract(
    Action = "CalculateDerivative")]
decimal CalculateDerivative(
    string[] symbols,
    decimal[] parameters,
    string[] functions);
```

   Whatever value is assigned to the `Action` parameter of a
   `System.ServiceModel.OperationContract` attribute must serve to uniquely identify
   the method to which the attribute is applied relative to the other methods of the
   service type. The reason is that the Windows Communication Foundation determines to which method of a service a message is to be directed by matching the
   `Action` header of the message to the value of the `Action` parameter of the method's
   `System.ServiceModel.OperationContract` attribute.

3. Look at how the client is configured by examining the app.config file of the Client
   project. The configuration is like the one shown in Listing 7.6, so the client will
   offer a username and password for the service to use for authentication.

4. Study the app.config file of the Host project to see how the service is configured. It
   is reproduced in Listing 7.12. The service is configured with a set of behaviors that
   has the arbitrary name DerivativesCalculatorService. That set includes a
   `System.ServiceModel.Description.ServiceCredentials` behavior with its
   `UserNameAuthentication` property set to authenticate the credentials provided by
   the client using a custom validation routine rather than simply validating the
   credentials against Windows account information. Therefore, however authorization
   will be accomplished in this case, the mechanism must not be one that is restricted
   to use with Windows accounts.

   How authentication is to be accomplished is defined by another behavior in the set,
   the `System.ServiceModel.Description.ServiceAuthorization` behavior. That
   behavior is configured to ignore any
   `System.Security.Permissions.PrincipalPermission` attributes that exist in the
   code, by virtue of having the value `System.ServiceModel.Description.`
   `PrincipalPermissionMode.None` assigned to its `PrincipalPermissionMode` property.
   The behavior also has a type assigned to its `ServiceAuthorizationManagerType`
   property. Any type assigned as the value of `System.ServiceModel.Description.`
   `ServiceAuthorization` behavior's `ServiceAuthorizationManagerType` property must
   derive from `System.ServiceModel.ServiceAuthorizationManager`. The type that is
   assigned in this case is the `DerivativesCalculator.MyServiceAuthorizationManager`
   type in the `CustomServiceAuthorizationManager` assembly.

LISTING 7.12   Service Configuration

```xml
<?xml version="1.0" encoding="utf-8" ?>
  <configuration>
    <system.serviceModel>
      <services>
        <service
name="DerivativesCalculator.DerivativesCalculatorServiceType"
          behaviorConfiguration="DerivativesCalculatorService">
          <endpoint
            address="Calculator"
            binding="wsHttpBinding"
            bindingConfiguration="SecureMessage"
            contract="DerivativesCalculator.IDerivativesCalculator"/>
            <host>
              <baseAddresses>
                <add
                  baseAddress="http://localhost:8000/Derivatives/" />
                <add
                  baseAddress="net.tcp://localhost:8010/Derivatives/" />
              </baseAddresses>
            </host>
        </service>
      </services>
      <bindings>
        <wsHttpBinding>
          <binding name="SecureMessage">
            <security mode="Message">
              <message clientCredentialType="UserName"/>
            </security>
          </binding>
        </wsHttpBinding>
      </bindings>
      <behaviors>
        <serviceBehaviors>
          <behavior name="DerivativesCalculatorService">
            <serviceCredentials>
            <userNameAuthentication
              userNamePasswordValidationMode="Custom"
              customUserNamePasswordValidatorType=
 "DerivativesCalculator.MyUserNamePasswordValidator,Host"/>
              <serviceCertificate
                findValue="CN=FabrikamEnterprises"/>
            </serviceCredentials>
            <serviceAuthorization
```

LISTING 7.12   Continued

```
                principalPermissionMode="None"
                serviceAuthorizationManagerType=
"DerivativesCalculator.MyServiceAuthorizationManager,
[ic:ccc] CustomServiceAuthorizationManager"/>
            <serviceMetadata
                httpGetEnabled="true" />
          </behavior>
        </serviceBehaviors>
      </behaviors>
    </system.serviceModel>
</configuration>
```

5. Look at the assemblies referenced by the Host project in the Authorization solution. An assembly called `CustomServiceAuthorizationManager` is not among them.

6. Look at the assemblies deployed in the same directory as the Host.exe assembly that is built from the Host project. That directory should be the WCFHandsOn\ SecurityBasics\Authorization\Host\bin directory, and it contains an assembly called `CustomServiceAuthorizationManager`. The CustomServiceAuthorizationManager project in the solution is configured to copy the assembly that it builds into that directory. So, evidently, the reference in the configuration of the service to the `DerivativesCalculator.MyServiceAuthorizationManager` type in the `CustomServiceAuthorizationManager` assembly could be a reference to a type in any assembly that the .NET common language runtime loader can locate.

7. Study the code of the class that is assigned as the value, in the configuration of the service, to the `ServiceAuthorizationManagerType` property of the `System.ServiceModel.Description.ServiceAuthorization` behavior. That code is in the MyServiceAuthorizationManager.cs file of the CustomServiceAuthorizationManager project. It is reproduced in Listing 7.13. The code defines a type that derives from `System.ServiceModel.ServiceAuthorizationManager` and overrides its virtual `CheckAccess()` method. Because the type has been assigned as the value of the `ServiceAuthorizationManagerType` property of the `System.ServiceModel.Description.ServiceAuthorization` behavior, its `CheckAccess()` override will be invoked whenever the service type with which the behavior is associated receives a request. The `CheckAccess()` method is passed a `System.ServiceModel.OperationContext` object that conveys information about the request. In particular, the code for the method can use the `System.ServiceModel.OperationContext` object to ascertain which operation will be executed in response to the request, and everything that is known about the user on whose behalf the request was sent. This expression yields the `Action` header of the message that identifies the operation to be executed:

```
operationContext.IncomingMessageHeaders.Action
```

This expression retrieves the information about the user:

```
operationContext.ServiceSecurityContext.AuthorizationContext.ClaimSets
```

That information is in the form of a collection of
`System.IdentityModel.Claim.ClaimSet` objects, and each of the objects in that
collection consists of an array of `System.IdentityModel.Claim.Claim` objects, each
of which represents some claim made about the user. Based on the operation that is
to be executed, and based on what is known about the user, the code for the
`CheckAccess()` method decides whether the user is authorized to have the operation
executed. If the user is authorized, the `CheckAccess()` method returns true, and
otherwise it returns false.

LISTING 7.13   ServiceAuthorizationManager Implementation

```
public class MyServiceAuthorizationManager: ServiceAuthorizationManager
{
    public override bool CheckAccess(OperationContext operationContext)
    {
        if (string.Compare(
                operationContext.IncomingMessageHeaders.Action,
                "CalculateDerivative",
                true) == 0)
        {

            ReadOnlyCollection<ClaimSet> claimSets =
operationContext.ServiceSecurityContext.AuthorizationContext.ClaimSets;

            ClaimSet claimSet = claimSets[0];
            foreach (Claim claim in claimSet)
            {
                if(string.Compare(
                  claim.ClaimType,
                  ClaimTypes.Name,
                  true)==0)
                {
                    if (string.Compare(
                    claim.Right,
"http://schemas.xmlsoap.org/ws/2005/05/identity/right/identity",
                    true) == 0)
                    {
                        if (string.Compare(
                        (string)claim.Resource,
                        "don",
                        true) == 0)
                        {
```

LISTING 7.13   Continued

```
                            return true;
                        }
                    }
                }
            }
        }
        return false;
    }
}
```

8. Choose Debug, Start Debugging from the Visual Studio 2005 menus.

9. When the output in the console of the Host application confirms that the service is ready, enter a keystroke into the console of the Client application. The Client application should retrieve the value of a derivative from the service. It does so by offering a username and password to the service that the service authenticates using its custom validation routine. After authenticating the credentials proferred by the client, the service authorizes access to the derivatives calculation routine based on information from the authenticated credentials.

10. Choose Debug, Stop Debugging from the Visual Studio 2005 menus to terminate the applications.

The authorization mechanism seen at work in the preceding steps is, in its simplicity and its power, a key innovation of the Windows Communication Foundation. It is the core of the Windows Communication Foundation's Extensible Security Infrastructure (XSI).

XSI is conceptually very simple indeed. Whatever a client offers to a service to authenticate its user is considered to be credentials, and credentials consist of a number of claims made about the user of the client application by the issuer of the credentials. In the process of authentication, whatever form the credentials might take, the Windows Communication Foundation does two primary things: It decides whether it trusts the issuer of the credentials, and, if it does, it converts the credentials into a list of claims. Those claims can then be examined by a type that derives from System.ServiceModel.ServiceAuthorizationManager. That type can determine whether to authorize access by comparing the claims extracted from the credentials to the access requirements.

This simple solution for authorization is extremely powerful for several reasons. First, the same solution works regardless of the type of credentials used and irrespective of how those credentials are authenticated. In the case illustrated above, the user was authenticated from credentials consisting of a username and password by a custom routine that decided it trusted the issuer of those credentials—which was simply the user of the client application—because the password matched the username. The claim yielded from those credentials was a claim about the user's username. If the authentication mechanism was reconfigured so that the client offered Kerberos credentials instead, the authentication process would involve confirming that those credentials were issued by a trusted domain controller. In that case, the claims yielded from the credentials would be claims about the user's Windows security identifiers. Yet, whatever type of credentials are offered and however those credentials are authenticated, authenticated credentials are transformed into a list of claims that can be evaluated during the authorization process. The significance of this feat that XSI accomplishes becomes even more impressive when it is considered that the Windows Communication Foundation supports an unlimited variety of types of credentials. Among the types of credentials for which the Windows Communication Foundation provides inherent support are Kerberos credentials, NTLM credentials, username tokens, Security Assertion Markup Language (SAML) tokens, Windows CardSpace credentials, and X.509 certificates. However, the `System.ServiceModel.Description.ClientCredentials` class can be extended to accommodate additional types of credentials.

A second reason that XSI's authorization system is so powerful is because the code that does the authorization for the service can be connected to the service through configuration. Whereas `System.Security.Permissions.PrincipalPermission` attributes get embedded in the code for the service so that widening or narrowing the access requirements might require changes to the service's code and recompilation, the `System.ServiceModel.ServiceAuthorizationManager` type that a service is to use for authorization can be identified through configuration. Moreover, that type does not have to be in the service's assembly or in any assembly referenced in the compilation of the service's assembly. The type can be in any assembly that the .NET common language runtime loader can find on behalf of the Windows Communication Foundation at runtime. Therefore, changes can be made to the authorization process without the code for the service having to be modified or even recompiled.

A third reason that XSI's authorization system is impressively powerful is that it does not restrict the definition of trusted issuers of credentials in any way. Whereas `System.Security.Permissions.PrincipalPermission` attributes are limited to evaluating access based on Kerberos or NTLM credentials, and the boundary of trusted issuers for those extends no further than the boundary of trust of the domain, XSI is not restricted to accepting credentials issued within the boundary of trust of the domain. It allows for more flexible definitions of trust. Therefore, it can provide the foundation for federated security, a prospect that will be explored further in the other chapters in this section.

Reversing the Changes to Windows

This chapter opened with some instructions for installing sample certificates, for configuring IIS and HTTP.SYS for SSL, and for configuring an identity for the server. Examples in some subsequent chapters will require those same steps to be executed, so one might choose not to reverse those steps right away. However, restoring Windows to its original security configuration after working through all of the examples in the book would be advisable.

Uninstalling the Certificates

Follow these steps to uninstall the certificates:

1. Open the Microsoft Management Console by choosing Run from the Windows Start menus and entering

   mmc

2. Choose File, Add/Remove Snap-In from the Microsoft Management Console menus.

3. Click Add on the Add/Remove Snap-In dialog that opens.

4. Choose Certificates from the list of available standalone snap-ins presented and click the Add button.

5. Select Computer Account on the Certificates snap-in dialog and click the Next button.

6. Accept the default on the Select Computer dialog and click the Finish button.

7. Click the Close button on the Add Standalone Snap-In dialog.

8. Click the OK button on the Add/Remove Snap-In dialog.

9. Expand the Certificates node that now appears in the left panel of the Microsoft Management Console.

10. Expand the Personal child-node of the Certificates node.

11. Select the Certificates child-node of the Personal node.

12. Select the FabrikamEnterprises certificate that should now have appeared in the right panel, and press the Delete key.

13. If a confirmation dialog appears, click Yes.

14. Select the Woodgrove certificate in the right panel, and press the Delete key.

15. If a confirmation dialog appears, click Yes.

16. In the left panel, Expand the Trusted Root Certification Authorities child node of the Certificates node.

17. Select the Certificates child-node of the Trusted Root Certification Authorities node.

18. Locate and select the Root Agency node in the right panel, and press the Delete key.

19. If a configuration dialog appears, click Yes.

20. Close the Microsoft Management Console.

Removing the SSL Configuration from IIS

To remove the SSL configuration from IIS do as follows:

1. Choose Control Panel, Administrative Tools, Internet Information Services (IIS) Manager from the Windows Start menus.

2. Expand the nodes of the tree control in the left pane until the node named Default Web Site becomes visible.

3. Right-click on that node and choose Properties from the context menus that appear.

4. Select the Directory Security tab.

5. Click the Server Certificate button.

6. Click Next on the first dialog of the Web Service Certificate Wizard.

7. Select Remove the Current Certificate and click Next.

8. Click Next on the Remove a Certificate dialog.

9. Click Finish to complete the Wizard.

10. Click OK on the Web Site Properties dialog.

11. Close the IIS Manager.

Removing the SSL Configuration from HTTP.SYS

Follow these instructions to remove the SSL configuration from HTTP.SYS. The easiest tool to use to configure HTTP.SYS is Steve Johnson's HTTP configuration utility, which has a graphical user interface. His utility is available at http://www.StevesTechSpot.com. Follow these instructions to use that tool to identify the certificate that HTTP.SYS is to use for SSL exchanges:

1. Start the HTTP Configuration Utility available from http://www.StevesTechSpot.com.

2. Choose the SSL Certs tab.

3. Select the entry for IP address 127.0.0.1 and port 8020 and click the Remove button.

4. Click OK on the main window of the HTTP Configuration Utility to close it.

Restoring the Identity of the Server

To restore the identity of the server, follow these steps:

1. Use Notepad to open the hosts file in the System32\drivers\etc subfolder of the system directory.

2. Delete the line

```
127.0.0.1 fabrikamenterprises
```

3. Save the hosts file.

4. Close the hosts file.

Summary

The basic tasks involved in securing communications are entity authentication, assuring the confidentiality, integrity and nonrepudiability of transmissions, potentially impersonating the source, and authorizing access. The Windows Communication Foundation can rely on SSL for entity authentication, confidentiality, integrity, and nonrepudiability—an option referred to as *transport security*. It can also accomplish those tasks using the mechanisms defined by the WS-Security specification. That option is referred to as *message security*. When the source of a transmission is authenticated as a Windows user, the Windows Communication Foundation can have a service impersonate that user, provided the client grants permission for the service to do so. For authorization, the Windows Communication Foundation supports the use of the `System.Security.Permissions.PrincipalPermission` attributes that were introduced in the very first version of the .NET Framework. However, the Windows Communication Foundation's alternative XSI mechanism for authentication, although simple to use, is much more flexible.

References

Kaler, Chris, ed. 2002. *Web Services Security (WS-Security)*. http://msdn.microsoft.com/library/default.asp?url=/library/en-us/dnglobspec/html/ws-security.asp. Accessed October 8, 2005.

Microsoft Press Computer Dictionary. 1997. S.v. "authorization." Redmond, WA: Microsoft.

Tulloch, Mitch. 2003a. *Microsoft Encyclopedia of Security*. S.v. "authentication." Redmond, WA: Microsoft.

_____. 2003b. *Microsoft Encyclopedia of Security*. S.v. "confidentiality." Redmond, WA: Microsoft.

_____. 2003c. *Microsoft Encyclopedia of Security*. S.v. "integrity." Redmond, WA: Microsoft.

_____. 2003d. *Microsoft Encyclopedia of Security*. S.v. "nonrepudiation." Redmond, WA: Microsoft.

_____. 2003e. *Microsoft Encyclopedia of Security*. S.v. "impersonation." Redmond, WA: Microsoft.

_____. 2003f. *Microsoft Encyclopedia of Security*. S.v. "Secure Sockets Layer (SSL)." Redmond, WA: Microsoft.

CHAPTER 8

Windows CardSpace, Information Cards, and the Identity Metasystem

Introduction

Identity and access control is a fundamental part of building connected systems. This chapter looks at Windows CardSpace, a client-side technology that authenticates users to web services and websites. By providing a simple and secure alternative to usernames and passwords via a consistent user interface that anyone can use, CardSpace is destined to become the preferred way to provide identities on the Internet and in federated applications.

The Role of Identity

There are people in their 50s in parts of the American midwest who have worked for cash all their lives, never left the United States, and never applied for, or been given, a Social Security number. When, at last, they come into contact with officialdom—a visit to a bank, a hospital, or a mortuary—there is a problem, a big problem: They don't exist!

This is the exception, however. For most people in the developed world, it is only for the first few weeks of one's life that one has no identity. Then a birth certificate is issued, one officially exists, and one has taken one's first, baby step toward the modern world and delightful encounters with taxmen, banks, and utility companies.

Identity is a key part of everyday life. It's required—implicitly or explicitly—in almost every interaction one has. If it's taken away, misused, or abused, the consequences are frequently dire. Yet it's only recently that most people have begun to care deeply about how their identity is used and by whom. This is, of course, a direct consequence of connected computer systems and the Internet in particular.

Prior to the advent of the Internet, it wasn't really necessary to worry too much about one's identity information—it was locked away, accessed only by people one trusted. Today, however, things are radically different. Googling one's name can be an entertaining exercise—until one stops to consider that a potential employer will probably do exactly the same thing. Does one *really* want to publish details of what one gets up to in one's (hitherto) private life—with *photos*—on one's blog? People have been fired directly as a consequence of what they've put on their blog; managers are checking what employees put in their Facebook entries. Even if one has second thoughts and deletes a post, it's probably cached in a search engine archive, on a company server, or in the Internet archive. After something is posted it is, effectively, permanently public.

These problems arise precisely because the Internet is so powerful. It's easy to take for granted just how much it enriches everyone's life. It would be extremely inconvenient if it were no longer possible to access a bank account, pay bills, or buy anything online. The Long Tail of the Internet (see the "References" section) has enabled a powerful new business model ("selling less of more"). Innovations such as web services, Ajax, and Really Simple Syndication (RSS)—and broadband access—have introduced a new wave of applications that some have felt the need to dub a part of Web 2.0 to distinguish them from their static, HTML-based predecessors. And who can imagine what the future will bring? Will new innovations such as pervasive, free wireless access lead to the Internet being even more deeply woven into the fabric of everyday life?

Despite all this convenience, power, and potential, many people are actually cutting down their usage of the web or are stopping altogether, particularly with respect to online purchasing (see recent studies by Gartner). It seems that just as the usefulness of the Internet is increasing, confidence in it is *decreasing*! The cause is problems with online identity.

Online identity theft, fraud, and privacy concerns in general are on the rise. Phishing and pharming are two of the biggest problems on the Internet today. And it's not script kiddies having malicious fun; organized crime is reaping the misbegotten rewards. What are phishing and pharming? From www.antiphishing.org:

> Phishing attacks use both social engineering and technical subterfuge to steal consumers' personal identity data and financial account credentials. Social-engineering schemes use "spoofed" emails to lead consumers to counterfeit websites designed to trick recipients into divulging financial data such as credit card numbers, account usernames, passwords, and Social Security numbers. Hijacking brand names of banks, e-retailers, and credit card companies, phishers often convince recipients to respond. Technical subterfuge schemes plant crimeware onto PCs to steal credentials directly, often using Trojan keylogger spyware. Pharming crimeware misdirects users to fraudulent sites or proxy servers, typically through DNS hijacking or poisoning.

Research by Harvard University and the University of California at Berkeley found that good phishing websites fooled 90% of the participants on their study (see the "References" section). They also found that people are vulnerable, regardless of how computer-literate they are. In fact, it's worse even than that: It's currently possible to make a phishing site totally indistinguishable from a genuine site. One might be the foremost computer security expert in the world and still be fooled!

The severity of the problem has led to the Federal Financial Institutions Examination Council (FFIEC) recommending (see the "References" section) that banks and financial institutions should introduce multifactor authentication for high-risk transactions *by the end of 2006*. Their definition of a high-risk transaction is one that either allows funds to be transferred to other parties or that permits access to customer information. After these features have been removed from a bank's website, there's not much left! FFIEC field examiners will be measuring compliance.

A multi-factor authentication protocol requires more than one method of establishing the user's identity. For example, instead of just entering a username and password one might also use a smartcard. Authentication methods are usually categorized as "something one knows" (for example, a PIN), "something one has" (for example, a card) or "something one is" (for example, a fingerprint). There are other categories but these are by far the most common. Combining different categories of authentication allows one to mitigate weaknesses in any particular method.

At the root of these problems is a flaw in the design of the Internet. There is no built-in system to handle identity, no "identity layer." The Internet was built without a way to know who and what one is connecting to.

Consequently, everyone offering an Internet service has had to provide a workaround and we've ended up with a patchwork of one-off identity solutions. Personal information becomes bound to these islands of identity. There is no way to move Amazon.com book-purchasing history or Netflix.com preferences to, say, Barnesandnoble.com. A hard-earned eBay reputation cannot be used with other sites.

One might argue that although portability of personal data has clear benefits for the user, the island rulers will want to keep the information to themselves. This is probably a correct assessment in the short term, but in the long term, the benefits to sharing will outweigh those of hoarding.

At each site, one is obliged to use a new username and password combination in an attempt to be secure. (Don't forget to look for an https: URL and a padlock symbol. It helps to know when one is securely connected to a phishing site!) One is trapped by the password paradox: The more secure the password, the more difficult it is to remember! Incidentally, the normal recommendation is to not write down passwords, but a strong password written on a Post-It is difficult to attack remotely. Anyone who gets hold of the Post-It can use the password, but this might be an acceptable risk. As always, security is about careful risk management rather than blindly following a set of rules.

The lack of a consistent way to handle identity has had dire effects in the enterprise arena, too. Whereas enterprises typically try to limit themselves to one central directory service, for example Active Directory, it is common to have hundreds of line-of-business applications, each with its own way of authenticating and authorizing the user (and storing the user data). Consequently, an astonishing amount of time and effort are spent on *single sign-on* (SSO): affording users the simple luxury of having to provide their user-name and password only once rather than for every single system they use.

Regulatory compliance also plays its part in the identity pain. A company's information technology systems directly affect how the company controls financial reporting. Thorough financial auditing requires identity management and correlation of what users did and when they did it.

The emergence of service-oriented architecture in the enterprise—this is a book about connected systems technology after all—begs the question: "If, by using web services protocols, potentially anyone or anything with an Internet connection can access my application, how do I identify users and control access?"

How can this situation be improved? How can the Internet be made safer? How can phishing be prevented? How can a user determine that a site is trustworthy? How can the user securely and reliably authenticate without having to remember usernames and pass-words? How can users' privacy be protected, allowing them to control how and when personal information is disclosed? And how can business users authenticate to connected systems?

What's needed is a simple, consistent, secure way of handling identity, one that is usable by everyone, that puts users in control of their identity and removes the walls between systems.

Microsoft Passport and Other Identity Solutions

The obvious solution is for everyone to agree on just one way of handling identity. Fat chance? The industry has a history of moving away from proprietary technologies such as X.400 and token ring toward standardized, simple, open protocols such as TCP/IP (Transmission Control Protocol/Internet Protocol), HTML (Hypertext Markup Language), and SMTP (Simple Mail Transfer Protocol). The WS-* protocols have broad industry support; why can't someone just devise an identity system for the Internet and have done with it?

Although this would be a great relief for everybody, it is important to realize that each of the technologies available today has its compelling use cases, its merits, and its faults. In short, it is an extremely difficult task to select a single identity technology that can satisfy all existing scenarios and, furthermore, anticipate every future scenario.

There are two classic approaches to complex computing problems like this. One is to have a very simple system with an extensibility mechanism so that it can be adapted to each problem domain (for example, SOAP [Simple Object Access Protocol]). The other approach is to add a level of indirection—an abstraction—that provides a consistent expe-rience and hides multiple underlying technology implementations (for example, TCP/IP over Ethernet and token ring).

But before deciding which fundamental approach to take—and each has its advocates—it would be wise to examine previous efforts at solving the identity problem. One can learn from their successes and their failures—both technological and sociological—in a range of contexts. From that analysis, one can identify the characteristics that an identity system must possess in order to be successful.

Although there have been a number of efforts in this area, the two that spring to mind are Microsoft's (much-maligned) Passport and Public Key Infrastructure (PKI). What prevented the Passport identity system from being successful? Well, that question's a bit harsh: At the time of writing there are more than 300 million Passport users and more than a billion logons per day (Passport has been rebranded Windows LiveId). So, it *is* a success as an identity provider for MSN. However, as an identity provider for the Internet, it didn't gain acceptance. For example, eBay used it for a while, but ultimately dropped it.

The problem is that Microsoft is the identity provider for every transaction. Regardless of whether one trusts the company—or believes it to be the very incarnation of evil—this arrangement is not always appropriate or desirable. When a user discloses his digital identity, only those parties whose presence is truly justified should be involved. One can formalize this requirement as follows:

> Digital identity systems must be designed so that the disclosure of identifying information is limited to parties having a necessary and justifiable place in a given identity relationship.

This is referred to as the law of justifiable parties and it is one of seven "laws of identity" published and refined online at www.identityblog.com. Identity experts across the industry have directly influenced the formation of these laws via the blogosphere, helping to produce an industry-wide consensus that the laws are sound, accurate, and complete. This set of laws is one of the best tools available for evaluating new and existing identity systems.

The rest of the laws will be examined in a moment, but first stop to consider the case of PKI. PKI, as many of those immersed in it will vouch, is a wonderful technology that is set to take the world by storm. Unfortunately, PKI's advocates have been saying this for a long time! There is no doubt that it is an extremely powerful and useful technology, but it can be costly, it can be complex to manage, and it is overkill in simple contexts.

Despite its flaws, PKI is the nearest thing to a universal identity system today. It is PKI that provides the security backbone of the Internet. SSL certificates allow secure transactions over the Web. If one were to build an Internet identity layer and were not averse to a bit of reuse, it might be prudent to take advantage of this existing infrastructure—provided it doesn't cause one to fall foul of the laws of identity (see the next section).

It is revealing that even a strong technology like PKI, with a choice of vendors and identity providers (namely the certificate authorities), has not been universally deployed. Without being overly pessimistic, there probably isn't a one-size-fits-all identity solution. For instance, it's not possible to have a central authority for peer-to-peer systems.

It is this point, combined with the reality of a large existing installed base of identity technologies, that helps decide whether the "simple and extensible" or the "level of indirection" approach is most likely to gain traction and succeed.

In short, the indirection method has the greater potential. What's more, it has the advantage of not precluding the simple/extensible approach. Nascent identity technologies can evolve under the all-encompassing wing of indirection. Perhaps, over time, one simple/extensible solution will become dominant—but it will still be able to interoperate with legacy technologies.

Therefore, what's required is an identity metasystem or system of systems that provides that level of indirection, encompasses existing identity technologies, and obeys the laws of identity.

The Laws of Identity

The Laws of Identity are an attempt to identify and formalize the characteristics required for any particular identity system to be successful. They have been derived by looking at many existing systems, examining their strengths and weaknesses, successes and failures.

Here are the seven laws of identity as stated at www.identityblog.com:

1. **User Control and Consent**—Technical identity systems must reveal information identifying a user only with the user's consent.

2. **Limited Disclosure for a Constrained Use**—The solution that discloses the least amount of identifying information and best limits its use is the most stable long-term solution.

3. **Justifiable Parties**—Digital identity systems must be designed so that the disclosure of identifying information is limited to parties having a necessary and justifiable place in a given identity relationship.

4. **Directed Identity**—A universal identity system must support both omnidirectional identifiers for use by public entities and unidirectional identifiers for use by private entities, thus facilitating discovery while preventing unnecessary release of correlation handles.

5. **Pluralism of Operators and Technologies**—A universal identity system must channel and enable the interworking of multiple identity technologies run by multiple identity providers.

6. **Human Integration**—The universal identity metasystem must define the human user to be a component of the distributed system integrated through unambiguous human-machine communication mechanisms offering protection against identity attacks.

7. **Consistent Experience Across Contexts**—The unifying identity metasystem must guarantee its users a simple, consistent experience while enabling separation of contexts through multiple operators and technologies.

The laws are reasonably self-explanatory, but I'll attempt to clarify or emphasize where appropriate. For a detailed explanation, take a look at the Laws of Identity whitepaper (see the "References" section).

The first law states that the user must be in control, be informed, and give consent before the system releases personal information. This law is at the heart of the oft-used term *user-centric* identity management (as opposed to domain-centric).

The second law and third laws are common sense: Identity information is sensitive, so reveal the minimal amount to the fewest parties necessary (this can apply to storage of identity data, too). For example, it is not a great idea to use Social Security numbers as student identifiers at U.S. universities. In fact, U.S. social security numbers can themselves disclose the year and state an individual was born in!

The fourth law says that an identity system should support both public and private identities. A website such as Amazon has a public identity. The more people who know that identity, the better. A private individual, on the other hand, might want to share her identity only in a point-to-point fashion, not broadcast it to the whole world. An example of getting this wrong is unencrypted radio frequency identification (RFID) tags in passports with a demonstrated reading range of 30 feet. Fortunately, the U.S. government is rethinking this bright idea.

The fifth law we've already covered. The sixth law emphasizes that the user is a fundamental part of the system, not an afterthought. A computer system that is in all other ways perfectly secure is fallible if it doesn't account for the user.

The seventh law derives from the two laws that precede it. If one accepts that the human factor is crucial and there will be a mixture of operators and technologies, there must be a unified experience across contexts for the system to be usable. Even with multiple operators, technologies, and scenarios, one must try to have a consistent user experience.

The Identity Metasystem

So an identity metasystem is required. What does it look like? Well, it has to obey the laws of identity, expose the strengths of its constituent identity systems, provide interoperability between them, and enable the creation of a consistent and straightforward user interface over all of them. To be successful, it should also be completely open and nonproprietary: It is "the Identity Metasystem" not "the Microsoft or IBM or whoever Identity Metasystem."

The Identity Metasystem is an abstraction of identity, a level of indirection above all the underlying identity systems. So, starting at the beginning, how does one abstract identity itself?

There are a myriad of different ways to identify someone or something and a multitude of different contexts. An identity can include physical appearance, beliefs, interests, likes and dislikes, reputation, and history. It might include such self-evident attributes as name, age, and address, but equally it could cover favorite author, eBay reputation, or purchasing history.

Key identifying characteristics can vary from one system and one context to another. To illustrate how one person's identity information varies by context, consider that bank cards are appropriate at an ATM or a shop, passports at immigration control, and a coffee card (Your 12th cup is free!—an anonymous form of identity information) in a particular coffee shop. Try interchanging these! The key point is that each of us has many identities (or "personas"), depending on the context—and the abstraction should handle this. As simple as life would be with just one identity, in reality one needs different identities from different providers, and identity management involves context switching and maintaining multiple personas for the different relationships one develops and sustains.

Despite all this potential complexity, identity can be abstracted very simply. The identity of a subject can be always be expressed via a set of *claims*. Or, more formally:

> *A digital identity is a set of claims made by one digital subject about itself or another digital subject.*

If one tests this abstraction against all the types of identity mentioned earlier—or anything else one can think of—one can see that it fits very well: "Peter Pan is over 21," "Bob's Kerberos domain and principal are MS\bob," "Bill's credit limit is $5,000," or "Alice knows symmetric key <x>."

Incidentally, does one believe these claims? Why? Why not? Would showing a passport or driver's license increase one's level of belief in someone's age? What if the Human Resources department at Microsoft were asserting that someone was a Microsoft employee?

The use of the word *claim* in the definition of digital identity is a subtle but deliberate choice. In a closed directory-based domain (for example, a Windows Server 2003 domain), one typically deals in security *assertions*, meaning "confident and forceful statements of fact or belief." This confidence is well-merited: It is a closed, administered system. However, if one wants to have an open and broad-reaching identity system, it helps to reflect the element of doubt inherent in dealing with parties on the Internet. How confident one is in the veracity of a set of claims depends on who the identity provider is, their reputation, and one's relationship to them. Oh, and also whether the claims have arrived intact, without being tampered with.

This claim model is extremely flexible—one can express a subject's identity in pretty much any way one chooses to. This enables one to tackle the concerns of the general public around privacy and anonymity. On the Internet—even more than elsewhere— one's natural desire is to remain anonymous until the moment one chooses to reveal one's identity, and even then one wants to disclose the minimum amount of information possible (for example, revealing that one is over 18 without revealing one's precise age). But how can an identity system preserve anonymity? Surely *anonymous identity* is an oxymoron?!

Well, anonymity is as much a part of identity as recognition. Many existing identity systems rely on unique identifiers (for example, security identifiers, or SIDs, in Windows). This is a critically useful constraint (to say the least), but not necessarily a constraint one always wants to apply. This is a flaw in uniform resource locator (URL)–based systems—by their very definition, they resolve to a location.

The key idea is that identifying a subject needn't have anything to do with knowing who that subject is in the real world. One can use a pseudo-identity to represent a user, not a real identity, and associate that with zero or more claims. The fact that a certain user has a consistent pseudo-identity over time allows one to learn about that user without having any idea of who he really is.

Summarizing, a subject's digital identity is going to be represented by using a set of claims supplied in a secure and verifiable way by an identity provider. The claims are packaged in a security token that can travel over process and machine boundaries to wherever they are required.

There are three roles in the metasystem:

▶ **Subjects**—Entities about whom claims are made

▶ **Identity Providers** (IPs or IdPs)—Issue digital identities

▶ **Relying Parties** (RPs)—Require digital identities

To give but one example to illustrate the roles, when one buys a book online one is the subject, one's bank is the identity provider giving one's credit card details, and the online bookstore is the relying party consuming those details, enabling one to buy a copy of *The Idiot's Guide to PKI*.

An identity is packaged in a security token containing claims made by an identity provider. In the preceding example, the online bookstore might specify that it requires a token that contains one's name, address, and credit-card claims. One can then ask one's bank to provide the required security token with proof that it was issued by them plus a way to prove one is the rightful possessor of the token. When one gives this token to the online bookstore, it verifies that it came from one's bank and that one is the rightful purchaser, and then it extracts the claims and completes the transaction.

Notice here that the user is at the center. Potentially the token could have gone directly from bank to bookstore—from Identity Provider to Relying Party—but instead it goes via the user so that the user has control and consent over the release of identity information. There might be other communications between the Identity Provider and the Relying Party, but the flow of identity information should be under the control of the user, as per the first law of identity. In essence, what one is trying to do is to get a security token containing claims from the Identity Provider to the Relying Party under the consent and control of the user. The protocol at its simplest is

1. The user is asked for his identity.

2. The user selects an Identity Provider.

3. The Identity Provider gives the user a security token.

4. The user passes the token to the requestor.

In traditional models, the Identity Provider and Relying Party are confined to the same domain, but this model is more generic. Here is the Identity Metasystem protocol in more detail (Figure 8.1).

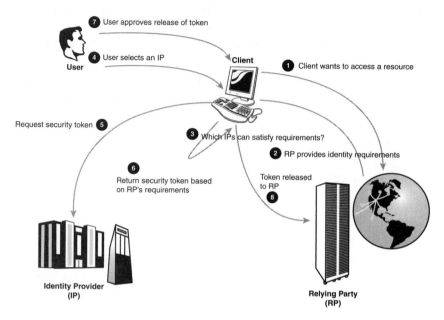

FIGURE 8.1   Identity Metasystem architecture.

Note that everything is abstract here—nothing has been said yet about how one might implement this using specific technologies. The token can be in any format. There is no dependency on the client, so provided that the Relying Party can understand the token (and ask for it) and the Identity Provider can supply the token (and say that it can), we're OK.

Step 5 deserves further explanation. When the user requests a security token, he has to authenticate to the Identity Provider in some way. The Identity Provider does not simply give a token to anyone who asks (imagine one's bank is being asked for one's account checking balance, for example). The client has to have the right to ask for the token. This step of providing a set of credentials to an Identity Provider to get another set of credentials for a relying party can be confusing, but it is straightforward to understand when one considers a few examples. It's what happens when one applies for a passport: one has to provide one's birth certificate or other documents to prove one's nationality; one set of credentials (birth certificate) is exchanged for another (passport).

Drilling a little deeper into the model, there are a number of requirements for the system to work. Firstly, the Relying Party needs a way to specify the claims it requires in a way that everyone understands: "I need first name, surname, and address claims." Likewise, the Identity Provider needs a way to specify the claims it is able to supply.

Secondly, the Relying Party and potential Identity Providers might use completely different identity systems with different token formats—this is a metasystem, remember! So, both types of entity need a technology-agnostic way to express the kinds of security tokens that they understand: "I need a SAML (Security Assertion Markup Language) 1.1 or Kerberos token."

Furthermore, it would be useful if the Identity Provider and Relying Party could negotiate the types of claims they can use: "I can provide tokens of these types: X, Y"; " I can receive tokens of these types: Y, Z"—"Okay, let's use token type Y because we both understand that."

This is a bit like people communicating via languages and raises an interesting idea. If one person speaks English and French, and another speaks only Japanese, Swedish, and German, they can still communicate provided they can find someone who can understand, say, French and Japanese. Provided they can trust that person to translate accurately, they can interoperate perfectly well.

Within the context of an identity system, one might have to translate not only the type of token but also the claims themselves. For example, an Identity Provider might provide a "date of birth" claim, but the Relying Party might require an "older than 21" claim (information minimalization). Or a company might provide an "is at job level 1000" claim, but the Relying Party needs an "is a manager" or "is an executive" claim. This can all be handled by the Identity Provider.

What's needed is a kind of token translation service: a trusted service that can receive security tokens of one type and convert them to security tokens of another type. One can refer to it as a security token service or STS.

Meanwhile, at the center of everything lies the user. Regardless of the complex flow of claims, tokens, and token types between the different systems within the metasystem, the user should have a simple, consistent, and comprehensible experience. One must be able to control the release of one's identity information. Every time a user provides their identity online he should be able to use the same, familiar process.

These requirements can be summarized as follows:

- ▶ **Negotiation**—A way to enable the relying party, subject, and Identity Provider to negotiate technical policy requirements

- ▶ **Encapsulation**—A technology-agnostic way to exchange policies and claims between the Identity Provider and the Relying Party

- ▶ **Claims transformation**—A trusted way to change one set of claims into another, regardless of token format

- ▶ **User experience**—A consistent user interface across multiple systems and technologies

Notice that up to this point, everything has been abstract. The Identity Metasystem is an abstract concept, but now it's time to make some implementation choices.

The obvious choice for a set of open protocols that satisfy all the above requirements is some subset of the web services protocols (http://msdn.microsoft.com/webservices/). In particular, WS-Security, WS-SecurityPolicy, WS-MetadataExchange (WS-MEX), and WS-Trust. The WS-* protocols have wide support across the industry and, following the publication of the Microsoft Open Specification Promise (OSP; see the "References" section), they are available for anyone to utilize.

Some people ask about the Liberty identity protocols as an alternative to WS-*. There is a general convergence in the industry towards the WS-* protocols for web services. Unfortunately, these protocols simply were not available when Liberty developed its identity protocols. Liberty is developing their work to embrace the WS protocol suite and it is very much in the interests of everyone to make sure the WS protocols work across implementations. The question is becoming moot.

The interactions between the user, Relying Party, and Identity Provider can be implemented as a set of SOAP messages. WS-Security defines how to secure those messages and attach security tokens. WS-SecurityPolicy describes the security token and claim requirements of the Relying Party and capabilities of the Identity Provider. WS-MetadataExchange allows the querying and retrieval of these service policies.

WS-Trust is what breathes life into the Identity Provider. It extends WS-Security, facilitating trust between parties by propagating security tokens and performing claims transformation. The manifestation of WS-Trust is the Security Token Service, a web service that issues security tokens. In other words, to accept requests for security tokens, perform claim transformation, and issue security tokens, an Identity Provider needs to build a security token service implementing WS-Trust.

The following diagram (Figure 8.2) shows how the specifications relate to each role in the metasystem. The subject is typically the user but could be any entity.

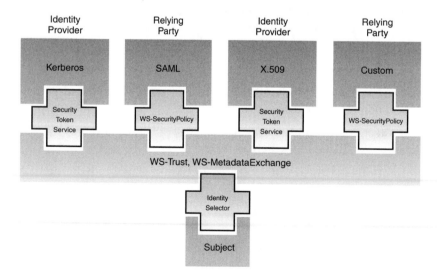

FIGURE 8.2   Identity Metasystem architecture implemented with web services protocols.

There can be many relying parties, each with different token and claim requirements expressed using WS-SecurityPolicy. To access one of these relying parties, one can discover the corresponding policy using WS-MEX. Once one knows the requirements, one can choose an appropriate Identity Provider.

For example, a relying party might require SAML 1.1 tokens containing the user's name and Social Security number from "any" Identity Provider. One selects one of the Identity Providers that is able to provide this kind of token.

The *Identity Selector* part of the metasystem has not been mentioned up until now. This is the consistent user experience part of the metasystem, interacting with the user, matching a Relying Party's requirements to Identity Providers' capabilities, making all the necessary web service calls, and allowing the user to be in complete control of how his identity is exposed and consumed. Windows CardSpace is an identity selector.

Information Cards and CardSpace

The Identity Selector is invoked by a client application when a Relying Party requires the user's identity. The Identity Selector determines the Relying Party's requirements and helps the user choose an appropriate Identity Provider. It sends that Identity Provider a request for a security token with the user's credentials. When the response comes back, the Identity Selector asks the user to confirm the release of the token. It then passes the token back to the client application to be sent to the Relying Party.

So, what does the user interface (UI) of an Identity Selector look like? At a minimum, it has to help the user choose an identity provider that can meet the Relying Party's requirements, and prompt the user for release of the token. So, each Identity Provider has to be represented in the user interface in some way and those that can meet the RP requirements should be distinguished from those that can't. Hence the Identity Selector must have a way of knowing the capabilities of the IP.

One could just display the IPs in a couple of list boxes (matching and nonmatching), but it would be good for this to be as intuitive and user friendly as possible (law 6). Turning to the physical world for ideas, when asked for one's identity, how does one provide it? By using business cards, credit cards, passports, driving licenses, identity cards, and employee (smart) cards. The blindingly obvious way to represent Identity Providers (and thus the user's identities) is by using a card-based UI. Rather than a list box of names, have a bunch of images of cards for the user to choose from. Each card has a name and an image to make it clear which Identity Provider it represents and the ones that don't meet the RP's requirements can be grayed out. To know which IPs can meet those requirements, include some *metadata* (data about data) with the card that describes which claims it can provide, which token formats, where the security token service is, and so on. Now choose a file format for the card: Because everything has to be completely open (law 5), the obvious way to represent the card is via an XML document containing the metadata and an image of the card, signed by the identity provider who supplies the card to the user using XMLDSIG (XML digital signature). One can publish the schema, give it a .crd extension, and call it an Information Card.

8

And that, essentially, is it: an *Information Card* is an XML document containing identity metadata created and signed by an Identity Provider (Figure 8.3). It represents the relationship between the user and the Identity Provider. The card does not contain data about the user; it contains data about the Identity Provider: which identity claims the IP can provide ("SSN" not "123-45-6789") and how to get a security token containing those claims. Signed, encrypted security tokens are what carry the user's identity back to the client and on to the Relying Party. The only time a card travels anywhere is when the IP gives it to the user and the user imports it into the Identity Selector.

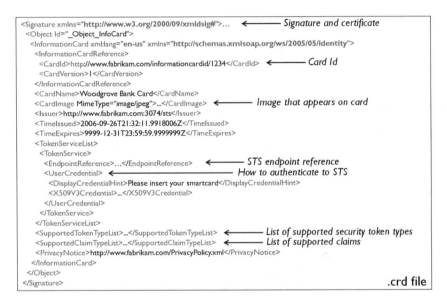

FIGURE 8.3   An Information Card (simplified for clarity).

Everything about the Identity Metasystem is designed to be completely inclusive, open, and nonproprietary. Anyone can build an Identity Selector—using whichever platform or technology he prefers—and many people are building them (for example, OSIS, Higgins and Bandit; see the "References" section). There will be identity selectors for Linux, Macintosh, and other operating systems, each taking advantage of native features and APIs. Indeed, an important measure of success for the metasystem will be its capability to build an end-to-end solution (Relying Party, client, Identity Selector, and Identity Provider) without using any Microsoft software whatsoever.

Windows CardSpace is an Identity Selector built by Microsoft for Windows operating systems, namely Windows Vista, Windows XP SP2, and Windows Server 2003 SP1. Version 1.0 ships as a part of .NET Framework 3.0 (Figure 8.4).

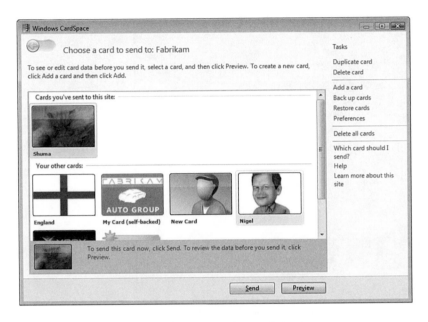

FIGURE 8.4   The UI of a card-based Identity Selector.

While it was in development, the codename for CardSpace was *InfoCard*. Many people became attached to the name, but it had one weakness (apart from being trademarked by someone else!). The term *InfoCard* was ambiguous: It could mean either the identity selector or the card. CardSpace has the virtue of being unambiguous. Windows CardSpace is an Identity Selector for Windows; an *Information Card* is the bundle of metadata (about an identity provider) that users import into whichever Identity Selector they happen to be using.

Managing Information Cards

CardSpace can be launched by a client application via the GetToken() or GetBrowserToken() functions or by the user via a Control Panel applet (Figure 8.5). In Category View, it can be found under User Accounts.

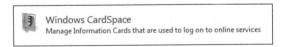

Windows CardSpace
Manage Information Cards that are used to log on to online services

FIGURE 8.5   The CardSpace icon as it appears in the Control Panel's Category view.

When this is launched, after an initial splash screen the Select a Card to Preview dialog appears (Figure 8.6).

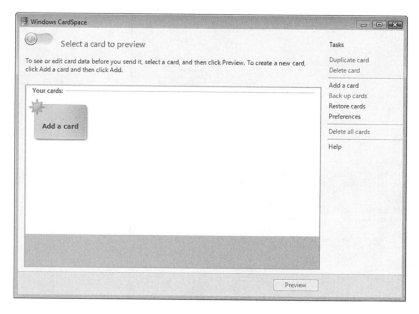

FIGURE 8.6   The initial card preview dialog.

This window and the other CardSpace windows are running on a randomly created, private desktop, in much the same way that the Windows Security dialog runs in a separate desktop (that is, the UI that appears when one uses the secure attention sequence, Ctrl+Alt+Del). This is a desktop in the Windows security architecture sense, not the normal "created by Explorer" sense.

It appears as if the normal desktop is grayed out and disabled in the background. However, it is in fact a bitmap of the screen captured when CardSpace was launched (with a mask applied). No matter how long one waits, the clock in the background will not update until one exits the UI! By running on a separate Windows desktop and limiting access rights, the bar is raised for the bad guys, making it more difficult to emulate the user experience, especially from within a browser.

CardSpace consists of two processes: icardagt.exe, running as the logged-on user, and infocard.exe, running as SYSTEM. The icardagt.exe process renders the CardSpace user interface and the infocard.exe process is the main CardSpace engine; they communicate with each another using a randomly created remote procedure call (RPC) channel. If Task Manager is visible when CardSpace is launched, these processes should be listed before the background is "frozen."

Clicking on Add a Card *gives* the following dialog (Figure 8.7).

There are two types of card: Personal Cards and Managed Cards. *Personal Cards*—also known as *Self-Issued Cards*—are created and maintained by the user in the CardSpace UI. In other words, the *user* is the Identity Provider. This addresses a very common scenario: When one first registers at many websites, one creates a set of credentials: a username and a password. Likewise, CardSpace gives one the ability to log on and register using a self-asserted identity.

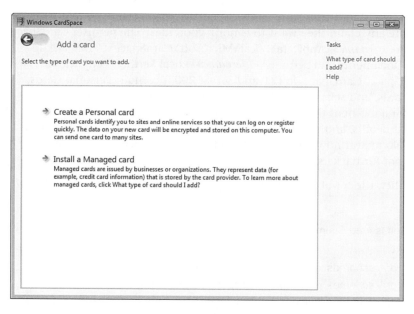

FIGURE 8.7   Add a Personal Card or install a Managed Card.

Managed Cards—also referred to as *Provider Cards*—are supplied to the user as a signed .CRD file by a third-party Identity Provider. This might be an employer, a financial institution, a government, or any other appropriate body. Cards are installed into CardSpace using the Install a Managed Card button or by simply double-clicking on the .crd file. How the .crd file gets from the IP to the user is left to the discretion of the IP (for v1.0, at least). It could be by email or by web download or a CD in the mail.

After installation, Managed Cards are stored locally in the user's CardSpace store but the personally identifiable information associated with a card is *not* stored locally. The data is owned, stored, and managed by the Identity Provider who supplied the card. With Self-Issued Cards, both the card *and* the personal identity information associated with the card are stored in the user's CardSpace store.

Semantically, Personal Cards and Managed Cards are identical. They both contain metadata that describes where and how the subject's identity data can be retrieved. It's just that for one type of card, that identity data is created by the user and stored locally; for the other type of card, the data is created and stored by a third party. In neither case does the card itself contain any personally identifiable information (PII) (for example, "Bill Gates," "One Microsoft Way," "Male," or "+1 425 555 8080"). Cards contain metadata about where and how to obtain security tokens. It is the security tokens that contain the PII and are protected accordingly.

Although Personal and Managed Cards are conceptually identical, the difference in where the PII is stored has an important consequence for the implementation details. In principle, a user could provide any of the claims that a third-party Identity Provider might offer, they would just be self-asserted claims rather than IP-asserted claims. In practice, allowing users to create any claim they want to is not a good idea. The per-user CardSpace stores *<Drive>*:\Users*<username>*\AppData\Local\Microsoft\CardSpace\CardSpace.db (Vista) and *<Drive>*:\Documents and Settings*<username>*\Local Settings\Application Data\Microsoft\CardSpace\CardSpace.db (XP and Server 2003) contain Personal Cards, imported Managed Cards, and self-asserted PII. Of course the store is encrypted and ACL'd, but imagine for a moment that a user decides to store their Social Security number, bank account details, and pension information as self-asserted claims—it's jolly convenient after all! No matter how hard it might be to break the security, the user has just created a honey pot for hackers.

To avoid this eventuality, the set of self-issued claims is useful but uninteresting and *fixed* (see Table 8.1).

TABLE 8.1   List of Self-Issued Claims and Their URIs

Claim	URI
Given Name	http://schemas.xmlsoap.org/ws/2005/05/identity/claims/givenname
Surname	http://schemas.xmlsoap.org/ws/2005/05/identity/claims/surname
Email Address	http://schemas.xmlsoap.org/ws/2005/05/identity/claims/emailaddress
Street Address	http://schemas.xmlsoap.org/ws/2005/05/identity/claims/streetaddress
Locality	http://schemas.xmlsoap.org/ws/2005/05/identity/claims/locality
State/Province	http://schemas.xmlsoap.org/ws/2005/05/identity/claims/stateorprovince
Postal Code	http://schemas.xmlsoap.org/ws/2005/05/identity/claims/postalcode
Country	http://schemas.xmlsoap.org/ws/2005/05/identity/claims/country
Home Phone	http://schemas.xmlsoap.org/ws/2005/05/identity/claims/homephone
Other Phone	http://schemas.xmlsoap.org/ws/2005/05/identity/claims/otherphone
Mobile Phone	http://schemas.xmlsoap.org/ws/2005/05/identity/claims/mobilephone
Date of Birth	http://schemas.xmlsoap.org/ws/2005/05/identity/claims/dateofbirth
Gender	http://schemas.xmlsoap.org/ws/2005/05/identity/claims/gender
Web page	http://schemas.xmlsoap.org/ws/2005/05/identity/claims/webpage
PPID	http://schemas.xmlsoap.org/ws/2005/05/identity/claims/privatepersonalidentifier

None of the self-issued claims are particularly sensitive. It would be far easier for a bad guy to find this information in a phone book or a search engine than by trying to hack a user's machine! The set of claims associated with a Managed Card is not limited in any way. It is for the Identity Provider to decide which claims are made available and how the data is stored and accessed.

Users can create as many Personal Cards as they want to. Typically, different cards will be used for different contexts. For example, the identities one might use at Xbox Live, Amazon.com, and commenting on online forums are going to be different. As reputation services begin to take advantage of Information Cards, users will choose carefully which cards they use to build a positive reputation.

Users can use many different cards at the same RP or one card at many RPs. The only things that restrict card usage are the policies of the RP and IP (and one's own good sense).

Each claim has a URI to uniquely identify it. This is used in security policy, security tokens, and token-processing code. Note that the chosen namespace is not affiliated to any particular company (such as Microsoft) because many identity providers—including the self-asserted IPs of other Identity Selectors—will want to reuse these standard claims while adding other claims relevant to their domain (for example, healthcare or government).

Go ahead and create some Personal Cards (Figure 8.8) and experiment by exporting and importing them. Open the exported .crds file in Notepad to see what it looks like (it's encrypted). In version 1.0 of CardSpace, exporting and importing like this is the only way to roam cards from one machine to another. Later versions will have more sophisticated provisioning and roaming capabilities. The .crds file format is documented in the CardSpace Technical Reference on MSDN (see the "References" section) enabling compatibility with other identity selectors. It is perhaps worth pointing out that after a Managed Card has been imported into CardSpace, the XML digital signature in the .crd file is no longer meaningful and is discarded. The .crds file has its own signature.

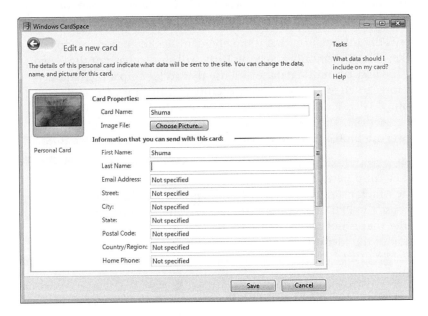

FIGURE 8.8   The CardSpace Edit a New Card dialog.

The user decides what values to assign the self-asserted claims. However, there is one claim in the table that doesn't appear when one types claim values in the UI: the

PrivatePersonalIdentifier (PPID) claim. This is not entered by the user, it is generated by CardSpace.

CardSpace and the Identity Metasystem can be used to provide any claim whatsoever. That said, which claim or claims should be used to uniquely identify a user? When someone registers with eBay or Amazon, how does the site know that it is the same person returning to the site each time? How can it customize pages for individual users, provide a purchasing history, and so on? Well, until the advent of Information Cards at least, it is the username that uniquely identifies a user, and it is the password that authenticates that user. Knowledge of a {username, password} pair "proves" that someone is the rightful user (probably).

With CardSpace, it's slightly different. The Relying Party asks for and receives a security token signed by an Identity Provider. The user is uniquely identified by a combination of who the IP is (by means of the public key or certificate used to sign the token) and whichever claim that IP chooses to uniquely identify its users (a "user Id"). For example, the IP and user Id could be {government, SSN} or {employer, employee number}. This means the Relying Party has to know which claim the IP uses as a unique identifier for the user. The important point is that a Relying Party knows who the user is by knowing who the IP is and the user Id claim used by that IP.

Consider the case where the user is the Identity Provider, using self-issued claims and tokens. To be consistent with third party Identity Providers, a public key and a user Id claim is required. A 2048-bit RSA key pair is generated by the CardSpace system for signing tokens. The user Id claim is the PPID, also generated by CardSpace.

Thus for self-issued cards the information that uniquely identifies the user to relying parties is {RSA public key, PPID}. Typically a Relying Party will store a hash of these two values in a column of the user account database and use that to look up a user and his account history. Therefore, a Relying Party can consistently identify a user, regardless of the values of other claims. This, actually, is the true value of self-issued cards: an asymmetric key-based user credential. The other self-issued claims are useful, but claims from an IP other than the user are probably more valuable since they are asserted by a third party.

So, which claim should a third-party IP use to uniquely identify the user and how does the Relying Party know which claim is being used? The simplest solution is for an Identity Provider to re–use the PPID claim, particularly if it wants to adhere to law 2 (that is, choosing an identifier that is not overloaded with another meaning). However, it is entirely at the discretion of the Identity Provider which claim set it provides just as it is at the discretion of the Relying Party which claim set is demanded. The Identity Metasystem is as inclusive as possible.

On the other hand, a Relying Party might not need to uniquely identify a user at all. Maybe it just needs to know the user is over 21. In which case it can ask for an Age claim or perhaps an Over 21 claim, specify the IP as a government-run STS, and be done with it.

Information Cards contain metadata describing which claims can be retrieved from an IP, where they are, and how to get them. For self-issued cards, the security token service is local and the data is stored on a local storage device. For Managed Cards, the security token service is hosted by the Identity Provider. The card and STS model can also be extended in other ways.

Future versions of CardSpace will support security token services on devices such as USB keys, smart cards, and mobile phones. These portable security token services (pSTSes) will provide a robust solution for roaming scenarios. Another potential implementation is to have "Information Cards in the cloud" where one's cards are stored online—either by oneself or a third party—instead of on a hard disk. However, that begs the question, "How does one authenticate to the cloud?" That one is left as an exercise to the reader!

The portable STS solution is useful because it offers true portability plus greater security when using an untrusted client machine. Suppose that someone leaves on vacation just in the midst of a bidding war for a pair of Elvis' pants on eBay. While travelling, the person decides to go into an Internet café and use one of the machines to place a new bid. The problem is that one knows nothing about the machine. It could have root kits and keyboard loggers installed and be lying in wait for someone fool enough to use Outlook Web Access, eBay, or whatever and have their credentials stolen. Therefore, anyone would be understandably reluctant to import their information cards onto this potentially compromised machine. With a portable STS, one doesn't need to. Whether it's via a USB port, or a smart card reader, or a wireless connection, one can use CardSpace to approve the release of a signed, encrypted security token from the pSTS. It is *this* that travels through the compromised Internet café machine (or via some other channel) and onward to the Relying Party. The malware on the machine is left impotent.

Architecture, Protocols, and Security

CardSpace consists of three main parts (Figure 8.9):

- ▶ A service that does the core work
- ▶ A user interface component that handles interaction with the user
- ▶ A data store containing cards and the self-issued PII

The central part of the system is the infocard.exe service, which handles all token and management requests and runs as Local System. On startup it creates the UI Agent process, icardagt.exe, and this runs as the user on a private desktop, communicating with infocard.exe via a randomly created RPC channel. Running the UI in a separate desktop helps protect personal identity information, mitigating phishing and shatter attacks and preventing disclosure of personal information. The UI process runs with an augmented access token (special logon SID) so that only that process can access the desktop. The UI is minimally functional to reduce the attack surface. For example, it does not render rich text and there is strict boundary-checking to prevent overflows. Likewise, it is not skin-able: It is not intended to be a general purpose programming surface.

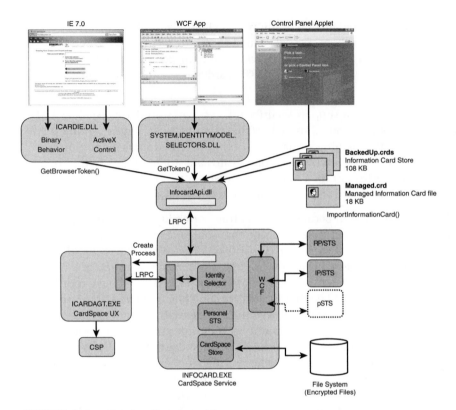

FIGURE 8.9   The CardSpace architecture.

The store, cardspace.db, is ACL'd for Local System access only, and stored in the user's profile. If the store is not present, such as when the user runs CardSpace for the first time, it is created automatically. CardSpace allows only that user account to have access. If several people share the same user profile, individual information cards can be PIN-protected.

Data in the store is encrypted. The store and individual cards can be backed up and moved onto other machines using the UI. When the user exports cards he or she is prompted for a password, which CardSpace uses to protect the exported .crds file.

One component, infocardapi.dll, handles all entry points into the CardSpace system and is loaded into the client application process. It intentionally has a very limited API. There are only four interesting methods (the others are Windows Communication Foundation [WCF] callbacks): ImportInformationCard(), GetToken(), GetBrowserToken(), and ManageCardSpace(). *None* of these functions outputs any information without the user's consent. CardSpace is designed to be an *interactive* rather than a *programmatic* system. It will not release PII without explicit user approval.

When a client application uses WCF to access a service endpoint (Figure 8.10), WCF will retrieve the relevant policy (steps 1 and 2). CardSpace is just one way of providing credentials to a WCF service. A service specifies which type of credentials the client should use via the client credential type. There are several options depending on which binding one uses. When using message security, the options are None (anonymous), Windows, Username, Certificate, and IssuedToken.

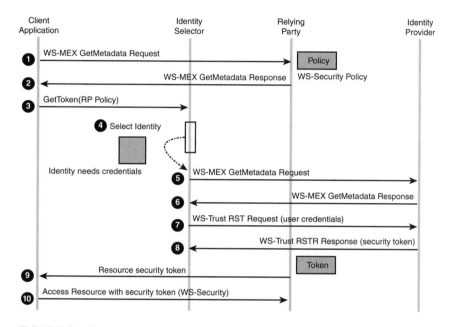

FIGURE 8.10   Swim lanes for a Windows Communication Foundation client.

The IssuedToken policy assertion indicates that user credentials should be in the form of a signed token issued by a security token service. WCF will use CardSpace to get this security token if the transport is HTTP, HTTPS, or net.tcp and one of the following is true:

- ▶ <Issuer> is empty or absent

- ▶ <Issuer> is set to the self-issued token URI

- ▶ <Issuer> points to an IP whose policy has the
  <RequireFederatedIdentityProvisioning> assertion

If this is the case, WCF will launch CardSpace automatically via the GetToken() method, passing in the RP's policy (step 3). After CardSpace has interacted with the user and an STS to get a signed, encrypted security token, GetToken() returns the token for WCF to send to the Relying Party web service (step 9). Note that developers don't call GetToken() directly, it is done for them by WCF.

GetToken() causes CardSpace and the CardSpace UI to be launched but before selecting a card and authenticating to a particular Relying Party, one first has to agree to release information to it. CardSpace checks the card usage history (aka the *CardSpace ledger*) to see whether the user has agreed to provide personal information to the site. If not, a special dialog appears—an "introduction ceremony"—providing information from the

Relying Party's SSL or Extended Validation (EV) SSL certificate (Figures 8.11 and 8.12). The dialog also appears when the user imports a managed card (Figure 8.13).

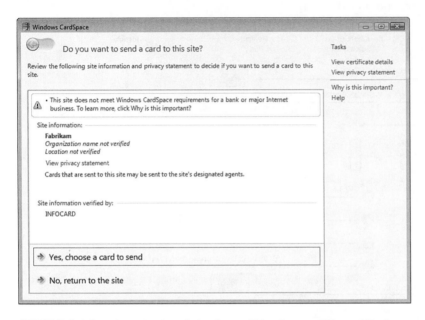

FIGURE 8.11   Introduction dialog for an RP using an SSL certificate.

This Introduction dialog is a vital cog in the defense against phishing attacks. CardSpace will *only* work with Relying Parties and Identity Providers that identify themselves with an SSL certificate, and one can only import a card or choose a card if one first makes an explicit choice to trust the associated organization and its certificate via the Introduction dialog.

If the certificate is a simple SSL certificate, the Introduction dialog will display the text `This site does not meet Windows CardSpace requirements for a bank or major Internet business...` and it will say that the organization name and the location are unverified (Figure 8.11). If, on the other hand, the certificate is an Extended Validation certificate, no such apocalyptic message appears (Figure 8.12). In the future, there will be additional information to help the user's decision such as data from reputation services.

How does this help against phishing? Put simply, a certificate authority (CA) will issue an EV certificate to an organization only after it (the organization) has passed a rigorous, industry-defined validation process. Therefore, if one knows the website or service one is using is backed by an EV certificate, one can be confident that the site is genuine (incompetent CAs and software bugs notwithstanding). As the Introduction dialog indicates, banks and major Internet businesses will use extended validation certificates.

Internet Explorer 7 and contemporary browsers recognize EV certificates and make the address bar glow green as feedback to the user. CardSpace goes one step further by making the decision to send a card explicit and keeping track of which certificates the user has accepted.

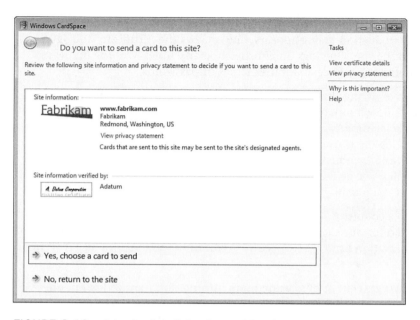

FIGURE 8.12   Introduction dialog for an RP using an EV SSL certificate.

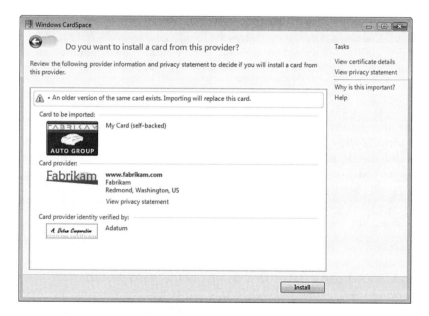

FIGURE 8.13   Introduction dialog when importing an updated version of an information card signed with the Identity Provider's EV certificate.

Making this more concrete, suppose that a bank uses an EV certificate. When logging on to the bank's website, the login page is secured using the EV certificate (via SSL) and the address bar glows a reassuring green. One can choose to log on using an Information Card and when the Introduction dialog appears, one reviews the certificate, and agrees to release information to the site. One logs on effortlessly many times over the following weeks without taxing the brain once about usernames or passwords.

One day an email arrives saying that one's bank account information might have been compromised and to follow a link to the bank website to check the account. Of course, it's a phishing email. A legitimate email should never have a link to the website in it but simply ask the user to log on as usual (whilst reminding them not to click on any links in emails). However, in haste, one makes a mistake—as happens to most of us from time to time—and with one click one arrives at a web page that looks exactly like the bank website's login page. It is a phish!

At this point there are a couple of ways for the bad guys to get hold of the user's credentials: Either one is asked for one's username and password, or it's an HTTPS page and one is asked for one's Information Card (CardSpace v1.0 will not function with an HTTP web page).

In the first case, following weeks of bliss using one's Information Card to log on, one doesn't want to use username and password. If this site says information cards aren't available, one's suspicions should start to grow. Furthermore, without an EV certificate, the browser address bar will no longer be green.

> **TIP**
>
> Extended Validation (EV) certificates should be available as of February 2007. Internet Explorer 7.0's recognition of EV certificates and modification of the appearance of the address bar will be enabled in the same time frame.

If the bad guys support Information Cards (and face it, they're usually technically advanced), they must identify their site with an SSL certificate. Because one hasn't been to that site before, when one tries to use a card, the Introduction dialog will appear. One is alerted that something is phishy on three counts: The dialog has appeared even when one has already agreed to release identity information to the bank; the information from the certificate won't match the bank's details or logos; and unless it's an EV certificate, there will be the This site does not meet Windows CardSpace requirements... message.

Suppose that one is having a real off day and releases one's credentials to the site. In the Choose a Card to Send dialog, none of the cards will have been used at the site before, but one goes ahead and chooses one anyway. One doesn't bother to look at the site history of the card showing the date and time when one last visited the genuine site. And so a signed, encrypted security token is sent to the bad guys who decrypt the contents using their SSL certificate. However, it's still not much use to them because although they have access to the claim values if they try to repurpose the token to log on to the bank website proper (backed by a different certificate), they'll break the signature.

Furthermore, if the card selected is backed by a smart card or other device—and it should if it's a bank card, according to the FFIEC—the bad guy has to steal that, too. Therefore, even if the bad guy manages to persuade a user to back up all their information cards to a .crds file and email it to him (with the PIN) or he steals a laptop, he *still* won't be able to gain access to one's bank account.

This touches on the topic of card revocation. If a machine is stolen, Vista's BitLocker feature will make it more difficult for the bad guy to gain access to data but one should still revoke one's cards, in much the same way that cards are revoked in the physical world when they are lost. For Managed Cards, one simply contacts the IP. It will then block all access using the stolen card's card ID and issue a replacement .crd file. For Personal Cards, the thief will have both the card and the IP. In that case, the RP will need to be contacted to remove the stolen card's public key and PPID from the associated user account.

When contacting the RP or IP to revoke one's cards, typically using a Lost or Stolen Cards web page, it will be necessary to authenticate oneself. If one's cards are backed up somewhere they can be used on another machine. Otherwise some fallback mechanism is required, such as supplying an email address and answering a security question or two. Associating a new card with an account is straightforward.

And now back to the Introduction dialog...

Once the user has explicitly agreed to release their credentials to a Relying Party, the Choose a Card dialog will appear directly on each subsequent occasion unless either the RP's certificate details change or its privacy terms have changed.

The Identity Selector module in infocard.exe uses the RP policy to determine which cards match the RP's requirements. The UI process, icardagt.exe, displays the cards to the user with nonmatching cards grayed out. The ledger keeps track of the sites where a card is used with the date and time of last usage. Cards that have been used at the RP in the past appear at the top of the Choose a Card dialog.

When the user selects a card, CardSpace knows which Identity Provider to contact from the card's metadata. Included in the metadata is a MEX endpoint and CardSpace retrieves the IP/STS's security policy via a WS-MEX request and response (steps 5 and 6). It then sends a Request for a Security Token (RST) message to an STS endpoint asking for a security token matching the Relying Party's policy and providing the user's credentials (step 7).

Whereas the Identity Metasystem will accommodate any method of authenticating to a security token service—including round-tripping—CardSpace version 1.0 is limited to four authentication methods for external STSes. Naturally, for self-issued tokens, the local STS doesn't require an additional authentication step and the MEX and RTS/RSTR messages are optimized. If the user chooses a Personal Card, infocard.exe goes ahead and creates a SAML 1.0 or 1.1 security token (which version depends on RP policy) using data stored locally in the CardSpace store.

The four methods of authentication for Managed cards in CardSpace version 1.0 are

- ▶ Kerberos

- ▶ X.509 certificate (hardware– and software–based)

▶ Personal information card

▶ Username and password

Some of these credential types require additional user interaction. With Kerberos and personal information card authentication, the user simply chooses the card. With a hardware-based X.509 certificate, the user will be prompted to engage the device (for example, insert a smart card into a smart card reader and type a PIN). With username and password, the user will be prompted for his password. *Hardware-based X.509 certificate* means any certificate-based device that has a Cryptographic Service Provider available for it.

All communications between CardSpace and other parties are encrypted as appropriate (including MEX calls). How the contents of the RST and RSTR messages are encrypted depends on the credential type used. The Information Card contains metadata about the security binding, and the security policy is also retrieved via the MEX exchange prior to sending the RST (steps 5 and 6).

When username and password credentials are used, the channel is secured using SSL. For Kerberos, a symmetric key is used (included in a Kerberos V5 session ticket). For X.509 certificates, an asymmetric key pair is used. Authentication to an STS using a Personal Card can use either a symmetric or an asymmetric key pair for the security binding. For in-depth details on how this is implemented, please refer to the CardSpace Technical Reference and the WS-SecurityPolicy specification.

The Kerberos authentication method will dovetail nicely with Microsoft's Active Directory Security Token Service (AD/STS)—or ADES 2.0—when it is released. System administrators will use an admin console to set up trust relationships with STSes outside the Enterprise domain, define which Active Directory attributes are exposed as claims, and define claim transformation. When a user wants to authenticate to a business partner's site or service, she simply selects a company information card. All the necessary authentication and access control are done seamlessly via federated security token services.

After authenticating the user using the credentials in the RST and retrieving the required PII from its user database, the IP/STS creates a security token containing the required claims and a proof key for the RP if required. (See the text following Figure 8.14 for more information on proof keys.)

CardSpace can include the Relying Party's identity (that is, its endpoint and public key) in an <AppliesTo> element in the RST, in which case the token is encrypted with the RP's public key. However, the default is to conceal the RP's identity from the IP in order to protect the user's privacy.

If the RP wants its identity to be given to the IP, it can put an <AppliesTo> element in its security policy. The IP, on the other hand, can specify that an RP's identity is mandatory (as per an "auditing STS") or optional by putting a <requireAppliesTo> element in its Information Card.

The RP's identity is *always* sent in the case of an auditing STS (unless the user cancels) and it is also sent if the RP identity is optional for the IP but the RP wants it included.

CardSpace alerts the user if the IP will be given the RP's identity, allowing her to cancel before the RST is sent (Figure 8.14). For full details on token scope, please refer to the CardSpace Technical Reference.

There is a classic trade-off here: increased security versus increased privacy. The benefits of providing the RP's identity are that the security token can be encrypted using the RP's public key so that only the RP can access the contents, and the IP can track where tokens are used. The benefit of not providing the RP's identity is that the user could, for example, use her government IP to prove she is of a legal age at verystrongalcohol.com, but the IP will be unaware that the user identity was used for that purpose.

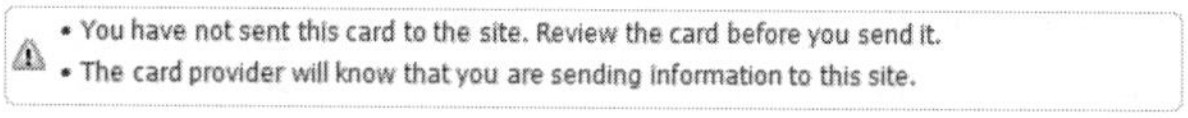

> ⚠ • You have not sent this card to the site. Review the card before you send it.
> • The card provider will know that you are sending information to this site.

FIGURE 8.14   Alerting the user when the RP's identity will be sent to the IP.

After the signed security token has been created, containing claims and a proof key for the RP, it is packaged into the RST Response (RSTR) message with, optionally, a display token to show the user what's in the security token.

As the name implies, a *proof key* enables the user to prove to the relying party that she is the rightful bearer of the security token (it's also known as a *subject confirmation key*). Between them, the client and the IP securely establish either a shared symmetric key or an asymmetric key pair with the private key held by the client. The IP includes its key (symmetric or public) in the security token intended for the RP. The client signs the message to the RP—which includes the token—using its key (symmetric or private). The Relying Party checks the message signature using the key the IP provides. If the signature is okay, the client possesses the key agreed with the IP and therefore must be the rightful bearer of the token.

Entropy for creating the symmetric key can be provided by the client and/or the IP. Asymmetric proof keys are always generated by the client. The only restriction is that tokens not encrypted with the RP's public key cannot use a symmetric proof key because if the proof key were a shared, symmetric key, the RP would be able to reuse the token elsewhere without breaking the IP's signature—and thus pretend to be the client! By default CardSpace asks for an asymmetric proof key unless the RP policy specifically requests a symmetric key.

For CardSpace v1.0, proof of possession with websites is determined by maintaining an HTTPS session between the client and the Relying Party (that is, proof is supplied at the transport level) and the token returned from the STS is a raw token (there is no proof key). The STS is asked for a token with no proof key and if it issues a SAML token, it is marked as a *bearer token* and includes an `<AudienceRestrictionCondition>` element restricting the token to the target site. After the CardSpace system has received a security token from the IP via an RSTR, the user is prompted whether to send the token to the Relying Party.

Relying Parties are required to have an X.509 certificate (preferably an EV certificate) to identify themselves and to allow security tokens to be encrypted using a session key protected by the certificate's public key. This means that the security token is totally opaque to CardSpace! This is by design: Identity selectors need to be security token-agnostic. There shouldn't be a requirement for CardSpace to understand every token that passes by. However, for users to give fully informed consent to the release of the token, they need to know what personally identifiable information is being sent to the RP.

The solution is for the IP to send an additional (and optional) display token to the user. When the user chooses a card, he knows which claims will be sent—it's in the metadata of the card and displayed in the UI. If he wants to know the values of those claims, he can click on the Retrieve button. In that case, the RSTR includes the display token, secured using the IP's security binding, and is displayed to the user. The question that invariably crops up at this point is, "if the security token is opaque, how does the user know that its contents are the same as what's in the display token?"

Technically, it's impossible for CardSpace to check that the two match because the claims can use any encoding whatsoever and are encrypted using keys that only the RP can decrypt. It's those very properties (encapsulation) that let the Metasystem transmit claims from any one system to another. However, the display token and the security token are cryptographically bound together by the IP's signature. The IP cannot repudiate claims after the fact (that is, they can't say, "We didn't send that"). If the claims shown to the user and the claims sent to the RP don't match, the Identity Provider can be held accountable via human/reputation/legal processes. In other words, this is one for the lawyers and this is where real-world solutions to breach-of-trust will have to reside.

After the user has approved the release of the token, it is handed back to the client application via an out parameter of the `GetToken()` method (step 9). WCF then sends the token to the Relying Party (step 10). The recipient of the security token can be a service endpoint or an STS. The token is cracked open, the signature verified, and the user is authenticated and authorized using claims in the token.

For browser applications the flow is very similar (Figure 8.15): steps 4 through 8—how CardSpace operates—is identical.

For websites, the canonical scenario is that the client—the browser—will try to access a protected web page (step 1a) and will be redirected to a login page (step 1b). The browser retrieves this page over HTTPS (steps 2a and 2b); there's nothing new yet!

If the login page supports Information Cards, it will include a button bound to a particular `<object>` element:

```
<object type="application/x-informationcard" name="…">
  <param name="tokenType" value="…" >
  <param name="issuer" value="…" >
  <param name="requiredClaims"
    value="http://.../claims/givenname, http://.../claims/
➥privatepersonalidentifier">
</object>
```

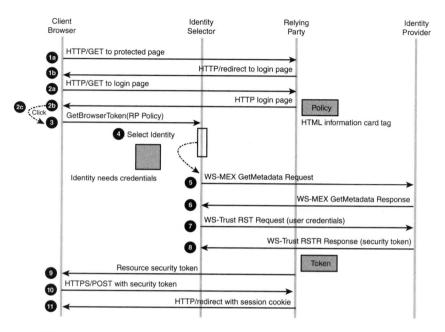

FIGURE 8.15   Swim lanes for a browser client.

The `type` attribute is the key here, indicating that the `object` element represents an Information Card Identity Selector. This tells the browser to launch whichever Identity Selector is on the machine. One could use the `classid` attribute, but that would limit one to one specific identity selector (assuming the same classid wasn't used elsewhere). The `param` elements contain the RP policy.

If the Relying Party doesn't want to use an `<object>` element (for example, if the browser has disabled ActiveX support), the following binary behavior format is equivalent:

```
<ic:informationCard  name="…"
  style="behavior:url(#default#informationCard) "
  issuer="…"
  tokenType="…">
    <ic:add claimType="http://…/claims/privatepersonalidentifier" optional
➥="false"/>
<ic:/informationCard>
```

Both formats make it incredibly simple to add information card support to an existing login page. The RP's policy is described not in WS-SecurityPolicy, but in simple HTML within the main element tags.

All that's required now is a browser, or browser add-in/extension, that recognizes this format. IE 7.0, for example, ships with an icardie.dll file that handles this. Browsers that don't recognize the format, such as IE 6 and earlier, will ignore the element completely. Likewise, if the .NET Framework 3.0 is not installed, icardie.dll fails graciously.

When the user clicks on the Information Card button (step 2c), the browser calls the GetBrowserToken() method, passing in the RP policy as an input parameter (step 3). Like GetToken(), GetBrowserToken() returns a signed and encrypted security token. However, unlike GetToken(), the token returned has no proof key; it is a raw token. All that the browser has to do when it receives the token (step 9) is to post it to the website (step 10). The Relying Party processes the token in the usual way (validation, claim extraction, lookup, authorization) and then it allows the user website access in precisely the same way that it does for users authenticating with a username and password. The most common method is to issue a session cookie (step 11).

This is the simplest scenario, but there are others. If the RP doesn't want to do token processing on its front-end servers, it can specify a resource STS as the issuer and get the STS to do the token processing and cookie issuance (or whatever token the front-end servers require). Of course, if the resource STS supports information cards (that is, it has the <RequireFederatedIdentityProvisioning> assertion in its policy), the Relying Party can be its own Identity Provider and the user simply chooses the Relying Party's Information Card. If it has an IssuedToken policy assertion with <Issuer> missing, empty, or set to self-issued token, CardSpace will ask the user to choose an information card (and an IP) to get a token to authenticate to the resource STS. One can have any number of STSs chained together in this way; WCF simply traverses the chain.

Identity Providers sign their security tokens with a private key so that the token recipient can validate the token and the issuer using the corresponding public key. Third-party IPs do this using an X.509 certificate. For self-issued tokens, CardSpace creates an RSA key pair.

However, if there is one key pair and one PPID per card, the user has the same unique identifier wherever she uses that card. This creates a privacy problem because any two Relying Parties can determine whether they have the same user and potentially collude.

To mitigate this, when the user creates a Personal Card, CardSpace generates a 256-bit random number called the *master key* and a globally unique URI called *CardId*. (Managed Cards also contain a unique CardId generated by the Identity Provider.)

When the user selects a Personal card to authenticate to an RP, the master key is hashed with either the RP's public key if it's an SSL certificate, or the OLSC (Organization, Location, State, Country) ID if it's an EV cert. This hash is used as the seed for the Crypto API to generate a per-card, per-site RSA key pair, thus solving the collusion problem.

The Crypto API uses an ANSI X9.31-compliant algorithm to generate the RSA key pair so that the same master key and RP certificate will always produce the same RSA key pair. This means that when the card (including the master key) is backed up to a .crds file and imported to a different machine, the RP sees exactly the same user.

Similarly, the PPD is created by hashing the CardID with the RP's public key or OLSC ID. This means a user can use the same card at multiple sites and there will be a different PPID and a different RSA key pair for each one. Relying Parties are unable to collude and track the user. In fact, this feature can be extended to external Identity Providers. A

PPIDSeed can be sent in the RST so that IPs can present a different PPID to different Relying Parties even though the user selects the same card.

CardSpace displays the PPID to the user in a human-friendly form (Figure 8.16). The algorithm that converts the PPID into this form is very simple (Listing 8.1) and can be used by Relying Party sites to display PPIDs to the user. This is useful when the user has more than one card associated with an account and wants to delete one of them; for example, when the user wants to use a different card and/or revoke an existing one.

LISTING 8.1   Code to Convert PPID to Human-Friendly Form

```
public static string CalculateSiteSpecificID(string ppid)
{
    int CallSignChars = 10;
    char[] CharMap = "QL23456789ABCDEFGHJKMNPRSTUVWXYZ".ToCharArray();
    int CharMapLength = CharMap.Length;

    byte[] raw = Convert.FromBase64String(ppid);
    raw = SHA1.Create().ComputeHash(raw);

    string callSign = "";

    for (int i = 0; i < CallSignChars; i++)
    {
        // after char 3 and char 7, place a dash
        if (i == 3 || i == 7)
        {
            callSign += '-';
        }
        callSign += CharMap[raw[i] % CharMapLength];
    }
    return callSign;
}
```

One final note on security: Information Cards and CardSpace make life more difficult for the bad guys, but one shouldn't make the mistake of thinking one is 100% safe: there is no such thing. No software is without bugs and no software is without security bugs. CardSpace is no exception: It will have bugs, security bugs, and vulnerabilities. As they are discovered, they will be patched and updates sent out via Windows Update. Computer security is about continually trying to keep one step ahead of the bad guys. However, CardSpace does represent a significant step forward in the fight against cybercrime and after people become accustomed to the convenience and the increased security that it offers, there will be no looking back.

That's enough on architecture. For fine details on interactions between the Identity Provider, the user, and the Relying Party, the best place to look is in the CardSpace Technical Reference and the Integration Guide (see the "References" section).

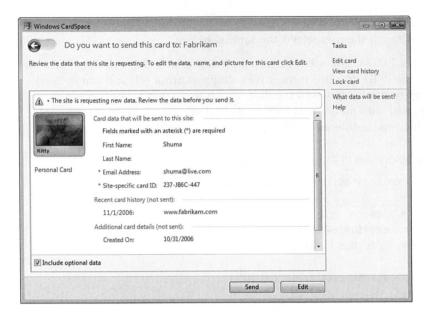

FIGURE 8.16   Human-readable version of the PPID.

CardSpace and the Enterprise

The consumer value of information cards is blindingly obvious, but where do they fit in the enterprise space? Does "user-centric" identity have a place in the enterprise?

Within corporations, the success of a particular technology depends on how well it meets business needs. Some of the business needs *du jour* are regulatory compliance, security, and business process efficiency. CardSpace and the Metasystem have a strong part to play in this world above and beyond the simple fact that almost all enterprises have relationships with consumers and small businesses.

Historically, most applications have been built as stove-pipe solutions with their own methods of authentication and authorization. The result has been a mess, and companies have spent a small fortune on Single Sign-On (SSO) solutions just so that their users can log on once and not have to use a separate username and password for every line-of-business application.

When companies get beyond the issues of SSO, they can look at how they might integrate internal applications to enable new interaction channels adding additional business value. For example, they can composite applications made up of components from existing applications and combined with new business logic.

They also consider how they might integrate with external organizations using federation. Examples here include business partners accessing enterprise applications, employees using Application Service Providers (ASPs), and portals integrating with third-party services.

This thinking has led to an upsurge in service-based architectures and is quite possibly the reason many are reading this book! At a time when people are turning to services to solve their integration issues, it is natural to think of identity as a service. An identity service layer, integrating with other identity service layers, makes a lot of sense! The technologies that enable this are WS-Trust and the Security Token Service.

Figure 8.17 is the classic Identity Metasystem "triangle" of trust. This can scale easily because the user is at the center and the Relying Party and Identity Provider are loosely coupled. The RP could be just one website or hundreds of sites and services. Trust is mutual between all parties in the Metasystem, not just the IP and RP. The underlying protocols have the advantage of being very simple and flexible and the whole architecture is easily managed and scales well.

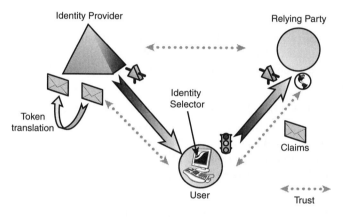

FIGURE 8.17   The Identity Metasystem "Triangle of Trust."

Identity in the enterprise follows a far more rigid model: the domain model (Figure 8.18). The Identity Provider, the domain controller, *creates* the users and services (security principals) and makes all the trust decisions for everyone. This is a world of absolute authority and sharply defined lines of trust: a world where the user—and the business unit—are disenfranchised.

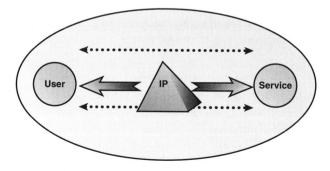

FIGURE 8.18   Domain model trust: a totalitarian regime.

Federation is a set of agreements, standards, and technologies that enables one to make identity and entitlements portable across autonomous security domains. A lot of value can be derived by federating the domain model. For example, if one is using Active Directory, one can extend it using Active Directory Federation Services (ADFS) and the WS-Federation Passive Requestor Profile protocol. This enables one to have web SSO with one's business partners but it does not support active clients. In other words, it allows federated browser applications but not web services applications.

The problem is that the simplistic domain model makes the job of controlling access to resources inefficient and unreliable (and therefore unsafe). As the domain model is federated outwards via acquisitions and partnerships, one ends up with a mesh of many, many enterprise domains, each stuck with a central IP making all the decisions. One can try building circles of trust, but ultimately one ends up with a complex and difficult-to-manage mishmash of policy.

The key is to realize that it is the owner of a resource that should be making the trust decisions, not centralized IT. It is a business decision, not an IT decision (although they should still have a say). In other words, the Relying Party should control access to its resource(s), not the Identity Provider.

This is an age in which IT departments are devolving power to end users to reduce support costs—for example, allowing users to manage their own PCs and controlling network access through policy enforcement. Why not allow the owners of a resource—that is, the business unit or individual—decide who should have access while under the aegis of enterprise policy? Why not let the employee agree to privacy and consent policies during the federation process?

CardSpace offers many things to the enterprise: a standardized and ubiquitous means of providing credentials, flexible user-driven relationships, multiple user roles, antiphishing features, multifactor authentication, information minimalization, active federation and, not least, easy implementation. But perhaps the greatest gift is the ability to devolve access control to the true resource owners. And the way it does this is via security token services.

In Figure 8.19, there are two enterprises: Contoso and Fabrikam. Contoso is a Microsoft shop using Active Directory; Fabrikam prefers to use Linux-based servers. Two business groups, C from Contoso and F from Fabrikam, meet up and strike a deal where members of C can access one of F's services. They agree to a set of claims that will be exposed and F modifies the policy of the resource STS to authorize the C group; that is, a trust relationship is set up.

Lisa, who works in C group, has been sent an email describing the deal. Sure enough in her WCF client application there is a new option to use the F service. When she selects the option, WCF accesses the F service policy (step 1) and gets redirected to the resource STS, which passes back its policy (step 2). WCF sees that the `<issuer>` element is empty so it launches CardSpace (step 3). The only Information Card that is lit up is her employee card because that is the card with an IP that can provide a SAML token (say) and the Employer and Group claims. In any case, she knows she has to select her company information card—it is her online employee badge.

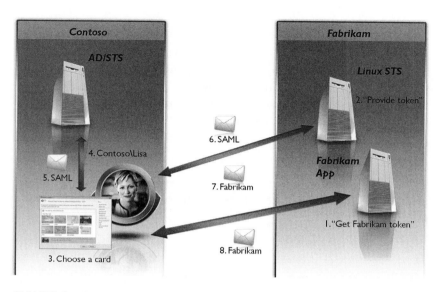

FIGURE 8.19   Federation using Security Token Services.

When Lisa chooses her employee card, an RST containing her Kerberos credentials and F's STS policy are sent to the Contoso Active Directory STS (step 4). It authenticates her and sends an RSTR containing a signed SAML token (step 5). Lisa confirms the release of the token and an RST is sent on to the Fabrikam resource STS (step 6). The token is validated—the signature proves it comes from Contoso—and the group claim (which has been transformed to the department claim) shows that Lisa works for C. This matches the policy, so the STS issues a Fabrikam token (step 7), which happens to be a special token format that only Fabrikam applications use and understand. WCF presents this to F group's application (step 8), and the application gives back to Lisa exactly the information she needed to do her job.

Clearly this model is extremely powerful and encompasses many interesting scenarios, such as mergers and acquisitions. STSs are destined to become the cornerstones of IT infrastructure—they are the identity layer. This is why many companies are anxious for the release of AD/STS and other STS solutions, and the vendors are anxious to get their STS products to market.

Ultimately, the interesting question here is not "Where do information cards fit in enterprise scenarios?" but rather "Where does the domain model fit?" If information cards become increasingly ubiquitous for both consumers on the Web and for employees using federated business applications, is it desirable to maintain two enterprise architectures? Companies are already moving toward security "de-perimeterization." Will they move to one unified identity architecture? Only time will tell.

In any case, anyone using WCF is in good shape. It's a simple change of client credential type from Windows to IssuedToken and a different token handler.

Summary

Windows CardSpace and the Identity Metasystem provide users with a simple, consistent, and secure way to handle their online identities. They no longer have to remember usernames and passwords, and are protected against phishing attacks. Built-in support for additional authentication factors such as smart cards allows banks and others to improve levels of security while providing a consistent and familiar user experience.

Information cards can be used with both websites and web services. The protocols are simple and open, allowing them to be used in a broad range of contexts with different vendor offerings to choose from.

Very little developer effort is required—but to truly believe that, one needs to take a look at the next chapter...

References

FFIEC Guidance: Authentication in an Internet Banking Environment

http://www.fdic.gov/news/news/financial/2005/fil10305.html

CardSpace Community Site

http://cardspace.netfx3.com

Design Rationale Behind the Identity Metasystem Architecture

http://research.microsoft.com/~mbj/papers/Identity_Metasystem_Design_Rationale.pdf

Firefox Identity Selector Extension

http://perpetual-motion.com/

Get Safe Online

http://www.getsafeonline.org/

A Guide to Interoperating with the Information Card Profile v1.0

http://www.identityblog.com/wp-content/resources/profile/Infocard-Profile-v1-Guide.pdf

Higgins Trust Framework Project

http://www.eclipse.org/higgins/

Kim Cameron's Identity Weblog

http://www.identityblog.com/

Laws of Identity

http://www.identityblog.com/?page_id=352

Long Tail of the Internet

http://en.wikipedia.org/wiki/Long_tail

The Meta-Identity System

Bob Blakley

http://notabob.blogspot.com/2006/07/meta-identity-system.html

Microsoft Live Labs Security Token Service

http://sts.labs.live.com/

Microsoft Open Specification Promise (OSP)

http://www.microsoft.com/interop/osp/

Novell Bandit

http://www.bandit-project.org/

Open Source Identity System (OSIS)

http://osis.netmesh.org/wiki/Main_Page

Sun's Project Tango

http://java.sun.com/developer/technicalArticles/glassfish/ProjectTango/

Why Phishing Works

Rachna Dhamija, J. D. Tygar, and Marti Hearst

http://people.deas.harvard.edu/~rachna/papers/why_phishing_works.pdf

Windows LiveId

http://msdn.microsoft.com/library/default.asp?url=/library/en-us/dnlive/html/WinLiveIDServ.asp

8

CHAPTER 9

Securing Applications with Information Cards

Introduction

This chapter shows how one can build applications that use Information Cards. More specifically, it covers how to implement the different roles in the Identity Metasystem: how one might build a client, a Relying Party (RP), or an Identity Provider (IP). Both Windows Communication Foundation (WCF) applications and browser-based applications are covered.

Developing for the Identity Metasystem

There are three roles in the Identity Metasystem: Client (Subject), Relying Party, and Identity Provider. Developers can plug in at any point. One can build client applications that allow users to provide their credentials using Windows CardSpace or another identity selector. One can build websites and web services that accept security tokens generated when a user selects an information card. And one can become an identity provider, issuing cards to users and allowing them to authenticate using identity data one supplies.

To build an **Identity Provider**, a developer needs to build or buy the following:

▶ A Secure Sockets Layer (SSL) certificate; preferably an EV (Extended Validation) SSL certificate

Identifies the IP to the user and the key pair signs/validates security tokens

- ▶ A Security Token Service (STS)

  Web service that issues security tokens via the WS-Trust protocol (RST/RSTR)

- ▶ A policy document giving the security policy of the IP

  Described using WS-SecurityPolicy and exposed via a secure metadata exchange (MEX) endpoint

- ▶ An Information Card for each user

  XML document signed with the IP's private key

- ▶ Software and/or hardware related to the user authentication method used

  For example, a smart card for each user

- ▶ A data store to store the users' identity data

  For example, Active Directory, Active Directory Application Mode, or SQL Server

To build a **Relying Party** web service, a developer needs

- ▶ An SSL certificate; preferably an EV SSL certificate

  Identifies the RP to the user and the key pair encrypts/decrypts security tokens

- ▶ Service endpoints

  Exposed services that do work for the user

- ▶ A policy document

  Described using WS-Security Policy and exposed via a secure MEX endpoint

- ▶ Token-processing code

  Validates and decrypts token, extracts claims, authenticates and authorizes user

- ▶ A user account store

  Holds user Id (IP public key + PPID [`PrivatePersonalIdentifier`]) and per-user account information

To build a **Relying Party** website, one needs

- ▶ An SSL certificate; preferably an EV SSL certificate

  Identifies the RP to the user and encrypts/decrypts security tokens

- ▶ Modified login and registration pages

  Information Card HTML tag with policy, accepts posted token, issues cookie (or similar)

▶ Token-processing code

Validates and decrypts token, extracts claims, authenticates and authorizes user

▶ A user account store

Holds user Id (IP public key + PPID) and per-user account information

To build a **rich Windows client that uses CardSpace**, one needs

▶ The .NET Framework 3.0 or Windows Vista

Ship vehicle for CardSpace and WCF

▶ An application using WCF

WCF invokes CardSpace

To use **CardSpace in a browser on a Windows client**, one needs

▶ The .NET Framework 3.0 or Windows Vista

Ship vehicle for CardSpace

▶ A CardSpace-cognizant browser (for example, Internet Explorer [IE] 7)

Browser recognizes Information Card tag, calls `GetBrowserToken()`, *posts token to site*

Identity Providers, Relying Parties, and Clients—and Identity Selectors—can be implemented using any technology stack on any operating system as long as they implement the correct web and web services protocols and can do the appropriate X.509-based cryptographic operations.

The last two client scenarios listed concern using Windows CardSpace with Windows client applications. To build a client application that uses Information Cards and runs on the Mac, Linux, or any other platform, one has to use an identity selector other than CardSpace and a web services stack other than WCF since CardSpace, WCF, and the .NET Framework 3.0 run on only Windows. This software is outside the scope of this book.

Simple Demonstration of CardSpace

The simplest way to see the user experience of CardSpace is to create a Personal Card and use it to log on to a website that supports Information Cards. One needs to have .NET Framework 3.0 and IE 7.0 (or another Information Card–aware browser) installed. Windows Vista RC1 or later includes both.

One such site is http://www.netfx3.com. This is the community site for the .NET Framework 3.0 technologies. It is run by the authors of this book and others from the product groups at Microsoft. There is lots of useful information there related to CardSpace development, specifically at the http://cardspace.netfx3.com subdomain. At the time of writing, one can use http://sandbox.netfx3.com to log in with a Personal Information Card using the Join and Sign In links in the top-right corner of the page. Other features will be added over time.

For something a little more exotic, try logging in to Kim Cameron's website: http://www.identityblog.com. Kim is the chief identity architect at Microsoft and his website and blog is implemented using WordPress running on LAMP (Linux, Apache, MySQL, and PHP). Using open source software helps illustrate the openness and viability of the Identity Metasystem. To register at the site, one needs to provide a Personal Card with a *real* email address. An email is sent to that address, and registration is completed by clicking on a link in the email (a simple precaution against spam bots). The PHP code used to implement the Information Card login is published there.

Prerequisites for the CardSpace Samples

The CardSpace samples in this book use WCF and ASP.NET 2.0. These are not the only ways to add Information Card support to applications, but other methods are outside the scope of this book. One should be able to use browsers other than IE 7 provided that they have Information Card support. For example, one could use FireFox and an identity selector extension (see references). Please make certain that both IIS and ASP.NET 2.0 are enabled. The Service Model Metadata Utility Tool, svcutil.exe, used to configure WCF services, ships in the Windows SDK.

For the samples in this chapter to run correctly one first needs to do some simple machine configuration. One needs to install some certificates to do the cryptographic operations such as signing and encryption of messages, update the hosts file to resolve full web URLs to the local machine, and create some virtual directories for the web applications that will do the work. The simplest way to do this is to download the Zip file from http://www.cryptmaker.com/WindowsCommunicationFoundationUnleashed and extract the CardSpace-related content to C:\WCFHandsOn\CardSpaceOne. One can then run the setup script to configure one's machine automatically.

That said, working through the manual steps detailed below helps one understand what is required to set up a CardSpace application. Reading through them will be beneficial even if running the setup script.

Familiarity with Windows XP and Windows Server 2003 is assumed, but more detailed steps are provided for Windows Vista because it is likely that readers may be less familiar with that operating system. There are some compatibility issues with Visual Studio 2005 and SQL Server 2005 on Vista (resolved in various service packs), but the CardSpace samples have been fully tested and work correctly.

All sample files are assumed to be installed under C:\WCFHandsOn\CardSpace.

1) Enable Internet Information Services and ASP.NET 2.0

In Vista, one enables IIS via Control Panel, Programs, Programs and Features, Turn Windows Features On or Off (optionalfeatures.exe). Click on Internet Information

Services and under World Wide Web Services, Application Development Features, click on the ASP.NET check box (this will select .NET extensibility, ASP.NET, ISAPI [Internet Server API] extensions, and ISAPI filters) .

2) Get X.509 Certificates

CardSpace requires Relying Parties and Identity Providers to identify themselves using X.509 certificates and to use them as the basis for cryptographic operations. In which case one needs to create, find, or buy some SSL certificates. SSL certificates can be created using the makecert.exe utility (one of the .NET Framework security tools one can download from the Web) or Certificate Services, but these tools cannot create Extended Validation certificates. One can see how EV certificates work with CardSpace by downloading the sample EV certificates from this book's website or from http://cardspace.netfx3.com. To generate basic SSL certificates with makecert use the following format:

```
makecert -sv ContosoRoot.pvk -r -n "CN=ContosoRoot" ContosoRoot.cer
makecert -ic ContosoRoot.cer -iv ContosoRoot.pvk -n "CN=ContosoLeaf" -sv
➥ContosoLeaf.pvk ContosoLeaf.cer
```

The first command creates the certificate root and the second command the certificate itself. The options are

```
-sv  <pvkFile>      Subject's PVK file; to be created if not present
-r                  Create a self-signed certificate
-n   <X509name>     Certificate subject X500 name (for example, CN=Fred Dews)
-ic  <file>         Issuer's certificate file
-iv  <pvkFile>      Issuer's PVK file
```

3) Import the Certificates Into the Certificate Store

Import the certificates into the certificate store using the Microsoft Management Console and the Certificates snap-in. Run mmc from a command prompt and choose File, Add/Remove Snap-in, Add, Certificates, Computer Account, Local Computer (the computer this console is running on).

Then import the certificates (select Store and right-click; select All Tasks, Import) as per Table 9.1.

TABLE 9.1   Sample Certificates and Their Intended Locations

Certificate	Store location	Store	Password
adatum.sst	Local Computer (Local Machine)	Trusted Root CAs	[None]
www.adatum.com.pfx	Local Computer (Local Machine)	Personal ("My")	[Blank]

TABLE 9.1   Continued

www.fabrikam.com.pfx	Local Computer (Local Machine)	Personal ("My")	[Blank]
www.contoso.com.pfx	Local Computer (Local Machine)	Personal ("My")	[Blank]
www.woodgrovebank.com.pfx	Local Computer (Local Machine)	Personal ("My")	[Blank]

4) Update the Hosts File with DNS Entries to Match the Certificates

The website addresses used must match those listed in the certificates to avoid warning messages about non–matching certificates and to enable the certificate images to display correctly. Put some entries into the hosts file so that the domain name server (DNS) names being used resolve to the local machine. With purchased certificates, this isn't necessary since they would be bought to match the domain being used.

Add the following entries to C:\Windows\System32\drivers\etc\hosts using Notepad (run as Administrator on Vista):

```
127.0.0.1        www.adatum.com
127.0.0.1        adatum.com
127.0.0.1        www.contoso.com
127.0.0.1        contoso.com
127.0.0.1        www.fabrikam.com
127.0.0.1        fabrikam.com
127.0.0.1        www.woodgrovebank.com
127.0.0.1        woodgrovebank.com
```

Important: If one is using IE 7, the proxy settings have to be turned off for DNS resolution to work correctly. That is, select Tools, Internet Options, Connections. The LAN settings Automatically Detect Settings and Use Automatic Configuration must be off. The Use a Proxy Server for Your LAN option should also be unchecked. This will probably disable Internet access, but it is only required while running the samples.

5) Internet Information Services Setup

Run inetmgr.exe and add the three web applications with the aliases and physical directories given in Table 9.2. Do it by right-clicking Default Web Site and choosing Add Application.

TABLE 9.2   Web Application Locations

Alias	Physical directory	Notes
Cardspace	C:\WCFHandsOn\Cardspace\Website\Cardspace	Samples
Crldata	C:\WCFHandsOn\Cardspace\Website\Crldata	Certificate revocation list data
Images	C:\WCFHandsOn\Cardspace\Website\Images	Certificate images

Adatum.crl should be placed in the Crldata folder.

Adatum.gif, Contoso.gif, Fabrikam.gif, and Woodgrovebank.gif should be placed in the Images folder.

All the code samples will be in the Cardspace folder (under Website) and TokenProcessor.cs should be placed in an App_Code folder within that folder.

Next add an HTTPS binding with the www.fabrikam.com certificate bound to port 443. CardSpace v1.0 requires communication to a website to be over HTTPS.

To do this in Vista, right-click Default Web Site and choose Edit Bindings... Then select HTTPS as the type of binding, 443 as the port, and Fabrikam as the SSL certificate (it will appear in the drop-down list only if it is in the Local Computer Personal [Local Machine "My"] store).

To do this in XP, right-click Default Web Site and choose Properties, Directory Security, Server Certificate, Assign an Existing Certificate, and choose the www.fabrikam.com certificate.

6) Certificate Private Key Access

For the website examples, a TokenProcessor class performs token validation, decryption, and claim extraction. To decrypt tokens, the ASP.NET worker thread executing this code must have access to the www.fabrikam.com certificate's private key. By default, on Vista and Windows Server 2003, ASP.NET worker threads run as NETWORK SERVICE; on Windows XP, they run as ASPNET. So one needs to find the private key and allow this account read access to the appropriate file on disk.

To find the private key, use the Windows SDK tool findprivatekey.exe, which returns the absolute location of the www.fabrikam.com certificate. This tool is included in the Zip file. One can search for the key using certificate store name, location, thumbprint and subject name. For instance, one can find the key location by looking up the www.fabrikam.com certificate's thumbprint in the certificate properties and entering the following at the command prompt (the thumbprint appears inside the quotes):

```
findprivatekey.exe My LocalMachine -t "d4 7d e6 57 fa 49 02 55 59 02 cb 7f
➥0e dd 2b a9 b0 5d eb b8" -a
```

However, there is an easier way:

```
findprivatekey.exe My LocalMachine
```

Simply choose the Fabrikam certificate in the dialog box that appears.

Once the location of the Fabrikam private key is known, one can use Windows Explorer to add read access (that is, Read and Execute) for NETWORK SERVICE or ASPNET (right-click the file, select Properties, Security, Edit, Add). Alternatively, one can use the CACLS tool to do it programmatically. On Vista, one can use the ICACLS tool, which is an improved, marginally more user-friendly version (CACLS is deprecated on Vista):

```
cacls C:\ProgramData\Microsoft\Crypto\RSA\MachineKeys\<privatekeyfilename>
➥/E /G "NETWORK SERVICE":R
icacls C:\ProgramData\Microsoft\Crypto\RSA\MachineKeys\<privatekeyfilename>
➥/grant "NETWORK SERVICE":RX
```

So the code running under ASP.NET has read access to the certificate's private key. The WCF code will need to do the same. There is no need to do anything when running the samples in Visual Studio when logged in with an account that has Administrator privileges. However, if one is using a non-administrator account to run the WCF code, please remember to give that account access to the private key or there will be an error ("Keyset not found" is one such error).

7) HTTP Configuration

By default Windows Vista with User Account Access turned on will give the following error when running the WCF samples:

```
HTTP could not register URL http://+:8000/Derivatives/. Your process does not
have access rights to this namespace (see
http://go.microsoft.com/fwlink/?LinkId=70353 for details).
```

On Vista, listening at an HTTP address (via HTTP.sys) is a privileged operation. The account used to run the samples must be given the correct privilege to access the URLs used in the samples using either netsh or the httpcfg.exe tool (included in the Zip file or available via the XP/2003 Support Tools). Whereas the httpcfg tool requires one to use Security Descriptor Definition Language (SDDL) to set ACLs, netsh is more user-friendly. From a command prompt, and running as Administrator, type

```
netsh http add urlacl url=http://+:8000/Derivatives/ user=MYMACHINE\MyUsername
netsh http add urlacl url=http://+:7000/ user=MYMACHINE\MyUsername
netsh http add urlacl url=https://+:7001/ user=MYMACHINE\MyUsername
```

Where MYMACHINE and MyUsername are placeholders for the user account one wants to use. Check that the entries are set correctly using the following:

```
netsh http show urlacl
```

To delete them one can enter the following:

```
netsh http delete urlacl url=http://+:8000/Derivatives/
netsh http delete urlacl url=http://+:7000/
netsh http delete urlacl url=https://+:7001/
```

CardSpace requires WS-MetadataExchange queries to an STS to be secured using an SSL channel. The sample STS is configured to use port 7000 for service endpoints and port 7001 for MEX endpoints. Therefore port 7001 must be configured to use SSL. This can be done using netsh on Vista, but in this instance the syntax is simpler using the HTTP configuration utility, httpcfg.exe. The Fabrikam certificate is being used again (that is, the IP and the RP will be the same entity). First one deletes any existing SSL binding to that port. From a command prompt, type

> **NOTE**
>
> The HTTP configuration utility httpcfg is provided in source code form. It is necessary to build it using Visual Studio or MSBUILD to use the executable.

```
httpcfg delete ssl -i 0.0.0.0:7001
httpcfg set ssl -i 0.0.0.0:7001 -h
➥"d47de657fa4902555902cb7f0edd2ba9b05debb8"
```

One can use

```
httpcfg query ssl
netsh http show sslcert
```

to check that everything is correct. The SSL binding on port 443 for the web server should be visible as well.

Adding Information Cards to a WCF Application

To illustrate CardSpace and Information Cards with web services, one can take the DerivativesCalculator sample and add Information Card support to it. For the benefit of those who have leapt straight to the CardSpace chapter, here is the WCF code in its entirety, listed by project, *without* Information Card support. One can either take the BasicDerivativesCalculator solution from the downloaded Zip file or create a new solution and create each of the following projects (Listings 9.1–9.3) in turn.

LISTING 9.1   DerivativesCalculator.csproj Class Library

No external references are required for this project.

Calculator.cs:

```
namespace DerivativesCalculator
{
    public class Calculator
    {
        public decimal CalculateDerivative(
            string[] symbols,
            decimal[] parameters,
            string[] functions)
        {
            return (decimal)(System.DateTime.Now.Millisecond);
        }
    }
}
```

LISTING 9.2   DerivativesCalculatorService.csproj Class Library

The references required for this project are System.ServiceModel and the
DerivativesCalculator project. Add them using

IDerivativesCalculator.cs:

```
using System.ServiceModel;

namespace DerivativesCalculator
{
    [ServiceContract]
    public interface IDerivativesCalculator
    {
        [OperationContract]
        decimal CalculateDerivative(
            string[] symbols,
            decimal[] parameters,
            string[] functions);

        void DoNothing();
    }
}
```

LISTING 9.2   Continued

DerivativesCalculatorServiceType.cs:

```
namespace DerivativesCalculator
{
    public class DerivativesCalculatorServiceType: IDerivativesCalculator
    {
        #region IDerivativesCalculator Members

        decimal IDerivativesCalculator.CalculateDerivative(
            string[] symbols,
            decimal[] parameters,
            string[] functions)
        {

            return new Calculator().CalculateDerivative(
                symbols, parameters, functions);
        }

        void IDerivativesCalculator.DoNothing()
        {
            return;
        }

        #endregion
    }
}
```

LISTING 9.3   Host.csproj Console Application

The references required for this project are System, System.ServiceModel, and the DerivativesCalculatorService project.

Program.cs:

```
using System;
using System.ServiceModel;

namespace DerivativesCalculator
{
    public class Program
    {
        public static void Main(string[] args)
        {
            Type serviceType = typeof(DerivativesCalculatorServiceType);
```

LISTING 9.3   Continued

```
            using(ServiceHost host = new ServiceHost( serviceType ))
            {
                host.Open();

                Console.WriteLine(
                    "The derivatives calculator service is available."
                );
                Console.ReadKey(true);

                host.Close();
            }
        }
    }
}
```

App.config:

```xml
<?xml version="1.0" encoding="utf-8" ?>
<configuration>
  <system.serviceModel>
    <services>
      <service
        name="DerivativesCalculator.DerivativesCalculatorServiceType"
        behaviorConfiguration="DerivativesCalculatorService">
        <host>
          <baseAddresses>
            <add baseAddress="http://localhost:8000/Derivatives/"/>
          </baseAddresses>
        </host>
        <endpoint
          address="Calculator"
          binding="wsHttpBinding"
          contract="DerivativesCalculator.IDerivativesCalculator">
        </endpoint>
      </service>
    </services>
    <behaviors>
      <serviceBehaviors>
        <behavior name="DerivativesCalculatorService">
          <serviceMetadata httpGetEnabled="true" />
        </behavior>
      </serviceBehaviors>
```

LISTING 9.3   Continued

```
    </behaviors>
  </system.serviceModel>
</configuration>
```

Build the entire solution, run the host (right-click, Debug, Start New Instance) and then browse to http://localhost:8000/Derivatives/ to check that the service is functioning correctly.

While the service is running, create a client proxy and configuration file by using the service model metadata utility tool, svcutil.exe, from a command prompt:

svcutil /out:proxy.cs /config:app.config http://localhost:8000/Derivatives/

One can then create a Client.csproj console application and add the Proxy.cs and app.config files. Next one just needs some code in the Client project to instantiate the proxy and call the service. This is shown in Listing 9.4.

LISTING 9.4   Client.csproj Console Application

The references required for this project are System and System.ServiceModel.

Program.cs:

```
using System;

namespace Client
{
    public class Program
    {
        public static void Main(string[] args)
        {
            Console.WriteLine("Press any key when the service is ready.");
            Console.ReadKey(true);

            decimal result = 0;
            using (DerivativesCalculatorClient proxy =
                new DerivativesCalculatorClient())
            {
                result = proxy.CalculateDerivative(
                    new string[] { "MSFT" },
                    new decimal[] { 3 },
                    new string[] { });
                proxy.Close();
            }
            Console.WriteLine(string.Format("Result: {0}", result));
```

LISTING 9.4   Continued

```
            Console.WriteLine("Press any key to exit.");
            Console.ReadKey(true);


        }
    }
}
```

At this point build everything and run the host and client console applications to check that everything works correctly. One can edit the solution properties to make Host and Client the startup projects so that one just needs to press F5 to get both to run automatically.

After everything compiles and runs successfully, the next step is to set about adding Information Cards.

Adding Information Cards

What is required to add Information Cards to a WCF-based application? In short, one needs to set the client credential type on the client and service, use a certificate to identify the service to the client and enable cryptographic operations, express in policy the type of token and claims the service requires, and add some code to the service to process the token when it arrives.

Changing client credential type is a trivial operation that a system administrator can do in the app.config file. A conscientious developer can build a service that exposes one endpoint to authenticate internal users with Windows client credentials—for that much sought-after SSO (single signon) feel–good factor—and one endpoint using a token issued from an STS. Note that everything one can do in a config file—and more—one can do in code should one want to.

With the DerivativesCalculator solution, one first needs to update the host's endpoint to use message-level security and a client credential type of IssuedToken in the endpoint binding.

In the host app.config file, add a <bindings> configuration section as a peer of <services> and <behaviors>:

```
</behaviors>
<bindings>
  <wsHttpBinding>
    <binding name="cardspaceBinding">
      <security mode="Message">
        <message clientCredentialType="IssuedToken"/>
      </security>
    </binding>
  </wsHttpBinding>
```

```
</bindings>
  </system.serviceModel>
</configuration>
```

One refers to this binding configuration in the `endpoint` element:

```
<endpoint
    address="Calculator"
    binding="wsHttpBinding"
    bindingConfiguration="cardspaceBinding"
    contract="DerivativesCalculator.IDerivativesCalculator">
</endpoint>
```

This specifies that the client should use an issued token to pass credentials to the host endpoint. *Issued token* normally refers to a security token generated by an STS. Whether an identity selector is used to select the STS depends on the `<Issuer>` assertion in the service policy. If any one of the following is true

▶ `<Issuer>` is empty or absent

▶ `<Issuer>` is set to the self-issued token URI

▶ `<Issuer>` points to an STS whose policy has the `<RequireFederatedIdentityProvisioning>` assertion

WCF will launch an identity selector and the user will choose an STS by virtue of selecting a card representing that STS. Because the `wsHttpBinding` has no issuer specified, CardSpace will be launched by default. Other bindings have more fine-grained policy settings.

How does the service identify itself to the client application? How are security tokens encrypted to protect privacy? One of the requirements of CardSpace is that any potential recipients of the user's identity must identify themselves using cryptographically verifiable but human-friendly means. Only then can users make a rational decision on whether to provide the recipient with their information.

Web servers identify themselves on the Internet today using *X.509v3 certificates*—SSL certificates typically purchased from certificate authorities such as VeriSign and Thawte—and CardSpace v1.0 takes advantage of this. The public key infrastructure is subsumed by the flexible, web services–based architecture called the *Identity Metasystem*. A service must identify itself using an X.509 certificate. It's conceivable that another method might be used in the future, but SSL is used for CardSpace v1.

The first time a service requires the user's identity CardSpace displays a mutual authentication dialog displaying information from the certificate. (CardSpace keeps track of where the user's digital identities are used.) Ideally, this certificate should be an EV certificate—also referred to as a *high assurance* or *high value assurance certificate*—which the CardSpace user interface will reflect.

The certificate identifies the organization behind the service and, to help the human in the process, the certificate should utilize logotypes (RFC 3709) for the issuer (the certificate authority) and the subject (the Relying Party). Logotypes provide a mechanism wherein signed JPEG or GIF images are bound to the certificate to help users recognize the relevant parties and make an informed trust decision. One can see the logotype references by looking at an EV certificates properties (Figure 9.1).

The certificate in this lab to identify the service, www.fabrikam.com, is an EV certificate with logotypes associated with it. The images are placed in the C:\WCFHandsOn\ Cardspace\Website\Images folder and accessed via http://www.fabrikam.com/images/ fabrikam.gif and http://www.fabrikam.com/images/adatum.gif.

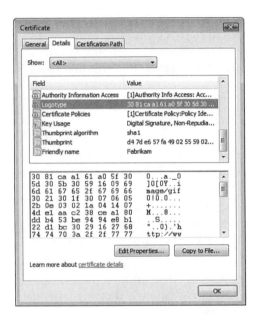

FIGURE 9.1 Logotypes in the certificate.

WCF needs access to the service certificate on both the client and the host. On the client, one can access the certificate either statically via the certificate store or dynamically by retrieving it from the service's MEX endpoint. With browser applications, there is a well-established mechanism for the browser to access the certificate.

One can modify the host's app.config file so that WCF can locate and use the www.fabrikam.com certificate. WCF accesses a resource on the local machine via a behavior. There is a behavior for the service already, which exposes service metadata (WSDL). Now one can add a serviceCredentials element to reference the www.fabrikam.com service certificate:

```
<behavior name="DerivativesCalculatorService">
  <serviceMetadata httpGetEnabled="true" />
  <serviceCredentials>
```

```
    <issuedTokenAuthentication allowUntrustedRsaIssuers="true" />
    <serviceCertificate
      findValue="www.fabrikam.com"
      storeLocation="LocalMachine"
      storeName="My"
      x509FindType="FindBySubjectName"/>
  </serviceCredentials>
</behavior>
```

The www.fabrikam.com certificate is located in the Local Machine Personal ("My") store. One could store the certificate in any of the certificate stores, but this is an appropriate place for a service. Make sure that the account the service runs under has access to the private key as detailed in the prerequisites.

WCF needs the allowUntrustedRsaIssuers flag when one is not using a fully trusted certificate. This might be because the certificate has expired or a certificate revocation list is inaccessible.

Now that WCF on the host knows how to access the service's certificate, host configuration is complete. Now regenerate the client app.config file by using svcutil.exe when the host is running:

svcutil.exe /config:app.config http://localhost:8000/Derivatives/

Note that no code has been recompiled—only configuration files have been changed, not source files. Try running the client and the host applications and see if there is a prompt for an Information Card. Take a look at the client app.config file generated by svcutil.exe. It should be similar to Listing 9.5.

LISTING 9.5   Client app.config File Generated by svcutil.exe (Simplified)

```
<?xml version="1.0" encoding="utf-8"?>
<configuration>
  <system.serviceModel>
    <bindings>
      <wsHttpBinding>
        <binding name="WSHttpBinding_IDerivativesCalculator"
          …>
          <readerQuotas maxDepth="32" maxStringContentLength="8192"
            maxArrayLength="16384" maxBytesPerRead="4096"
            maxNameTableCharCount="16384" />
          <reliableSession ordered="true" inactivityTimeout="00:10:00"
            enabled="false" />
          <security mode="Message">
            <transport clientCredentialType="Windows"
              proxyCredentialType="None"
              realm="" />
```

LISTING 9.5   Continued

```
                <message clientCredentialType="IssuedToken"
                  negotiateServiceCredential="true"
                  algorithmSuite="Default" establishSecurityContext="true" />
              </security>
            </binding>
          </wsHttpBinding>
        </bindings>
        <client>
          <endpoint
            address="http://localhost:8000/Derivatives/Calculator"
            binding="wsHttpBinding"
            bindingConfiguration="WSHttpBinding_IDerivativesCalculator"
            contract="IDerivativesCalculator"
            name="WSHttpBinding_IDerivativesCalculator">
            <identity>
              <certificate encodedValue="AwAAAAEAAAAUAAAA…Vo/O4R0=" />
            </identity>
          </endpoint>
        </client>
      </system.serviceModel>
    </configuration>
```

Notice that the client app.config file does not reference the certificate using a behavior, but has an identity element instead. This comes directly from the WSDL exposed by the service (http://localhost:8000/Derivatives/?wsdl):

```
<wsdl:service name="DerivativesCalculatorServiceType">
  <wsdl:port name="WSHttpBinding_IDerivativesCalculator"
    binding="tns:WSHttpBinding_IDerivativesCalculator">
    <soap12:address location="http://localhost:8000/Derivatives/Calculator" />
    <wsa10:EndpointReference>
      <wsa10:Address>http://localhost:8000/Derivatives/Calculator
      </wsa10:Address>
      <Identity xmlns="http://schemas.xmlsoap.org/ws/2006/02/
➥addressingidentity">
        <KeyInfo xmlns="http://www.w3.org/2000/09/xmldsig#">
          <X509Data>
            <X509Certificate>MIIGRDCCBSyg…PzuEd</X509Certificate>
          </X509Data>
        </KeyInfo>
      </Identity>
    </wsa10:EndpointReference>
  </wsdl:port>
</wsdl:service>
```

When a service endpoint uses a client credential type of IssuedToken, WCF exposes the service certificate via an identity element in the WSDL and an identity element in the service endpoint itself. One can explicitly include the service endpoint identity in the app.config file but it's not necessary:

```
<endpoint
    address="Calculator"
    binding="wsHttpBinding"
    bindingConfiguration="cardspaceBinding"
    contract="DerivativesCalculator.IDerivativesCalculator">
    <identity>
      <certificateReference
        findValue="www.fabrikam.com"
        storeLocation="LocalMachine"
        storeName="My"
        x509FindType="FindBySubjectName" />
    </identity>
</endpoint>
```

The identity element enables the client to authenticate the service *before sending any messages to it* and to determine the service's authenticity. In the handshake process between a client and the service—that is, when a secure channel is being established—the WCF infrastructure will check that the identity exposed through the service endpoint matches the identity retrieved from the service's metadata and used to configure the client. A message will be sent to the service only if these identities match. One can think of this identity processing as the client equivalent of the authentication a secure service does. In the same way that a service shouldn't do any work until the client's credentials have been authenticated, a client shouldn't send a message to a service until the service has been authenticated based on what is known in advance from the service's metadata.

Using a Federation Binding

So far, the WCF policy has not specified the type of token, claims, or issuer required (and there is no code to process the token when it arrives). The wsFederationBinding allows one to have this level of control.

Open the service app.config file and add the following to the <bindings> section as a peer of wsHttpBinding:

```
<wsFederationHttpBinding>
  <binding name="cardspaceFederatedBinding">
    <security mode="Message">
      <message
        algorithmSuite="Basic128"
        issuedTokenType="urn:oasis:names:tc:SAML:1.0:assertion"
        issuedKeyType="SymmetricKey">
        <claimTypeRequirements>
```

```
        <clear />
        <add claimType="http://schemas.xmlsoap.org/ws/2005/05/
➥identity/claims/emailaddress" />
      </claimTypeRequirements>
    </message>
  </security>
 </binding>
</wsFederationHttpBinding>
```

Change the endpoint binding and binding configuration:

```
<endpoint
    address="Calculator"
    binding="wsFederationHttpBinding"
    bindingConfiguration="cardspaceFederatedBinding"
    contract="DerivativesCalculator.IDerivativesCalculator">
```

Run the host and regenerate the client app.config file by running svcutil.exe from a command prompt:

```
svcutil /config:app.config http://localhost:8000/Derivatives/
```

Run the application to check that it works and experiment further by using different claims. Here is the set of self-issued claims:

```
http://schemas.xmlsoap.org/ws/2005/05/identity/claims/givenname
http://schemas.xmlsoap.org/ws/2005/05/identity/claims/surname
http://schemas.xmlsoap.org/ws/2005/05/identity/claims/emailaddress
http://schemas.xmlsoap.org/ws/2005/05/identity/claims/streetaddress
http://schemas.xmlsoap.org/ws/2005/05/identity/claims/locality
http://schemas.xmlsoap.org/ws/2005/05/identity/claims/stateorprovince
http://schemas.xmlsoap.org/ws/2005/05/identity/claims/postalcode
http://schemas.xmlsoap.org/ws/2005/05/identity/claims/country
http://schemas.xmlsoap.org/ws/2005/05/identity/claims/homephone
http://schemas.xmlsoap.org/ws/2005/05/identity/claims/otherphone
http://schemas.xmlsoap.org/ws/2005/05/identity/claims/mobilephone
http://schemas.xmlsoap.org/ws/2005/05/identity/claims/dateofbirth
http://schemas.xmlsoap.org/ws/2005/05/identity/claims/gender
http://schemas.xmlsoap.org/ws/2005/05/identity/claims/webpage
http://schemas.xmlsoap.org/ws/2005/05/identity/claims/
➥privatepersonalidentifier
```

One can mark claims as optional or required:

```
<add claimType="http://schemas.xmlsoap.org/ws/2005/05/identity/claims/
➥emailaddress"
  isOptional="false"/>
```

```
<add claimType="http://schemas.xmlsoap.org/ws/2005/05/identity/claims/
➥givenname"
  isOptional="true"/>
```

Or one can use a different issued token type (the self-issued tokens generated by CardSpace can be SAML 1.0 or 1.1):

```
issuedTokenType="http://docs.oasis-open.org/wss/
➥oasis-wss-saml-token-profile-1.1#SAMLV1.1"
```

Or one can specify that one only wants a self-issued token:

```
<issuer address="http://schemas.xmlsoap.org/ws/2005/05/identity/issuer/self"/>
```

One can also specify the key type and algorithm suite. Go ahead and experiment!

Catching Exceptions

When CardSpace fails, it will throw an exception that can be caught in client code and handled appropriately. If a severe error occurs, always remember to check the application event log (using eventvwr.exe) because typically there is more detailed information recorded there.

In the Client project, add a reference to System.IdentityModel.Selectors and open Program.cs. Add the following:

```
using System.IdentityModel.Selectors;
```

Then in the body of Program.cs, modify Main() so that it looks like the following:

```
public static void Main(string[] args)
{
    Console.WriteLine("Press any key when the service is ready.");
    Console.ReadKey(true);
    try
    {
        decimal result = 0;
        using (DerivativesCalculatorClient proxy =
            new DerivativesCalculatorClient())
        {
            result = proxy.CalculateDerivative(
                new string[] { "MSFT" },
                new decimal[] { 3 },
                new string[] { });
            proxy.Close();
        }
```

```
        Console.WriteLine(string.Format("Result: {0}", result));
    }
    catch (System.IdentityModel.Selectors.CardSpaceException cse)
    {
        Console.WriteLine("Generic Cardspace exception:" + cse.Message);
    }
    catch (IdentityValidationException)
    {
        Console.WriteLine("Recipient's certificate was not valid");
    }
    catch (System.IdentityModel.Selectors.UserCancellationException)
    {
        Console.WriteLine("User cancelled");
    }
    catch (UntrustedRecipientException)
    {
        Console.WriteLine("User does not trust the recipient");
    }
    catch (ServiceNotStartedException)
    {
        Console.WriteLine("Cardspace service not started");
    }
    catch (Exception e)
    {
        Console.WriteLine("Other exceptions :" + e.Message);
    }
    finally
    {
        Console.WriteLine("Press any key to exit.");
        Console.ReadKey(true);
    }
}
```

Try a few different permutations and see whether the exceptions are caught as expected.

Processing the Issued Token

The next step is to write some service code to crack open the security token that has been generated by the Identity Provider and sent to the recipient service. So far one has been using self-issued tokens generated by the CardSpace system, but the same process applies to tokens generated by third party Identity Providers.

WCF and the System.IdentityModel namespace have some very useful classes for security token processing on the server-side. It is much harder to process the tokens on .NET Framework 1.1.

In the DerivativesCalculatorService project, add a reference to System.IdentityModel.
Next modify DerivativesCalculatorServiceType.cs to look like Listing 9.6.

LISTING 9.6   DerivativesCalculatorServiceType.cs

```csharp
using System;
using System.ServiceModel;
using System.IdentityModel.Policy;
using System.IdentityModel.Claims;

namespace DerivativesCalculator
{
    public class DerivativesCalculatorServiceType : IDerivativesCalculator
    {
        #region IDerivativesCalculator Members

        decimal IDerivativesCalculator.CalculateDerivative(
            string[] symbols,
            decimal[] parameters,
            string[] functions)
        {
            AuthorizationContext ctx =
                OperationContext.Current.ServiceSecurityContext.
➥AuthorizationContext;
            foreach (ClaimSet claimSet in ctx.ClaimSets)
            {
                foreach (Claim claim in claimSet)
                {
                    Console.WriteLine();
                    Console.WriteLine("ClaimType: " + claim.ClaimType);
                    Console.WriteLine("Resource: " + claim.Resource);
                    Console.WriteLine("Right: " + claim.Right);
                }
            }
            return new Calculator().CalculateDerivative(
                symbols, parameters, functions);
        }

        void IDerivativesCalculator.DoNothing()
        {
            return;
        }

        #endregion
    }
}
```

This code simply outputs the claims provided in the token to the console. Run the application and see which claims are displayed. It is very simple to gain access to claims and make authorization decisions, such as whether the client can use the DerivativesCalculator, based on those claims. Token processing will be covered again in the "Adding Information Cards to Browser Applications" section.

Using the Metadata Resolver

Everything one can put in an app.config file, one can choose to implement in code instead. However, the converse is not true. There are certain things one can only do in code. One example on the client is to avoid having a client configuration file entirely. Instead one generates the client proxy dynamically using the MetadataResolver class. It is this class that the service model metadata utility tool (Svcutil.exe) uses when it generates client proxies.

Whereas app.config files are useful for being able to make changes to a WCF client or service configuration without having to recompile, this code enables one to do away with client configuration altogether. The only things one needs to know about a particular service *a priori* to using this code are the MEX endpoint reference for the service and its type. However, these also might be supplied at runtime. The MEX endpoint for a service is not exposed by default. One has to put the following in the service app.config file as a peer of the exiting calculator endpoint:

```
<endpoint

  contract="IMetadataExchange"

  binding="mexHttpBinding"

  address="mex" />
```

Delete the client project's app.config file and add a reference to DerivativesCalculatorService. Next modify the client's Program.cs so that it has a couple of extra using statements

```
using System.ServiceModel;
using System.ServiceModel.Description;
```

and the `try` block looks like the following:

```
try
{
    decimal result = 0;
    Uri mexUri = new Uri("http://localhost:8000/Derivatives/mex");
    ContractDescription contract =
        ContractDescription.GetContract(typeof(
➥DerivativesCalculator.IDerivativesCalculator));
```

```
    EndpointAddress mexEndpointAddress = new EndpointAddress(mexUri);
    ServiceEndpointCollection endpoints = MetadataResolver.Resolve(
➥contract.ContractType, mexEndpointAddress);
    foreach (ServiceEndpoint endpoint in endpoints)
    {
        if (endpoint.Contract.Namespace.Equals(contract.Namespace) &&
            endpoint.Contract.Name.Equals(contract.Name))
        {
            ChannelFactory<DerivativesCalculator.IDerivativesCalculator> cf =
➥ new ChannelFactory<DerivativesCalculator.IDerivativesCalculator>(
➥endpoint.Binding, endpoint.Address);
            cf.Credentials.ServiceCertificate.Authentication.RevocationMode =
                System.Security.Cryptography.X509Certificates.
➥X509RevocationMode.NoCheck;
            DerivativesCalculator.IDerivativesCalculator chn =
➥cf.CreateChannel();
            result = chn.CalculateDerivative(
                new string[] { "MSFT" },
                new decimal[] { 3 },
                new string[] { });
            cf.Close();
        }
    }
    Console.WriteLine(string.Format("Result: {0}", result));
}
```

Looking through the code, one can see that the service endpoints are retrieved from the MEX address and service contract, and then one loops through the endpoints looking for "the" endpoint—the one corresponding to DerivativesCalculator.IDerivativesCalculator—and then one constructs the channel and invokes the method as usual.

Adding Information Cards to Browser Applications

Now we turn to websites. All the sample web files will be in the C:\WCFHandsOn\Cardspace\Website\Cardspace folder. For CardSpace to be launched and for the samples to work as intended, use IE 7. Other browsers that understand Information Card tags should work, but they have not been tested for the book.

The Identity Selector can be invoked in a browser application by using either a particular <object> element or binary behavior object. Essentially, the browser—or an add-in— needs to recognize the object tag/binary behavior and invoke the CardSpace system in much the same way that WCF invokes the CardSpace system when it sees the IssuedToken client credential type.

https://www.fabrikam.com/CardSpace/sample1.htm (Listing 9.7) uses the simplest option, which is to include the object element in the body of a form element. This activates the

Identity Selector when the form is submitted (make sure it says https in the browser address bar).

LISTING 9.7   Sample1.htm

```
<!DOCTYPE html PUBLIC "-//W3C//DTD XHTML 1.0 Transitional//EN"
➥"http://www.w3.org/TR/xhtml1/DTD/xhtml1-transitional.dtd">
<html xmlns="http://www.w3.org/1999/xhtml" >
<head>
  <title>Sample 1</title>
</head>
<body>
  <form id="form1" method="post" action="login1.aspx">
    <div>
      <button type="submit">Click here to sign in with your
➥Information Card</button>
      <object type="application/x-informationcard" name="xmlToken">
        <param name="tokenType"
          value="urn:oasis:names:tc:SAML:1.0:assertion" />
        <param name="issuer"
          value="http://schemas.xmlsoap.org/ws/2005/05/identity/issuer/self"/>
        <param name="requiredClaims"
          value="http://schemas.xmlsoap.org/ws/2005/05/identity/claims/
➥givenname
            http://schemas.xmlsoap.org/ws/2005/05/identity/claims/surname
            http://schemas.xmlsoap.org/ws/2005/05/identity/claims/emailaddress
            http://schemas.xmlsoap.org/ws/2005/05/identity/claims/
➥privatepersonalidentifier" />
      </object>
    </div>
  </form>
</body>
</html>
```

The important elements of the object element are shown in Table 9.3.

TABLE 9.3   Elements of the Object Element

type="application/x-informationcard"	Tells the browser to launch an Identity Selector.
param name="tokenType"	Controls the token type the Identity Selector will emit; in this case, a SAML 1.0 token.
param name="issuer"	The Identity Provider's URL that will provide the identity. In this case, the Identity Provider is the built-in self-issued token provider.
param name="requiredClaims"	The claims that the Relying Party is asking for.

When the button is pressed, the Identity Selector will display. The user experience is the same as with web services applications. The user chooses a card; a request is made to the corresponding Identity Provider for a security token meeting the website's requirements; and, in the browser case, the encrypted token is posted to the login1.aspx page shown in Listing 9.8.

LISTING 9.8   Login1.aspx

```
<%@ Page Language="C#"  Debug="true" ValidateRequest="false"%>

<!DOCTYPE html PUBLIC "-//W3C//DTD XHTML 1.0 Transitional//EN"
➥"http://www.w3.org/TR/xhtml1/DTD/xhtml1-transitional.dtd">

<script runat="server">

    protected void Page_Load(object sender, EventArgs e)
    {
        string xmlToken;
        xmlToken = Request.Params["xmlToken"];
        if (xmlToken == null ¦¦ xmlToken.Equals(""))
        {
            xmlToken = "*NULL*";
        }
        Label1.Text = xmlToken;
    }
</script>

<html xmlns="http://www.w3.org/1999/xhtml" >
<head runat="server">
    <title>Login Page</title>
</head>
<body>
    <form id="form1" runat="server">
    <div>
        The value of the token is:
        <asp:Label ID="Label1" runat="server" Text="Label"></asp:Label></div>
    </form>
</body>
</html>
```

The login1.aspx page simply displays the encrypted token, which will look something like Figure 9.2.

https://www.fabrikam.com/CardSpace/sample1b.htm (Listing 9.9) is similar to the first sample, but uses the binary behavior format instead of the object tag format. It still posts the token to login1.aspx.

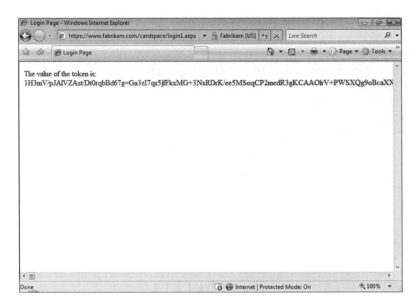

FIGURE 9.2 Login1.apsx showing the encrypted token.

LISTING 9.9 Sample1b.htm (Binary Behavior)

```
<!DOCTYPE html PUBLIC "-//W3C//DTD XHTML 1.0 Transitional//EN"
➥"http://www.w3.org/TR/xhtml1/DTD/xhtml1-transitional.dtd">
<html XMLNS:ic>
<head>
  <title>Sample 1b</title>
</head>
<body>
  <form id="form1" method="post" action="login1.aspx" >
    <ic:informationCard name="xmlToken"
      style="behavior:url(#default#informationCard)"
      issuer="http://schemas.xmlsoap.org/ws/2005/05/identity/issuer/self"
      tokenType="urn:oasis:names:tc:SAML:1.0:assertion" >
      <ic:add claimType="http://schemas.xmlsoap.org/ws/2005/05/identity/
➥claims/givenname"
        optional="false"/>
      <ic:add claimType="http://schemas.xmlsoap.org/ws/2005/05/identity/
➥claims/surname"
        optional="false"/>
      <ic:add claimType="http://schemas.xmlsoap.org/ws/2005/05/identity/
➥claims/privatepersonalidentifier"
        optional='false'/>
    <ic:/informationCard>
```

LISTING 9.9   Continued

```
    <input type='submit' value='Click here to sign in with your
➥Information Card'   />
  </form>
</body>
</html>
```

https://www.fabrikam.com/CardSpace/sample2.htm (Listing 9.10) activates the Identity
Selector on demand. Developers might want more flexibility around the timing and
handling of the invocation of the Identity Selector. In this instance, the <object> element
is scripted to return the encrypted token on request.

LISTING 9.10   Sample2.htm

```
<!DOCTYPE html PUBLIC "-//W3C//DTD XHTML 1.0 Transitional//EN"
➥"http://www.w3.org/TR/xhtml1/DTD/xhtml1-transitional.dtd">
<html xmlns="http://www.w3.org/1999/xhtml" >
<head>
  <title>Authenticate</title>
  <object type="application/x-informationcard" name="_xmlToken">
    <param name="tokenType" value="urn:oasis:names:tc:SAML:1.0:assertion" />
    <param name="issuer" value="http://schemas.xmlsoap.org/ws/2005/05/
➥identity/issuer/self" />
    <param name="requiredClaims"
      value="http://schemas.xmlsoap.org/ws/2005/05/identity/claims/givenname
      http://schemas.xmlsoap.org/ws/2005/05/identity/claims/surname
      http://schemas.xmlsoap.org/ws/2005/05/identity/claims/emailaddress
      http://schemas.xmlsoap.org/ws/2005/05/identity/claims/
➥privatepersonalidentifier" />
  </object>
  <script language="javascript">
    function GoGetIt()
    {
      var xmltkn=document.getElementById("_xmlToken");
      var thetextarea = document.getElementById("xmlToken");
      thetextarea.value = xmltkn.value ;
    }
  </script>
</head>
<body onload="GoGetIt()">
  <form id="form1" method="post" action="login2.aspx">
    <div>
      <button name="go" id="go" onclick="javascript:GoGetIt();">
        Click here to get the token.</button>
      <button type="submit">Click here to send the card to the server</button>
```

LISTING 9.10   Continued

```
        <textarea cols=100 rows=20 id="xmlToken" name="xmlToken" ></textarea>
    </div>
  </form>
</body>
</html>
```

The `<object>` element is placed in the header of the HTML document, and the Identity Selector is invoked when the `value` property is accessed. The script in this example places the token XML into a `<textarea>` (Figure 9.3), allowing the developer to view the contents before the `<form>` is submitted.

The token text in the text area will not exactly match the token text in the login2.aspx page because the browser is suppressing the display of the XML tags.

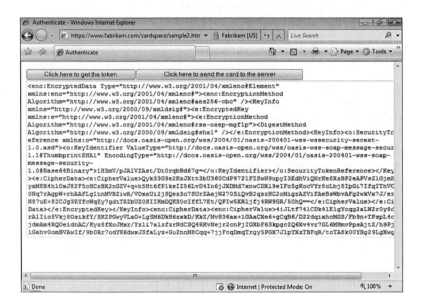

FIGURE 9.3   Sample2.htm.

https://www.fabrikam.com/CardSpace/sample3.htm (Listing 9.11) shows how to extract claims from the encrypted security token on the server by using the `TokenProcessor` class. This class handles all the decryption and verification of the token, using WCF classes. `TokenProcessor` is used in the target page of the post; in this case, the login3.aspx page.

LISTING 9.11   Sample3.aspx

```
<%@ Page Language="C#"  Debug="true" ValidateRequest="false" %>
<%@ Import Namespace="System.IdentityModel.Claims" %>
<%@ Import Namespace="Microsoft.IdentityModel.TokenProcessor" %>

<!DOCTYPE html PUBLIC "-//W3C//DTD XHTML 1.0 Transitional//EN"
➥"http://www.w3.org/TR/xhtml1/DTD/xhtml1-transitional.dtd">

<script runat="server">
  protected void ShowError(string text)
  {
    fields.Visible = false;
    errors.Visible = true;
    errtext.Text = text;
  }
  protected void Page_Load(object sender, EventArgs e)
  {
    string xmlToken;
    xmlToken = Request.Params["xmlToken"];
    if (xmlToken == null || xmlToken.Equals(""))
    {
      ShowError("Token presented was null");
    }
    else
    {
      Token token= new Token(xmlToken);
      givenname.Text = token.Claims[ClaimTypes.GivenName];
      surname.Text   = token.Claims[ClaimTypes.Surname];
      email.Text     = token.Claims[ClaimTypes.Email];
    }
  }
</script>

<html xmlns="http://www.w3.org/1999/xhtml" >
<head runat="server">
  <title>Login Page</title>
</head>
<body>
  <form id="form1" runat="server">
    <div runat="server" id="fields">
      Given Name:<asp:Label ID="givenname" runat="server" Text="">
              </asp:Label><br/>
      Surname:<asp:Label ID="surname" runat="server" Text=""></asp:Label><br/>
      Email Address:<asp:Label ID="email" runat="server" Text="">
                  </asp:Label><br/>
```

9

LISTING 9.11   Continued

```
    </div>
    <div runat="server" id="errors" visible="false">
      Error:<asp:Label ID="errtext" runat="server" Text=""></asp:Label><br/>
    </div>
    </form>
</body>
</html>
```

To get the claims out of the token, use the `Claims` property, passing it the claim URI one is looking for.

There is one piece of configuration data that goes along with the `TokenProcessor`. In a web.config file, one can put the following:

```
<appSettings>
  <add key="MaximumClockSkew" value="60"/>
</appSettings>
```

`MaximumClockSkew` specifies the maximum number of seconds the client and the server can be out of skew. The default is 10 seconds.

When the token is posted to the login page and decrypted, one can see the claim values (Figure 9.4).

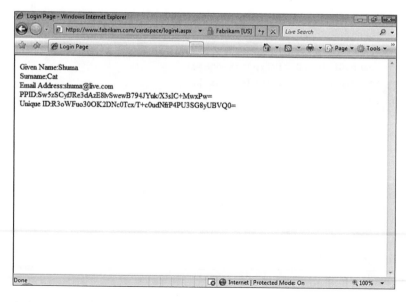

FIGURE 9.4   Login4.apsx showing the claim values.

https://www.fabrikam.com/CardSpace/sample4.htm (Listing 9.12) shows how to uniquely identify the user using the `TokenProcessor` class.

As explained in Chapter 8, "Windows CardSpace, Information Cards, and the Identity Metasystem," to uniquely identify the user of a card requires two things: a key representing the token issuer, and a claim that issuer maintains is unique users at that IP. For example, two companies, Fabrikam and Contoso, could both use a sequential employee ID to uniquely identify their employees. Fabrikam employee #1 is different from Contoso employee #1 because they both have different employers with different keys.

The simplest way to store this pair of values is hash them together. `TokenProcessor` generates a `UniqueID` by hashing together the key and the unique user claim supplied in the token. With self-issued cards and tokens, the unique user claim is the `PrivatePersonalIdentifier` claim. The `TokenProcessor` uses this claim by default, but it can be changed through a configuration setting. All the developer has to do is store this 20-character, base64-encoded hash value in the user account database table or, as a better alternative, in a separate table, to allow a user to associate more than one Information Card with their account.

LISTING 9.12   Login4.aspx

```
<%@ Page Language="C#" Debug="true" ValidateRequest="false" %>
<%@ Import Namespace="System.IdentityModel.Claims" %>
<%@ Import Namespace="Microsoft.IdentityModel.TokenProcessor" %>

<!DOCTYPE html PUBLIC "-//W3C//DTD XHTML 1.0 Transitional//EN"
➥"http://www.w3.org/TR/xhtml1/DTD/xhtml1-transitional.dtd">

<script runat="server">
  protected void ShowError(string errtext)
  {
    divFields.Visible = false;
    divErrors.Visible = true;
    lblErrtext.Text   = errtext;
  }
  protected void Page_Load(object sender, EventArgs e)
  {
    string xmlToken;
    xmlToken = Request.Params["xmlToken"];
    if ( xmlToken == null || xmlToken.Equals("") )
    {
      ShowError("Token presented was null");
    }
    else
    {
      Token token = new Token(xmlToken);
      lblGivenname.Text = token.Claims[ClaimTypes.GivenName];
```

LISTING 9.12   Continued

```
        lblSurname.Text    = token.Claims[ClaimTypes.Surname];
        lblEmail.Text      = token.Claims[ClaimTypes.Email];
        lblPpid.Text       = token.Claims[ClaimTypes.PPID];
        lblUid.Text        = token.UniqueID;
    }
  }
</script>

<html xmlns="http://www.w3.org/1999/xhtml" >
  <head id="Head1" runat="server">
    <title>Login Page</title>
  </head>
  <body>
    <form id="form1" runat="server">
      <div runat="server" id="divFields">
        <table runat="server" id="tblClaims" border="1"
➥summary="Claim Values">
          <tr><th>Claim</th><th>Value</th></tr>
          <tr>
            <td>Given Name</td>
            <td><asp:Label ID="lblGivenname" runat="server" Text="">
                </asp:Label></td>
          </tr>
          <tr>
            <td>Surname</td>
            <td><asp:Label ID="lblSurname" runat="server" Text="">
                </asp:Label></td>
          </tr>
          <tr>
            <td>Email Address</td>
            <td><asp:Label ID="lblEmail" runat="server" Text="">
                </asp:Label></td>
          </tr>
          <tr>
            <td>PPID</td>
            <td><asp:Label ID="lblPpid" runat="server" Text="">
                </asp:Label></td>
          </tr>
          <tr>
            <td>Unique ID</td>
            <td><asp:Label ID="lblUid" runat="server" Text="">
                </asp:Label></td>
          </tr>
        </table>
```

LISTING 9.12   Continued

```
        </div>
        <div runat="server" id="divErrors" visible="false">
            Error:<asp:Label ID="lblErrtext" runat="server" Text="">
                    </asp:Label><br/>
        </div>
    </form>
  </body>
</html>
```

To change the claim used for uniqueness, add the following key to the web.config file and change the value to a different claim URI:

```
<add key="IdentityClaimType"
    value="http://schemas.xmlsoap.org/ws/2005/05/identity/claims/
➥privatepersonalidentifier"/>
```

There is one last thing that is useful when one is adding information card support to web pages. If the user does not have a browser that supports information cards, one may want to modify the way the login page displays. For example, instead of having a "Login here with your information card" button, one might direct the user to a page that explains information cards and how to get them. The javascript function in Listing 9.13 detects and returns true when information cards are supported.

LISTING 9.13   Detecting Information Card Support in the Browser

```
function AreCardsSupported()
{
  var IEVer = -1;
  if (navigator.appName == 'Microsoft Internet Explorer')
    if (new RegExp("MSIE ([0-9]{1,}[\.0-9]{0,})")
        .exec(navigator.userAgent) != null)
      IEVer = parseFloat( RegExp.$1 );

  // Look for IE 7+.
  if( IEVer >= 7 )
  {
    var embed = document.createElement("object");
    embed.setAttribute("type", "application/x-informationcard");

    if(  ""+embed.issuerPolicy != "undefined" )
      return true;
    return false;
  }
  // not IE (any version)
```

9

LISTING 9.13   Continued

```
if( IEVer < 0 && navigator.mimeTypes && navigator.mimeTypes.length)
{
  // check to see if there is a mimeType handler.
  x = navigator.mimeTypes['application/x-informationcard'];
  if (x && x.enabledPlugin)
    return true;

  // check for the IdentitySelector event handler is there.
  var event = document.createEvent("Events");
  event.initEvent("IdentitySelectorAvailable", true, true);
  top.dispatchEvent(event);

  if( top.IdentitySelectorAvailable == true)
    return true;
}
return false;
}
```

Creating a Managed Card

Included in the Zip file for the book is a simple Managed Card creator that one can build using Visual Studio or msbuild. When CardWriter.exe is run from a command prompt, one supplies a customizable .ini file as an argument. The CardWriter will produce a .crd file with the same name in the same directory.

Here are the steps to create a Managed Card where the credential that authenticates the user to the IP is a self-issued PPID. Look for the FabrikamSelfIssued.ini file in the SampleCards folder. Its contents will look something like Listing 9.14.

LISTING 9.14   FabrikamSelfIssued.ini

```
[CARD]
; type is one of UserNamePassword,KerberosAuth,SelfIssuedAuth,SmartCard,
TYPE=SelfIssuedAuth

[Details]
Name=My Fabrikam Card (self-backed)
ID=http://www.fabrikam.com/card/self/sequentialnumber1
version=1
image=images\fabrikam.jpg

[Issuer]
Name=Fabrikam Auto Group
Address=http://www.fabrikam.com:7000/sample/trust/selfissuedsaml/sts
```

LISTING 9.14   Continued

```
MexAddress=https://www.fabrikam.com:7001/sample/trust/selfissuedsaml/mex
PrivacyPolicy=http://www.fabrikam.com/PrivacyPolicy.xml
; certificate should be either a STORELOCATION/STORE/Subject name
; or
; c:\path\to\cert.pfx -- in which case you also need a CertificatePassword=
Certificate=LOCALMACHINE/MY/www.fabrikam.com
;CertificatePassword=foo

[Claims]
; add claims required for card. standard (self issued) are listed below.
; keynames are not important (just don't duplicate them)
1=http://schemas.xmlsoap.org/ws/2005/05/identity/claims/givenname
2=http://schemas.xmlsoap.org/ws/2005/05/identity/claims/surname
3=http://schemas.xmlsoap.org/ws/2005/05/identity/claims/emailaddress
;3=http://schemas.xmlsoap.org/ws/2005/05/identity/claims/streetaddress
;4=http://schemas.xmlsoap.org/ws/2005/05/identity/claims/locality
;5=http://schemas.xmlsoap.org/ws/2005/05/identity/claims/stateorprovince
;6=http://schemas.xmlsoap.org/ws/2005/05/identity/claims/postalcode
;7=http://schemas.xmlsoap.org/ws/2005/05/identity/claims/country
;8=http://schemas.xmlsoap.org/ws/2005/05/identity/claims/homephone
;9=http://schemas.xmlsoap.org/ws/2005/05/identity/claims/otherphone
;10=http://schemas.xmlsoap.org/ws/2005/05/identity/claims/mobilephone
;11=http://schemas.xmlsoap.org/ws/2005/05/identity/claims/dateofbirth
;12=http://schemas.xmlsoap.org/ws/2005/05/identity/claims/gender
13=http://schemas.xmlsoap.org/ws/2005/05/identity/claims/
➥privatepersonalidentifier
;4=http://my-uri.com/test


;[http://my-uri.com/test]
;display=My Super Claim
;description=A claim for all to see

[TokenTypes]
; add token types.
; keynames are not important (just don't duplicate them)
1=urn:oasis:names:tc:SAML:1.0:assertion
;2=http://docs.oasis-open.org/wss/oasis-wss-saml-token-profile-1.1#SAMLV1.1

[Token Details]
RequiresAppliesTo=false

[Credentials]
; if the Auth type is UserNamePassword the value is the Username
```

LISTING 9.14   Continued

```
; if the Auth type is SmartCard the value is the Certificate
➥Path(Localmachine/my/www.fabrikam.com), hash, filename
➥(in which case you may need certificatepassword=)
; if the Auth type is SelfIssuedAut the value is the PPID
value=yfVRWjKItIwGtpK1ZFecf4d5CHryps+hjWJpXGReVaw=
Hint=
```

The .ini file has several sections, each of which can be modified to create different flavors of the Managed Card.

```
[CARD]
TYPE=SelfIssuedAuth
```

In this instance, the Card section indicates that a self-issued card will be used to authenticate to the STS as opposed to either username and password, Kerberos, or certificate–based (soft certificates or hardware-based certificates).

```
[Details]
Name=My Fabrikam Card (self-backed)
ID=http://www.fabrikam.com/card/self/sequentialnumber1
version=1
image=images\fabrikam.jpg
```

The Details section gives the initial name of the card (the user can change it after the card has been imported), the unique ID of the card, the card version number, and the card image.

```
[Issuer]
Name=Fabrikam Auto Group
Address=http://www.fabrikam.com:7000/sample/trust/selfissuedsaml/sts
MexAddress=https://www.fabrikam.com:7001/sample/trust/selfissuedsaml/mex
PrivacyPolicy=http://www.fabrikam.com/PrivacyPolicy.xml
Certificate=LOCALMACHINE/MY/www.fabrikam.com
```

The Issuer section supplies the name of the IP and endpoints for the service, MEX, and the site's privacy policy, plus the location of the certificate whose private key will be used to sign the card.

```
[Claims]
1=http://schemas.xmlsoap.org/ws/2005/05/identity/claims/givenname
2=http://schemas.xmlsoap.org/ws/2005/05/identity/claims/surname
3=http://schemas.xmlsoap.org/ws/2005/05/identity/claims/emailaddress
4=http://my-uri.com/identity/claims/customclaim
```

The `Claims` section lists the URIs of the claims that the IP can provide. To include some custom claims, one must define each one:

```
[http://my-uri.com/identity/claims/customclaim]
display=My Custom Claim
description=A non-self-issued claim
```

The display name and the description are displayed to the user in the CardSpace user interface.

```
[TokenTypes]
1=urn:oasis:names:tc:SAML:1.0:assertion
```

The `TokenTypes` section states the types of the tokens that the STS will support.

```
[Token Details]
RequiresAppliesTo=false
```

The `TokenDetails` section specifies whether the Relying Party's identity must be provided to the STS in an `<AppliesTo>` element.

```
[Credentials]
value=yfVRWjKItIwGtpK1ZFecf4d5CHryps+hjWJpXGReVaw=
Hint=
```

The credentials section provides the credentials that can be included in the card and a hint for those that can't:

▶ For self-issued card authentication, the value is the PPID claim as given to the Identity Provider (and unique to their certificate). The hint is superfluous.

▶ For username/password authentication, the value is the username (optional), and the hint would be something like `"Enter your password"`.

▶ For certificate–based authentication, the value can be the certificate thumbprint, the certificate hash, or a certificate store location (for example, CurrentUser/My/JohnDoe)

So, to create a Managed Card that uses a self-issued token to authenticate, one has to know what the PPID is for that recipient. Because in this case the www.fabrikam.com certificate will be used to identify the IP, one can use https://www.fabrikam.com/CardSpace/sample4.htm to discover the PPID to use in the .ini file. Once one has it one can put it in the .ini file and run the CardWriter:

```
C:\WCFHandsOn\CardSpace\Cards>bin\CardWriter SampleCards\
➥FabrikamSelfIssued.ini
Reading card config from
```

6

```
    C:\WCFHandsOn\CardSpace\Cards\SampleCards\FabrikamSelfIssued.ini
Card written to
    C:\WCFHandsOn\CardSpace\Cards\SampleCards\FabrikamSelfIssued.crd
```

Now one can double-click on the card (the .crd file) to import it into CardSpace or use the CardSpace control panel applet and import from there.

Building a Simple Security Token Service

Now that one has a card that points to some STS endpoints it's time to build an STS! A simplre STS is included in the Zip file and can be found in C:\WCFHandsOn\CardSpace\Sts.

The STS is already configured for use with the Fabrikam sample website. The following settings are adjustable in the app.config file to enable it to be used for other sites:

```
<appSettings>
  <!-- The Identity Provider -->
  <add key="issuer" value="www.fabrikam.com" />
  <!-- The Thumbprint of the certificate to sign the RSTR-->
  <add key="certificateThumbprint"
    value="D47DE657FA4902555902CB7F0EDD2BA9B05DEBB8" />
  <!-- The Base address of the WS-Trust endpoint -->
  <add key="baseAddress" value="http://www.fabrikam.com:7000/sample/trust" />
  <!-- The Base address of the MEX endpoint -->
  <add key="baseMexAddress"
    value="https://www.fabrikam.com:7001/sample/trust" />
</appSettings>
```

When the STS is built and run, one should see the following output:

```
Listener = http://www.fabrikam.com:7000/sample/trust/smartcard/sts,
➥State = Opened
Listener = https://www.fabrikam.com:7001/sample/trust/smartcard/mex,
➥State = Opened
Listener = http://www.fabrikam.com:7000/sample/trust/smartcard,
➥State = Opened
Listener = http://www.fabrikam.com:7000/sample/trust/selfissuedsaml/sts,
➥State = Opened
Listener = https://www.fabrikam.com:7001/sample/trust/selfissuedsaml/mex,
➥State = Opened
Listener = http://www.fabrikam.com:7000/sample/trust/selfissuedsaml,
➥State = Opened
Listener = http://www.fabrikam.com:7000/sample/trust/usernamepassword/sts,
➥State = Opened
```

```
Listener = https://www.fabrikam.com:7001/sample/trust/usernamepassword/mex,
➥State = Opened
Listener = http://www.fabrikam.com:7000/sample/trust/usernamepassword,
➥State = Opened


Press <ENTER> to terminate services
```

After the STS is running, choose one of the samples, making sure that the claim set, token type, and issuer are suitable for the managed card used. By default, the STS provides only one claim—the PPID—so make sure that the Relying Party has only that as a required claim. Run the sample, choose the managed card, and examine the output.

The STS is simple but extensible. There are four sections marked /// SAMPLE EXTENSIBILITY TASK. They allow one to plug in one's own method of selecting a certificate for signing tokens and a way to specify the issuer ID, but the most important parts allow one to plug in additional user authentication and claim values.

The user authentication piece is here:

```
public Message Issue(Message request)
{
    try
    {
        if (request == null)
        {
            throw new ArgumentNullException("request");
        }
        // Parse the incoming request, an RST
        RST rst = new RST(request.GetReaderAtBodyContents());

        // SAMPLE EXTENSIBILITY TASK:
        //
        // You could add code here to further check the validity of
        // the incoming identity
        // by examining the claims in the AuthorizationContext
        //
        AuthorizationContext ctx =
          OperationContext.Current.ServiceSecurityContext.AuthorizationContext;

        // Process the request and generate an RSTR
        RSTR rstr = new RSTR(rst);

        // Generate a response message
        Message response = Message.CreateMessage(MessageVersion.Default,
            Constants.WSTrust.Actions.IssueResponse, rstr);
```

```
        // Set the RelatesTo
        if ( request.Headers.MessageId != null )
        {
            response.Headers.RelatesTo = request.Headers.MessageId;
        }
        else
        {
            // not supported in this sample
            throw new NotSupportedException("Caller must provide a
➥Message Id");
        }

        // Send back to the caller
        return response;
    }
```

One plugs in claim values here:

```
/// <summary>
/// SAMPLE EXTENSIBILITY TASK:
///
/// Returns the SAML attributes to insert into the token
///
/// Add your own claims into the token in this method
///
/// </summary>
/// <returns></returns>
protected List<SamlAttribute> GetTokenAttributes()
{
    List<SamlAttribute> result = new List<SamlAttribute>();

    result.Add(new SamlAttribute(new Claim(ClaimTypes.PPID ,
      "*Fill in this field*", Rights.PossessProperty)));

    return result;
}
```

This is a simple but well-written STS that encourages experimentation. Enjoy!

Summary

Very little developer effort is required to add Information Card support to a website or a web service, and the benefits to users are tangible. By the time this book has been published, there should be some standard images that one can use to indicate to the user that an application supports Information Cards.

Security Token Services take more effort to build and industrial-strength STSs will be supplied by software vendors. In the meantime, one can use simple STSs like the one used in this chapter to try out the technology and see how it might be exploited.

References

The TokenProcessor, STS, and Managed Card Writer are all taken from the samples on http://cardspace.netfx3.com.

Advanced Security

Prelude

Driving south from the city of Seattle in Washington State towards Oregon, one is faced with a choice of route shortly after passing the impressive State Capitol building in Olympia. One can continue on Interstate 5 or head west and then south again on U.S. Highway 101.

Interstate 5 offers a superb driving experience. With multiple lanes in each direction most of the way to Portland, it is amply wide for the density of traffic, and there are well-appointed gas stations, restaurants, shops, and accommodation all along the way.

U.S. Highway 101, by contrast, has just a single lane in each direction for most of the journey. There are tight turns with little or no room for error, and it is not uncommon to be stuck behind a truck going up a steep incline with no opportunity to overtake. The roadside amenities are fewer and further between and often not in good repair.

Yet the beauty of that road leaves one breathless. The tight turns are bounded by dense forests of evergreen on one side, and the Pacific Ocean on the other.

Also, shortly after branching off onto the 101, one gets to stop at Clarks Restaurant in Grays Harbor county. There, if one asks the waitress what is good on the voluminous menu of guilty pleasures, she'll reply, somewhat taken aback, that everything is, and she will be prove to be quite right.

Most important, after a few hours, one will reach the enclave of Cannon Beach. There, a few miles of wind and rain-swept coastline and mountain views stretch natural splendor far out beyond the reach of any language one might try using to describe it.

The journey toward software security is currently like the choice between Interstate 5 and U.S. Highway 101. Interstate 5 is Windows security as it exists today. There are facilities galore, and it will take one to one's destination much more quickly. US 101 is claims-based security. It is not only beautiful, but also leads to Paradise, yet the journey will be longer, and the facilities much less frequent and somewhat poorly equipped. This chapter, though, purports to be like Clarks Restaurant, showing hardy travelers a menu of things that it thinks are all wonderful, and fortifying them for the road ahead.

Introduction

The notion of claims has been stalking through the woods of the last few chapters. In Chapter 7, "Security Basics," it was explained that the Windows Communication Foundation's Extensible Security Infrastructure (XSI) takes all the different kinds of credentials that users might offer to authenticate themselves, and translates those into a set of claims. Then in Chapters 8, "Using Windows CardSpace to Secure Windows Applications," and 9, "Using Windows CardSpace to Secure Web Applications," which introduced Windows CardSpace, it was proposed that digital identity is nothing more than a collection of claims that might be believed or not, with CardSpace providing a way for users to manage their multiple digital identities. Now the notion of claims will emerge from the trees into a clearing where it can be seen for what it is.

Securing Resources with Claims

Consider this scenario. A man walks into a bar, places his driver's license and a small sum of money on the bar, and asks the bartender for a beer. The bartender looks at the driver's license, takes the money, and serves the man a beer.

Here, the bar represents a service. The serving of beer is an operation. The beer is a protected resource. To access it, a person must be of legal drinking age, and must pay a sum of money for it.

The driver's license and the money both represent claim sets. A claim set is a number of claims provided by the same issuer. In the case of the driver's license, the issuer is a government department that licenses drivers, and in the case of the money, the issuer is a country's central bank. However, those issuers are themselves present merely as sets of claims: as logos, signatures, and images on the driver's license and the money.

Claims consist of a type, a right, and a value. One of the claims in the set of claims represented by the driver's license is the driver's date of birth. The type of that claim is *date of birth*, and the value of that claim is the driver's birth date. The right that a claim confers on the bearer specifies what the bearer can do with the claim's value. In the case of the claim of the driver's date of birth, the right is simply possession. The driver possesses that date of birth but cannot, for example, alter it.

In examining the driver's license and the money, the bartender translates the claim about the bearer's date of birth provided by the driver's license into a claim about the bearer's age. The bartender also translates the value of each of the proffered items of money on the bar into a claim about the total sum of money offered. The rules by which the bartender performs these translations from an input claim set to an output claim set constitute the bartender's authorization policy. The input claim set of an authorization policy is referred to as the evaluation context, and the output claim set is referred to as the authorization context. A set of authorization policies constitute an authorization domain.

In taking the money and serving the beer, the bartender compares the claim about the age of the person asking for a beer to the minimum drinking age, and compares the total sum of money offered to the price of the requested beer. In that process, the bartender is comparing the authorization context claim set yielded by the authorization policy, to the access requirements for the operation of serving a beer. It so happened that the authorization context claim set of the age of the man asking for the beer, and the total sum of money offered, satisfied the access requirements for the operation, so the bartender served the man a beer.

This is how the claims-based security system provided by XSI works. Access to an operation on a protected resource is authorized based on claims. Claims have a type, a right, and a value. A claim set is a number of claims provided by the same issuer. The issuer of a claim set is itself a claim set. Authorization based on claims is accomplished in two steps. First, an authorization policy is executed, which takes an evaluation context claim set as input and translates that into an authorization context claim set that it outputs. Then the claims in the authorization context claim set are compared to the access requirements of the operation, and, depending on the outcome of that comparison, access to the operation is denied or granted.

Claims-Based Authorization Versus Role-Based Authorization

How does this claims-based approach to authorization compare to role-based authorization, which is a fairly common approach to controlling what users can do with software applications? A definition of role-based authorization would be helpful in answering that question.

"Role-based authorization is a mechanism that uses roles to assign users suitable rights for performing system tasks and permissions for accessing resources" (Tulloch 2003, 281). A role is a "symbolic category that collects together users who share the same levels of security privileges" (Tulloch 2003, 281).

Role-based authorization requires first identifying the user, and then ascertaining the roles to which the user is assigned, and finally comparing those roles to the roles that are authorized to access a resource. Therefore, in the role-based authorization system provided by Microsoft .NET role-based security, for example, the most important element is the principal object, which incorporates a user's identity and any roles to which the user belongs (.NET Framework Class Library 2006; Freeman and Jones 2003, 249).

By contrast, if one recalls what the bartender did in deciding whether to serve a beer to the man requesting one in the previous scenario, it is noteworthy that identifying the man was not important. Certainly, the proffered driver's license could also be used to establish the man's identity because driver's licenses do typically make claims about the bearer's identity, but those claims were not important to the bartender; the bartender was interested only in the license's claim about the date of birth of the bearer. If the man proceeded to rob the bartender, identifying him would no doubt become important.

In general, claims-based authorization subsumes role-based authorization. To be precise, identity is just one sort of right to the value of a claim—the right of using the value of the claim to identify oneself. A birth date is not a value of a claim that you have the right to use to identify yourself because many people share the same birth date, whereas a photographic portrait is a value of a claim that you have the right to use to identify yourself. In addition, a role is just one type of claim.

Claims-Based Authorization Versus Access Control Lists

How does the claims-based approach to authorization provided by XSI compare to controlling the use of resources with access control lists (ACLs), an approach that is common in administering access to network resources? Once again, having a definition of ACLs would be useful in answering the question.

"ACLs are composed of a series of Access Control Entries (ACEs) that specify which operations [a user or group] can perform on [a resource]" (Tulloch 2003, 7). An ACE consists of a security identifier (SID) identifying a user or group, and a set of access rights defining which operations the user or group is allowed or not allowed to perform on the resource (Tulloch 2003, 7).

ACLs "are used on Microsoft Windows platforms to control access to securable [resources] such as files, processes, services, shares, [and] printers" (Tulloch 2003, 7). Specifically, "[w]hen a user account is created on a Microsoft Windows platform, it is assigned a [SID] that uniquely identifies the account to the operating system" (Tulloch 2003, 7). When the user logs on using that account, an access token is created that contains the SID for that account and the SIDs of the groups to which the account belongs. That token "is then copied to all processes and threads owned by the account" (Tulloch 2003, 7). When the user tries to access a resource secured using an ACL, the SIDs in the token are compared with the SIDs in each ACE of the ACL, until a match is found, and access is either granted or denied (Tulloch 2003, 7).

Once again, claims-based authorization subsumes access control lists as a special case. The credentials by which a user logs on to an operating system, and the SIDs contained in the access token, are both claim sets. The process by which the operating system exchanges the credentials by which the user logs on for the SIDs in the access token that it issues is simply one case of the execution of an authorization policy. Comparing the SIDs in an access token with the SIDs in an ACL is merely an instance of comparing the claims in an authorization context claim set to the access requirements of whatever operation the user wants to perform on the resource secured by the ACL.

However, the more general model provided by XSI works far better than ACLs to accommodate the requirements of authorizing access to a distributed system. There are three reasons.

First, access tokens were never designed to be exchanged across platforms. Claims, by contrast, can be readily expressed in standard, interoperable formats like the one defined by the Security Assertion Markup Language (SAML). Second, access tokens are issued by operating systems. Claims, however, can be issued by any source. Third, and most important, the SIDs in access tokens and ACLs are generally useful only within the scope of the operating system issuing the access tokens. If that operating system is a domain controller, the utility of its SIDs will extend as far as the domain does. In contrast, a claim can be meaningful wherever the issuer of the claim is trusted.

Adopting Claims-Based Authorization

However, despite these advantages of claim-based authorization over role-based authorization and access control lists, you should not necessarily eschew role-based authorization and access control lists in favor of claims-based authorization. The use of role-based authorization and access control lists is supported by a vast number of powerful tools. Many such tools are built into Microsoft Windows and their use is customary among network administrators. Support for claims-based authorization is limited to XSI, Windows CardSpace, and Active Directory Federation Services.

So, instead of seeing claims-based authorization as a superior alternative to role-based authorization and access control lists, a wiser approach would be to use them together, leveraging their respective strengths where it is most appropriate to do so. Claims-based authorization is especially effective for controlling access to resources across platforms and between organizations. Therefore, in cases in which the users of one organization need to access resources managed by the systems of another organization, have them exchange their access tokens for claims that the other organization can use to decide whether to grant the users access.

How exactly might such a solution be implemented? The Web Services Trust Language (WS-Trust) is a standard language for requesting and issuing claim sets. A system that issues claim sets in accordance with that language is called a security token service (STS) (Gudgin and Nadalin 2005, 7; Cabrera and Kurt 2005, 24-27). An organization whose users need to access the facilities of another organization's systems could provide their users with an STS from which they could request claim sets that the other organization's systems would understand. That STS would take the claims constituted by the SIDs in the users' access tokens and apply an authorization policy that would yield claims with types, rights, and values agreed on with the other organization. That other organization would provide a second STS to accept those claims and apply an authorization policy of its own to yield claims that the other systems within that organization could then use to decide whether to grant a user access to their resources. This solution is depicted in Figure 10.1. The approach has several important virtues.

First, trust relationships are minimized and the management of them is centralized. Specifically, the services with resources to protect need to trust the claims from only a single issuer; namely, their own organization's STS. That STS can be configured to trust claims issued by any number of other organizations' STSs. Configuring an STS to trust claims issued by another organization's STS is simply a matter of giving it access to the other organization's public key.

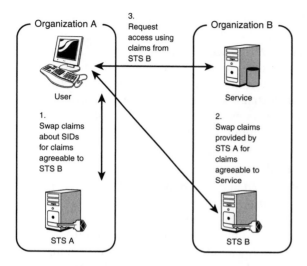

FIGURE 10.1   Cross-organization claims-based authorization.

Second, the claims that one organization makes about its users attempting to access another organization's services are also hidden from the services by the authorization policy of the STS they trust. That STS applies the authorization policy to translate the claims made by the other organizations into claims that are familiar to the services. That process of translating the diverse sorts of claims that various organizations might make into the sorts of claims that are familiar to a suite of services is commonly referred to as *claim normalization*.

Third, the administration of access to services is truly federated. Federation is the formation of a unity in which the participants retain control over their internal affairs (*Oxford Dictionary of Current English* 2001), thereby minimizing the cost of maintaining the unity. In this case, the addition or removal of users and the elevation or reduction in users' privileges by the system administrators in one organization will determine their rights to access the services of the other organization, without the system administrators of that other organization needing to be involved. This benefit will be quite vividly demonstrated in the following exercise.

Leveraging Claims-Based Security Using XSI

The exercise begins with a Windows Communication Foundation solution in which access to an intranet resource is controlled using role-based authorization. That solution will show how the securing of Windows Communication Foundation applications simply leverages existing, familiar facilities of Microsoft Windows and Microsoft .NET, saving system administrators from having to learn new concepts and tools and saving software developers from having to learn new concepts and class libraries.

The exercise then proceeds to show how, with XSI, the same resource can be accessed from the same client deployed in a separate, federated organization, with the access being authorized based on claims. What should be impressive is that neither the code of the client nor the code of the service managing the resource will need to be altered to accomplish a fundamental change in how access to the resource is controlled. That should serve as yet another eloquent demonstration of the power of the software factory template for software communications that the Windows Communication Foundation provides, allowing you to fundamentally alter the behavior of an application by making some changes to a model while leaving its code intact.

Authorizing Access to an Intranet Resource Using Windows Identity

This first step will demonstrate a Windows Communication Foundation solution in which access to an intranet resource is controlled using role-based authorization. The role-based authorization is accomplished using .NET Role-Based Security, the ASP.NET 2.0 AuthorizationStoreRoleProvider, and the Windows Server 2003 Authorization Manager.

Readers using Windows XP Service Pack 2 can install the Windows Server 2003 Authorization Manager onto their systems by installing the Windows Server 2003 Service Pack 1 Administration Tools Pack. That can be obtained by searching for "Windows Server 2003 SP1 Administration Tools Pack" from the Microsoft Downloads Center.

Follow these steps to get started:

1. Copy the code associated with this chapter downloaded from http://www.crypt-maker.com/WindowsCommunicationFoundationUnleashed to the folder C:\WCFHandsOn. The code is all in a folder called AdvancedSecurity, which contains two subfolders, one of which is called IntranetSecurity. That subfolder contains a single Visual Studio solution: Security.sln.

2. Open that solution in Visual Studio 2005. It contains two projects. The Service project is for building a console application that hosts a Windows Communication Foundation service. The Client project is for building a Windows Forms client application that attempts to access the resources provided by the service.

3. If, for some reason, the solution was not placed in the folder C:\WCFHandsOn\AdvancedSecurity\IntranetSolution, open the App.config file of the Service project and modify the entry

   ```
   connectionString="msxml://C:\WCFHandsOn\
   ➥AdvancedSecurity\IntranetSolution\AuthorizationStore.xml" />
   ```

   so that it refers to the actual path to the AuthorizationStore.xml file that is in the same folder as the Security.sln solution file itself.

4. Choose Debug, Start debugging from the Visual Studio 2005 menus. The console application of the service should appear, as well as the user interface of the Resource Access client application, which is shown in Figure 10.2. That user interface has two large buttons. The button on the left has a picture of coal on its face, and the one on the right has a picture of a more valuable resource, a diamond, on its face.

FIGURE 10.2   The Resource Access client user interface.

5. After the console application of the service has shown some activity, click on the coal button. A message box should appear confirming that the less valuable resource, coal, has been accessed, as shown in Figure 10.3.

FIGURE 10.3   Successfully accessing coal.

6. Now click on the diamond button. Alas, access to the more valuable resource of a diamond should be denied. Specifically, a message box like the one shown in Figure 10.4 should appear.

FIGURE 10.4   Unsuccessfully attempting to access a diamond.

7. Choose Debug, Stop Debugging from the Visual Studio 2005 menus, and close the console of the service.

The next few steps will explain why the coal was accessible but the diamond was not. Begin by following these instructions to open the Windows Server 2003 Authorization Manager user interface:

1. Open the Microsoft Management Console by choosing Run from the Windows Start menu, and entering this command in the Run dialog box:

    mmc

2. Select File, Add/Remove Snap-in from the Microsoft Management Console's menus.

3. Click on the Add button on the Add/Remove Snap-in dialog.

4. Select Authorization Manager from the Add Standalone Snap-in dialog; click on the Add button, and then the Close button.

5. Back on the Add/Remove Snap-in dialog, click on the OK button.

   Now the Windows Server 2003 Authorization Manager user interface should be open, as shown in Figure 10.5. Proceed to examine the authorization store used to control access to the service's resources.

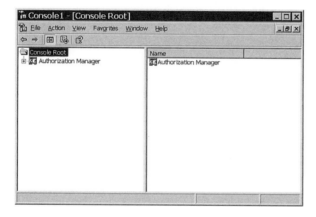

FIGURE 10.5   The Windows Server 2003 Authorization Manager user interface.

6. In the tree in the left pane of the Authorization Manager user interface in the Microsoft Management Console, right-click on Authorization Manager, and choose Open Authorization Store from the context menu.

7. Click Browse in the Open Authorization Store dialog shown in Figure 10.6, browse to the file C:\WCFHandsOn\AdvancedSecurity\IntranetSolution\AuthorizationStore.xml in the file dialog that appears, and click on the Open button.

FIGURE 10.6   Opening an authorization store.

10

8. Expand the Authorization Manager tree in the left pane as shown in Figure 10.7. Select the StaffMember node in the tree on the left, and observe, in the pane on the right, that the users in the Everyone group are assigned to the StaffMember role.

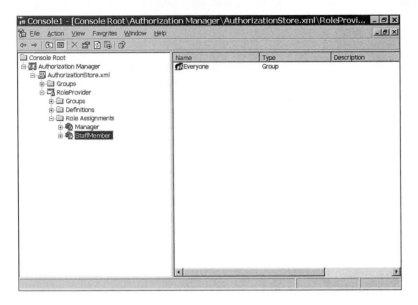

FIGURE 10.7   Role assignments.

9. Select the Manager node and see that no user is assigned to the Manager role.

10. Right-click on the Manager node, and select Assign Windows Users and Groups from the context menu. Enter the username of the currently logged-on user in the Select Users and Groups dialog, and click OK.

11. Start debugging the application again.

12. When the console of the service shows some activity, click on the diamond button in the Resource Access client user interface. The message shown in Figure 10.8 should confirm that diamonds are now accessible.

FIGURE 10.8   Successfully accessing diamonds.

13. Choose Debug, Stop Debugging from the Visual Studio 2005 menus, and close the console of the service.

14. Return to the authorization store console, and select the `Manager` node under `Role Assignments`. Right-click on the Administrator entry in the panel on the right, and choose Delete from the context menu to restore the access of the currently logged-on user to its original state.

Evidently, access to resources managed by the Windows Communication Foundation service is being controlled based on the roles to which the user of the client application is assigned within the Windows Server 2003 Authorization Manager authorization store, C:\WCFHandsOn\AdvancedSecurity\IntranetSolution\AuthorizationStore.xml. The next few steps will reveal how that is being done:

1. In the Security solution in Visual Studio 2005, open the ResourceAccessServiceType.cs code module of the Service project. The content of the module is shown in Listing 10.1. There it is apparent that access to the operations of the service by which resources are made available is controlled by .NET Role-Based Security `System.Security.Permissions.PrincipalPermission` attributes that specify that only users assigned to the role of Manager can access the more valuable resource of diamonds.

LISTING 10.1   Using `PrincipalPermission` Attributes

```
using System;
using System.Collections;
using System.Collections.Generic;
using System.Security.Permissions;
using System.Runtime.Serialization;
using System.ServiceModel;
using System.Text;
using System.Web;
using System.Web.Security;


namespace Service
{
    public class ResourceAccessServiceType: IResourceAccessContract
    {
        #region IResourceAccessContract Members

        [PrincipalPermission(SecurityAction.Demand, Role = "StaffMember")]
        [PrincipalPermission(SecurityAction.Demand, Role = "Manager")]
        string IResourceAccessContract.AccessCoal()
        {
            return "Here is your coal!";
        }
```

LISTING 10.1   Continued

```
    [PrincipalPermission(SecurityAction.Demand, Role = "Manager")]
    string IResourceAccessContract.AccessDiamond()
    {
        return "Here is your diamond!";
    }

    #endregion
}
}
```

2. Open the App.config file in the Service project. Its contents are reproduced in Listing 10.2.

The binding for the Windows Communication Foundation service that has the resources is the netTcpBinding. By default, that binding uses Windows credentials via Kerberos or NTLM to identify those users to the service.

The service has a System.ServiceModel.Description.ServiceAuthorization with the arbitrary name ServiceBehavior associated with it. That behavior is configured so that its PrincipalPermissionMode property is assigned the value System.ServiceModel.Description.PrincipalPermissionMode.UseAspNetRoles, and its RoleProviderName property is assigned the name of the Role Provider with the arbitrary name, AuthorizationStoreRoleProvider.

That Role Provider is defined lower down in the configuration file. It is configured to use C:\WCFHandsOn\AdvancedSecurity\IntranetSolution\AuthorizationStore.xml as its authorization store.

So, by virtue of this configuration, the service is configured to authenticate users based on their Windows credentials, and then to determine whether the users are authorized to access the resources they request based on their membership in groups maintained in that authorization store. This approach to authorization was explained in Chapter 7 and merely serves to illustrate it.

LISTING 10.2   Service Configuration

```
<configuration>
  <system.serviceModel>
    <behaviors>
      <serviceBehaviors>
        <behavior name='ServiceBehavior'>
          <serviceAuthorization
            principalPermissionMode='UseAspNetRoles'
```

LISTING 10.2   Continued

```
          roleProviderName='AuthorizationStoreRoleProvider' />
          <serviceMetadata
            httpGetEnabled ='true'/>
        </behavior>
      </serviceBehaviors>
    </behaviors>
    <services>
      <service
        name="Service.ResourceAccessServiceType"
        behaviorConfiguration='ServiceBehavior'>
        <host>
          <baseAddresses>
            <add baseAddress='net.tcp://localhost:9000/Woodgrove'/>
            <add baseAddress='http://localhost:8000/Woodgrove'/>
          </baseAddresses>
        </host>
        <endpoint address="ResourceAccess"
          binding="netTcpBinding"
          contract="Service.IResourceAccessContract" />
        <endpoint address="mex"
          binding="mexHttpBinding"
          contract="IMetadataExchange" />
      </service>
    </services>
  </system.serviceModel>
  <system.web>
    <roleManager defaultProvider="AuthorizationStoreRoleProvider"
      enabled="true"
      cacheRolesInCookie="true"
      cookieName=".ASPROLES"
      cookieTimeout="30"
      cookiePath="/"
      cookieRequireSSL="false"
      cookieSlidingExpiration="true"
      cookieProtection="All" >
    <providers>
      <clear />
      <add
        name="AuthorizationStoreRoleProvider"
        type="System.Web.Security.AuthorizationStoreRoleProvider"
        connectionStringName="AuthorizationServices"
        applicationName="RoleProvider" />
```

10

LISTING 10.2   Continued

```
      </providers>
    </roleManager>
  </system.web>
  <connectionStrings>
    <add
      name="AuthorizationServices"
      connectionString="msxml://C:\WCFHandsOn\
➥AdvancedSecurity\IntranetSolution\AuthorizationStore.xml" />
    </connectionStrings>
  </configuration>
```

Improving the Initial Solution

The shortcoming of this solution for authorization is in its ultimate dependency on
`System.Security.Permissions.PrincipalPermission` attributes to control access to the
service's operations. Those attributes have the effect of winding the code for authenticating users into code of the service itself.

As explained in Chapter 7, XSI allows you to do better. It can translate whatever credentials are used to authenticate users into a list of claims and isolate the evaluation of those
claims into a separate assembly that is identified by the configuration of the service.

That will benefit the design of the service in two ways at once. First, it has the more
obvious effect of disentangling the programming of the business logic from the programming and management of access to the service. Second, it has the more subtle yet significant effect of disentangling access to the service from any single issuer of credentials, or,
to use the terminology of the Web Services Federation Language specification, from any
single security realm (Kaler and Nadalin 2003). Where access to the service was formerly
tied to the credentials of a particular Windows domain, now it will be evaluated based on
claims that might have originated from any issuer, and not even necessarily claims about
the user's identity.

The following steps demonstrate how easily that profound transformation can be accomplished by modifying the service to use an XSI Service Authorization Manager to authorize access to its resources:

1. Open the ResourceAccessServiceType.cs code module of the Service project, and
   comment out the `System.Security.Permissions.PrincipalPermission` attributes,
   as shown in Listing 10.3.

LISTING 10.3   Foregoing `PrinciplePermission` Attributes

```
using System;
using System.Collections;
using System.Collections.Generic;
```

LISTING 10.3   Continued

```
using System.Security.Permissions;
using System.Runtime.Serialization;
using System.ServiceModel;
using System.Text;
using System.Web;
using System.Web.Security;

namespace Service
{
    public class ResourceAccessServiceType: IResourceAccessContract
    {
        #region IResourceAccessContract Members

        //[PrincipalPermission(SecurityAction.Demand, Role = "StaffMember")]
        //[PrincipalPermission(SecurityAction.Demand, Role = "Manager")]
        string IResourceAccessContract.AccessCoal()
        {
            return "Here is your coal!";
        }

        //[PrincipalPermission(SecurityAction.Demand, Role = "Manager")]
        string IResourceAccessContract.AccessDiamond()
        {
            return "Here is your diamond!";
        }

        #endregion
    }
}
```

2. Modify the App.config file of the Service project to look like the configuration in Listing 10.4. To save you from having to make the changes manually, a copy of the configuration file is in the folder C:\WCFHandsOn\AdvancedSecurity\IntranetSolution\Listing10.4 folder.

   The key alteration made is in how the System.ServiceModel.Description.ServiceAuthorization behavior is configured. Now it is configured so as to delegate the management of authorization to an XSI Service Authorization Manager—in this case, the Service.AccessChecker type in the assembly with the arbitrary name, ServiceAuthorizationManager:

```
<behavior name='ServiceBehavior'>
        <serviceAuthorization
serviceAuthorizationManagerType='Service.AccessChecker,
➥ServiceAuthorizationManager'
```

10

```
                      principalPermissionMode='None'  />
            [...]
      </behavior>
```

LISTING 10.4   ServiceAuthorizationManagerType Configuration

```
<?xml version="1.0" encoding="utf-8" ?>
<configuration>
  <configSections>
    <section
      name="operationRequirements"
      type="Service.OperationRequirementsConfigurationSection,
➥ServiceAuthorizationManager" />
  </configSections>
  <operationRequirements>
    <operation
    identifier="http://tempuri.org/IResourceAccessContract/AccessCoal">
      <role name="Manager"/>
      <role name="StaffMember"/>
    </operation>
    <operation
    identifier="http://tempuri.org/IResourceAccessContract/AccessDiamond">
      <role name="Manager"/>
    </operation>
  </operationRequirements>
  <system.serviceModel>
    <behaviors>
      <serviceBehaviors>
        <behavior name="'ServiceBehavior'">
          <serviceAuthorization
          serviceAuthorizationManagerType=
➥"Service.AccessChecker,ServiceAuthorizationManager"
          principalPermissionMode="None" />
          <serviceMetadata httpGetEnabled ="true"/>
        </behavior>
      </serviceBehaviors>
    </behaviors>
    <services>
      <service
        name="Service.ResourceAccessServiceType"
        behaviorConfiguration="ServiceBehavior">
        <host>
          <baseAddresses>
            <add baseAddress="net.tcp://localhost:9000/Woodgrove"/>
```

LISTING 10.4   Continued

```
            <add baseAddress="http://localhost:8000/Woodgrove"/>
          </baseAddresses>
        </host>
        <endpoint address="ResourceAccess"
        binding="netTcpBinding"
        contract="Service.IResourceAccessContract"/>
        <endpoint address="mex"
        binding="mexHttpBinding"
        contract="IMetadataExchange" />
      </service>
    </services>
  </system.serviceModel>
  <!— Role Provider Configuration —>
  <system.web>
    <roleManager defaultProvider="AuthorizationStoreRoleProvider"
    enabled="true"
    cacheRolesInCookie="true"
    cookieName=".ASPROLES"
    cookieTimeout="30"
    cookiePath="/"
    cookieRequireSSL="false"
    cookieSlidingExpiration="true"
    cookieProtection="All" >
      <providers>
        <clear />
        <add
        name="AuthorizationStoreRoleProvider"
        type="System.Web.Security.AuthorizationStoreRoleProvider"
        connectionStringName="AuthorizationServices"
        applicationName="RoleProvider" />
      </providers>
    </roleManager>
  </system.web>
  <!— Connection Strings —>
  <connectionStrings>
    <add
    name="AuthorizationServices"
    connectionString="msxml://C:\WCFHandsOn\
➥AdvancedSecurity\IntranetSolution\AuthorizationStore.xml" />
  </connectionStrings>
</configuration>
```

10

3. Add the project for building the `ServiceAuthorizationManager` assembly to the solution now by choosing File, Add, Existing Project from the Visual Studio 2005 menus, and selecting ServiceAuthorizationManager.csproj from the C:\WCFHandsOn\AdvancedSecurity\IntranetSolution\IntranetServiceAuthorization Manager folder. Be careful not to select the similarly named project from the InternetServiceAuthorizationManager folder—that one will be used later.

4. Study the code of the `System.AccessChecker` class in the AccessChecker.cs file of the ServiceAuthorizationManager project. It is reproduced in Listing 10.5. The `System.AccessChecker` class is an XSI Service Authorization Manager because it derives from derives from XSI's `System.ServiceModel.ServiceAuthorizationManager` base class, and overrides its virtual `CheckAccess()` method. That method is invoked for every inbound request. By that time, XSI has performed its magic of translating the Windows credential authenticated via the `NetTcpBinding` into a set of claims. The `System.ServiceModel.ServiceAuthorizationManager` subclass that is the `System.AccessChecker` examines those claims. It decides whether the claims satisfy the requirements for processing the request, the nature of the request being identified by its `Action` header. In this particular case, the requirements for processing each request are defined in a custom section of the configuration file

```
<operationRequirements>
  <operation
  identifier="http://tempuri.org/IResourceAccessContract/AccessCoal">
    <role name="Manager"/>
    <role name="StaffMember"/>
  </operation>
  <operation
  identifier="http://tempuri.org/IResourceAccessContract/AccessDiamond">
    <role name="Manager"/>
  </operation>
</operationRequirements>
```

although they could be defined anywhere. The decision about whether the claims submitted satisfy the request is made by selecting a claim about the user's name from among the claims, and querying the authorization store that was used previously, to determine whether the user is assigned to a specified role:

```
if (string.Compare(
    claim.ClaimType,
    "http://schemas.xmlsoap.org/ws/2005/05/identity/claims/name",
    true) == 0)
    {
```

```
            userName = (string)claim.Resource;
            foreach (string requiredRole in requiredRoles)
            {
                if (Roles.Provider.IsUserInRole(
                            userName,
                                requiredRole))
                {
                    return true;
                }
            }
        }
    }
```

However, the determination of the adequacy of the claims can be made in any fashion and based on any criteria whatsoever. Later, the determination will be made based on a Windows Workflow Foundation rule set.

LISTING 10.5   A ServiceAuthorizationManager

```
sing System;
using System.Collections.Generic;
using System.Configuration;
using System.IdentityModel.Claims;
using System.IdentityModel.Policy;
using System.IO;
using System.ServiceModel;
using System.Web.Security;

namespace Service
{

    public class AccessChecker : ServiceAuthorizationManager
    {
        private Dictionary<string, string[]> accessRequirements = null;

        public AccessChecker()
        {
            this.accessRequirements = new Dictionary<string, string[]>();

            OperationRequirementsConfigurationSection
                operationRequirementsConfigurationSection
                = ConfigurationManager.GetSection("operationRequirements")
                as OperationRequirementsConfigurationSection;
```

10

LISTING 10.5   Continued

```
            OperationRequirementsCollection requirements =
        operationRequirementsConfigurationSection.OperationRequirements;
        List<string> roles = null;
        foreach (OperationElement operationElement in requirements)
        {
            roles = new List<string>(operationElement.Roles.Count);
            foreach (RoleElement roleElement in operationElement.Roles)
            {
                roles.Add(roleElement.Name);
            }

            this.accessRequirements.Add(
                operationElement.Identifier,
                roles.ToArray());
        }
    }

    public override bool CheckAccess(OperationContext operationContext)
    {
        string header =
        operationContext.RequestContext.RequestMessage.Headers.Action;
        string[] requiredRoles = null;
        if (!(this.accessRequirements.TryGetValue(
                            header,
                            out requiredRoles)))
        {
            return false;
        }

        string userName = null;
        foreach(ClaimSet claimSet in
operationContext.ServiceSecurityContext.AuthorizationContext.ClaimSets)
        {
            foreach (Claim claim in claimSet)
            {
                if (string.Compare(
                claim.ClaimType,
    "http://schemas.xmlsoap.org/ws/2005/05/identity/claims/name",
                true) == 0)
                {
                    userName = (string)claim.Resource;
```

LISTING 10.5   Continued

```
                        foreach (string requiredRole in requiredRoles)
                        {
                            if (Roles.Provider.IsUserInRole(
                                                    userName,
                                                    requiredRole))
                            {
                                return true;
                            }
                        }
                    }
                }
            }
            return false;
        }
    }
}
```

Follow these steps to test the modified solution:

1. Choose Debug, Start Debugging to start debugging the application once again.

2. When the console of the service shows some activity, click on the coal button in the Resource Access client user interface. The message confirming access to the coal should appear, as before.

3. Click on the diamond button of the Resource Access client user interface. The message denying access to the diamonds should appear.

4. Choose Debug, Stop Debugging from the Visual Studio 2005 menus.

By virtue of these modifications to the original application facilitated by the Windows Communication Foundation, the authorization of the users is no longer entangled with the code of the service itself. The configuration of the application identifies a separate class, an XSI Service Authorization Manager, that is responsible for managing access to the service's operations. In addition, how the authorization is done is no longer tied to any particular type of credentials issued by any particular security realm. XSI is translating all varieties of credentials into a collection of claims that the authorization mechanism can evaluate. Although the particular XSI Service Authorization Manager used to do the authentication in this case is anticipating a claim about a Windows username, and is evaluating that claim based on a Windows Server 2003 Authorization Manager authorization store, a different authorization mechanism can be swapped in through a simple change in configuration. That change will be among the changes made as the chapter proceeds.

10

Adding STSs as the Foundation for Federation

Assume now that the intranet service used up to this point is deployed within an organization called Woodgrove. In the following steps, that service will be made accessible from within a partner organization called Fabrikam.

That feat will be accomplished in accordance with the architecture depicted in Figure 10.1. Both Fabrikam and Woodgrove will provide an STS. The Woodgrove STS will be configured to trust claims about users issued by the Fabrikam STS, and the Woodgrove service will be configured to trust claims about the users made by the Woodgrove STS.

When a user of the Resource Access client application within Fabrikam uses that application to make use of an operation provided by the Woodgrove service, the application will request a set of claims from the Fabrikam STS. That STS will execute an authorization policy to determine the claims it should issue for the user. That authorization policy authenticates the user from the user's Windows credentials and determines the roles to which the user is assigned using the ASP.NET 2.0 `AuthorizationStoreRoleProvider` and the Windows Server 2003 Authorization Manager. Based on the roles to which the user is assigned, the Fabrikam STS issues a set of claims about the user's roles to the Resource Access client application.

The Resource Access client application will submit the claim set obtained from the Fabrikam STS to the Woodgrove STS, which trusts claims issued by the Fabrikam STS. The Woodgrove STS will execute an authorization policy to translate the claims about the user's role made by the Fabrikam STS into a set of claims about the user's roles with which Woodgrove's service is familiar.

The Resource Access client application will submit the set of claims about the user's roles issued by the Woodgrove STS to the Woodgrove service, which trusts claims issued by that STS. The Woodgrove service will compare the Woodgrove STS's claims about the user's roles with the roles that are permitted access to the operation that the user is attempting to employ via the Resource Access client. By doing so, it will be able to determine whether the user should be granted access to the operation.

Certificate Installation

Configuring the Woodgrove STS to trust claims about users issued by the Fabrikam STS is a matter of ensuring that the Woodgrove STS can authenticate claims signed by the Fabrikam STS. To facilitate that, some X.509 certificates will need to be installed. Follow these steps to accomplish that task:

1. Follow the instructions in the "Installing Certificates" section in Chapter 7 to install X.509 certificates for Woodgrove and Fabrikam Enterprises.

2. The next few steps are for copying those certificates from the local machine's personal store to the local machine's Trusted People store. In reality, the Fabrikam Enterprises' certificate would be in the Trusted People store on the Woodgrove STS' machine, and the Woodgrove certificate would be in the Trusted People store on the

Fabrikam STS' machine, and, indeed, that is what configuring the two STSs to trust one another ultimately means. However, in this case, the Fabrikam STS and the Woodgrove STS are assumed to running on the same machine, so both certificates are going into the same Trusted People store. Just realize that the Woodgrove certificate is being put there so that the Fabrikam STS can trust the Woodgrove's STS' claims, and the Fabrikam Enterprises certificate is being put there so that the Woodgrove STS can trust the Fabrikam STS' claims. Proceed by opening the Microsoft Management Console by choosing Run from the Windows Start menus, and entering

mmc

3. Choose File, Add/Remove Snap-In from the Microsoft Management Console menus.

4. Click Add on the Add/Remove Snap-In dialog that opens.

5. Choose Certificates from the list of available standalone snap-ins presented, and click on the Add button.

6. Select Computer Account on the Certificates snap-in dialog, and click on the OK button.

7. Accept the default on the Select Computer dialog and click on the Finish button.

8. Click on the Close button on the Add Standalone Snap-In dialog.

9. Click on the OK button on the Add/Remove Snap-In dialog.

10. Expand the Certificates (Local Computer) node that now appears in the left panel of the Microsoft Management Console.

11. Expand the Personal child-node of the Certificates node.

12. Select the Certificates child-node of the Personal node.

13. Select both the FabrikamEnterprises certificate and the Woodgrove certificate that should now have appeared in the right panel. Do so by holding down a Shift key while clicking on first the FabrikamEnterprises certificate and then the Woodgrove certificate before releasing the Shift key.

14. Right-click on the selected certificates, and choose Copy from the context menu.

15. Right-click on the Trusted People child-node of the Certificates (Local Computer Node) and choose Paste from the context menu.

Adding the Fabrikam STS to the Solution

Now proceed to add the Fabrikam STS to the solution.

1. Add the project, FabrikamSecurityTokenService.csproj in the C:\WCFHandsOn\ AdvancedSecurity\IntranetSolution\FabrikamSecurityTokenService, to the Security solution. Do not risk building STSs from scratch, but rather use STSs that are widely

known to function correctly. Consequently, prebuilt STSs have been provided for use in this exercise. Those STSs have been programmed by Martin Gudgin, one of the two editors of the WS-Trust specification by which STSs are defined, so they could hardly have a finer lineage. The behavior of this particular STS will be customized in a later step.

2. Open the ISecurityTokenService.cs file of the FabrikamSecurityTokenService project in the Security solution, and examine the ISecurityTokenService service contract that the Fabrikam STS implements:

```
[ServiceContract(
        Name = "SecurityTokenService",
        Namespace = "http://tempuri.org")]
public interface ISecurityTokenService
{
    [OperationContract(Action = Constants.Trust.Actions.Issue,
                    ReplyAction = Constants.Trust.Actions.IssueReply)]
        Message ProcessRequestSecurityToken(Message rstMessage);
}
```

The important elements in the definition of this security contract are the terms `Constants.Trust.Actions.Issue` and `Constants.Trust.Actions.IssueReply`, which define the valid WS-Addressing Action header for a request message, and specify the WS-Addressing Action header for response messages. Those terms are defined in the Constants.cs file within the same project:

```
public const string Issue =
        "http://schemas.xmlsoap.org/ws/2005/02/trust/RST/Issue";
public const string IssueReply =
        "http://schemas.xmlsoap.org/ws/2005/02/trust/RSTR/Issue";
```

These values defined for the WS-Addressing Action headers are values defined in the Web Services Trust Language (WS-Trust) (Gudgin and Nadalin 2005) specification, which stipulates the WS-Addressing Action headers for SOAP messages exchanged with an STS. Consequently, the service contract defines an operation that can receive and return SOAP messages with the WS-Addressing Action headers defined by WS-Trust protocol for messages exchanged with an STS. Therefore, the service contract is, in effect, describing the interface of an STS as defined by the specification of the WS-Trust protocol. Or, in other words, the ISecurityTokenService contract defines the service contract of an STS as defined by the WS-Trust specification.

3. Open the App.config file of the FabrikamSecurityTokenService project in the Security solution to see how the Fabrikam STS is configured. The configuration is shown in Listing 10.6.

The appSettings included in that configuration are used by the code of the STS to identify the certificates to use to sign and encrypt the security tokens that it issues.

```
<appSettings>
        [...]
        <add key="ProofKeyCertificateIdentifier"
                value="CN=Woodgrove"/>
        <add key="IssuerCertificateIdentifier"
                value="CN=FabrikamEnterprises"/>
</appSettings>
```

The tokens will be signed with Fabrikam Enterprises' private key, and encrypted with Woodgrove's public key. The certificate of the recipient STS, Woodgrove's in this case, is referred to as the proof key, or more formally, in the WS-Trust Language as the proof-of-possession token (Gudgin and Nadalin 2005, 7), because it is only by possessing the private key corresponding to that certificate that the recipient will be able to decrypt the token and use it.

The binding specified in the configuration for the STS endpoint is the standard WSHttpBinding—it could be any binding. By default, services configured with the WSHttpBinding binding identify users by their Windows credentials.

LISTING 10.6   Fabrikam Configuration

```
<configuration>
  <appSettings>
    <add
      key="SecurityTokenServiceName"
      value="FabrikamEnterprises"/>
    <add
      key="ProofKeyCertificateIdentifier"
      value="CN=Woodgrove"/>
    <add
      key="IssuerCertificateIdentifier"
      value="CN=FabrikamEnterprises"/>
  </appSettings>
  <system.serviceModel>
    <services>
      <service
      name="SecurityTokenService.ConcreteSecurityTokenService"
      behaviorConfiguration="FabrikamSecurityTokenServiceBehavior">
        <host>
          <baseAddresses>
            <add baseAddress="http://localhost:8001/Fabrikam"/>
          </baseAddresses>
        </host>
        <endpoint
          address=""
```

10

LISTING 10.6   Continued

```
        binding="wsHttpBinding"
        contract="SecurityTokenService.ISecurityTokenService"/>
      <endpoint
        address="mex"
        binding="mexHttpBinding"
        contract="IMetadataExchange" />
    </service>
  </services>
  ...[]
  <system.serviceModel>
</configuration>
```

The Authorization Policy of the Fabrikam STS

In this particular case, users of the Resource Access client application seeking to use the Woodgrove Resource Access Service will be approaching the Fabrikam STS with their Windows credentials. The Fabrikam STS will issue them with a security token containing claims that the Woodgrove service will understand. In issuing those tokens, the Fabrikam STS will, in effect, be translating claims derived from the Windows credentials offered by the Fabrikam users into claims that the Woodgrove service can process.

Remember the analogy with the man attempting to access a drink in a bar using a driver's license and some money. What happened in that case? The bartender translated the claim about the bearer's date of birth provided by the driver's license into a claim about the bearer's age. The bartender also translated the value of each of the proffered items of money on the bar into a claim about the total sum of money being offered. The rules by which the bartender performs those translations from an input claim set to an output claim set was referred to as the bartender's *authorization policy*. The input claim set of an authorization policy was referred to as the *evaluation context*, and the output claim set was referred to as the *authorization context*.

Therefore, for the Fabrikam STS to do the translation from the Windows credentials of the Fabrikam users into claims that the Woodgrove service can process, it must implement some authorization policy.

1. Look again at the App.config file of the FabrikamSecurityTokenService project. It defines an authorization policy for the STS using the System.ServiceModel.Description.ServiceAuthorization behavior.

```
<behaviors>
        <serviceBehaviors>
                <behavior name='FabrikamSecurityTokenServiceBehavior'>
                        [...]
                        <serviceAuthorization>
                                <authorizationPolicies>
                                        <add
```

```
policyType=
➥'SecurityTokenService.AuthorizationPolicy, FabrikamSecurityTokenService'/>
                        </authorizationPolicies>
                    </serviceAuthorization>
                </behavior>
            </serviceBehaviors>
        </behaviors>
```

2. Study that authorization policy, which is in the AuthorizationPolicy.cs file of the project. The code is reproduced in Listing 10.7.

Authorization policies are defined by implementing the System.IdentityModel.Policy.IAuthorizationPolicy interface. The key member defined by that interface is the Evaluate() method.

The implementation of that method receives a set of claims that XSI has extracted from the user's credentials and incorporated into a System.IdentityModelPolicy.EvaluationContext object. What the code by which the Evaluate() method is implemented is required to do is examine the inbound claims in the System.IdentityModelPolicy.EvaluationContext object and decide on a set of claims to issue. Whatever claims are in the System.IdentityModelPolicy.EvaluationContext object when the Evaluate() method returns are the claims that the STS will include in the token that it issues to the user.

In this particular case, the implementation of the Evaluate() method takes the inbound claims extracted from the user's Windows credentials, looks up the roles to which the user is assigned in an Authorization Manager authorization store, and issues claims that the user is in those roles. Any translation mechanism could be programmed instead—the only constraint is that the claims that are issued must be claims that the Woodgrove STS will recognize.

LISTING 10.7   Fabrikam STS Authorization Policy

```
public class AuthorizationPolicy : IAuthorizationPolicy
{
        [...]

    bool IAuthorizationPolicy.Evaluate(
        EvaluationContext evaluationContext,
        ref object state)
    {
        List<Claim> claimsToAdd = new List<Claim>();
        ReadOnlyCollection<ClaimSet> inputClaims =
            evaluationContext.ClaimSets;
        for (int index = 0; index < inputClaims.Count; index++)
        {
```

10

LISTING 10.7   Continued

```
    foreach (Claim claim in
                    inputClaims[index].FindClaims(ClaimTypes.Name, null))
    {
        string[] roles = Roles.Provider.GetRolesForUser(
            (string)claim.Resource);
        foreach (string role in roles)
        {
            claimsToAdd.Add(
                new DefaultClaimSet(
                    ClaimSet.System,
                    new Claim[] {
                new Claim(
                    "http://schemas.fabrikam.com/2005/05/ClaimType/Role",
                    role,
                    Rights.PossessProperty) })[0]);
        }
    }
}

if (claimsToAdd.Count > 0)
{
    evaluationContext.AddClaimSet(
        this, new DefaultClaimSet(
        this.Issuer, claimsToAdd));
}

return true;
}

[...]

}
```

Adding the Woodgrove STS to the Solution

The Woodgrove STS will receive requests from Fabrikam users to issue them with security tokens by which they can make use of Woodgrove's Resource Access Service. In requesting security tokens from the Woodgrove STS, the Fabrikam users will be authenticated by the tokens issued by the Fabrikam STS. So, the task of the Woodgrove STS is to examine the inbound claims issued by the Fabrikam STS and decide what claims of its own to issue, claims that Woodgrove's Resource Access Service will be able to understand.

It would be natural to assume that Woodgrove's STS is providing tokens for use not only with the Resource Access Service but for use with any service deployed within Woodgrove. It is also natural to assume that it is managing access not just by Fabrikam users, but also by users within any of Woodgrove's partners. In that case, the Woodgrove STS will be responsible for claim normalization, translating the claims that each partner organization's STS makes about its users into claims understood by all of the services deployed within Woodgrove.

Like any claims translation work done by an STS, the Woodgrove STS's claim normalization is programmed into an authorization policy, and the Woodgrove STS could be programmed to do it in a variety of ways. It happens to use the Windows Workflow Foundation to accomplish the task. More specifically, the rules for translating inbound claims into the claims that it will issue are defined as a set of Windows Workflow Foundation rules. The translation of the inbound claims is done by executing a sequential workflow containing a policy activity that executes the rules.

Before adding the project by which the Woodgrove STS itself is constructed, one must add the projects for building the policy activity and the workflow that the STS project references:

1. Add the project, ClaimMappingActivity.csproj in the folder C:\WCFHandsOn\AdvancedSecurity\IntranetSolution\ClaimMappingActivity, to the solution.

2. Select the ClaimMappingActivity.cs file in that project and choose View, Designer from the Visual Studio 2005 menus.

3. On the designer surface, right-click on the ClaimMappingPolicy activity shown highlighted in Figure 10.9, and choose Properties from the context menu.

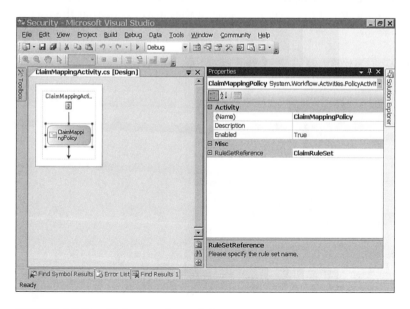

FIGURE 10.9   Claim-mapping activity.

4. In the property editor, click on the ellipsis button—also visible in Figure 10.9—next to the `RuleSetReference` property value. The Select Rule Set dialog shown in Figure 10.10 should open.

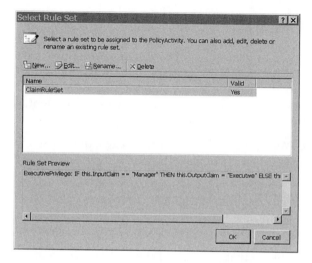

FIGURE 10.10 The Select Rule Set dialog.

5. Click on the Edit Rule Set button to open the Rule Set Editor shown in Figure 10.11. The Rule Set Editor shows the rule by which the Woodgrove STS will translate an inbound claim that a user is a manager into a claim that it will issue that the user is an executive.

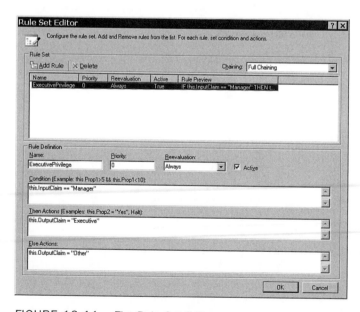

FIGURE 10.11 The Rule Set Editor.

6. Click Cancel to close the Rule Set Editor.

7. Click Cancel to close the Select Rule Set dialog.

8. Add the project, ClaimMappingWorkflow.csproj in the folder
   C:\WCFHandsOn\AdvancedSecurity\IntranetSolution\ClaimMappingWorkflow, to
   the solution.

9. Select the ClaimMappingWorkflow.cs file in that project, and choose View Designer
   from the Visual Studio 2005 menus. The sequential workflow shown in Figure 10.12
   should appear. That workflow consists of a
   System.Workflow.Activities.Replicator activity that contains the custom claim
   mapping activity constructed from the ClaimMappingActivity project. The
   System.Workflow.Activities.Replicator activity is for the purpose of executing
   another activity multiple times. It is required in this case because there may be
   several claims in a set of inbound claims. Therefore, the claim-mapping activity will
   need to be executed once for each of those claims so that all of them can be translated into output claims.

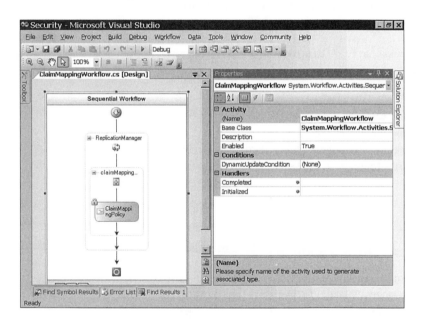

FIGURE 10.12   Claim-mapping workflow.

Now that the Windows Workflow Foundation components on which the Woodgrove STS
depends have been added to the solution, the Woodgrove STS itself can be added by
following these steps:

1. Add the project, WoodgroveSecurityTokenService.csproj from the folder
   C:\WCFHandsOn\AdvancedSecurity\IntranetSolution\WoodgroveSecurityTokenSer
   vice, to the solution.

2. Open the App.config file of the WoodgroveSecurityTokenService project to see how the Woodgrove STS is configured. The configuration is reproduced in Listing 10.9.

The Woodgrove STS is configured to use the predefined `WSFederationHttpBinding`, by which a service can be configured to authenticate requestors based on security tokens issued by a trusted STS. In this case, the Fabrikam STS is identified as a trusted issuer of security tokens.

As in the case of the Fabrikam STS, the authorization policy of the Woodgrove STS is configured using the `System.ServiceModel.Description.ServiceAuthorization` behavior. The authorization policy is the `SecurityTokenService.AuthorizationPolicy` class.

LISTING 10.8   Woodgrove STS Configuration

```
<services>
  <service
  name="SecurityTokenService.ConcreteSecurityTokenService"
  behaviorConfiguration="WoodgroveSecurityTokenServiceBehavior">
    <host>
      <baseAddresses>
        <add baseAddress="http://localhost:8002/Woodgrove"/>
      </baseAddresses>
    </host>
    <endpoint
      address=""
      binding="wsFederationHttpBinding"
      bindingConfiguration="WoodgroveSecurityTokenServiceBinding"
      contract="SecurityTokenService.ISecurityTokenService"  />
    <endpoint address="mex"
    binding="mexHttpBinding"
    contract="IMetadataExchange" />
  </service>
</services>
<bindings>
  <wsFederationHttpBinding>
    <binding name="'WoodgroveSecurityTokenServiceBinding'">
      <security mode="'Message'">
        <message>
          <issuerMetadata
          address="http://localhost:8001/Fabrikam/mex" >
          <identity>
            <dns value ="FabrikamEnterprises"/>
          </identity>
          </issuerMetadata>
        </message>
```

LISTING 10.8   Continued

```
      </security>
    </binding>
  </wsFederationHttpBinding>
</bindings>
<behaviors>
  <serviceBehaviors>
    <behavior name="WoodgroveSecurityTokenServiceBehavior">
      [...]
      <serviceAuthorization>
        <authorizationPolicies>
          <add
            policyType="SecurityTokenService.AuthorizationPolicy,
➥WoodgroveSecurityTokenService"/>
        </authorizationPolicies>
      </serviceAuthorization>
    </behavior>
  </serviceBehaviors>
</behaviors>
```

3. Examine that authorization policy, which is in the project's AuthorizationPolicy.cs file. It is reproduced in Listing 10.9.

Like any authorization policy type, this one implements the `System.IdentityModel.Policy.IAuthorizationPolicy` interface. The important work is done by the code that implements the interface's `Evaluate()` method.

By the time that code executes, XSI has extracted a set of claims from the security token accompanying the request to the Woodgrove STS—a security token that, in this particular case, will have been the security token issued by the Fabrikam STS. The set of claims extracted by XSI from the inbound security token is passed to the `Evaluate()` method, which in turn passes it to an instance of the claim-mapping workflow. The claim-mapping policy activity incorporated in that workflow executes the rules for translating an inbound claim to an outbound claim once for each inbound claim. The code in the authorization policy's `Evaluate()` method takes the claims yielded from the execution of the rules, and adds them to the evaluation context object. The STS takes the claims in the evaluation context object and issues a security token incorporating those claims to the requestor.

10

LISTING 10.9   Woodgrove STS Authorization Policy

```
public class AuthorizationPolicy : IAuthorizationPolicy
{
    [...]

    private string[] MapClaims(string[] inputClaims)
    {
        if (Thread.CurrentThread.Name == null)
        {
            Thread.CurrentThread.Name = Guid.NewGuid().ToString();
        }

        using (WorkflowRuntime workflowRuntime = new WorkflowRuntime())
        {
            workflowRuntime.StartRuntime();

            workflowRuntime.WorkflowCompleted += this.ClaimMappingCompleted;

            Type type = typeof(ClaimMappingWorkflow);

            Dictionary<string, object> parameters =
                new Dictionary<string, object>();
            parameters.Add(
                "RequestIdentifier",
                Thread.CurrentThread.Name);
            parameters.Add(
                "InputClaims",
                inputClaims);

            AutoResetEvent waitHandle = new AutoResetEvent(false);

            lock (this.waitHandlesLock)
            {
                this.waitHandles.Add(Thread.CurrentThread.Name, waitHandle);
            }

            workflowRuntime.CreateWorkflow(type, parameters).Start();

            waitHandle.WaitOne();

            workflowRuntime.StopRuntime();
        }
```

LISTING 10.9   Continued

```
        string[] outputClaims = null;
        lock (this.outputClaimsLock)
        {
            this.outputClaims.TryGetValue(
                Thread.CurrentThread.Name,
                out outputClaims);
            this.outputClaims.Remove(
                Thread.CurrentThread.Name);
        }

        return outputClaims;
    }


    #region IAuthorizationPolicy Members

    bool IAuthorizationPolicy.Evaluate(
                EvaluationContext evaluationContext,
        ref object state)
    {
        List<Claim> claimsToAdd = new List<Claim>();

        List<string> inputClaims = new List<string>();

        for (
                        int index = 0;
                        index < evaluationContext.ClaimSets.Count;
                        index++)
        {
            foreach (Claim claim in
                            evaluationContext.ClaimSets[index].FindClaims(
"http://schemas.fabrikam.com/2005/05/ClaimType//Role", null))
            {
                inputClaims.Add(claim.Resource.ToString());
            }
        }

        string[] roleClaims = this.MapClaims(inputClaims.ToArray());
        Claim targetClaim = null;
        foreach (string roleClaim in roleClaims)
        {
            targetClaim = new DefaultClaimSet(
                ClaimSet.System,
                new Claim[] {
```

10

LISTING 10.9   Continued

```
                    new Claim(
                        "http://schemas.woodgrove.com/2005/05/ClaimType/Role",
                        roleClaim,
                        Rights.PossessProperty) })[0];
            claimsToAdd.Add(targetClaim);
        }

        if (claimsToAdd.Count > 0)
        {
            evaluationContext.AddClaimSet(this, new DefaultClaimSet(
                this.Issuer, claimsToAdd));
        }


        return true;
    }
}
```

Reconfiguring the Resource Access Service

Now that the Woodgrove STS has been deployed, the Resource Access Service can be
reconfigured to demand that its users authenticate themselves with a security token
issued by that STS by following these steps.

1. Replace the contents of the App.config file of the Service project with the configuration in Listing 10.10. For convenience, the contents of that listing can be found in
   the App.config file in the folder
   C:\WCFHandsOn\AdvancedSecurity\IntranetSolution\Listing10.10.

   The new configuration selects the predefined WSFederationHttpBinding as the
   binding for the service. To reiterate, that is a binding by which a service can be
   configured to authenticate requestors based on security tokens issued by a trusted
   STS, and in this case, the trusted STS is identified as the Woodgrove STS.

LISTING 10.10   Service Reconfiguration

```
<?xml version="1.0" encoding="utf-8" ?>
<configuration>
  <configSections>
    <section name="operationRequirements"
    type="Service.OperationRequirementsConfigurationSection,
➥ServiceAuthorizationManager" />
  </configSections>
  <!— Operation Requirements —>
  <operationRequirements>
```

LISTING 10.10   Continued

```
    <operation
    identifier="http://tempuri.org/IResourceAccessContract/AccessCoal">
      <role name="Executive"/>
      <role name="Other"/>
    </operation>
    <operation
identifier="http://tempuri.org/IResourceAccessContract/AccessDiamond">
      <role name="Executive"/>
    </operation>
  </operationRequirements>
  <!— Service Configuration —>
  <system.serviceModel>
    <services>
      <service name="Service.ResourceAccessServiceType"
      behaviorConfiguration="'ServiceBehavior'">
        <host>
          <baseAddresses>
            <add baseAddress="http://localhost:8000/Woodgrove"/>
          </baseAddresses>
        </host>
        <endpoint
          address="ResourceAccess"
          binding="wsFederationHttpBinding"
          bindingConfiguration="ResourceAccessBinding"
          contract="Service.IResourceAccessContract"/>
        <endpoint
          address="mex"
          binding="mexHttpBinding"
          contract="IMetadataExchange" />
      </service>
    </services>
    <bindings>
      <wsFederationHttpBinding>
        <binding name="'ResourceAccessBinding'">
          <security mode="Message">
            <message>
              <issuerMetadata
              address="http://localhost:8002/Woodgrove/mex">
              <identity>
                <dns value="Woodgrove"/>
              </identity>
              </issuerMetadata>
            </message>
          </security>
```

LISTING 10.10   Continued

```
                </binding>
            </wsFederationHttpBinding>
        </bindings>
        <behaviors>
            <serviceBehaviors>
                <behavior name="ServiceBehavior">
                    <serviceAuthorization
                    serviceAuthorizationManagerType=
➥"Service.AccessChecker,ServiceAuthorizationManager" />
                    <serviceCredentials>
                        <serviceCertificate
                        findValue="CN=Woodgrove"
                        x509FindType="FindBySubjectDistinguishedName"
                        storeLocation="LocalMachine"
                        storeName="My" />
                        <issuedTokenAuthentication>
                            <knownCertificates>
                                <add
                                findValue="CN=Woodgrove"
                                x509FindType="FindBySubjectDistinguishedName"
                                storeLocation="LocalMachine"
                                storeName="TrustedPeople" />
                            </knownCertificates>
                        </issuedTokenAuthentication>
                    </serviceCredentials>
                    <serviceMetadata
                    httpGetEnabled ="'true'"/>
                </behavior>
            </serviceBehaviors>
        </behaviors>
    </system.serviceModel>
</configuration>
```

2. Now that requestors are to be authenticated by security tokens issued by the Woodgrove STS, one other change to the Resource Access Service is required. The XSI Service Authorization Manager that the service was configured to use—the one for which the code was shown in Listing 10.5—is more suitable for the original intranet scenario than the new one in which the service is to be used by other organizations via the Internet.

The existing XSI Service Authorization Manager takes claims extracted by XSI from Windows credentials. It evaluates the sufficiency of those claims against data in a Windows Server 2003 Authorization Manager authorization store.

The new XSI Service Authorization Manager shown in Listing 10.11 is more suitable for the Internet scenario. It simply takes the claims extracted by XSI from the security tokens issued by the Woodgrove STS, and determines whether those claims meet the requirements for accessing the service.

Because the service has already been enhanced to use an XSI Service Authorization Manager, the particular one that is used can be changed very easily. Indeed, that is one of the virtues of using XSI Service Authorization Managers instead of System.Security.Permissions.PrincipalPermission attributes. In this case, the change will be accomplished simply by replacing the assembly containing the Service Authorization Manager. Remove the ServiceAuthorizationManager project from the solution, and add the ServiceAuthorizationManager project in the C:\WCFHandsOn\AdvancedSecurity\IntranetSolution\InternetServiceAuthorization Manager folder. Be careful not to add the project from the C:\WCFHandsOn\AdvancedSecurity\IntranetSolution\IntranetServiceAuthorization Manager—that is the very one that was just removed.

LISTING 10.11   New Service Authorization Manager

```
public class AccessChecker : ServiceAuthorizationManager
{
    public AccessChecker()
    {
        [...]

    }

    public override bool CheckAccess(OperationContext operationContext)
    {
        string header =
            operationContext.RequestContext.RequestMessage.Headers.Action;
        Claim[] requiredClaims = null;
        if (!(accessRequirements.TryGetValue(header, out requiredClaims)))
        {
            return false;
        }

        AuthorizationContext authorizationContext =
            operationContext.ServiceSecurityContext.AuthorizationContext;

        foreach (Claim requiredClaim in requiredClaims)
        {
            for (
                int index = 0;
                index < authorizationContext.ClaimSets.Count;
```

10

LISTING 10.11   Continued

```
                index++)
        {
            if (
                authorizationContext.ClaimSets[index].
                ContainsClaim(requiredClaim))
            {
                return true;
            }
        }
    }
        return false;
    }
}
```

Reconfiguring the Client

Now the Resource Access Service is configured so that it requires users to identify themselves with security tokens issued by the Woodgrove STS. The Woodgrove STS is configured so that it will issue those security tokens in response to requests accompanied by security tokens issued by the Fabrikam STS. So, Fabrikam users who want to make use of the Resource Access Service can do so by requesting security tokens from the Fabrikam STS that they can then exchange for the security tokens they need from the Woodgrove STS. All that remains to be done is the reconfiguration of the Resource Access client application to reflect this new arrangement:

1. Right-click on the Security solution in the Visual Studio Solution Explorer and choose Set Startup Projects from the context menu.

2. Modify the startup project property of the solution as shown in Figure 10.13.

3. Start debugging the solution.

4. Open the Microsoft Windows Vista Debug Build Environment prompt by choosing All Programs, Microsoft Windows SDK, CMD Shell from the Windows Start menu.

5. Use the cd command at the prompt to make C:\WCFHandsOn\AdvancedSecurity\IntranetSolution the prompt's current directory.

6. Enter this command to have the Windows Communication Foundation's Service Metadata Tool generate the necessary configuration for the client application:

```
svcutil /config:app.config http://localhost:8000/Woodgrove
```

7. Choose Debug, Stop Debugging.

8. Delete the existing configuration for the client by deleting the file App.config from the Client project of the Security solution.

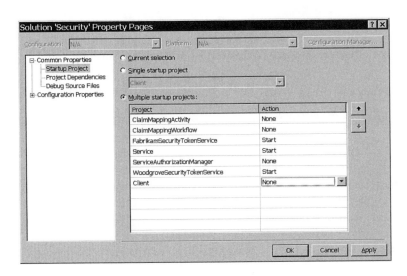

FIGURE 10.13   Security solution startup project property.

9. Replace that configuration with the configuration file generated using the Service Metadata Tool by adding the file C:\WCFHandsOn\AdvancedSecurity\IntranetSolution to the Client project of the Security solution.

10. Some modifications need to be made to the generated configuration file. Open the App.config file in the Client project of the Security solution, and modify the definition of the Woodgrove service's endpoint therein, providing a name for the endpoint, changing how the contract is identified, and specifying a behavior configuration, so that the endpoint configuration looks like this:

```
<client>
        <endpoint
        address="http://localhost:8000/Woodgrove/ResourceAccess"
        binding="wsFederationHttpBinding"
        bindingConfiguration="WSFederationHttpBinding_IResourceAccessContract"
        contract="Client.IResourceAccessContract"
        behaviorConfiguration ="ResourceAccessClientBehavior"
        name="ResourceService">
                <identity>
                        <certificateReference
                                storeLocation="LocalMachine"
                                storeName="TrustedPeople"
                                findValue="CN=Woodgrove"/>
                </identity>
        </endpoint>
</client>
```

10

11. Add the behavior configuration named in the previous step as shown in Listing 10.12. The behaviors in this configuration specify how the client is to validate the certificate that the Woodgrove Resource Access Service will offer to authenticate itself.

LISTING 10.12   Internet Client Configuration

```
<client>
        <endpoint
        address="http://localhost:8000/Woodgrove/ResourceAccess"
        binding="wsFederationHttpBinding"
        bindingConfiguration="WSFederationHttpBinding_IResourceAccessContract"
        contract="Client.IResourceAccessContract"
        behaviorConfiguration ="ResourceAccessClientBehavior"
        name="ResourceService">
                <identity>
                        <certificateReference
                                storeLocation="LocalMachine"
                                storeName="TrustedPeople"
                                findValue="CN=Woodgrove"/>
                </identity>
        </endpoint>
</client>
<behaviors>
        <endpointBehaviors>
                <behavior name="ResourceAccessClientBehavior">
                        <clientCredentials>
                                <serviceCertificate>
                                        <authentication
                                        certificateValidationMode="PeerOrChainTrust" />
                                </serviceCertificate>
                        </clientCredentials>
                </behavior>
        </endpointBehaviors>
</behaviors>
```

Experiencing the Power of Federated, Claims-Based Identity with XSI

To see what has been accomplished, follow these steps:

1. Right-click on the Security solution in the Visual Studio Solution Explorer and choose Set Startup Projects from the context menu.

2. Modify the startup project property of the solution so that the Client project is now added to the list of projects that will start.

3. Choose Debug, Start Debugging from the Visual Studio 2005 menus.

4. When the console of the Fabrikam STS, the Woodgrove STS, and the Resource Access Service all show some activity, click on the coal button in the Resource Access client user interface. You should see some activity in the console of the Fabrikam STS as it responds to a request to grant the client application a Fabrikam security token. Then you should see some activity in the console of the Woodgrove STS as it responds to a request to issue the client application a Woodgrove security token. Finally, based on the claims incorporated in the Woodgrove security token, access to the coal should be granted.

5. Click on the diamond button in the Resource Access client user interface. Access to the diamond resource should be denied. The reason is that the user is not assigned to the role of Manager within Fabrikam. As a result, the Fabrikam STS includes a claim in the security token it issues that the user is a staff member. The Woodgrove STS translates that claim into one that says that the user is in some role other than an executive role. The Woodgrove Resource Access Service grants access to the diamond only to those requestors for whom the Woodgrove STS claims executive privilege.

6. Choose Debug, Stop Debugging from the Visual Studio 2005 menus.

The full benefit of claims-based security will become apparent in these remaining steps. The user of the Resource Access client will be promoted within the Fabrikam organization, and instantly experience the benefit of enhanced access to resources within Woodgrove:

1. Promote the current user to the Manager role within Fabrikam. Do so by using the Windows Server 2003 Authorization Manager user interface to add the user to the Manager role in the Authorization Manager authorization store, according to the instructions for doing so provided earlier in this chapter.

2. Choose Debug, Start Debugging from the Visual Studio 2005 menus.

3. When the console of the service, the Woodgrove STS, and the Fabrikam STS all show some activity, click on the diamond button in the Resource Access client user interface. Because the user has been promoted within Fabrikam, the user now has access to the more valuable diamond resource in Woodgrove that the user was previously prevented from accessing.

With that click on the diamond button in the Resource Access client user interface, the possibilities for commerce offered by XSI should be clear. Without having to write any code, an application that was designed for use within an intranet has been upgraded for access by external partners via the Internet. That application is, moreover, highly configurable. The authorization mechanisms in both organizations are available for modification by administrators using the Windows Server 2003 Authorization Manager user interface and the Windows Workflow Foundation Rule Set Editor.

Claims-Based Security and Federated Security

This chapter has illustrated claims-based security. The Windows Communication Foundation documentation refers to *federated security*. What is the difference?

In the sense in which the term *federation* is used in the WS-Federation Language specification, where it refers to the establishment of trust between realms, federation is accomplished through claims, those being what one realm trusts from another (Kaler and Nadalin 2003). Claims, though, can be also be used within a given realm—a SID, for instance, which has meaning only within the context of the domain where it was issued, can plausibly be described as a claim. Therefore, claims-based security is more general than federation, which is only one application for claims-based security, albeit the canonical one.

Correspondingly, the class `System.Security.IdentityModel.Claims.Claim` is more fundamental to XSI than `System.ServiceModel.WSFederationBinding`. As shown in Chapter 7, you can use XSI for authorizing access to an endpoint and, in so doing, evaluate a set of `System.Security.IdentityModel.Claims.Claim` objects, without using as the binding for the endpoint `System.ServiceModel.WSFederationBinding`.

Yet consider how the term *federated security* is defined in the Windows Communication Foundation documentation: "[f]ederated security is a mechanism that allows for clean separation of concerns between a service and its associated authentication and authorization procedures for clients consuming the service" (Microsoft Corporation 2006). How is that "clean separation of concerns" achieved? By having the service trust some mechanism for authentication and authorization. As soon as the service entrusts its security to some truly separate mechanism, the security of the service is federated in much the same way that the security of a political entity is federated when it trusts another such entity to provide a military and to manage citizenship.

By virtue of federating its security, access to the service is made decidedly more flexible, yet, at the same time, more manageable. Access can be extended through to any parties that are vouched for by an authority that the authentication and authorization mechanism is configured to trust. Conversely, access is restricted to those parties. The separate authentication and authorization mechanism serves as a central access management point for the service and potentially for any number of other services as well.

That the federation of its security is accomplished by having the service trust the determinations of the separate authentication and authorization mechanism is what makes a federated security system also a claims-based system. What users get from the separate authentication and authorization mechanism is some thing that the service will trust or not, based on its configuration, and that thing is a claim. So, in the sense in which the term *federated security* is used in the Windows Communication Foundation documentation, it is interchangeable with how the term *claims-based security* was used here.

Summary

The concept of claims that had appeared throughout the chapters in this section was the focus of this one. Claims consist of a type, a right, and a value. Claims are made about the bearer by some issuer that may be trusted to some degree or not at all.

The Windows Communication Foundation's Extensible Security Infrastructure (XSI) provides a foundation for claims-based security. It translates credentials of various types from various sources into sets of claims. Those claims can be translated from the language of one organization into the languages of another by XSI authorization policies. Services can evaluate the sufficiency of claims to access requested resources using XSI authorization managers. Both authorization policies and authorization managers can be identified through configuration, thereby making the process by which access to resources is authorized entirely independent from the resources themselves.

The power of claims-based security using XSI was demonstrated by an exercise in which access to an intranet service controlled using role-based authorization was extended to permit controlled claims-based access by the users of another organization. In the process, no changes had to be made to the code of either the client or the service, which is an eloquent demonstration of the power that the Windows Communication Foundation can bring to bear on complex business scenarios.

Yet it is important to remember that although the virtues of claims-based security are readily apparent, one shortcoming is that support for it is still quite limited. Therefore, you should not overlook the fact that, in the sample application within the hypothetical Fabrikam organization that was studied throughout this chapter, security was still based on Windows credentials—those were how the users of the Resource Access client application identified themselves to the Fabrikam STS. This hybrid approach to security might be the wisest one to adopt, relying on established security tools within the organization, but leveraging claims-based security where it is especially powerful, in the space between organizations. For although claims-based security may be the road to Paradise, that road is still being paved.

References

.NET Framework Class Library. 2006. S.v. "IPrincipal Interface." http://msdn. microsoft.com/library/default.asp?url=/library/en-us/cpref/html/ frlrfsystemsecurityprincipaliprincipalclasstopic.asp. Accessed January 1, 2006.

Cabrera, Luis Felipe and Chris Kurt. 2005. *Web Services Architecture and Its Specifications: Essentials for Understanding WS-**. Redmond, WA: Microsoft.

Freeman, Adam and Allen Jones. 2003. *Programming .NET Security*. Sebastopol, CA: Wiley.

Gudgin, Martin and Anthony Nadalin, eds. *Web Services Trust Language (WS-Trust)*. http://msdn.microsoft.com/library/en-us/dnglobspec/html/WS-trust.pdf. Accessed January 1, 2006.

10

Kaler, Chris and Anthony Nadalin, eds. *Web Services Federation Language (WS-Federation)*. http://msdn.microsoft.com/library/default.asp?url=/library/en-us/dnglobspec/html/ws-federation.asp. Accessed October 26, 2006.

McPherson, Dave. 2005. Role-Based Access Control for Multi-tier Applications Using Authorization Manager. http://www.microsoft.com/technet/prodtechnol/windowsserver2003/technologies/management/athmanwp.mspx. Accessed January 2, 2006.

Microsoft Corporation. 2005. *Federation*. http://msdn.microsoft.com/library/default.asp?url=/library/en-us/WCF_Con/html/2f1e646f-8361-48d4-9d5d-1b961f31ede4.asp?frame=true. Accessed October 26, 2006.

Oxford Dictionary of Current English. 2001 ed. S.v. "Federation."

Tulloch, Mitch. 2003. *Microsoft Encyclopedia of Security*. Redmond, WA: Microsoft.

PART IV

Integration and Interoperability

IN THIS PART

CHAPTER 11

Legacy Integration

Introduction

Windows Communication Foundation provides a unified messaging API that provides the capability to integrate with a number of legacy technologies. This chapter focuses on the Windows Communication Foundation's capability to integrate with COM+ and non–Windows Communication Foundation MSMQ (Microsoft Message Queuing) applications.

COM+ Integration

Windows Communication Foundation provides a rich environment for creating distributed applications. If one has a substantial investment in component-based application logic hosted in COM+, one can use the Windows Communication Foundation to extend one's existing logic rather than having to rewrite it. A common scenario is when one wishes to expose existing COM+ or Enterprise Services business logic through web services.

When an interface on a COM+ component is exposed as a web service, the specification and contract of that service are determined by an automatic mapping to be performed at application initialization time. The conceptual model for this mapping is as follows:

▶ There is one service for each exposed COM class.

▶ The contract for the service is derived directly from the selected component's interface definition.

▶ The operations in that contract are derived directly from the methods on the component's interface definition.

▶ The parameters for those operations are derived directly from the COM interoperability type corresponding to the component's method parameters.

▶ Default addresses and transport bindings for the service are provided in a service configuration file, but these can be reconfigured as required.

NOTE

The contracts for the generated Windows Communication Foundation services are tied to the underlying COM+ application's interfaces and configuration.

Modifying the COM+ component methods automatically results in an updated service when the application is next started. However, a modification to the number of interfaces does *not* automatically update the available services. In the latter scenario, one will need to rerun the COM+ Service Model Configuration tool (`ComSvcConfig.exe`).

The authentication and authorization requirements of the COM+ application and its components continue to be enforced when used as a web service. If the caller initiates a web service transaction, components marked as transactional enlist within that transaction scope.

The steps that are required to expose a COM+ component's interface as a web service without modifying the component are as listed here:

1. Determine whether the COM+ component's interface can be exposed as a web service.

2. Select an appropriate hosting mode.

3. Use the COM+ Service Model Configuration tool (`ComSvcConfig.exe`) to add a web service for the interface.

Supported Interfaces

Not all types of interfaces can be exposed as a web service. Here is a list of the types that cannot be exposed:

▶ Interfaces that accept object references as parameters

▶ Interfaces that accept types that are not compatible with the .NET Framework COM Interop conversions

▶ Interfaces for applications that have application pooling enabled when hosted by COM+

▶ Interfaces of components that are marked as "private" to the application

▶ COM+ infrastructure interfaces

▶ Interfaces from the system application

▶ Interfaces from managed components that have not been added to the Global Assembly Cache (GAC)

Selecting the Hosting Mode

As is stated in the documentation, COM+ can expose web services in one of the following three hosting modes.

COM+ Hosted

The web service is hosted within the application's dedicated COM+ server process (Dllhost.exe). This mode requires the application to be explicitly started before it can receive web service requests. The COM+ options Run as an NT Service and Leave Running When Idle can be used to prevent idle shutdown of the application and its services. This mode has the benefit that it provides both web service and DCOM access to the server application.

Web Hosted

The web service is hosted within a web server worker process. This mode does not require the COM+ application to be active when the initial request is received. If the application is not active when this request is received, it is automatically activated before the request is processed. This mode also provides both web service and DCOM access to the server application, but it incurs a process hop for web service requests. This typically requires the client to enable impersonation. In the Windows Communication Foundation, this can be done with the SetSspiSettings method and the Impersonation enumeration value.

> **NOTE**
>
> Like other Windows Communication Foundation services, the security settings for the exposed service are administered through roles and web host settings. COM+ application roles are enforced, whereas traditional DCOM security settings such as the DCOM machinewide permissions settings are not.

Web Hosted In-Process

The web service and the COM+ application logic are hosted within the web server worker process. This provides automatic activation of the web hosted mode without incurring the process hop for web service requests. The disadvantage is that the server application cannot be accessed through DCOM.

Using the COM+ Service Model Configuration Tool

The mechanism used to configure COM+ interfaces to be exposed as web services is the COM+ Service Model Configuration command-line tool (ComSvcConfig.exe). This tool will be used in this exercise to expose a COM+ business object.

The calling convention and command-line switches for ComSvcConfig are as shown here:

```
ComSvcConfig.exe /install ¦ /list ¦ /uninstall [/application:<ApplicationID
➥ ¦ ApplicationName>] [/contract<ClassID ¦ ProgID ¦ *,InterfaceID ¦
➥ InterfaceName ¦ *>] [/hosting:<complus ¦ was>] [/webSite:<WebsiteName>]
➥ [/webDirectory:<WebDirectoryName>] [/mex] [/id] [/nologo] [/verbose]
➥ [/help]
```

> **NOTE**
>
> One must be an administrator on the local computer to use `ComSvcConfig.exe`.

Table 11.1 describes the modes that can be used with ComSvcConfig.exe.

TABLE 11.1   Modes That Can Be Used with `ComSvcConfig.exe`

Option	Description
/install	Configures a COM+ interface for Service Model integration. Short form /i.
/uninstall	Removes a COM+ interface from Service Model integration. Short form /u.
/list	Queries for information about COM+ applications and components that have interfaces that are configured for Service Model integration. Short form /l.

Table 11.2 describes the option flags that can be used with ComSvcConfig.exe.

TABLE 11.2   Flags That Can Be Used with `ComSvcConfig.exe`

Option	Description
/application:< ApplicationID ¦ ApplicationName >	Specifies the COM+ application to configure. Short form /a.
/contract:< ClassID ¦ ProgID ¦ *, InterfaceID ¦ InterfaceName ¦ * >	Specifies the COM+ component and interface to configure as a service contract. Short form /c. Although the wildcard character (*) can be used when one specifies the component and interface names, doing so is not recommended because one might expose interfaces one did not intend to expose.
/allowreferences	Specifies that object reference parameters are allowed. Short form /r.

TABLE 11.2   Continued

Option	Description
/hosting:< *complus* ¦ *was* >	Specifies whether to use the COM+ hosting mode or the web hosting mode.
	Short form /h.
	Using the COM+ hosting mode requires explicit activation of the COM+ application. Using the web hosting mode allows the COM+ application to be automatically activated as required. If the COM+ application is a library application, it runs in the Internet Information Services (IIS) process. If the COM+ application is a server application, it runs in the Dllhost.exe process.
/webSite:< *WebsiteName* >	Specifies the website for hosting when web hosting mode is used (see the /hosting flag).
	Short form /w.
	If no website is specified, the default website is used.
/webDirectory:< *WebDirectoryName* >	Specifies the virtual directory for hosting when web hosting is used (see the /hosting flag).
	Short form /d.
/mex	Adds a Metadata Exchange (MEX) service endpoint to the default service configuration to support clients that want to retrieve a contract definition from the service.
	Short form /x.
/id	Displays the application, component, and interface information as IDs.
	Short form /k.
/nologo	Prevents ComSvcConfig.exe from displaying its logo.
	Short form /n.
/verbose	Outputs additional tool progress information.
	Short form /v.
/help	Displays the usage message.
	Short form /?.

Exposing a COM+ Component as a Windows Communication Foundation Web Service

This series of exercises will focus on a scenario in which a school has an application for registering students. The business logic for this application resides within an Enterprise Service component hosted in COM+. The goal is to expose that component as a web service that can be consumed both by the school's web-based management application and from a Windows Forms-based smart client application.

This exercise involves taking a legacy COM+ component and exposing it as a Windows Communication Foundation service that is consumed in the smart client application. To begin, examine the COM+ component to understand its functionality.

> **NOTE**
>
> Because projects in this exercise require strong names, several of the projects are signed. When opening the solution, one might be prompted for the passwords for the key files used. The password for these files is PERCY123marta.

1. Copy the code associated with this chapter downloaded from http://www.crypt-maker.com/WindowsCommunicationFoundationUnleashed to the folder `C:\WCFHandsOn`. The code is all in a folder called `LegacyIntegration`, which has three subfolders: `COM`, `COMPlus`, and `MSMQ`.

2. Open the solution `COMPlus.sln` in the `Before` subdirectory of the `COMPlus` subfolder.

3. Open the `Students.cs` file of the Student Management Application that is included in that solution. The contents are reproduced in Listing 11.1.

Because this component is being placed within COM+, it contains several attributes. The `ApplicationName` attribute identifies the name for the COM+ application this class will be installed into. Also note that the interface and the class are attributed with GUIDs, and the class is attributed with a ProgID. Even though this was written in .NET, the component will live in COM+ with the attributes providing the information necessary for consistent Interop registration.

This class provides methods to the user interface for additions, updates, and retrieval of basic student information. For additions and updates, the changes are sent to an MSMQ using the `System.Messaging` libraries. In this exercise, only the `Add` method will be invoked.

LISTING 11.1   The COM+ Code

```
using System;
using System.Collections.Generic;
using System.Text;
using System.Messaging;
```

LISTING 11.1   Continued

```csharp
using System.Data;
using System.Data.SqlClient;
using System.EnterpriseServices;
using System.Runtime.InteropServices;


[assembly: ApplicationName("StudentManagement")]
[assembly: ApplicationID("2C9BFEA5-005D-4218-8C69-A03F6B9037BA")]
[assembly: ApplicationActivation(ActivationOption.Server)]
[assembly: ApplicationAccessControl(false, AccessChecksLevel =
➥  AccessChecksLevelOption.Application)]

namespace WCFHandsOn
{
    [Guid("1C5677EC-8046-4c5b-B361-BA354CFA3DB3")]
    public interface IStudents
    {
        string Add(string FirstName, string LastName, string PhoneNumber);
        bool Update(string ID, string FirstName, string LastName,
➥ string PhoneNumber);
        bool Delete(string ID);
        System.Collections.ArrayList GetAll();

    }

    [Guid("E4A5D9FD-3B5F-4598-9E42-EC8D1329EE9D")]
    [ProgId("StudentManagement.Students")]
    public class Students : ServicedComponent, IStudents
    {
        public Students() { }

        string qPath = @"FormatName:DIRECT=OS:w2k3ee\private$\school";
        public string Add(
            string FirstName,
            string LastName,
            string PhoneNumber)
        {
            //For any modifications to the data, we place the
            //request on a queue.

            //First we generate a System.Messaging.Message for the queue.
            try
            {
                string ID = Guid.NewGuid().ToString();
```

LISTING 11.1   Continued

```
            Student student = new Student(ID, FirstName, LastName,
➥ PhoneNumber);
            System.Messaging.Message msg = GenerateAddMessage(student);

            //Now we place it to the queue
            PlaceMessageOnQueue(msg);

            //This is a new student, return the GUID
            return ID;
        }
        catch (Exception e)
        {
            //Debug.WriteLine(e.ToString());
            throw e;
        }
    }
}
```

In the next few steps, the IStudents interface is to be exposed from the COM+ application as a web service using the Windows Communication Foundation. That will enable it to be used as a WS-*–compatible service from clients on any platform. To expose this as a Windows Communication Foundation service, the ComSvcConfig utility will be used. To use that utility, one will need to create a virtual directory to house the service:

1. Choose Start, Programs, Administrative Tools, Internet Information Services Manager.

2. Create a directory at C:\WCFHandsOn\LegacyIntegration\ ComPlus\ Before\StudentManagementService.

3. Navigate to the default website and create a new Virtual Directory. The alias for the directory should be WCFHandsOn_StudentMgmt, and the path for the directory is C:\WCFHandsOn\LegacyIntegration\Complus\Before\StudentManagementService.

Now the ComSvcConfig utility can be used:

1. Open the SDK Command Prompt by choosing All Programs, Microsoft Windows SDK, CMD Shell.

2. Navigate to C:\WCFHandsOn\LegacyIntegration\ComPlus\Before\.

3. Run the following script to register the COM+ component. It configures the IStudents interface on the component from the StudentManagement application,

hosts it using IIS (as opposed to COM+), and places the files in the virtual directory WCFHandsOn_StudentMgmt:

```
C:\Windows\Microsoft.NET\Framework\v3.0\Windows Communication Foundation\
➥ComSvcConfig.exe
➥ /i
➥ /application:StudentManagement
➥ /contract:StudentManagement.Students,Students* /hosting:was
➥ /webDirectory:WCFHandsOn_StudentMgmt /mex
```

4. Navigate to the virtual directory created earlier and confirm that a service—named after the interface—was generated and placed there.

5. Examine the web.config file that was generated. Its contents should be similar to the configuration shown in Listing 11.2. It includes a section called comContracts, which includes the GUID for the contract, the interface name, and lists the exposed methods. The name of the service references GUIDs as well:

LISTING 11.2   The Generated Configuration <?xml version="1.0" encoding="utf-8"?>

```xml
<configuration>
    <system.serviceModel>
        <behaviors>
            <serviceBehaviors>
                <behavior name="ComServiceMexBehavior">
                    <serviceMetadata httpGetEnabled="true" />
                    <serviceDebug includeExceptionDetailInFaults="false" />
                </behavior>
            </serviceBehaviors>
        </behaviors>
        <bindings>
            <wsHttpBinding>
                <binding name="comNonTransactionalBinding">
                    <reliableSession enabled="true" />
                </binding>
                <binding
                    name="comTransactionalBinding"
                    transactionFlow="true">
                    <reliableSession enabled="true" />
                </binding>
            </wsHttpBinding>
        </bindings>
        <comContracts>
```

LISTING 11.2   Continued

```
            <comContract contract="{1C5677EC-8046-4C5B-B361-BA354CFA3DB3}"
                name="IStudents"
                namespace="http://tempuri.org/1C5677EC-8046-4C5B-B361-
➥BA354CFA3DB3"
                requiresSession="true">
                <exposedMethods>
                    <add exposedMethod="Add" />
                    <add exposedMethod="Update" />
                    <add exposedMethod="Delete" />
                    <add exposedMethod="GetAll" />
                </exposedMethods>
            </comContract>
        </comContracts>
        <services>
            <service
                behaviorConfiguration="ComServiceMexBehavior"
                name="{2C9BFEA5-005D-4218-8C69-A03F6B9037BA},
➥ {E4A5D9FD-3B5F-4598-9E42-EC8D1329EE9D}">
                <endpoint
                    address="IStudents"
                    binding="wsHttpBinding"
                    bindingConfiguration="comNonTransactionalBinding"
                    contract="{1C5677EC-8046-4C5B-B361-BA354CFA3DB3}" />
                <endpoint
                    address="mex"
                    binding="mexHttpBinding" bindingConfiguration=""
                    contract="IMetadataExchange" />
            </service>
        </services>
    </system.serviceModel>
</configuration>
```

To test the service, open the service file in your web browser. Navigate to http://local-host/WCFHandsOn_StudentMgmt/Service.svc. If the service is functioning properly, a page is displayed that identifies the location of the WSDL and how to consume the service, as in Figure 11.1.

Record the address of the WSDL specified in the first box on this screen because it is used in the next part of the exercise.

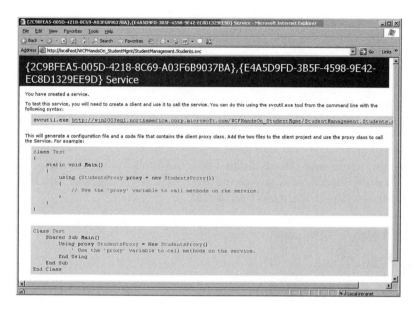

FIGURE 11.1   Web page generated from the metadata of the new Windows Communication Foundation service.

Referencing in the Client

The next step in the exercise is to connect the service to a Windows Forms client. While a Windows Forms client is used here, the service can be consumed by any application that can interact with a web service. Proceed as follows:

1. Open the SDK Command Prompt by choosing All Programs, Microsoft Windows SDK, CMD Shell.

2. Run the following script to generate proxy code and a configuration file that can be used:

    ```
    "C:\Program Files\Microsoft SDKs\Windows\v6.0\Bin\svcutil.exe "
    ➥ http://localhost/WCFHandsOn_StudentMgmt/StudentManagement.Students.svc
    ➥ /out:proxy.cs
    ```

    This generates two files: proxy.cs and output.config.

3. Add both files to the Teacher Application project.

4. Rename the configuration file to Web.Config for the website and App.Config for the Windows Forms application.

    The application provides an interface that gives the capability to add new students to the system.

5. Open the `Proxy.cs` file and note the name of the new proxy class that was created. This class will be referenced in the code for executing the service.

6 Modify the code for the button to add the students using the new web service. This is done by adding the following code to the `btnUpdate_Click` method:

```
StudentsClient proxy = new StudentsClient("Students");
string result = proxy.Add(tbFirstName.Text,tbLastName.Text,tbPhone.Text);
MessageBox.Show("Student Added!");
```

7. Enter a first name, last name, and phone number into the application, and click Add to test it. The results should be as shown in Figure 11.2. A message box will be displayed identifying that the student has been added.

FIGURE 11.2   The user interface for the sample.

The preceding steps confirm successful integration with a legacy COM+ application, and the provision of a platform-agnostic web service. They also confirm the successful use of the SvcUtil tool to generate proxies for that new service, proxies that have been incorporated into a Windows Forms client.

Calling a Windows Communication Foundation Service from COM

In addition to exposing COM+ applications as Windows Communication Foundation services, there's also a need to expose Windows Communication Foundation services to legacy COM applications. Whether it's a legacy application such as Lotus Notes, a custom application written in Visual Basic 6 or VBScript, there are a number of COM centric scenarios where the ability to call Windows Communication Foundation services from COM clients could prove useful.

In this next exercise, a Windows Communication Foundation service will be exposed via COM and consumed by a VBScript component.

Building the Service

Follow these steps to create the Windows Communication Foundation service:

1. Create a new Console Application project named service in `C:\WCFHandsOn\LegacyIntegration\COM\Before\`.

2. Add a reference to `System.Configuration`.

3. Add a reference to `System.ServiceModel`.

4. Add a referemce to `System.Runtime.Serialization`.

5. Add a new class and name it `ICreditCheck.cs`.

6. Populate `ICreditCheck.cs` with the following code to create the service interface:

```csharp
using System;
using System.Collections.Generic;
using System.Text;
using System.ServiceModel;

namespace WCFHandsOn
{
        [ServiceContract]
    public interface ICreditCheck
    {
        [OperationContract]
        int CheckCredit(
            string socialSecurityNumber,
            string firstName,
            string lastName);
    }
}
```

7. Add a new class and name it `service.cs`.

8. Populate `service.cs` with the following code to create the service interface:

```csharp
using System;
using System.ServiceModel;
using System.Runtime.Serialization;

namespace WCFHandsOn
{
```

```
public class CreditCheck : WCFHandsOn.ICreditCheck
{
    public int CheckCredit(
            string socialSecurityNumber,
            string firstName,
            string lastName)
    {
        //650 is the average US Credit Score
        return 650;

    }
}

}
```

9. Rename program.cs to servicehost.cs.

10. Populate servicehost.cs with the following code to create the service interface:

```
using System;
using System.Collections.Generic;
using System.Text;
using System.Configuration;
using System.ServiceModel;

namespace WCFHandsOn
{
    class CustomServiceHost
    {
      static void Main(string[] args)
      {

            Uri baseAddress = new Uri(
               ConfigurationManager.AppSettings["baseAddress"]);
            // Instantiate new ServiceHost

            ServiceHost service = new ServiceHost(
               typeof(CreditCheck), baseAddress);


            service.Open();

            Console.WriteLine("Credit Check Service is online.");

            Console.ReadLine();
```

```
            }
        }
    }
```

11. Add a new Application Configuration file.

12. Populate the configuration file with the configuration shown in Listing 11.3:

LISTING 11.3   Service Configuration

```xml
<?xml version="1.0" encoding="utf-8" ?>
<configuration>
  <appSettings>
    <!-- use appSetting to configure base address provided by host -->
    <add key="baseAddress" value="http://localhost:8080/WCFHandsOn" />
  </appSettings>
  <system.serviceModel>
    <services>
      <service
          name="WCFHandsOn.CreditCheck"
          behaviorConfiguration="CreditCheckServiceBehavior">
        <endpoint address="CreditCheck"
                  binding="wsHttpBinding"
                  bindingNamespace="http://WCFHandsOn.Samples.ChapterSix"
                  contract="WCFHandsOn.ICreditCheck" />

        <endpoint address="mex"
                  binding="mexHttpBinding"
                  contract="IMetadataExchange" />
      </service>
    </services>


    <behaviors>
      <serviceBehaviors>
        <behavior name="CreditCheckServiceBehavior">
          <serviceMetadata httpGetEnabled="True"/>
          <serviceDebug includeExceptionDetailInFaults="False" />
        </behavior>
      </serviceBehaviors>
    </behaviors>

  </system.serviceModel>

</configuration>.
```

Building the Client

These next few steps are for constructing the client:

1. Start the service created in the first part of the exercise.

2. Open the SDK Command Prompt by choosing All Programs, Microsoft Windows SDK, CMD Shell.

3. Create a proxy for the service using SvcUtil.exe:

   ```
   C:\Program Files\Microsoft SDKs\Windows\v6.0\Bin\svcutil.exe "
   ➥ http://localhost/WCFHandsOn/mex_/out:CreditCheckClient.cs
   ```

   This will generate two files: CreditCheckClient.cs and output.config. For a COM client, only the CreditCheckClient.cs file will be used.

4. Create a new class library project named Client.

5. Delete Class1.cs from the project.

6. Add the CreditCheckClient.cs file to the project.

7. In the property folder for the Client project, open the AssemblyInfo.cs file, reproduced in Listing 11.4, and assign the guid EE540164-B991-4600-83D2-1A66EC5DE20A and set ComVisible = true.

LISTING 11.4   Assembly Information Fileusing System;

```
using System.Reflection;
using System.Runtime.CompilerServices;
using System.Runtime.InteropServices;


// General Information about an assembly is controlled through the following
// set of attributes. Change these attribute values to modify the information
// associated with an assembly.
[assembly: AssemblyTitle("client")]
[assembly: AssemblyDescription("")]
[assembly: AssemblyConfiguration("")]
[assembly: AssemblyCompany("")]
[assembly: AssemblyProduct("client")]
[assembly: AssemblyCopyright("Copyright ©  2005")]
[assembly: AssemblyTrademark("")]
[assembly: AssemblyCulture("")]


// Setting ComVisible to false makes the types in this assembly not visible
// to COM componenets.  If one needs to access a type in this assembly from
// COM, set the ComVisible attribute to true on that type.
[assembly: ComVisible(true)]
[assembly: CLSCompliant(true)]
```

LISTING 11.4   Continued

```
// The following GUID is for the ID of the typelib
// if this project is exposed to COM
[assembly: Guid("EE540164-B991-4600-83D2-1A66EC5DE20A")]

// Version information for an assembly consists of the following four values:
//
//        Major Version
//        Minor Version
//        Build Number
//        Revision
//
// One can specify all the values or
// one can default the Revision and Build Numbers
// by using the '*' as shown below:
[assembly: AssemblyVersion("1.0.0.0")]
[assembly: AssemblyFileVersion("1.0.0.0")]
```

8. Right-click on the Client project and select Properties.

9. Click on the Signing tab.

10. Under Choose a Strong Name Key File, select New from the drop-down list.

11. Name the key file CreditCheckClient.

12. Build the client.

13. Open the SDK Command Prompt by choosing All Programs, Microsoft Windows SDK, CMD Shell.

14. Navigate to the bin directory for the Client project.

15. Run the regasm tool against the client library:

    ```
    regasm /tlb:CreditCheckClient client.dll
    ```

16. Install the assembly into the GAC. Type the following at the SDK Command Prompt:

    ```
    gacutil /i client.dll
    ```

Building the VBScript File

The next task is to build a VBScript file that will use the client to call the service. In the last exercise, the client.dll assembly was placed in the GAC and registered. In the next few steps, a VBScript file will be created that will use COM to call the CreditCheck service.

1. Run Notepad.exe.

2. Enter the following script into the new Notepad document:

```
Set proxy = GetObject(
➥ "service:address=http://localhost:8080/WCFHandsOn/CreditCheck,
➥ binding=wsHttpBinding, contract={D144C6BB-0C7B-3671-846C-
➥AE1EEBFD3FA4}")

WScript.Echo
➥ "Credit Score: "
➥ & cstr(proxy.CheckCredit("123456789", "John", "Smith"))

Set proxy = nothing
```

The service is called from script code using GetObject. This is a latebound call created by passing in the service address, the binding, and the contract. The contract is identified by a GUID.

The GUID is not the same GUID that was specified in the assembly. This GUID is the one that is attached to the ICreditCheck interface in the Windows Registry. This can be found with the regedit tool by searching for the interface name (in this case, ICreditCheck).

After creating the proxy, one can call CheckCredit() passing the expected information: Social Security number, first name, and last name.

3. Save the file as CreditCheckClient.vbs.

Now the solution is ready to be tested.

Testing the Solution

Follow these steps to test the solution:

1. Start the service.

2. Run the CreditCheckClient.vbs file.

A message box that displays **Credit Score: 650** should appear.

Using COM, the CreditCheckClient.vbs file makes a call into the proxy client assembly, which calls through to the service. This serves to demonstrate a means by which one can empower legacy applications and languages to participate as clients not only to classic web services, but also to services using transports, such as TCP.

Integrating with MSMQ

The next exercise will be to create a Windows Communication client for a System.Messaging service. The client application will use the Windows Communication

Foundation to send messages to an MSMQ queue. The service uses the facilities of `System.Messaging` to detect and retrieve the incoming messages. In scenarios like this one, in which the Windows Communication Foundation is used to exchange messages via MSMQ with non-Windows Communication Foundation applications, the Windows Communication Foundation's `MsmqIntegrationBinding` is used to transmit the messages.

The client Windows Communication Foundation application has a dummy contract to mimic invoking a service operation, but, in reality, the message is consumed by an MSMQ service. The service contract is `IStudent`, which defines a one-way service that is suitable for use with queues. An MSMQ message does not have an `Action` header. It is not possible to map different MSMQ messages to operation contracts automatically. Therefore, there can be only one operation contract. If more than one operation contract is to be defined for the service, the application must provide information as to which header in the MSMQ message (for example, the `Label` or `correlationID`) can be used to decide which operation contract to dispatch.

The MSMQ message also does not contain information about which headers are mapped to the different parameters of the operation contract. So, there can be only one parameter in the operation contract. The parameter is of type generic `MsmqMessage` (`MsmqMessage<T>`) and contains the underlying MSMQ message. The type `T` in the generic `MsmqMessage` (`MsmqMessage<T>`) class represents the data that is serialized into the MSMQ message body. In this exercise, a `Student` type is serialized into the MSMQ message body.

Creating a Windows Communication Foundation Service That Integrates with MSMQ

In this scenario, a Windows Communication Foundation service will be created that provides the capability to update student records. The first step will be to create a struct that will contain the student information used when adding or updating a record. That step will be followed by the creation of the service and client.

The result will be a Windows Communication client that posts a message to MSMQ that is later received by a non–Windows Communication Foundation application monitoring the queue. That receiving application will process the message in the appropriate way, modifying the student records as needed.

Creating the Request

For the purposes of this exercise, a student will be represented by four pieces of information: `studentID`, `firstName`, `lastName`, and `phoneNumber`. All these pieces of information will need to be conveyed in the body of a message when a student is added or updated. These first few steps are for defining a struct with the four student information items:

1. Create a new class library project named `StudentManagementRequest` in `C:\Apps\WCFHandsOn\ExerciseThree\Before`.

2. Delete `Class1.cs`.

3. Using Solution Explorer, add a new class named `StudentManagementRequest.cs`.

4. Populate the new class with the following code to create the struct:

```
using System;
using System.Collections.Generic;
using System.Text;

namespace WCFHandsOn
{
    [Serializable]
    public struct StudentManagementRequest
    {
        public string studentID;
        public string firstName;
        public string lastName;
        public string phoneNumber;
    }
}
```

Creating the Service

The next steps are for building the non-Windows Communication Foundation student information service. It is to receive messages requesting updates to student records via System.Messaging:

1. Create a new class library project named Service in C:\WCFHandsOn\LegacyIntegration\MSMQ\Before.

2. Delete Class1.cs.

3. Add a reference to System.Messaging.

4. Add a reference to System.Configuration.

5. Add a reference to the StudentManagementRequest project created earlier.

6. Using Solution Explorer, add a new Application Configuration file to identify the queue by which the application will receive messages, a private queue on the local machine named *school:*

```
<?xml version="1.0" encoding="utf-8" ?>
<configuration>
    <appSettings>
        <!-- use appSetting to configure MSMQ queue name -->
        <add key="queueName" value=".\private$\school" />

    </appSettings>
</configuration>
```

7. Using Solution Explorer, add a new class to the project named `Program.cs`.

    Open `Program.cs`, and add the following namespaces to the top of the file:

    ```
    using System;
    using System.Collections.Generic;
    using System.Text;
    using System.Messaging;
    using System.Configuration;
    using System.Data;
    using System.Data.SqlClient;
    namespace WCFHandsOn
    ```

8. Now proceed to add the code that forms the core of the service. The code reads the queueName specified in the `App.config` file and confirms that a queue with that name exists. If the queue does not exist, a transactional queue with the specified name is created. After designating a method called *ProcessMessage* as the one to be called when a message arrives, the code calls the `BeginReceive()` method of the `System.Messaging` `MessageQueue` object to start monitoring the queue for incoming messages.

    ```
    static void Main(string[] args)
    {
        // Create a transaction queue using System.Messaging API
        // You could also choose to not do this and instead create the
        // queue using MSMQ MMC--make sure you create a transactional queue
        if (!MessageQueue.Exists(ConfigurationManager.AppSettings["queueName"]))
          MessageQueue.Create(ConfigurationManager.AppSettings["queueName"], true);
        //Connect to the queue
        MessageQueue Queue = new
    ➥ MessageQueue(ConfigurationManager.AppSettings["queueName"]);
        Queue.ReceiveCompleted += new ReceiveCompletedEventHandler(ProcessMessage);
        Queue.BeginReceive();
        Console.WriteLine("Message Processing Service is running");
        Console.ReadLine();
    }
    ```

9. Next, add the code for the aforementioned `ProcessMessage()` method, shown in Listing 11.5. The method reads the body of each received message into a StudentManagementRequest object and inspects the message label. The Windows Communication Foundation client, which will be programmed next, uses the message label to indicate what action the service is to take in processing the message:

LISTING 11.5   The ProcessMessage() Method

```
public static void ProcessMessage(Object source,
    ReceiveCompletedEventArgs asyncResult)
{
    try
      {
          // Connect to the queue.
          MessageQueue Queue = (MessageQueue)source;

          // End the asynchronous receive operation.
          System.Messaging.Message msg =
➥ Queue.EndReceive(asyncResult.AsyncResult);

            msg.Formatter = new System.Messaging.XmlMessageFormatter(new
➥ Type[] { typeof(StudentManagementRequest) });
            StudentManagementRequest request =
➥ (StudentManagementRequest)msg.Body;
          switch (msg.Label)
          {
              case "Add":
                  AddStudent(request);
                  break;
              case "Update":
                  UpdateStudent(request);
                  break;
              case "Delete":
                  DeleteStudent(request.studentID);
                  break;
              default:
                  Console.WriteLine("The label of the message is of
➥ an unknown type or not set correctly.");
                  break;

          }

          Queue.BeginReceive();
      }
      catch (System.Exception ex)
      {
          Console.WriteLine(ex.Message);
      }
}
```

10. Add the code for the methods, `UpdateStudent()`, `AddStudent()` and `DeleteStudent()` that the `ProcessMessage()` method uses in dealing with incoming requests:

```
private static void UpdateStudent(StudentManagementRequest s)
{
    Console.WriteLine("Just updated student {0} {1} with a phone number of
➥ {2}", s.firstName, s.lastName, s.phoneNumber);
}


private static void AddStudent(StudentManagementRequest s)
{
    Console.WriteLine("Just added student {0} {1} with a phone number of
➥ {2}", s.firstName, s.lastName, s.phoneNumber);
}


private static void DeleteStudent(string studentID)
{
    Console.WriteLine("Just deleted student with ID {0}", studentID);
}
```

Creating the Client

These next few steps are for creating the client application that will use the student information service to maintain student records:

1. Open the Client application found at `C:\WCFHandsOn\LegacyIntegration\MSMQ\Before`.

2. Add a reference to `System.ServiceModel`.

3. Using Solution Explorer, add a reference to the StudentManagementRequest project that contains the struct by which student records are defined.

4. Using Solution Explorer, add a new class called `StudentManagementProxy.cs`. That class will contain the service interface and proxy code for communicating with the student information service.

5. Add the code shown in Listing 11.6 to the `StudentManagementProxy` class, taking note of several key elements. The service interface provides only a single operation: `ProcessMessage`. This might seem odd because there are `Add`, `Update`, and `Delete` operations on the service. When using the Windows Communication Foundation to integrate with non-Windows Communication Foundation applications via MSMQ, it is not possible to map different MSMQ messages to operation contracts automatically. Instead, one defines a single operation that takes an MSMQ message of a particular type as a parameter. In this case, the parameter is the `StudentManagmentRequest` defined earlier. How the message is to be processed by the application that receives the message is identified by the label on the message.

LISTING 11.6   Code for the Client of the Student Information Service

```
using System.ServiceModel;
using System.ServiceModel.Channels;
using System.ServiceModel.MsmqIntegration;

namespace WCFHandsOn
{

    [System.ServiceModel.ServiceContractAttribute(
      Namespace = "http://www.tempuri.org")]
    public interface IStudentManagement
    {

        [System.ServiceModel.OperationContractAttribute(
            IsOneWay = true, Action = "*")]
        void ProcessMessage(MsmqMessage<StudentManagementRequest> msg);
    }

    public interface IStudentManagementChannel:
      IStudentManagement,
      System.ServiceModel.IClientChannel
    {
    }

    public partial class StudentManagementProxy:
      System.ServiceModel.ClientBase<IStudentManagement>,
      IStudentManagement
    {

        public StudentManagementProxy()
        {
        }

        public StudentManagementProxy(string configurationName)
            :
                base(configurationName)
        {
        }

        public StudentManagementProxy(
          System.ServiceModel.Channels.Binding binding)
            :
```

LISTING 11.6   Continued

```
                base(binding.Name.ToString())
    {
    }

    public StudentManagementProxy(
      System.ServiceModel.EndpointAddress address,
➥System.ServiceModel.Channels.Binding binding)
        :
            base(address.Uri.ToString(), binding.Name.ToString())
    {
    }

    public void ProcessMessage(MsmqMessage<StudentManagementRequest> msg)
    {
        base.Channel.ProcessMessage(msg);
    }
  }
}
```

5. Using Solution Explorer, add a new Application Configuration file.

   Populate the configuration file as shown in the following code:

```xml
<?xml version="1.0" encoding="utf-8" ?>
<configuration xmlns="http://schemas.microsoft.com/.NetConfiguration/v2.0">


    <system.serviceModel>

        <client>
            <!-- Define NetProfileMsmqEndpoint -->
            <endpoint       name="StudentManagementEndpoint"
                            address="msmq.formatname:DIRECT=OS:
➥.\private$\school"
                            binding="msmqIntegrationBinding"
                bindingConfiguration="Binding2"
                contract="WCFHandsOn.IStudentManagement">
            </endpoint>
        </client>

        <bindings>
            <msmqIntegrationBinding>
                <binding name="Binding2">
                    <security mode="None" />
```

```
            </binding>
              </msmqIntegrationBinding>
          </bindings>

      </system.serviceModel>

  </configuration>
```

6. Modify the `Program.cs` file to include the code in Listing 11.7. The code generates a
   message from the information entered into the user interface and sends it to the
   queue. Messages that arrive on the queue are processed by the student information
   service:

LISTING 11.7   Client User Interface Code

```
static void Main(string[] args)
    {
    Console.WriteLine("Student Management Client is Now Online");
    Console.WriteLine("-------------------------------------");
    AddStudent("Marc", "Mercuri", "123456789");

        Console.WriteLine();
        Console.WriteLine("Press <ENTER> to terminate client.");
        Console.ReadLine();
    }

  private static void AddStudent(
    string firstName,
    string lastName,
    string phoneNumber)
  {
      using (StudentManagementProxy p = new
        StudentManagementProxy(
          "StudentManagementEndpoint"))
      {

          using (TransactionScope tx = new
            TransactionScope(
              TransactionScopeOption.Required))
          {
              // Submit a job to add two numbers
              StudentManagementRequest request =
                new StudentManagementRequest();
```

LISTING 11.7   Continued

```
                MsmqMessage<StudentManagementRequest> msg =
                  new MsmqMessage<StudentManagementRequest>(
                    request);

                request.firstName = firstName;
                request.lastName = lastName;
                request.phoneNumber = phoneNumber;
                request.studentID = System.Guid.NewGuid().ToString();
                msg.Label = "Add";
                msg.Body = request;
                Console.WriteLine(
                  "Client attempting to add student "
                  + firstName
                  + " "
                  + lastName
                  + " with phone number :"
                  + phoneNumber);
                p.ProcessMessage(msg);

                //Commit the transaction
                tx.Complete();

            }


        }



        }
```

Testing

With the code completed, it is time to test the application.

1. Using Solution Explorer, right-click on the Client project and select Debug, New Instance.

2. Using Solution Explorer, right-click on the Service project and select Debug, New Instance.

The client and server consoles will be displayed. The information entered in the client's Main method will send a message to the queue using the Windows Communication Foundation, which will be received by the waiting service using MSMQ.

To verify that the message was transferred, check the window of the Service application. The information provided should be displayed as in Figure 11.3.

FIGURE 11.3   Service output indicating that a student has been added.

Summary

Very few enterprises start from scratch; they've evolved over time and have multiple legacy systems in place. Leveraging the information and business processes in these legacy applications is of keen interest to the enterprise. This chapter demonstrated how well the Windows Communication Foundation works with two of the most popular types of legacy applications, those that utilize COM+ and MSMQ.

CHAPTER 12

Interoperability

The World Wide Web Consortium defines a *web service* as

> ...a software system designed to support interoperable
> machine-to-machine interaction over a network. It has an
> interface described in a machine-processable format
> (specifically WSDL). Other systems interact with the Web
> service in a manner prescribed by its description using
> SOAP messages, typically conveyed using HTTP with an
> XML serialization in conjunction with other Web-related
> standards (Booth and others; 2004).

Those other web-related standards are designed to be
composable, meaning that any one or more of them can be
selected for use in a given case. That the standards are
composable in that way was intended from the outset
because "SOAP's [very] architecture anticipates the composition of infrastructure protocols through the use of a flexible header mechanism" (Cabrera, Kurt, and Box; 2004). The
protocol defined by each standard specifies the format and
use of a separate header of a SOAP message. The compos-
ability of the web service specifications is in contrast to

> ...[n]umerous domain-specific communication protocols
> [that] are effectively "silos" in which protocol designers
> find themselves coining new mechanisms for dealing with
> security, reliability, error reporting, etc. ...[T]his approach
> to defining an entire protocol for each vertical domain
> breaks when domains overlap and becomes extremely
> costly in terms of both initial development and ongoing
> support costs (Cabrera, Kurt, and Box; 2004).

The Windows Communication Foundation is designed to
facilitate interoperability via the web services standards.
Specifically, it provides implementations of a great many of

those standards, and developers can use those implementations to achieve interoperability with other systems that implement a subset of those same specifications.

The complete list of specifications implemented by the Windows Communication Foundation is included in the documentation, and made available on the Internet. To locate it, search for "Web Services Protocols Supported by System-Provided Interoperability Bindings" in the Microsoft Developer Network Library at http://msdn.microsoft.com/library/default.asp.

The predefined `BasicHttpBinding` binding implements a profile—the WS-I Basic Profile 1.1—that specifies how a small subset of the web services protocols can be used to maximize the likelihood of interoperability. `WSHttpBinding` and `WSFederationBinding` bindings incorporate implementations of a number of communications protocols for which profiles do not yet exist, including WS-Security, WS-ReliableMessaging, WS-SecurityPolicy, WS-AtomicTransaction, WS-Coordination, and WS-Trust. Although communication via those protocols with non–Windows Communication Foundation applications using other implementations of the same protocols can be accomplished using the `WSHttpBinding` and `WSFederationBinding` as a foundation, doing so might require considerable effort. As developers create profiles for additional protocols, versions of `WSHttpBinding` and `WSFederationBinding` with the appropriate defaults will likely become available, and interoperability with other software that conforms to the same profiles should be easy to achieve.

Chapter 2, "The Fundamentals," showed that by virtue of the WS-I Basic Profile 1.1, it is possible to build a Java client for a Windows Communication Foundation service. To see that a Windows Communication Foundation client can also readily interoperate with a non–Windows Communication Foundation service, follow these steps to build a client for Sun Microsystems' public services for interoperability testing:

1. Create a new Visual Studio 2005 C# Console Application project called *SunClient* in the folder C:\WCFHandsOn\Interoperability.

2. Open the SDK Command Prompt by choosing All Programs, Microsoft Windows SDK, CMD Shell.

3. Use the `cd` command at the prompt to make C:\WCFHandsOn\Interoperability\SunClient the prompt's current directory.

4. Enter this command at the prompt to generate a Windows Communication Foundation client in a file that should be named InteropTest.cs, and a Windows Communication Foundation configuration file named App.config:

   ```
   svcutil http://soapinterop.java.sun.com/round2/base?WSDL /config:App.config
   ```

5. Add the generated files C:\WCFHandsOn\Interoperability\SunClient\InteropTest.cs and C:\WCFHandsOn\Interoperability\SunClient\App.config to the Visual Studio project.

6. Open the Interop.cs file and look at the list of types defined therein to find one

with the suffix *Client*. That will be the Windows Communication Foundation client that you can use for communication with the Sun Microsystems' service. It should be a class named `RIBaseIFClient`.

7. Choose Project, Add Reference from the Visual Studio 2005 menus and add a reference to the Windows Communication Foundation's `System.ServiceModel` assembly.

8. Open the Program.cs file and add this code to the `Main()` method defined therein:

```
RIBaseIFClient client = new RIBaseIFClient();
client.Open();
foreach (string currentString in
        client.echoStringArray(
                new string[] { "Hello", ",", " ", "World!" }))
{
    Console.Write(currentString);
}
Console.Write("\n");
client.Close();


Console.Write("Done!");
Console.ReadKey();
```

Notice that in writing

```
RIBaseIFClient client = new RIBaseIFClient();
```

no information about the endpoint with which the client is to communicate is specified. This phrase takes advantage of a convenience provided by the Windows Communication Foundation by which, if the code does not explicitly identify an endpoint configuration, the Windows Communication Foundation uses the first endpoint configuration it finds in the configuration file. Because the configuration file should have only the configuration for the Sun Microsystems service endpoint for which it was generated, that convenience provides a suitable result in this case.

9. Choose Debug, Start Debugging from the Visual Studio 2005 menus. The console should show the application using the Windows Communication Foundation client to send an array of strings to the Sun Microsystems service, which echoes them back to the client for display in the console.

10. Choose Debug, Stop Debugging from the Visual Studio 2005 menus.

Summary

This chapter covered the Windows Communication Foundation's facilities for interoperating with applications on other platforms. The Windows Communication Foundation provides for interoperability through its implementation of various web services protocols. The WS-I Basic Profile 1.1 defines how you can use a subset of those protocols to maximize the likelihood of interoperability. Thus it was possible to show how a Windows Communication Foundation client can easily be made to communicate with a non–Windows Communication Foundation service that conforms to the profile.

References

Booth, David, Hugo Hass, Francis McCabe, Eric Newcomer, Michael Champion, Chris Ferris, and David Orchard. 2004. *Web Services Architecture*. http://www.w3.org/TR/ws-arch/. Accessed October 26, 2006.

Cabrera, Luis Felipe, Christopher Kurt, and Don Box. 2004. *An Introduction to the Web Services Architecture and Its Specifications*. http://msdn.microsoft.com/webservices/webservices/understanding/advancedwebservices/default.aspx?pull=/library/en-us/dnwebsrv/html/introwsa.asp. Accessed October 26, 2006.

PART V

Extending the Windows Communication Foundation

IN THIS PART

Custom Behaviors

Introduction

This chapter is the first of three on how to customize the Windows Communication Foundation. It begins by describing how the Windows Communication Foundation can be extended, before going on to describe one category of customizations in detail: extensions to the Windows Communication Foundation Service Model that are accomplished using custom behaviors.

Extending the Windows Communication Foundation

The Windows Communication Foundation is meant to be, or at least to become, the single best way of getting pieces of software to communicate under any circumstances. For it to achieve that ambitious objective, it must be possible to customize the technology to cover cases that the designers of the Windows Communication Foundation may not have anticipated. Therefore, the designers worked hard to ensure that the Windows Communication Foundation was extensible.

In doing so, they followed the layered approach to framework design that Krzysztof Cwalina and Brad Abrams recommend based on their experience working on the design of the .NET Framework itself (Cwalina and Abrams 2006, 29). The objective of a layered approach to framework design is to make the most common scenarios very easy, while still making it possible to cover all the less common scenarios that are meant to be accommodated. The general guidelines for achieving that objective "is to factor [the] API set into low-level types that expose all of the richness and power and high-level types that wrap the lower layer with convenience APIs" (Cwaline and Abrams 2006, 29–30). One approach to accomplishing that factoring is to "put the high-level and low-level types in different but related namespaces. This has the advantage of hiding the low-level types from the main-stream scenarios without putting them too far out of reach when developers need to implement more complex scenarios" (Cwalina and Abrams 2006, 30).

That is precisely how the Windows Communication Foundation types are organized. The high-level types needed for the commonplace scenarios are in the primary `System.ServiceModel` namespace, whereas the low-level types needed for extending the Windows Communication Foundation to accommodate less common cases are primarily in the `System.ServiceModel.Dispatcher` and `System.ServiceModel.Channels` namespace.

The low-level types in the `System.ServiceModel.Dispatcher` namespaces are for defining custom behaviors that extend the Windows Communication Foundation's Service Model. The low-level types in the `System.ServiceModel.Channels` namespace are for defining custom binding elements that extend the Windows Communication Foundation's Channel Layer.

Behaviors control internal communication functions, whereas binding elements create channels that control external communication functions. For example, a behavior controls the internal function of serializing outbound data into a message, whereas a channel created from a binding element controls the external function of sending the message to its destination.

Extending the Service Model with Custom Behaviors

Within Windows Communication Foundation clients, behaviors modify the operation of components that are primarily responsible for serializing outbound data into messages and de-serializing the responses. The Windows Communication Foundation provides a client runtime component for each endpoint. Each of those components has a number of client operation runtime components associated with it—one for each of the operations included in the endpoint's contract. When an operation is invoked, the client operation runtime component for that operation takes the outbound data and serializes it into a message. That message is then passed to the client runtime component for the endpoint, which passes it on to the Windows Communication Foundation's Channel Layer.

Within Windows Communication Foundation services, behaviors modify the functioning of components called *dispatchers*. Dispatchers are responsible for taking incoming messages and passing the data therein to the appropriate method of a service.

Three kinds of dispatchers participate in that process. The channel dispatcher reads inbound messages from the channel layer, determines the endpoint to which each message is directed toward based on address of the message, and passes each message to the appropriate endpoint dispatcher. The endpoint dispatcher determines the operation to which each message corresponds based on the Action header of the message, and passes the messages to the appropriate operation dispatcher. The operation dispatcher deserializes each incoming message into parameters, and passes those parameters to the method of the service that corresponds to the operation. It also serializes outbound responses into messages.

So, within both clients and services, there are components that correspond to endpoints and others that correspond to operations. The latter perform, as one might expect, functions that are operation specific. For example, the task of serializing outbound data into a message is an operation-specific one, for the way in which the data for one operation has to be serialized might be different from how it has to be done for another operation. The task of passing the messages into which outbound data has been serialized to the channel layer for transmission, however, is not an operation-specific function: It is performed in the same way for all of an endpoint's operations.

The implementation of custom behaviors to modify the workings of the client runtime components and the dispatchers usually involves three steps. Here is an explanation of each step.

Declare What Sort of Behavior You Are Providing

The first step in the implementation of a custom behavior is to declare what sort of behavior one is providing—one that works inside clients to serialize outgoing data into messages, for instance, or one that works inside services to manage instances of service types, perhaps. Declaring what sort of behavior one is providing is easily accomplished by implementing the appropriate interface. Those interfaces are almost all defined in the `System.ServiceModel.Dispatcher` namespace. So, for example, declaring that one is providing a behavior to work inside clients to customize the serialization of outgoing data is done by implementing the interface `System.ServiceModel.Dispatcher.IClientMessageFormatter` interface. Declaring that one is providing a behavior to work inside services to manage instances of service types is done by implementing the interface `System.ServiceModel.Dispatcher.IInstanceProvider`.

One might ask, "How is one to know what kinds of behaviors one can provide, and how is one to know which interface to implement to provide a particular kind of behavior?" The answer is that to ascertain what kinds of behaviors one can provide, one can examine the properties of the client runtime and dispatcher classes, for it is by assigning values to their properties that one attaches custom behaviors to them. The data types of those properties also indicate the interfaces that each type of custom behavior must implement.

Starting that process of examination with the client runtime, the client runtime components are defined by two classes. The class `System.ServiceModel.Dispatcher.ClientOperation` represents the client runtime components at the operation level, whereas the class `System.ServiceModel.Dispatcher.ClientRuntime` represents the client runtime at the endpoint level.

The `System.ServiceModel.Dispatcher.ClientOperation` class has two properties for attaching operation-specific behaviors:

▶ The first property is `ParameterInspectors`, which is a collection of `System.ServiceModel.Dispatcher.IParameterInspector` objects. So, one can create a custom parameter inspector behavior by implementing the `System.ServiceModel.Dispatcher.IParameterInspector` interface. A parameter inspector gets to examine and optionally modify outgoing data as well as incoming response data.

▶ The second property of the `System.ServiceModel.Dispatcher.ClientOperation` class by which one can attach a custom behavior to an operation is the `Formatter` property. Objects that implement the `System.ServiceModel.Dispatcher.IClientMessageFormatter` interface can be assigned to that property. Such objects, which are referred to as *client message formatters,* are for serializing outgoing data into messages, or, more precisely, into the bodies of `System.ServiceModel.Channels.Message` objects.

The `System.ServiceModel.Dispatcher.ClientRuntime` class also has two properties for attaching endpoint behaviors:

▶ The first property of the `System.ServiceModel.Dispatcher.ClientRuntime` class by which one can attach a custom behavior to an endpoint is the `OperationSelector` property. Objects that implement the `System.ServiceModel.Dispatcher.IClientOperationSelector` interface can be assigned to that property. Those client operation selector objects determine to which operation of a service a request is to be directed based on the particular method of the client that was invoked.

▶ The second property is `MessageInspectors`, which is a collection of `System.ServiceModel.Dispatcher.IClientMessageInspector` objects. The client message inspector objects one can create by implementing that interface allow one to examine, and, optionally, modify outgoing request messages and incoming response messages. Being able to do so is useful for, among other things, making copies of outbound messages for later auditing.

Within a service, the dispatchers are defined by three classes. The class `System.ServiceModel.Dispatcher.DispatchOperation` represents the operation-specific dispatcher components. The class `System.ServiceModel.Dispatcher.DispatchRuntime` represents the dispatcher components at the endpoint level. The class `System.ServiceModel.Dispatcher.ChannelDispatcher` defines the service-level channel dispatchers.

Among the several properties of the `System.ServiceModel.Dispatcher.DispatchRuntime` class for attaching endpoint behaviors are these:

▶ The `InstanceContextProvider` property can be assigned an instance of a class that implements `System.ServiceModel.Dispatcher.IInstanceContextProvider`, which can be used for managing state information.

▶ An object that implements the `System.ServiceModel.Dispatcher.IDispatchOperationSelector` interface can be assigned to the `OperatonSelector` property to determine, based on the addressing of a request message, the operation to which that message is to be dispatched.

▶ `MessageInspectors` property can be used to attach message inspectors to examine incoming request messages. Those message inspectors would implement the `System.ServiceModel.Dispatcher.IDispatchMessageInspector` interface.

▶ The `InstanceProvider` property can be assigned an instance of a class that implements `System.ServiceModel.Dispatcher.IInstanceProvider`, which can be used to manage instances of service types.

The `System.ServiceModel.Dispatcher.DispatchOperation` class has three properties for attaching operation-specific behaviors:

▶ Objects that implement the `System.ServiceModel.Dispatcher.IDispatchMessageFormatter` interface can be assigned to the `Formatter` property to deserialize incoming messages into data items and to serialize outbound responses into messages. Such objects are referred to as *dispatch message formatters*.

▶ The `ParameterInspectors` property is a collection of `System.ServiceModel.Dispatcher.IParameterInspector` objects. Those parameter inspector objects can be used to examine and optionally modify the data deserialized from incoming messages by the dispatch message formatter, as well as to examine and possibly modify outbound response data.

▶ A custom operation invoker can be assigned to the `OperationInvoker` property. An operation invoker implements the `System.ServiceModel.Dispatcher.IOperationInvoker` interface. It is used to invoke the method of the service that implements the operation, passing it the data deserialized from the incoming message as parameters.

This analysis of the kinds of behaviors one can provide also yields an understanding of how the Windows Communication Foundation's service model works. Starting from the point at which a Windows Communication Foundation developer's code invokes a method of a Windows Communication Foundation client, the following sequence of events occurs:

1. The client operation selector determines to which operation of the service to direct a request, based on which method of the client was invoked.

2. Any parameter inspectors attached to the client runtime components specific to that operation get to see the data that the developer's code is passing as arguments

to the operation, and can modify that data, too. Parameter inspectors might be used to confirm that the values of outbound data items fall within a specific range, and to adjust them if they do not. They might also perform transformations on the values of certain data items.

3. The client message formatter serializes the data items into XML, and writes the XML into the body of a Windows Communication Foundation message.

4. The `System.ServiceModel.Channels.Message` object representing the message is passed to the client runtime component at the endpoint level.

5. The client message inspector is permitted to examine and optionally modify the `System.ServiceModel.Channels.Message` object representing the message.

6. The message is passed to the Windows Communication Foundation's Channel Layer for delivery. More specifically, it is passed to the top channel in the stack of channels that the Windows Communication Foundation assembled in accordance with the binding selected for the endpoint.

7. The message is received by the service and passed from the Channel Layer to the channel dispatcher, which passes it on to the dispatcher component of the appropriate endpoint.

8. The instance context provider retrieves any state information.

9. Based on the addressing of the message, the dispatch operation selector determines to which operation, among those defined by the service contract, the message pertains.

10. The dispatch message inspector is permitted to examine and optionally modify the `System.ServiceModel.Channels.Message` object representing the incoming message.

11. The instance provider creates or retrieves the instance of the service type that will be passed the data extracted from the message.

12. The message is passed to the dispatcher component for the operation identified by the dispatch operation selector.

13. The dispatch message formatter for the operation deserializes the body of the message into an array of data items.

14. Parameter inspectors attached to the dispatcher components for the operation are permitted to examine and optionally modify the data items.

15. The operation invoker for the operation invokes the method of the service by which the operation is implemented, passing the data items deserialized from the body of the message as arguments to the method.

16. If the method returns data, the parameter inspectors attached to the dispatcher components for the operation are allowed to look at and modify that data.

17. The dispatch message formatter for the operation serializes the data returned by the method into a `System.ServiceModel.Channels.Message` object that represents the response to the message received from the client.

18. That response message is passed to the dispatcher component at the endpoint level.

19. The dispatch message inspector is permitted to examine and modify the response message.

20. The instance context provider is allowed to persist or discard the state information.

21. The instance provider is given the opportunity to dispose of the instance of the service type that it created or retrieved to process the message.

22. The response message is passed to the channel dispatcher, which passes it on for transmission to the uppermost channel in the hierarchy of channels that the Windows Communication Foundation builds in accordance with the binding selected for the endpoint.

23. The response message is received by the client and passed from its Channel Layer to the client runtime component for the receiving endpoint.

24. The client message inspector of that client runtime component examines and optionally modifies the response message.

25. The client operation selector identifies the operation to which the response message pertains based on the addressing of the message.

26. The response message is passed to the client runtime component for that operation.

27. The client message formatter deserializes the body of the response message into an array of data items.

28. That array of data items is passed to any parameter inspectors attached to the client runtime component of the operation for examination and optional modification.

29. The data items are provided to the client developer's code as values returned by the operation that code invoked.

Attach the Custom Behavior to an Operation or Endpoint

The second step in implementing a custom behavior is to attach the custom behavior to an operation, if it is operation specific, or to an endpoint if it is not operation specific. To attach a custom behavior to an operation, implement the `System.ServiceModel.Description.IOperationBehavior` interface. To attach a custom behavior to an endpoint, implement the `System.ServiceModel.Description.IEndpointBehavior` interface.

One might ask, "If the `System.ServiceModelDispatcher.IClientMessageFormatter` interface, for example, signifies that a behavior serializes outgoing data, and if that is, by definition, an operation-specific function, why doesn't the System.ServiceModelDispatcher. IClientMessageFormatter interface derive from the System.ServiceModel.Description. IEndpointBehavior interface?" The answer is that by keeping the two interfaces separate, one class that implements the System.ServiceModelDispatcher. IClientMessageFormatter interface can be attached to an operation by another class that implements the System.ServiceModel.Description.IEndpointBehavior interface. Of course, one class could also implement both interfaces, and attach itself to the operation.

Inform the Windows Communication Foundation of the Custom Behavior

For the behavior to attach itself to a client runtime component or to a dispatcher at either the operation or endpoint level, the behavior must be given access to the client runtime components and the dispatchers. Informing the Windows Communication Foundation Service Model of a custom behavior will cause it to pass the appropriate client runtime component or dispatcher to the custom behavior so that it can attach itself to one of them.

Implementing a Custom Behavior

The preceding steps for implementing a custom behavior are actually very simple to execute. As an example, consider writing a class that is to serve as a client message inspector.

Declare

The first step would be to have the class declare what sort of behavior it will be providing. It is meant to be a message inspector, and classes declare themselves to be client message inspectors by implementing the System.ServiceModel.Dispatcher.IClientInspector interface:

```
public class MyMessageInspector:
        IClientMessageInspector
{
        public void AfterReceiveReply(
                ref System.ServiceModel.Channels.Message reply,
                object correlationState)
        {
        }

        public object BeforeSendRequest(
                ref System.ServiceModel.Channels.Message request,
                System.ServiceModel.IClientChannel channel)
        {
                return null;
        }
}
```

Attach

The second step in implementing a client message inspector is to attach it to the client runtime. Message inspectors attach to the client runtime components at the endpoint level. That is accomplished by implementing the System.ServiceModel.Description.IEndpointBehavior interface, as illustrated in Listing 13.1. That interface has an ApplyClientBehavior() method for attaching to the client endpoint runtime, as well as an ApplyDispatchBehavior() method for attaching to the endpoint dispatcher.

Listing 13.1   Attaching a Behavior to the Client Endpoint Runtime

```
public class MyMessageInspector:
      IClientMessageInspector,
      IEndpointBehavior
{
    public void AddBindingParameters(
            ServiceEndpoint serviceEndpoint,
            BindingParameterCollection bindingParameters)
    {
    }

    public void ApplyClientBehavior(
            ServiceEndpoint serviceEndpoint,
            ClientRuntime behavior)
    {
            behavior.MessageInspectors.Add(this);
    }

    public void ApplyDispatchBehavior(
            ServiceEndpoint serviceEndpoint,
            EndpointDispatcher endpointDispatcher)
    {
    }

    public void Validate(ServiceEndpoint serviceEndpoint)
    {
    }

    [...]
}
```

Inform

The remaining step in implementing a client behavior is to inform the Windows Communication Foundation Service Model of the existence of the behavior. That step is required in order for the Windows Communication Foundation to give the custom behavior access to the client runtime so that the custom behavior can attach itself to the client runtime. The step can be accomplished in code or through configuration.

Informing the Windows Communication Foundation of a Custom Behavior in Code

The constructor of this Windows Communication Foundation client informs the Windows Communication Foundation service model of the existence of a custom behavior that is to be attached to the client endpoint runtime:

```
public class Client: ClientBase<ISimple>, ISimple
{
    public Client(string endpointConfigurationName)
        : base(endpointConfigurationName)
    {
        IEndpointBehavior endpointBehavior = new MyMessageInspector();
        base.Endpoint.Behaviors.Add(endpointBehavior);
    }

    [...]
}
```

Having been thus informed, the Windows Communication Foundation Service Model will pass the custom behavior the client endpoint runtime via that custom behavior's implementation of the ApplyClientBehavior() method of the System.ServiceModel.Description.IEndpointBehavior interface.

In the statement that informs the Windows Communication Foundation Service Model of the behavior

```
base.Endpoint.Behaviors.Add(endpointBehavior);
```

the expression, Endpoint, is an object of the type System.ServiceModel.Description.ServiceEndpoint. The object represents the Windows Communication Foundation's description of the endpoint. Remember that when a Windows Communication Foundation application starts, the Windows Communication Foundation examines the code and the configuration to determine how the application is to communicate. The information gleaned from that examination is stored in a System.ServiceModel.Description.ServiceDescription object, which represents a description of how a Windows Communication Foundation client or service is to communicate. A System.ServiceModel.Description.ServiceEndpoint is an element of that description. As its name suggests, it is an element that describes an endpoint. From this snippet,

```
public class Client: ClientBase<ISimple>, ISimple
{
    public Client(string endpointConfigurationName)
```

```
        : base(endpointConfigurationName)
    {
        [...]
        base.Endpoint.Behaviors.Add(endpointBehavior);
    }

    [...]
}
```

it should be evident that the ClientBase<T> generic makes the description of the endpoint available to the client programmer. Developers writing services can access the Windows Communication Foundation's description of the service via the Description property of the System.ServiceModel.ServiceHost class, thus:

```
ServiceHost host = new ServiceHost(typeof(Service));
host.Description.Endpoints[0].Behaviors.Add(
    new MyMessageInspector());
```

How would the developer of a service to be hosted in IIS access the description, then, for when a service is hosted in IIS one does not need to construct an instance of the System.ServiceModel.ServiceHost class? To access the properties of the service's host when a service is hosted in IIS, one refers, in the .svc file for the service, not directly to the service type, as one usually does

```
<%@ServiceHost Service="MyServiceType" %>
```

but rather to a type that derives from the abstract class, System.ServiceModel.Activation.ServiceHostFactoryBase:

```
<%@ServiceHost Factory="MyServiceHostFactory" %>
```

Types that derive from that abstract base must override its abstract method, CreateServiceHost():

```
public class MyServiceHostFactory: ServiceHostFactoryBase
{
    public override ServiceHostBase CreateServiceHost(
                string constructorString,
                Uri[] baseAddresses)
    {
        ServiceHost host = new ServiceHost(baseAddresses);
        return host;
    }

        [...]
}
```

In overriding that method, one is able to construct the host for the service, and access the members thereof.

Informing the Windows Communication Foundation of a Custom Behavior Through Configuration

To inform the Windows Communication Foundation Service Model of the existence of a custom behavior through configuration, it is necessary to provide a class that derives from the abstract base class System.ServiceModel.Configuration.BehaviorExtensionElement. Listing 13.2 provides an example.

Listing 13.2   A Behavior Extension Element

```
public class MyBehaviorExtensionElement:
        BehaviorExtensionElement
{
        public override Type BehaviorType
    {
        get
        {
            return typeof(MyMessageInspector);
        }
    }

        protected override object CreateBehavior()
        {
            return new MyMessageInspector(this.MyProperty);
        }
}
```

The abstract members of System.ServiceModel.Configuration.BehaviorExtensionElement, the ones that must be implemented, are the BehaviorType property and the CreateBehavior() method. The BehaviorType property informs the Windows Communication Foundation of the type of a custom behavior, and the CreateBehavior() method provides an instance of that type, an instance of the custom behavior.

Given an implementation of the abstract base class, System.ServiceModel.Configuration.BehaviorExtensionElement, one can use it to inform the Windows Communication Foundation of a custom behavior through configuration. A sample configuration is provided in Listing 13.3. In that configuration, the behaviorExtensions element

```
<behaviorExtensions>
        <add
                name="myCustomElement"
```

```
          type="Extensibility.MyBehaviorExtensionElement,
        ➥ BehaviorExtensionElement,
        ➥ Version=1.0.0.0,
        ➥ Culture=neutral,
        ➥ PublicKeyToken=null" />
</behaviorExtensions>
```

defines an extension to the Windows Communication Foundation configuration language for identifying an endpoint behavior. That extension takes the form of a new element called myCustomElement. The element is implemented by the type, Extensibility.MyBehaviorExtensionElement, the definition of which was shown in Listing 13.2. It is identified in the configuration by a complete assembly-qualified name. In this case, a complete assembly-qualified name is mandatory, and that name must be on a single, unbroken line, which is impossible to reproduce here.

Having defined an extension to the Windows Communication Foundation configuration language for identifying an endpoint behavior, that extension can be used to configure a Windows Communication Foundation client, which, in the configuration in Listing 13.3, is done in this way:

```
<client>
        <endpoint
                address="http://localhost:8000/SimpleService/Endpoint"
                binding="basicHttpBinding"
                contract="Extensibility.ISimple"
                behaviorConfiguration="SimpleServiceEndpointBehavior"
                name="SimpleService" />
</client>
<behaviors>
        <endpointBehaviors>
                <behavior
                        name="SimpleServiceEndpointBehavior">
                        <myMessageInspector/>
                </behavior>
        </endpointBehaviors>
</behaviors>
```

Here, the expression

```
<client>
        <endpoint
                [...]
                behaviorConfiguration="SimpleServiceEndpointBehavior"
```

signifies that a set of behaviors with the arbitrary name SimpleServiceEndpointBehavior apply to the client endpoint that is being configured. The inclusion of the previously defined extension to the Windows Communication Foundation configuration language, the element called `myCustomElement`, within that set of behaviors, performs the crucial step of informing the Windows Communication Foundation Service Model of the existence of the custom behavior.

```
<behaviors>
        <endpointBehaviors>
                <behavior
                        name="SimpleServiceEndpointBehavior">
                        <myCustomElement/>
```

When the Windows Communication Foundation parses the configuration and finds that element, it loads the type associated with the element, which is the type `Extensibility.MyBehaviorExtensionElement`. Knowing that the type derives from `System.ServiceModel.Configuration.BehaviorExtensionElement`, the Windows Communication Foundation calls the type's `CreateBehavior()` method, and is given an instance of the custom endpoint behavior, `MyMessageInspector`. Because that type is indeed a custom endpoint behavior, and because it was applied to the configuration of a client endpoint, the client runtime components for that endpoint will be passed to the `ApplyClientBehavior()` method of `MyMessageInspector`. When that method is called, the `MyMessageInspector` object attaches itself to the client endpoint runtime.

Listing 13.3   Informing of a Custom Behavior Through Configuration

```
<?xml version="1.0" encoding="utf-8" ?>
<configuration>
  <system.serviceModel>
    <extensions>
      <behaviorExtensions>
        <add
          name="myCustomElement"
          type="Extensibility.MyBehaviorExtensionElement,
➥BehaviorExtensionElement,
➥Version=1.0.0.0,
➥Culture=neutral,
➥PublicKeyToken=null" />
      </behaviorExtensions>
    </extensions>
    <client>
      <endpoint
        address="http://localhost:8000/SimpleService/Endpoint"
        binding="basicHttpBinding"
        contract="Extensibility.ISimple"
        behaviorConfiguration="SimpleServiceEndpoint
➥Behavior"
```

Listing 13.3   Continued

```
        name="SimpleService"/>
    </client>
    <behaviors>
      <endpointBehaviors>
        <behavior
          name="SimpleServiceEndpointBehavior">
          <myCustomElement/>
        </behavior>
      </endpointBehaviors>
    </behaviors>
    <bindings>
      <customBinding>
        <binding name="SimpleServiceBinding">
          <httpTransport/>
        </binding>
      </customBinding>
    </bindings>
  </system.serviceModel>
</configuration>
```

If the foregoing explanation of how to identify custom behaviors to the Windows Communication Foundation was complicated to follow, then, alas, there are some additional details of which one should be aware. First, it might be necessary to pass data to a custom behavior through the configuration. In that case, the class that derives from `System.ServiceModel.Configuration.BehaviorExtensionElement` must define those data items as `System.Configuration.ConfigurationProperty` members, and is responsible for passing the values of members to the instance of the custom behavior that it supplies to the Windows Communication Foundation, as shown in Listing 13.4. In this way, any data items can be passed to a custom behavior through configuration, as in this example:

```
<behaviors>
        <endpointBehaviors>
                <behavior
                        name="SimpleServiceEndpointBehavior">
                        <myMessageInspector myProperty="whatever"/>
                </behavior>

        </endpointBehaviors>
</behaviors>
```

Listing 13.4   Defining Custom Configurable Properties in a Behavior Extension Element

```
public class MyBehaviorExtensionElement: BehaviorExtensionElement
{
    private ConfigurationPropertyCollection properties = null;

    [ConfigurationProperty(
                "myProperty",
                DefaultValue = "",
                IsRequired = true)]
    public string MyProperty
    {
        get
        {
            return (string)base["myProperty"];
        }

        set
        {
            base["myProperty"] = value;
        }
    }

    protected override ConfigurationPropertyCollection Properties
    {
        get
        {
            if(this.properties == null)
            {
                this.properties = new ConfigurationPropertyCollection();
                this.properties.Add(
                    new ConfigurationProperty(
                        "myProperty",
                        typeof(string),
                        "",
                        ConfigurationPropertyOptions.IsRequired));
            }
            return properties;
        }
    }

    public override void CopyFrom(ServiceModelExtensionElement from)
    {
        base.CopyFrom(from);
```

13

Listing 13.4   Continued

```
        MyBehaviorExtensionElement element = (MyBehaviorExtensionElement)from;
        this.MyProperty = element.MyProperty;
    }

    protected override object CreateBehavior()
    {
        return new MyMessageInspector(this.MyProperty);
    }

    [...]
}
```

A further detail is that only behaviors that apply to endpoints can be directly identified to the Windows Communication Foundation through configuration, not behaviors that apply to operations. To identify a custom operation behavior to the Windows Communication Foundation through configuration, have the behavior implement the System.ServiceModel.Description.IEndpointBehavior as an endpoint behavior would. Then identify it to the Windows Communication Foundation through configuration as if it were an endpoint behavior. When the Windows Communication Foundation invokes the behavior's implementation of the System.ServiceModel.Description.IEndpointBehavior interface's ApplyClientBehavior() or ApplyDispatchBehavior(), one has the opportunity to attach the custom behavior to the client operation runtime or the operation dispatcher:

```
public void ApplyClientBehavior(
            ServiceEndpoint serviceEndpoint,
            ClientRuntime behavior)
{
  behavior.Operations[0].ParameterInspectors.Add(
    this);
}

public void ApplyDispatchBehavior(
        ServiceEndpoint serviceEndpoint,
        EndpointDispatcher endpointDispatcher)
{
  endpointDispatcher.DispatchRuntime.Operations[0].ParameterInspectors.Add(
    this);
}
```

Implementing Each Type of Custom Behavior

Now the three steps for implementing a custom behavior—declaring what type of behavior it is, attaching it to a client runtime component or a dispatcher, and informing the

Windows Communication Foundation of its existence—will be shown for each of the various types of custom behaviors. For the simplicity of the exposition, in each case, the simpler option of informing the Windows Communication Foundation of the existence of the custom behavior through code will be illustrated, rather than the option of doing so through configuration.

Operation Selector

Operation selectors can be applied to both clients and services.

Client

Here are the steps for applying an operation selector to a client.

Declare   Implement the `System.ServiceModel.Dispatcher.IClientOperationSelector` interface:

```
public class MyOperationSelector:
        IClientOperationSelector
{
    public string SelectOperation(
      MethodBase method,
      object[] parameters)
    {
      //Select the operation based on the name of the method.
    }
    [...]
}
```

Attach   Implement the `ApplyClientBehavior()` method of the `System.ServiceModel.Description.IEndpointBehavior` interface:

```
public class MyOperationSelector:
        IClientOperationSelector,
        IEndpointBehavior
{
    public void ApplyClientBehavior(
                ServiceEndpoint serviceEndpoint,
                ClientRuntime behavior)
        {
                behavior.OperationSelector = this;
        }
        [...]
}
```

Inform   In the code for a Windows Communication Foundation client, add the operation selector to the Behaviors collection of a System.ServiceModel.Description.ServiceEndpoint object:

```
public class Client: ClientBase<ISimple>, ISimple
{
    public Client(string endpointConfigurationName)
        : base(endpointConfigurationName)
    {
        base.Endpoint.Behaviors.Add(
                        new MyOperationSelector());
    }

    [...]
}
```

Service

Here are the steps for applying an operation selector to a service.

Declare   Implement the System.ServiceModel.Dispatcher.IDispatchOperationSelector interface:

```
public class MyOperationSelector :
        IDispatchOperationSelector
{
    public string SelectOperation(
        refMessage message)
    {
        //Select the operation based on the Action header of the message.
    }
}
```

Attach   Implement the ApplyDispatchBehavior() method of the System.ServiceModel.Description.IEndpointBehavior interface:

```
public class MyOperationSelector :
        IDispatchOperationSelector,
        IEndpointBehavior
{
    public void ApplyDispatchBehavior(
      ServiceEndpoint serviceEndpoint,
      EndpointDispatcher endpointDispatcher)
    {
      endpointDispatcher.DispatchRuntime.OperationSelector = this;
    }
}
```

Inform   In the code for a Windows Communication Foundation service host, add the
instance context provider to the Behaviors collection of a System.ServiceModel.
Description.EndpointDescription object:

```
ServiceHost host = new ServiceHost(typeof(Service));
host.Description.Endpoints[0].Behaviors.Add(
    new MyOperationSelector());
```

Parameter Inspector

Parameter inspectors can be applied to both clients and services.

Client

Here are the steps for applying a parameter inspector to a client.

Declare   Implement the System.ServiceModel.Dispatcher.IParameterInspector interface:

```
public class MyParameterInspector:
        IParameterInspector
{
        public void AfterCall(
                string operationName,
                object[] outputs,
                object returnValue,
                object correlationState)
        {
                //Inspect return values here.
        }

        public object BeforeCall(
                string operationName,
                object[] inputs)
        {
                //Inspect parameters here.
                return null;
        }
}
```

Attach   Implement the ApplyClientBehavior() method of the System.ServiceModel.
Description.IOperationBehavior interface:

```
public class MyParameterInspector:
        IParameterInspector,
        IOperationBehavior
{
        public void ApplyClientBehavior(
                OperationDescription description,
```

```
                        ClientOperation proxy)
        {
                proxy.ParameterInspectors.Add(this);
        }

        [...]
}
```

Inform   In the code for a Windows Communication Foundation client, add the parameter inspector to the Behaviors collection of the System.ServiceModel.Description. OperationDescription object corresponding to whichever operation's parameters are to be inspected:

```
public class Client: ClientBase<ISimple>, ISimple
{
    public Client(string endpointConfigurationName)
        : base(endpointConfigurationName)
    {
        base.Endpoint.Contract.Operations[0].Behaviors.Add(
                        new MyParameterInspector());
    }

    [...]
}
```

Service

Here are the steps for applying a parameter inspector to a service.

Declare   Parameter inspectors are declared in the same way for services as they are for clients: by implementing the System.ServiceModel.Dispatcher.IParameterInspector interface.

Attach   Implement the ApplyDispatchBehavior() method of the System.ServiceModel. Description.IParameterInspector() interface:

```
public class MyParameterInspector:
        IOperationBehavior,
        IParameterInspector
{
        public void ApplyDispatchBehavior(
                OperationDescription description,
                DispatchOperation dispatch)
        {
                dispatch.ParameterInspectors.Add(this);
        }

        [...]
}
```

Inform   In the code for a Windows Communication Foundation host, add the parameter inspector to the Behaviors collection of the System.ServiceModel.Description.OperationDescription object corresponding to whichever operation's parameters are to be inspected:

```
ServiceHost host = new ServiceHost(typeof(Service));
host.Description.Endpoints[0].Contract.Operations[0].Behaviors.Add(
    new MyParameterInspector());
```

Message Formatter

Message formatters can be applied to both clients and services.

Client

Here are the steps for applying a message formatter to a client.

Declare   Implement the System.ServiceModel.Dispatcher.IClientMessageFormatter interface:

```
public class MyMessageFormatter:
    IClientMessageFormatter
{
    public Message SerializeRequest(
        MessageVersion messageVersion,
        object[] parameters)
    {
        //Serialize request data items into a request message here.
    }

    public object DeserializeReply(
        Message message,
        object[] parameters)
    {
        //De-serialize response message here.
    }
}
```

Attach   Implement the ApplyClientBehavior() method of the System.ServiceModel.Description.IOperationBehavior interface:

```
public class MyMessageFormatter:
    IClientMessageFormatter,
    IOperationBehavior
{
    public void ApplyClientBehavior(
        OperationDescription description,
        ClientOperation proxy)
    {
```

```
                proxy.Formatter = this;
        }


        [...]
}
```

Inform   In the code for a Windows Communication Foundation client, add the message formatter to the Behaviors collection of the System.ServiceModel.Description.OperationDescription object corresponding to whichever operation's parameters are to be serialized by the message formatter:

```
public class Client: ClientBase<ISimple>, ISimple
{
    public Client(string endpointConfigurationName)
        : base(endpointConfigurationName)
    {
        base.Endpoint.Contract.Operations[0].Behaviors.Add(
                    new MyMessageFormatter());
    }

    [...]
}
```

Service

Here are the steps for applying a message formatter to a service.

Declare   Implement the System.ServiceModel.Dispatcher.IDispatchMessageFormatter interface:

```
public class MyMessageFormatter:
        IDispatchMessageFormatter
{
        public void DeserializeRequest(
                Message message,
                object[] parameters)
        {
                //De-serialize request message here.
        }

        public Message SerializeReply(
                MessageVersion messageVersion,
                object[] parameters,
                object result)
        {
                //Serialize response data items into a response message here.
        }
}
```

Attach   Implement the ApplyDispatchBehavior() method of the
System.ServiceModel.Description.IOperationBehavior interface:

```
public class MyMessageFormatter:
        IDispatchMessageFormatter,
        IOperationBehavior
{
        public void ApplyDispatchBehavior(
                OperationDescription description,
                DispatchOperation dispatch)
        {
                dispatch.Formatter = this;
        }

        [...]
}
```

Inform   In the code for a Windows Communication Foundation service host, add the
message formatter to the Behaviors collection of the
System.ServiceModel.Description.OperationDescription object corresponding to
whichever operation's parameters are to be serialized by the message formatter:

```
ServiceHost host = new ServiceHost(typeof(Service));
host.Description.Endpoints[0].Contract.Operations[0].Behaviors.Add(
    new MyMessageFormatter());
```

Message Inspector

Message inspectors can be applied to both clients and services.

Client

Here are the steps for applying a message inspector to a client.

Declare   Implement the System.ServiceModel.Dispatcher.IClientMessageInspector
interface:

```
public class MyMessageInspector:
        IClientMessageInspector
{
            public object BeforeSendRequest(
                ref Message request,
                IClientChannel channel)
        {
                //Inspect outbound request message here.
        }
```

```
        public void AfterReceiveReply(
                Message reply,
                object correlationState)
        {
                //Inspect inbound response message here.
        }
}
```

Attach   Implement the `ApplyClientBehavior()` method of the
`System.ServiceModel.Description.IEndpointBehavior` interface:

```
public class MyMessageInspector:
        IClientMessageInspector,
        IEndpointBehavior
{
    public void ApplyClientBehavior(
                ServiceEndpoint serviceEndpoint,
                ClientRuntime behavior)
        {
                behavior.MessageInspectors.Add(this);
        }

        [...]
}
```

Inform   In the code for a Windows Communication Foundation client, add the message
inspector to the `Behaviors` collection of the
`System.ServiceModel.Description.EndpointDescription` object corresponding to
whichever endpoint's messages are to be inspected:

```
public class Client: ClientBase<ISimple>, ISimple
{
    public Client(string endpointConfigurationName)
        : base(endpointConfigurationName)
    {
        base.Endpoint.Behaviors.Add(
                        new MyMessageInspector());
    }

    [...]
}
```

Service
Here are the steps for applying a message inspector to a service.

Declare   Implement the `System.ServiceModel.Dispatcher.IDispatchMessageInspector` interface:

```
public class MyMessageInspector:
        IDispatchMessageInspector
{
        public object AfterReceiveRequest(
                ref Message request,
                IClientChannel channel,
                InstanceContext instanceContext)
        {
                //Inspect inbound request message here.
        }

        public void BeforeSendReply(
                ref Channels.Message reply,
                object correlationState)
        {
                //Inspect outbound response message here.
        }
}
```

Attach   Implement the `ApplyDispatchBehavior()` method of the `System.ServiceModel.Description.IEndpointBehavior` interface:

```
public class MyMessageInspector:
        IDispatchMessageInspector,
        IEndpointBehavior
{
        public void ApplyDispatchBehavior(
                ServiceEndpoint serviceEndpoint,
                EndpointDispatcher endpointDispatcher)
        {
           endpointDispatcher.DispatchRuntime.MessageInspectors.Add(this);
        }

        [...]
}
```

Inform   In the code for a Windows Communication Foundation service host, add the message inspector to the `Behaviors` collection of the `System.ServiceModel.Description.EndpointDescription` object corresponding to whichever endpoint's messages are to be inspected:

```
ServiceHost host = new ServiceHost(typeof(Service));
host.Description.Endpoints[0].Behaviors.Add(
    new MyMessagInspector());
```

Instance Context Provider

Instance context providers can be applied to services.

Service

Here are the steps for applying an instance context provider to a service.

Declare   Implement the `System.ServiceModel.Dispatcher.IInstanceContextProvider` interface:

```
public class MyInstanceContextProvider :
        IInstanceContextProvider
{
    public InstanceContext GetExistingInstanceContext(
                Message message,
                IContextChannel channel)
    {
        //Retrieve previously initialized instance context.
    }

    public void InitializeInstanceContext(
                InstanceContext instanceContext,
                Message message,
                IContextChannel channel)
    {
        //Initialize instance context.
    }
    [...]
}
```

Attach   Implement the `ApplyDispatchBehavior()` method of the `System.ServiceModel.Description.IEndpointBehavior` interface:

```
public class MyInstanceContextProvider :
        IInstanceContextProvider,
        IEndpointBehavior
{
    public void ApplyDispatchBehavior(
      ServiceEndpoint serviceEndpoint,
      EndpointDispatcher endpointDispatcher)
    {
      endpointDispatcher.DispatchRuntime.InstanceContextProvider = this;
    }
    [...]
}
```

Inform   In the code for a Windows Communication Foundation service host, add the
instance context provider to the `Behaviors` collection of a `System.ServiceModel.`
`Description.EndpointDescription` object:

```
ServiceHost host = new ServiceHost(typeof(Service));
host.Description.Endpoints[0].Behaviors.Add(
    new MyInstanceContextProvider());
```

Instance Provider

Instance providers can be applied to services.

Service

Here are the steps for applying an instance provider to a service.

Declare   Implement the `System.ServiceModel.Dispatcher.IInstanceProvider` interface:

```
public class MyInstanceProvider :
        IInstanceProvider
{
    public object GetInstance(
                InstanceContext instanceContext,
                Message message)
    {
        //Retrieve or create the service instance here.
    }

    public object GetInstance(
                InstanceContext instanceContext)
    {
                //Retrieve or create the service instance here.
    }

    public void ReleaseInstance(
                InstanceContext instanceContext,
                object instance)
    {
        //Store or dispose of the service instance.
    }
}
```

Attach   Implement the `ApplyDispatchBehavior()` method of the `System.ServiceModel.`
`Description.IEndpointBehavior` interface:

```
public class MyInstanceProvider :
        IInstanceProvider,
        IEndpointBehavior
{
```

```
    public void ApplyDispatchBehavior(
      ServiceEndpoint serviceEndpoint,
      EndpointDispatcher endpointDispatcher)
    {
      endpointDispatcher.DispatchRuntime.InstanceProvider = this;
    }
    [...]
}
```

Inform   In the code for a Windows Communication Foundation service host, add the instance context provider to the `Behaviors` collection of a `System.ServiceModel.Description.EndpointDescription` object:

```
ServiceHost host = new ServiceHost(typeof(Service));
host.Description.Endpoints[0].Behaviors.Add(
    new MyInstanceProvider());
```

Operation Invokers

Operation invokers can be applied to services.

Service

Here are the steps for applying an operation invoker to a service.

Declare   Implement the `System.ServiceModel.Dispatcher.IOperationInvoker` interface:

```
public class MyOperationInvoker:
    IOperationInvoker
{
    public object Invoke(
        object instance,
        object[] inputs,
        out object[] outputs)
    {
      //Invoke a method of the service.
    }
    [...]
}
```

Attach   Implement the `ApplyDispatchBehavior()` method of the `System.ServiceModel.Description.IOperationBehavior` interface:

```
public class MyOperationInvoker :
        IOperationInvoker,
        IOperationBehavior
{
    public void ApplyDispatchBehavior(
      OperationDescription description,
```

```
    DispatchOperation dispatch)
  {
    dispatch.Invoker = this;
  }
  [...]
}
```

Inform   In the code for a Windows Communication Foundation service host, add the instance context provider to the Behaviors collection of a System.ServiceModel.Description.OperationDescription object:

```
ServiceHost host = new ServiceHost(typeof(Service));
host.Description.Endpoints[0].Contract.Operations[0].Behaviors.Add(
        new MyOperationInvoker());
```

Implementing a WSDL Export Extension

The custom behaviors dealt with thus far in this chapter have all been behaviors applied to a client runtime component or a dispatcher at either the endpoint or operation level. However, there is a useful type of custom behavior that is a little different. It is a WSDL export extension, which is useful for modifying the WSDL that the Windows Communication Foundation generates to describe a service.

A WSDL export extension gets attached to the description of either a contract or an endpoint. When a request for the metadata of a service is received, the Windows Communication Foundation generates that metadata using a System.ServiceModel.Description.WsdlExporter object. That object identifies any WSDL export extensions attached to the service's endpoints or to any of the contracts thereof, and gives them the opportunity to add to or modify the WSDL that gets provided in response to the request.

Implementation Steps

Here are the steps for implementing a WSDL export extension.

Declare That a Type Is a WSDL Export Extension

To provide a WSDL export extension, create a class and declare that it is a WSDL export extension by implementing the System.ServiceModel.Description.IWsdlExportExtension interface:

```
public class MyContractBehavior: IWsdlExportExtension, IContractBehavior
{
        public void ExportContract(
                WsdlExporter exporter,
                WsdlContractConversionContext context)
        {
```

```
                //Modify the WSDL represented by the context parameter here.
        }

        public void ExportEndpoint(
                WsdlExporter exporter,
                WsdlEndpointConversionContext context)
        {
                //Modify the WSDL represented by the context parameter here.
        }
}
```

Specify Whether the WSDL Export Extension Attaches to an Endpoint or to a Contract
Specify that the WSDL export extension attaches to an endpoint by having it implement
the System.ServiceModel.Description.IEndpointBehavior interface, or specify that it
attaches to a contract by having it implement the
System.ServiceModel.Description.IContractBehavior interface.

```
public class MyContractBehavior:
        IWsdlExportExtension,
        IContractBehavior
{
        public void AddBindingParameters(
                ContractDescription contractDescription,
                ServiceEndpoint endpoint,
                BindingParameterCollection bindingParameters)
    {
    }

        public void ApplyClientBehavior(
                ContractDescription contractDescription,
                ServiceEndpoint endpoint,
                ClientRuntime clientRuntime)
    {
    }

        public void ApplyDispatchBehavior(
                ContractDescription contractDescription,
                ServiceEndpoint endpoint,
                DispatchRuntime dispatchRuntime)
    {
    }

        public void Validate(
                ContractDescription contractDescription,
```

```
                    ServiceEndpoint endpoint)
   {
   }

   [...]
}
```

In this case, no code needs to be written in the implementations of any of the methods of the interfaces. The WSDL export extension does not have to actively attach itself to an endpoint or contract in the way that the custom behaviors discussed previously in this chapter did. Implementing the interface simply declares whether it is to an endpoint, or to a contract, or to both of those, that the WSDL export extension attaches.

Inform the Windows Communication Foundation of the WSDL Export Extension

If the WSDL export extension is to be attached to an endpoint, it implements the System.ServiceModel.Description.IEndpointBehavior interface, and the Windows Communication Foundation can be informed of it in code or in configuration in the same way as the other endpoint-level behaviors described in this chapter. However, if the WSDL export extension is to be attached to a contract, it is a contract behavior, and the Windows Communication Foundation cannot be informed about those through configuration. It can be informed of them through imperative code:

```
host.Description.Endpoints[0].Contract.Behaviors.Add(
  new MyContractBehavior());
```

The other option is to have the contract behavior also be a custom attribute by having it derive from System.Attribute

```
[AttributeUsage(AttributeTargets.Interface)]
public class MyContractBehavior:
        Attribute,
        IWsdlExportExtension,
        IContractBehavior
{
        [...]
}
```

and then it can be applied to the contract declaratively:

```
[MyContractBehavior]
[ServiceContract]
public interface ISimple
{
        [...]
}
```

Custom Behaviors in Action

The sample code provided for this chapter provides a simple implementation of every type of custom behavior that has been described. So, to see all the custom behaviors at work, follow these steps:

1. Copy the code associated with this chapter downloaded from http://www.crypt-maker.com/WindowsCommunicationFoundationUnleashed to the folder C:\WCFHandsOn. The code is all in a folder called `CustomBehaviors`.

2. Open the Visual Studio 2005 solution, CustomBehaviors.sln. The solution contains a project called ServiceHost for building a console application to host the Windows Communication Foundation service built from the project called Service. The project called Client is for building a console application that is a Windows Communication Foundation client of the service. The projects called CustomServiceBehaviors and CustomClientBehaviors are for building class libraries that contain the custom behaviors applied to the service and the client. A project called BehaviorExtensionElement is for building a class library that contains a class used for identifying one of the custom client behaviors to the Windows Communication Foundation through configuration.

3. Choose Build, Build Solution from the Visual Studio 2005 menus.

4. Choose Debug, Start Debugging from the Visual Studio 2005 menus. Consoles for the ServiceHost and Client applications should open.

5. When the output in the console of the service host indicates that the service is ready, navigate a browser to the address http://localhost:8000/SimpleService?wsdl. Doing so will generate a request for the service's metadata, and in the process of responding, the Windows Communication Foundation will use a WSDL export extension that adds this WSDL import statement to the WSDL that gets produced:

```
<wsdl:import
  namespace="http://someorganization.org/somenamespace/"
  location="http://someorganization.org/somenamespace/their.wsdl"/>
```

The WSDL export extension also announces its having been used in the console of the service host.

6. Enter a keystroke into the console of the client application, and observe the output in the both the console of the client application and the console of the service host. What will have happened is that a request will have been sent from the client to the service, and each custom behavior attached to the client runtime components and the dispatchers will have reported its involvement in the process with output to the console. Thus, one can see not only the evidence of the custom behaviors having been used, but also the order in which they are activated.

7. Choose Debug, Stop Debugging from the Visual Studio 2005 menus to terminate the applications.

Summary

This chapter has presented the first set of options for extending the Windows Communication Foundation—the addition of custom behaviors to the Windows Communication Foundation Service Model. All the various types of custom behaviors that can be attached to clients and services were enumerated. The role of each custom behavior was explained, and its sequential position within the Service Model's processing was identified. The steps for implementing each type of custom behavior were explained and demonstrated.

References

Cwalina, Krzysztof and Brad Abrams. 2006. *Framework Design Guidelines: Conventions, Idioms, and Patterns for Reusable .NET Libraries*. Upper Saddle River, NJ: Addison Wesley.

CHAPTER 14

Custom Channels

Introduction

This chapter continues the exposition of opportunities for customizing the Windows Communication Foundation. As explained in Chapter 13, "Custom Behaviors," there are two primary ways of extending the technology to accommodate scenarios for which it does not explicitly provide. The first is through the addition of custom behaviors that control the Windows Communication Foundation's internal communication functions, such as the function of serializing outbound data into messages.

The second primary way of extending the technology is through the addition of custom bindings. Custom bindings supplement the Windows Communication Foundation's external communication capabilities, increasing the variety of protocols it supports for exchanging messages with external parties. The subject of extending the Windows Communication Foundation through the addition of custom binding elements will be covered in two parts. This chapter covers the implementation of generic custom binding elements. Chapter 15, "Custom Transports," deals with the construction of a special category of custom binding element, the custom transport binding element.

Binding Elements

In developing a Windows Communication Foundation application, one uses the Windows Communication Foundation's Service Model language to create a model of how one's application is to communicate with other software entities. When the application prepares to send or receive data, the Windows Communication Foundation examines the model that the developer has created, and constructs the runtime components necessary to facilitate the communication.

A model of how an application is to communicate that is expressed in the language of the Windows Communication Foundation Service Model consists, at a minimum, of an address, a binding, and a contract. The binding constituent defines the protocols the application is to use to communicate. The binding constituent consists of nothing more than a list of binding elements. A *binding element* is a piece of software provided by the Windows Communication Foundation's channel layer that knows how to construct runtime components that implement a particular protocol. So, in implementing a model for communication created by a Windows Communication Foundation developer, the Windows Communication Foundation examines the binding included in that model, and retrieves from it a list of binding elements. Then it has the first of those binding elements construct the runtime components it provides for supporting some protocol. That binding element is responsible for having the next binding element in the list construct its runtime components, and so on.

The runtime components that a binding element creates to provide support for a protocol are channel factories and channel listeners. Channel factories create channels for outbound communication, whereas channel listeners provide channels for inbound communication.

It is those channels that actually implement a protocol. Messages pass through the channels, and each channel manipulates the messages passing through it in accordance with the protocol that the channel implements.

Outbound Communication

When the binding element that is first in the list of binding elements specified in a binding is told by the Windows Communication Foundation to construct its runtime components in preparation for outbound communication, it creates its channel factory. In the process of initializing itself, that channel factory tells the binding element that is next in the list to create its channel factory, and that next channel factory will instruct any subsequent binding element to do the same, and so on. Consequently, what the Windows Communication Foundation receives in response to its instruction to the first binding element to prepare for outbound communication is the first in a stack of channel factories that the binding elements have cooperated in constructing.

The Windows Communication Foundation then instructs that first channel factory to create a channel for outbound communication. The channel factory responds by telling the next channel factory in the stack to create a channel, and that channel factory instructs the subsequent channel factory to construct a channel, and so on. Each channel factory takes the channel provided by the channel factory beneath, and passes that subordinate channel to the channel that it itself constructs.

That channel now has two responsibilities. Its first responsibility is to pass instructions and outbound messages on to the subordinate channel, which will in turn pass them on to its own subordinate channel. The channel's second responsibility is to implement whatever protocol it is meant to support by performing operations on the outbound messages passing through it.

Having told the first channel factory in the stack of channel factories to create a channel for outbound communication, the Windows Communication Foundation will have received in response an outbound channel that is the first in a stack of outbound channels that the channel factories have cooperated in building. Outbound channels have standard methods for sending messages, so when a message is to be transmitted, the Windows Communication Foundation will be able to use a method of that first channel to send the message. That first channel will do to the message whatever the protocol that it implements dictates should be done, and then it will pass the message on to the next channel in the stack.

When the application that sent the message wants to dispose of the resources that the Windows Communication Foundation has provided for outbound communication, the Windows Communication Foundation instructs the first channel in the stack of channels to close, which is that channel's opportunity to dispose of its resources. That channel will in turn tell the next channel in the stack to dispose of its resources, and that next channel will pass the instruction along to the next channel in the stack, and so on. When the first channel has finished disposing of its own resources, and detects that its subordinate channel has finished closing as well, it reports to the Windows Communication Foundation that it is indeed closed. More generally, channels are state machines, and the Windows Communication Foundation can have the channels in a stack transition to a new state by instructing the first channel in the stack to make the transition, and that first channel will pass the instruction along to the next channel, and so on.

Inbound Communication

When the binding element that is first in the list of binding elements specified in a binding is told by the Windows Communication Foundation to construct its runtime components in preparation for inbound communication, it creates its channel listener. In the process of initializing itself, that channel listener tells the binding element that is next in the list to create its channel listener, and that channel listener instructs any subsequent binding element to do the same, and so on. Consequently, what the Windows Communication Foundation receives in response to its instruction to the first binding element to prepare for inbound communication is the first in a stack of channel listeners that the binding elements have cooperated in constructing. The Windows Communication Foundation constructs a channel dispatcher to use that channel listener.

The channel dispatcher proceeds to ask the first channel listener for an inbound communication channel from which it will be able to read incoming messages. The channel listener responds by asking the next channel listener in the stack for an inbound communication channel, and so on. Each channel listener takes the channel provided by the channel listener beneath, and passes that subordinate channel to the channel that it itself constructs.

That new inbound channel now has three responsibilities. Its first responsibility is to pass on instructions to its subordinate channel, which will in turn pass them on to its own subordinate channel, and so on. Its second responsibility is to pass on incoming messages received from its subordinate channel. The inbound channel's third responsibility is to implement whatever protocol it is meant to support by performing some operation on the incoming messages that pass through it.

Having told the first channel listener in the stack of channel listeners to provide a channel for inbound communication, the channel dispatcher will have received in response an inbound channel that is first in the a stack of inbound channels that the channel listeners have cooperated in building. Inbound channels have standard asynchronous methods for waiting for incoming messages, methods that complete when a message arrives. So, the channel dispatcher is able to use a method of the first inbound channel in the stack to wait for an incoming message. When that method completes, there will be an inbound message to process. The channel dispatcher immediately has the first inbound channel in the stack go back to waiting for the subsequent messages. Meanwhile, the channel dispatcher takes the message that it already received, determines from its address the endpoint to which the message is directed, and passes the message to the appropriate endpoint dispatcher. The endpoint dispatcher will determine the operation to which the message corresponds based on the message's action header, and pass over to the appropriate operation dispatcher. That operation dispatcher will deserialize the message into data items, and pass those data items to an instance of a service type for processing.

When the application that is hosting the service that was receiving communications no longer wants to do so, the Windows Communication Foundation instructs the channel dispatcher to close, which in turn tells the first channel in the stack of inbound channels to close. That channel disposes of its resources, and tells the next channel in the stack of channels to dispose of its resources too. That channel will in turn tell the next channel in the stack to dispose of its resources, and so on. When the first channel has finished disposing of its own resources, and detects that its subordinate channel has finished closing as well, it reports to the channel dispatcher that it is indeed closed. Other instructions for state transitions from the channel dispatcher to the stack of inbound channels are passed on in the same way.

Channels Have Shapes

The foregoing explanation of how binding elements work used the notion of inbound communication channels and outbound communication channels for simplicity. It is more correct to say that channels have shapes. Being able to receive messages is one shape that a channel might have, whereas being able to send messages is another, and being able to reply directly to messages that have been received is yet another, and there are other shapes, too.

The fundamental shapes that a channel can assume are defined by a family of interfaces that derive from the `System.ServiceModel.Channels.IChannel` interface:

▶ `System.ServiceModel.Channels.IInputChannel` is the shape of a channel for receiving messages.

▶ `System.ServiceModel.Channels.IOutputChannel` is the shape of a channel for sending messages.

▶ System.ServiceModel.Channels.IRequestChannel is the shape of a channel for sending a message for which a response is expected.

▶ System.ServiceModel.Channels.IReplyChannel is the shape of a channel for sending messages in reply to request messages.

▶ System.ServiceModel.Channels.IDuplexChannel implements both System.ServiceModel.Channels.IOutputChannel and System.ServiceModel.Channels.IInputChannel to define the shape of a channel that can both send and receive messages.

A channel declares its shape by implementing one or more of those interfaces:

```
public class MyCustomRequestChannel: IRequestChannel
```

Crucially, the shapes of the channels that a Windows Communication Foundation application will need for sending and receiving its messages are implied by Windows Communication Foundation contracts. For example, this contract

```
[ServiceContract]
public interface IEcho
{
    [OperationContract]
    string Echo(string input);
}
```

has an operation by which some data is received in response to data that is sent. A channel with only the shape defined by the System.ServiceModel.Channels.IOutputChannel interface would not suffice for the exchange of messages required by that operation because such a channel could not convey the response. A channel with only the shape defined by the System.ServiceModel.Channels.IInputChannel interface would not suffice either because such a channel could not transmit the data to be sent. A channel with the shape defined by the System.ServiceModel.IRequestChannel interface would be sufficient, as would a channel with the shape defined by the System.ServiceModel.Channels.IDuplexChannel interface.

In general, one can say that contracts describe a *message exchange pattern*—a pattern for the exchange of messages between applications. The variety of message exchange patterns that a channel can support is determined by its shape, which is defined by the System.ServiceModel.Channels.IChannel interfaces that it implements.

Channels Might Be Required to Support Sessions

Besides describing a particular message exchange pattern that the channels defined by a binding must be able to support, service contracts might or might not require that the

14

exchange of messages take place within the context of a session. Whether or not a contract requires a session is determined by the `SessionMode` property of the contract:

```
[ServiceContract(SessionMode=SessionMode.Required)]
public interface IExchange
{
    [OperationContract(IsInitiating=true,IsTerminating=false)]
    string Start(string input);
    [OperationContract(IsInitiating=true,IsTerminating=true)]
    string Stop(string input);
}
```

If a contract requires that an exchange of messages takes place within the context of a session, the messages will have to convey the state of the session. For that to be possible, at least one channel through which messages are sent will have to be capable of writing information about the session into those messages, and at least one channel through which messages are received will have to be capable of reading information about the sessions from the messages. Channels that are capable of supporting sessions signal that by implementing an interface derived from the `System.ServiceModel.Channels.ISession` interface—`System.ServiceModel.Channels.IOutputSession` or `System.ServiceModel.Channels.IInputSession`. Versions of the shape-defining `System.ServiceModel.Channels.IChannel` interfaces that implement the `System.ServiceModel.Channels.ISession` interfaces are predefined in the `System.ServiceModel.Channels` namespace. For example, there is a predefined `System.ServiceModel.Channels.IRequestSession` interface that implements both `System.ServiceModel.Channels.IRequestChannel` and `System.ServiceModel.Channels.IOutputSession`.

Matching Contracts to Channels

So, evidently, how a contract is defined has implications for the types of channels that can be used for exchanging messages in accordance with it. Those implications of the contract are referred to as its *implicit communication requirements*, whereas the exchange of messages described by its operations are referred to as its *explicit communication semantics*.

When a Windows Communication Foundation application is preparing to send or receive data, the Windows Communication Foundation determines the implicit communication requirements of the contract, and ascertains whether those can be satisfied by the channels that can be constructed from the selected binding's binding elements. If those requirements cannot be met, the Windows Communication Foundation throws a `System.InvalidOperation` exception.

How does the Windows Communication Foundation determine whether the implicit communication requirements of a contract can be satisfied by the channels that can be constructed from a binding's binding elements? It calls the generic `CanBuildChannelFactory<T>()` and `CanBuildChannelListener<T>()` methods of the first binding element, using, as *T*, one of the interfaces that a channel could implement that would satisfy the contract's implicit communication requirements. If that first binding element can construct channels that implement that interface, the first binding element calls the CanBuildChannelFactory<*T*>() and CanBuildChannelListener<*T*>() methods of the next binding element, which will then call the same methods of the next binding element, and so on. The first binding element reports the consensus back to the Windows Communication Foundation. Here are sample implementations of CanBuildChannelFactory<*T*>() and CanBuildChannelListener<*T*>():

```
public override bool CanBuildChannelFactory<TChannel>(BindingContext context)
{
    if (typeof(TChannel) == typeof(IRequestChannel))
    {
        return context.CanBuildInnerChannelFactory<TChannel>();
    }
    else
    {
        return false;
    }
}


public override bool CanBuildChannelListener<TChannel>(BindingContext context)
{
    if (typeof(TChannel) == typeof(IReplyChannel))
    {
        return context.CanBuildInnerChannelListener<TChannel>();
    }
    else
    {
        return false;
    }
}
```

In this case, the implementation implies that the binding element can only provide output channels with the shape defined by System.ServiceModel.Channels.IRequestChannel, and can only provide input channels with the shape defined by System.ServiceModel.Channels.IReplyChannel. The System.ServiceModel.Channels.BindingContext object that is passed to both methods as a parameter provides the current binding element access to the next one.

The Windows Communication Foundation invokes the CanBuildChannelFactory<*T*>() and CanBuildChannelListener<*T*>() methods for each of the interfaces that a channel could implement to satisfy the implicit communication requirements of the contract. After having done so, it knows whether those requirements can be met by the binding elements of the selected binding.

Assuming that the implicit communication requirements of the contract can be satisfied by the binding elements, the Windows Communication Foundation then selects one of the interfaces that could be used to satisfy those requirements, and that is supported by the binding elements. In the case of a client that is preparing to send a message to a service, the Windows Communication Foundation then tells the first of the binding elements to provide a channel factory that can create channels that conform to the selected interface. To do so, it calls that binding element's `BuildChannelFactory<T>()` method, using the selected interface as *T*:

```
public override IChannelFactory<TChannel> BuildChannelFactory<TChannel>(
        BindingContext context)
{
    return (IChannelFactory<TChannel>)
                (object)new MyCustomChannelFactory<TChannel>(
                        this,context);
}
```

In the case of a service that is preparing to listen for messages, the Windows Communication Foundation tells the first of the binding elements to provide a channel listener that can provide input channels that conform to the selected interface. To do so, it calls the binding element's `BuildChannelListener<T>()` method, using the selected interface as *T*:

```
public override IChannelListener<TChannel> BuildChannelListener<TChannel>(
        BindingContext context)
{
    return(IChannelListener<TChannel>)
                (object)new MyCustomChannelListener<TChannel>(
                        this,context);
}
```

It should be apparent that in providing custom binding elements, a key decision is which implicit communication requirements of contracts will be accommodated. Some binding elements might not be compatible with some contracts.

Communication State Machines

Channels, channel factories, and channel listeners are all state machines. More specifically, the Windows Communication Foundation defines a communication state machine in its `System.ServiceModel.Channels.ICommunicationObject` interface, and channels, channel factories, and channel listeners all implement that interface.

The interface defines a property, `State`, for ascertaining the current state of a communication state machine. The states are defined as `Created`, `Opening`, `Opened`, `Faulted`, `Closing`, and `Closed`.

Three methods, `Open()`, `Close()`, and `Abort()`, are provided for initiating state transitions. It is via these methods that the Windows Communication Foundation is able to communicate the state of an application to channel factories, channel listeners, and channels, and have them respond appropriately. In particular, the `Open()` method signifies that the application is preparing to send or receive messages, so a stack of channels for sending or receiving messages needs to be constructed. The `Close()` method is the signal to dispose of resources. The `Abort()` method indicates that not only should resources be disposed of, but any outstanding operations should be cancelled immediately. All communication state machines are responsible for passing on instructions to perform state transitions to the subordinate communication state machines in their stack.

The `System.ServiceModel.Channels.ICommunicationObject` interface also defines several events by which a communication state machine can signal a state transition. Those events are `Opening`, `Opened`, `Faulted`, `Closing`, and `Closed`.

Building Custom Binding Elements

To create a custom binding element to support a protocol for outbound communication, it is necessary to implement, at a minimum, the binding element itself, a channel factory, and an outbound communication channel. To support a protocol for input communication, the binding element is required along with a channel listener and an inbound communication channel.

The steps for implementing a custom binding element to support both outbound and inbound communication will be presented in the pages that follow. The starting point will be a simple Windows Communication Foundation client that sends a message to a service.

Understand the Starting Point

These steps are for getting acquainted with the starting point:

1. Copy the code associated with this chapter downloaded from http://www.crypt-maker.com/WindowsCommunicationFoundationUnleashed to the folder C:\WCFHandsOn. The code is all in a folder called `CustomChannels`. The completed solution is the subfolder called `CompletedSolution`, and the starting point for the step-by-step instructions that follow is in the subfolder called `StartingPoint`.

2. Open the solution `CustomChannels.sln` in the `StartingPoint` subfolder. It consists of four projects. The Service project is for building a simple Windows Communication Foundation service. The ServiceHost project is for building a console application for hosting that service. The Client project is for building a console application that is a client of the service. The project called MyCustomBindingElement is a blank class library project to which the classes required for the custom binding element will be added.

3. Examine the service contract in the `ISimple.cs` file of the Service project. It has a single operation that anticipates a reply in response to a request:

```
[ServiceContract]
public interface ISimple
{
```

```
      [OperationContract]
      string AcceptRequest(string someRequest);
   }
```

4. Study the code for the client application in the Program.cs file of the Client project. The application constructs a Windows Communication Foundation client using a custom binding consisting solely of an instance of one of the predefined transport binding elements, System.ServiceModel.Channels.HttpTransportBindingElement. The application then calls the client's Open() method, and pauses for input. Then the application proceeds to use the client to send two messages to the service before calling the client's Close() method.

```
public class Program
{
  static void Main(string[] args)
  {
    Console.WriteLine("Press any key when the service is ready.");
    Console.ReadKey(true);
    Client client = new Client(
      new CustomBinding(
        new BindingElement[]{new HttpTransportBindingElement()}),
      new EndpointAddress(
        "http://localhost:8000/SimpleService/Endpoint"));
    client.Open();
    Console.WriteLine("The client is open: press any key to continue.");
    Console.ReadKey(true);
    Console.WriteLine(client.AcceptRequest("Hello, World!"));
    Console.WriteLine(client.AcceptRequest("Hello, World!"));
    client.Close();
    Console.WriteLine("Done.");
    Console.ReadKey(true);
  }
}
```

5. Choose Debug, Start Debugging from Visual Studio 2005's menus.

6. When the console of the ServiceHost application confirms that the service is ready, enter a keystroke into the console of the client application.

7. When the console of the client application confirms that the Windows Communication Foundation client is open, enter a keystroke into the console of the client application. The output in both consoles should confirm that the service received both messages from the client and responded to each of them.

8. Enter a keystroke into both consoles to close the applications.

Provide a Custom Binding Element That Supports Outbound Communication

Now a custom binding element will be constructed by which some protocol could be applied to outbound messages. Code for the binding element itself, a channel factory, and a channel for outbound communication will be required.

1. Add a class called `MyCustomBindingElement.cs` to the MyCustomBindingElement project.

2. Modify the contents of the class to look like this:

```
using System;
using System.Collections.Generic;
using System.ServiceModel;
using System.ServiceModel.Channels;
using System.Text;

namespace Extensibility
{
    public class MyCustomBindingElement: BindingElement
    {
    }
}
```

By deriving from `System.ServiceModel.Channels.BindingElement`, the class signifies that it is in fact a binding element.

3. Add a default constructor and a copy constructor:

```
public MyCustomBindingElement()
{
    Console.WriteLine("Constructing binding element.");
}

public MyCustomBindingElement(MyCustomBindingElement original)
{
    Console.WriteLine("Copying binding element.");
}
```

4. Implement the abstract `Clone()` method using the copy constructor. That method allows the Windows Communication Foundation to make deep copies of the binding element:

```
public override BindingElement Clone()
{
    Console.WriteLine("Cloning binding element.");
    return new MyCustomBindingElement(this);
}
```

5. Implement the abstract, generic GetProperty<T>() method by which the Windows Communication Foundation can query the stack of binding elements for the values of properties:

```
public override T GetProperty<T>(BindingContext context)
{
    return context.GetInnerProperty<T>();
}
```

6. Provide an override for the key CanBuildChannelFactory<T>() method, the significance of which was explained earlier in this chapter:

```
public override bool CanBuildChannelFactory<TChannel>(BindingContext context)
{
    Console.WriteLine(
"Querying if the binding element can build a channel factory of type {0}.",
            typeof(TChannel).Name);

    if (typeof(TChannel) == typeof(IRequestChannel))
    {
        return context.CanBuildInnerChannelFactory<TChannel>();
    }
    else
    {
        return false;
    }
}
```

7. Add a class called MyCustomChannelFactory.cs to the MyCustomBindingElement project.

8. Modify the contents of that class to look like this:

```
using System;
using System.Collections.Generic;
using System.ServiceModel;
using System.ServiceModel.Channels;
using System.Text;

namespace Extensibility
{
```

```
class MyCustomChannelFactory<TChannel> :
            ChannelFactoryBase<IRequestChannel>
{
}
}
```

By deriving from
`System.ServiceModel.Channels.ChannelFactoryBase<IRequestChannel>`, the class
signifies that it is in fact a channel factory, and that it can provide channels with
the shape defined by the `System.ServiceModel.Channels.IRequestChannel` interface.

9. Recall that a channel factory is responsible for having the next binding element
   after its own create another channel factory—the next channel factory in the stack
   of channel factories that the binding elements construct. Recall, as well, that when
   a channel factory creates a channel, it has the next channel factory in the stack
   create a channel that it then provides to its own channel, so that its own channel
   can pass messages through to a subordinate channel. So, a channel factory has need
   of a reference to the next channel factory in the stack. Add a member by which to
   maintain that reference:

```
class MyCustomChannelFactory<TChannel>:
        ChannelFactoryBase<IRequestChannel>
{
    IChannelFactory<TChannel> innerChannelFactory = null;
}
```

10. Add a constructor that has the next channel factory in the stack constructed as well,
    and that stores the reference to that next channel factory in the member that was
    added in the previous step:

```
public MyCustomChannelFactory(
        MyCustomBindingElement bindingElement,
        BindingContext context)
    : base(context.Binding)
{
    Console.WriteLine("Constructing the channel factory.");
    this.innerChannelFactory =
                context.BuildInnerChannelFactory<TChannel>();
    if (this.innerChannelFactory == null)
    {
        throw new InvalidOperationException(
        "MyCustomChannelFactory requires an inner IChannelFactory.");
    }
}
```

11. Right-click on the term `ChannelFactoryBase<IRequestChannel>` in the declaration of the class, and choose Implement Abstract Class from the context menu. Visual Studio will create stubs for the `OnCreateChannel()`, `OnBeginOpen()`, `OnEndOpen()`, and `OnOpen()` methods.

12. Modify the implementation of the `OnOpen()` method so that when the Windows Communication Foundation tells the channel factory that the host application has called the `Open()` method of the Windows Communication Foundation client in preparation for outbound communication, the channel factory passes that information on to the next channel factory:

```
protected override void OnOpen(TimeSpan timeout)
{
        Console.WriteLine("Channel factory OnOpen() method.");
        this.innerChannelFactory.Open(timeout);
}
```

13. Add a class called `MyCustomRequestChannel.cs` to the solution, and modify the contents to look like this:

```
using System;
using System.Collections.Generic;
using System.ServiceModel;
using System.ServiceModel.Channels;
using System.Text;

namespace Extensibility
{
    class MyCustomRequestChannel: IRequestChannel
    {
    }
}
```

By implementing the `System.ServiceModel.Channels.IRequestChannel` interface, the class signifies that it is a channel with the shape defined by that interface.

14. As a channel, it is responsible for passing instructions and messages along to the channel beneath itself in a stack of channels. Define a member for maintaining a reference to that next channel:

```
class MyCustomRequestChannel: IRequestChannel
{
        private IRequestChannel innerChannel = null;
}
```

15. Provide a constructor by which the channel will accept a reference to the channel beneath itself from the channel factory, and store that in the member defined in the

previous step. Also have the constructor monitor events of the subordinate channel so as to be notified of changes in that channel's state:

```
public MyCustomRequestChannel(IRequestChannel innerChannel)
{
        Console.WriteLine("Constructing request channel.");
        this.innerChannel = innerChannel;

        this.innerChannel.Closed += new EventHandler(innerChannel_Closed);
}
```

16. Add the handler for the subordinate channel's `Closed` event, referred to in the constructor. Have that handler signify that because the subordinate channel is finished closing, the current channel can be considered to have closed as well.

```
protected void innerChannel_Closed(object sender, EventArgs e)
{
    Console.WriteLine("Inner request channel closed.");
    if (this.Closed != null)
    {
        this.Closed(this, e);
    }
}
```

17. Right-click on the term `IRequestChannel` in the declaration of the class and choose Implement Interface, Implement Interface from the context menu to create stubs for the methods of the `System.ServiceModel.Channels.IRequestChannel` interface.

18. Replace the stub for the `State` property defined by the `System.ServiceModel.Channels.ICommunicationObject` interface from which the `System.ServiceModel.Channels.IRequestChannel` interface ultimately derives. That interface defines the Windows Communication Foundation communication state machine, and its `State` property is for retrieving the current state of such a state machine.

```
public CommunicationState State
{
    get
    {
        Console.WriteLine("Retrieving request channel state.");
        return this.innerChannel.State;
    }
}
```

19. Replace the stub for the `Open()` method of the `System.ServiceModel.Channels.ICommunicationObject` interface, by which a Windows Communication Foundation communication state machine can be instructed to transition into the `Opened` state.

Recall that a channel like the one being programmed here is responsible for passing on state transition instructions from the Windows Communication Foundation to subordinate channels.

```
public void Open(TimeSpan timeout)
{
    Console.WriteLine("Request channel Open");
    this.innerChannel.Open(timeout);
}
```

20. Replace the stub for the Close() method of the System.ServiceModel.Channels.ICommunicationObject interface, by which a Windows Communication Foundation communication state machine can be instructed to transition into the Closed state.

```
public void Close(TimeSpan timeout)
{
    Console.WriteLine("Request channel Close");
    this.innerChannel.Close(timeout);
}
```

21. Replace the stub for the Request() method of the System.ServiceModel.Channels.IRequestChannel interface. It is by implementing this method that the channel will be able to serve its function of implementing some communication protocol. The method is passed an outbound message as a parameter and is able to transform the message as the protocol dictates.

```
public Message Request(Message message, TimeSpan timeout)
{
    Console.WriteLine("Request channel request.");
    Console.WriteLine("This is where I can implement my protocol.");
    return this.innerChannel.Request(message,timeout);
}
```

22. Now that the coding of the channel has been finished, the channel factory can be completed by having it construct an instance of the channel on cue. The channel factory must have the next channel factory in the stack create a channel that can then be passed to its own channel as the subordinate channel to which messages and instructions must be passed on. Replace the stub for the OnCreateChannel() method of the Extensibility.MyCustomChannelFactory class in the MyCustomChannelFactory.cs file:

```
protected override IRequestChannel OnCreateChannel(
        EndpointAddress address,
        Uri via)
{
    Console.WriteLine("Channel factory OnCreateChannel event.");
```

```
IRequestChannel innerChannel =
            (IRequestChannel)this.innerChannelFactory.CreateChannel(
                address,
                via);
    return new MyCustomRequestChannel(innerChannel);
}
```

23. With the channel factory finished, the binding element can be completed by providing an override of the important `BuildChannelFactory<T>()` method. That is the method by which it will be able to respond to an instruction to create the channel factory that will provide channels to participate in outbound communications. So, add this override to the `Extensibility.MyCustomBindingElement` class in the `MyCustomBindingElement.cs` file:

```
public override IChannelFactory<TChannel> BuildChannelFactory<TChannel>(
        BindingContext context)
{
    Console.WriteLine(
"Asking the binding element for a channel factory of type {0}.",
                typeof(TChannel).Name);
    return (IChannelFactory<TChannel>)
                (object)new MyCustomChannelFactory<TChannel>(
                        this,context);
}
```

24. The binding element is now fully capable of supporting outbound communications. Choose Build, Build Solution from the Visual Studio 2005 menus to confirm that there are no errors in the code.

25. Now proceed to edit the client application to use the binding element. Specifically, edit the statement in the `Program.cs` file of the Client project by which the Windows Communication Foundation client is created. Have that statement add an instance of the binding element into the list of binding elements by which the binding is defined:

```
Client client = new Client(
    new CustomBinding(
        new BindingElement[] {
            new MyCustomBindingElement(),
            new HttpTransportBindingElement() }),
        new EndpointAddress(
        "http://localhost:8000/SimpleService/Endpoint"));
```

26. Choose Debug, Start Debugging from Visual Studio 2005's menus.

27. When the console of the ServiceHost application confirms that the service is ready, enter a keystroke into the console of the client application.

28. When the console of the client application confirms that the Windows Communication Foundation client is open, enter a keystroke into the console of the client application. The output in both consoles should show that the service received both messages from the client and responded to each of them. Examine the output in the client application console to confirm that, this time, each message from the client passed through the Request() method of the custom channel Extensibility.MyCustomRequestChannel. That method will have output this statement to the client application's console, confirming that it has the opportunity to transform the outbound message in accordance with some protocol:

```
This is where I can implement my protocol.
```

29. Enter a keystroke into both consoles to close the applications.

Amend the Custom Binding Element to Support Inbound Communication

Follow the next set of instructions to enhance the custom binding element so that it could apply some protocol to inbound messages. It will be necessary to add some code to the binding element, and also to add a channel listener and an inbound communication channel. Do that now by following these steps:

1. Start by adding this override to the binding element defined in the MyCustomBindingElement.cs file of the MyCustomBindingElement project. The override has the binding element assert that it is capable of constructing channel listeners that can provide channels that conform to the shape defined by the System.ServiceModel.Channels.IReplyChannel interface.

```
public override bool CanBuildChannelListener<TChannel>(
        BindingContext context)
{
    Console.WriteLine(
  "Querying if the binding element can build a listener of type {0}.",
                typeof(TChannel).Name);

    if (typeof(TChannel) == typeof(IReplyChannel))
    {
        return context.CanBuildInnerChannelListener<TChannel>();
    }
    else
    {
        return false;
    }
}
```

2. For that assertion to be valid, it will be necessary to program the channel listener. Add a class called MyChannelListener.cs to the MyCustomBindingElement project and modify the contents to look like this:

```
using System;
using System.Collections.Generic;
using System.ServiceModel.Channels;
using System.Text;

namespace Extensibility
{
    class MyCustomChannelListener<TChannel> :
        ChannelListenerBase<IReplyChannel>
            where TChannel : class, IChannel
    {
    }
}
```

By deriving from System.ServiceModel.Channels.ChannelListenerBase<IReplyChannel>, the class declares that it is in fact a channel listener and that it provides channels that conform to the shape defined by the System.ServiceModel.Channels.IReplyChannel interface.

3. Give the channel listener a member by which it can maintain a reference to the next channel listener in the stack:

```
class MyCustomChannelListener<TChannel> :
    ChannelListenerBase<IReplyChannel>
        where TChannel : class, IChannel
{
        IChannelListener<TChannel> innerChannelListener = null;
}
```

4. Provide a constructor by which the channel listener can obtain a reference to the next channel listener from the binding element that follows its own:

```
public MyCustomChannelListener(
        MyCustomBindingElement bindingElement,
        BindingContext context)
    : base(context.Binding)
{
    Console.WriteLine("Constructing the channel listener.");
    this.innerChannelListener =
                context.BuildInnerChannelListener<TChannel>();
    if (this.innerChannelListener == null)
    {
        throw new InvalidOperationException(
```

```
                        "MyCustomChannelListener requires an inner IChannelFactory.");
        }
    }
```

5. Right-click on the term `ChannelListenerBase<IReplyChannel>` in the declaration of the class, and choose Implement Abstract Class from the context menu that appears. Visual Studio 2005 will create stubs for a number of abstract methods of the base class.

6. Replace the stub for the `OnOpen()` method with this implementation by which the channel listener passes on notification that the host application has transitioned into the `Opened` state that is defined by the Windows Communication Foundation communication state machine:

```
protected override void OnOpen(TimeSpan timeout)
{
    Console.WriteLine("Channel listener OnOpen.");
    this.innerChannelListener.Open(timeout);
}
```

7. Replace the stub for the `OnClose()` method with an implementation that does the same for notifications of transitions into the `Closed` state:

```
protected override void OnClose(TimeSpan timeout)
{
    Console.WriteLine("Channel listener OnClose.");
    this.innerChannelListener.Close(timeout);
}
```

8. Replace the stub for the `Uri` property with this implementation by which the Windows Communication Foundation can retrieve the URI on which the stack of listeners is listening for incoming messages:

```
public override Uri Uri
{
    get
    {
        Console.WriteLine("Retrieving channel listener URI.");
        return this.innerChannelListener.Uri;
    }
}
```

9. The remainder of the work to be done in programming the channel listener is to override the methods by which it provides inbound communication channels: `OnBeginAcceptChannel()` and `OnEndAcceptChannel()`. However, before those methods can be implemented, it will be necessary to define the channel itself. Begin that task now by adding a class called `MyCustomReplyChannel.cs` to the MyCustomBindingElement project.

10. Modify the contents of that class to look like this:

```
using System;
using System.Collections.Generic;
using System.ServiceModel;
using System.ServiceModel.Channels;
using System.Text;

namespace Extensibility
{
    class MyCustomReplyChannel : IReplyChannel
    {
    }
}
```

By implementing the `System.ServiceModel.IReplyChannel` interface, the channel declares that it is a channel with the shape defined by that interface.

11. Add a member by which the channel can maintain a reference to the next channel in the channel stack:

```
class MyCustomReplyChannel : IReplyChannel
{
        private IReplyChannel innerChannel = null;
}
```

12. Add a constructor by which the channel accepts a reference to the next channel in the channel stack from the channel listener and stores that reference. Also have the constructor monitor the subordinate channel's state changes to detect that channel transitioning into the Closed state.

```
public MyCustomReplyChannel(IReplyChannel innerChannel)
{
    Console.WriteLine("Constructing reply channel.");
    this.innerChannel = innerChannel;
    this.innerChannel.Closed += new EventHandler(innerChannel_Closed);
}

protected void innerChannel_Closed(object sender, EventArgs e)
{
    Console.WriteLine("Inner reply channel closed.");
    if (this.Closed != null)
    {
        this.Closed(this, e);
    }
}
```

14

13. Right-click on the term `IReplyChannel`, in the declaration of the class, and choose Implement Interface, Implement Interface from the context menu that appears. Visual Studio 2005 will create stubs for the methods defined by the `System.ServiceModel.Channels.IReplyChannel` interface.

14. Replace the stub for the `System.ServiceModel.Channels.ICommunicationObject`'s `State` property with this implementation that reports the state of the channel's state machine to be whatever state its subordinate channel is in:

```
public CommunicationState State
{
    get
    {
        Console.WriteLine("Retrieving reply channel state.");
        return this.innerChannel.State;
    }
}
```

15. Replace the stub for the `Open()` method of the `System.ServiceModel.Channels.ICommunicationObject` with this implementation that passes on the instruction to transition to the `Opened` state to the next channel in the stack:

```
public void Open()
{
    Console.WriteLine("Reply channel Open");
    this.innerChannel.Open();
}
```

16. Do the same for the instruction to transition to the `Closed` state passed on by the `Close()` method the `System.ServiceModel.Channels.ICommuncationObject` interface:

```
public void Close(TimeSpan timeout)
{
    Console.WriteLine("Reply channel Close.");
    this.innerChannel.Close(timeout);
}
```

17. Replace the stubs for the important `BeginTryReceiveRequest()` and `EndTryReceiveRequest()` methods defined by the `System.ServiceModel.Channels.IReplyChannel` interface. The `BeginTryReceiveRequest()` method is the asynchronous method by which the channel will wait on an inbound message to be passed on by its subordinate channel. That `EndTryReceiveRequest()` method will execute when that happens, providing the channel with the opportunity to apply whatever protocol it implements to the inbound message. That message is available via the `RequestMessage` property of the context parameter.

```
public IAsyncResult BeginTryReceiveRequest(
        TimeSpan timeout,
        AsyncCallback callback,
        object state)
{
    Console.WriteLine("Reply channel BeginTryReceiveRequest.");
    return this.innerChannel.BeginTryReceiveRequest(
                timeout,
                callback,
                state);
}

public bool EndTryReceiveRequest(
        IAsyncResult result,
        out RequestContext context)
{
    Console.WriteLine("Reply channel EndTryReceiveRequest.");

    bool outcome = this.innerChannel.EndTryReceiveRequest(
                result,
                out context);

    Console.WriteLine(
"This is where I can apply my protocol to the inbound message.");
    return outcome;
}
```

18. Now that the coding of the channel has been finished, the channel listener can be completed by programming the methods by which it will provide the channel. In the MyChannelListener.cs file of the MyCustomBindingElement project, replace the stubs for OnBeginAcceptChannel() and OnEndAcceptChannel() with these implementations. The channel listener retrieves a channel from the next listener in the stack, which is then passed to the listener's own channel as the subordinate channel, the channel to which it is responsible for passing on instructions and from which it will receive incoming messages:

```
protected override IAsyncResult OnBeginAcceptChannel(
        TimeSpan timeout,
        AsyncCallback callback,
        object state)
{
    Console.WriteLine("Channel listener BeginAcceptChannel.");
    return this.innerChannelListener.BeginAcceptChannel(
                timeout,
                callback,
```

```
                    state);
    }


    protected override IReplyChannel OnEndAcceptChannel(
            IAsyncResult result)
    {
        Console.WriteLine("Channel listener EndAcceptChannel.");
        IReplyChannel replyChannel =
                    ((IReplyChannel)this.innerChannelListener.EndAcceptChannel(
                        result));

        if (replyChannel == null)
        {
            return null;
        }
        return new MyCustomReplyChannel(replyChannel);
    }
```

19. The channel listener is now complete, which allows one to add the method to the binding element by which it will create instances of the channel listener. Go to the MyCustomBindingElement.cs file of the MyCustomBindingElement project, and provide this override of the BuildChannelListener<*T*>() method:

```
public override IChannelListener<TChannel> BuildChannelListener<TChannel>(
        BindingContext context)
{
    Console.WriteLine(
                "Asking the binding element for a listener of type {0}.",
                        typeof(TChannel).Name);
    return (IChannelListener<TChannel>)
                (object)new MyCustomChannelListener<TChannel>(this, context);
}
```

20. Choose Build, Build Solution from the Visual Studio 2005 menus to ensure that no syntactical errors have been made.

Applying a Custom Binding Element Through Configuration

Earlier, the custom binding element was added to the client application's binding using code. It is more customary for bindings to be defined using configuration. To be able to refer to a custom binding element in the configuration of a Windows Communication Foundation application, it is necessary to extend the Windows Communication Foundation's configuration language. Follow these steps by which it will be possible to add the newly constructed custom binding element to the binding of the service through configuration:

1. Examine the current configuration of the service in the `App.config` file of the ServiceHost project of the CustomChannels solution. It is reproduced in Listing 14.1. The configuration defines a custom binding that has the arbitrary name, `MyCustomBinding`. That binding has a single binding element, `System.ServiceModel.Channel.HttpTransportBindingElement`, which is referred to by the element `httpTransport` in the configuration.

LISTING 14.1   Initial Service Configuration

```
<?xml version="1.0" encoding="utf-8" ?>
<configuration>
    <system.serviceModel>
        <services>
            <service name="Extensibility.Service">
                    <host>
                            <baseAddresses>
                                    <add
baseAddress="http://localhost:8000/SimpleService"/>
                            </baseAddresses>
                    </host>
                <endpoint address="Endpoint"
                    binding="customBinding"
                                    bindingConfiguration="MyCustomBinding"
                                    contract="Extensibility.ISimple" />
            </service>
        </services>
                <bindings>
                        <customBinding>
                                <binding name="MyCustomBinding">
                                        <httpTransport/>
                                </binding>
                        </customBinding>
                </bindings>
    </system.serviceModel>
</configuration>
```

2. Add a class called `MyBindingExtensionElement.cs` to the MyCustomBindingElement project.

3. Modify its contents to look like this:

```
using System;
using System.Collections.Generic;
using System.Configuration;
using System.ServiceModel;
```

```
using System.ServiceModel.Channels;
using System.ServiceModel.Configuration;
using System.Text;

namespace Extensibility
{
    public class MyBindingElementExtension : BindingElementExtensionElement
    {
        public override Type BindingElementType
        {
            get
            {
                return typeof(MyCustomBindingElement);
            }
        }

        protected override BindingElement CreateBindingElement()
        {
            return new MyCustomBindingElement();
        }
    }
}
```

Having the class derive from
`System.ServiceModel.Configuration.BindingElementExtensionElement` signifies
that it is a class that can be referred to by a custom configuration element in a
Windows Communication Foundation configuration, a custom configuration
element that can be used to signify a binding element. The class overrides the
`CreateBindingElement()` method. When the Windows Communication Foundation
parses the configuration and finds the custom configuration element, it will invoke
that method to retrieve an instance of the binding element to which the custom
configuration element is meant to refer.

4. Now modify the `App.config` file of the ServiceHost project so that it looks like the
   configuration shown in Listing 14.2. That configuration uses a
   `bindingElementExtension` element to define a new configuration element with the
   arbitrary name `myElement`. That new configuration element is associated with the
   `System.ServiceModel.Configuration.BindingElementExtensionElement` defined in
   the previous step, and it is used in the new definition of the service's binding to
   include the custom binding in the list of binding elements.

LISTING 14.2   Extended Service Configuration

```
<?xml version="1.0" encoding="utf-8" ?>
<configuration>
        <system.serviceModel>
```

LISTING 14.2   Continued

```
            <services>
                    <service name="Extensibility.Service">
                            <host>
                                    <baseAddresses>
                                            <add

baseAddress="http://localhost:8000/SimpleService"/>
                                    </baseAddresses>
                            </host>
                            <endpoint address="Endpoint"
                    binding="customBinding"
                                    bindingConfiguration="MyCustomBinding"
                                    contract="Extensibility.ISimple" />
                    </service>
            </services>
            <bindings>
                    <customBinding>
                            <binding name="MyCustomBinding">
                                    <myElement/>
                                    <httpTransport/>
                            </binding>
                    </customBinding>
            </bindings>
            <extensions>
                    <bindingElementExtensions>
                            <add name="myElement"
type="Extensibility.MyBindingElementExtension, MyCustomBindingElement"/>
                    </bindingElementExtensions>
            </extensions>
        </system.serviceModel>
</configuration>
```

5. Now modify the App.config file of the ServiceHost project so that it looks like the configuration shown in Listing 14.2. That configuration uses a bindingElementExtension element to define a new configuration element with the arbitrary name myElement. That new configuration element is associated with the System.ServiceModel.Configuration.BindingElementExtensionElement defined in the previous step, and it is used in the new definition of the service's binding to include the custom binding in the list of binding elements.

6. Choose Debug, Start Debugging from Visual Studio 2005's menus.

7. When the console of the ServiceHost application confirms that the service is ready, enter a keystroke into the console of the client application.

8. When the console of the client application confirms that the Windows Communication Foundation client is open, enter a keystroke into the console of the client application. The output in both consoles should show that the service received both messages from the client and responded to each of them. Examine the output in the service host application console to confirm that, this time, each message from the client passed through the `EndTryReceiveRequest()` method of the custom channel, `Extensibility.MyCustomReplyChannel`. That method will have output this statement to the client application's console, confirming that it has the opportunity to transform the inbound message in accordance with some protocol:

```
This is where I can apply my protocol to the inbound message.
```

Also notice that directly after that statement, and before the incoming message is actually passed to the instance of the service type, the Windows Communication Foundation has the channel go back to listening for further incoming messages.

9. Enter a keystroke into both consoles to close the applications.

Although the custom binding element constructed in this chapter works for both inbound and outbound communication, it is not complete. In particular, its channels do not implement all the state transitions defined by the Windows Communication Foundation's communication state machine, most notably transitions to the `Faulted` state. The sample, should, however, have served its purpose of showing how custom binding elements are constructed, and how they can provide channels for applying protocols to both inbound and outbound messages.

Summary

Custom bindings supplement the Windows Communication Foundation's external communication capabilities, increasing the variety of protocols it supports for exchanging messages with external parties. New protocols are implemented in channels, but it is binding elements that are used to incorporate those channels into the stack of channels that a Windows Communication Foundation application uses to communicate. The Windows Communication Foundation examines the binding defined for an application, either through code or through configuration, and derives from that a list of binding elements. It calls on the first binding element to provide a channel factory for creating outbound communication channels, or a channel listener for providing inbound communication channels.

The channel factory and the channel listener will have the next binding element in the list provide a channel factory or a channel listener as well. In that way, channel factories get to add their outbound communication channels into a stack of such channels that the Windows Communication Foundation will use to send messages. Channel listeners add their inbound communications to a stack of channels, too, and each channel in the stack waits to receive a message from the channel beneath. When a message is sent, each outbound channel gets to apply its protocol to the message, and is responsible for passing it on to the next channel in the stack. Similarly, when a message arrives, each inbound channel applies its protocol to the incoming message, and passes the message along.

CHAPTER 15

Custom Transports

Introduction

This chapter completes the series covering the various ways of extending the Windows Communication Foundation. There are two primary ways of extending the technology to accommodate scenarios for which it does not explicitly provide: by adding custom behaviors and by adding custom bindings. Custom behaviors control the Windows Communication Foundation's internal communication functions, such as the function of serializing outbound data into messages. Custom bindings supplement the Windows Communication Foundation's external communication capabilities by providing channels that implement additional protocols for exchanging messages with external parties. Chapter 14, "Custom Channels," introduced the subject of extending the Windows Communication Foundation through the addition of custom binding elements. This chapter goes on to cover the construction of a special category of custom binding element—custom binding elements that provide channels to implement protocols for transporting data.

Transport Channels

The International Organization for Standardization's Open Systems Interconnection Basic Reference Model defines seven networking layers (ISO/IEC 1994, 28). The transport layer "provides transparent transfer of data between [...]entities and relieves them from any concern with the detailed way in which [the] transfer of data is achieved" (ISO/IEC 1994, 43). Within Windows Communication Foundation applications, data is transferred in the form of messages, and the transfer of messages between applications—from clients to services and back—is achieved by transport channels.

Inbound Communication

In the case of inbound communication, a transport channel will receive a stream of bytes from some source that it has been monitoring. It will determine where individual messages in that stream of bytes begin and end, a process referred to as *framing* messages. The array of bytes corresponding to each individual message is passed to an instance of whatever message encoder was specified in the binding. The message encoder will return a `System.ServiceModel.Channels.Message` object that the Windows Communication Foundation passes to the next channel in the stack of inbound communication channels, or directly to the channel dispatcher if there are no other channels in the stack.

Outbound Communication

For outbound communication, a transport channel will receive a `System.ServiceModel.Channels.Message` object from the next channel in the stack of outbound channels, or directly from the channel dispatcher if there are no other channels in the stack. The transport channel will pass the `System.ServiceModel.Channels.Message` object to an instance of whatever message encoder was specified in the binding, and the message encoder will translate the object into an array of bytes. The transport channel will send the array of bytes to a remote destination.

Message Encoders

Transport channels rely on message encoders to assemble inbound arrays of bytes into messages and to represent outbound messages as arrays of bytes. Although a transport channel can always construct a message encoder of its own choosing to do that work on its behalf, it is customary for the transport channel to first check the binding and use whatever message encoder the binding specifies. Doing so permits the transport channel to be used together with any number of different message encoders through the binding.

Therefore, in extending the Windows Communication Foundation to support a new transport protocol, one typically implements both a new binding element to provide a transport channel and a new binding element to provide a message encoder. The transport channel implements the parts of the protocol that pertain to the sending and receiving of bytes, and the framing of messages, whereas the message encoder implements the parts of the protocol that pertain to mapping an array of received bytes that represent a single message into a `System.ServiceModel.Channels.Message` object.

Completing the Stack

Chapter 14 explained that the Windows Communication Foundation examines the binding specified for an application and derives from that a list of binding elements. The binding elements are made to construct a stack of channel factories for outbound communication, and a stack of channel listeners for inbound communication. The stack of channel factories provides a stack of outbound channels and the stack of channel listeners provides a stack of inbound channels. Outbound messages are passed to the topmost channel in the stack of outbound channels, and that channel passes the message on to the next one, and so on. When a message is received, each channel in the stack of inbound channels passes the message through to the channel above until the message reaches the channel dispatcher within the Windows Communication Foundation's Service Model, which will have the message deserialized into data items that get passed to a service's method.

This explanation left at least one key question unanswered: *What happens at the bottom of a stack?* The binding elements, channel factories, listeners, and channels all relied on their counterparts beneath them. When they received instructions or messages, they passed them down—indeed, that behavior is required of them in order for Windows Communication Foundation applications to work. Yet what happens when a listener is asked for a channel, but there is no listener beneath it in the stack to which it can delegate the request?

```
protected override IAsyncResult OnBeginAcceptChannel(
        TimeSpan timeout,
        AsyncCallback callback,
        object state)
{
    return this.innerChannelListener.BeginAcceptChannel(
                timeout,
                callback,
                state);
}


protected override IReplyChannel OnEndAcceptChannel(
        IAsyncResult result)
{
    IReplyChannel replyChannel =
                ((IReplyChannel)this.innerChannelListener.EndAcceptChannel(
                        result));

    if (replyChannel == null)
    {
        return null;
    }
    return new MyCustomReplyChannel(replyChannel);
}
```

Where do the channels that are getting passed up to each listener from the bottom of the stack originate? What do they ultimately represent? Also, how exactly are those inbound messages that get passed through the channels received from clients? And when outbound messages are sent, what happens when they reach the bottom of a stack of outbound channels?

All of these questions will be answered through the following explanation of transport binding elements, transport listeners, transport channel factories, and transport channels.

Those are, by definition, at the bottom of their respective stacks. When the Windows Communication Foundation examines the binding for an application and derives a list of binding elements from it, it confirms that the last binding element in that list is indeed a transport binding element, and neither it nor the channel factories and listeners it provides are permitted to refer to counterparts beneath them.

Implementing a Transport Binding Element and an Encoder Binding Element

Seeing how transport binding elements, transport listeners, transport factories, transport channels, and message encoders work will be facilitated by studying an example incorporating custom implementations of those components. To follow the example, copy the code associated with this chapter downloaded from http://www.cryptmaker.com/WindowsCommunicationFoundationUnleashed to the folder C:\WCFHandsOn. All the code is in a folder called CustomTransport, which has two subfolders: CustomTransportSolution and TCPSocketPair.

The Scenario

The scenario illustrated in the example is actually quite common. A Windows Communication Foundation application must exchange information with some other application that can send and receive data in a proprietary format via TCP.

The exchange over TCP would typically take the form of a protracted conversation, with data going back and forth over time. A simple way of representing that conversation in the form of a Windows Communication Foundation contract is shown in Listing 15.1. There

```
SessionMode=SessionMode.Required
```

signifies that the two applications will be exchanging information to and fro as part of the same conversation. The expression

```
CallbackContract=typeof(IMyClientContract))
```

applies to the service contract defined by the interface, IMyServiceContract, which indicates that the Windows Communication Foundation application receiving data via an endpoint with that contract may respond to the sender using the message defined by the IMyClientContract. So, the contract shown in Listing 15.1 describes the sort of bidirectional exchange that one might expect between the Windows Communication Foundation application and its counterpart, although the messages defined by the contract in this case are, for the sake of clarity, very simple ones.

LISTING 15.1   Contract Representing a Conversation over TCP

```
[ServiceContract(
        Namespace = "any.tcp://www.fabrikam.com",
        SessionMode = SessionMode.Required,
```

LISTING 15.1   Continued

```
        CallbackContract = typeof(IMyClientContract))]
public interface IMyServiceContract
{
    [OperationContract(Action="*",IsOneWay = true)]
    void Receive(Message request);
}

public interface IMyClientContract
{
    [OperationContract(Action="*",IsOneWay = true)]
    void Respond(string response);
}
```

The Requirements

The Windows Communication Foundation provides the predefined `NetTcpBinding` to allow for communication over TCP between two Windows Communication Foundation applications. That binding implements its own rules for framing and its own rules for demarcating messages within streams of bytes. The SOAP specification provides a SOAP HTTP binding that defines a standard way of demarcating SOAP messages within HTTP transmissions, but there is no corresponding standard with similarly broad acceptance for demarcating messages within TCP transmissions. So, the `NetTcpBinding` has its own rules for demarcating messages within TCP transmissions, rules that, therefore, only other Windows Communication Foundation applications using the `NetTcpBinding` know how to apply. Consequently, the predefined `NetTcpBinding` does not provide a means for communicating with some non–Windows Communication Foundation application via TCP.

For that purpose, a Windows Communication Foundation implementation of the protocols for communicating with that other application would be required. More specifically, a custom Windows Communication Foundation transport binding element would be needed, one that is capable of providing channels that implement the other application's protocols for sending and receiving data over TCP and for demarcating messages within TCP streams. Also, a custom message encoder binding element would be needed that could translate the other application's way of addressing and structuring messages into Windows Communication Foundation `System.ServiceModel.Channels.Message` objects.

The `TcpListener` and the `TcpClient` Classes

In the example, the .NET classes `System.Net.Sockets.TcpListener` and `System.Net.Sockets.TcpClient` are used to implement a Windows Communication Foundation transport binding element that can provide channels for communicating over TCP. To understand how they are used within the Windows Communication Foundation components, it helps to understand how they are used normally. Follow these steps to study a simple application that uses them.

1. Open the solution `TCPSocketPair.sln` that is in the `TCPSocketPair` folder referred to previously. The solution includes a project called Server for building a console application that uses the `System.Net.Sockets.TcpListener` class to receive data via TCP and the `System.Net.Sockets.TcpClient` class to reply. The other project is called Client, and it is for building a console application that uses the `System.Net.Sockets.TcpClient` class to send data via TCP to the Server application. The code for both applications is copied with very little alteration from the samples in the .NET Framework Class Library documentation.

2. Choose Debug, Start Debugging from the Visual Studio 2005 menus.

3. When the output in the console of the Server application shows that it is waiting for a connection, enter a keystroke into the Client application's console. The output in the consoles should show that the Client application sent a message to the Server application, which received the message and echoed it back.

4. Choose Debug, Stop Debugging from the Visual Studio 2005 menus to terminate the applications.

5. Examine the code in the `Program.cs` file of the Server project. The essence of it is reproduced in Listing 15.2. The statements

```
TcpListener server = new TcpListener(IPAddress.Any, port);
server.Start();
```

start an instance of the `System.Net.Sockets.TcpListener` class listening for attempts to connect to any of the host machine's Internet Protocol (IP) addresses, on the port with the number specified by the `port` variable. The statement

```
TcpClient client = server.AcceptTcpClient();
```

returns a `System.Net.Sockets.TcpClient` class that can be used to communicate with a client that has connected. If no client has connected yet, the `AcceptTcpClient()` method blocks until one does. After a client has connected, these next two statements are able to use the `System.Net.Sockets.TcpClient` object to retrieve a `System.Net.Sockets.NetworkStream` object from which data sent by the client can be read into a buffer:

```
byte[] bytes = new byte[1024];
NetworkStream stream = client.GetStream();
dataLength = stream.Read(bytes, 0, bytes.Length);
```

The same `System.Net.Sockets.NetworkStream` object can then be used to respond to the client.

```
stream.Write(msg, 0, msg.Length);
```

The `System.Net.Socket.NetworkStream` class's `Read()` method used in this code returns immediately if there is no data available to be read. However, the

BeginRead() method takes a delegate of a callback method as a parameter, and waits on a separate thread until data is received or an error occurs, after which it sends notification via the callback method.

LISTING 15.2   Using the TcpListener and TcpClient Classes

```
int port = 13000;
TcpListener server = new TcpListener(IPAddress.Any, port);

server.Start();

byte[] bytes = new byte[1024];
string data;

while (true)
{
    TcpClient client = server.AcceptTcpClient();

    NetworkStream stream = client.GetStream();

    int dataLength;

    dataLength = stream.Read(bytes, 0, bytes.Length);

    while (i != 0)
    {
        data = Encoding.ASCII.GetString(bytes, 0, dataLength);
        Console.WriteLine(String.Format("Received: {0}", data));

        data = data.ToUpper();

        byte[] msg = System.Text.Encoding.ASCII.GetBytes(data);

        stream.Write(msg, 0, msg.Length);
        Console.WriteLine(String.Format("Sent: {0}", data));

        dataLength = stream.Read(bytes, 0, bytes.Length);

    }

    client.Close();
}
```

6. Close the TCPSocketPair solution.

Implementing Custom Binding Elements to Support an Arbitrary TCP Protocol

Now that the tools that will be used within custom Windows Communication Foundation components for communicating over TCP have been introduced, the custom components themselves can be examined. They enable the Windows Communication Foundation to support communication using an arbitrary protocol over TCP.

The Configuration

Follow these instructions to begin that examination:

1. Open the solution `CustomTransport.sln`, which is in the `CustomTransportSolution` folder referred to previously. The solution has a project called Service for building a class library containing a Windows Communication Foundation service type that implements the contract, `Extensibility.IMyServiceContract`, that was shown in Listing 15.1. As has already been explained, that contract describes a conversation back-and-forth between two applications over the sort of persistent connection that is provided by TCP. The project called ServiceHost is for building a console application to host an instance of the service type. The projects called MyCustomTransportBindingElement and MyCustomMessageEncoderBindingElement are for building class libraries that provide a custom Windows Communication Foundation transport binding element, and a custom Windows Communication Foundation message encoder binding element. The remaining project in the solution, which is called TCPServer, is for building a console application that communicates via TCP but not SOAP or XML, and certainly not the Windows Communication Foundation.

2. Open the `App.config` file in the ServiceHost project. The content thereof is reproduced in Listing 15.3. A custom binding is defined with the arbitrary name `MyCustomBinding`. That binding incorporates two custom binding configuration elements: `myMessageEncoderElement` and `myTransportElement`. Those custom binding configuration elements are defined in the `extensions` section as referring to the binding elements provided by the `Extensibility.MyCustomMessageEncoderBindingElement` and `Extensibility.MyCustomTransportBindingElementExtension` classes. This mechanism for extending the Windows Communication Foundation configuration language to allow one to refer to custom binding elements in configuration was explained in Chapter 14.

LISTING 15.3   Configuring a Service to Use Custom Binding Elements

```
<?xml version="1.0" encoding="utf-8" ?>
<configuration>
    <system.serviceModel>
        <services>
            <service name="Extensibility.Service">
```

LISTING 15.3   Continued

```
                              <host>
                                  <baseAddresses>
                                      <add
                                          baseAddress=
"any.tcp://127.0.0.1:8000/SimpleService"/>
                                  </baseAddresses>
                              </host>
                <endpoint address="Endpoint"
                              binding="customBinding"
                              bindingConfiguration="MyCustomBinding"
                              contract="Extensibility.IMyServiceContract" />
            </service>
        </services>
                <bindings>
                    <customBinding>
                        <binding name="MyCustomBinding">
                              <myMessageEncoderElement/>
                              <myTransportElement/>
                        </binding>
                    </customBinding>
                </bindings>
                <extensions>
                    <bindingElementExtensions>
                        <add
                            name="myMessageEncoderElement"
type="Extensibility.MyCustomMessageEncoderBindingElementExtension,
                            MyCustomMessageEncoderBindingElement"/>
                    </bindingElementExtensions>
                        <add
                            name="myTransportElement"
type="Extensibility.MyCustomTransportBindingElementExtension,
                            MyCustomTransportBindingElement"/>
                </extensions>
        </system.serviceModel>
</configuration>
```

3. Look at the Extensibility.MyCustomMessageEncoderBindingElementExtension class that is specified in the configuration file as providing the binding element referred to by the custom configuration element, myMessageEncoderElement. It is in the MyCustomMessageEncoderBindingElement project. Its CreateBindingElement() method, which the Windows Communication Foundation will use to get an instance of the binding element to which the custom configuration element myMessageEncoderElement refers, returns an instance of Extensibility. MyCustomMessageEncoderBindingElement. That is the custom binding element that

was built to provide a custom message encoder for mapping data received via TCP from the TCPServer application to a Windows Communication Foundation System.ServiceModel.Channels.Message object.

```
protected override BindingElement CreateBindingElement()
{
    return new MyCustomMessageEncoderBindingElement();
}
```

4. Look at the Extensibility.MyCustomTransportBindingElementExtension class that is specified in the configuration file as providing the binding element referred to by the custom configuration element, myTransportElement. The class is in the MyCustomTransportBindingElement project. Its CreateBindingElement() method, which the Windows Communication Foundation will use to get an instance of the binding element to which the custom configuration element myTransportElement refers, returns an instance of Extensibility.MyCustomTransportBindingElement. That is the custom transport binding element that was built to provide channels for exchanging data with the TCPServer application using TCP.

```
protected override BindingElement CreateBindingElement()
{
    return new MyCustomTransportBindingElement();
}
```

The Custom Transport Binding Element

These steps trace the implementation of the custom transport binding element:

1. Study the Extensibility.MyCustomTransportBindingElement class in the MyCustomTransportBindingElement.cs file of the MyCustomTransportBindingElement project. The class derives from System.ServiceModel.Channels.TransportBindingElement.

```
public class MyCustomTransportBindingElement: TransportBindingElement
```

That code line declares to the Windows Communication Foundation that the class represents a binding element that can accept the responsibility of being at the bottom of a stack of binding elements. Remember that, in the configuration of the application shown in Listing 15.3, the custom configuration element, myTransportElement, which refers to the Extensibility.MyCustomTransportBindingElement class, was indeed the lowest in the list of binding elements.

```
<binding name="MyCustomBinding">
  <myMessageEncoderElement/>
  <myTransportElement/>
</binding>
```

The Windows Communication Foundation validates that the last binding element in the list of binding elements by which any binding is defined is a binding that implements System.ServiceModel.Channels.TransportBindingElement.

2. Look at the implementation of the Scheme property. It is the only member that the System.ServiceModel.Channels.TransportBindingElement base class defines that is abstract, and that classes deriving from it must therefore implement. The Scheme property is for a derived transport binding element to specify the scheme that must be used in any addresses provided for Windows Communication Foundation endpoints that have bindings incorporating the transport binding element. The Extensibility.MyCustomTransportBindingElement class provides the arbitrary value, any.tcp, for the Scheme property:

```
public override string Scheme
{
    get
    {
        return "any.tcp";
    }
}
```

Referring back once again to the configuration of the Windows Communication Foundation application in Listing 15.3, one can confirm that the address provided for the endpoint defined there has the scheme any.tcp.

```
<baseAddresses>
        <add
                baseAddress="any.tcp://localhost:8000/SimpleService"/>
</baseAddresses>
```

3. Study the overrides that the Extensibility.MyCustomTransportBindingElement provides for the four key methods of any binding element: CanBuildChannelFactory<*T*>(), CanBuildChannelListener<*T*>(), BuildChannelFactory<*T*>(), and BuildChannelListener<*T*>(). Those are shown in Listing 15.4. The significance of those methods was explained in Chapter 14. The methods indicate the kinds of channels that its channel factories and channel listeners can provide.

The implementations of these methods by the Extensibility.MyCustomTransportBindingElement class differ from those of the custom binding element described in the previous chapter in only one important way. As a transport binding element, it does not have to query the binding elements beneath it to determine the kinds of channels that those other binding elements can support. Indeed, it cannot query any binding elements beneath it because it is a transport binding element, and so there are no binding elements beneath it.

By its implementations of CanBuildChannelFactory<*T*>() and
CanBuildChannelListener<*T*>(), the Extensibility.
MyCustomTransportBindingElement class indicates that it can support channels that
implement the System.ServiceModel.Channels.IDuplexSessionChannel interface.
In the previous chapter it was explained that the kinds of channels supported by
the binding elements of a binding must satisfy the implicit communication requirements of any contracts associated with that binding in the definition of a Windows
Communication Foundation endpoint. In this case, the contract, which was shown
in Listing 15.1, describes an ongoing two-way conversation between two endpoints,
and that is precisely the sort of communication that channels implementing the
System.ServiceModel.Channels.IDuplexSessionChannel interface are claiming to
support. In the name, IDuplexSessionChannel, Duplex signifies communication that
can be initiated from either direction, and Session signifies an ongoing exchange
over the same connection. In the discussion of the contract, it was explained that
this form of communication is characteristic of communications over TCP.

LISTING 15.4   Overrides of Binding Element Methods

```
public override bool CanBuildChannelFactory<TChannel>(
        BindingContext context)
{
    if (typeof(TChannel) == typeof(IDuplexSessionChannel))
    {
        return true;
    }
    else
    {
        return false;
    }
}


public override bool CanBuildChannelListener<TChannel>(
        BindingContext context)
{
    if (typeof(TChannel) == typeof(IDuplexSessionChannel))
    {
        return true;
    }
    else
    {
        return false;
    }
}
```

LISTING 15.4   Continued

```
public override IChannelFactory<TChannel> BuildChannelFactory<TChannel>(
        BindingContext context)
{
    return (IChannelFactory<TChannel>)
            (object)new MyCustomChannelFactory<TChannel>(this,context);
}

public override IChannelListener<TChannel> BuildChannelListener<TChannel>(
        BindingContext context)
{
    return(IChannelListener<TChannel>)
            (object)new MyCustomChannelListener<TChannel>(this,context);
}
```

The Channel Listener

In its implementation of the BuildChannelListener() method, the custom transport binding provides an instance of the Extensibility.MyCustomChannelListener<T> generic. Follow these steps to study that channel listener:

1. Look at the constructor of the Extensibility.MyCustomChannelListener class in the MyCustomChannelListener.cs file of the MyCustomTransportBindingElement project. That constructor is shown in Listing 15.5.

   An instance of the System.ServiceModel.Channels.BufferManager class is constructed. Objects of that type manage a pool of buffers. In reviewing the use of the System.Net.Sockets.TcpListener and System.Net.Sockets.TcpClient classes in Listing 15.3, it was pointed out that incoming data is read from the System.Net.Sockets.NetworkStream object into a buffer. Using the buffer manager will reduce the overhead that would by incurred by constantly having to allocate and deallocate buffers for incoming data by using buffers from the buffer manager's pool instead.

   ```
   this.bufferManager = BufferManager.CreateBufferManager(
           bindingElement.MaxBufferPoolSize,
           (int)bindingElement.MaxReceivedMessageSize);
   ```

   Earlier in this chapter, it was explained that it is customary for the components of a transport binding element to attempt to use whatever message encoder is specified in the binding because doing so permits the transport binding element to be used together with any number of different message encoders through the binding. With these lines of code, the listener is able to retrieve, from the binding of the endpoint, the binding element that specifies which message encoder to use:

```
MessageEncodingBindingElement encodingBindingElement =
        context.BindingParameters.
                Remove<MessageEncodingBindingElement>();
if (encodingBindingElement != null)
{
    this.encoderFactory =
                encodingBindingElement.CreateMessageEncoderFactory();
}
```

It uses that binding element to obtain a reference to a message encoder factory from which a message encoder for processing incoming messages can be obtained.

The last few lines of code in the constructor obtain information about the address specified for the endpoint that the listener is to service:

```
this.uri = new Uri(
            context.ListenUriBaseAddress,
            context.ListenUriRelativeAddress);
```

LISTING 15.5   Channel Listener Constructor

```
public MyCustomChannelListener(
      TransportBindingElement bindingElement,
      BindingContext context)
    : base(context.Binding)
{
    this.bindingElement = bindingElement;

    this.bufferManager = BufferManager.CreateBufferManager(
                bindingElement.MaxBufferPoolSize,
                (int)bindingElement.MaxReceivedMessageSize);

    MessageEncodingBindingElement encodingBindingElement =
                context.BindingParameters.
                        Remove<MessageEncodingBindingElement>();
    if (encodingBindingElement != null)
    {
        this.encoderFactory =
                    encodingBindingElement.CreateMessageEncoderFactory();
    }
    else
    {
        this.encoderFactory =
                    new MyCustomMessageEncoderBindingElement()
                            .CreateMessageEncoderFactory();
    }
```

LISTING 15.5   Continued

```
    this.uri = new Uri(
                context.ListenUriBaseAddress,
                context.ListenUriRelativeAddress);
}
```

2. Examine the listener's implementation of the OnOpen() method that the Windows
   Communication Foundation will invoke as the host application prepares to receive
   incoming data. The listener starts an instance of the
   System.Net.Sockets.TcpListener class listening for attempts to connect on the
   port identified by the endpoint address:

```
protected override void OnOpen(TimeSpan timeout)
{
    [...]

    IPEndPoint ipEndpoint = new IPEndPoint(
                IPAddress.Parse(uri.Host), uri.Port);
    this.tcpListener = new TcpListener(ipEndpoint);
    this.tcpListener.Start();
}
```

3. Look at how the listener implements the OnBeginAcceptChannel() method that the
   Windows Communication Foundation will call next after calling OnOpen(). The
   listener calls the BeginAcceptTcpClient() method of its
   System.Net.Sockets.TcpListener class that will wait on a separate thread until a
   client has connected.

```
protected override IAsyncResult OnBeginAcceptChannel(
        TimeSpan timeout,
        AsyncCallback callback,
        object state)
{
    return this.tcpListener.BeginAcceptTcpClient(callback, state);
}
```

When a client connects, the listener's OnEndAcceptChannel() method will be called,
where it obtains a reference to a System.Net.Sockets.TcpClient object for exchanging data with that client. That object is passed to the constructor of a custom
channel. Earlier in this chapter, it was pointed out that although Chapter 14
showed custom listeners higher in the listener stack accepting channels, there was
no explanation of where the channels originated, nor any clear definition of what a
channel represents. This code for the transport listener's OnEndAcceptChannel()
method fills in those gaps in the understanding of listeners and channels. A transport listener waits for clients to connect, and when a client does connect, the
transport listener provides a channel that represents the connection with that

client. The Windows Communication Foundation passes that channel up to the listeners above the transport listener in the stack so that each listener can connect a channel of its own to the one provided by the transport listener. Then the Windows Communication Foundation Service Model's channel dispatcher can pull messages from the topmost channel, and, in doing so, each message is pulled in through the transport listener's channel—the channel that represents the connection with the client—and passed up through the intermediate channels, being transformed by them in the process.

```
protected override IDuplexSessionChannel OnEndAcceptChannel(
        IAsyncResult result)
{
    if (this.state != CommunicationState.Closed)
    {
        TcpClient client =
                        this.tcpListener.EndAcceptTcpClient(result);
        return new MyCustomDuplexSessionChannel(
                        this.uri,
                        this.bindingElement,
                        this.encoderFactory,
                        this.bufferManager,
                        client);
    }
    else
    {
        return null;
    }
}
```

The Transport Channel

Follow these steps to see how the transport channel provided by the transport channel listener works:

1. Examine the constructor of the Extensibility.MyCustomDuplexSessionChannel class in the MyCustomDuplexSessionChannel.cs file of the MyCustomTransportBindingElement project. Among other things, it receives the references to the buffer manager and the message encoder factory that the channel listener had obtained, as well as a reference to the System.Net.Sockets.TcpClient object representing the connection with the client. The reference to the message encoder factory is used to obtain a reference to a message encoder.

```
public MyCustomDuplexSessionChannel(
        Uri uri,
        TransportBindingElement bindingElement,
        MessageEncoderFactory encoderFactory,
```

```
        BufferManager bufferManager,
        TcpClient tcpClient)
{
    this.uri = uri;
    this.bindingElement = bindingElement;
    this.tcpClient = tcpClient;
    this.state = CommunicationState.Created;
    this.bufferManager = bufferManager;

    this.encoder = encoderFactory.CreateSessionEncoder();

    this.pendingReads = new Dictionary<IAsyncResult, PendingRead>();
}
```

2. Next, look at the implementation of the BeginTryReceive() method that will be invoked when the channel dispatcher starts pulling messages from the channel stack. The channel dispatcher would call BeginTryReceive() on the topmost System.ServiceModel.Channels.IDuplexSessionChannel in the stack of channels, and each of those channels would call BeginTryReceive() on the channel beneath itself, until the call reached this transport channel. This particular transport channel, which is meant for communicating with another application over TCP, retrieves a System.Net.Sockets.NetworkStream object from the System.Net.Sockets.TcpClient object passed to the constructor and calls the BeginRead() method on that stream. That method, as explained earlier in this chapter, waits on a separate thread for data to arrive from a source represented by a System.Net.Sockets.TcpClient object.

```
public IAsyncResult BeginTryReceive(
        TimeSpan timeout,
        AsyncCallback callback,
        object state)
{
    if (this.state == CommunicationState.Opened)
    {
        byte[] buffer =
          this.bufferManager.TakeBuffer(this.tcpClient.Available);
        NetworkStream stream = this.tcpClient.GetStream();
        IAsyncResult result =
          stream.BeginRead(
            buffer,
            0,
            buffer.Length,
            callback,
            state);

        [...]
```

```
            return result;
        }
        else
        {
            return null;
        }
    }
```

When data arrives, the transport channel's `EndTryReceive()` method is invoked. In this implementation, any data received is passed directly to the message encoder. In a more complete implementation, the framing logic would be here, separating out the bytes corresponding to individual messages from the bursts of bytes received, and passing the bytes of each message to the encoder.

```
public bool EndTryReceive(
        IAsyncResult result,
        out Message message)
{
    message = null;

    NetworkStream stream;

    [...]

    int size = stream.EndRead(result);

    [...]

    byte[] data = this.bufferManager.TakeBuffer(size);
    Array.Copy(pendingRead.Buffer, data, size);
    this.bufferManager.ReturnBuffer(pendingRead.Buffer);

    message = encoder.ReadMessage(
      new ArraySegment<byte>(data, 0, size),
      this.bufferManager);
    message.Headers.To = this.uri;

    return true; ;
}
```

3. Examine the transport channel's `Send()` method by which outbound messages passed down through the stack of channels are sent to their destination. The method passes the outbound message to the message encoder, which yields an array of bytes that is sent to the client via the client's `System.Net.Sockets.NetworkStream` object.

```
public void Send(
        Message message,
        TimeSpan timeout)
{
    ArraySegment<byte> bytes =
                this.encoder.WriteMessage(
                    message,
                    (int)this.bindingElement.MaxReceivedMessageSize,
                    this.bufferManager);
    NetworkStream stream = this.tcpClient.GetStream();
    stream.Write(bytes.Array, 0, bytes.Count);
    stream.Flush();
    bufferManager.ReturnBuffer(bytes.Array);
}
```

The Message Encoder

Follow these steps to understand the operation of the message encoder that the transport channel relies on.

15

1. Examine the declaration of the class Extensibility.MyCustomMessageEncoder, which is in the MyCustomMessageEncoder.cs file of the MyCustomMessageEncoder project. The class derives from System.ServiceModel.Channels.MessageEncoder, which, as its name suggests, is the base class for message encoders provided by the Windows Communication Foundation. The most important members of that class are its ReadMessage() and WriteMessage() methods. The ReadMessage() method takes an array of bytes received by a transport channel as input and yields an inbound System.ServiceModel.Channels.Message object as output. The WriteMessage() method takes an outbound System.ServiceModel.Channels.Message as input and yields an array of bytes for a transport channel to transmit as output.

```
public class MyCustomMessageEncoder : MessageEncoder
```

2. Look at the override of the ReadMessage() method. It is very simple, merely interpreting the received bytes as an ASCII string and writing those into the body of a System.ServiceModel.Channels.Message object.

```
public override Message ReadMessage(
        ArraySegment<byte> buffer,
        BufferManager bufferManager,
        string contentType)
{
    return Message.CreateMessage(
            this.MessageVersion,
            "*",
            Encoding.ASCII.GetString(
```

```
                    buffer.Array,
                    0,
                    buffer.Array.Length));
    }
```

3. The override of the `WriteMessage()` method does the same in reverse, producing the array of bytes representing the ASCII encoding of the outbound message's content:

```
public override ArraySegment<byte> WriteMessage(
        Message message,
        int maxMessageSize,
        BufferManager bufferManager,
        int messageOffset)
{
    string messageBody = message.GetBody<XmlElement>().InnerText;
    return new ArraySegment<byte>(
                ASCIIEncoding.ASCII.GetBytes(messageBody),
                messageOffset,
                messageBody.Length);
}
```

Using the Custom Transport Binding Element

Execute these steps to see the custom transport binding element in action:

1. Choose Debug, Start Debugging from the Visual Studio 2005 menus.

2. When there is activity in the console of ServiceHost application, enter a keystroke into the console of the TCPServer application. The two applications—one a Windows Communication Foundation application, and the other an application that simply knows how to send and receive via TCP—will cycle through an exchange of messages back and forth over a single connection.

   The console of the ServiceHost application will show some output, in the course of that exchange, from a message inspector behavior that is attached to the endpoint dispatcher of the Windows Communication Foundation service. The operation of message inspector behaviors was explained in Chapter 13, "Custom Behaviors." A message inspector is used here to illustrate that they are particularly useful in the debugging of custom binding elements in general and of custom transport binding elements in particular. The reason is that a message that has been formatted incorrectly due to errors that are usually within the message encoder will at least proceed as far as a message inspector behavior. That will serve to confirm that messages are being received by the transport components and pulled up through the channel stack, even if they cannot be deserialized, or if the operation to which they pertain cannot be identified.

3. Choose Debug, Stop Debugging from the Visual Studio 2005 menus.

Summary

This chapter concludes the section on customizing the Windows Communication Foundation. It completes the account of what goes on within the Windows Communication Foundation and how its mechanisms can be extended to cover new scenarios.

The Windows Communication Foundation receives incoming messages by having transport listeners wait for clients to connect. When a client does connect, the transport listener provides a channel that represents the connection with that client. The Windows Communication Foundation passes that channel up to listeners above the transport listener in the stack so that each of those listeners can connect a channel of its own to the one provided by the transport listener. Then the Windows Communication Foundation Service Model's channel dispatcher pulls messages from the topmost channel, and in doing so, data is pulled in through the transport listener's channel, the channel that represents the connection to the client. That client uses a message encoder to assemble the data into messages, and then each message is passed up through the intermediate channels, being transformed by them in the process. The channel dispatcher passes the messages on to the endpoint dispatcher that identifies the operation to which the message pertains. An operation dispatcher then deserializes the message into data items that it passes to the method of the service by which the service implements the operation.

Outbound data is serialized into messages by client runtime components corresponding to the operation that the client has invoked. The message is passed down through a stack of outbound channels to a transport channel. That channel uses a message encoder to convert the outbound message into an array of bytes that the transport channel then transmits.

To extend the Windows Communication Foundation to support new kinds of solutions, one can add transport binding elements that can provide channels to accommodate additional protocols for transporting data. Message encoder binding elements can be implemented to handle new ways of representing messages within transmissions. Other custom binding elements can be used to implement additional message handling protocols. Also, a variety of custom behaviors can be attached to the client runtime components and to the dispatchers of services so as to modify the processing with the Windows Communication Foundation Service Model of messages received via the Channel Layer.

References

ISO/IEC. 1994. *International Standard 7498-1: Information technology - Open Systems Interconnection - Basic Reference Model: The Basic Model.* http://standards.iso.org/ittf/PubliclyAvailableStandards/s020269_ISO_IEC_7498-1_1994(E).zip. Accessed October 18, 2006.

PART VI
Special Cases

IN THIS PART

Publish/Subscribe Systems

Introduction

In "publish/subscribe systems[...]processes can subscribe to messages containing information on specific subjects, while other processes produce (that is, publish) such messages" (Tannenbaum and van Steen 2002, 701). Publish/subscribe systems are required in many scenarios. In the financial industry, subscriptions to prices are needed. Subscriptions to sensor data and to information about other equipment are required in manufacturing. In computer systems administration, the administrators need to subscribe to information about the security and states of the systems.

Web Services Eventing and Web Services Notification are competing protocols pertinent to publish/subscribe systems. Both specify formats for subscription messages and for publication messages. Neither format is likely to become very important until at least both International Business Machines (IBM) and Microsoft endorse just one of the protocols.

The Web Services Notification specification provides a handy description of some of the various ways in which publishers can provide updates to subscribers (Graham, Hull and Murray 2005, 24). In *push-style notification*, subscribers send subscription messages to publishers, who then send publication messages to the subscribers. In *pull-style notification*, subscribers send subscription messages to publishers, who send publication messages to a pull-point that is known to the subscribers, from which the subscribers retrieve the publication messages. In *brokered notification*, subscribers send subscription messages to brokers, who retrieve publication messages sent by publishers and make them available to the subscribers.

There are various ways of constructing publish/subscribe systems with the Windows Communication Foundation. This chapter describes several of them.

Publish/Subscribe Using Callback Contracts

A simple way of building a publish/subscribe system with the Windows Communication Foundation is to use callback contracts. This service contract, IPublisher,

```
[ServiceContract(Session=true,CallbackContract=typeof(ISubscriber))]
public interface IPublisher
{
    [OperationContract]
    KnownDataPoint[] GetKnownDataPoints();

    [OperationContract]
    void Subscribe(
        KnownDataPoint[] dataPoints,
        out bool subscriptionAccepted);
}
```

identifies a callback contract, ISubscriber, that clients of the service are required to implement:

```
[ServiceContract]
public interface ISubscriber
{
    [OperationContract(IsOneWay=true)]
    void Notify(Guid dataPointIdentifier, byte[] value);
}
```

Because all clients of a service that implements IPublisher must implement ISubscriber, which exposes a one-way operation called Notify(), the service can rely on being able to use the client's Notify() operation to publish data to the client. The callback contract can include any number of operations, but they must all be one-way operations.

Note that the IPublisher service contract also has the value of the Session parameter of the ServiceContract attribute set to true. That signifies that the messages exchanged between a client and a service for the duration of a connection between them will be grouped together by the Windows Communication Foundation into a session, and that the Windows Communication Foundation will maintain some information about the state of each session. Having the Windows Communication Foundation do that is a prerequisite for using callback contracts.

Using callback contracts requires not only the obvious task of specifying a callback contract for a service contract, but also the task of selecting a binding for the service by which the service can initiate transmissions to the client. For a binding to allow for that possibility, it must either use a transport protocol that supports communication initiated from both ends of a connection—such as TCP—or incorporate the composite duplex binding element, `System.ServiceModel.Channels.CompositeDuplexBindingElement`. A predefined binding that incorporates that binding element is the `WSDualHttpBinding`.

To use the operations of the callback contract implemented by the client, the service requires a means for communicating with the client. The means of communicating with the client is referred to as a *callback channel* in the language of the Windows Communication Foundation. A callback channel is obtained using the `GetCallbackChannel<T>()` generic method of the Windows Communication Foundation's `System.ServiceModel.OperationContext` class. That class is a static one that is always available to the code of any method that implements an operation of Windows Communication Foundation service contract:

```
ISubscriber callback =
    OperationContext.Current.GetCallbackChannel<ISubscriber>();
callback.Notify(...);
```

To see how to use the `ISubscriber` callback contracts in a publish/subscribe solution, follow these steps:

1. Copy the code associated with this chapter downloaded from http://www.cryptmaker.com/WindowsCommunicationFoundationUnleashed to the folder `C:\WCFHandsOn`. The code is all in a folder called `PublishSubscribe`, which has several subfolders.

2. Open the solution `CallbackContract.sln` that is in the `Callbacks` subfolder of the `PublishSubscribe` folder.

3. The solution consists of six projects:

   ▶ The RandomDataPoint project is for building a class library with a class called `RandomDataPoint` that represents the source of the information that subscribers want to receive.

   ▶ The `RandomDataPoint` class derives from the `DataPoint` class provided by the class library built from the DataPoint project.

   ▶ The PublisherService project is for building a class library incorporating the `IPublisher` service contract, which has `ISubscriber` as a callback contract. The class library also includes the `PublisherService` class, a service type that implements the `IPublisher` service contract.

   ▶ The PublisherServiceHost project provides a console application to serve as the host for the `PublisherService` service type.

   ▶ SubscriberOne and SubscriberTwo are both console applications with clients of `PublisherService` service that implement the `ISubscriber` callback contract.

4. Examine the IPublisher service contract in the IPublisher.cs module of the PublisherService project in the CallbackContract solution:

```
[ServiceContract(Session=true,CallbackContract=typeof(ISubscriber))]
public interface IPublisher
{
    [OperationContract]
    KnownDataPoint[] GetKnownDataPoints();

    [OperationContract]
    void Subscribe(KnownDataPoint[] dataPoints,
                        out bool subscriptionAccepted);
}
```

The IPublisher interface is a Windows Communication Foundation service contract that designates ISubscriber as its callback contract. The service contract provides the GetKnownDataPoints() operation for retrieving the identifiers of the data items about which a service that implements the contract can publish information. The Subscribe() operation is provided for clients to subscribe to information about one or more of those data items.

5. Look at the ISubscriber callback contract in the ISubscriber.cs module of the PublisherService project:

```
public interface ISubscriber
{
    [OperationContract(IsOneWay=true)]
    void Notify(Guid dataPointIdentifier, byte[] value);
}
```

Although ISubscriber is not marked as a service contract, it does incorporate operation contracts. All of those operation contracts define one-way operations. Actually, there is just one operation, called Notify(), by which the service can push the current values of a data item to the client.

6. Look at the definition of the subscribers in the Subscriber.cs class of the SubscriberOne project. The subscribers implement the ISubscriber interface:

```
public class Subscriber: ISubscriber, IDisposable
```

7. Study the client classes that the subscribers use for sending messages to the publisher service. That class derives from System.ServiceModel. DuplexClientBase<*T*> rather than System.ServiceModel.ClientBase<*T*>. The constructor for System.ServiceModel.DuplexClientBase<*T*> takes an instance of a class that implements the callback contract of *T* as a parameter. That will be the instance to which inbound messages from the service will be directed.

```
private class PublisherClient : DuplexClientBase<IPublisher>, IPublisher
{
    public PublisherClient(
                InstanceContext callbackInstance,
                string endpointConfigurationName)
        : base(callbackInstance, endpointConfigurationName)
    {
    }

    public KnownDataPoint[] GetKnownDataPoints()
    {
        return base.Channel.GetKnownDataPoints();
    }

    public void Subscribe(
                KnownDataPoint[] dataPoints,
                out bool subscriptionAccepted)
    {
        base.Channel.Subscribe(dataPoints, out subscriptionAccepted);
    }
}
```

8. Examine the implementation of the IPublisher contract's Subscribe() method by
   the publisher service's service type, in the PublisherService.cs module of the
   PublisherService project:

```
void IPublisher.Subscribe(
    KnownDataPoint[] dataPoints, out bool subscriptionAccepted)
{
    Console.WriteLine("Received subscription request.");
    subscriptionAccepted = false;
    string dataPointIdentifier = null;
    if (dataPoints.Length == 1)
    {
        dataPointIdentifier = dataPoints[0].Identifier;
        this.ValidateDataPoint(dataPointIdentifier, out subscriptionAccepted);
    }

    if (subscriptionAccepted)
    {
        if (!(this.randomDataPoint.Active))
        {
            this.randomDataPoint.Active = true;
        }
        lock (this.subscribersLock)
        {
```

16

```
            this.subscribers.Add(
                OperationContext.Current.GetCallbackChannel<ISubscriber>());
        }
    }
}
```

After confirming that the subscription request is for information about a data item of which the service is aware, the method retrieves a callback channel by which it can communicate with the subscriber using the Windows Communication Foundation's System.ServiceModel.OperationContext class. Then it adds that callback channel to a list of callback channels.

9. Study the NextValueHandler() method of the PublisherService service type, which is also in the PublisherService.cs module of the PublisherService project:

```
private void NextValueHandler(IDataPoint sender, byte[] newValue)
{
    lock(this.subscribersLock)
    {
        for(int index = this.subscribers.Count - 1; index >= 0; index--)
        {
            try
            {
                this.subscribers[index].Notify(sender.Identifier, newValue);
            }
            catch (Exception exception)
            {
                Console.WriteLine(
                    "Removing subscriber due to exception {0}.",
                    exception.ToString());
                this.subscribers.RemoveAt(index);
            }
            if (this.subscribers.Count <= 0)
            {
                this.randomDataPoint.Active = false;
            }
        }
    }
}
```

This method is the one by which the service type is notified of a change in the value of the data item about which it publishes information. The service type iterates through its list of callback channels, using each to publish a message concerning the fluctuation in the value of the data item to a subscriber.

10. Look at the subscribers' implementation of the `Notify()` operation of the
    `ISubscriber` callback contract, which is in the `Subscriber.cs` module of the
    SubscriberOne project of the `CallbackContract` solution. It simply outputs the
    content of messages published by the client to the console:

```
void ISubscriber.Notify(Guid dataPointIdentifier, byte[] value)
{
    Console.WriteLine(
        "Notified of value {0} of data point {1}.",
            BitConverter.ToInt32(value,0),
            dataPointIdentifier.ToString());
}
```

11. Compare the configuration of the publisher service in the `App.config` file of the
    PublisherServiceHost project

```
<system.serviceModel>
  <services>
    <service
      name="PublicationSubscription.PublisherService">
      <host>
        <baseAddresses>
          <add baseAddress="http://localhost:9000/Server/"/>
        </baseAddresses>
      </host>
      <endpoint
      address="Publisher"
      binding="wsDualHttpBinding"
      contract="PublicationSubscription.IPublisher"/>
    </service>
  </services>
</system.serviceModel>
```

with the configuration of a subscriber, such as the one in the `App.config` file of the
SubscriberOne project:

```
<system.serviceModel>
  <client>
    <endpoint name="SubscriptionService"
    address="http://localhost:9000/Server/Publisher"
    binding="wsDualHttpBinding"
    bindingConfiguration="SubscriberBindingConfiguration"
    contract="PublicationSubscription.IPublisher"/>
```

16

```
    </client>
    <bindings>
      <wsDualHttpBinding>
        <binding
        name="SubscriberBindingConfiguration"
        clientBaseAddress="http://localhost:9001/Subscriber"/>
      </wsDualHttpBinding>
    </bindings>
  </system.serviceModel>
```

The publisher service is configured to use the predefined WSDualHttpBinding, and therefore, so is the subscriber. However, the configuration of the subscriber incorporates a customization to the predefined WSDualHttpBinding that is necessary only on the Windows XP SP2 operating system. That operating system does not support sharing HTTP ports. So, to ensure the default port by which the subscriber is to receive messages from the publisher service, it is necessary to specify an unused one. That is done by providing a base address for the client:

```
<binding
        name="SubscriberBindingConfiguration"
        clientBaseAddress="http://localhost:9001/Subscriber"/>
```

12. Choose Debug, Start Debugging from the Visual Studio 2005 menus. Console windows for the PublisherServiceHost and for the two subscribers should appear.

13. When there is activity in the console of the PublisherServiceHost, enter a keystroke into the console windows of both subscribers' consoles.

    After a few moments, the service should begin publishing messages about fluctuations in the value of a data item to both of the subscribers, as shown in Figure 16.1. It may take a moment after the first published message is received by the first subscriber before the first published message is received by the second subscriber.

14. Choose Debug, Stop debugging from the Visual Studio 2005 menus.

Callback contracts provide a very easy way of implementing publish/subscribe with the Windows Communication Foundation. As is true of push-style notification solutions generally (Graham, Hull and Murray 2005, 24), the technique presupposes the network being configured to allow the publisher to transmit messages to the client.

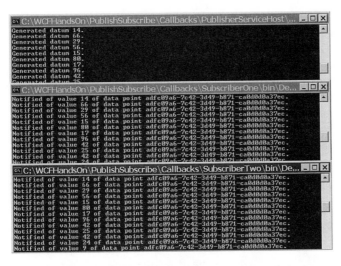

FIGURE 16.1   Publish/Subscribe using callback contracts.

Publish/Subscribe Using MSMQ Pragmatic Multicasting

Version 3 of Microsoft Message Queuing (MSMQ), a technology provided free of charge with Microsoft Windows operation systems, added support for the pragmatic multicasting (PGM) protocol. As shown in Figure 16.2, a nontransactional queue can be associated with a PGM address, and any number of queues can be associated with the same PGM address.

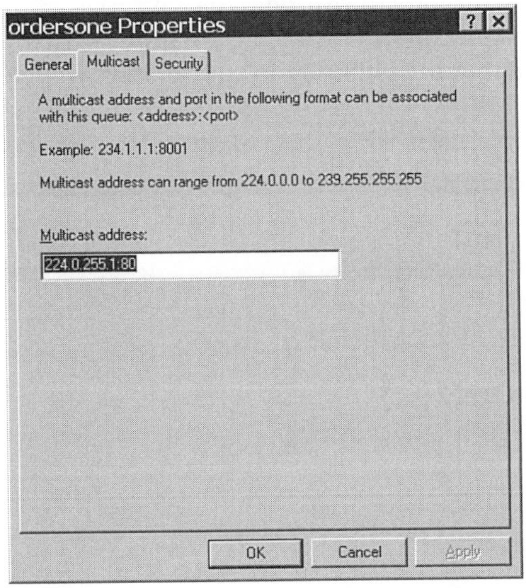

FIGURE 16.2   Associating a PGM address with an MSMQ queue.

As Anand Rajagopalan points out, this new facility of MSMQ provides a simple way of doing publish/subscribe with pull-style notification (Rajagopalan 2005). A publisher can direct publication messages to a PGM address via MSMQ, which will result in those messages being added to all the subscriber queues associated with that address. Subscribers can then pull the messages from their respective queues. Because, as Rajagopalan further points out, the Windows Communication Foundation provides the `MsmqIntegrationBinding` for exchanging messages with MSMQ applications, this way of doing publish/subscribe can also be implemented with the Windows Communication Foundation. Follow these steps to accomplish that:

1. Open the solution, `MSMQPragmaticMulticasting.sln`, that is in the `MSMQPragmaticMulticasting` subfolder of the `PublishSubscribe` folder. The solution consists of four projects:

   ▶ The Order project is for building a class library with a class called `PurchaseOrder`.

   ▶ The Publisher project provides a console application that publishes information about incoming purchase orders to a PGM address via MSMQ, using the Windows Communication Foundation's `MsmqIntegrationBinding`.

   ▶ SubscriberOne and SubscriberTwo are console applications that subscribe to notifications of incoming purchase orders, using the Windows Communication Foundation's `MsmqIntegrationBinding` to pull the notifications from queues associated with the PGM address to which the Publisher sends the notifications.

2. Look at the `PurchaseOrder` class in the `Order.cs` module of the Order project in the MSMQPragmaticMulticasting project, reproduced in Listing 16.1. The class claims to be serializable by having the `Serializable` attribute. It overrides the `ToString()` method of the base class, `Object`, to provide an informative representation of itself as a string. It will be instances of this class that the publisher in this solution will be sending to the subscribers.

LISTING 16.1   Notification Class

```
[Serializable]
public class PurchaseOrder
{
    public string orderIdentifier;
    public string customerIdentifier;
    public PurchaseOrderLineItem[] orderLineItems;
    private OrderStates orderStatus;

    public float TotalCost
    {
        get
        {
```

LISTING 16.1   Continued

```
            float totalCost = 0;
            foreach (PurchaseOrderLineItem lineItem in orderLineItems)
                totalCost += lineItem.TotalCost;
            return totalCost;
        }
    }

    public OrderStates Status
    {
        get
        {
            return orderStatus;
        }
        set
        {
            orderStatus = value;
        }
    }

    public override string ToString()
    {
        StringBuilder buffer =
            new StringBuilder("Purchase Order: " + orderIdentifier + "\n");
        buffer.Append("\tCustomer: " + customerIdentifier + "\n");
        buffer.Append("\tOrderDetails\n");

        foreach (PurchaseOrderLineItem lineItem in orderLineItems)
        {
            buffer.Append("\t\t" + lineItem.ToString());
        }

        buffer.Append("\tTotal cost of this order: $" + TotalCost + "\n");
        buffer.Append("\tOrder status: " + Status + "\n");
        return buffer.ToString();
    }
}
```

3. Examine the IOrderSubscriber interface in the Publisher.cs module of the
   Publisher project, and in the Subscriber.cs module of the SubscriberOne project:

   ```
   [ServiceContract(Namespace = "http://Microsoft.ServiceModel.Samples")]
   [KnownType(typeof(PurchaseOrder))]
   public interface IOrderSubscriber
   {
   ```

```
    [OperationContract(IsOneWay = true, Action = "*")]
    void Notify(MsmqMessage<PurchaseOrder> message);
}
```

This .NET interface is designated as a Windows Communication Foundation service contract by the ServiceContract attribute. It includes a single operation, Notify(), that accepts a single parameter of the type MsmqMessage<PurchaseOrder>. MsmqMessage<T> is a generic type provided by the Windows Communication Foundation for which any serializable type can serve as the type argument. It allows data to be marshaled in and out of MSMQ messages sent or received via the MSMQ integration binding.

As explained in Chapter 10, "Advanced Security," the value of the Action parameter of the OperationContract attribute is used to correlate messages with operations. A value usually does not have to be provided for that parameter because the Windows Communication Foundation automatically and invisibly supplies appropriate default values.

However, the value "*" is provided for the Action parameter of the OperationContract attribute on the IOrderSubscriber contract's Notify() operation. Specifying Action="*" as the parameter to the OperationContract attribute signifies that the operation with that attribute is the default operation, which means that operation will be used to process all messages not matched with another operation. All messages received via the MSMQ integration binding are dispatched to the default operation of the receiving service. In this case, all such messages will be dispatched to the method by which the IOrderSubscriber contract's Notify() operation is implemented.

4. Study the static Main() method of the Publisher class in the Publisher.cs module of the Publisher project:

```
static void Main(string[] args)
{
    [...]

    PurchaseOrder order = new PurchaseOrder();
    order.customerIdentifier = "somecustomer.com";
    order.orderIdentifier = Guid.NewGuid().ToString();

    PurchaseOrderLineItem firstLineItem = new PurchaseOrderLineItem();
    [...]

    PurchaseOrderLineItem secondLineItem = new PurchaseOrderLineItem();
    [...]

    order.orderLineItems =
        new PurchaseOrderLineItem[] {firstLineItem,    secondLineItem };
```

```
OrderSubscriberClient orderSubscriberClient =
    new OrderSubscriberClient(
        "OrderPullPoint");

proxy.Notify(new MsmqMessage<PurchaseOrder>(order));
((IChannel)proxy).Close();

[...]
}
```

The method sends notification of a purchase order to the subscribers using a client class that is defined in the usual way by deriving from the Windows Communication Foundation's ClientBase<T> generic.

```
private class OrderSubscriberClient:
        ClientBase<IOrderSubscriber>,
        IOrderSubscriber
{
    public OrderSubscriberClient(string endpointConfigurationName)
        : base(endpointConfigurationName)
    {
    }

    public void Notify(MsmqMessage<PurchaseOrder> message)
    {
        base.Channel.Notify(message);
    }
}
```

The Publisher code simply invokes the Notify() operation of an instance of the client class, passing an instance of MsmqMessage<PurchaseOrder> created from the purchase order about which it wants to notify the subscribers.

5. Look at the configuration of the Publisher in the App.config file of the Publisher project to see the OrderPullPoint configuration referred to in the construction of the proxy:

```
<system.serviceModel>
  <client>
    <endpoint name="OrderPullPoint"
    address="msmq.formatname:MULTICAST=224.0.255.1:80"
    binding="msmqIntegrationBinding"
    bindingConfiguration="OrderPublicationBinding"
    contract="Microsoft.ServiceModel.Samples.IOrderSubscriber">
    </endpoint>
  </client>
```

```
<bindings>
  <msmqIntegrationBinding>
    <binding
      name="OrderPublicationBinding"
      exactlyOnce="false">
      <security mode="None" />
    </binding>
  </msmqIntegrationBinding>
</bindings>
</system.serviceModel>
```

That configuration selects the Windows Communication Foundation's predefined MsmqIntegrationBinding as the binding to use in publishing the service. The settings of that predefined binding are modified so as to not require the assurance of messages being delivered exactly once. That assurance, which is provided by default by the MsmqIntegrationBinding, is not possible in this case because the destination queues are not transactional queues. They are not transactional queues because MSMQ queues associated with PGM addresses cannot be transactional.

The address provided as the destination of the messages is msmq.formatname: MULTICAST=224.0.255.1:80. In that address, msmq is the scheme associated with the MSMQ-integration transport protocol by the MSMQ integration binding. The expression formatname:MULTICAST signifies that the destination for messages is to be identified by a PGM address. The PGM address given is 224.0.255.1. The component 80 of the address is a port number.

6. Compare the configuration of the Publisher with the configuration of a subscriber, such as the configuration of the first subscriber, in the App.config file of the SubscriberOne project:

```
<configuration>
        <appSettings>
                <add key="orderQueueName" value=".\private$\WCFHandsOnOne" />
                <add key="multicastAddress" value="224.0.255.1:80"/>
        </appSettings>
        <system.serviceModel>
    <services>
      <service
        name="Microsoft.ServiceModel.Samples.OrderSubscriber">
        <endpoint address="msmq.formatname:DIRECT=OS:.\private$\WCFHandsOnOne"
                            binding="msmqIntegrationBinding"
                bindingConfiguration="OrderSubscriptionBinding"
                contract="Microsoft.ServiceModel.Samples.IOrderSubscriber">
        </endpoint>
      </service>
    </services>
    <bindings>
```

```
<msmqIntegrationBinding>
  <binding name="OrderSubscriptionBinding" exactlyOnce="false" >
    <security mode="None" />
  </binding>
</msmqIntegrationBinding>
        </bindings>
    </system.serviceModel >
</configuration>
```

The subscriber configuration defines the configuration of a Windows
Communication Foundation service that receives messages via MSMQ. The selection
and configuration of the binding corresponds exactly with the selection and configuration of the binding for the publisher. Whereas the address provided as the destination of the publisher's messages was a PGM address, the address provided as the
source of messages for the subscriber service is the name of an MSMQ queue associated with that PGM address.

7. Examine the static Main() method of the OrderSubscriber class of one of the
   subscribers in the Subscriber.cs module of the SubscriberOne project:

```
public static void Main()
{
    string queueName = ConfigurationManager.AppSettings["orderQueueName"];

    if (!(MessageQueue.Exists(queueName)))
    {
        MessageQueue.Create(queueName);
        MessageQueue queue = new MessageQueue(queueName);
        queue.MulticastAddress =
            ConfigurationManager.AppSettings["multicastAddress"];
    }

    using (ServiceHost serviceHost = new ServiceHost(typeof(OrderSubscriber)))
    {
        serviceHost.Open();

        Console.WriteLine("The service is ready.");
        Console.WriteLine("Press any key to terminate the service.");
        Console.ReadKey(true);

        serviceHost.Close();
    }
}
```

16

The method creates the queue that serves as the subscriber's pull-point if it does not already exist. In creating the queue, it associates the queue with the PGM address to which the publisher directs its messages.

An instance of the OrderSubscriber class, which implements the IOrderSubscriber service contract, is then loaded into an application domain using an instance of the Windows Communication Foundation's System.ServiceModel.ServiceHost class. Then the Open() method of the System.ServiceModel.ServiceHost instance is invoked, whereupon the Windows Communication Foundation's channel layer will begin watching for messages delivered to the queue specified in the subscriber's configuration file. Such messages will be dispatched by the Windows Communication Foundation to the implementation of the default operation, the Notify() operation, of the IOrderSubscriber service contract.

8. Look at the OrderSubscriber class's implementation of the Notify() operation of the IOrderSubscriber contract:

```
public void Notify(MsmqMessage<PurchaseOrder> message)
{
    PurchaseOrder order = (PurchaseOrder)message.Body;
    Random statusIndexer = new Random();
    order.Status = (OrderStates)statusIndexer.Next(3);
    Console.WriteLine("Processing {0} ", order);
}
```

Recall that the Notify() operation is designated as the default operation of the IOrderSubscriber contract, and also that all messages received via the MSMQ integration binding are dispatched to the method that implements the default operation. In this case, that method is the Notify() method of the OrderSubscriber class. The received messages are dispatched to the Notify() method as instances of the MsmqMessage<PurchaseOrder> type, from which instances of the PurchaseOrder class are extracted with this simple statement:

```
PurchaseOrder order = (PurchaseOrder)message.Body;
```

9. Choose Debug, Start Debugging from the Visual Studio 2005 menus. Console windows for the two subscriber applications should appear, as well as the console window of the publisher.

10. When there is activity in both of the subscriber application's console windows, enter a keystroke into the console window of the publisher. The results should appear as shown in Figure 16.3. Notifications of incoming purchase orders are published to the subscriber's pull-points by the publisher, from which they are retrieved by the subscribers.

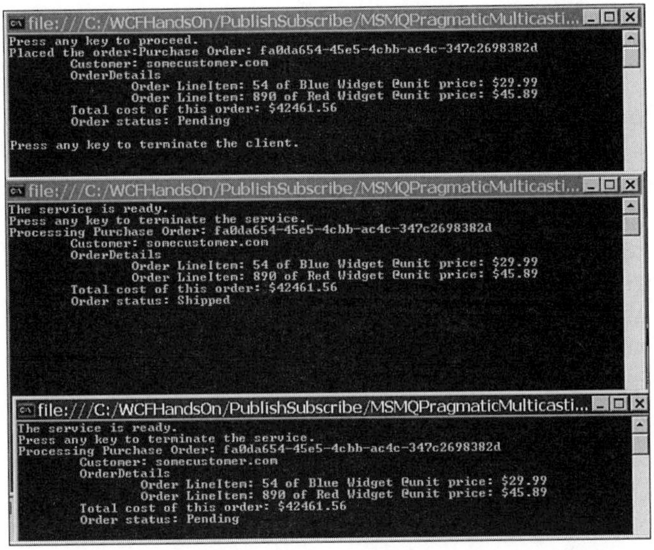

FIGURE 16.3   Publish/Subscribe using MSMQ PGM.

11. Choose Debug, Stop debugging from the Visual Studio 2005 menus.

Generally, when Windows Communication Foundation applications send messages to other Windows Communication Foundation applications via MSMQ queues, one uses the Windows Communication Foundation's predefined `NetMsmqBinding`, rather than `MsmqIntegrationBinding`. `NetMsmqBinding` has the virtue of being more flexible, not requiring messages to be sent and received in the form of instances of `MsmqMessage<T>` types, and allowing messages to be dispatched to operations other than the unmatched message handler. Usually, one must resort to using the `MsmqIntegrationBinding` only when a Windows Communication Foundation application must communicate with a non–Windows Communication Foundation application via MSMQ. In this case, however, all the applications communicating via MSMQ are Windows Communication Foundation applications, so what is the reason for using the `MsmqIntegrationBinding` rather than the `NetMsmqBinding`? The reason is that the implementation of the PGM protocol in MSMQ represents, in effect, a non–Windows Communication Foundation application interposed between the Windows Communication Foundation applications.

Publish/Subscribe Using Streaming

In using either callback contracts or MSMQ PGM to do publish/subscribe with the Windows Communication Foundation, there is the shortcoming of incurring the cost of sending an entire message with each notification from the publisher to the subscribers. That price is more acceptable when the size of the notification in proportion to the total size of the messages is larger, and when notifications are required less frequently. However, the requirement to publish frequent notifications of small items of information is commonplace. You can use the Windows Communication Foundation's streamed transfer mode to avoid having to create an entire message for each notification in such cases.

The Streamed Transfer Mode

The Windows Communication Foundation uses a buffered transfer mode by default. That means that the entire contents of an outgoing message must have been written into a buffer before the message is sent, and that the entire contents of an incoming message must be read from a buffer before the message is dispatched for processing. However, the Windows Communication Foundation provides the option of a streamed transfer mode by which the content of an incoming message can be dispatched for processing by the receiver even before the entire content of the message has been formulated by the source. Follow these steps to send a message using the streamed transfer mode:

1. Open the solution Streaming.sln in the Streaming subfolder of the PublishSubscribe directory. It consists of two projects. The Client project is for building a Windows Forms application that displays an image retrieved from a Windows Communication Foundation service. That service is built using the other project in the solution, called Service.

2. Examine the interface IPictureServer in the Program.cs module of the Service project. It is designated as a Windows Communication Foundation service contract, of which the only notable feature is that its sole operation, GetPicture(), is defined as returning a Stream object:

```
[ServiceContract]
public interface IPictureServer
{
    [OperationContract]
    Stream GetPicture(string pictureName);
}
```

3. Look at the PictureServer class, which is a service type that implements the IPictureServer contract. It returns the image requested by a client as a FileStream object:

```
internal class PictureServer: IPictureServer
{
    Stream IPictureServer.GetPicture(string pictureName)
    {
        try
        {
            return new FileStream(pictureName, FileMode.Open);
        }
        catch (Exception)
        {
```

```
                return null;
        }
    }


}
```

4. See how the service is configured in the `App.config` file of the PictureService project:

```
<system.serviceModel>
        <services>
                <service name="Server.PictureServer">
                        <host>
                          <baseAddresses>
                           <add baseAddress="http://localhost:8000/Server"/>
                          </baseAddresses>
                        </host>
                        <endpoint        address="Picture"
                                        binding="basicHttpBinding"
                                        bindingConfiguration="StreamedHttp"
                                        contract="Server.IPictureServer"/>
                </service>
        </services>
        <bindings>
                <basicHttpBinding>
                        <binding
                                name="StreamedHttp"
                                transferMode="StreamedResponse"/>
                </basicHttpBinding>
        </bindings>
</system.serviceModel>
```

The predefined Windows Communication Foundation `BasicHttpBinding` is selected for the service, but the value of the `transferMode` property of that binding is set to `StreamedResponse`.

5. Examine the client application's use of the `GetPicture()` operation of the service in the `RetrievePicture()` method of the `MainForm.cs` module of the Client project:

```
private void RetrievePicture(object state)
{
        if (this.InvokeRequired)
        {
                PictureClient pictureClient =
                        new PictureClient("PictureServer");
                Stream pictureStream =
                    pictureClient.GetPicture(ConfigurationManager.AppSettings[
```

```
                            "PictureName"]);
                pictureClient.Close();

                this.Invoke(
                        new RetrievePictureDelegate(
                                this.RetrievePicture),
                        new object[]{pictureStream});
        }
        else
        {
                Bitmap bitMap = new Bitmap((Stream)state);
                this.Picture.Image = bitMap;

        }
}
```

The PictureClient class referred to in this code is an ordinary Windows Communication Foundation client derived from System.ServiceModel.ClientBase<*T*>:

```
public class PictureClient : ClientBase<IPictureServer>, IPictureServer
{
    public PictureClient(string endpointConfigurationName)
        : base(endpointConfigurationName)
    {
    }

    public Stream GetPicture(string pictureName)
    {
        return base.Channel.GetPicture(pictureName);
    }
}
```

The Stream object retrieved from the service via the GetPicture() operation using an instance of this client class is marshaled onto the user interface thread. Then it is displayed in the PictureBox control of the client application's form.

6. Compare the configuration of the client, which is in the App.config file of the Client project, with the configuration of the service examined earlier:

```
<system.serviceModel>
        <client>
                <endpoint name="PictureServer"
                                address="http://localhost:8000/Server/Picture"
                                binding="basicHttpBinding"
                                bindingConfiguration="StreamedHttp"
                                contract="Client.IPictureServer"/>
        </client>
```

```
<bindings>
    <basicHttpBinding>
        <binding
            name="StreamedHttp"
            transferMode="StreamedResponse"
            maxReceivedMessageSize="9223372036854775807" />
    </basicHttpBinding>
</bindings>
</system.serviceModel>
```

The predefined `BasicHttpBinding` is selected and the value of the `TransferMode` property is set to `StreamedResponse` as it was for the server. Note, though, that the value of the `MaxReceivedMessageSize` property is set to a very large number, which happens to be the maximum value.

7. Choose Debug, Start Debugging from the Visual Studio 2005 menus. The console window of the service should appear, along with the client application's form.

8. When there is activity in the console window of the service, click the Get the Picture! button on the client application's form. After a moment, a picture, retrieved from the service, should appear on the client application's form, as shown in Figure 16.4.

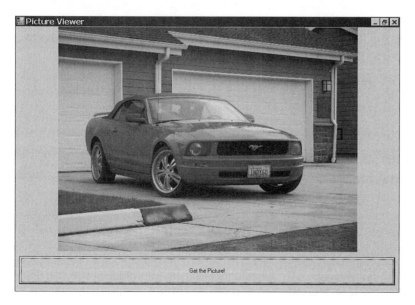

FIGURE 16.4   Retrieving a picture from a service using the streamed transfer mode.

9. Choose Debug, Stop Debugging from the Visual Studio 2005 menus.

The message by which the service responds to the client's request for a picture would look like this, with the stream object incorporated in the body of a SOAP message:

```
<s:Envelope
    xmlns:a="http://schemas.xmlsoap.org/ws/2004/08/addressing"
    xmlns:s="http://schemas.xmlsoap.org/soap/envelope/">
    <s:Header>
        <a:Action s:mustUnderstand="1">
        http://tempuri.org/IPictureServer/GetPictureResponse</a:Action>
        <a:To s:mustUnderstand="1">
        http://schemas.xmlsoap.org/ws/2004/08/addressing/role/anonymous
        </a:To>
        </s:Header>
        <s:Body>... stream ...</s:Body>
</s:Envelope>
```

Remember that, in the configuration of the client, it was necessary to set the value of the `MaxReceivedMessageSize` property of the binding to a large value. Specifically, the value assigned to the `MaxReceivedMessageSize` property has to be at least equal to the size of the incoming response message incorporating the picture stream.

This solution has demonstrated how to select the streamed transfer mode for the `BasicHttpBinding`. It has also shown that one can transmit a `Stream` object using the Windows Communication Foundation. However, the effect of the streamed transfer mode has remained mostly invisible. It has not yet been made apparent that the initial content of the stream was available to the client before the entire content of the stream was received.

Most important, this crucial line of code by which the service returned the stream to the client

```
return new FileStream(pictureName, FileMode.Open);
```

does not reveal how individual data items can be sent progressively via a stream. That is what would be required to implement publish/subscribe using the Windows Communication Foundation's streamed transfer mode.

Transmitting a Custom Stream with the Streamed Transfer Mode

To see how individual data items can be fed through a stream, follow these steps:

1. Open the solution `CustomStream.sln` in the `CustomStream` subfolder of the `PublishSubscribe` directory. It consists of two projects. The Client project is for building a console application that retrieves an image from a Windows Communication Foundation service. The service is built using the other project in the solution, called Service.

2. Examine the interface IPictureServer in the Program.cs module of the Service project. It represents the same service contract that was used previously, with a single operation, GetPicture(), that returns a stream object:

```
[ServiceContract]
public interface IPictureServer
{
    [OperationContract]
    Stream GetPicture(string pictureName);
}
```

3. See, however, that the PictureServer class that implements the IPictureServer contract is slightly altered from the earlier version. This time the stream that it returns is an instance of the CustomStream() class:

```
internal class PictureServer: IPictureServer
{
    Stream IPictureServer.GetPicture(string pictureName)
    {
        try
        {
            CustomStream customStream = new CustomStream(pictureName);
            return customStream;

        }
        catch (Exception)
        {
            return null;
        }
    }
}
```

4. Study the definition of the CustomStream class in the CustomStream.cs module of the Service project, which is reproduced in Listing 16.2.

LISTING 16.2   A Custom Stream Class

```
public class CustomStream: Stream
{
    private string backingStore = null;
    private FileStream backingStream = null;
    private bool initialRead = true;
    private DateTime startRead;
    private long totalBytes = 0;
```

LISTING 16.2   Continued

```csharp
private CustomStream()
{
}

public CustomStream(string fileName)
{
    this.backingStore = fileName;
}

[...]

public override int Read(byte[] buffer, int offset, int count)
{
    TimeSpan duration;

    if (this.initialRead)
    {
        this.startRead = DateTime.Now;
        this.initialRead = false;
    }
    else
    {
        Thread.Sleep(100);
    }

    Console.WriteLine(string.Format(
        "Reading {0} bytes from backing store.", count));

    if (this.backingStream == null)
    {
        this.backingStream = new FileStream(
            this.backingStore,
            FileMode.Open);
    }

    int bytesRead = this.backingStream.Read(buffer, offset, count);

    if (bytesRead <= 0)
    {
        this.backingStream.Close();
    }
```

LISTING 16.2   Continued

```
        this.totalBytes += bytesRead;

        duration = (DateTime.Now - this.startRead);

        Console.WriteLine(
            "Sent {0} bytes in {1}:{2}.",
            this.totalBytes,
            duration.Seconds,
            duration.Milliseconds);

        return bytesRead;
    }

    [...]
}
```

The CustomStream class derives from the abstract Stream class. Although it is required to override all the latter's abstract methods, it really provides a substantive override for only the Read() method. What the CustomStream class's Read() method does is return a chunk of the image requested by the client application, the maximum size of the chunk being specified by a parameter passed to the Read() method.

5. Choose Debug, Start Debugging from the Visual Studio 2005 menus. The console window of the service application should appear, followed by the console window of the client application.

6. When there is activity in the console window of the service application, enter a keystroke into the console window of the client application. The results should be as shown in Figure 16.5: As chunks of the image requested by the client are still being retrieved from the CustomStream object within the service, the chunks already transmitted to the client are being retrieved from the CustomStream object within the client.

7. Stop debugging the solution.

This makes the effect of the streamed transfer mode readily apparent. In response to a single request from a client, data is being transmitted to the client in chunks. The chunks received by the client are immediately available for processing, before all the chunks have been sent by the service.

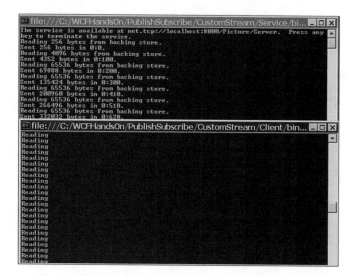

FIGURE 16.5   Using the streamed transfer mode with a custom stream class.

In the service's implementation of the operation used by the client to retrieve the picture

```
internal class PictureServer: IPictureServer
{
    Stream IPictureServer.GetPicture(string pictureName)
    {
        try
        {
            CustomStream customStream = new CustomStream(pictureName);
            return customStream;

        }
        catch (Exception)
        {
            return null;
        }
    }
}
```

this single line of code

```
return customStream;
```

causes the Windows Communication Foundation to send the initial parts of the response message to the client

```
<s:Envelope
    xmlns:a="http://schemas.xmlsoap.org/ws/2004/08/addressing"
    xmlns:s="http://schemas.xmlsoap.org/soap/envelope/">
```

```
<s:Header>
    <a:Action s:mustUnderstand="1">
    http://tempuri.org/IPictureServer/GetPictureResponse</a:Action>
    <a:To s:mustUnderstand="1">
    http://schemas.xmlsoap.org/ws/2004/08/addressing/role/anonymous
    </a:To>
    </s:Header>
    <s:Body>
```

and then calls the Read() method of the stream iteratively, requesting up to 1KB of data from it on each iteration. Each chunk of data retrieved in that manner is transmitted to the client:

```
... stream ...
```

When the Read() method returns zero bytes, the Windows Communication Foundation closes the stream and transmits the remainder of the message:

```
            </s:Body>
</s:Envelope>
```

Implementing Publish/Subscribe Using the Streamed Transfer Mode and a Custom Stream

Now it should be evident how to use the Windows Communication Foundation's streamed transfer mode to implement publish/subscribe. When the data to be published consists of small data items, and the subscribers require notifications with minimal delay, the publisher can send a stream to each of its subscribers using the Windows Communication Foundation's streamed transfer mode. The streams should be custom streams. The Windows Communication Foundation will invoke the Read() methods of the custom streams iteratively, requesting kilobytes of data to transmit to the subscribers. If the custom stream objects have updates available, they can provide those to the Windows Communication Foundation to publish to the subscribers. If no updates are available, the Read() methods of the streams can sleep until updates occur, or until some configurable timeout expires. If the timeout expires, zero bytes can be returned to the Windows Communication Foundation, which will close the stream. The subscriber can then choose to renew the subscription. The publisher buffers updates pertinent to the subscriber for a configurable period so that if the subscription is renewed, updates that occurred between the closing of the initial stream and the renewal of the subscription can be sent to the subscriber immediately upon the renewal.

If updates continue to be available, so that the custom streams continue to make data available to the Windows Communication Foundation as it iteratively calls their Read() method, the maximum sizes for the messages into which the Windows Communication Foundation is embedding the data retrieved from the custom streams will eventually be exceeded. So, there should be logic in the custom streams that detects when the maximum message size is about to be exceeded. That logic will have the Windows

Communication Foundation close the current stream and then immediately open a new stream to the subscriber.

All of these capabilities are implemented in a reusable library called StreamingPublicationSubscription that is included in the solution StreamedPublishSubscribe.sln in the StreamedPublishSubscribe subdirectory of the PublishSubscribe folder. The key classes that it provides are the BufferedSubscriptionManager class and the NotificationStreamWriter class. The former is programmed to buffer data items to which subscriptions have been received for configurable periods, whereas the latter is programmed to retrieve data items from the BufferedSubscriptionManager and make them available to the Windows Communication Foundation. The NotificationStreamReader class is programmed to read the streams output by the NotificationStreamWriter class.

To see these classes in action, and to understand how to use them to implement publish/subscribe solutions, follow these steps:

1. Open the solution, StreamedPublishSubscribe.sln, in the StreamedPublishSubscribe subdirectory of the PublishSubscribe folder. In addition to the project for building the StreamingPublicationSubscription library, the solution also has the Subscriber project, for building a subscriber console application, and the PublisherServiceHost project, for building a console application to host the publisher built from the PublisherService project.

2. Examine the ISubscriber interface in the ISubscriber.cs module of the PublisherService project. That interface defines the service contract that all subscribers are expected to implement. It defines a single operation, Notify(), that takes a Stream object as a parameter:

```
[ServiceContract]
public interface ISubscriber
{
    [OperationContract(IsOneWay=true)]
    void Notify(Stream stream);
}
```

3. Look at the Subscribe() method of the PublisherService class in the PublisherService.cs module of the PublisherService project. That method, shown in Listing 16.3, executes when subscribers submit subscription requests. After validating the subscription and the subscriber, the method invokes the Activate() method of the PublishingAgent class on a background thread.

LISTING 16.3   Method for Processing Subscription Requests

```
void IPublisher.Subscribe(
  KnownDataPoint[] dataPoints,
  out bool subscriptionAccepted)
{
    subscriptionAccepted = false;
```

LISTING 16.3   Continued

```
    string dataPointIdentifier = null;
    if (dataPoints.Length == 1)
    {
        dataPointIdentifier = dataPoints[0].Identifier;
        this.ValidateDataPoint(dataPointIdentifier, out subscriptionAccepted);
    }

    string configuration = null;
    if(subscriptionAccepted)
    {
        this.ValidateSubscriber(
        OperationContext.Current.ServiceSecurityContext.WindowsIdentity.Name,
            out subscriptionAccepted,
            out configuration);
    }

    if (subscriptionAccepted)
    {

        ThreadPool.QueueUserWorkItem(
            new WaitCallback(
                ((IPublishingAgent)new PublishingAgent(
                    configuration,
                    dataPointIdentifier)).Activate
                ),null);
    }
}
```

4. See what is done by the Activate() method of the PublishingAgent class, in the PublishingAgent.cs module of the PublisherService project. The method is reproduced in Listing 16.4.

LISTING 16.4   Activating a Publication Agent

```
void IPublishingAgent.Activate(object state)
{
    this.randomDataPoint.Active = true;

    NotificationStreamWriter writer = null;

    IBufferedSubscriptionManager bufferedDataSubscriptionManager
        = new BufferedSubscriptionManager(
          this.subscriberConfiguration,
          100);
    bufferedDataSubscriptionManager.AddSubscription(this.randomDataPoint);
```

16

LISTING 16.4   Continued

```
    while (true)
    {
        using (SubscriberProxy subscriberProxy
            = new SubscriberProxy(this.subscriberConfiguration))
        {
            ISubscriber subscriber = (ISubscriber)subscriberProxy;
            writer = new NotificationStreamWriter(
                bufferedDataSubscriptionManager,
                long.Parse(
                  ConfigurationManager.AppSettings[
                    "MessageCapacity"]),
                new TimeSpan(
                    0,
                    0,
                    0,
int.Parse(
    ConfigurationManager.AppSettings["UpdateFrequencyInSeconds"])),
                new TimeSpan(
                    0,
                    0,
                    0,
                    0,
int.Parse(
    ConfigurationManager.AppSettings["DataSourceTimeoutInMilliseconds"]))));
            subscriber.Notify(writer);
            subscriberProxy.Close();
            Console.WriteLine("Batch completed.");
        }
    }
}
```

The method adds details of the subscription to an instance of the
BufferedDataSubscriptionManager class, which will begin buffering updates to the
values of the data point to which the subscription pertains. Then the method
invokes the subscriber's Notify() operation, passing an instance of a
NotificationStreamWriter, which will then proceed to read updates from the
BufferedDataSubscriptionManager and pass them to the Windows Communication
Foundation for transmission.

5. Choose Debug, Start Debugging from the Visual Studio 2005 menus. The console
   windows of the Subscriber application and the PublisherServiceHost application
   should appear.

6. When there is activity in the console window of the PublisherServiceHost application, enter a keystroke into the console of the Subscriber application. After a moment, updates from the publisher will begin to register in the console window of the subscriber.

7. Watch for notification in the console window of the subscriber that the maximum size of a message incorporating a stream was about to be exceeded, resulting in that stream being closed and a new one automatically being provided by the publisher. This effect is shown in Figure 16.6.

FIGURE 16.6   Implementing publish/subscribe with the
`StreamingPublicationSubscription` library.

8. Choose Debug, Stop Debugging from the Visual Studio 2005 menus.

Summary

There are various ways of implementing publish/subscribe solutions with the Windows Communication Foundation. Callback contracts and MSMQ PGM are suitable for scenarios in which the size of notifications is larger and the required frequency for updates is lower. When the notifications are smaller and more frequent, one can use the streamed transfer mode with a custom stream class to stream the notifications to the subscribers.

References

Graham, Steve, David Hull, and Bryan Murray. 2005. *Web Services Base Notification 1.3 (WS-BaseNotification)*. Billerica, MA: OASIS.

Rajagopalan, Anand. 2005. *Building Pub-sub applications using MSMQ.* http://blogs.msdn.com/solutions/archive/2005/09/20/471615.aspx. Accessed January 9, 2006.

Tannenbaum, Andrew and Maarten van Steen. 2002. *Distributed Systems: Principles and Paradigms.* Upper Saddle River, NJ: Prentice Hall.

Peer Communication

Introducing Peer Channel

As explained in Chapter 14, "Custom Channels," Windows Communication Foundation protocols are implemented as channels. A transport channel called Peer Channel is provided for multiparty, peer-to-peer communication.

Peer Channel is a significant innovation of the Windows Communication Foundation that provides two very important benefits. First, it enables the construction of sophisticated peer-to-peer applications involving the exchange of structured data. More generally, though, Peer Channel provides simply the easiest way to leverage the new Windows Peer-to-Peer Networking facilities available in Windows XP Service Pack 2 and later Windows client operating systems.

Using Structured Data in Peer-to-Peer Applications

Today, on Windows XP and later Windows operating systems, the Windows application programming interface (API) incorporates a real-time communications client API. That API enables one to develop applications incorporating facilities for real-time human communications in a variety of forms: instant messaging, two-way voice and video, and application sharing. The various Microsoft instant messaging solutions are built using the real-time communications client API.

Although one can certainly construct powerful and interesting applications with that API, those applications rely on the human participants to structure the data that is being exchanged. When one is doing instant messaging or conversing verbally with someone via one's computer over a network, one relies on one's linguistic and verbal abilities to be understood. Yet there are many circumstances in which the computer could assist considerably in structuring the data being passed around. For example, in the species of file-sharing application exemplified by the original Napster, users provide some input every now and then, but the bulk of the activity is done by the application that accepts the user's input, puts it into a form meaningful to its peers, and then goes about getting what the user wanted. Here is another example: It is becoming increasingly common for technology companies to offer technical support via instant messaging. Users of those technical-support instant messaging applications do want to start exchanging free-form text messages with one another. However, before they reach that point, they must generally identify themselves, and describe their needs so that the appropriate support person can be engaged to assist them, which is a process wherein structured data must be gathered from them, exchanged between applications, and processed. The Windows Communication Foundation's Peer Channel facility is the right technology to choose in any scenario like that, in which computer software applications need to exchange structured data with one another on behalf of their respective human users.

Leveraging the Windows Peer-to-Peer Networking Development Platform

Windows XP Service Pack 2 and later Windows client operating systems provide Windows Peer-to-Peer Networking as an optional Windows Networking Services component. Windows Peer-to-Peer Networking is a developer platform for building secure, scalable, and autonomic peer-to-peer applications of any kind. Its key components are these:

▶ The Peer Name Resolution Protocol (PNRP) as a solution to the problem of resolving the name of network peers to network addresses in scenarios in which there is no central domain name server or in which the network addresses assigned to the peers change relatively frequently

▶ Teredo as an implementation of IPv6 NAT Traversal or NAT-T, a proposed standard solution to the problem of traversing Network Address Translators (NATs)

▶ Graphing, a mechanism for maintaining paths, ideally as short as possible, between every two peers in the network, and sustaining the graph as peers leave and join the network

▶ Facilities for securing the network: controlling which peers are permitted to communicate, and ensuring the confidentiality and integrity of the communication

Peer Channel is the very easiest way to leverage all the capabilities of Windows Peer-to-Peer Networking to build server-less applications.

Understanding Windows Peer-to-Peer Networks

Computers communicating via Windows Peer-to-Peer Networking constitute a mesh. A *mesh* is a network in which

> "information typically has more than one route it can take between any two end stations [which] works to provide fault tolerance—if a wire hub, switch or other component fails, data always reaches its destination by traveling along an alternate path." (Tulloch and Tulloch 2002, 753)

This network topology is appropriate for peer-to-peer communication. In a network of servers, the servers and their network are maintained by administrators. By contrast, the nodes in a network of peers, as well as any single path among those nodes, must be assumed to be transient.

Communications in a Windows Peer-to-Peer network are via TCP/IP. If each node in the network had to maintain a TCP/IP connection with every other node in the mesh, the size of the mesh would be severely constrained by the resources of the nodes. So, instead, each node maintains a connection with only some other nodes, which in turn maintain a connection to a few others, and so on. Thus, each node can respond to a PNRP query on the name of the mesh with the physical network addresses of the nodes to which it is connected. Therefore, the topology of a network of Windows Peer-to-Peer applications is more properly described as *partially meshed*, where there are some redundant data paths among nodes, but not a direct link between every pair of nodes (Tulloch and Tulloch 2002, 754).

Using Peer Channel

As in the case of other software communication solutions, those involving the exchange of structured data via Windows Peer-to-Peer Networking can be described using the terms of the Windows Communication Foundation Service Model. In that language, communication is via endpoints, each of which is defined by an address, a binding, and a contract.

Endpoints

Usually, services provide endpoints with which clients can communicate. In the case of peer-to-peer applications, the applications are, by definition, peers, and so it is not appropriate to differentiate one as the service to which others are clients. Instead, in defining peer nodes in the language of the Windows Communication Foundation Service Model, one represent all the nodes as clients of one another:

```
<system.serviceModel>
      <client>
            <endpoint
                  name="MyPeerEndpoint"
                  [...]/>
      </client>
</system.serviceModel>
```

Binding

To indicate that a peer node is to use Peer Channel to communicate via Windows Peer-to-Peer Networking, one selects as the binding for the peer node endpoint the predefined NetPeerTcpBinding. As the name of the binding implies, communications via the NetPeerTcpBinding use TCP. The reliance on TCP simply reflects that of Windows Peer-to-Peer Networking.

The NetPeerTcpBinding can be selected in the configuration of an endpoint in the usual way,

```
<system.serviceModel>
        <client>
                <endpoint
                        name="MyPeerEndpoint"
                        binding="netPeerTcpBinding"
                    [...]/>
        </client>
</system.serviceModel>
```

although a port must be specified, and that is done through a customization of the binding, rather than via the address:

```
<system.serviceModel>
        <client>
                <endpoint
                        name="MyPeerEndpoint"
                        binding="netPeerTcpBinding"
                        bindingConfiguration="PeerBinding"
                        [...]/>
        </client>
        <bindings>
          <netPeerTcpBinding>
            <binding
              name="PeerBinding"
              port="8090"
            </binding>
          </netPeerTcpBinding>
        </bindings>
</system.serviceModel>
```

If it is desirable to authenticate the source of communication, that option can also be selected via a customization of the binding. The source can be authenticated using a password or an X.509 certificate. If a certificate is to be used, it is also necessary to configure a behavior, as shown in Listing 17.1. That behavior must specify the certificate to be used to identify the source of outbound communications, and also specify the store of trusted certificates to be used to authenticate the sources of inbound communications.

LISTING 17.1   Securing Peer Channel Communications

```xml
<system.serviceModel>
        <client>
                <endpoint
                        name="MyPeerEndpoint"
                        binding="netPeerTcpBinding"
                        bindingConfiguration="PeerBinding"
                        behaviorConfiguration="PeerEndpointBehavior"
                        [...]/>
        </client>
        <bindings>
    <netPeerTcpBinding>
        <binding
          name="PeerBinding"
          port="8090"
        </binding>
    </netPeerTcpBinding>
    </bindings>
    <behaviors>
      <endpointBehaviors>
        <behavior name="PeerEndpointBehavior">
          <clientCredentials>
            <peer>
              <certificate
                              findValue="CN=FabrikamEnterprises"
                              storeLocation="LocalMachine" />
              <peerAuthentication
                              certificateValidationMode="PeerTrust"
                              trustedStoreLocation="CurrentUser"
                              revocationMode="NoCheck"   />
            </peer>
          </clientCredentials>
        </behavior>
      </endpointBehaviors>
    </behaviors>
</system.serviceModel>
```

If the solution is to be used exclusively on machines that have Windows Peer-to-Peer Networking installed, no further configuration of the binding is necessary. However, Windows Peer-to-Peer Networking is not available on the Windows Server operating systems. The primary significance of that is that there will be no implementation of PNRP to supply the physical network addresses of the nodes within a mesh. It is still possible to deploy Peer Channel solutions on Windows Server 2003, but in that case, it is necessary to have the resolution of the physical network addresses of peers done by a peer name resolver.

A peer name resolver is a class that derives from the abstract base
System.ServiceModel.PeerResolver. As shown in Listing 17.2, that base class defines a
handful of abstract methods. Peer Channel will invoke those methods to add the current
peer node to a mesh, and to ascertain the physical addresses of the other nodes in the
mesh when the current node is to send outbound messages. One identifies one's peer
name resolver, one's implementation of System.ServiceModel.PeerResolver through a
customization of the NetPeerTcpBinding configuration, as shown in Listing 17.3. There,
the custom peer name resolver is identified as the class, MyResolverClass, in the
MyResolverAssembly assembly.

LISTING 17.2   System.ServiceModel.PeerResolver

```
public abstract class PeerResolver
{
    public abstract bool CanShareReferrals { get; }

    public virtual void Initialize(
                EndpointAddress address,
                Binding binding,
                ClientCredentials credentials,
                PeerReferralPolicy referralPolicy);
    public abstract object Register(
                string meshId,
                PeerNodeAddress nodeAddress,
                TimeSpan timeout);
    public abstract ReadOnlyCollection<PeerNodeAddress> Resolve(
                string meshId,
                int maxAddresses,
                TimeSpan timeout);
    public abstract void Update(
                object registrationId,
                PeerNodeAddress updatedNodeAddress,
                TimeSpan timeout);
}
```

LISTING 17.3   Identifying a Custom Peer Resolver

```
<system.serviceModel>
  <client>
    <endpoint
      name="MyPeerEndpoint"
      binding="netPeerTcpBinding"
      bindingConfiguration="PeerBinding"
      [...] />
    <endpoint
```

LISTING 17.3   Continued

```
      name="CustomPeerResolverEndpoint"
      address="net.tcp://localhost:8089/MyResolverService"
      binding="wsHttpBinding"
      contract="IMyPeerResolverContract"/>
  </client>
  <bindings>
    <netPeerTcpBinding>
      <binding
        name="PeerBinding"
        port="8090">
        <resolver mode="Custom">
          <custom
            resolverType="MyResolverClass,MyResolverAssembly"/>
        </resolver>
      </binding>
    </netPeerTcpBinding>
  </bindings>
</system.serviceModel>
```

How would a custom peer name resolver accomplish the tasks of adding a node to a mesh, and retrieving the addresses of the peer nodes within a mesh? Typically, it would do so by contacting a peer name resolution service—an otherwise ordinary Windows Communication Foundation service that keeps track of the peer nodes joining the mesh. So, in Listing 17.3, a client endpoint and the peer node endpoint are configured to define how the custom peer name resolver would communicate with the peer name resolution service. Notice that the binding selected for the communication between the custom peer name resolver and the peer name resolution service in that case is the predefined wsHttpBinding. It could be any binding except NetPeerTcpBinding because the communication between the custom peer name resolver and the peer name resolution service is not peer-to-peer communication, but rather the communication of a client with a service. However, an HTTP binding is selected in this case to emphasize that the peer name resolution service does not have to maintain a TCP connection with every peer node. If it did, the resources of the peer name resolution service's host would restrict the number of peer nodes that could be included in the mesh.

Address

Addresses used for endpoints configured with the NetPeerTcpBinding must have the scheme, net.p2p:

```
<system.serviceModel>
    <client>
        <endpoint
```

17

```
                name="MyPeerEndpoint"
                address="net.p2p://MyMeshIdentifier/MyEndpointName"
                  binding="netPeerTcpBinding"
                [...]/>
        </client>
</system.serviceModel>
```

The next segment of the address, MyMeshIdentifier, in this example, is the identifier of the mesh of peers in which the node is to participate. The remainder of the address is the address of the endpoint relative to the base address constituted by the mesh identifier.

Contract

With Peer Channel, a message sent by any node in the peer-to-peer mesh is sent asynchronously, and delivered to every other node in the mesh, including itself. Hence, the pattern for the exchange of messages among peer applications via Peer Channel is always asynchronous and bidirectional. That message exchange pattern is represented in code using the Windows Communication Foundation by defining a service contract that identifies itself as its own callback contract:

```
[ServiceContract(CallbackContract = typeof(IMyContract))]
public interface IMyContract
{
    [OperationContract(IsOneWay = true)]
    void OneMessage(MyDataType data);

    [OperationContract(IsOneWay = true)]
    void AnotherMessage(string otherData);
}
```

That location signifies that any application sending a message defined by that service contract must also be prepared to receive that message.

Implementation

Service contracts with callback contracts are referred to as *duplex contracts* in the language of the Windows Communication Foundation. Windows Communication Foundation clients for sending messages defined by such contracts are derived from System.ServiceModel.DuplexClientBase<*T*> rather than System.ServiceModel.ClientBase<*T*>:

```
public class MyClient : DuplexClientBase<IMyContract>, IMyContract
{
  [...]
}
```

Peer Channel in Action

The example that will be used to show Peer Channel in action is an application for conducting a quiz in a classroom. In the scenario, each pupil has a computer program that can receive the questions in the quiz from a software application that the teacher has. The pupils respond to the quiz questions using their program, and their responses are transmitted to the teacher, who can grade the pupils' answers as they come in, and transmit grades back to each individual class member. The teacher can also broadcast instructions to the entire class.

This scenario is not a good one in which to apply an instant-messaging solution. Besides the tedium involved in the teacher having to type out each question, the pupils' application could do little more than simply show the pupil what the teacher typed. It would be better for the teacher's application to transmit structured data to the pupils' application, which could then meaningfully process the information that it received and display it accordingly. Of course, one could transmit strings of XML between the applications via an instant messaging API like the real-time communications client API, but then one would have to write code to parse the XML. As will become apparent, considerable effort will be saved when the Windows Communication Foundation's Peer Channel is used to implement the solution.

Be aware that to use Peer Channel, one's computer system must have a network connection. That is necessary even for communication among applications residing together on that system.

Envisaging the Solution

Figure 17.1 shows the user interface of the teacher's application. As the pupils start their applications, each pupil's application transmits the pupil's name and photograph to the teacher's application, which displays the photographs in the area at the top. When the teacher sees that all the pupils have started their applications, and are therefore ready to begin the quiz, the teacher clicks on the Start button to transmit the quiz questions to the students. There is a box for text entry along with a Send button for broadcasting announcements to the class. As the students answer the quiz questions, their responses are displayed in the box in the Grading section of the screen. The teacher can scroll backward and forward through the responses that have been received, and indicate, for each response, whether it is correct or incorrect. The teacher can then click the Grade button to send a message to the application of the pupil who submitted the response, indicating whether the pupil's response was correct.

The user interface of the pupils' application is shown in Figure 17.2. It has an area on the left to display a picture, an area at the top to display an instruction, and a set of radio buttons to show the possible answers, with a button to submit a selected answer. When the teacher has graded a particular answer, a check mark shows up next to the radio buttons if the answer is correct and a cross shows up if the answer is incorrect. There are buttons to navigate back and forth through the questions.

FIGURE 17.1   The teacher's application.

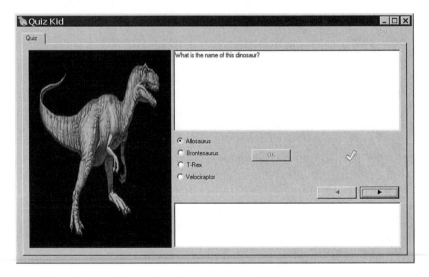

FIGURE 17.2   The pupil's application.

Figure 17.3 depicts one possible sequence of messages that could be exchanged. There are really only two rules, though, governing the sequence of messages. The first rule is that the pupils' application must send the teacher's application a Join message before the teacher's application can begin transmitting AddItem messages to the pupils with the quiz questions. The second rule is that the pupils' application must send a Response message with the answer to a question before the teacher's application can send a Response message with the teacher's assessment of the answer.

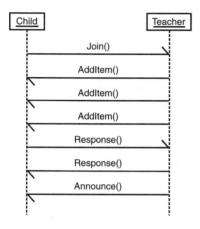

FIGURE 17.3   One possible sequence of messages.

Almost all the data exchanged between the teacher's application and the pupils' application via these messages is structured:

▶ The message that each pupil's application transmits to the teacher's application when it starts consists of a picture and a name. The teacher's application unpacks that message and displays the picture, while using the name, in the background, to open a private connection with that pupil's application.

▶ Each quiz question that the teacher's application transmits to the pupils' application consists of a picture, an instruction, and set of possible answers for the pupil to choose from. The pupils' application unpacks the messages containing the questions, and displays each element in the appropriate area of the pupils' user interface.

▶ When a pupil's application conveys an answer to a question to the teacher's application, the message consists of the pupil's name, the identifier of the question being answered, and the answer itself. The teacher's response to the pupil indicating whether the response was correct or incorrect conveys the identifier of the question that the pupil answered and whether the pupil's answer was correct. The pupil's application reads that message, identifies the quiz item to which it pertains, and updates it with the teacher's evaluation of the pupil's answer.

Only the announcements that the teacher broadcasts to the class during the quiz constitute unstructured data.

To prepare for an exploration of Peer Channel as a way of implementing the classroom quiz solution, follow these steps:

1. Copy the code associated with this chapter downloaded from http://www.crypt-maker.com/WindowsCommunicationUnleashed to the folder C:\WCFHandsOn. The code is all in a folder called PeerChannel.

2. Open the solution C:\WCFHandsOn\PeerChannel\PeerChannel.sln. It consists of four projects. The project called Child is for building the pupils' application, and the project called Teacher is for building the teacher's application. The project called ResolverClient is for building the custom peer name resolver that is used by both the pupils' application and the teacher's. The CustomPeerResolverService project is for building a peer name resolution service that the custom peer name resolvers of both the pupils' application and the teacher's application will use.

3. Follow the instructions under the heading "Installing Certificates" in Chapter 7, "Security Basics," to install X.509 certificates. One of those certificates, the one for Fabrikam Enterprises, will be used by the peer nodes in the example to authenticate one another.

4. The next few steps are for copying that certificate from the local machine's personal store to the current user's personal store and to the current user's Trusted People store. To begin doing that, open the Microsoft Management Console by choosing Run from the Windows Start menus, and entering

   mmc

5. Choose File, Add/Remove Snap-In from the Microsoft Management Console menus.

6. Click Add on the Add/Remove Snap-In dialog that opens.

7. Choose Certificates from the list of available standalone snap-ins presented, and click the Add button.

8. Select Computer Account on the Certificates snap-in dialog, and click the OK button.

9. Accept the default on the Select Computer dialog and click the Finish button.

10. Click Add again on the Add Standalone Snap-In dialog.

11. Choose Certificates again from the list of available standalone snap-ins, and click the Add button.

12. Select My User Account on the Certificates snap-in dialog, and click the Finish button.

13. Click the Close button on the Add Standalone Snap-In dialog.

14. Click the OK button on the Add/Remove Snap-In dialog.

15. Expand the Certificates (Local Computer) node that now appears in the left panel of the Microsoft Management Console.

16. Expand the Personal child node of the Certificates node.

17. Select the Certificates child node of the Personal node.

18. Right-click on the FabrikamEnterprises certificate that should now have appeared in the right panel, and choose Copy from the context menu.

19. Expand the Certificates - Current User node in the left panel of the Microsoft Management Console.

20. Expand the Personal child node of the Certificates node.

21. Right-click on that node and choose Paste from the context menu.

22. Expand the Trusted People child node of the Certificates node.

23. Right-click on that node and choose Paste from the context menu.

Designing the Data Structures

Because Peer Channel is properly used for the exchange of structured data between peers, the first step in constructing a Peer Channel solution is to design the data structures to be exchanged among the peers. The representation of the data to be exchanged in messages via Peer Channel is done in the same way as it usually is with the Windows Communication Foundation—preferably by designing data contracts, or alternatively by designing XML-serializable types.

To see the data structures defined for use with the classroom quiz application, examine the data contracts in the file `Quiz.cs` of the Teacher project, which is shared with the Child project. They are reproduced in Listing 17.4. These data contracts represent the messages to be exchanged between the teacher's application and the students' application.

LISTING 17.4   Data Contracts

```
[DataContract]
public struct QuizResponse
{
    [DataMember]
    public Student Responder;
    [DataMember]
    public QuizItem Item;
    [DataMember]
    public string ResponseText;
    [DataMember]
    public string ResponseIdentifier;
    [DataMember]
    public bool? Correct;
    public bool Submitted;
}
```

17

LISTING 17.4   Continued

```
[DataContract]
public struct QuizItem
{
    [DataMember]
    public string Identifier;
    [DataMember]
    public byte[] ItemImage;
    [DataMember]
    public string Text;
    [DataMember]
    public QuizResponse[] Responses;
    public bool Submitted;

    public string ResponseText
    {
        get
        {
            foreach (QuizResponse response in Responses)
            {
                if (response.Submitted)
                {
                    return response.ResponseText;
                }
            }

            return null;
        }
    }

    public bool? Correct
    {
        get
        {
            foreach (QuizResponse response in Responses)
            {
                if (response.Submitted)
                {
                    return response.Correct;
                }
            }
```

LISTING 17.4   Continued

```
            return null;
        }
    }
}

[DataContract]
public struct Student
{
    [DataMember]
    public string Name;
    [DataMember]
    public byte[] Image;
}
```

The Student class represents the message that the pupil's application will send to the teacher's application to signal that the pupil has started the application. It contains the pupil's name and photograph.

The QuizItem class represents the message that the teacher's application will send to the pupils' application containing a quiz question. The Identifier, ItemImage, Text, and Responses members of that class represent the identifier of the quiz question, the picture to which the question pertains, the instruction, and various possible responses. The Submitted member will be used internally in the pupils' application to track whether the response to the question that the pupil selected has been submitted to the teacher.

The QuizResponse class represents the message from the pupils' application to the teacher's application conveying the pupil's response, as well as the message from the teacher's application to the pupils' application with the teacher's assessment of the response. The Responder member identifies the pupil who is responding to the question. The Item member indicates which quiz question is being answered. The ResponseText member contains the pupil's answer. The Correct member contains the teacher's evaluation of the pupil's answer. The Submitted member will be used internally in the pupil's application to track whether the response is the pupil's chosen response, and by the teacher's application to track whether the teacher's assessment of the response has been transmitted to the pupil who submitted it.

Defining the Service Contracts

Look at the service contracts defined in the code from the Quiz.cs module of the Teacher project:

```
[ServiceContract(CallbackContract = typeof(IQuizManagement))]
public interface IQuizManagement
{
```

17

```
    [OperationContract(IsOneWay = true)]
    void Join(Student student);

    [OperationContract(IsOneWay = true)]
    void Announce(string announcement);
}


[ServiceContract(CallbackContract = typeof(IQuizQuestion))]
public interface IQuizQuestion
{
    [OperationContract(IsOneWay = true)]
    void AddItem(QuizItem item);
}

[ServiceContract(CallbackContract = typeof(IQuizResponse))]
public interface IQuizResponse
{
    [OperationContract(IsOneWay = true)]
    void SendResponse(QuizResponse response);
}
```

These service contracts define the messages and the message exchange patterns required for the classroom quiz solution. The messages they define are

▶ The Announce message, by which each pupil's application will indicate to the teacher's application that the pupil is ready for the quiz

▶ The AddItem message by which the teacher's application will send a quiz question to the pupil's application

▶ The SendResponse message by which the pupil's application will send answers to the teacher's, and the teacher's application will send the evaluation of the answer to the pupil's

Crucially, each service contract identifies itself as its own callback contract, which, as explained already, is a requirement of service contracts used with Peer Channel, signifying that any application sending a message defined by the service contract must also be prepared to receive that message.

Clients for sending messages defined by the service contracts are also in the Quiz.cs file. The code for those clients is shown in Listing 17.5.

LISTING 17.5   Client Classes

```csharp
public class QuizQuestionClient :
    DuplexClientBase<IQuizQuestion>,
    IQuizQuestion
{
    public QuizQuestionClient(
                InstanceContext callbackInstance,
                string endpointConfigurationName)
        : base(
                    callbackInstance,
                    endpointConfigurationName)
    {
    }

    #region IQuizQuestion Members

    public void AddItem(QuizItem item)
    {
        base.Channel.AddItem(item);
    }

    #endregion
}

public class QuizResponseClient :
    DuplexClientBase<IQuizResponse>,
    IQuizResponse
{
    public QuizResponseClient(
                InstanceContext callbackInstance,
                Binding binding,
                EndpointAddress address)
        : base(
                    callbackInstance,
                    binding, address)
    {
    }

    #region IQuizResponse Members

    public void SendResponse(QuizResponse response)
    {
        base.Channel.SendResponse(response);
    }
```

LISTING 17.5   Continued

```
    #endregion
}


public class QuizManagementClient :
    DuplexClientBase<IQuizManagement>,
    IQuizManagement
{
    public QuizManagementClient(
                InstanceContext callbackInstance,
                string endpointConfigurationName)
        : base(
                    callbackInstance,
                    endpointConfigurationName)
    {
    }

    #region IQuizManagement Members

    public void Join(Student student)
    {
        base.Channel.Join(student);
    }

    public void Announce(string announcement)
    {
        base.Channel.Announce(announcement);
    }

    #endregion
}
```

Implementing the Service Contracts

Usually, in building solutions using the Windows Communication Foundation, after one
has defined the service contracts—the interfaces that describe how messages are to be
exchanged—the next step is to write classes that implement those interfaces. The same
procedure applies when using Peer Channel. Usually, though, it is only an application
that is to function as a service that will implement a service contract. By contrast, because
Peer Channel applications must also be able to receive the messages that they send, all
the applications that are to exchange data with one another via Peer Channel implement
all the service contracts defining the messages they are to exchange. Follow these steps to
examine the implementations of the service contracts:

1. Look at the definition of the QuizTeacher class in QuizTeacher.cs file of the Teacher project. It implements the IQuizManagement, IQuizQuestion, and IQuizResponse service contracts by which the message exchanges for the classroom quiz solution are defined:

```
public class QuizTeacher :
        IQuizQuestion,
        IQuizResponse,
        IQuizManagement,
        IDisposable
{
        [...]
}
```

2. Also look at the definition of the QuizChild class in the QuizChild.cs file of the Child project. It implements the same interfaces:

```
public class QuizChild:
        IQuizQuestion,
        IQuizResponse,
        IQuizManagement,
        IDisposable
{
        [...]
}
```

Configuring the Endpoints

To see how the predefined NetPeerTcpBinding is used in the classroom quiz application, follow these steps:

1. Examine the constructor of the QuizChild class in the QuizChild.cs file of the Child project. That is the code by which a pupil's application prepares to announce the presence of the pupil to the teacher's application. The code simply constructs instances of the QuizManagementClient and QuizQuestionClient classes defined in Listing 17.5. The System.ServiceModel.InstanceContext object passed to the constructors specifies the object to which inbound messages are to be directed, and in this case, that object is simply the current QuizChild object. The names QuizManagementEndpoint and QuizQuestionEndpoint simply identify the Windows Communication Foundation endpoint configurations. When the Open() method of the client object is invoked, it is readied to receive messages from its peers, as well as to send messages to them.

```
this.site = new InstanceContext(this);

//Management
this.managementClient =
```

17

```
            new QuizManagementClient(
                    this.site,
                    "QuizManagementEndpoint");
    this.managementClient.Open();

    //Question
    this.questionClient =
            new QuizQuestionClient(
                    this.site,
                    "QuizQuestionEndpoint");
    this.questionClient.Open();
```

2. Look for the client endpoint configurations in the App.config file of the client project. Taking one of them, the endpoint configuration named QuizManagementEndpoint, as an example,

```
<endpoint
    name="QuizManagementEndpoint"
    address="net.p2p://Classroom_3A_ManagementMesh/QuizManagement"
    behaviorConfiguration="PeerEndpointBehavior"
    binding="netPeerTcpBinding"
    bindingConfiguration="PeerBinding"
    contract="WindowsCommunicationFoundationHandsOn.School.IQuizManagement"/>
```

it specifies the NetPeerTcpBinding as the binding of the endpoint. The address it provides, net.p2p://Classroom_3A_ManagementMesh/QuizManagement, conforms to the requirement of using the scheme, net.p2p, in the addresses of endpoints associated with the NetPeerTcpBinding. The next portion of the address, Classroom_3A_ManagementMesh, identifies the name of the Windows Peer-to-Peer Networking mesh to which messsages are to be directed and from which messages may be received. The final portion, QuizManagement, is the name of the endpoint relative to the base addresses constituted by the mesh name.

The customization specified for the predefined NetPeerTcpBinding identifies a port as well as a custom peer resolver—the ResolverClient class that is defined in the ResolverClient project. It also indicates that the pupil's application and the teacher's application are to authenticate one another's users by means of a certificate.

```
<netPeerTcpBinding>
        <binding
                name="PeerBinding"
                port="8090"
                [...]
                <security mode="Transport">
                        <transport credentialType="Certificate"/>
                </security>
```

```
                    <resolver mode="Custom">
                            <custom
                                    resolverType=
"WindowsCommunicationFoundationHandsOn.School.ResolverClient,ResolverClient"/>
                            </resolver>
            </binding>
</netPeerTcpBinding>
```

The behavior identified in the configuration of the endpoint specifies the certificate to use to identify the user, and the certificate store to use in authenticating the senders of inbound messages:

```
<behaviors>
  <endpointBehaviors>
    <behavior name="PeerEndpointBehavior">
      <clientCredentials>
        <peer>
          <certificate
                        findValue="CN=FabrikamEnterprises"
                        storeLocation="LocalMachine" />
          <peerAuthentication
                        certificateValidationMode="PeerTrust"
                        revocationMode="NoCheck" />
          <messageSenderAuthentication
                        certificateValidationMode="PeerTrust"
              revocationMode="NoCheck" />
        </peer>
      </clientCredentials>
    </behavior>
  </endpointBehaviors>
</behaviors>
```

A second endpoint is configured to define how the custom peer resolver is to locate and communicate with the peer name resolution service. An HTTP binding is selected in that case, which, of course, matches the choice of binding in the configuration of the peer name resolution service itself—a fact that can be confirmed by examining the App.config file of the custom peer resolver service project.

```
<endpoint
    name="CustomPeerResolverEndpoint"
    address="http://localhost:8089/School/PeerResolverService"
    binding="wsHttpBinding"
    contract="WindowsCommunicationFoundationHandsOn.School.IPeerResolver">
</endpoint>
```

Directing Messages to a Specific Peer

Remember that messages sent via Peer Channel are delivered to every node in the mesh. Yet, there might be cases in which one node has a message that is intended for a specific other node rather than for every node in the mesh. The closest one can come to satisfying that requirement with Peer Channel is to create a mesh consisting of those two nodes only. Then messages from either node, in being delivered to every node in the mesh, will be delivered to only two nodes—the sender and the intended recipient.

In the classroom quiz scenario, each pupil's answers to the quiz questions are meant to be communicated only to the teacher, and the teacher's evaluation of each pupil's answers is meant to be communicated only to that pupil. To see how that requirement is satisfied in the classroom quiz application, follow these steps:

1. Look again at the constructor of the QuizChild class in the QuizChild.cs file of the Teacher project. A QuizResponse object is constructed that the pupil's application will use to send quiz responses to the teacher's application and receive evaluations. The endpoint to be used by that object is defined in code rather than through configuration, and the address that is used identifies a mesh that is named for the pupil:

```
string endpoint =
    ConfigurationManager.
    AppSettings[QuizChild.QuizResponseEndpointKey];
EndpointAddress address =
    new EndpointAddress(
        string.Format("{0}{1}{2}/{3}",
            QuizChild.PeerChannelAddressPrefix,
            ConfigurationManager.AppSettings[
                            QuizChild.MeshIdentifierKey],
            this.student.Name,
            endpoint));

this.responseClient = new QuizResponseClient(
        this.site,
        new NetPeerTcpBinding(QuizChild.PeerBindingKey),
        address);
ClientCredentials credentials = this.responseClient.ClientCredentials;
credentials.Peer.SetCertificate(
    StoreLocation.LocalMachine,
    StoreName.My,
    X509FindType.FindBySubjectDistinguishedName,
    QuizChild.CertificateSubjectDistinguishedName);
credentials.Peer.PeerAuthentication.CertificateValidationMode
        = X509CertificateValidationMode.PeerTrust;
credentials.Peer.PeerAuthentication.TrustedStoreLocation
        = StoreLocation.CurrentUser;

responseClient.Open();
```

2. Study the code for the Join() method of the QuizTeacher class in the QuizTeacher.cs file of the Teacher project, reproduced in Listing 17.6. That is the method to which messages from the pupils' applications are directed, announcing that a pupil is ready for the test. The teacher's application creates an instance of the QuizResponse client class for communicating exclusively with each pupil, defining an endpoint with an address identifying a mesh named for the pupil. Thus, for each pupil participating in the quiz, the teacher's application is joined to a mesh consisting of just the teacher's application and the application used by that pupil. Hence, while the teacher's application can broadcast quiz questions to all the pupils via the mesh to which the teacher's application and the application of every pupil belongs, the teacher's application can also communicate privately with each pupil's application via another mesh to which only the two of them belong.

In this case, the QuizResponse objects for communicating with each pupil individually are cached, and that is suitable where the number of private conversations is small. For larger meshes where one node is required to communicate privately with every other node, the connections to the private mesh of each of those other nodes will have to be more transient. When a node needs to send a message to one particular other node, it would have to join that other node's private mesh, send the message, and then leave the private mesh. The same would have to happen in reverse if the other node wanted to respond.

LISTING 17.6   Joining a Mesh with a Specific Other Node

```
void IQuizManagement.Join(Student student)
{
    if (!(this.responseClients.ContainsKey(student.Name)))
    {
        if(this.meshIdentifier == null)
        {
            this.meshIdentifier =
                        ConfigurationManager.AppSettings[
                                QuizTeacher.MeshIdentifierKey];
        }
        string endpoint =
            ConfigurationManager.
            AppSettings[QuizTeacher.QuizResponseEndpointKey];
        EndpointAddress address =
            new EndpointAddress(
                string.Format("{0}{1}{2}/{3}",
                    QuizTeacher.PeerChannelAddressPrefix,
                    this.meshIdentifier,
                    student.Name,
                    endpoint));
```

LISTING 17.6   Continued

```
if(this.binding == null)
{
    binding =
                    new NetPeerTcpBinding(
                            QuizTeacher.PeerBindingKey);
}

QuizResponseClient responseClient = new QuizResponseClient(
                this.site,
                this.binding,
                address);
        Credentials credentials = responseClient.ClientCredentials;
credentials.Peer.SetCertificate(
    StoreLocation.LocalMachine,
    StoreName.My,
    X509FindType.FindBySubjectDistinguishedName,
    QuizTeacher.CertificateSubjecDistinguishedName);

credentials.Peer.PeerAuthentication.CertificateValidationMode =
                X509CertificateValidationMode.PeerTrust;
credentials.Peer.PeerAuthentication.TrustedStoreLocation =
                StoreLocation.CurrentUser;

responseClient.Open();

this.responseClients.Add(student.Name, responseClient);

[...]
    }
}
```

Custom Peer Name Resolution

Custom peer name resolution is necessary only on operating systems like Windows Server 2003 on which the .NET Framework 3 can be installed, but Windows Peer-to-Peer Networking is not avaiable. To see how custom peer name resolution is accomplished in the classroom quiz application, follow these steps:

1. Examine the code for the ResolverClient class in the ResolverClient.cs file of the ResolverClient project, shown in Listing 17.7. The class implements the abstract methods of its System.ServiceModel.PeerResolver base. Peer Channel will invoke those methods to add the current node to a mesh, to retrieve the physical network addresses of the other nodes in the mesh, and to remove the node from the mesh.

The `ResolverClient` class accomplishes those tasks by calling on a custom peer resolver service.

Notice that the `Resolve()` method by which Peer Channel retrieves the physical network addresses of the other nodes in a mesh accepts a `maxAddresses` value as a parameter to restrict the number of addresses of other nodes of which the current node will be aware. Thus, no single node will necessarily know about every other node. More generally, the same algorithm that Windows Peer-to-Peer Networking uses to scale indefinitely large meshes across a partially meshed network is being used in this case, and no single node will be required to maintain a connection with every other node.

LISTING 17.7   Custom Peer Name Resolver

```
public class ResolverClient : PeerResolver
{
    private const string endpointConfigurationName
            = "CustomPeerResolverEndpoint";

    public override bool CanShareReferrals
    {
        get { return true; }
    }

    public override object Register(
            string meshId,
            PeerNodeAddress nodeAddress,
            TimeSpan timeout)
    {
        using (ChannelFactory<ICustomPeerResolverChannel> factory
                    = new ChannelFactory<ICustomPeerResolverChannel>(
                        endpointConfigurationName))
        {
            using (ICustomPeerResolverChannel client =
                        factory.CreateChannel())
            {
                foreach (IPAddress address in ipAddresses)
                  {
                    if (address.AddressFamily == AddressFamily.InterNetworkV6)
                      address.ScopeId = 0;
                  }
                int registrationId = client.Register(meshId, nodeAddress);
                return registrationId;
            }
        }
    }
```

17

LISTING 17.7   Continued

```
public override void Unregister(object registrationId, TimeSpan timeout)
{
    using (ChannelFactory<ICustomPeerResolverChannel> factory =
                new ChannelFactory<ICustomPeerResolverChannel>(
                    endpointConfigurationName))
    {
        using (ICustomPeerResolverChannel client = factory.CreateChannel())
        {
            client.Unregister((int)registrationId);
        }
    }
}

[...]

public override ReadOnlyCollection<PeerNodeAddress> Resolve(
            string meshId,
            int maxAddresses,
            TimeSpan timeout)
{
    PeerNodeAddress[] addresses = null;

    using (ChannelFactory<ICustomPeerResolverChannel> factory =
                new ChannelFactory<ICustomPeerResolverChannel>(
                    endpointConfigurationName))
    {
        using (ICustomPeerResolverChannel client =
                        factory.CreateChannel())
        {
            addresses = client.Resolve(
                            meshId,
                            maxAddresses);
        }
    }

    // If addresses couldn't be obtained, return empty collection
    if (addresses == null)
        addresses = new PeerNodeAddress[0];

    return new ReadOnlyCollection<PeerNodeAddress>(addresses);
}

}
```

2. Look at the code of the peer name resolution service in the `PeerResolver.cs` file of the CustomPeerResolverService project. The code there is provided as a sample in the Windows SDK for the .NET Framework 3.0, and reproduced in Listing 17.8. The peer name resolution service defines a custom set of operations that a peer name resolver can use to add a node to a mesh, retrieve the physical network addresses of nodes in the mesh, and to remove a node from the mesh. The service simply maintains a hashtable of the nodes that have registered in a given mesh, and returns information from that hashtable in response to queries for the addresses of the nodes in the mesh. In this implementation, if the number of nodes in the mesh exceeds the number of addresses that a peer name resolver can accommodate, the peer name resolution service returns the addresses of a random subset of nodes. In a more robust implementation, it would be necessary for the peer name resolution service to ensure that the address of every node in the mesh has been provided to at least some of the other nodes.

LISTING 17.8   Peer Name Resolution Service

```
[ServiceContract([...])]
public interface IPeerResolver
{
    [OperationContract]
    int Register(string meshId, PeerNodeAddress nodeAddresses);
    [OperationContract]
    void Unregister(int registrationId);
    [OperationContract]
    void Update(int registrationId, PeerNodeAddress updatedNodeAddress);
    [OperationContract]
    PeerNodeAddress[] Resolve(string meshId, int maxAddresses);
}

[ServiceBehavior(InstanceContextMode = InstanceContextMode.Single)]
public class CustomPeerResolverService : IPeerResolver
{
    [...]

    static Dictionary<int, Registration>
            registrationTable = new Dictionary<int, Registration>();
    static Dictionary<string, Dictionary<int, PeerNodeAddress>> meshIdTable =
            new Dictionary<string, Dictionary<int, PeerNodeAddress>>();
    static int nextRegistrationId = 0;

    [...]

    public int Register(string meshId, PeerNodeAddress nodeAddress)
    {
```

17

LISTING 17.8   Continued

```
        bool newMeshId = false;
        int registrationId;
        Registration registration = new Registration(meshId, nodeAddress);

        lock (registrationTable)
        {
            registrationId = nextRegistrationId++;
            lock (meshIdTable)
            {
                Dictionary<int, PeerNodeAddress> addresses;
                if (!meshIdTable.TryGetValue(meshId, out addresses))
                {
                    newMeshId = true;
                    addresses = new Dictionary<int, PeerNodeAddress>();
                    meshIdTable[meshId] = addresses;
                }
                addresses[registrationId] = nodeAddress;

                registrationTable[registrationId] =
                                    new Registration(meshId, nodeAddress);

            }
        }

        return registrationId;
    }

    public void Unregister(int registrationId)
    {
        [...]

        registration = registrationTable[registrationId];
        registrationTable.Remove(registrationId);

        [...]
    }

    [...]

    public PeerNodeAddress[] Resolve(string meshId, int maxAddresses)
    {
        Console.WriteLine("Resolving the addresses of the mesh {0}.", meshId);

        [...]
```

LISTING 17.8   Continued

```
    PeerNodeAddress [] copyOfAddresses;
    lock (meshIdTable)
    {
        Dictionary<int, PeerNodeAddress> addresses;

        if (meshIdTable.TryGetValue(meshId, out addresses))
        {
            copyOfAddresses = new PeerNodeAddress[addresses.Count];
            addresses.Values.CopyTo(copyOfAddresses, 0);
        }
        else
            copyOfAddresses = new PeerNodeAddress[0];
    }

    if (copyOfAddresses.Length <= maxAddresses)
    {
        return copyOfAddresses;
    }
    else
    {
        List<int> indices = new List<int>(maxAddresses);
        while (indices.Count < maxAddresses)
        {
            int listIndex =
                this.random.Next() % copyOfAddresses.Length;
            if (!indices.Contains(listIndex))
                indices.Add(listIndex);
        }
        PeerNodeAddress[] randomAddresses =
                        new PeerNodeAddress[maxAddresses];
        for (int i = 0; i < randomAddresses.Length; i++)
            randomAddresses[i] = copyOfAddresses[indices[i]];
        return randomAddresses;
    }
}

[...]
}
```

17

Seeing Peer Channel Work

Follow these steps to witness Peer Channel at work in the classroom quiz solution:

1. Right-click on the CustomPeerResolverService project and choose Debug, Start New Instance from the context menu. A console for the CustomPeerResolverService application should open.

2. Wait until output in the console for the CustomPeerResolverService application indicates that the custom peer resolver service is ready, and then right-click on the Teacher project and choose Debug, Start New Instance from the context menu. The teacher's application should appear, as shown in Figure 17.4.

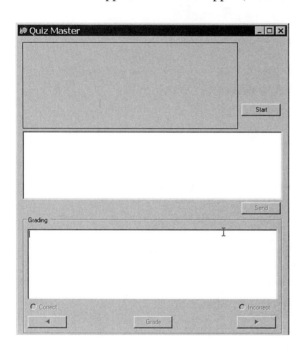

FIGURE 17.4   Teacher's application.

3. Notice the output in the console of the CustomPeerResolverService application. It shows that as the teacher's application started, it registered itself in the mesh, and retrieved the addresses of the other nodes in the mesh.

4. Wait for a few moments, continuing to watch the output in the console of the CustomPeerResolverService application. Soon, the teacher's application will be seen querying the addresses of the other nodes in the mesh once again as Peer Channel keeps its record of the other nodes in the mesh up to date.

5. Right-click on the Child project in the Visual Studio Solution Explorer, and choose Debug, Start New Instance from the context menu. The pupil's application should appear, as shown in Figure 17.5.

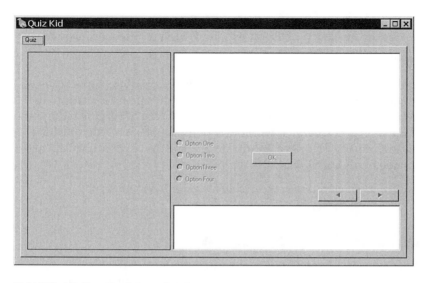

FIGURE 17.5   Pupils' application.

6. Look again at the output in the console of the CustomPeerResolverService application. As the pupil's application started, it registered itself in the mesh, and retrieved the addresses of the other nodes in the mesh.

7. Switch back to the main form of the teacher's application. At the top of that form, there should be the picture of a pupil transmitted by the pupil's application as that application started, as shown previously in Figure 17.1.

8. Click on the Start button on the main form of the teacher's application, and switch to the main form of the pupil's application. The pupil's application should now have received a quiz question from the teacher's application. In fact, if one were to use the buttons labeled with arrows to navigate forward and backward through the quiz questions, one should find that several quiz questions have been received by the pupil's application.

9. Examine the output in the console of the CustomPeerResolverService application. When the teacher's application sent the quiz questions to the other nodes in the mesh, there was no exchange with the peer name resolution service. That indicates that when a peer channel node sends a message, the message is propagated among the nodes via the connections that each node already has with some of the other nodes in the mesh. The nodes do not query for the addresses in the mesh each time they send a message, and the messages themselves do not go via the peer name resolution service.

10. Select an answer for any one of the questions, and click on the OK button.

11. Switch back to the teacher's application, and, in the Grading section, the response chosen in the pupil's application should be shown in the teacher's application.

12. Choose whether the answer is correct, and click on the Grade button.

13. Switch to the pupil's application, and a check mark or a cross will have appeared to signify whether the answer to the question was judged to be correct or incorrect.

14. Close the teacher's application.

15. Look at the output in the console of the CustomPeerResolverService application. As the only two nodes in the mesh, the pupil's application and the teacher's application were maintaining a TCP connection between themselves. When the teacher's application shut down, Peer Channel, within the pupil's application, detected the loss of that connection, and requested an update of the nodes currently in the mesh from the peer name resolution service.

16. Choose Debug, Stop Debugging from the Visual Studio 2005 menus.

Peer Channel and People Near Me

People Near Me is the name of a new technology incorporated in the Windows Vista operating system (Smith 2006) that provides a user-friendly way of managing Windows Peer-to-Peer Networking meshes. So, users of the Vista operating system will be able to invite one another to participate in a mesh via an ad hoc peer-to-peer network. The technology incorporates an unmanaged API by which applications can register themselves to exchange data with other nodes in meshes created using People Near Me.

Summary

The Windows Communication Foundation's Peer Channel makes it easy to use the facilities of the Windows Peer-to-Peer Networking infrastructure to construct applications involving the exchange of structured data among peers. Peer Channel applications, like any Windows Communication Foundation application, are defined by an address, a binding, and a contract. The addresses must have net.p2p as the scheme. The binding is the NetPeerTcpBinding. The contracts must be defined with themselves as their callback contracts. On Windows XP SP2, and other operating systems with the Windows Peer-to-Peer Networking infrastructure, peer name resolution can be left to that infrastructure. On other operating systems, such as Windows Server 2003, it is necessary to provide a custom peer name resolver that will typically work together with a peer name resolution service.

References

Smith, Justin. 2006. "Peer to Peer: Harness the Power of P2P Communication in Windows Vista and WCF." *MSDN Magazine* (October).

Tulloch, Mitch and Ingrid Tulloch. 2002. *Microsoft Encyclopedia of Networking*. Redmond, WA: Microsoft.

CHAPTER 18

Representational State Transfer and Plain XML Services

Introduction

This chapter shows how the Windows Communication Foundation can be used to build and use Representational State Transfer services and also services that communicate with XML files, rather than SOAP messages. A good example of a Representational State Transfer service that provides XML files rather than SOAP messages to its clients is a Really Simple Syndication (RSS) server, and that is indeed what this chapter shows how to build.

Representational State Transfer

Representational State Transfer, commonly referred to as *REST*, is sometimes misrepresented, as it is by Paul Prescod (2002) as a "new model for [W]eb services construction." Actually, it is an architectural pattern that was first formally described by Dr. Roy Fielding in his 2000 Ph.D. dissertation at the University of California at Irvine (Fielding 2000). Dr. Fielding is a co-author, along with Sir Timothy Berners-Lee, of many of the core specifications of the World Wide Web, and a co-founder of the Apache Foundation. In his dissertation, he was attempting to describe the architecture of an application for using the World Wide Web, and, as he himself points out, "the most common example [of such an application] is a Web browser" (Fielding 2000). So, Dr. Fielding was not proposing a way of building web services; he was providing a formal description of the architecture of a web browser.

What is the architecture of a web browser, according to Fielding? There are two fundamental elements that he highlights in his analysis.

First, a web browser retrieves representations of content:

> REST components perform actions on a resource by using a representation to capture the current or intended state of that resource and transferring that representation between components. A representation is a sequence of bytes, plus representation metadata to describe those bytes. ... The data format of a representation is known as a media type (Fielding 2000).

In other words, what a web browser requests from a server is some content that the server has, presented in some format. If that observation seems trivial that might be because its significance is in the behavior that it implicitly excludes. A web browser does not, for example, send input data to the server that the server is expected to perform some operations on and send back. The significant transfer of data is in one direction, from the server to the browser, and the data that is transferred is some representation of content on the server that the web browser knows how to render to the user.

The second fundamental element of the architecture of a web browser that Fielding identifies is that "each request from client to server must contain all of the information necessary to understand the request, and cannot take advantage of any stored context on the server. Session state is therefore kept entirely on the client" (Fielding 2000). Although the data transferred from the server determines the state of the web browser—its cache, its history, and the links it has to new data—the state of the server is unaffected by the exchange, and the content requested by the web browser remains as it was.

Thus, the term *Representational State Transfer* describes an architecture of an application with a client that behaves like a like a web browser does. Such a client requests representations of content from a server, and provides, in its requests, all the state information that the server might require to satisfy them.

REST Services

A *REST service* is one that responds to an HTTP request with a plain text document. The request method together with the query string determines the content of the response document.

REST Services and Plain XML

A natural format for the plain text documents provided by web services is XML. Typically, those XML documents are not in the SOAP format. The term *Plain Old XML* or *POX* is sometimes used to refer to XML messages that are not in the SOAP format (Box 2005, Wikipedia 2005).

The Virtues and Limitations of REST Services

A common notion is that a REST service that provides POX responses is simpler than a SOAP service. "Any developer can figure out how to create and modify a URI to access different Web resources. SOAP, on the other hand, requires specific knowledge of a new XML specification, and most developers will need a SOAP toolkit to form requests and parse the results" (Asaravala, 2002). That perceived simplicity is sometimes put forward as a justification for building a REST service rather than a SOAP service.

In practice, though, building a REST POX service is not simpler than building a SOAP service. It is true that the specifications pertaining to a REST POX service are merely the specifications for HTTP and XML, whereas those pertaining to SOAP services have become quite voluminous. Furthermore, the view has been expressed, most notoriously and amusingly by Tim Bray, that the specifications for SOAP services are "bloated, opaque, and insanely complex" (Bray 2004). Yet, because good tools for building SOAP services are so ubiquitous, developers of SOAP services have as little need to read all those specifications as .NET or Java developers have a need to know the assembly languages of the processors on which their applications will be executing. Indeed, precisely because the SOAP specifications include a metadata specification—the WSDL specification—SOAP toolkits can download descriptions of services and generate the code required for communicating with them. The only way of describing how to use a REST POX service is with prose and samples. On the other hand, the need for tools arguably creates a dependency on "large software vendors or integrators" (Wikipedia 2006).

More important, though, is that REST POX services and SOAP services should not be seen as two alternative ways of implementing the same solution, because, in fact, REST POX services are clearly suited to certain scenarios for which SOAP services really are not, and the other way around. Specifically, REST POX services are, not surprisingly, ideal for the kind of solutions that Fielding (2000) described in articulating the REST pattern in his dissertations: solutions in which the client is simply requesting a copy of some content to be transferred to the service, as opposed to solutions in which the client is relying on the service to process data provided by the client. By contrast, using SOAP simply as a container for data is not only overkill, but positively unsuitable in cases where larger quantities of data are being requested. That is evident from there having been several specifications for how to supply large amounts of binary data with SOAP messages, the most recent being the specification for MTOM, and none of those specifications has been widely implemented yet. Sanjiva Weerawarana, Francisco Curbera, Frank Leymann, Tony Storey, and Donald F. Ferguson share this view of when to use REST POX services and when to use SOAP services:

> From an architectural perspective, it is not "either REST or Web services." Both technologies have areas of applicability. As a rule of thumb, REST is preferable in problem domains that are query intense or that require exchange of large grain chunks of data. SOA in general and Web service technology [...] in particular is preferable in areas that require asynchrony and various qualities of services. [...] You can even mix both architectural styles in a pure Web environment (Weerawarana and others 2005, 57).

18

Building REST POX Services with the Windows Communication Foundation

The Windows Communication Foundation Service Model is a language for describing the solution to any kind of software communication problem. It can certainly be used to describe a REST POX service.

Remember that in the language of the Service Model, a piece of software that responds to communications over a network is a service, a service has one or more endpoints to which communications can be directed, and an endpoint consists of an address, a binding, and a contract.

The Address of a REST POX Service Endpoint

In describing a REST POX service in the language of the Windows Communication Foundation Service Model, you must specify an HTTP address. As indicated previously, a REST service responds to HTTP requests.

```
<services>
     <service
          name="MyRESTPOXService"
          <host>
               <baseAddresses>
                  <add baseAddress="http://localhost:8000/Derivatives/"/>
               </baseAddresses>
          </host>
          [...]
     </service>
<services>
```

The Binding of a REST POX Service Endpoint

The binding for a service specifies the protocols to be used for communication. A protocol for encoding messages and a protocol for transporting messages must be identified.

A POX service is one that responds with plain text XML messages with no SOAP wrappers. To select that kind of encoding for messages in a Windows Communication Foundation, you can write

```
<customBinding>
  <binding name="PlainXMLRepresentationalStateTransferBinding">
    <textMessageEncoding messageVersion="None"/>
    [...]
  </binding>
</customBinding>
```

Here, the expression, `messageVersion="None"` signifies that no version of SOAP is to be used.

Because a REST service responds to HTTP requests, the transport protocol selected by the binding must be HTTP. Thus, the complete definition of the binding for a REST POX service would look like this:

```
<customBinding>
  <binding name="PlainXMLRepresentationalStateTransferBinding">
    <textMessageEncoding messageVersion="None"/>
    <httpTransport/>
  </binding>
</customBinding>
```

The Contract of a REST POX Service Endpoint

SOAP provides a standard way of expressing the invocation of an operation in XML—of identifying the operation to be invoked, and the parameter values to be passed to it. So, given an inbound SOAP message, the Windows Communication Foundation can determine the operation to which the message refers, and it can deserialize the payload of the message into the values of the parameters that are to be passed to the method that implements the operation.

There is no way of identifying a particular operation to be invoked from a POX message, though, and no way of identifying the values for particular parameters of an operation from among its content. A POX message is simply any XML document—one cannot assume that it contains any reference to an operation to be invoked or parameter values to be passed. Hence, the contract for any endpoint of a POX service must always be defined in such a way as to signify that all requests to an endpoint are to be processed by the same operation, and that inbound messages are to be passed to the method by which the operation is implemented in their entirety, without being deserialized into parameters. Such a contract looks like this:

```
[ServiceContract]
public interface IPOXService
{
    [OperationContract(Action = "*",ReplyAction="*")]
    Message Resource(Message input);
}
```

Here, `Action="*"` signifies that the operation called `Resource` is the default operation of the endpoint—the operation to which all messages are to be passed if the message cannot be matched to any other operation. Because POX messages cannot be matched to operations, all POX messages would indeed get passed to the default operation. The expression `ReplyAction="*"` signifies that response messages are not to incorporate addresses because the standard ways of incorporating addresses into SOAP messages would not apply to POX messages. The input to the operation is specified as being of the `System.ServiceModel.Channels.Message` type signifying that any inbound message is to be passed to the operation as a single parameter, there being no way of deserializing a POX message into separate parameters.

Implementation

Remember that a REST service can determine how it should respond to a client based on the HTTP request method and the query string. This code shows how, in implementing a REST POX service, one can extract the HTTP request method and the query string from an inbound message:

```
Message IReallySimpleSyndication.Resource(Message input)
{
    HttpRequestMessageProperty httpRequestProperty
        = (HttpRequestMessageProperty)
            input.Properties[HttpRequestMessageProperty.Name];

        string method = httpRequestProperty.Method;
        string query = httpRequestProperty.QueryString;

        switch(method)
        {
            case "GET":
                    [...]
                    break;
            case "POST":
                    [...]
                    break;
            case "PUT":
                    [...]
                    break;
            case "DELETE":
                    [...]
                    break;
            default:
                    [...]
        }
}
```

A Sample Application

Really Simple Syndication aggregation is a common, and ideal, application of REST and POX. The aggregating application retrieves data via an HTTP GET method, which it is able to display and manipulate because the data conforms to a known RSS XML format. Users of RSS aggregators benefit by receiving a feed of information from the World Wide Web, rather than having to expend effort to retrieve information through browsing. RSS aggregation has already dramatically democratized and increased the flow of information and opinion to private individuals, and it is poised for application to the burgeoning problem of knowledge management within organizations.

To provide an RSS feed using a REST POX service built with the Windows Communication Foundation, follow these steps:

1. Open Microsoft Visual Studio 2005, choose File, New, Project from the menus, and create a C# Console Application project called RESTPOXService in the folder `C:\WCFHandsOn\RESTPOX`.

2. Choose Project, Add Reference from the Visual Studio 2005 menus, and add references to the `System.ServiceModel` assembly and the `System.Runtime.Serialization` assemblies, two of the core assemblies of the Windows Communication Foundation.

3. Add using statements for the `System.IO`, `System.ServiceModel`, `System.ServiceModel.Channels`, and `System.Xml` namespaces to the list of using statements in the `Program.cs` file of the RESTPOXService project:

```
using System;
using System.Collections.Generic;
using System.IO;
using System.ServiceModel;
using System.ServiceModel.Channels;
using System.Text;
using System.Xml;
```

4. Add this definition of the arbitrarily named `IReallySimpleSyndication` service contract to the `RESTPOXService` namespace in the `Program.cs` file of the RESTPOXService project:

```
namespace RESTPOXService
{
    [ServiceContract]
    public interface IReallySimpleSyndication
    {
        [OperationContract(Action = "*", ReplyAction = "*")]
        Message Resource(Message input);
    }

    class Program
    {
        static void Main(string[] args)
        {
        }
    }
}
```

This contract conforms to the pattern for REST POX service contracts described earlier in this chapter.

5. Add the implementation of `IReallySimpleSyndication` service contract shown in Listing 18.1 to the `RESTPOXService` namespace in the `Program.cs file`. The code for the service obtains the HTTP method and the query string from the request and uses those to contact the service. Specifically, in response to HTTP GET requests, the service uses the query string to identify a file of RSS that is being requested, incorporates that file into the body of `System.ServiceModel.Channels.Message` object, and returns that object in response to the request. The version specified for the `System.ServiceModel.Channels.Message` is `System.ServiceModel.Channels.MessageVersion.None`, signifying that the object represents, not any kind of a SOAP message, but a POX message instead.

LISTING 18.1   A Really Simple Syndication Service

```
[ServiceBehavior(
    InstanceContextMode = InstanceContextMode.Single,
    ConcurrencyMode=ConcurrencyMode.Multiple)]
public class ReallySimpleSyndicationServer : IReallySimpleSyndication
{

    Message IReallySimpleSyndication.Resource(Message input)
    {
        HttpRequestMessageProperty httpRequestProperty
            = (HttpRequestMessageProperty)
            input.Properties[HttpRequestMessageProperty.Name];
        string query = httpRequestProperty.QueryString;
        string fileName = string.Format("{0}.xml", query);
        switch (httpRequestProperty.Method)
        {
            case "GET":
                Message message = null;
                if (File.Exists(fileName))
                {
                    XmlDocument document = new XmlDocument();
                    document.Load(fileName);

                    message = Message.CreateMessage(
                        MessageVersion.None,
                        "*",
                        new XmlNodeReader(document.DocumentElement));

                }
                else
                {
                    message = Message.CreateMessage(
```

LISTING 18.1   Continued

```
                            MessageVersion.None,
                            "*");
                }

                return message;

            default:
                return Message.CreateMessage(
                    MessageVersion.None, "*");

        }

    }
}
```

6. Add this code for hosting the service to the `Main()` method of the `Program` class in the `Program.cs` file of the `RESTPOXService` project:

```
class Program
{
    static void Main(string[] args)
    {
        using (ServiceHost host =
                    new ServiceHost(typeof(ReallySimpleSyndicationServer)))
        {
            host.Open();
            Console.WriteLine("The service is ready.");

            Console.ReadKey(true);
            host.Close();
        }
    }
}
```

7. Choose Project, Add New Item from the Visual Studio 2005 menus, and add an application configuration file named `App.config` to the `RESTPOXService` project.

8. Modify the contents of the `App.config` file to conform to Listing 18.2. The configuration shown in that listing specifies an HTTP address for the service because REST POX services like the one being built respond to HTTP requests. A custom binding with the arbitrary name `RESTPOXBinding` specifies HTTP as the transport protocol for the same reason. The encoding protocol specified by the binding

```
<textMessageEncoding messageVersion="None"/>
```

18

indicates that the service's responses are to be encoded as POX: text XML with no SOAP message envelope.

LISTING 18.2   REST POX Service Configuration

```xml
<?xml version="1.0" encoding="utf-8" ?>
<configuration>
  <system.serviceModel>
    <services>
      <service name=
        "RESTPOXService.ReallySimpleSyndicationServer">
        <host>
          <baseAddresses>
            <add baseAddress="http://localhost:8888/"/>
          </baseAddresses>
        </host>
        <endpoint
          address="Service"
          binding="customBinding"
          bindingConfiguration="RESTPOXBinding"
          contract=
            "RESTPOXService.IReallySimpleSyndication"/>
      </service>
    </services>
    <bindings>
      <customBinding>
        <binding name="RESTPOXBinding">
          <textMessageEncoding messageVersion="None"/>
          <httpTransport/>
        </binding>
      </customBinding>
    </bindings>
  </system.serviceModel>
</configuration>
```

To start the REST POX service, execute these two steps:

1. Choose Build, Build Solution from the Visual Studio 2005 menus.

2. Choose Debug, Start Debugging from the Visual Studio 2005 menus to start the REST POX RSS service.

Follow these next few steps to provide some RSS for the service to serve up in response to requests:

1. Open any two pages of RSS on the World Wide Web in a web browser. One particularly useful one can be found at http://www.identityblog.com/?feed=rss2. Another can be found at http://www.joelonsoftware.com/rss.xml.

2. Save the first page of RSS to a file named `0.xml` in the same folder as the service executable, which should be in
`C:\WCFHandsOn\RESTPOX\RESTPOXService\bin\Debug`.

3. Save the second page of RSS to a file named `1.xml` in the same folder.

To use the REST POX service, do as follows:

1. Point the browser at the REST POX RSS service and request RSS. Do so first by pointing the browser at `http://localhost:8888/Service?0`, and then at `http://localhost:8888/Service?1`. The pages of RSS should appear in the browser, retrieved from REST POX RSS service. In these uniform resource locators, `http://localhost:8888` is the base address of the REST POX RSS service, and `Service` is the address of its sole endpoint. The queries, `0` and `1`, serve to identify the resources being requested from the service.

2. Choose Debug, Stop Debugging from the Visual Studio 2005 menus.

It is likely that the next release of the Windows Communication Foundation that will ship with the next version of Visual Studio will provide enhanced support for the specific case of REST POX services functioning as RSS and Atom syndicators. In the steps for building a simple RSS syndicator, no code was written to construct or manipulate the RSS feed itself. The possible additions to the Windows Communication Foundation object model will support doing just that, by providing classes for working with feeds and built-in options for encoding the feed content as either RSS or ATOM.

Summary

The Windows Communication Foundation supports plain XML REST services in addition to services that communicate using SOAP messages. This chapter showed how to build REST POX services, and argued that those are suitable to cases where clients are simply requesting content, especially large amounts of content, from a service.

References

Asaravala, Amit. 2002. *Giving SOAP a REST*. http://www.devx.com/DevX/Article/8155. Accessed October 21, 2006.

Box, Don. 2005. *POX Enters the Lexicon*. http://pluralsight.com/blogs/dbox/archive/2005/02/10/5764.aspx. Accessed January 7, 2006.

Bray, Tim. 2004. *The Loyal WS-Opposition.* http://www.tbray.org/ongoing/When/200x/2004/09/18/WS-Oppo. Accessed October 26, 2006.

Fielding, Roy Thomas. 2000. Architectural Styles and the Design of Network-based Software Architectures. Ph.D. diss., University of California, Irvine. http://www.ics.uci.edu/~fielding/pubs/dissertation/top.htm. Accessed January 7, 2006.

Prescod, Paul. 2002. *REST and the Real World.* http://webservices.xml.com/pub/a/ws/2002/02/20/rest.html. Accessed January 7, 2006.

Wikipedia. 2005. S.v. "POX." http://en.wikipedia.org/wiki/POX. Accessed January 7, 2006.

Wikipedia. 2006. S.v. "Web service." http://en.wikipedia.org/wiki/Web_Services#Criticisms. Accessed October 26, 2006.

Weerawarana, Sanjiva, Francisco Curbera, Frank Leymann, Tony Storey, and Donald F. Ferguson. 2005. *Web Services Platform Architecture: SOAP, WSDL, WS-Policy, WS-Addressing, WS-BPEL, WS-Reliable Messaging, and More.* Upper Saddle River, NJ: Prentice Hall.

Winer, Dave. 2005. *RSS 2.0 Specification.* http://blogs.law.harvard.edu/tech/rss. Accessed January 7, 2006.

PART VII

The Lifecycle of Windows Communication Foundation Applications

IN THIS PART

Manageability

Introduction

For any software to be an asset that the system administrators can manage effectively—can confirm that it is in a healthy state and take effective remedial action if it is not—the software must provide at least four layers of management facilities.

The first layer is instrumentation, which consists of data points and control points. Data points provide information about the state of the software, whereas control points allow one to make adjustments to it to apply remedies for problems divined from the data points.

The second layer consists of tools for reading from the data points and for manipulating the control points. The third layer provides a management model. Given sufficient instrumentation and good tools for using it, a management model provides the system administrators with knowledge of how to use the tools to maintain the health of the system. That is, how to determine whether the system is in a healthy state or an unhealthy one, what actions to take to maintain the health of the system, and how to remedy its maladies.

The fourth layer of management facilities an application should provide consists of a control panel integrated into the administrator's preferred integrated management environment—an environment such as IBM's Tivoli Software, Hewlett-Packard's HP OpenView, or Microsoft Operations Manager (MOM). Having such a control panel integrated into a familiar integrated management environment not only serves to automate the processes described in the management model, but also to translate the elements of the management model that are specific to an application into the standard terms of the integrated management environment.

There is a comprehensive set of instrumentation and tooling for the Windows Communication Foundation. The chapter describes those facilities in detail, and goes on to show how developers can use those instruments and tools as the foundation of management models specific to their own applications, as well as how to incorporate those management models into a control panel within an integrated management environment.

Instrumentation and Tools

The Windows Communication Foundation provides the following instrumentation:

- A configuration system for deployment and for post-deployment control and tuning
- Security event logging
- Message logging
- The tracing of internal activities, and of sequences of activities across nodes
- Performance counters for key operational, security, reliability, and transaction statistics for services, for the various endpoints of a service, for the individual operations of an endpoint
- A Windows Management Instrumentation (WMI) provider for querying and modifying the properties of running systems

Familiar tools already exist for accessing and using some of this instrumentation. For example, the Windows operating system provides a Performance Monitor by which the new performance counters of the Windows Communication Foundation can be examined. In a few cases, new tools had to be provided. Table 19.1 identifies the tools, new and familiar, available for monitoring and controlling the Windows Communication Foundation through its instrumentation.

TABLE 19.1   Management Tools

Instrumentation	Tools
Configuration System	New Windows Communication Foundation Service Configuration Editor
Security Event Logging	Familiar Windows Event Viewer
Message Logging	New Windows Communication Foundation Service Trace Viewer
Activity Tracing	New Windows Communication Foundation Service Trace Viewer
Performance Counters	Familiar Windows Performance Monitor
WMI Provider	Many familiar tools including WMI CIM Studio, ScriptOMatic, and Windows PowerShell

To prepare for the introduction to the Windows Communication Foundation's instrumentation and tooling provided in this chapter, follow these steps:

1. Copy the code associated with this chapter downloaded from http://www.crypt-maker.com/WindowsCommunicationFoundationUnleashed to the folder `C:\WCFHandsOn`. The code is all in a folder called `Management`, which has three subfolders, one called `CompletedSolution`, another called `StartingPoint`, and a third one called `Logs`.

2. Open the solution `C:\WCFHandsOn\Management\StartingPoint\TradingService.sln`.

The solution is for building a derivatives trading system. Derivatives were introduced in Chapter 2, "The Fundamentals," and the derivatives trading system manages the risk in buying them.

The TradingService project in the solution builds a trading service for pricing and purchasing derivatives. The TradingServiceHost project constructs the host for that service.

The TradeRecordingService project builds a trade-recording service that the trading service uses to execute the purchase of derivatives. The TradeRecordingServiceHost project constructs the host of the recording service.

The client project in the solution is for building a risk management system. That risk management system uses the trading service to price and execute two derivatives purchases at a time: a primary purchase, and another one that is intended as a hedge against the possibility of losses on the first purchase. Depending on the difference in the prices of the primary and hedge purchases, the risk management system will commit either to both purchases together or to neither. If the risk management system chooses not to commit to the purchases, the records of those purchases in the recording service are erased; otherwise, those records are kept.

The Configuration System and the Configuration Editor

At the management instrumentation layer, the Windows Communication Foundation provides a configuration system by which administrators can control the endpoints of Windows Communication Foundation applications. The Service Configuration Editor is provided as a tool for them to use in doing so.

The Configuration System

Windows Communication Foundation services are defined by an address that specifies where they are located, a binding that specifies how to communicate with them, and a contract that specifies what they can do. The internal operations of Windows Communication Foundation services and clients can be controlled through properties called *behaviors*. Although one can write code to specify the addresses, bindings, and contracts of services, and to modify the behaviors of services and clients, the Windows Communication Foundation allows one to instead specify addresses, bindings, and contracts and to modify behaviors in configuration files.

19

The Windows Communication Foundation's configuration system is made fully programmable via the classes of the `System.ServiceModel.Configuration` namespace. Those classes allow developers to create their own tools for interrogating and modifying the configurations of Windows Communication Foundation applications. The code in Listing 19.1 is for a method that adds the Windows Communication Foundation endpoint to a specified .NET application configuration file.

LISTING 19.1   Writing a Windows Communication Foundation Configuration

```
void WriteConfiguration(string configurationFilePath)
{
    ServiceEndpointElement endpointElement =
        new ServiceEndpointElement(
            new Uri(@"Calculator",UriKind.Relative),
            @"DerivativesCalculator.IDerivativesCalculator");
    endpointElement.Binding = @"netTcpBinding";

    ServiceElement serviceElement =
        new ServiceElement(
@"DerivativesCalculator.DerivativesCalculatorServiceType");
    serviceElement.Endpoints.Add(endpointElement);

    BaseAddressElement baseAddressElement =
        new BaseAddressElement();
    baseAddressElement.BaseAddress =
        @"net.tcp://localhost:8000/Derivatives/";

    serviceElement.Host.BaseAddresses.Add(baseAddressElement);

    ExeConfigurationFileMap fileMap = new ExeConfigurationFileMap();
    fileMap.ExeConfigFilename =
        configurationFilePath;
    Configuration configuration =
        ConfigurationManager.OpenMappedExeConfiguration(
            fileMap,
            ConfigurationUserLevel.None);

    ServiceModelSectionGroup sectionGroup =
        (ServiceModelSectionGroup)configuration.GetSectionGroup(
            "system.serviceModel");

    ServicesSection servicesSection =
        (ServicesSection)sectionGroup.Sections["services"];
    servicesSection.Services.Add(serviceElement);

    configuration.Save();
```

LISTING 19.1   Continued

```
    Console.WriteLine("Done");
    Console.ReadKey(true);
}
```

The classes of the Windows Communication Foundation's `System.ServiceModel.Configuration.Namespace` rely on the facilities of the .NET Framework's configuration system for loading and applying configuration data to an application, though, and those facilities have important limitations. In particular, applying configuration data from any given file is not supported, yet less being able to apply configuration data in a database.

Of course, the primary benefit of the Windows Communication Foundation's configuration system is not that it allows developers to read and write the configuration of Windows Communication Foundation applications programmatically. The primary benefit is that it allows system administrators to control how services behave without requiring programming modifications. Indeed, using configuration files to specify addresses, bindings, and contracts is preferred to using code.

The Windows Communication Foundation's configuration system simply extends that of Microsoft .NET. Therefore, it should be familiar to any administrator of .NET applications. The language of the Windows Communication Foundation's configuration system is defined in the file `\Program Files\Microsoft Visual Studio 8\Xml\Schemas\DotNetConfig.xsd`, on the disc where Visual Studio 2005 resides after the .NET Framework 3 Development Tools have been installed.

The Service Configuration Editor

The Windows Communication Foundation provides the Service Configuration Editor to ease, and give guidance for, the task of editing configuration files. The Service Configuration Editor is `SvcConfigEditor.exe`. It should be found in the folder `\Program Files\Microsoft SDKs\Windows\v1.0\Bin`, assuming a complete and normal installation of the Microsoft Windows SDK for the .NET Framework 2.0. If the .NET Framework 3.0 Development Tools have also been installed, the Service Configuration Editor is also accessible right from within Visual Studio.

Configuring the Trade Recording Service with the Configuration Editor

Recall that the trade-recording service of the trading service solution is a service for recording the purchase of derivatives. That service is not currently in a working state. To confirm that, do the following:

1. Right-click on the TradeRecordingServiceHost project of the trading service solution in Visual Studio 2005, and choose Debug, Start New Instance from the context menu. An exception should be thrown with this error message:

Service 'Fabrikam.TradeRecorder' has zero application (non-infrastruc-
ture) endpoints. This might be because no configuration file was found
for your application, or because no service element matching the service
name could be found in the configuration file, or because no endpoints
were defined in the service element.

The message is quite accurate: The service cannot start because no endpoints have
been defined for it. There is indeed no configuration file with endpoint definitions.

2. Choose Debug, Stop debugging from the Visual Studio 2005 menus to terminate the
   application.

Follow these steps to use the Configuration Editor to configure an endpoint for the trade
recording service:

1. Right-click on the TradeRecordingServiceHost project and choose Add, New Item
   from the context menu, and proceed to add an application configuration file called
   App.config to the project.

2. Right-click on the new App.config file and choose Edit WCF Configuration from
   the context menu. The Service Configuration Editor will open, as shown in
   Figure 19.1.

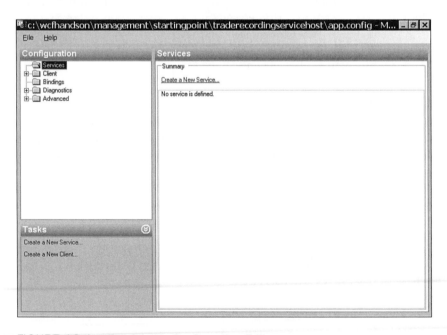

FIGURE 19.1   The Service Configuration Editor.

3. Click on the Create a New Service link in the right pane to start the New Service
   Element Wizard.

4. The first step in the wizard is to identify the service type of the service. To do that for the trade-recording service, start by clicking on the Browse button to open the Type Browser dialog.

5. In the Type Browser dialog, locate the `TradeRecordingService.dll` assembly in the `bin\debug` subdirectory of the `TradeRecordingServiceHost` project directory.

6. Double-click on that assembly to see a list of the service types defined in that assembly. Select the `Fabrikam.TradeRecordingService` type, and click Open. The Type Browser dialog will close and the New Service Element Wizard will be back in the foreground.

5. Click Next. A list of Windows Communication Foundation service contracts implemented by the `Fabrikam.TradeRecordingService` type is displayed.

6. There is only one such contract, so there is no need, in this case, to select one. Simply click Next.

7. The next dialog asks what mode of communication is to be used, as shown in Figure 19.2. The trade-recording service receives requests via a Microsoft Message Queue, so choose MSMQ from among the options displayed, and click Next.

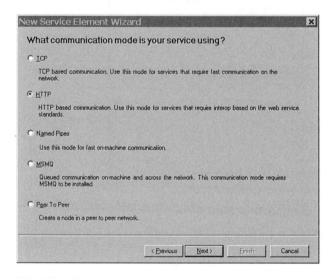

FIGURE 19.2   The communication mode dialog of the New Service Element Wizard.

8. The next dialog is for the New Service Element Wizard to choose between the predefined bindings `NetMsmqBinding` and `LegacyMsmqBinding`. To do so, it asks the user whether Windows Communication Foundation clients for MSMQ clients will be connecting to the service. Select the former option, and click Next.

9. Now the address for the endpoint is to be entered. Enter **net.msmq://localhost/ private/TradeRecording** as the address and click Next.

10. Click Finish on the final screen of the New Service Element Wizard.

11. The binding for the newly defined endpoint will need to be modified slightly to accommodate the possibility of the host system not being attached to a Windows domain. To initiate that modification, click on the link labeled Click to Create opposite the Binding Configuration label on the right pane of the Service Configuration Editor, shown in Figure 19.3. A panel for configuring the NetMsmqBinding opens in the right pane of the Editor, as shown in Figure 19.4.

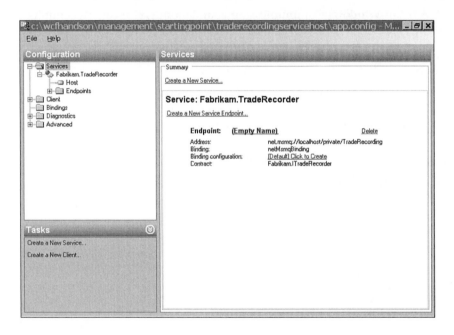

FIGURE 19.3   Service endpoint configuration.

12. Enter **MyMSMQBindingConfiguration** as the name of the binding configuration opposite the Name label in the right pane of the editor.

13. Click on the Security tab.

14. Select None as the mode from the list of security modes opposite the Mode label on the right pane of the editor.

15. Choose File, Save from the Service Configuration Editor menus.

16. Choose File, Exit to close the Service Configuration Editor.

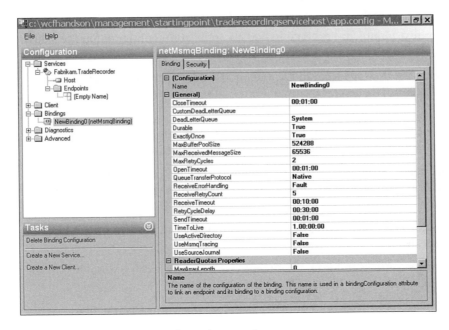

FIGURE 19.4   Binding Configuration panel.

Now that an endpoint has been defined in the configuration of the Trade Recording Service Host, that application should be able to start properly. Confirm that by following these steps:

1. Right-click on the TradeRecordingServiceHost project of the trading service solution in Visual Studio 2005, and choose Debug, Start New Instance from the context menu. A console window for the application should open, and after a few moments, a message should appear confirming that the trade-recording service is available.

2. Choose Debug, Stop Debugging from the Visual Studio 2005 menus to terminate the application.

Configuring a Client Application with the Configuration Editor

The client risk management application communicates with the trading service, which, in turn, uses the trade-recording service to record derivatives purchases. The trading service has an endpoint at the address http://localhost:8000/TradingService. That endpoint uses the Windows Communication Foundation's standard WSHttpBinding. The WSHttpBinding is customized to include information about the state of transactions within messages, and to ensure that the messages are delivered exactly once, and in order. Follow these steps to configure the client risk management application appropriately to communicate with the trading service:

1. Right-click on the Client project within the trading service solution, and choose Build from the context menu.

2. Right-click on the TradeRecordingServiceHost project and choose Add, New Item from the context menu, and proceed to add an application configuration file called App.config to the project.

3. Right-click on the new App.config file and choose Edit WCF Configuration from the context menu. The Service Configuration Editor will open as shown in Figure 19.1.

4. Click on the Create a New Client link on the Tasks panel on the bottom left of the Service Configuration Editor. The New Client Element Wizard opens.

5. On the first dialog, select the option to configure the client manually using the wizard, rather than have the wizard configure the client from the configuration file of the service.

6. The next dialog is for identifying the service contract. Click Browse to open the Type Browser dialog.

7. Use the dialog's controls to locate the Client.exe assembly, which should be in the bin\debug subdirectory of the Client project directory.

8. Double-click on that assembly to display a list of service contracts it defines.

9. Select the Client.ITradingService contract, and click Open, which should serve to close the Type Browser dialog, and bring the New Client Element Wizard back to the foreground.

10. Click Next to proceed to a selection of communication modes.

11. Select HTTP from the list, and click Next.

12. The next screen is for the wizard to choose between the predefined BasicHttpBinding and the predefined WSHttpBinding. It displays that choice to the user as a choice between Basic Web Services Interoperability and Advanced Web Services Interoperability. Opt for the latter, and click Next.

13. Enter **http://localhost:8000/TradingService** as the address on the subsequent dialog, and click Next.

14. Enter **TradingServiceConfiguration** as the name for the client endpoint configuration, and click Next.

15. Click Finish to complete the wizard's steps.

16. The binding for the newly defined endpoint will need to be modified slightly to add the assurance of the messages being delivered exactly once and in order. To initiate that modification, click on the link labeled Click to Create opposite the Binding Configuration label on the right pane of the Service Configuration Editor. A panel for configuring the WSHttpBinding opens in the right pane of the Editor.

17. Enter **MyReliableBindingConfiguration** as the name of the binding configuration opposite the Name label in the right pane of the editor.

18. Scroll down to the `ReliableSession` properties section.

19. Select `True` as the value for the `Enabled` property in that section, as shown in Figure 19.5.

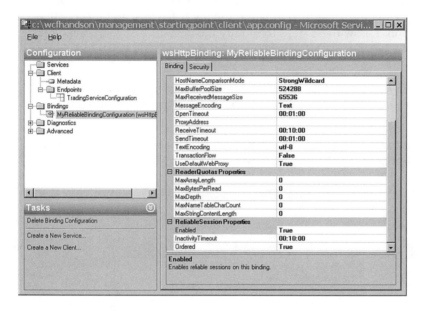

FIGURE 19.5   Enabling a Reliable Session.

20. Choose File, Save from the Service Configuration Editor menus.

21. Choose File, Exit to close the Service Configuration Editor.

Test the newly configured solution by following these steps:

1. Choose Debug, Start Debugging from the Visual Studio 2005 menus.

2. Choose Debug, Start Debugging from the menus.

3. When there is activity in the console application windows of the Trade Recording Service Host and the Trading Service Host applications confirming that the services they host are ready, enter a keystroke into the console application window of the client application.

   After a few moments, activity should start to appear in the console application window of the trading service host, as the client risk management system begins pricing and purchasing a derivative. There might be a pause as the trading service loads the Microsoft Distributed Transactions Coordinator for the first time. Then the pricing and purchasing of primary and hedging derivatives purchases should proceed.

4. Choose Debug, Stop Debugging from the Visual Studio 2005 menus.

Configurable Auditing of Security Events

The Windows Communication Foundation records security events in the Windows event log—a management instrumentation facility that is complemented by the Windows Event Viewer as a tool for examining the entries made in the log. The security auditing facility is one of the Windows Communication Foundation's many behaviors, and it is configurable. To see it in action, follow these steps to modify the default configuration so that not only authentication failures, but also authentication successes will be recorded in the log:

1. Right-click on the App.config file of the TradingServiceHost project and choose Edit WCF Configuration from the context menu. The Service Configuration Editor opens.

2. To proceed to edit a behavior, in the top-left pane, expand the Advanced node of the tree, and select Service Behaviors as shown in Figure 19.6.

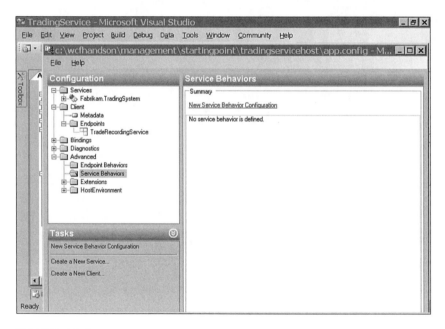

FIGURE 19.6   Preparing to edit service behaviors.

3. Click on the New Service Behavior Configuration link that will have appeared in the right pane.

4. Enter **TradingServiceBehaviors** as the name for a behavior configuration as shown in Figure 19.7.

5. Click on the Add button in the Behavior Element Extension Position section.

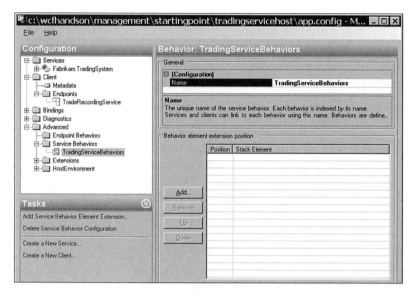

FIGURE 19.7   Naming a behavior configuration.

6. Choose serviceSecurityAudit from the list of behaviors in the Adding Behavior
   Element Extension dialog that appears, and click the Add button. An entry for the
   serviceSecurityAudit behavior should appear in the list of behavior elements as
   shown in Figure 19.8.

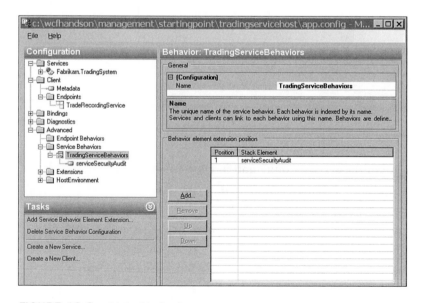

FIGURE 19.8   List of behaviors.

7. Double-click on the entry to be able to modify the properties of the security-auditing behavior.

8. In the property editor for the behavior, select `Security` as the `AuditLogLocation`.

9. Choose `SuccessOrFailure` as the value for the `MessageAuthenticationAuditLevel`.

10. Choose `SuccessOrFailure` as the value for the `ServiceAuthenticationAuditLevel`.

11. Now a behavior configuration has been created that includes the configuration of the security-auditing behavior. That behavior configuration now has to be associated with the trading service. To do so, select `Fabrikam.TradingSystem` under the Services node in the tree in the left pane, and then select the `TradingServiceBehaviors` configuration from the list opposite the `BehaviorConfiguration` label on the right pane, as shown in Figure 19.9.

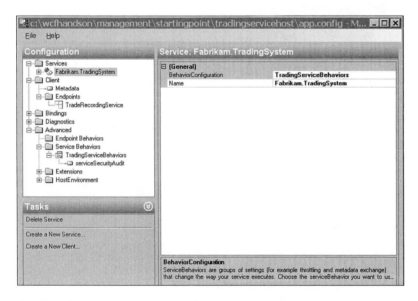

FIGURE 19.9   Associating a behavior configuration with a service.

12. Choose File, Save from the Service Configuration Editor menus.

13. Choose File, Exit to close the Service Configuration Editor.

Follow these steps to see the effect of the new configuration of the security-auditing behavior:

1. In Visual Studio 2005, in the trading service solution, choose Debug, Start Debugging from the menus.

2. When there is activity in the console application windows of the trade recording service host and the trading service host, confirming that the services they host are ready, enter a keystroke into the console application window of the client application.

3. After seeing activity in the console application windows of the trading service host and the client as they price and purchase derivatives, choose Debug, Stop Debugging from the Visual Studio 2005 menus.

4. Open the Windows Event viewer.

5. Refresh the security log.

6. Locate and examine events with the source ServiceModel Audit. Those are the Windows Communication Foundation's security audit events. They should look like the event shown in igure 19.10.

FIGURE 19.10   Windows Communication Foundation security audit event.

Message Logging, Activity Tracing, and the Service Trace Viewer

At the management instrumentation layer, the Windows Communication Foundation applications can be configured to log messages, and to record traces of their activities. Those facilities can assist administrators in diagnosing problems with the applications. The Service Trace Viewer is provided as a tool for them to use in doing so.

Message Logging

Windows Communication Foundation applications can be configured to log incoming and outgoing messages. Messages can be logged not only at the point at which they are transported, but also as they proceed through the channel layer.

The message-logging facility is implemented using the trace-listening mechanism already incorporated in .NET, in the `System.Diagnostics` namespace. A *trace listener* is a class that knows how to output diagnostic information to a particular destination, such as an event log, or a file of a particular format. When particular categories of diagnostic information are directed to a trace listener, the information in that category is dispatched to the destination to which the trace listener sends its output. The same diagnostic information can be recorded in various ways when information is directed to multiple trace listeners.

Message logging is a particular type of diagnostic information that can be sent to a trace listener for recording. By providing message logging via trace listeners, the Windows Communication Foundation not only uses a mechanism with which .NET developers will already be familiar, but also allows developers, enterprises, and other software vendors that might have developed custom trace listeners to use them for logging messages.

To see how to configure Windows Communication Foundation applications to log messages, follow these steps:

1. Right-click on the `App.config` file of the TradingServiceHost project and choose Edit WCF Configuration from the context menu. The Service Configuration Editor opens.

2. Click on the `Diagnostics` node in the tree in the left pane. The right pane should now show links for configuring message logging and other diagnostic facilities, as shown in Figure 19.11.

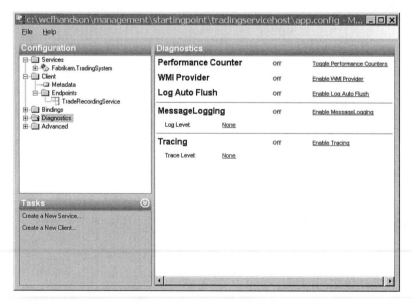

FIGURE 19.11   Diagnostics configuration.

3. Click on the Enable Message Logging link.

4. Click on the ServiceModelMessageLoggingListener link that will have appeared, to configure the trace listener to which logged messages will be directed.

5. In the Listener Settings window, observe that the trace listener will, by default, be writing the logged messages to a file called `app_messages.svclog` in the same folder as the Trading Service Host project.

6. Click OK to close the Listener Settings dialog and return to the Diagnostics Configuration pane.

7. Click the link labeled Malformed, Transport opposite the Log Level label. The Message Logging Settings dialog appears, which allows one to determine which messages will be captured.

8. Selecting Transport Messages on that dialog will mean that messages will be logged as they are sent or received, which would mean that if the messages being exchanged are encrypted, the logged messages will be encrypted. Selecting Service Messages will mean that messages are logged as they pass in or out of the Windows Communication Foundation Service model layer, at which point they would usually no longer be encrypted. Select all the options on the dialog and click OK.

9. Click on the Enable Log Auto Flush link which will ensure that any message log data cached by the trace listener will be flushed to the message log.

10. Choose File, Save from the Service Configuration Editor menus.

11. Choose File, Exit to close the Service Configuration Editor.

To see messages being logged, do the following:

1. In Visual Studio 2005, in the trading service solution, choose Debug, Start Debugging from the menus.

2. When there is activity in the console application windows of the trade recording service host and the trading service host, confirming that the services they host are ready, enter a keystroke into the console application window of the client application.

3. Wait until the console application window of the client application confirms that it is done pricing and purchasing derivatives.

4. Choose Debug, Stop Debugging from the Visuals Studio 2005 menus.

5. Execute the Windows Communication Foundation's Trace Viewer, which is `SvcTraceViewer.exe`. It should be found in the `bin` subdirectory of the installation of folder of the .NET Framework 3 SDK. The Trace Viewer is shown in Figure 19.12.

6. Choose File, Open from the menus, and open the file `app_messages.svclog`, which should be found in the same folder as the TradingServiceHost project file.

7. Select the first entry in the activity list on the left of the Trace Viewer.

19

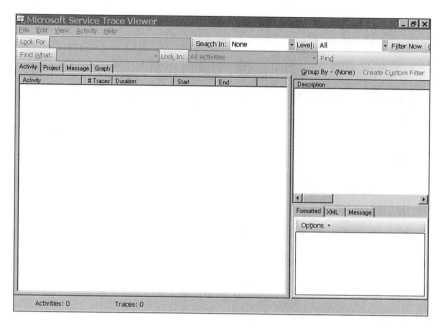

FIGURE 19.12   The Trace Viewer.

8. Select the XML tab on the lower right, and scroll through the entry on that tab. It contains a record of a message, as shown in Figure 19.13.

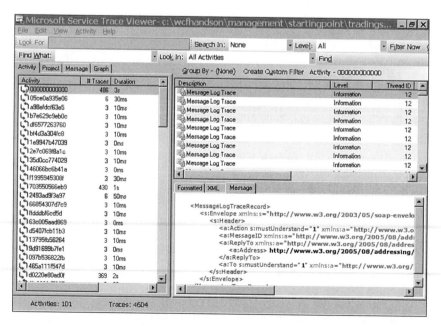

FIGURE 19.13   A logged message.

Activity Tracing

Wikipedia defines a trace as "a detailed record of the steps a computer program executes during its execution, used as an aid in debugging" (Wikipedia 2006). The Windows Communication Foundation generates traces for internal processing milestones, events, exceptions, and warnings. The traces are intended to enable administrators to see how an application is behaving and understand why it might be misbehaving without having to resort to using a debugger. In fact, the members of the Windows Communication Foundation development team are encouraged to diagnose unexpected conditions they encounter using the traces rather than a debugger, and to file a bug report demanding additional traces if the existing traces are not sufficient to allow them to render a diagnosis.

The Microsoft .NET Framework Class Library 2.0 provides an enhanced tracing infrastructure in the form of classes that have been added to the System.Diagnostics namespace, and the Windows Communication Foundation leverages those new classes. The most important of them is the TraceSource class that allows one to generate traces associated with a named source:

```
private static TraceSource source = new TraceSource("ANamedSource");
source.TraceEvent(TraceEventType.Error,1,"Trace error message.");
```

Given a named source of traces, one can configure trace listeners to listen for traces from that particular source:

```
<configuration>
  <system.diagnostics>
    <sources>
      <source name="ANamedSource"
        switchValue="Warning"
        <listeners>
          <add name="AListener"/>
          <remove name="Default"/>
        </listeners>
      </source>
    </sources>
    <sharedListeners>
      <add name="AListener"
        type="System.Diagnostics.TextWriterTraceListener"
        initializeData="myListener.log">
        <filter type="System.Diagnostics.EventTypeFilter"
          initializeData="Error"/>
      </add>
    </sharedListeners>
  </system.diagnostics>
</configuration>
```

19

The name of the source of traces emitted by the Windows Communication Foundation's Service Model is System.ServiceModel. Thus, one might configure a trace listener to listen for traces emitted by the Service Model in this way:

```
<configuration>
  <system.diagnostics>
    <sources>
      <source name="System.ServiceModel"
        switchValue="Verbose"
        <listeners>
          <add name="xml"
            type="System.Diagnostics.XmlWriterTraceListener"
            initializeData="ClientTraces.svclog"
          />
        </listeners>
      </source>
    </sources>
  </system.diagnostics>
</configuration>
```

Trace sources have a Switch property for filtering traces emanating from that source according to their level of importance. Traces emitted by the Windows Communication Foundation can be filtered by six levels of importance, as shown, in descending order, in Table 19.2. Filtering a source for traces with a given level of importance will exclude traces with a lower level of importance and include any traces in which the level of importance is of the specified level or higher.

TABLE 19.2   Windows Communication Foundation Trace Levels

Level	Description
Critical	Traces of catastrophic errors that cause an application to cease functioning
Error	Traces of exceptions
Warning	Traces of conditions that might subsequently cause an exception, such as a limit having been reached or credentials having been rejected
Information	Traces of milestones significant for monitoring and diagnosis
Verbose	Traces of processing milestones interesting to developers for diagnosis and optimization
ActivityTracing	Traces of activity boundaries

The Windows Communication Foundation does not emit traces by default. Activating tracing is easily done using the Configuration Editor:

1. Right-click on the App.config file of the TradingServiceHost project and choose Edit WCF Configuration from the context menu. The Service Configuration Editor opens.

2. Click on the Diagnostics node in the tree in the left pane. The right pane should now show links for configuring message logging and other diagnostic facilities, as shown in Figure 19.11.

3. Click on the Enable Tracing link.

4. Click on the ServiceModelTraceListener link that will have appeared to configure the trace listener to which activity traces will be directed.

5. In the Listener Settings window, observe that the trace listener will, by default, be writing the logged messages to a file called app_tracelog.svclog in the same folder as the Trading Service Host project.

6. Click OK to close the Listener Settings dialog and return to the Diagnostics Configuration pane.

7. Click the link labeled Warning, Activity Tracing, Propagate Activity opposite the Trace Level label. The Tracing Settings dialog appears, which allows one to set the trace level.

8. Choose Verbose from the list of options, and click OK.

9. Choose File, Save from the Service Configuration Editor menus.

10. Choose File, Exit to close the Service Configuration Editor.

After traces have been recorded, they can be examined using the Service Trace Viewer, SvcTraceViewer.exe. An example of what might be seen is displayed in Figure 19.14.

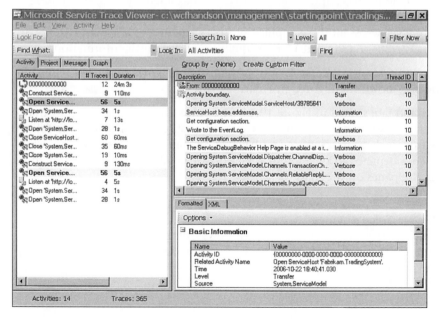

FIGURE 19.14   Viewing traces.

The Trace Viewer

The Windows Communication Foundation's Trace Viewer has already been introduced. As can be seen in Figure 19.14, the Trace Viewer displays a list of activities in a pane on the left, and all the traces pertaining to a selected activity in the pane on the upper right. The lower-right pane shows the details of a particular trace. As shown in Figure 19.13, the Trace Viewer can also be used to view logs of messages.

The most impressive capability of the Trace Viewer, though, is in allowing one to examine the flow of an activity across network nodes. Windows Communication Foundation traces have a globally unique identifier, and whenever a Windows Communication Foundation application is configured to emit traces, the activity identifiers are included in any messages it sends. To see the significance of that, follow these steps:

1. Open the Service Trace Viewer, SvcTraceViewer.exe, in the bin subdirectory of the Windows SDK installation folder.

2. Choose File, Open from the menus.

3. In the File Open dialog, select all the trace files in the Logs subdirectory of the Management folder that contains the code associated with this chapter.

4. Click on the Open button.

5. If the Partial Loading Dialog appears, click OK to dismiss it.

6. A progress bar might appear at the bottom of the Service Trace Viewer. Wait until it disappears and the counts of traces and activities appear. These activities were recorded from all three components of the trading system that has been used as an example throughout this chapter: the client risk management system, the trading service, and the trade-recording service. The total number of traces recorded at the verbose trace level across all three applications over a period of less than two minutes was 72,980—a quite considerable quantity of diagnostic information.

7. Select any activity labeled Process Action in the list of activities in the left pane, such as the one shown highlighted in Figure 19.15.

8. Select the Graph tab, shown in Figure 19.16. The Trace Viewer is able to show transfers of activity between the endpoints of a system! That feature allows one to follow an activity from a client to a service and back. For instance, one can select any step in the sequence depicted in the graphical view to see details of the traces emitted in that step in the panes on the right.

Incorporating Custom Trace Sources

One can direct one's own activity traces to the Windows Communication Foundation's trace listener. By doing so, one can see one's own activity traces included among those in the service Trace Viewer.

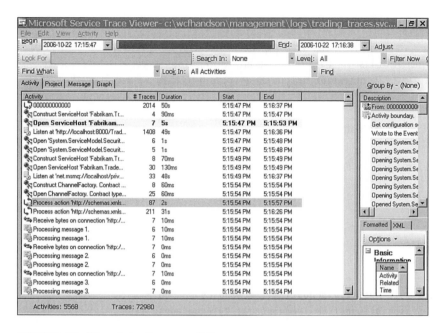

FIGURE 19.15   Selecting an activity.

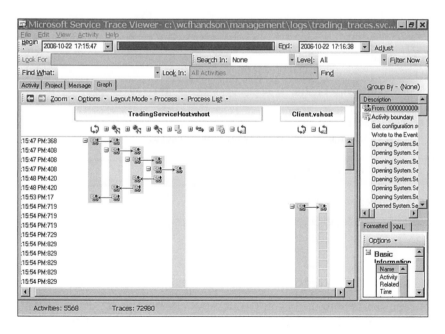

FIGURE 19.16   The Graph tab.

Follow these steps to see how to take advantage of that capability:

1. Open the `Program.cs` file of the Trading Service Host project, and modify the code therein as shown in Listing 19.2. The two additional lines serve to define a trace source with the arbitrary name, `MyTraceSource`, and to emit a trace from that source.

LISTING 19.2   Emitting a Custom Trace

```
using System;
using System.Collections.Generic;
using System.ServiceModel;
using System.Text;

namespace Fabrikam
{
    public class Program
    {
        private static System.Diagnostics.TraceSource source =
            new System.Diagnostics.TraceSource("MyTraceSource");

        public static void Main(string[] args)
        {
            using (ServiceHost host = new ServiceHost(typeof(TradingSystem)))
            {
                host.Open();

                Console.WriteLine("The trading service is available.");

                source.TraceEvent(
                    System.Diagnostics.TraceEventType.Verbose,
                    1,
                    "My trace message.");

                Console.ReadKey(true);
            }
        }
    }
}
```

2. Right-click on the `App.config` file of the TradingServiceHost project and choose Edit WCF Configuration from the context menu. The Service Configuration Editor opens.

3. Proceed to identify the new trace source to the Windows Communication Foundation. Begin by expanding the `Diagnostics` node in the tree in the left pane.

4. Right-click on the `Sources` child node and choose New Source from the context menu.

5. Enter **MyTraceSource** as the name of the source—the name of the trace source to which the activity trace emitted by the code in Listing 19.2 is ascribed.

6. Select Verbose as the trace level.

7. Now that the new trace source has been identified to the Windows Communication Foundation, traces from that source have to be directed to the Windows Communication Foundation's trace listener. To begin doing that, expand the `Listeners` child node of the `Diagnostics` node.

8. Select the `ServiceModelTraceListener` child node.

9. Click Add on the right pane, and, from the Add Tracing Source dialog, select `MyTraceSource` from the list of defined trace sources, and click OK.

10. Choose File, Save from the Service Configuration Editor menus.

11. Choose File, Exit to close the Service Configuration Editor.

12. Delete the `app_tracelog.svclog` file in the same folder as the TradingServiceHost project so that a new trace file will be created in which the custom trace emitted by the code in Listing 19.2 will be easier to pick out.

13. Right-click on the TradingServiceHost project, and choose Debug, Start New Instance from the context menu.

14. When the output in the console of the TradingServiceHost application confirms that the trading service is ready, enter a keystroke into the console to terminate the application.

15. Open the Service Trace Viewer, `SvcTraceViewer.exe`, in the `bin` subdirectory of the Windows SDK installation folder.

16. Choose File, Open from the Service Trace Viewer menus.

17. In the File Open dialog, select the `app_tracelog.svclog` that is in the same folder as the TradingServiceHost project, and click the Open button.

18. Select the first activity in the pane on the left, and the trace emitted by the code in Listing 19.2 will appear in the list of traces associated with that activity, as shown in Figure 19.17.

19. Choose File, Exit from the Service Trace Viewer menus.

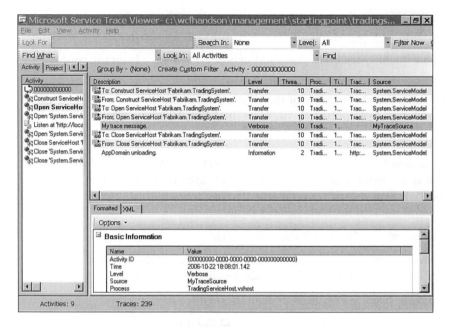

FIGURE 19.17   A trace from a custom source in the Service Trace Viewer.

Performance Counters

At the management instrumentation layer, the Windows Communication Foundation provides a rich variety of performance counters for the monitoring, diagnosis, and optimization of applications. There are performance counters for monitoring services, the individual endpoints of a service, and the individual operations exposed at an endpoint. The performance counter instrumentation is accessible via the Windows Performance Monitor, among other tools.

To examine the performance counters, follow these steps:

1. Right-click on the App.config file of the TradingServiceHost project and choose Edit WCF Configuration from the context menu. The Service Configuration Editor opens.

2. Select the Diagnostics node from the tree in the left pane.

3. Click twice on the Toggle Performance Counters link on the right pane to cycle through the performance counter settings. The first click turns on the performance counters for monitoring the service, whereas the second click turns on the performance counters for individual endpoints and operations as well.

4. Choose File, Save from the Service Configuration Editor menus.

5. Choose File, Exit to close the Service Configuration Editor.

6. Choose Debug, Start Debugging from the Visual Studio 2005 menus.

7. Wait until there is activity in the console window of the trade recording service host.

8. Choose Run from the Windows Start menu; then enter

   perfmon

   and click OK.

9. In the Performance console, right-click on the graph on the right side, and choose Add Counters from the context menu, as shown in Figure 19.18.

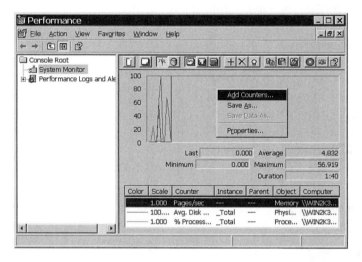

FIGURE 19.18   Adding performance counters to the Performance console.

10. Select `ServiceModelService` from the Performance Object list, as shown in Figure 19.19.

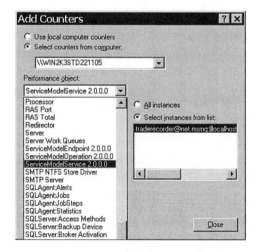

FIGURE 19.19   Selecting a Windows Communication Foundation performance counter category.

19

ServiceModelService is the name of the category of Windows Communication Foundation performance counters at the service level. Note that there are also categories for performance counters at the level of both endpoints and operations. When the ServiceModelService category is selected, the trade-recording service shows up in the list of instances on the right, as shown in Figure 19.19, because that is a service for which performance counters have been enabled.

11. Scroll through the extensive list of performance counters in the ServiceModelService category, as shown in Figure 19.20.

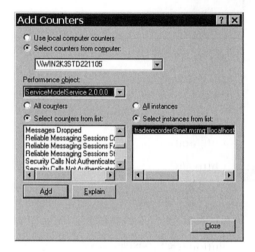

FIGURE 19.20   Examining the Windows Communication Foundation performance counters.

12. Click on the Close button.

13. Choose File, Exit from the Performance Console's menus to close it.

14. In Visual Studio 2005, choose Debug, Stop Debugging.

WMI Provider

WMI is Microsoft's implementation of the Web-Based Enterprise Management architecture defined by the Desktop Management Task Force. The purpose of the architecture is to define a unified infrastructure for managing both computer hardware and software.

WMI is now built into Windows operating systems, and since its introduction as an add-on for Windows NT version 4.0, not only has it become very familiar to Windows systems administrators, but it also is the foundation for many computer management products. If a piece of software can be examined and manipulated via WMI, system administrators will be able to monitor and adjust it using their preferred computer management tools.

The Windows Communication Foundation takes advantage of that situation, incorporating, at the management instrumentation layer, a WMI provider. By virtue of that, Windows Communication Foundation applications become accessible via any WMI-enabled tools, of which there are a great many.

Accessing Data from the WMI Provider via WMI CIM Studio

Follow these steps to observe the effects of the WMI provider through WMI CIM Studio, a simple WMI explorer provided free of charge by Microsoft as part of its WMI toolkit:

1. Right-click on the App.config file of the TradingServiceHost project and choose Edit WCF Configuration from the context menu. The Service Configuration Editor opens.

2. Select the Diagnostics node from the tree in the left pane.

3. Click on the link labeled Enable WMI Provider on the right pane to activate the WMI provider.

4. Choose File, Save from the Configuration Editor menus to save the configuration.

5. Select File, Exit from the menus to close the Configuration Editor.

6. Download the WMI Administrative Tools from http://www.microsoft.com/downloads/details.aspx?displaylang=en&FamilyID=6430F853-1120-48DB-8CC5-F2ABDC3ED314.

7. Install the WMI Administrative Tools.

8. In Visual Studio 2005, in the trading service solution, choose Debug, Start Debugging from the menus.

9. Wait until there is activity in the console window of the trade-recording service host.

10. Choose WMI Tools, WMI CIM Studio from the Windows Start menu.

11. Enter **root\ServiceModel** into the Connect to Namespace dialog that appears, as illustrated in Figure 19.21. root\ServiceModel is the namespace of the classes that the Windows Communication Foundation exposes to WMI.

12. Click OK on the WMI CIM Studio Login dialog to log in as the current user.

13. The classes that the Windows Communication Foundation exposes to WMI are enumerated in the pane on the left. Select Endpoint, as shown in Figure 19.22.

19

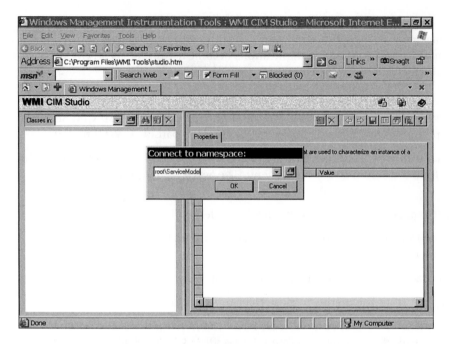

FIGURE 19.21   Connecting to the root\ServiceModel namespace.

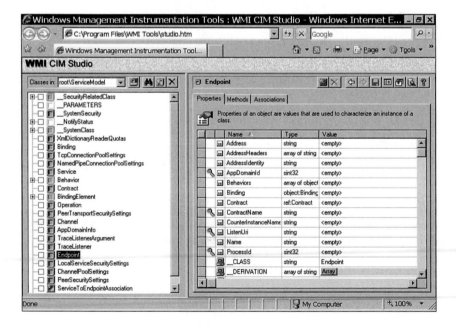

FIGURE 19.22   Selecting a class.

14. Click on the Instances button, which is the fourth button from the left in the row of buttons at the top of the right-hand pane. Information is displayed for each endpoint of any running Windows Communication Foundation application for which the WMI provider is enabled, as shown in Figure 19.23. The WMI CIM Studio retrieves that information via WMI, which, in turn, retrieves it using the Windows Communication Foundation's WMI provider.

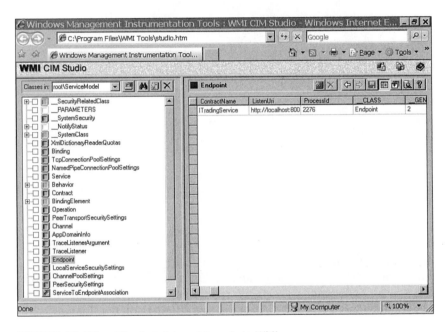

FIGURE 19.23   Viewing data retrieved via WMI.

15. Select the AppDomainInfo class in the pane on the right. As illustrated in Figure 19.24, one can modify properties of that class, such as the LogMessagesAtServiceLevel property, which configures message logging for a service. This facility allows one to configure properties of services while they are executing. Any modifications made in this way are made to the running instances only and are not persisted in any configuration file. To persist configuration elements in configuration files, use the Service Configuration Editor.

16. Choose File, Close from the WMI CIM Studio menus to close WMI CIM Studio.

17. Choose Debug, Stop Debugging from the Visual Studio 2005 menus.

19

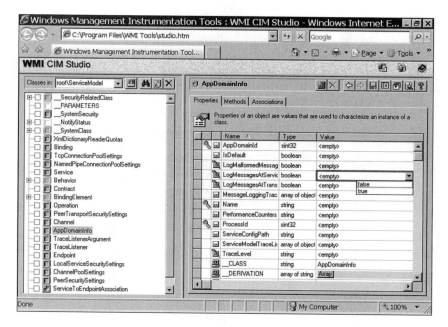

FIGURE 19.24   Configuring running services.

Accessing Data from the WMI Provider Using Windows PowerShell

Windows PowerShell is another WMI-enabled management tool. The next few steps show how Windows PowerShell can be used to access information about running Windows Communication Foundation services via the Windows Communication Foundation WMI provider:

1. Download Windows PowerShell from the Microsoft Downloads site, http://www.microsoft.com/downloads.

2. Install Windows PowerShell.

3. In Visual Studio 2005, in the trading service solution, choose Debug, Start Debugging from the menus.

4. Wait until there is activity in the console window of the trade recording service host.

5. Choose Programs, Windows PowerShell 1.0, Windows PowerShell from the Windows Start menu.

6. Enter the following command at the Windows PowerShell command prompt:

```
get-wmiobject endpoint -n root\ServiceModel ¦ft name
```

Windows PowerShell displays the names of each Windows Communication Foundation endpoint on the local machine by querying WMI for the data for all endpoint objects in the root\ServiceModel namespace, and displaying the name property of each one.

7. Close the Windows PowerShell console.

8. In Visual Studio 2005, choose Debug, Stop Debugging from the menus.

Using the WMI Provider to Add Custom Performance Counters

The WMI provider allows one to add custom performance counters to monitor data points unique to a system. This section shows how one can accomplish that.

In the trading service solution, a natural quantity for business administrators to want to monitor is the volume of trades. Among various ways in which that quantity could be exposed for examination, adding a performance counter for trade volume to the trade recording service would allow it to be monitored using the Performance Console that is built into Windows operating systems.

Remember that the Windows Communication Foundation performance counters can be monitored for each individual instance of a service, as shown in Figure 19.19, as well as for individual endpoints and operations. To associate the trace volume performance counter with a particular instance of a Windows Communication Foundation application, it is necessary to access the running instance of the application via WMI. To see how to do this, follow these steps:

1. Right-click on the App.config file of the TradeRecordingServiceHost project and choose Edit WCF Configuration from the context menu. The Service Configuration Editor opens.

2. Select the Diagnostics node from the tree in the left pane.

3. Click on the link labeled Enable WMI Provider on the right pane to activate the WMI provider.

4. Click twice on the Toggle Performance Counters link on the right pane to cycle through the performance counter settings to the setting by which all the performance counters are enabled.

5. Choose File, Save from the Configuration Editor menus to save the configuration.

6. Select File, Exit from the menus to close the Configuration Editor.

7. Open the Program.cs file of the TradeRecordingServiceHost project in the trading service solution. After initializing the host of the trade recording service, the code in that file calls a custom IntializeCounters() method of the trading service's service type:

```
public static void Main(string[] args)
{
    if (!(MessageQueue.Exists(queueName)))
    {
        MessageQueue.Create(queueName, true);
    }

    TradeRecorder tradeRecorder = new TradeRecorder();
    using (ServiceHost host = new ServiceHost(tradeRecorder))
    {
        host.Open();
        tradeRecorder.InitializeCounters(host.Description.Endpoints);
        Console.WriteLine("The trade recording service is available.");
        Console.ReadKey();
    }
}
```

8. Examine that method, which is in the `TradeRecorder.cs` module of the
   TradeRecordingService project. It is reproduced in Listing 19.3. The code for the
   method assembles a list of the names for the service's endpoints:

```
foreach (ServiceEndpoint endpoint in endpoints)
{
  names.Add(
  string.Format("{0}@{1}",
  this.GetType().Name, endpoint.Address.ToString()));
}
```

Then it uses those names to retrieve the WMI objects corresponding to the
endpoints of the running instance of the service:

```
string condition = string.Format(
    "SELECT * FROM Service WHERE Name=\"{0}\"", name);
SelectQuery query = new SelectQuery(condition);
ManagementScope managementScope =
    new ManagementScope(
        @"\\.\root\ServiceModel",
        new ConnectionOptions());
ManagementObjectSearcher searcher =
    new ManagementObjectSearcher(managementScope, query);
ManagementObjectCollection instances = searcher.Get();
```

Those objects are then used to add the trade volume counter to that instance of the
service:

```
    foreach (ManagementBaseObject instance in instances)
    {
        PropertyData data =
            instance.Properties["CounterInstanceName"];

        this.volumeCounter = new PerformanceCounter(
            TradeRecorder.CounterCategoryName,
            TradeRecorder.VolumeCounterName,
            data.Value.ToString());
        this.volumeCounter.ReadOnly = false;
        this.volumeCounter.RawValue = 0;
        break;
    }
```

LISTING 19.3   InitializeCounters() Method

```
public void InitializeCounters(ServiceEndpointCollection endpoints)
{
    List<string> names = new List<string>();
    foreach (ServiceEndpoint endpoint in endpoints)
    {
        names.Add(
            string.Format("{0}@{1}",
                this.GetType().Name, endpoint.Address.ToString()));
    }

    while (true)
    {
        try
        {
            foreach (string name in names)
            {
                string condition = string.Format(
                    "SELECT * FROM Service WHERE Name=\"{0}\"", name);
                SelectQuery query = new SelectQuery(condition);
                ManagementScope managementScope =
                    new ManagementScope(
                        @"\\.\root\ServiceModel",
                        new ConnectionOptions());
                ManagementObjectSearcher searcher =
                    new ManagementObjectSearcher(managementScope, query);
                ManagementObjectCollection instances = searcher.Get();
                foreach (ManagementBaseObject instance in instances)
                {
```

LISTING 19.3   Continued

```
                    PropertyData data =
                        instance.Properties["CounterInstanceName"];

                    this.volumeCounter = new PerformanceCounter(
                        TradeRecorder.CounterCategoryName,
                        TradeRecorder.VolumeCounterName,
                        data.Value.ToString());
                    this.volumeCounter.ReadOnly = false;
                    this.volumeCounter.RawValue = 0;

                    break;
                }
            }
            break;
        }
        catch(COMException)
        {

        }

    }

    if(this.volumeCounter != null)
    {
        Console.WriteLine("Volume counter initialized.");
    }
    Console.WriteLine("Counters initialized.");

}
```

9. Look at the RecordTrades() method of the trade-recording service's service type, which is in the same module:

```
void ITradeRecorder.RecordTrades(Trade[] trades)
{
    Console.WriteLine("Recording trade ...");
    return;
    lock (this)
    {
        while (this.volumeCounter == null)
        {
            Thread.Sleep(100);
        }
    }
```

```
foreach(Trade trade in trades)
{
    this.tradeCount+=((trade.Count != null)?trade.Count.Value:0);

    this.volumeCounter.RawValue = this.tradeCount;

    Console.WriteLine(string.Format("Recorded trade for {0}",trade));
}
}
```

The method updates the trading volume performance counter with the value of each trade the service records. Currently, however, this return statement

```
Console.WriteLine("Recording trade ...");
return;
```

causes the method to exit prematurely. The reason is that the performance counter would not have been available until the WMI provider was activated for the service according to the instructions given previously. Only after the WMI provider was activated for the service would the InitializeCounters() method have been able to retrieve the running instance of the service to which to add the performance counter.

10. Because the WMI provider has now been activated for the service, comment out the return statement:

```
Console.WriteLine("Recording trade ...");
//return;
```

11. Choose Debug, Start Debugging from the menus.

12. Wait until there is activity in the console window of the trade-recording service host.

13. Choose Run from the Windows Start menu; then enter

    perfmon

    and click OK.

14. In the Performance console, right-click on the graph on the right side, and choose Add Counters from the context menu, as shown in Figure 19.18.

15. Select TradeRecording from the Performance Object list, TradeRecording being the name provided by the InitializeCounters() method for a custom performance counter category for the trade volume counter. As shown in Figure 19.25, the Trade Volume counter is shown as being available for the running instance of the trade recording service.

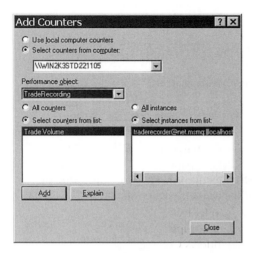

FIGURE 19.25   Adding the Trade Volume performance counter.

16. Click the Add button on the Add Counters dialog, and then the Close button.

17. Enter a keystroke into the console application window of the client application.

18. Observe, in the Performance Console, the movement of the custom trade volume performance counter, as depicted in Figure 19.26.

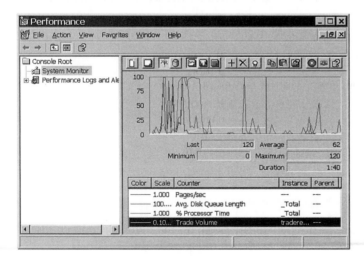

FIGURE 19.26   Monitoring the Trade Volume performance counter.

19. In Visual Studio 2005, choose Debug, Stop Debugging from the menus.

20. In the Performance Console, choose File, Exit from the menus to close it.

Completing the Management Facilities

It should be apparent from the foregoing that there is ample instrumentation and tooling for Windows Communication Foundation applications. However, it must remain a task for developers to provide management models specific to their particular applications—because what needs to be monitored, what the values of instruments signify, and what remedial action needs to be taken, will be specific to each application.

A tool to assist in the process of building management models is the Microsoft Management Model designer, which is available free of charge from the Microsoft Downloads site, http://www.microsoft.com/downloads. A paper that describes how to use the tool to define normal and abnormal states for one's application, and to specify the remedial actions to be taken is available at http://www.microsoft.com/windowsserversystem/dsi/designwp.mspx. In using the Management Model Designer to build a management model for a Windows Communication Foundation application, one will be specifying for administrators how to interpret the Windows Communication Foundation's instrumentation in divining the health of the application, and how to use the Windows Communication Foundation's management tools to sustain normal operation.

An especially useful feature of the Management Model Designer is that it allows one to export a management model as a Microsoft Operations Manager management pack. By importing the management pack in Microsoft Operations Manager 2003, one can achieve the integration of a particular application's management model into an integrated management environment familiar to administrators.

Summary

The Windows Communication Foundation is designed to provide manageable software services. It offers a rich variety of instrumentation and tools for systems administrators to use to manage Windows Communication Foundation solutions, and it allows software developers to add their own. The administration facilities offered by the Windows Communication Foundation all build on familiar management components of the Windows platform, such as WMI and the .NET configuration system, thereby reducing what administrators and developers have to learn about managing Windows Communication Foundation applications.

References

Wikipedia. 2006. S.v. "Trace." http://en.wikipedia.org/wiki/Trace. Accessed January 26, 2006.

19

Versioning

Introduction

Microsoft's field personnel often express interest in hearing about how to manage the lifecycle of a service and, in particular, how to deal with the changes that will inevitably need to be made to services over time. The reason for their interest is that their customers are seeking guidance on the matter. Unfortunately, the literature on service-oriented programming, including the first edition of this book, neglects to pay any attention to the topic. One book that devotes a few paragraphs to the subject is *Service-Oriented Architecture Compass: Business Value, Planning, and Enterprise Roadmap*, by Norbert Bieberstein and others (Bieberstein and others 2006, 39). The brief discussion there refers to the most useful contribution on the subject of service version management hitherto: the article, *Best Practices for Web services versioning* by Kyle Brown and Michael Ellis (Brown and Ellis 2004). They make an observation that might well explain why so little has been written about versioning services when so much has been written about building them:

> [T]he brutal fact [...] is that versioning has not been built into the Web services architecture. Current products from [the leading vendors] do not directly address the versioning issue, requiring developers to solve the problem through the application of patterns and best practices (Brown and Ellis 2004).

The Windows Communication Foundation actually does have some versioning facilities. This chapter will cover those mechanisms, of course. However, its main purpose is to remedy the shortage of guidance on managing the versioning of services. The chapter aims to do so by using the language the Windows Communication Foundation provides for modeling services, to yield a logically complete set of versioning problems, with the solutions to each one of them.

Versioning Nomenclature

The challenge in managing modifications to a service over time is to limit the cost the changes incur. The obvious way of accomplishing that is to avoid having to change any existing client applications as a consequence of changing the service.

Brown and Ellis refer to changes to services that would not require changes to existing clients as *backwards-compatible changes*, and changes to services that would require changes to existing clients as *non-backwards-compatible changes* (Brown and Ellis 2004). The same nomenclature will be used here.

The Universe of Versioning Problems

A versioning decision tree is presented in Figure 20.1. It depicts all of the logically possible ways in which one might have to modify a service, how to implement each change, and what the consequences will be.

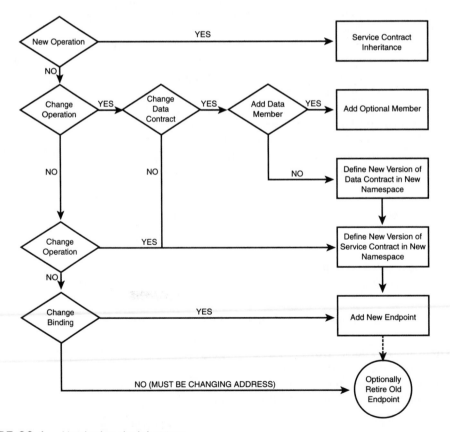

FIGURE 20.1   Versioning decision tree.

The diamonds represent alternative ways in which a service might have to change. The rectangles and the circle represent procedures for implementing changes. The procedures represented by the rectangles yield backwards-compatible changes, whereas the procedure represented by the circle results in a non-backwards-compatible change.

Thus, the versioning decision tree provides two interesting insights at a glance. The first is that there is exactly one thing one might do that would result in a non-backwards-compatible change. The second is that one can have considerable leeway to modify one's services while still avoiding that outcome.

Trace the routes through the decision tree now to understand the implications of each alternative. Start by imagining that there is a service that has to be modified.

Adding a New Operation

The first decision that the decision tree requires one to make is whether it will suffice to simply add a new operation to the service. If that is indeed all that is required, that change can be accomplished using a procedure called *service contract inheritance*, and the result will be a backwards-compatible change.

To understand service contract inheritance, suppose that the service that has to be modified has an endpoint with this service contract:

```
[ServiceContract]
public interface IEcho
{
    [OperationContract]
    string Echo(string input);
```

Assume that this service contract is implemented by this service type:

```
public class Service : IEcho
{
    public string Echo(string input)
    {
        return input;
    }
}
```

The first step in service contract inheritance is to define a new service contract, with the new operations to be added to the service, that derives from the original service contract:

```
[ServiceContract]
public interface IExtendedEcho: IEcho
{
    [OperationContract]
    string[] ExtendedEcho(string[] inputs);
```

The next step is to have the service type implement the new contract in addition to the original one:

```
public class Service : IEcho, IExtendedEcho
{
    public string Echo(string input)
    {
        return input;
    }
    public string[] ExtendedEcho(string[] input)
    {
        return input;
    }
}
```

The final step is to modify the configuration of the service endpoint so that where it referred to the original contract

```
<endpoint
        address="Echo"
        binding="basicHttpBinding"
        contract="IEcho"
/>
```

it now refers to the derived contract with the additional methods:

```
<endpoint
        address="Echo"
        binding="basicHttpBinding"
        contract="IExtendedEcho"
/>
```

Now new clients that are aware of the additional operations of the derived contract can make use of those operations. Yet existing clients, which might know about only the original service contract, could still have the operations of that original contract executed at the same endpoint. Thus, service contract inheritance has the happy consequence of a backwards-compatible change.

Changing an Operation

The second decision posed by the versioning decision tree is whether or not an existing operation of a service has to be modified. If so, the next decision to make is whether or not the change that is required is a change to the data contracts of one or more parameters.

Changing the Data Contract of a Parameter

If the change that has to be made to an existing operation is a change to the data contracts of one or more parameters, the versioning decision tree asks whether that change is restricted to the addition of data members to those data contracts. As the decision tree shows, that change can be accomplished by adding optional members to the data contracts, and the change is a backwards-compatible one.

Adding Optional Members to Data Contracts   To add an optional member to a data contract, add the member and set the value of the `IsRequired` property of its `System.Runtime.Serialization.DataMember` attribute to `false`. Thus, given an original data contract

```
[DataContract]
public class DerivativesCalculation
{
    [DataMember(IsRequired=true)]
    public string[] Symbols;
    [DataMember(IsRequired=true)]
    public decimal[] Parameters;
    [DataMember(IsRequired=true)]
    public string[] Functions;
    public DataTime Date
}
```

one could add a new optional member:

```
[DataContract]
public class DerivativesCalculation
{
    [DataMember(IsRequired=true)]
    public string[] Symbols;
    [DataMember(IsRequired=true)]
    public decimal[] Parameters;
    [DataMember(IsRequired=true)]
    public string[] Functions;
    public DataTime Date
    [DataMember(IsRequired=false)]
    public decimal LastValue;
}
```

The addition of optional data members is a backwards-compatible change. The Windows Communication Foundation's `System.Runtime.Serialization.DataContractSerializer` can deserialize from XML streams that omit values for the optional members. It can also deserialize from XML streams that have values for optional members into instances of types that do not include the optional members. Thus, if new optional members get added to the data contracts of a service, clients using versions of those data contracts that do not have the new optional members will still be able to send messages to the service, and even receive responses that might include values for the optional members, values that the Windows Communication Foundation will quietly ignore.

20

Consider this case, though. Messages are being passed from one node through an intermediary node to a third node. The first and third nodes have been modified so that their versions of the data contracts that define the messages include optional members of which the intermediary node is unaware. In that case, it would be desirable for the values of those optional members of which the intermediary node is unaware, to still pass from the first node, through the intermediary node, and on to the third. All that is required for that to happen is for the data contracts of the intermediary node to implement the System.Runtime.Serialization.IExtensibleDataObject interface. Implementing that simple interface ensures that memory is set aside where the System.Runtime.Serialization.DataContractSerializer can store data in from an input XML stream that is not defined by a data contract, so that the data can later be reserialized into an output XML stream. A data contract that implements the System.Runtime.Serialization.IExtensibleDataObject interface is shown in Listing 20.1. It is always wise to implement that interface on data contracts so as to anticipate the possibility of the values of unknown members having to pass through them.

LISTING 20.1   A Data Contract that Implements IExtensibleDataObject

```
[DataContract]
public class DerivativesCalculation: IExtensibleDataObject
{
        [DataMember(IsRequired=true)]
        public string[] Symbols;
        [DataMember(IsRequired=true)]
        public decimal[] Parameters;
        [DataMember(IsRequired=true)]
        public string[] Functions;
        public DataTime Date

        private ExtensionDataObject unknownData = null;

        public ExtensionDataObject ExtensionData
        {
                get
                {
                        return this.extensionData;
                }

                set
                {
                        this.extensionData = value;
                }
        }
}
```

Other Changes to Data Contracts   As the versioning decision tree shows, any change to a data member other than the addition of an optional member would require the definition of a new version of the data contract. Such changes would include altering the name or the type of a member, or deleting a member.

A new version of a data contract would have to be disambiguated from the original. Disambiguation is necessary so that references to the new version of the data contract in the metadata for the modified service would not be mistaken by clients as references to the original version. That mistake could result in an error if the client was to send a message incorporating data that was structured in accordance with the original version of the data contract to the service when data structured in accordance with the revised version was expected.

Brown and Ellis offer sound advice on how to disambiguate versions of contracts: "[t]o ensure that the various editions of a [contract] are unique, we would recommend a simple naming scheme that appends a date or version stamp to the end of a namespace definition. This follows the general guidelines given by the W3C for XML namespace definitions" (Brown and Ellis 2004). Following that advice, starting with this contract

```
namespace Fabrikam.Derivatives
{
        [DataContract(
                Namespace="http://www.fabrikam.com/derivatives/v1.0.0.0",
                Name="DerivativesCalculation")]
        public class DerivativesCalculation
        {
                [DataMember(IsRequired=true)]
                public string[] Symbols;
                [DataMember(IsRequired=true)]
                public decimal[] Parameters;
                [DataMember(IsRequired=true)]
                public string[] Functions;
                public DataTime Date
        }
}
```

one could unambiguously define a new version, modified by the omission of one of the original members, in this way, using a version-specific namespace:

```
namespace Fabrikam.Derivatives
{
        [DataContract(
                Namespace="http://www.fabrikam.com/derivatives/v2.0.0.0",
                Name="DerivativesCalculation")]
        public class SimplifiedDerivativesCalculation
        {
                [DataMember(IsRequired=true)]
                public string[] Symbols;
```

```
                [DataMember(IsRequired=true)]
                public decimal[] Parameters;
                public DataTime Date

        }

}
```

The versioning decision tree shows that once a new version of a data contract has had to be defined, that new version will have to be incorporated into the definition of a revised service contract. Just as new versions of data contracts should be disambiguated from earlier versions by defining them in new version-specific namespaces, so too should revised versions of service contracts.

After a new version of a service contract has been defined, then, as the versioning decision tree shows, it should be exposed at a new service endpoint. So, to summarize the complete sequence of steps through the tree, if a service has to be modified, and the modification requires some change to a data contract other than the addition of an optional member, a new data contract and service contract must be defined, and the new service contract exposed at a new service endpoint. Interestingly, as the tree shows, none of this would entail a non-backwards-compatible change. The original client applications, unaware of the modified data contract, would continue to use the original service endpoint, whereas new client applications that are aware of the new version of the data contract would use the new service endpoint.

Other Changes to Operations

Changes to existing operations that are not restricted to changing the data contracts of one or more parameters—changing the name of the operation or adding or deleting a parameter—can be dealt with by defining a new service contract incorporating the modified operation. As indicated already, revised versions of service contracts must be disambiguated from earlier versions by defining them in new version-specific namespaces. Also as indicated before, after a new version of a service contract has been defined, it should be exposed at a new service endpoint. Again, exposing a new service endpoint is a backwards-compatible change.

Deleting an Operation

The versioning decision tree shows that deciding to delete an operation from a service contract has the same benign consequences. The backwards-compatible consequences are having to define to a new service contract that omits the deleted operation, within a new, version-specific namespace, and exposing that service contract at a new service endpoint.

Changing a Binding

If the change to be made to a service requires changing the binding of one its endpoints, the versioning decision tree indicates that the modified binding should be exposed at a new service endpoint. As noted several times, exposing a new service endpoint is a backwards-compatible change.

Deciding to Retire an Endpoint

The most important insight offered by the versioning decision tree is that there is exactly one type of change that one might decide to make that would be non-backwards-compatible, and that is the decision to retire an existing endpoint. Furthermore, the only change that necessarily entails the retiring of an existing endpoint is changing an endpoint's address. Changes to the operations of service contracts and changes to bindings do not require that existing endpoints which use those contracts and bindings be retired—the modified contracts and bindings can be exposed at new endpoints alongside the existing ones.

If an endpoint is to be retired, there are two ways of easing the consequences of this non-backwards-compatible change to a service. However, both require anticipating having to make that change and planning ahead.

The first alleviator is to add a System.ServiceModel.FaultContract attribute to all the operations of a contract to indicate that the operation might return a fault indicating that the endpoint has been retired:

```
[DataContract]
public class RetiredEndpointFault
{
        [DataMember]
        public string NewEndpointMetadataLocation;
}


[ServiceContract]
public interface IEcho
{
    [FaultContract(typeof(RetiredEndpointFault))]
    [OperationContract]
    string Echo(string input);
}
```

Doing so will ensure that the possibility of the endpoint being retired will be described in the metadata for the service as a potential cause of a fault from the outset. Consequently, developers building clients will be able to anticipate the prospect of the endpoint being retired at some point. To retire the existing endpoint, the service developer would have the methods implementing the operations exposed at that endpoint do nothing more than throw the fault exceptions indicating that the endpoint was no longer in use.

The second way of alleviating the consequences of retiring an endpoint is to closely monitor the use of a service. One should know the number of clients using an endpoint and also the operators of those clients. Then the implications of retiring the endpoint can be properly assessed and the parties that will be affected can be notified.

Changing the Address of a Service Endpoint

Deciding to change the address of a service endpoint is equivalent to deciding to retire an existing endpoint. However, if all one was doing was changing the address of an endpoint, the cost of that non-backwards-compatible change would be alleviated by having the clients locate the service via a UDDI registry rather than relying on an address that might vary. Chapter 2, "The Fundamentals," explained how to write Windows Communication Foundation clients that use address and binding information retrieved from metadata, and that metadata could be indeed be retrieved from a UDDI registry.

Centralized Lifecycle Management

In Chapter 2, *service-oriented architecture* was defined as an approach to organizing the software of an enterprise by providing service facades for all of that software, and publishing the WSDL for those services in a central repository. Among the perceived virtues of that approach is the prospect of centralized lifecycle management. Specifically, proponents of service-oriented architecture anticipate the registry serving as a central point of control through which system administrators could determine how the software entities in their organizations function by associating policies with the services that provide facades for all of the other software resources.

For that prospect to be realized, it would be necessary for services to monitor the registry for changes in policy applicable to them, and then automatically reconfigure themselves in accordance with those policies. As remarkable as that might sound, the Windows Communication Foundation actually can be made to reconfigure itself according to stipulated policies.

A *policy*, in the sense in which that term is being used here, refers to a collection of policy assertions, and a *policy assertion* is a nonfunctional requirement of a service endpoint (Weerawarana and others 2005, 128). WS-Policy provides an interoperable, standard way of expressing policies.

Because policies define the nonfunctional requirements of a service endpoint, they pertain to the binding of the endpoint, in Windows Communication Foundation terms, rather than to the contract, which defines the functional characteristics. So, for Windows Communication Foundation applications to be able to configure themselves in accordance with policies retrieved from a registry, they would have to be able to convert policies into bindings. They can. Follow these steps to learn how.

1. Copy the code associated with this chapter downloaded from http://www.cryptmaker.com/WindowsCommunicationFoundationUnleashed to the folder `C:\WCFHandsOn`. The code is all in a folder called `Versioning`.

2. Open the Visual Studio 2005 solution, `Versioning.sln`. This solution contains a single project, called Host. The project is for building a console application that is to serve as the host of a derivatives calculator service like the one described in Chapter 2.

3. Note that the project does not include any application configuration file.

4. Examine the code in the static `Main()` method of the console application, which is in the `Program.cs` of the Host project. It is reproduced in Listing 20.2. A single state-

ment that uses the Windows Communication Foundation's `System.ServiceModel.WsdlImporter` class, reads a stream of metadata that includes policy assertions expressed using WS-Policy, and yields from that stream a collection of binding objects. That collection of endpoints is then used to add service endpoints to the host programmatically.

LISTING 20.2   A Host that Configures Itself from Metadata

```
using (ServiceHost host = new ServiceHost(
    serviceType,
    new Uri[] { new Uri("http://localhost:8000/Derivatives/")}
    ))
{
    Collection<Binding> bindings =
                new WsdlImporter(
                        MetadataSet.ReadFrom(
                            new XmlTextReader(
                                new FileStream(
                                    "metadata.xml",
                                    FileMode.Open)))).ImportAllBindings();
    int index = 0;
    foreach (Binding binding in bindings)
    {
        host.AddServiceEndpoint(
                        typeof(IDerivativesCalculator),
                        binding,
                        string.Format("Calculator{0}",index++));
    }

    [...]
    host.Open();

    Console.WriteLine(
        "The derivatives calculator service is available."
    );
    Console.ReadKey(true);
    host.Close();
}
```

5. Choose Debug, Start Debugging from the Visual Studio 2005 menus, to start the service host application.

6. When that application's console asserts that the service is available, confirm that it is by directing a browser to the service's base address, http://localhost:8000/Derivatives/. A page describing the service should appear.

7. Choose Debug, Stop Debugging from the Visual Studio 2005 menus to terminate the host application.

In this case, the stream of metadata from which the Windows Communication Foundation's `System.ServiceModel.WsdlImporter` retrieved a collection of bindings included policies, and those policies consisted of standard policy assertions defined by the WS-SecurityPolicy specification. The `System.ServiceModel.WsdlImporter` has the facilities for understanding such standard policy assertions and configuring bindings accordingly. However, the WS-Policy language allows one to formulate an unlimited variety of policy assertions, and the `System.ServiceModel.WsdlImporter` is naturally not inherently capable of understanding every policy assertion one might devise. One can readily extend its capabilities to understand any given policy assertion, though. To do so, one creates a type that implements the `System.ServiceModel.Description.IPolicyImportExtension` interface that can read the policy assertion and apply it to a binding, and then one adds an instance of that type to the `System.ServiceModel.WsdlImporter` object's `PolicyImportExtensions` collection.

It should be apparent, then, that the Windows Communication Foundation does allow services to reconfigure themselves in accordance with stipulated policies. However, while the notion of services being able to do this has some currency, it is ill-advised. It has already been explained that having a service reconfigure itself to conform to new policies means having the service change its binding. The versioning decision tree showed that the least costly way to implement a change to a binding is to expose a new endpoint with the modified binding, and to avoid the option of retiring the old endpoint. However, when a service reconfigures its binding to conform to a new policy, the existing endpoint is changed, and any clients that used that endpoint will very likely no longer be able to do so until they are reconfigured as well. Chapter 2 already showed that Windows Communication Foundation clients can configure themselves dynamically from updated binding information that they could retrieve from the metadata of the modified service, but one must consider how many potential points of failure this scenario incorporates.

Summary

This chapter provided a versioning decision tree that depicts all the logically possible ways in which one might have to modify a service, how to implement each change, and what the consequences will be. The tree shows that one has considerable leeway to modify a service without incurring the cost of having to update all its clients.

References

Bieberstein, Norbert, Sanjay Bose, Marc Fiammante, Keith Jones, and Rawn Shah. 2006. *Service-Oriented Architecture Compass: Business Value, Planning, and Enterprise Roadmap.* Upper Saddle River, NJ: IBM.

Brown, Kyle and Michael Ellis. 2004. *Best practices for Web services versioning: Keep your Web services current with WSDL and UDDI.* www.ibm.com/developerworks/webservices/library/ws-version/. Accessed October 10, 2006.

Weerawarana, Sanjiva, Francisco Curbera, Frank Leymann, Tony Storey, and Donald F. Ferguson. 2005. *Web Services Platform Architecture: SOAP, WSDL, WS-Policy, WS-Addressing, WS-BPEL, WS-Reliable Messaging, and More.* Upper Saddle River, NJ: Prentice Hall.

PART VIII

Guidance

IN THIS PART

CHAPTER 21

Guidance

Introduction

This chapter provides a list of things to do and things to
avoid doing in building solutions with the Windows
Communication Foundation. The list has been assembled
over the course of nearly two years of working with the
technology, and assisting early adopters to use it.

Adopting the Windows
Communication Foundation

✗ **DO NOT** plan to rebuild existing applications so as to
use the Windows Communication Foundation.

Planning to rebuild existing applications to make use of a
new technology fails to take into account that there are
always new technologies emerging and new ideas about
how to build software. It yields a view of the future of one's
software with artificial milestones of accomplishment in
migrating from one new technology to the next. It post-
pones the delivery of new functionality while existing
functionality is re-engineered.

✓ **DO** develop a detailed vision of how one's software
should ideally be constructed that takes into account
the capabilities of new technologies as well as current
design principles.

✓ **DO** build exemplars based on that vision.

Given a vision of how one would like one's software to
work, one proceeds to build exemplars. An *exemplar* is a
solution to a small set of new functional requirements that
is constructed in accordance with the tenets of the vision
of how one's software should be constructed. Thus, in

building an exemplar, one aims to develop a solution to a small new set of requirements, rather than merely reproduce a solution to an existing set of requirements using new technologies and ideas. Further, whereas a pilot is typically something that is hastily constructed to confirm some possibility and then discarded, an exemplar is built very carefully as an example that one would like all of the software developers in one's organization to follow, using pieces that one would like them to be able to re-use. Therefore, in building an exemplar, one also builds or extends a reusable framework, and the utility of that framework will be proven through the construction of the exemplar.

The framework will typically hide the native interfaces of new vendor technologies away behind interfaces of one's own design, interfaces that reduce the surface area of the vendors' technologies to the set of options that one's developers actually need. So, by virtue of such a framework, one's developers would not use the Windows Communication Foundation directly, but only the pertinent elements thereof surfaced through the framework. Having such a framework accelerates the productivity of one's developers, saving them from having to learn all about a new technology, and it constrains them to follow techniques that are in accordance with one's vision, and proven through the construction of the exemplar.

✓ **DO** consider how to integrate one's existing software with new software built using the reusable framework developed in the construction of the exemplar.

Asking how to integrate one's existing software with a proven, reusable framework developed precisely in accordance with one's own requirements and one's own vision of how one's software should be constructed is entirely different from asking how to migrate one's existing software to use the Windows Communication Foundation. First, it is a question that one generally finds oneself better equipped to answer, because it is not a question of moving to a vast and unfamiliar new technology, but rather a question of integrating with a framework that is well-understood because one built and used it oneself. Second, it does not presuppose discarding existing technologies, but merely allows one's existing software to work properly with one's new software. Third, it is a question about how to progress with the delivery of new functionality, rather than a question about how to re-engineer the delivery of existing functionality.

✓ **DO** delegate the maintenance of one's vision, the construction of new exemplars, and the concomitant evolution of one's framework to one team of software developers.

✓ **DO** delegate the work of using the framework to deliver solutions over to the majority of one's software developers.

Of course, one's vision of how one's software should ideally be constructed will continue to evolve, and it should do so as new technologies and new design principles emerge. One should delegate the work of maintaining that vision and one's framework for implementing it over to one team of software developers that is tasked with absorbing new technologies and ideas and progressively incorporating them into the framework through the construction of new exemplars. The majority of the software developers should have the task of using the existing framework to deliver new functionality to users. This way of organizing one's development team is used by several successful software vendors.

A different organizational pattern is to allow one group of developers the leeway of using new technologies that emerge, but constraining other groups to using an existing framework, while charging both groups with delivering new functionality to end users. That organization does not provide for the systematic absorption of new technologies and ideas, and leads to the stagnation of the framework. It also leads to resentment of the group that gets to play with the new technologies. The pattern recommended here, where one group maintains the framework, absorbing new technologies, while everyone else delivers solutions for end users, does not necessarily lead to the same resentment. Some developers enjoy working on frameworks, whereas others enjoy delivering finished products, and provided they are assigned to do what they enjoy, they can be happy in their work.

Yet another organizational pattern delegates the maintenance of the framework to one group of developers, and the delivery of end user solutions to everyone else, but tasks the latter group with the absorption of new technologies. When a new technology is found to work for a particular type of solution, the maintainers of the framework extend the framework so that it can be used to reproduce that solution. This organizational pattern is typically used to reduce the cost of maintaining the framework by having it done by a team of capable developers that are less expensive because they work in a third-world country with a lower cost of living. Developers close to the high-paying customers in the first-world countries use whatever new technologies and design principles are available to them to give those customers what they want as quickly as possible. This organizational pattern can work, provided the groups working on new customer solutions are coordinated with one another so that they do not reproduce one another's efforts.

Working with Windows Communication Foundation Addresses

✓ **DO** specify base addresses for services that are not hosted within IIS.

✓ **DO** specify base addresses for all the transport protocols that one might want the service to support.

✓ **DO** specify endpoint addresses that are relative to the base addresses.

✗ **DO NOT** use absolute addresses for endpoints.

Compare this undesirable configuration that uses an absolute address for an endpoint

```
<!-- This is an example of what not to do: -->
<service
        name="DerivativesCalculator.DerivativesCalculatorServiceType">
        <endpoint
            address="http://localhost:8000/Derivatives/Calculator"
```

```
            binding="wsHttpBinding"
            contract="DerivativesCalculator.IDerivativesCalculator" />
</service>
```

with this desirable configuration that uses an address for an endpoint that is relative to a base address:

```
<service
        name="DerivativesCalculator.DerivativesCalculatorServiceType"
        <host>
                <baseAddresses>
                  <add baseAddress="http://localhost:8000/Derivatives/" />
                  <add baseAddress="net.tcp://localhost:8010/Derivatives/" />
                 </baseAddresses>
        </host>
        <endpoint
                address="Calculator"
                binding="wsHttpBinding"
                contract="DerivativesCalculator.IDerivativesCalculator" />
</service>
```

The latter, desirable configuration has two virtues.

First, if one changes the binding to one that uses a different transport protocol, one simply has to alter the name of the binding specified in the configuration, with no change to the endpoint address being required:

```
<service
        name="DerivativesCalculator.DerivativesCalculatorServiceType"
        <host>
                <baseAddresses>
                  <add baseAddress="http://localhost:8000/Derivatives/" />
                  <add baseAddress="net.tcp://localhost:8010/Derivatives/" />
                 </baseAddresses>
        </host>
        <endpoint
                address="Calculator"
                binding="netTcpBinding"
                contract="DerivativesCalculator.IDerivativesCalculator" />
</service>
```

In the former, undesirable configuration, two changes would have been required to achieve the same objective: a change to the name of the binding and a change to the scheme of the endpoint address:

```
<service
        name="DerivativesCalculator.DerivativesCalculatorServiceType"
        <endpoint
```

```
          address="net.tcp://localhost:800/Derivatives/Calculator"
          binding="nettcpBinding"
          contract="DerivativesCalculator.IDerivativesCalculator" />
</service>
```

The second virtue of the recommended configuration is that directing a browser to the specified HTTP base address will yield a page confirming the availability of the service. Being able to do that can be very useful for debugging.

Working with Windows Communication Foundation Bindings

✓ **DO** use the predefined `BasicHttpBinding` to interoperate with software that was not developed using Microsoft .NET, or that was developed using .NET web services.

✓ **DO** anticipate having to expend considerable effort getting the predefined `WSHttpBinding` and `WS-FederationBinding` to work with software that was not developed using Microsoft .NET and that uses implementations of one or more WS-* protocols for communication.

The predefined `BasicHttpBinding` implements a profile—the WS-I Basic Profile 1.1, which specifies how a small set of communications protocols can be used to maximize the likelihood of interoperability. `WSHttpBinding` and `WSFederationBinding` incorporate implementations of a number of communication protocols for which profiles do not yet exist, including WS-Security, WS-ReliableMessaging, WS-SecurityPolicy, WS-AtomicTransaction, WS-Coordination, and WS-Trust. Those bindings could be used as a basis for communication using those protocols with other implementations of the same protocols, but accomplishing that might require considerable effort. Anticipate that as profiles for those protocols are developed, versions of the bindings with the appropriate defaults will be made available, and then interoperability with other software that conforms to the profiles should be easy to achieve.

✓ **DO** analyze the solution to identify services with contended resources.

✓ **DO** use the predefined `NetMsmqBinding` to manage access to that service's resources.

If there are any services with resources to which access will be contended by clients, it is hard to imagine any reason sufficient to justify not having requests for those resources come via a queue. Using a queue for access to the service and its contended resources will ensure that the servicing of one client's request will not interfere with the servicing of another's—by causing a deadlock, for example—because each client's requests will be dealt with in sequence. More important, the developers of the service's clients will know to accommodate their requests for access to the service's resources being dealt with as the resources become available rather than right away.

The easiest way to have requests to a service go via a queue is to have them sent via the Windows Communication Foundation's predefined `NetMsmqBinding`. There are two limitations to be aware of in using that binding, though. First, messages conveyed via the `NetMsmqBinding` pass through an MSMQ queue, and MSMQ can only accommodate messages up to 4MB in size. Second, Windows Communication Foundation services that receive messages via the `NetMsmqBinding` must be deployed on the same computer system as the MSMQ queue from which the incoming messages are read.

✓ **DO** use the predefined `NetMsmqBinding` to guarantee message delivery.

✓ **DO** use the predefined `NetTcpBinding` for communication between applications built using the Windows Communication Foundation that are deployed on different computer systems, except if one of the preceding guidelines about bindings applies.

The predefined `NetTcpBinding` offers a great many configuration options by which it can be adapted to different scenarios. More important, it can accommodate duplex communication, by which a client can send a request to a service, and the service can respond asynchronously.

✓ **DO**, however, use an HTTP binding for scenarios where scaling out over load-balanced instances of services is required.

The following advice, written about how to load-balance .NET Remoting servers using Network Load Balancing, applies to Windows Communication Foundation servers as well:

> You cannot load balance across a serve farm [when using TCP], due to the machine affinity of the underlying TCP connection. This severely limits your application's ability to scale out. To provide an architecture that can scale out, use IIS as the host, combined with [communication via HTTP]. This configuration provides the greatest scale out ability, because each method call over [HTTP] only lives for the life of the method call and maintains no machine affinity (Meier, Vasireddy, Babbar, and Mackman 2004, 497).

✓ **DO** use a custom HTTP binding rather than a predefined HTTP binding for scenarios where scaling out over load-balanced instances of services is required.

The predefined HTTP bindings include a connection HTTP header in messages with the value `Keep-Alive`. That enables clients to create persistent, reusable connections to services that support doing so. That behavior can create a machine affinity that can interfere with load-balancing. The `System.ServiceModel.Channels.HttpTransportBindingElement` has a `KeepAliveEnabled` property that can be assigned a value of `false` to disable support for persistent connections. So, for load-balancing, use a custom binding that incorporates an instance of `System.ServiceModel.Channels.HttpTransportBindingElement` with the value of its `KeepAliveEnabled` property set to `false`.

✓ **DO** use the predefined `NetNamedPipeBinding` for communication between applications built using the Windows Communication Foundation that will execute within different processes on the same computer system, except if one of the preceding guidelines about bindings applies.

The predefined `NetNamedPipeBinding` offers all the benefits that the `NetTcpBinding` does. However, it yields better throughput between applications in different processes on the same computer system than the `NetTcpBinding` does. Switching to the `NetTcpBinding` if the applications are redeployed onto separate computer systems should entail a change only to the choice of binding in configurations of the applications.

> ✗ **DO NOT** use the Windows Communication Foundation in the .NET Framework 3.0 for communication between different application domains in the same process.

The .NET Common Language Runtime uses .NET Remoting to allow objects in one application domain access to objects in another application domain in the same process (Box and Sells 2003, 274). The version of the Windows Communication Foundation in the .NET Framework 3.0 is not optimized for communication between different application domains in the same process.

> ✓ **DO** use the predefined `NetPeerTcpBinding` for communication when no Domain Name Service (DNS) is available.

> ✓ **DO** provide a custom peer resolver service, if necessary, to help ensure messages reach their destinations.

On Windows XP SP2 and Windows Vista, the predefined `NetPeerTcpBinding` relies on the implementation of the Peer Name Resolution Protocol in Windows Peer-to-Peer Networking as a substitute for DNS. That protocol relies on peers running a consumer operating system to do name resolution, as opposed to relying on, say, Internet root name servers maintained by the Internet Network Information Center and agencies of the United States military. Therefore, although it is perfectly suitable for casual endeavors such as Internet gaming, it is unsuitable for critical communications. A more certain degree of reliability can be accomplished using a custom peer resolver service, at an address known to all the peers, that will do the peer name resolution.

> ✗ **AVOID** using the `WSDualHttpBinding`.

The `WSDualHttpBinding` provides for duplex communication over HTTP. As explained already, *duplex communication* involves clients sending requests to a service, and the service responding asynchronously. That form of communication will not usually work over HTTP when the client is behind a firewall because firewalls are customarily configured to block inbound HTTP connections. If one has the flexibility to modify the configuration of the firewall, it is preferable to open a port for use by the `NetTcpBinding` because doing so will yield better performance with at least as much flexibility. If the firewall cannot be reconfigured, the clients will have to poll the service for responses to their requests. Clients used by people from within their homes will typically be behind some network address translator and will not have a routable Internet Protocol address to which the server's responses can be delivered. They too will have to poll the service for responses to their requests. If the clients and the service are all deployed on the same local area network with no firewalls or network address translators, the

WSDualHttpBinding would work properly, but the NetTcpBinding would yield better performance.

> ✗ **DO NOT** activate unnecessary binding features.
>
> ✓ **DO** deactivate unnecessary binding features.

Securing the exchange of messages reduces message throughput, so do not secure the exchange of messages unless doing so is warranted by one's threat model. Reliable sessions also reduce message throughput, especially over HTTP, so do not use that binding option either unless it satisfies an explicit nonfunctional requirement.

One must not only avoid using unnecessary binding features, but also take care to deactivate unnecessary ones that are on by default to maximize security and robustness. For instance, comparing the performance of the Windows Communication Foundation's predefined NetTcpBinding with its default settings to the performance of ASP.NET web services is meaningless. The former is a secure, reliable, duplex communication channel, whereas the latter is an unsecured, request-response channel with no reliability assurances. However, the NetTcpBinding can readily be configured to outperform ASP.NET web services.

> ✓ **DO**, in constructing custom binding elements, use custom operation selector and message inspector behaviors to facilitate debugging.

Adding a custom operation selector and a custom message inspector behavior to the endpoint dispatcher for a service can be very helpful in debugging custom binding elements. The Windows Communication Foundation will pass messages received from the Channel Layer through a custom operation selector and a custom message inspector before attempting to deserialize the messages and invoke the methods of a service. So, those custom behaviors are useful for confirming that the messages are in fact passing through the custom channel, and for examining the messages themselves to diagnose any errors that the channel might have introduced. How to add custom operation selectors and custom message inspectors is covered in Chapter 13, "Custom Behaviors."

Working with Windows Communication Foundation Contracts

> ✓ **DO** design contracts using scenarios.

A question that is often asked but seldom properly answered is how to know which services to build. Given a set of requirements, for instance, how is one to identify the services needed to implement the solution?

One view is that attempts "to take a set of business requirements and from them derive a technology model" are often doomed because in "failing to work closely enough with the business, there is often a large disconnect between the business and the IT solution provided" (Sehmi and Schwegler 2006, 34). Proponents of this view argue that the analysis should begin with a business model that identifies the capabilities of the organization as well as its processes and service level expectations (Sehmi and Schwegler 2006, 34–35). The next step is to define a service model that identifies, in particular, "[e]xternally consumable service interfaces" mapped to the business capabilities (Sehmi and Schwegler 2006, 35–36). In arguing for this approach, which is a reasonable one, Arvindra Sehmi and Beat Schwegler pose this key question: "Given a business model, [...] how can you translate that [...] into a service model that you can ultimately implement?" (Sehmi and Schwegler 2006, 40). The answer they offer is this:

> To identify and document the [...] items in a service model, you do not need to use radically new analysis techniques. Rather, you can use existing skills such as conventional object-oriented analysis and design skills (Sehmi and Schwegler 2006, 40).

This answer is very likely mistaken, which is most unfortunate because following this advice will likely still yield a poorly designed service model after the considerable expense of analyzing the business model. Why is the answer mistaken? Well, compare it with the insightful guidance formulated by Krzysztof Cwalina and Brad Abrams based on their experience in developing the .NET Framework:

> DO NOT rely on standard design methodologies when designing the public APIs layer of a framework. Standard design methodologies (including object-oriented design methodologies) are optimized for the maintainability of the resulting implementation, not for the usability of the resulting APIs. Scenario-driven design together with prototyping, usability studies, and some amount of iteration is a much better approach (Cwalina and Abrams 2006, 16).

Cwalina and Abrams' remarkable book, *Framework Design Guidelines: Conventions, Idioms, and Patterns for Resuable .NET Libraries*, while reflecting on what they learned building a class library framework rather than a set of services, still offers wonderful guidance for designers of services. For after all, a set of services does indeed constitute, in their words, a "public API[] layer" and their book provides a rare distillation of the wisdom accrued by a large number of people engaged in the development of a modern and extremely popular programming framework. The very fine level of detail in their work provides abundant evidence that the authors have had considerable experience successfully solving very concrete engineering problems. More important, the fact that they frequently indicate and analyze shortcomings in the design of the .NET Framework indicates that much of the wisdom they offer is of the most precious kind: the kind that is acquired by learning from mistakes.

The most important lesson that they offer is that design of programming interfaces should follow the "Principle of Scenario-Driven Design" (Cwalina and Abrams 2006, 13). They write:

> To optimize the overall productivity of the developers using a framework, [...] framework design should be focused around a set of common scenarios to the point where the

whole design process is scenario-driven. We recommend that framework designers first write code that the users of the framework will have to write in the main scenarios, and then design the object model to support these code samples. [...] Frameworks must be designed starting from a set of usage scenarios and code samples implementing these scenarios (Cwalina and Abrams 2006, 13).

They note that this approach "is similar to processes based on test-driven development (TDD) or on use cases," but correctly point out that "TDD is more heavyweight as it has other objectives beyond driving the design of APIs. Users are describing scenarios on a higher level than individual API calls" (Cwalina and Abrams 2006, 13).

The steps that they propose, in articulating this approach, are the ones to follow in designing service contracts:

1. "[S]tart with producing a scenario-driven API specification" containing a listing of "the top five to ten scenarios for a given technology area and show code samples that implement these scenarios [...] in at least two programming languages" (Cwalina and Abrams 2006, 14).

2. "[D]esign APIs by first writing code samples for the main scenarios and then defining the object model to support the code samples (Cwalina and Abrams 2006, 15).

3. "[O]rganize usability studies to test APIs in main scenarios" (Cwalina and Abrams 2006, 19).

This guidance, which focuses the effort in designing an interface primarily toward its perspicacity and usability, is actually especially relevant to the task of designing service contracts. Developers writing clients for services very often have to figure out how to use the services from the metadata alone, without the luxury of extensive installed documentation and samples. Designers of services must therefore do their utmost not only to simplify the interfaces, but also to ensure that how they are meant to be used is conveyed through the design of the interface itself—that the interface must be self-documenting. Here are some specific guidelines offered by Cwalina and Abrams for accomplishing those objectives:

▶ "It has to be easy to identify the right set of types and members for common programming tasks" (Cwalina and Abrams 2006, 20).

▶ Provide convenience overloads that require setting fewer parameter values (Cwalina and Abrams 2006, 21).

▶ Ensure that the default values are the right ones (Cwalina and Abrams 2006, 21).

▶ "Think of the object model as a map—you have to put clear signs about how to get from one place to another. You want a property to clearly point people to what it does, what values it takes, and what will happen if you set it" (Anderson 2006, 21).

▶ "[E]nsure that the main [...] namespace contains only types that are used in the most common scenarios. Types used in advanced scenarios should be placed in subnamespaces" (Cwalina and Abrams 2006, 21).

▶ "Do not have members intended for advanced scenarios on types intended for mainline scenarios" (Cwalina and Abrams 2006, 1, emphasis omitted).

▶ "[E]xceptions should clearly describe their cause and the way the developer should modify their code to get rid of the problem" (Cwalina and Abrams 2006, 23).

▶ "Do not be afraid to use verbose identifier names. Most identifier names should clearly state what each method does and what each type and parameter expects" (Cwalina and Abrams 2006, 26, emphasis omitted).

▶ "[I]nvolve user education experts early in the design process. They can be a great resource for spotting designs with bad name choices and designs that would be difficult to explain" (Cwalina and Abrams 2006, 26).

▶ Reserve "the best type names for the most commonly used types" (Cwalina and Abrams 2006, 26).

✓ **DO** provide explicit namespaces and names for service contracts, operation contracts, data contracts, and data members.

One might not like the defaults if one knew what they were. More importantly, if the defaults were to change in subsequent releases of the technology and a service was upgraded to use that new release but its clients were not, the clients' messages might no longer be formatted in the way that the service expects them to be formatted.

Working with Structural Contracts

✓ **DO** use data contracts rather than serializable types wherever possible.

The `System.Runtime.Serialization.DataContractSerializer` used for serializing and deserializing data contracts outperforms the `System.Xml.Serialization.XmlSerializer` used for serializing and deserializing serializable types. That performance difference is important because the serialization of data items into messages and the deserialization of messages into data items tend to be the biggest bottlenecks in service-oriented programming solutions. Furthermore, data contracts are explicit about what gets serialized, whereas it is solely the public fields of serializable types that are implicitly serializable.

✗ **DO NOT**, in defining data contracts, use any types except .NET value types as data members, unless the types are themselves data contracts composed of hierarchies of .NET value types.

.NET value types map to XML Schema data types, which, in turn, represent types that are commonly found in type systems. Therefore, data contracts that are nothing more than hierarchies of .NET value types can deserialized into meaningful data structures on other platforms. Types that .NET developers often want to use in defining data members, but that they should not use, are `System.Data.DataSet`, `System.Collections.Hashtable`, and `System.Collections.Generic.Dictionary<TKey,TValue>`. As explained in Chapter 2, "The Fundamentals," service-oriented programming aims at developing software entities that are loosely coupled to one another by their shared knowledge of explicitly defined message formats, rather than tightly coupled by their shared knowledge of the same types. Adding a data member that is a .NET reference type like `System.Data.DataSet`, `System.Collections.Hashtable`, or `System.Collections.Generic.Dictionary<TKey,TValue>` to a data contract defeats the purpose of using a data contract to define a message format because only software entities that are tightly coupled to one another by their shared knowledge of the same types could exchange the messages. If the ease of using types like `System.Data.DataSet`, `System.Collections.Hashtable`, or `System.Collections.Generic.Dictionary<TKey,TValue>` seems more important than the objective of creating loosely coupled software entities, one might want to reconsider using a service-oriented programming technology at all.

✓ **DO** use instance fields for data members regardless of whether they are public or private.

✓ **DO** have the data members, and any methods included in data contract classes, in separate partial types.

These recommendations are for enhancing the readability of data contracts. In evaluating them, consider the definition of a data contract in Listing 21.1.

The first of the two recommendations contravenes the familiar design guideline "that you should almost never use publicly exposed instance fields, but use properties instead" (Cwalina and Abrams 2006, 35). However, in working with data contracts, one would often like to know what members the data contract includes, and that is more easily ascertained by glancing at a list of instance fields than by scrolling through the code for a number of properties. That readability is further enhanced when the data member instance fields are all defined in a separate partial type, as they are in Listing 21.1, uncluttered by any of the data contract class's behavior.

LISTING 21.1   Data Contract Definition

```
//MyDataContract.cs
[DataContract(Name="...",Namespace="...")]
public partial class MyDataContract
{
        [DataMember(Name="...")]
        public XType MyField;
}


//MyDataContractBehavior.cs
public partial class MyDataContract
{
```

LISTING 21.1   Continued

```
    public MyDataContract()
    {
    }

    public MyDataContract(XType myField)
    {
        this.MyField = myField;
    }

    public MyDataContract(MyBusinessType myBusinessType)
    {
        [...]
    }

    public MyBusinessType CreateBusinessType()
    {
        [...]
    }
}
```

▶ **DO NOT** include any business logic in the definition of data contract classes.

Data contracts are meant for defining message formats, not business objects. Therefore, besides data members, data contracts should have only constructors, including constructors for creating instances from business objects, and methods for creating instances of business objects from instances of the data contracts.

✗ **AVOID** using message contracts.

Message contracts are for differentiating the data that should be among the headers of a message from the data that should be in the body. However, it has become customary to use headers only for information pertaining to communication protocols, rather than to use them for conveying substantive information. Therefore, unless one is defining a communication protocol or using one that defines message headers, one should have no use for message contracts.

✗ **DO NOT** have more than one message body member in a message contract.

If one is justified in using a message contract, that message contract should have just one message body member that is a data contract.

✓ **DO** always have data contracts implement System.Runtime.Serialization. IExtensibleDataObject.

Implementing that interface ensures that the data contract will be able to be used together with newer versions of the same contract that include optional members that the original version of the contract did not include. By implementing the `System.Runtime.Serialization.IExtensibleDataObject` interface, the data contract provides memory that the Windows Communication Foundation can use for storing additional data members defined in later versions of the same data contract. Thus, a newer version of the data contract with additional operational data members can be deserialized into an older version and when that older version is serialized again, none of the data for the additional data members of the newer version will be lost.

Working with Behavioral Contracts

✓ **DO** add appropriate fault contracts to each operation contract.

✓ **DO** include a fault contract defining a fault signifying that the endpoint has been retired on each operation contract.

Adding fault contracts to operation contracts serves to incorporate, into the metadata for a service, an indication of the faults that might occur in each of the operations. That allows developers writing code that invokes those operations to anticipate what could go wrong and to write their code accordingly.

One fault that could always occur would be due to the provider of the service retiring the endpoint that included an operation that the client has invoked. In anticipation of that, one should add to every operation contract a fault contract signifying the retirement of the endpoint. That would signal the possibility of the endpoint being retired to developers writing code to use the operations, and allow them to plan for it. When the endpoint is retired, one would modify the methods implementing the operations exposed at that endpoint to do nothing more than throw the fault exceptions indicating that the endpoint is no longer in use. The information included with those faults could indicate where the metadata for a replacement endpoint might be found.

✓ **DO** include a default operation in every service contract.

A default operation is defined by assigning the value `"*"` to the `Action` parameter of the `OperationContract` attribute. Here is an example of a default operation:

```
[OperationContract(Action="*")]
Message Default(Message input);
```

Any incoming message not addressed to one of the other operations of a contract will be directed to the default operation. A default operation is more useful if it takes a `System.ServiceModel.Channels.Message` object as its input parameter, as in the example above, for that enables the operation to accept incoming data in any format. The virtue of including a default operation in a contract is that when a client is attempting to connect, and the binding is configured properly but the format of the message is mistaken, the messages will at least be delivered to the default operation. This thereby confirms that the binding is correct and that the remaining defects are restricted to a mismatch in contract definitions.

✓ **DO** make service contracts duplex by default.

Duplex service contracts define one-way operations by which clients send requests to services, and one-way operations by which services can send to clients any number of responses to each request. Here is an example of one:

```
[ServiceContract(
        SessionMode=SessionMode.Required,
        CallbackContract=typeof(ICalculatorClient))]
public interface ICalculatorDuplex
{
    [OperationContract(IsOneWay = true)]
    void CalculateDerivative(
                        string requestIdentifier,
                        string[] symbols,
            decimal[] parameters,
            string[] functions);
}

public interface ICalculatorClient
{
    [OperationContract(IsOneWay = true)]
    void SendCalculationResult(
                string requestIdentifier,
                double result);
}
```

The asynchronous exchange of messages provided by duplex contracts gives one more flexibility in designing how services process requests. One reason is that the contract itself implies that no client thread will be blocked by a pending request. Another reason is that the service can apportion its response to the client, providing the most urgent data first, and the remainder in subsequent portions.

Duplex contracts are not supported by all bindings. Among the bindings that do support them are the NetTcpBinding and the NetNamedPipesBinding, and their support for duplex contracts is one of the reasons those bindings are recommended.

✗ **DO NOT** overload the names of the methods by which operation contracts are defined.

If the methods by which two operation contracts are defined have the same name, there must be different names assigned to the Name properties of the operation contracts:

```
[OperationContract(Name="FindUserByName")]
User FindUser(string username);
[OperationContract(Name="FindUserByIdentifier")]
User FindUser(Guid userIdentifier);
```

Working with Windows Communication Foundation Services

✓ **DO** reduce latency and maximize throughput by having all client requests to a service go to a single, multithreaded instance of one's service type.

Left to its own devices, the Windows Communication Foundation will create a new instance of a service type to process each client request. It does so in order for Windows Communication Foundation applications to be as robust as possible by default, with each request being handled by a thread-safe instance of the service type. To reduce latency and optimize throughput, it would be better for just a single instance of the service type to be created to handle all client requests, and for that instance to be multithreaded.

To specify that all client requests are to be directed to the same instance of a service type, assign a value of System.ServiceModel.InstanceContextMode.Single to the InstanceContextMode parameter of the service type's System.ServiceModel.ServiceContract attribute. To specify that the service type be multithreaded, assign a value of System.ServiceModel.ConcurrencyMode.Multiple to the ConcurrencyMode parameter of the attribute. Here is an example:

```
[ServiceContract(
        InstanceContextMode=InstanceContextMode.Single,
        ConcurrencyMode=ConcurrencyMode.Multiple)]
public class DerivativesCalculatorServiceType: IDerivativesCalculator
```

✓ **DO** use transactional types to synchronize access to shared data in multithreaded service types.

In a brilliant contribution to *MSDN Magazine*, Juval Lowy documented some conceptually very simple types that he designed using the .NET Framework 2.0's System.Transaction namespace that allow one to apply the transactional programming model to the problem of writing thread-safe code (Lowy 2005). Transactional programming is very familiar to software developers, easy to do, and implemented in very much the same way on different development platforms. By contrast, techniques for synchronizing the access of multiple threads to shared resources are less well known, less reliable for avoiding trouble, and vary more considerably from one development platform to another. Because of the negligible overhead of the Lightweight Transaction Manager provided by the System.Transaction namespace, Lowy was able to design types, shared access to which can be efficiently managed using transactions. Those types offer a more reliable way of avoiding thread synchronization problems, which are often very difficult to diagnose and fix. In addition, the technique for using those types will be familiar to any developer who has ever performed the very common task of programming a transaction.

✓ **DO** make the option of hosting services within IIS one's first choice.

IIS is engineered for scalability, reliability, and fault tolerance, and its security has been tested and reinforced. One good reason for not using IIS to host one's services is that on operating systems prior to Windows Vista, IIS can only host services that communicate over HTTP, and one's choice of communication protocols should take precedence over one's choice of host. A second reason for not using IIS to host one's service is if one is a software vendor seeking to simplify deployments onto customers' systems. Not having to deploy one's solution into IIS is easier, and that is important when the deployment has to be repeated for every customer. A third good reason for not using IIS is that IIS can recycle a process at any time, making it unsuitable for hosting services that maintain state in a nondurable store. Writing services that maintain state in a durable store will be made easier by the durable services feature that is to be included in the next release of the Windows Communication Foundation.

✓ **DO** explicitly call the `Close()` method of `System.ServiceModel.ServiceHost` when hosting a service within a .NET application.

Explicitly calling the `Close()` method of `System.ServiceModel.ServiceHost` when hosting a service within a .NET application, as in this code snippet, serves to terminate the service more quickly, which can expedite shutting down the .NET application:

```
using (ServiceHost host = new ServiceHost(
    serviceType)}
    ))
{
    try
    {
        host.Open(new TimeSpan(0,0,30));

        Console.WriteLine(
            "The service is available."
        );
        Console.ReadKey(true);

        host.Close(new TimeSpan(0,0,30));

    }
    catch(TimeoutException timeoutException)
    {
        ...
    }
}
```

✓ **DO** also specify explicit timeouts in calls to the Open() and Close() methods of System.ServiceModel.ServiceHost.

Otherwise, if the transition to the Open or Closed state waits on some long-running process, the calls to Open() and Close() might not complete in any definite amount of time.

✓ **DO** build service types into class libraries.

Building service types into class libraries makes it easy to redeploy them into different kinds of hosts. They can be hosted within .NET applications by having the .NET applications reference their class libraries. They can be hosted within IIS by copying them into the bin subdirectory of an IIS virtual directory along with a Web.config file with their configuration information.

✗ **AVOID** having to rely on session state information.

✓ **DO** incorporate smaller volumes of session state information into messages.

✓ **DO** use a database to store larger volumes of state information.

✓ **DO** use the Extension property of the System.ServiceModel.InstanceContext object to maintain smaller volumes of session state information when maintaining it outside of messages proves unavoidable.

✓ **DO** use the Extension property of the System.ServiceModel.ServiceHost object to store smaller volumes of application state information.

Listing 21.2 provides an example of using the Extension property of the System.ServiceModel.InstanceContext object to store session state information. Listing 21.3 provides an example of using the Extension property of the System.ServiceModel.ServiceHost object to maintain application state information.

LISTING 21.2   Using InstanceContext.Extension

```
public class MyExtension: IExtension<InstanceContext>
{
        public MyDataType MyData = null;
}


public void Initialize(MyDataType myData)
{
        MyExtension extension = new MyExtension();
        extension.MyDataType = myData;
        OperationContext.InstanceContext.Extensions.Add(myData);
}
```

LISTING 21.2   Continued

```
public MyDataType Use()
{
        MyExtension extension =
            OperationContext.InstanceContext.Extensions.Find<MyExtension>();
        return extension.MyData;
}
```

LISTING 21.3   Using ServiceHost.Extension

```
public class MyExtension: IExtension<InstanceContext>
{
        public MyDataType MyData = null;
}

public class Host
{
    public static void Main(string[] args)
    {
        Type serviceType = typeof(DerivativesCalculatorServiceType);

        using(ServiceHost host = new ServiceHost(
            serviceType
            ))
        {
                        MyExtension extension = new MyExtension();
                        extension.MyDataType = myData;
                        host.Extensions.Add(extension);

            host.Open();

            Console.WriteLine(
                "The derivatives calculator service is available."
            );
            Console.ReadKey(true);

            host.Close();
        }
    }
}

public class DerivativesCalculatorServiceType: IDerivativesCalculator
{
    decimal IDerivativesCalculator.CalculateDerivative(
        string[] symbols,
```

LISTING 21.3   Continued

```
        decimal[] parameters,
        string[] functions)
    {

        MyExtension extension =
                OperationContext.InstanceContext.Extensions.Find<MyExtension>();
            MyDataType myData = extension.MyData;
            [...]
    }
}
```

✓ **DO** consider using the Windows Communication Foundation's ASP.NET Compatibility Mode to leverage the rich session management options of ASP.NET when network load-balanced service instances have to maintain session state.

✓ **DO** use a type derived from System.ServiceModel.ServiceAuthorizationManager for authorization rather than System.Security.Permissions.PrincipalPermission attributes.

System.Security.Permissions.PrincipalPermission must be embedded in the code of a service type. The System.ServiceModel.ServiceAuthorizationManager type that is to be used to control authorization can be identified in the configuration of the service, and can be in any assembly that the .NET Common Language Runtime loader can locate when the service type is constructed.

✓ **DO** consider using Windows Workflow Foundation rules to program types derived from System.ServiceModel.ServiceAuthorizationManager to control authorization.

Expressing authorization criteria in the form of Windows Workflow Foundation rules offers considerable flexibility. Windows Workflow Foundation rules can be defined either in code or in XML, and editors are provided that can be used for creating, examining, and editing rules.

Ensuring Manageability

✓ **DO** have every service type implement a service contract for obtaining information to assist in the administration of the service, and by which administrators can control the service.

The Windows Communication Foundation provides a number of data and control points for service administrators in the form of performance counters, activity tracing, message logging, and the WMI provider. However, those data and control points are designed for the administration of generic services, and naturally cannot take into account the specific requirements of every actual service. Therefore, one should consider designing service contracts with operations for exposing data and control points that do take the specific administration requirements of one's services into account, and those service contracts should be implemented by those services.

- ✓ **DO** provide a comprehensive health model for one's service.

- ✓ **DO** document the proper configuration for the service in the health model, possibly with reference to the use of the Windows Communication Foundation's Service Configuration Editor.

- ✓ **DO** activate the built-in performance counters and make use of those in developing the health model.

- ✓ **DO** activate only the performance counters at the service level initially, and use the performance counters at the endpoint and operation level solely for diagnosing actual defects.

- ✓ **DO** activate the WMI provider and make use of the information it exposes in developing the health model.

- ✓ **DO** provide Windows PowerShell scripts to assist in the administration of one's service, especially to monitor performance counter values and data exposed through the WMI provider, and to monitor and manipulate the service through the administrative service contract that all services should implement.

- ✓ **DO** document the facilities provided by the PowerShell scripts in the health model.

- ✓ **DO** cover the activity tracing and message logging facilities of the Windows Communication Foundation in the health model.

- ✓ **DO** include in the health model information about the security auditing events that the Windows Communication Foundation emits into the Windows Event Log.

- ✓ **DO** integrate the health model into an integrated management environment familiar to administrators, such as Microsoft Operations Manager, IBM Tivoli, or HP OpenView. Otherwise, provide a custom management console for the service.

A health model defines what it means for a system to be operating normally and for it to be operating abnormally, and explains how to transition the system from an abnormal state back to a normal one. The Windows Communication Foundation provides many performance counters that should be very useful in detecting normal and abnormal states, as well as a WMI provider that not only offers additional information for that purpose, but some control points for restoring normal operation. The performance counters and WMI provider are disabled by default for security so that no information about a Windows Communication Foundation Service will be exposed that is not exposed deliberately. The performance counters and WMI provider can be turned on through configuration:

```xml
<?xml version="1.0" encoding="utf-8" ?>
<configuration>
  <system.serviceModel>
```

```
    <diagnostics
                wmiProviderEnabled="true"
                performanceCounters="ServiceOnly"/>
  </system.serviceModel>
</configuration>
```

Only the performance counters at the service level should be activated in general. Those at the endpoint and operation level should be used only to diagnose actual defects because they incur a considerable performance overhead.

When the WMI provider of a service has been activated, information about it can be retrieved through many WMI-enabled management tools, including Windows PowerShell. For example, this Windows PowerShell command will list the names of all the active Windows Communication Foundation endpoints on the local machine that are exposed through WMI:

```
get-wmiobject endpoint -n root\ServiceModel ¦ft name
```

Also useful for diagnosing problems in order to restore a service to a healthy state, and therefore worthwhile covering in the health model for the service, are the activity traces that a Windows Communication Foundation service can emit to show its internal operations, and its ability to log messages. Those facilities are also activated through configuration as shown in Listing 21.4. A Service Trace Viewer tool is provided for studying activity traces and message logs.

LISTING 21.4   Activating Activity Tracing and Message Logging

```
<?xml version="1.0" encoding="utf-8" ?>
<configuration>
  <system.serviceModel>
    <diagnostics>
      <messageLogging logEntireMessage="true"
                      maxMessagesToLog="300"
                      logMessagesAtServiceLevel="true"
                      logMalformedMessages="true"
                      logMessagesAtTransportLevel="true" />
    </diagnostics>
  </system.serviceModel>
  <system.diagnostics>
    <sources>
      <source
              name="System.ServiceModel"
              switchValue="Verbose,ActivityTracing"
          propagateActivity="true">
          <listeners>
            <add
```

21

LISTING 21.4   Continued

```
                        type="System.Diagnostics.DefaultTraceListener"
                        name="Default">
          <filter type="" />
        </add>
        <add name="xml">
          <filter type="" />
        </add>
      </listeners>
    </source>
    <source
            name="System.ServiceModel.MessageLogging">
      <listeners>
        <add
                        type="System.Diagnostics.DefaultTraceListener"
                        name="Default">
          <filter type="" />
        </add>
        <add
                        name="xml">
          <filter type="" />
        </add>
      </listeners>
    </source>
  </sources>
  <sharedListeners>
    <add
                initializeData="C:\logs\ServiceTraces.svclog"
                type="System.Diagnostics.XmlWriterTraceListener"
        name="xml"
        traceOutputOptions="Callstack">
        <filter type="" />
    </add>
  </sharedListeners>
  <trace autoflush="true" />
  </system.diagnostics>
</configuration>
```

Other data for determining the health of a service that the Windows Communication Foundation provides are the security audit events that it records in the Windows Event Log. That facility is also controlled by configuration, as shown in Listing 21.5.

LISTING 21.5   Configuring the Auditing of Security Events

```xml
<?xml version="1.0" encoding="utf-8" ?>
<configuration>
  <system.serviceModel>
    <services>
      <service
        name="DerivativesCalculator.DerivativesCalculatorServiceType"
        behaviorConfiguration="DerivativesCalculatorService">
        <endpoint
          address="Calculator"
          binding="netTcpBinding"
          contract="DerivativesCalculator.IDerivativesCalculator"
        />
      </service>
    </services>
    <behaviors>
      <serviceBehaviors>
        <behavior
          name="DerivativesCalculatorService">
          <serviceSecurityAudit
            auditLogLocation="Application"
            suppressAuditFailure="false"
            serviceAuthorizationAuditLevel="SuccessOrFailure"
            messageAuthenticationAuditLevel="SuccessOrFailure" />
        </behavior>
      </serviceBehaviors>
    </behaviors>
  </system.serviceModel>
</configuration>
```

Working with Windows Communication Foundation Clients

✓ **DO** use the asynchronous pattern for operation contracts in Windows Communication Foundation clients.

Assume that a service implements this operation contract:

```
[OperationContract]
string Echo(string input);
```

Then the operation contract used by the client could be expressed according to the asynchronous pattern in this way:

```
[OperationContract(AsyncPattern = true)]
IAayncResult asynchronousResult = BeginEcho(
        string input,
        AsyncCallback callback,
        object state);
string EndEcho(
        IAsyncResult asynchronousResult);
```

The operation would be invoked as shown in Listing 21.6. Understand that the exchange of messages here is synchronous, but the Windows Communication Foundation delivers the service's synchronous response to the client asynchronously. Also note that the typed proxy, the instance of `System.ServiceModel.ClientBase<T>`, is kept open until the response from the service is processed. That is done to keep the synchronous channel of communication with the service open until the response from the service has been received.

LISTING 21.6   Using the Asynchronous Pattern

```
public class EchoClient: ClientBase<IEcho>: IEcho
{
        public EchoClient(string endpointConfigurationName):
                base(endpointConfigurationName)
        {
        }

        public IAayncResult BeginEcho(
                string input,
                AsyncCallback callback,
                object state)
        {
                return base.Channel.BeginEcho(
                        input,
                        callback,
                        state);
        }

        string EndEcho(
                IAsyncResult asynchronousResult)
    {
                return base.Channel.EndEcho(asynchronousResult);
    }
}
```

LISTING 21.6   Continued

```
EchoClient client = new EchoClient("endpointConfigurationName");
client.Open();

client.BeginEcho(
        "Hello, World!",
        this.EchoCallback,
        client);

Console.WriteLine("Press any key after the service has responded.");
Console.ReadKey(true);

client.Close();

void EchoCallback(IAsyncResult asynchronousResult)
{
    string echo =
                ((EchoClient)asynchronousResult.AsyncState).EndEcho(
                        asynchronousResult);
    Console.WriteLine("Echoed: {0}", echo);
}
```

The asynchronous pattern could be used for the service's operation contracts, too, whether or not the asynchronous pattern is used at all in the programming of the client. However, it is only really useful to do so if the service, in responding to requests from clients, will be using objects with their own asynchronous programming interfaces.

✓ **DO** correctly handle those exceptions that should always be anticipated in Windows Communication Foundation client applications.

The exceptions that should always be anticipated in programming Windows Communication Foundation client applications are System.TimeoutException and System.ServiceModel.CommunicationException. The proper way of handling both of those types of exceptions is to call the Windows Communication Foundation client's Abort() method. Calling the Close() method after either of those exceptions has occurred will cause another exception to be thrown. This guidance is illustrated in Listing 21.7. Note that operation-specific exceptions of the type System.ServiceModel.FaultException<*T*> derive from System.ServiceModel.CommunicationException, so the handlers for those exceptions should precede the handler for the base System.ServiceModel.CommunicationException.

LISTING 21.7   Properly Anticipating Exceptions

```
public class EchoClient: ClientBase<IEcho>: IEcho
{
        public EchoClient(string endpointConfigurationName):
```

LISTING 21.7   Continued

```
                base(endpointConfigurationName)
        {
        }

        public string Echo(
                string input)
        {
                return base.Channel.Echo(
                        input);
        }

}

EchoClient client = new EchoClient();
client.Open();

try
{
    string echo = client.Echo("Hello, World!");
    client.Close();
}
catch (TimeoutException exception)
{
    client.Abort();
}
catch(FaultException<MyFaultException> exception)
{
    if(client.State != CommunicationState.Open)
    {
        client.Abort();
    }
    else
    {
        //Client is still usable.
    }
}
catch (CommunicationException exception)
{
    client.Abort();
}
```

✓ **DO** call the Open() method of Windows Communication Foundation clients before attempting to use them.

Before messages can pass through a Windows Communication Foundation client to a service endpoint, the Windows Communication Foundation must construct a stack of communication channels to implement the hierarchy of communication protocols implied by the binding. That takes time.

The construction of the stack of communication channels is initiated by a call to the client's Open() method. However, it is not necessary to call the Open() method explicitly. If the Open() method has not been called explicitly before the client is used to send a message, the Windows Communication Foundation will call the Open() method implicitly.

Calling the Open() method explicitly before attempting to use the client to send a message does tend to get the first message on its way more quickly, though. The reason is that the construction of the stack of communication channels initiated by the explicit call to the Open() method gets underway asynchronously, and has usually advanced somewhat by the time the client is used to send a message.

✓ **DO** manage the lifetimes of Windows Communication Foundation clients correctly.

The Windows Communication Foundation must construct the stack of communication channels required to implement the hierarchy of communication protocols implied by a binding before messages can pass through clients to services, and that is time-consuming. Consequently, those communication stacks are precious resources and should not be disposed of idly.

With that in mind, consider the scenario in which browser clients make requests of an ASP.NET application, which services those requests via a Windows Communication Foundation client that communicates with a remote service. Such an application should be designed in such a way that a single instance of a multithreaded Windows Communication Foundation client services all the requests from every browser client. The stack of communication channels required by the Windows Communication Client for sending messages to the remote service should be constructed ahead of the first request by constructing the client and calling its Open() method. Then the client should be cached and reused for each request.

On the other hand, the stack of communication channels used by a client to send messages to a service represents a finite resource that should be released as soon as it is no longer required. Explicitly call a client's Close() method to accomplish that.

✗ **AVOID** scoping Windows Communication Foundation service hosts and clients with the C# using statement or the Visual Basic Using block.

Scoping Windows Communication Foundation service hosts and clients with the C# using statement or the Visual Basic Using block does not easily allow for the correct handling of the expected exceptions illustrated in Listing 21.5. More precisely, those syntactical devices imply that the service host's or the client's Dispose() method will be called as the service host or client goes out of scope, and the Dispose() method implicitly calls the Close() method that will throw an exception if a System.TimeoutException or a System.ServiceModel.CommunicationException has occurred.

Scoping a Windows Communication Foundation client with the C# using statement or the Visual Basic Using block also implicitly devalues the client's communication stack, connoting that it is to be quickly disposed, rather than carefully cached.

> ✓ **DO** use the Microsoft.Web.UI.UpdatePanel control that is among the facilities of the Microsoft ASP.NET 2.0 Ajax Extensions to build interactive web clients for Windows Communication Foundation services.

Ajax is the acronym for the *Asynchronous JavaScript and XML* technique for programming more responsive web applications. Rather than posting an entire HTML form to an HTTP server in response to a user's input, and replacing or refreshing the whole form, Ajax applications exchange small quantities of data with the server invisibly and only update particular visual elements. Because of the difficulty of parsing XML with JavaScript, Ajax applications now more typically exchange data with the server in the JavaScript Object Notation (JSON) format, rather than XML. The requests to the server are usually accomplished using a scriptable XMLHttpRequest object provided by the browser.

Microsoft's support for Ajax programming includes the Microsoft.Web.UI.UpdatePanel control that is included among the Microsoft ASP.NET 2.0 Ajax Extensions. That control is used as a container for any number of other ASP.NET controls. Developers can use JavaScript to trigger an update to the content of Microsoft.Web.UI.UpdatePanel controls, which causes them to exchange data with the server. When the data arrives at the server, whatever code the developer has provided to handle the update to the Microsoft.Web.UI.UpdatePanel control executes on the server. That code can read data from any of the ASP.NET controls on the page and update any of the ASP.NET controls contained by the Microsoft.Web.UI.UpdatePanel object.

Programming Ajax applications using the Microsoft.Web.UI.UpdatePanel control has two highly desirable consequences. Most importantly, it yields the effect for which Ajax is intended: interactive web applications that update quickly in response to users' input, with exchanges back and forth with the server happening invisibly. However, it saves the developer from having to write much JavaScript. After the update to a Microsoft.Web.UI.UpdatePanel object is triggered, which might require a few simple lines of JavaScript, the Microsoft.Web.UI.UpdatePanel object handles the work of exchanging data with the server, and the developer's code that updates the display is code written in the developer's preferred .NET programming language, running on the server. Minimizing the dependence on JavaScript code executing in the browser is a boon for Ajax programming because such code is notoriously difficult to debug and manage.

As a tool for building interactive web clients for interacting with Windows Communication Foundation services, Microsoft.Web.UI.UpdatePanel controls send requests to the server that result in .NET event handlers executing. Those handlers can use Windows Communication Foundation clients to interact with services beyond the web application server, as shown in Figure 21.1.

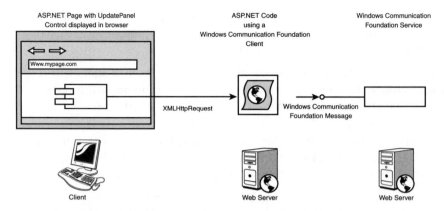

FIGURE 21.1   Using a `Microsoft.Web.UI.UpdatePanel` object as a client of a Windows Communication Foundation service.

A common question is how to have Ajax code executing in the browser use the Windows Communication Foundation to exchange secure messages directly with remote services. That sort of interaction is quite different from the exchange of data depicted in Figure 21.1, wherein the `Microsoft.Web.UI.UpdatePanel` object interacts with a server running code that in turn connects to a remote service via the Windows Communication Foundation.

There are several things to know in considering that question:

▶ There is no way of executing Windows Communication Foundation code within a standard browser.

▶ Although it is possible to have code executing in a standard browser communicate with services deployed on some arbitrary host, doing so violates the same origin policy. The same origin policy is "an important security measure for client-side scripting [that] prevents a document or script loaded from one 'origin' from getting or setting properties of a document from a different 'origin'" (Wikipedia 2006).

▶ One can use the Microsoft Ajax Library, the client-side scripting counterpart to the server-side Microsoft ASP.NET 2.0 Ajax Extensions, to manually exchange data directly with a service at the same origin. The `Microsoft.Web.UI.UpdatePanel` control just saves one from having to expend the effort of doing that.

▶ With the next release of the Windows Communication Foundation, concurrent with the next version of Microsoft Visual Studio, it will be possible for that service at the same origin with which the client-side script communicates directly to be a species of Windows Communication Foundation service—a species that can exchange JSON messages with XMLHttpRequest clients. Again, given that the `Microsoft.Web.UI.UpdatePanel` control saves one from having to write client-side script to communicate with services, the need for being able to write services that can exchange JSON messages with `XMLHttpRequest` clients is questionable.

▶ Communication between client-side scripts and the server via XMLHttpRequest objects can be secured using the Secure Sockets Layer (SSL) protocol over HTTP.

▶ It cannot be secured using any existing standard message security protocol because there simply is no such protocol for XMLHttpRequest objects and JSON.

Working with Large Amounts of Data

✓ **DO** determine exactly how large input and output messages can be.

✗ **DO NOT** provide operations that might return indefinite, potentially very large quantities of data in response to requests.

Providing operations that might return very large quantities of data in response to requests could severely compromise the throughput of a service. Moreover, the base class for Windows Communication Foundation transport-binding elements, System.ServiceModel.Channels.TransportBindingElement, has a configurable MaxReceivedMessageSize property, and if the size of a message exceeds the value assigned to that property, the receiver will fail. The default value of the property is 64KB, and the maximum value is 2^{64}.

✓ **DO** consider using the System.Net.FtpWebRequest class, rather than the Windows Communication Foundation, to transfer large amounts of data.

Service-oriented programming and development platforms for facilitating it, such as the Windows Communication Foundation, are meant for sending messages. Messages are meant to be like the things that get sent via postal services. Those are usually small enough to fit in envelopes that are just a little larger than the average adult's hand. On good, albeit infrequent days, the postal service does indeed deliver somewhat bigger and sturdier things from Amazon.com. Yet, although there is evidently considerable variation in the sizes of messages sent through the post, one can expect to pay dearly and even get into some trouble if one was to, say, change residences, and attempt to move all of one's belongings through the mail. One should also hesitate to send a lot of very sizeable things via a service-oriented programming technology.

By contrast, the File Transfer Protocol (FTP) is a venerable protocol that has been used for decades to transfer data of varying sizes and is widely supported on computing platforms. It supports authentication, and when used in conjunction with the SSL protocol, both the credentials for authenticating requestors and the data provided in response to requests can be transferred securely.

The System.Net.FtpWebRequest class allows one to write code that communicates with FTP servers to both uploading and downloading data. The EnableSsl property can be set to true to communicate via the SSL protocol with FTP servers that are configured to support that protocol.

✓ **DO** use the Windows Communication Foundation's implementation of the SOAP Message Transmission Optimization Mechanism (MTOM) for messages with binary constituents that must be transferred securely between platforms.

Binary data can be incorporated into XML messages for exchange across platforms via the Base64 Transfer-Content-Encoding. However, that encoding increases the size of the data by a third. According to MTOM, the binary data is first incorporated into the XML message using the Base64 Transfer-Content-Encoding, and then the protocols for securing XML messages are applied. Then the binary data is restored to its original format, and added along with the XML message to an XML-binary Optimized Packaging (XOP) package for transfer. The receiver reconstructs the secure XML message from the XOP package.

All the Windows Communication Foundation's HTTP bindings have a `MessageEncoding` property to which the value `System.ServiceModel.WSMessageEncoding.Mtom` can be assigned to signify that MTOM is to be used. In that case, byte arrays and types derived from `System.IO.Stream` will be treated as binary data in the MTOM encoding process.

✓ **DO** use a streaming transfer mode for messages that are too large to be buffered.

The Windows Communication Foundation buffers messages in their entirety by default. Doing so is essential to the application of certain protocols, WS-Security in particular. When the exchange of messages need not be secure, one can avoid the adverse implications for the application's working set that are entailed by the buffering of entire messages by using a streaming transfer mode. That option is available with the HTTP, TCP, and named pipes transport channels. Assigning the value `System.ServiceModel.TransferMode.Streamed` to their `TransferMode` properties causes byte arrays and types derived from `System.IO.Stream` that are incorporated in the message to be transmitted in chunks of a configurable size. The message is not buffered in its entirety, although the maximum size of the message is still restricted to the value assigned to the transport channel's `MaxReceivedMessageSize` property.

The option of using a streaming transfer mode is more useful if the data incorporated in the message is in a format that can be consumed as a stream. Such formats include those for digitally encoding audio and video. Being able to use a streaming transfer mode to avoid buffering the entire message in transmission is less valuable if the entire content of the message must be buffered anyway by the receiver for it to be processed.

✓ **DO** use a channel for chunking messages that are too large to be buffered, but which must be secured.

If the exchange of messages needs to be secure, but the messages are too large to be buffered in their entirety, one must provide a custom channel to break the messages into chunks and position that channel at the top of a Windows Communication Foundation channel stack. For each outbound message passed into it, the chunking channel would pass one or more messages representing chunks of the original outbound message into the channels beneath it. A channel implementing a secure messaging protocol that was lower down in the stack of channels could then secure each of those messages. On the receiving side, a corresponding channel would reassemble the original message from the chunks. Although there is no standard protocol for breaking messages into chunks and reassembling them, an ad hoc protocol for that purpose could certainly be implemented on any platform. A sample channel for breaking outbound messages into chunks and reassembling inbound messages from a series of chunks is included among the Windows Communication Foundation samples in the Software Development Kit for the .NET Framework 3.0. That sample relies on the chunks being transferred in order, and depends on the `System.ServiceModel.Channels.ReliableSessionBindingElement` to guarantee that ordering. That binding element is a constituent of the predefined `NetTcpBinding` and `WSHttpBinding`.

Debugging Windows Communication Foundation Applications

✓ **DO** first thoroughly test and debug service types by invoking their methods directly, before proceeding to invoke their methods via the Windows Communication Foundation.

✓ **DO** thoroughly test and debug services using Windows Communication Foundation clients deployed on the same computer system before testing and debugging services using clients on remote computers.

✓ **DO** thoroughly test and debug service types by hosting them within .NET applications before deploying and testing them within IIS.

Testing and debugging services hosted by .NET applications is easier than testing and debugging services hosted within IIS because, in the latter case, debugging requires attaching the debugger to an IIS process, which can be laborious if it has to be done repeatedly.

✓ **DO** rely on the Windows Communication Foundation samples in the Software Development Kit, especially when debugging.

The Windows Communication Foundation samples provided by the .NET Framework 3 Software Development Kit cover a great many scenarios, they have considerable documentation, and they do work. So, when one's own Windows Communication Foundation solution is not working properly for no apparent reason, systematically compare it to the corresponding samples to identify the problem. If the defect is not apparent by inspection, make a copy of the sample and modify it, proceeding step-by-step to match one's solution, and testing the modified sample after each step. That method will reveal the problem.

✓ **DO**, in debugging, use the `ReturnExceptionDetailInFaults` property of the `System.ServiceModel.ServiceDebugBehavior` class to have services include .NET exception information in faults returned to clients.

✗ **DO NOT** use that option in production.

Setting the value of the `ReturnExceptionDetailInFaults` property of the `System.ServiceModel.ServiceDebugBehavior` to `true` will cause the Windows Communication Foundation to include .NET exception information in any faults that a service returns to its clients. Having that information can be useful in debugging, although having it exposed in production compromises security.

✓ **DO** use message logging and activity tracing in debugging.

Summary

This chapter offered more than 80 points of guidance for using the Windows Communication Foundation. The guidance covers approaches to adopting the technology, how to work with endpoints, how to work with services and clients, how to design exchanges of large amounts of data, and how to debug.

References

Anderson, Chris. 2006. Annotation. In *Framework Design Guidelines: Conventions, Idioms, and Patterns for Reusable .NET Libraries*, Krzystof Cwalina and Brad Abrams, 21. Upper Saddle River, NJ: Addison Wesley.

Box, Don and Chris Sells. 2003. *Essential .NET Volume 1: The Common Language Runtime*. Boston, MA: Addison Wesley.

Cwalina, Krzysztof and Brad Abrams. 2006. *Framework Design Guidelines: Conventions, Idioms, and Patterns for Reusable .NET Libraries*. Upper Saddle River, NJ: Addison Wesley.

Lowy, Juval. 2005. Can't Commit? Volatile Resource Managers in .NET Bring Transactions to the Common Type. *MSDN Magazine* 58 (December).

Meier, J.D., Srinath Vasireddy, Ashish Babbar, and Alex Mackman. 2004. *Improving .NET Application Performance and Scalability*. Redmond, WA: Microsoft.

Sehmi, Arvindra and Beat Schwegler. 2006. Service-Oriented Modeling for Connected Systems—Part 1. *The Architecture Journal: Input for Better Outcomes* 7: 33–41.

Wikipedia. 2006. S.v. "Same origin policy." http://en.wikipedia.org/wiki/Same_origin_policy. Accessed October 13, 2006.

Index

A

D

E

EnableSsl property, 669

encapsulation, 19

encoders (message), 482

    binding elements, implementing, 484-487

    custom transports, 499

ending/initiating sessions, 114

EndpointBehaviors property, 425

endpoints. *See also* **Service Model [NPN]**

    adding programmatically, XmlFormatter example, 95-96

    attaching custom behaviors to, 425-427, 449-450

    Peer Channel, 539, 543-544, 555-557

    REST POX services, 572-573

    retiring, versioning, 631

    service endpoints, changing addresses of, 631

error handling, activities (Windows Workflow Foundation), 134

evaluation context (claim sets), 339, 362

EventDrivenActivity activity (Windows Workflow Foundation), state machine work-flows, 164

exception handling, data contracts, 103-107

exceptions

    anticipating, 664-665

    CardSpace (Windows), catching in, 313-314

exchange patterns, designing, 551

Execute() method, custom activities, 136

exemplars, Windows Communication Foundation integration, 639

explicit communication semantics, 458

export extension (WSDL)

    attaching to operations/endpoints, 449-450

    declaring, 448

    informing Windows Communication Foundation of, 450

Extension property, 656-658

F - G

Fabrikam certificates, 300, 309

fault contracts, 652

Faulty operation, exception handling, 105-106

federations (security), 342

    claim-based security versus, 380

    security token services, 288

FFIEC (Federal Financial Institutions Examination Council), authentication, 255

Fielding, Dr. Roy, web browser architectures, 570

formatname: MULTICAST, 518

Formatter property, 422-423

Forms client, COM+ integrations, 395-396

forward chaining, 186

frameworks

    API layers, designing public layers, 647

    layered designs, 419

    Principle of Scenario-Driven Design, 647-648

generics, 8

    base types, 10

    constructed types, 9

    methods, 9-10

How can we make this index more useful? Email us at indexes@samspublishing.com

IOrderSubscriber interface, 515

IOrderSubscriber service contract (MSMQ PGM), 520

IPictureServer

custom streams, 527-531

streamed transfer mode, 522-523, 526

IPublisher, callback contracts, 506-512

IPv6 NAT Traversal, Teredo, 538

ISecurityTokenService service contracts, STS addition process, 360

IssuedToken policy assertions (CardSpace), 275

Issuer section (.ini files), Managed Cards, 330

ISubscriber

callback contracts, 506-512

stream transfer mode, 532

Item member (Peer Channel example), 551

IUnknownSerializationData interface, XmlFormatter example, 99

J - K - L

Java clients, DerivativesCalculator example, 63-64

Java Virtual Machine Specification, class file format, 21

Justifiable Parties (Laws of Identity), 258

Kerberos authentication method, 280

KnownType attribute, XmlFormatter example, 102-103

Laws of Identity, 257-259

layered framework designs, 419

legacy integration

COM+, 385

authentication/authorization requirements, 386

calling Windows Communication Foundation services from, 397-402

component methods, 386

contacts, 386

hosting mode, 387

Service Model Configuration tool, 387-389

supported interfaces, 386

usage example, 390-396

web hosting mode, 387

Windows Forms client references, 395-396

MSMQ, 403

creating clients, 407-411

creating requests, 403-407

testing applications, 411

Liberty identity protocols, 264

Lightweight Transaction Manager, 13-14. *See also* Distributed Transaction Coordinator (Microsoft)

Limited Disclosure for a Constrained Use (Laws of Identity), 258

logotypes, adding Information Cards to WCF applications, 308

M

Main() method (MSMQ PGM), 516-520

maintenance, delegating (Windows Communication Foundation integration), 640-641

Managed Cards, 269, 328-332

N

X - Y - Z

Your Guide to Computer Technology

informIT

UNLEASHED

Unleashed takes you beyond the basics, providing an exhaustive, technically sophisticated reference for professionals who need to exploit a technology to its fullest potential. It's the best resource for practical advice from the experts, and the most in-depth coverage of the latest technologies.

Windows Presentation Foundation Unleashed
ISBN: 0672328917

OTHER UNLEASHED TITLES

Microsoft BizTalk Server 2006 Unleashed
ISBN: 0672329255

Microsoft SharePoint 2007 Development Unleashed
ISBN: 0672329034

Microsoft Exchange Server 2007 Unleashed
ISBN: 0672329204

Microsoft Small Business Server 2003 Unleashed
ISBN: 0672328054

Microsoft ISA Server 2006 Unleashed
ISBN: 0672329190

Microsoft Office Project Server 2007 Unleashed
ISBN: 0672329212

Microsoft Windows Server 2003 Unleashed (R2 Edition)
ISBN: 0672328984

Microsoft Windows Vista™ Unleashed
ISBN: 0672328941

Microsoft SQL Server 2005 Unleashed
ISBN: 0672328240

Microsoft Visual C# 2005 Unleashed
ISBN: 0672327767

ASP.NET 2.0 Unleashed
ISBN: 0672328232

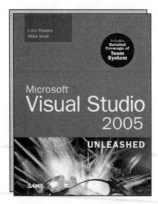

Microsoft Visual Studio 2005 Unleashed
ISBN: 0672328194

SAMS
www.samspublishing.com